AF686694

THE EFTA COURT

The EEA Agreement, which celebrates its 30th anniversary in 2024, extends the internal market of the EU to the participating EFTA States, Iceland, Liechtenstein and Norway. The successful operation of the EEA depends on a two-pillar system of judicial control and supervision. In respect of judicial control, the EFTA Court operates in parallel with the Court of Justice of the European Union and has jurisdiction vis-à-vis the three EFTA States. This collection of essays, celebrating the EFTA Court's 30th anniversary, reviews the success of the EEA and the Court, its interface with EU law and its future development.

The EFTA Court

Developing the EEA over Three Decades

To mark the 30th Anniversary of the EFTA Court

Edited by

Páll Hreinsson

Ólafur Jóhannes Einarsson

and

Bryndís Pálmarsdóttir

•HART•

OXFORD • LONDON • NEW YORK • NEW DELHI • SYDNEY

HART PUBLISHING

Bloomsbury Publishing Plc

Kemp House, Chawley Park, Cumnor Hill, Oxford, OX2 9PH, UK

1385 Broadway, New York, NY 10018, USA

29 Earlsfort Terrace, Dublin 2, Ireland

HART PUBLISHING, the Hart/Stag logo, BLOOMSBURY and the Diana logo are trademarks of Bloomsbury Publishing Plc

First published in Great Britain 2024

Copyright © The editors and contributors severally 2024

The editors and contributors have asserted their right under the Copyright, Designs and Patents Act 1988 to be identified as Authors of this work.

All rights reserved. No part of this publication may be reproduced or transmitted in any form or by any means, electronic or mechanical, including photocopying, recording, or any information storage or retrieval system, without prior permission in writing from the publishers.

While every care has been taken to ensure the accuracy of this work, no responsibility for loss or damage occasioned to any person acting or refraining from action as a result of any statement in it can be accepted by the authors, editors or publishers.

All UK Government legislation and other public sector information used in the work is Crown Copyright ©. All House of Lords and House of Commons information used in the work is Parliamentary Copyright ©. This information is reused under the terms of the Open Government Licence v3.0 (http://www.nationalarchives.gov.uk/doc/open-government-licence/version/3) except where otherwise stated.

All Eur-lex material used in the work is © European Union, http://eur-lex.europa.eu/, 1998–2024.

A catalogue record for this book is available from the British Library.

A catalogue record for this book is available from the Library of Congress.

Library of Congress Control Number: 2024937494

ISBN: HB: 978-1-50996-880-0
ePDF: 978-1-50996-882-4
ePub: 978-1-50996-881-7

Typeset by Compuscript Ltd, Shannon
Printed and bound in Great Britain by CPI Group (UK) Ltd, Croydon CR0 4YY

MIX
Paper | Supporting responsible forestry
FSC® C013604
www.fsc.org

To find out more about our authors and books visit www.hartpublishing.co.uk. Here you will find extracts, author information, details of forthcoming events and the option to sign up for our newsletters.

Foreword

The EFTA Court: Developing the EEA over Three Decades

PÁLL HREINSSON

THE THIRD DECADE in the EFTA Court's history has coincided with many historic events in Europe. For the first time in the more than 70-year history of the EU, a Member State, the UK, left the EU and consequently also the EEA Agreement. More recently, a pandemic of a magnitude unprecedented since the 1918 flu pandemic struck the globe. This was followed by the Russian invasion into Ukraine which brought war to Europe on a scale not seen since the Second World War. The occurrence of these events and the challenging times that have followed have demonstrated, now more than ever, the importance of European cooperation and unity. For Iceland, Norway and Liechtenstein, the EEA Agreement, the cornerstone of their special relationship with the EU, has played a pivotal role in safeguarding political and economic stability during these difficult times.

On 23 June 2016, the people of the UK voted to withdraw from the EU in a referendum on continued EU membership. Although the withdrawal officially took place on 31 January 2020, transitional arrangements under the Withdrawal Agreement[1] entailed that the UK remained a part of the internal market until 1 January 2021. What followed the UK's withdrawal from the internal market was political and economic instability. At the time, the Brexit movement in the UK was at the forefront of a wave of euroscepticism that seemed to be gaining traction throughout Europe. There were calls for such referendums in other EU Member States. However, since then, such discussions have faded away. The example of the UK has rather served as a cautionary tale, exposing the difficulties countries can face when exiting the EU and highlighting the importance of the internal market for economic and political stability.

Indeed, the importance for the economies of the EEA/EFTA States of the privileged access to the internal market of the EU under the EEA Agreement can hardly be overstated. Their economies rely on forming one internal market with the EU. It is also important to be cognisant of the fact that the economic relationship between the EFTA States and the EU does not exist in a vacuum. It occurs in the context of the global economy and economic development worldwide. In that respect, it should

[1] Agreement on the withdrawal of the United Kingdom of Great Britain and Northern Ireland from the European Union and the European Atomic Energy Community [2020] OJ L29/7.

be noted that in 2018, the EU imposed provisional safeguard measures with regard to imports of certain steel products due to developments on the global market.[2] These measures were adopted due to measures taken by the US, during the presidency of Donald Trump, against imports of steel and there was a high risk of further increase of imports into the EU resulting from trade diversion. These circumstances, in the context of persistent worldwide overcapacities, had the potential to jeopardise the EU steel industries.[3] The measures imposed an additional duty at the rate of 25 per cent on imports of specified steel products, except for such products originating from Norway, Iceland and Liechtenstein, which benefited from a special exception granted solely on the grounds of their participation in the EEA. Thus, while every other third country in the world was subject to those measures, regardless of whatever free trade agreements they might have concluded with the EU, the EFTA States, due to their special relationship with the EU, based on the EEA Agreement, were exempted. Indeed, the privileged trading relationship between the EFTA States and the EU on the basis of the EEA Agreement can only be compared to the relationship between the EU Member States themselves on the basis of the EU treaties.

The importance of the EEA Agreement was again demonstrated by the COVID-19 pandemic. This overwhelming health crisis brought with it an enormous impact on the economies and societies of states worldwide. The cherished freedom of movement under the EEA Agreement was sharply curtailed due to the risks posed by the pandemic. The increased interconnectedness and interdependence of the economies of EEA States, brought about by the EEA Agreement, also entail potential vulnerabilities in times of crisis. The EFTA States rely not only on exporting to the internal market, but also importing necessary goods and services as well as labour. Thus, in times of crisis, close cooperation is even more important. On 14 March 2020, during the early stages of the pandemic, the EU adopted a regulation making the exportation of personal protective equipment (PPE) subject to the production of an export authorisation due to the epidemiological crisis caused by COVID-19 and the concomitant significantly increased need for PPE.[4] In its original form, the export authorisation was required for any export outside of the EU, including to the EFTA States. Naturally, the haste with which such measures must necessarily be adopted in times of crisis means that they are not guaranteed to be flawless. However, a few days later, as swiftly as the measure had been adopted, this oversight was remedied.[5] The close integration brought about by the internal market in PPE meant that restricting exports in this area would be counterproductive.

Restrictions on the free movement of persons during the COVID-19 pandemic also demonstrated the benefits of cooperation within the framework of the EEA

[2] Commission Implementing Regulation (EU) 2018/1013 of 17 July 2018 imposing provisional safeguard measures with regard to imports of certain steel products [2018] OJ L181/39.

[3] Recitals 4 and 5 of Regulation (EU) 2018/1013.

[4] Commission Implementing Regulation (EU) 2020/402 of 14 March 2020 making the exportation of certain products subject to the production of an export authorisation [2020] OJ L177/1.

[5] Commission Implementing Regulation (EU) 2020/426 of 19 March 2020 amending Implementing Regulation (EU) 2020/402 making the exportation of certain products subject to the production of an export authorisation [2020] OJ L184/1. It should be noted that Switzerland was also included in the scope of the amending Regulation.

Agreement. Although there were restrictions on travel between EEA States, such restrictions were much more cumbersome vis-a-vis third countries, which the UK had become in the meantime. This was of major importance for the EFTA States, given the thousands of frontier workers crossing the borders between the EU and the EFTA States every day, including essential healthcare workers. The European Centre for Disease Prevention and Control (ECDC), an EU agency, proved to be pivotal in collecting and sharing information concerning the pandemic among EEA States. Furthermore, the close cooperation between the EU and the EFTA States during the pandemic, such as within the EEA Council, led to the participation of the EFTA States in the EU vaccine procurement scheme, demonstrating that there is strength in numbers and that unity in times of crisis brings about benefits for all. Indeed, one could say that the fundamental premise behind the close European cooperation embodied in the EEA Agreement is now stronger than ever.

Now turning to the case law of the EFTA Court in the last ten years, it can be said that in this respect too, these have been eventful years. From 2014 to the end of 2023, the Court registered 170 cases, which is close to half of all cases brought before the Court from the beginning of its operations in 1994. They are divided as follows: 87 are a request for an advisory opinion, 70 are infringement proceedings brought by the EFTA Surveillance Authority (ESA) against one of the EFTA States and 13 are actions for annulment of decisions adopted by the ESA. In the same period, the Court handed down judgments in over 150 cases.

Looking to the most noteworthy cases, I would like to start by mentioning a trio of judgments concerning the Citizenship Directive:[6] *Gunnarsson*, *Jabbi* and *Campbell*.[7] These cases all concerned the question of whether EFTA nationals could rely on their rights under the Directive vis-a-vis their home states. This was a question which the Court of Justice of the European Union (CJEU) had answered in the EU context in the negative. However, given the citizenship provisions in Articles 20 and 21 of the Treaty on the Functioning of the European Union (TFEU), the legal context under EU law was significantly different and, based on these provisions, EU citizens enjoy analogous protection as they would under the terms of the Directive with regard to their home state. The EFTA Court concluded that considerations of homogeneity and ensuring the effectiveness of free movement rights meant that, as a matter of EEA law, the Citizenship Directive laid down rights enforceable against the home state of the EFTA national. I consider this line of cases to provide an excellent example of the fact that adjudicating to ensure homogeneity within the EEA is far from being a mechanical exercise. The Grand Chamber of the CJEU also gave a very important ruling on the status of EFTA nationals under the EEA Agreement, and other agreements that the EFTA States have concluded with the EU in *IN*, holding that the combined

[6] Directive 2004/38/EC of the European Parliament and of the Council of 29 April 2004 on the right of citizens of the Union and their family members to move and reside freely within the territory of the Member States amending Regulation (EEC) No 1612/68 and repealing Directives 64/221/EEC, 68/360/EEC, 72/194/EEC, 73/148/EEC, 75/34/EEC, 75/35/EEC, 90/364/EEC, 90/365/EEC and 93/96/EEC [2004] OJ L158/77.

[7] Case E-26/13 *Atli Gunnarsson* [2014] EFTA Ct Rep 254; Case E-28/15 *Yankuba Jabbi* [2016] EFTA Ct Rep 575; and Case E-4/19 *Campbell*, judgment of 13 May 2020.

effect of these agreements 'renders the situation of that person objectively comparable with that of an EU citizen to whom, in accordance with Article 3(2) of the Treaty on European Union (TEU), the Union offers an area of freedom, security and justice without internal frontiers, in which the free movement of persons is ensured'.[8]

In my mind, there is no doubt that these judgments show that both courts are singing homogeneity from the same hymn sheet.

Scanteam also shows the complexities of homogeneity.[9] Ruling on a request for an advisory opinion from the Norwegian Complaints Board for Public Procurement, the EFTA Court had to decide on whether the Board fulfilled the conditions for being a court or tribunal within the meaning of Article 34 of the Agreement between the EFTA States on the Establishment of a Surveillance Authority and a Court of Justice (SCA). The judgment of the CJEU in *Banco Santander* left no doubt that under the more stringent application of the conditions, the CJEU would not consider such a body capable of requesting a preliminary ruling.[10] Nevertheless, the EFTA Court held the request admissible, relying primarily on the importance of such bodies in ensuring the application of EEA law in the EFTA States. The tightening of the admissibility criteria by the CJEU followed developments in its case law relating to rule of law concerns in some EU Member States. It goes without saying that the EFTA Court's decision not to follow suit in this respect as regards the admissibility criteria for requests for advisory opinions is not a signal to the effect that the rule of law is less important in the EFTA States. The rule of law is firmly anchored in EEA law. The seminal judgment of the European Court of Human Rights (ECtHR) in *Ástráðsson*, which concluded that the appointment of the judges to the newly constituted Court of Appeal in Iceland was in breach of Article 6 of the European Convention on Human Rights (ECHR), demonstrates that even established democracies such as the EFTA States cannot afford to rest on their laurels when it comes to compliance with the rule of law. Indeed, in *Pascal Nobile* the EFTA Court was confronted with irregularities in the appointment of the Norwegian judge, which thankfully had been rectified when the Court handed down its decision on the composition of the Court. Nevertheless, the Court seized the opportunity to emphasise that the principle of judicial independence is one of the fundamental values of the administration of justice. Moreover, maintaining judicial independence required strict observance of the applicable rules on judicial appointments.[11]

Any examination of the Court's judgments in the last decade would be incomplete without mentioning the NAV saga. In late 2019, it was revealed that a large number of benefit recipients in Norway had had their benefits suspended due to short stays in other EEA States. Some had been required to reimburse considerable amounts and there were even instances of people having been sentenced to imprisonment for social security fraud. The compatibility of this practice with EEA law was seriously called into question and the Norwegian Supreme Court reopened a criminal case and requested an advisory opinion from the EFTA Court.[12] We concluded that prior to the

[8] Case C-897/19 PPU *IN* ECLI:EU:C:2020:262, para 58.
[9] Case E-8/19 *Scanteam*, judgment of 16 July 2020.
[10] Case C-274/14 *Banco de Santander* ECLI:EU:C:2020:17.
[11] Case E-21/16 *Pascal Nobile* [2017] EFTA Ct Rep 554, Decision of the Court of 14 February 2017, para 16.
[12] Case E-8/20 *Criminal Proceedings against N*, judgment of 5 May 2021.

entry into force of the current Social Security Coordination Regulation 883/2004,[13] the Norwegian rules were in breach of the freedom to provide services under Article 36 EEA. Following the lead of the CJEU in its above-mentioned judgment in *IN*, the freedom to provide services was given a broad interpretation, effectively encompassing any travel to another EEA State. After Regulation 883/2004 came into force, the Norwegian rules were in breach of an explicit provision in that Regulation. The Supreme Court followed the EFTA Court's advisory opinion and acquitted the accused of the criminal charges brought against him. This judgment is examined in a chapter in this publication by Professors Halvard Haukeland Fredriksen and Christian NK Franklin, and I invite the reader to explore that chapter for an enlightening examination.

The Court also received requests for advisory opinions regarding the rules of the Social Security Coordination Regulation on the exportability of unemployment benefits. We found that these rules went beyond coordination of the social security legislation in the EEA States and constituted an independent body of rules upon which claimants could rely, irrespective of national law. As the export of the benefit was exhaustively regulated in the Regulation, the EFTA Court considered that it did not fall to be assessed whether there was a restriction of the freedom to provide services under Article 36 EEA.

These cases evidently demonstrate the complexity of social security law and I would like to note that, following on from the NAV cases, the EFTA Court has received several requests for advisory opinions concerning significant questions in the field of social security from courts in all three EFTA States.

The Norwegian Supreme Court made its first request for an advisory opinion to the EFTA Court for over 13 years in *Holship* in 2015.[14] Since then, the Supreme Court has submitted 10 requests for an advisory opinion, and it is worth highlighting that this is a higher number of cases than its sister court in Denmark has submitted to the CJEU in the same period. In addition to the cases already referred to above, I would like to mention its request in *Fosen II*, which concerned the threshold for liability under the Remedies Directive for breach of the public procurement rules.[15] The Frostating Court of Appeal had not followed the advisory opinion of the EFTA Court in *Fosen I*[16] and, rather than repeating the unfortunate episode of the *STX* case, the Supreme Court requested a new advisory opinion from the EFTA Court. For an account of the legal issues at stake and how the EFTA Court changed its approach, see the excellent contribution of Professor Albert Sanchez-Graells in this volume.

In the context of the EFTA Court's relationship with the highest judicial instances in the EFTA States, I would like to draw the reader's attention to the fact that this volume contains contributions from distinguished members of all these courts. These chapters discuss the relationship between these courts and the EFTA Court as well as their interaction with EEA law. The authors are Hilmar Hoch, President of the

[13] Regulation (EC) No 883/2004 of the European Parliament and of the Council of 29 April 2004 on the coordination of social security systems [2004] OJ L166/1.

[14] Case E-14/15 *Holship Norge* [2016] EFTA Ct Rep 240.

[15] Case E-7/18 *Fosen Linjen II*, judgment of 1 August 2019.

[16] Case E-16/16 *Fosen Linjen I* [2017] EFTA Ct Rep 617.

Liechtenstein Constitutional Court; Toril Marie Øie, President of the Norwegian Supreme Court, and Henrik Bull, judge at the Norwegian Supreme Court and former judge at the EFTA Court; and Benedikt Bogason, President of the Icelandic Supreme Court, and Þorgeir Örlygsson, its former President and also previously a member of the EFTA Court. Furthermore, Professor Ola Mestad's contribution is an interesting addition to this discussion, as he has examined how the Norwegian Supreme Court has dealt with the EFTA Court's advisory opinions from the beginning up to the present day.

In the context of discussing the EFTA Court's relationship with national courts, it is also important to bear in mind that EEA law may also create new possibilities for judges, particularly those in 'lower' national courts, to examine national legislation that might otherwise not have been subject to their judicial review. Indeed, the recent *RS*[17] case, for example, illustrates the 'judicial empowerment' that Protocol 35 EEA offers to 'lower' courts. In this case the Liechtenstein Constitutional Court had found a provision of tax law to be discriminatory and in breach of EEA law. Nonetheless, the Constitutional Court had suspended the annulment of the national law for reasons of legal certainty. The Administrative Court of the Principality of Liechtenstein was unsure how to treat this deferral under the terms of EEA law. Thus, the key issue was whether it was acceptable under Protocol 35 EEA to temporarily suspend the application of implemented EEA law, and thus allow EFTA States to maintain incompatible national legislation for a transitional period in order to bring it into conformity with EEA law. Following the case law of the CJEU, we found that national courts can only in very exceptional cases, for reasons of legal certainty, temporarily maintain the effects of a national rule that is contrary to EEA law, ie, when those concerned have acted in good faith and when there is a risk of serious difficulties if the annulment were to take effect immediately. Of particular interest in *RS* is the emphasis on the fact that not merely were the Liechtenstein rules incompatible with the free movement provisions, but that such incompatibility should already have been obvious from the CJEU's existing and indeed extensive case law on income tax. Thus, the EFTA Court found those cumulative conditions not to be fulfilled.

Earlier, I referred to *Holship* being the first request from the Norwegian Supreme Court for a long time and, as such, the case evidently constituted a milestone. However, the legal issues at stake were also highly significant. The case concerned a boycott directed against a Danish undertaking in the harbour of Drammen and thus the relationship between the right of establishment and the rights of trade unions derived from the freedom of association. In its judgment, the EFTA Court confirmed for the first time explicitly that fundamental rights are part of the general principles of EEA law. When the case came back to the Supreme Court, a majority of the Full Court concluded along the lines of the advisory opinion. However, that was not the end of the story as the case was brought before the ECtHR, whose judgment clarified both its position on the relationship between the fundamental freedoms and fundamental rights under the Convention, a subject on which we have certainly not heard the last word. Our colleagues in Strasbourg also provided a welcome clarification as to the

[17] Case E-11/22 *RS*, judgment of 4 July 2023.

status of fundamental rights protection under the terms of the EEA Agreement. This is explored in more detail in the chapter in this volume by Arnfinn Bårdsen, Section President at the ECtHR.

The Liechtenstein courts have on several occasions requested advisory opinions in the field of financial services law. To name but two cases, we have examined the notion of ultimate beneficial owner under the Anti-Money Laundering Directive and the scope of investor protection and the obligation to publish a prospectus.[18] Moreover, financial services provided the EFTA Court with the first ever request for an advisory opinion from Norway in criminal proceedings.[19] This request gave us an opportunity to provide guidance on the question of whether and in what circumstances real transactions (in the sense that they transfer risk between independent parties) can be deemed market manipulation. It is interesting to note that even though ensuring clarity in the rules on transactions with financial instruments is growing ever more important, this issue has not yet been dealt with by the CJEU. It is therefore a good example of the EFTA Court 'going first'. Our conclusion was that real transactions can be considered market manipulation, provided that they may be regarded as giving false or misleading signals regarding the marketing of financial instruments. This assessment was to be based on objective factors and the effects of the transactions to be taken into account.

The most politically significant case to come from Iceland in the last decade is the *Fresh Meat* case. It is also the only time to date where the same legal issue has arrived at the EFTA Court both via the advisory opinion procedure and as infringement proceedings brought by ESA against an EFTA State.[20] The case revolved around the legality of an authorisation scheme Iceland had in place for the import of fresh meat. Iceland had maintained this in force even after the entry into force of the decisions of the EEA Joint Committee incorporating the new veterinary acquis into the EEA Agreement. The EFTA Court held this to be a veterinary check which was not permitted by the applicable directive and that Iceland could neither rely on these products being outside the product scope as defined in Article 8 EEA nor the EEA not covering the EU's agricultural policy. These judgments demonstrate clearly that once legislation has been incorporated into the EEA Agreement, it is only in exceptional cases that the EFTA Court will deviate from homogeneity and interpret it differently from the CJEU.

Finally, I believe the *Telenor* case is worth mentioning.[21] ESA had fined Telenor almost €112 million for abusing its dominant position in breach of Article 54 EEA. The company brought an action for annulment against that decision. The abuse ESA had identified was a margin squeeze in the wholesale market for access to and handling of data on mobile networks. The case was the most voluminous ever dealt with by the EFTA Court. Following an extensive examination, the Court upheld ESA's

[18] Case E-10/19 *Bergbahn Aktiengesellschaft*, judgment of 22 December 2020; Case E-10/20 *ADCADA Immobilien AG PCC*, judgment of 18 June 2021.

[19] Case E-5/19 *Criminal Proceedings against F and G*, judgment of 4 February 2020.

[20] Case E-17/15 *Ferskar kjötvörur* [2016] EFTA Ct Rep 4 and Joined Cases E-2/17 and E-3/17 *ESA v Iceland* [2017] EFTA Ct Rep 727.

[21] Case E-12/20 *Telenor v ESA*, judgment of 5 May 2022.

decision on all accounts. The Court followed its previous judgment in *Posten Norge*,[22] emphasising the importance of robust judicial review and that ESA could not be considered to have any margin of discretion in its assessment of complex economic issues other than that which flows from the limitations inherent in a legality review such as that performed by the Court under Article 36 SCA.

Turning to the contents of this anniversary publication, I am delighted to note that we have been fortunate enough to receive contributions from both the President of the Court of Justice of the European Union, Koen Lenaerts, and the President of the General Court, Marc van der Woude. Interestingly, they both examine the CJEU's Opinion 1/91,[23] which rejected the original draft of the EEA Agreement as it considered the creation of the EEA Court incompatible with Community law and thus paved the way for the creation of the EFTA Court. There is even a further contribution on this groundbreaking opinion from Niilo Jääskinen, a judge at the CJEU, who recounts his experience leading up to this opinion as he was an official at the Finnish Ministry of Justice at the time. His chapter gives a unique perspective on the background which led to the proposed establishment of the EEA Court and its subsequent demise.

Of the other contributions, I would like to highlight the chapter by Thérèse Blanchet, Secretary-General of the Council, in which she explores whether using the surveillance mechanism of the EEA – ie, ESA and the EFTA Court – could help the EFTA States, as Schengen associates, to deepen their cooperation with the EU in matters relating to justice and home affairs. I, for one, find these ideas fully worth seriously considering. Should there not be an appetite for such a relatively extensive reform, a less ambitious option would be to at least extend the jurisdiction of the EFTA Court to also cover the Schengen *acquis* and other bilateral agreements the EFTA States have concluded with the EU, such as the Surrender Agreement, which replicates the European Arrest Warrant. It should be highlighted that, as a matter of EU law, there is no distinction made between these various agreements; they form a whole and constitute part of the privileged relationship between the EFTA States and the EU, which I discussed above.

The longevity of the EEA Agreement and the fact that it has proven as resilient, as practice over the last three decades has shown, has perhaps been a surprise to some. In 1994, Professor Marise Cremona wrote an article in the *European Law Review* about the Byzantine complexity of the EEA in which she was sceptical about its ability to achieve the objective of establishing a dynamic and homogeneous EEA as well as its longer-term prospects.[24] Therefore, it is particularly fascinating to read her re-appraisal of the EEA Agreement in her outstanding contribution to this publication, entitled 'Dynamism, Homogeneity and Byzantine Structures – A Reassessment of Integration in the EEA'.

In his thought-provoking book *What's Left of the Law of Integration?*, Julio Baquero Cruz wonders whether the fact that there are generations that have only

[22] Case E-15/10 *Posten Norge v ESA* [2012] EFTA Ct Rep 246.

[23] Opinion 1/91 ECLI:EU:C:1991:490.

[24] M Cremona, 'The "Dynamic and Homogeneous" EEA: Byzantine Structures and Variable Geometry' (1994) 19 *European Law Review* 508.

known peace has caused the impetus for European integration to be forgotten.[25] Since this book was published in 2018, events have very sadly revealed to us that war has most definitely not left the European continent. Moreover, the situation worldwide remains extremely uncertain in the near future. Even if the EEA Agreement and the EFTA States might not be at the heart of European integration, they make a valuable contribution to it and most importantly share with the EU and its Member States a commitment to peace, democracy, human rights and the rule of law. These fundamentals and a rule-based international order are crucial to securing a peaceful future.

[25] J Baquero Cruz, *What's Left of the Law of Integration? Decay and Resistance in European Union Law* (Oxford, Oxford University Press, 2018) ch 2.

Contents

THE INTERPRETATION AND APPLICATION OF INTERNAL MARKET LAW

EEA AGREEMENT AND FUNDAMENTAL RIGHTS

List of Contributors

Arnfinn Bårdsen – Vice-President of the European Court of Human Rights

Thérèse Blanchet – Secretary-General of the Council of the European Union

Benedikt Bogason – President of the Supreme Court of Iceland

Þorgeir Örlygsson – Former President of the Supreme Court of Iceland, former judge at EFTA Court

Graham Butler – Full Professor of Law, University of Southern Denmark

Marise Cremona – Emeritus Professor, European University Institute, Florence

Ólafur Jóhannes Einarsson – Registrar at the EFTA Court

Hilde K. Ellingsen – Partner, Lund & Co law firm and Associate Professor II at the University of Oslo

Karin Fløistad – Partner, Simonsen Vogt Wiig AS law firm

Halvard Haukeland Fredriksen – Professor and Vice Dean at the Faculty of Law, Co-Director of CENTENOL, University of Bergen

Christian NK Franklin – Professor at the Faculty of Law, Director of CENTENOL, University of Bergen

Bernd Hammermann – Judge at the EFTA Court

Kristín Haraldsdóttir – Director of the Judicial Administration, Iceland

Hilmar Hoch – President of the Constitutional Court of Liechtenstein

Páll Hreinsson – President of the EFTA Court

Niilo Jääskinen – Judge at the Court of Justice of the European Union

Koen Lenaerts – President of the Court of Justice of the European Union and Professor of European Union Law, Leuven University

Stanislas Adam – Legal secretary at the Court of Justice of the European Union and Professor of European Union Law, Ghent University (Ghent European Law Institute)

Gjermund Mathisen – Partner, Kvale law firm

Ola Mestad – Professor dr. juris, University of Oslo and ad-hoc judge at the EFTA Court

Gunnar Thor Pétursson – Dean and Professor of Law, School of Law, Reykjavik University, Iceland and ad-hoc judge at the EFTA Court

Michael Reiertsen – Judge at the EFTA Court

Ole-Andreas Rognstad – Professor at the Faculty of Law, Department of Private Law/ Centre for European Law, University of Oslo

Albert Sanchez-Graells – Professor of Economic Law, University of Bristol Law School

Romina Schobel – Deputy Director, EEA Coordination Unit of the Government of the Principality of Liechtenstein

Andrea Entner-Koch – Director, EEA Coordination Unit of the Government of the Principality of Liechtenstein

Wilhelm Ungerank – Presiding Judge at the Fürstliches Obergericht (Princely Court of Appeal)

Marc van der Woude – President of the General Court of the European Union

Joseph H. H. Weiler – Professor and holder of the European Union Jean Monnet Chair at New York University School of Law

Andreas P. Müller – Research assistant and doctoral candidate at Heinrich-Heine-University Düsseldorf

Toril Marie Øie – President of the Supreme Court of Norway

Henrik Bull – Judge at the Supreme Court of Norway, former judge at the EFTA Court

Judicial Architecture of the EEA Agreement: Past, Present and Future

1

The Foundations of the EFTA Court Looking Back at the Two EEA Opinions of the Court of Justice*

KOEN LENAERTS AND STANISLAS ADAM

WE ARE HONOURED to contribute to the anniversary that the EFTA Court celebrates this year. The almost 30 years of coexistence with the Court of Justice on the Kirchberg Plateau[1] have been marked by mutual respect and friendship. Our two Courts do not only neighbour one another geographically. That proximity also relates to the very substance of our judicial competences, as the EFTA Court primarily applies and interprets rules that are substantially identical to EU rules and that therefore also come within the jurisdiction of the Court of Justice. This cross-fertilisation goes far beyond those rules, as illustrated by the EFTA Court's case law on *locus standi* in actions for annulment against decisions of the EFTA Surveillance Authority concerning state aid,[2] on the right to access documents[3] or, to a certain extent, on the concept of a 'court or tribunal' entitled to request 'Advisory Opinions' from the EFTA Court.[4]

Celebrating an anniversary can be an occasion to leaf through a photo album with family and friends, containing pictures of the jubilee at different ages or of the future parents in the period preceding the birth of their child. The first pages of the EFTA Court's album would unmistakably have to display the two famous 'EEA' Opinions of

* All opinions expressed herein are personal to the authors.

[1] When it started to operate on 1 January 1994, the EFTA Court had its seat in Geneva. It moved to Luxembourg on 1 September 1996.

[2] See EFTA Court, judgment of 19 June 2003, E-2/02 *Technologien Bau- und Wirtschaftsberatung GmbH and Bellona Foundation v ESA*, [2003] EFTA Ct Rep 52, paras 38 and 39.

[3] See EFTA Court, judgment of 21 December 2012, E-14/11 *DB Schenker v EFTA Surveillance Authority*, [2012] EFTA Ct Rep 1178.

[4] See Art 34 of the Agreement between the EFTA States on the Establishment of a Surveillance Authority and a Court of Justice (hereinafter the 'Surveillance and Court Agreement'). The EFTA Court drew inspiration in that respect from the interpretation of the same term used in the context of the reference for a preliminary ruling governed by Art 267 TFEU. See EFTA Court, judgment of 16 December 1994, E-1/94, *Restamark*, [1994–95] EFTA Ct Rep 15, paras 24 et seq. See also EFTA Court, judgment of 16 June 1995, E-8/94 and E-9/94, *Mattel and Lego*, [1994–95] EFTA Ct Rep 113; K Lenaerts, 'On Judicial Independence and the Quest for National, Supranational and Transnational Justice', in G Selvik,

the Court of Justice.[5] They are indeed key to grasping the DNA of the EFTA Court and, by extension, that of the European Economic Area (EEA). Thus, in section I, we shall highlight the decisive influence that the Court of Justice has had through both Opinions on the inception of the EFTA Court as the judicial body ultimately responsible for the proper application of the EEA Agreement and internal market legislation in the EFTA EEA States. The present anniversary also gives the opportunity, in section II, to pay tribute to those Opinions for the lasting influence they have had on the EU's constitutional fabric itself.

I. FROM A 'NO' TO A CONDITIONAL 'YES': OPINIONS 1/91 AND 1/92 AS STEPPING STONES OF THE EEA AND ITS SYSTEM OF JUDICIAL SUPERVISION

A. The Objective of Creating a 'Dynamic and Homogeneous' EEA

The EEA Agreement was an alternative to EU membership for the states that wished to remain EFTA members, while benefiting from the ever-growing common, and subsequently internal, market. The objective was to make a large part of the Community's (now Union's) *acquis* on the internal market applicable in these states, thus forming a new area of cooperation with the Member States. The European states negotiating the EEA wished to establish a 'dynamic and homogeneous' area, based on 'common rules and equal conditions of competition' for economic operators.[6] That dynamic nature meant, in essence, that EU internal market rules[7] postdating the entry into force of the agreement would have to be made applicable in the participating EFTA States, as and when they were adopted. Homogeneity commands 'uniform interpretation and application of th[e EEA Agreement] and those provisions of [EU law] which

M-J Clifton, T Haas, L Lourenço and K Schwiesow (eds), *The Art of Judicial Reasoning: Festschrift in Honour of Carl Baudenbacher* (Cham, Springer, 2019) 160. However, this convergence is relative. In its judgment in *Scanteam*, the EFTA Court thus expressly departed from the examination of 'independence' of a referring body reflected in the judgment of the Court of Justice of 21 January 2020, *Banco de Santander* (C-274/14, EU:C:2020:17), referring in particular to the 'important role played by administrative appeal boards in the EFTA States'. See EFTA Court, judgment of 16 July 2020, E-8/19, *Scanteam AS v Norwegian Government*, paras 44–54.

[5] Opinion 1/91 (First Opinion on the EEA Agreement) of 14 December 1991 (EU:C:1991:490) and Opinion 1/92 (Second Opinion on the EEA Agreement) of 10 April 1992 (EU:C:1992:189). On these opinions, see: J Auvret-Finck, 'Les avis 1/91 et 1/92 relatifs au projet d'accord sur l'Espace économique européen' (1993) 38 *Cahiers de droit européen* 38–59; D Simon and A Rigaux, 'L'avis de la Cour de justice sur le projet d'accord CEE/AELE portant création de l'Espace économique européen (EEE)' (1992) *Europe* 1; M-A Gaudissart, 'La portée des avis 1/91 et 1/92 de la Cour de justice des Communautés européennes relatifs à la création de l'Espace Economique Européen. Entre autonomie et homogénéité : l'ordre juridique communautaire en péril' (1992) *Revue du marché unique Européen* 121–36; J Boulouis, 'Les avis de la Cour de justice des Communautés sur la compatibilité avec le traité CEE du projet d'accord créant l'espace économique européen' (1992) *Revue trimestrielle de droit européen* 457–63; HG Schermers, 'Comment. ECJ, Opinion 1/91, 14 December 1991; ECJ, Opinion 1/92, 10 April 1992' [1992] *CML Rev* 991–1009; N Burrows, 'The Second EEA Opinion' (1993) *EL Rev* 63–66; TC Hartley, 'The European Court and the EEA, (1992) 41 *ICLQ* 841–48; R Barents, 'The Court of Justice and the EEA-Agreement: Between Constitutional Values and Political Realities' in J Stuyck and A Looijestij-Clearie (eds), *The European Economic Area EC-EFTA: Institutional Aspects and Financial Services* (Deventer, Kluwer, 1994) 57–71.

[6] Preamble to the EEA Agreement, fourth recital.

[7] This reference to rules is deliberate, as it indicates from the outset that 'the EEA Agreement goes beyond simply taking over EC legislation'. See T van Stiphout, 'Homogeneity vs Decision-Making Autonomy in the EEA Agreement' (2007) 9(3) *European Journal of Law Reform* 431, 432.

are substantially reproduced in th[at] Agreement[,] to arrive at an equal treatment of individuals and economic operators as regards the four freedoms and the conditions of competition'.[8] In other words, that uniformity aims to ensure that individuals and economic operators are treated in the same manner regardless of whether EU law or EEA rules are applied.[9]

As the preamble to the EEA Agreement indicates, such objectives could only be achieved through 'adequate means of enforcement including at the judicial level'. However, a major legal difficulty arose in this respect from the need to establish a system of judicial supervision that would at the same time ensure homogeneity in an effective manner and not undermine the autonomy of the (then) Community legal order. That autonomy could already be inferred at that time, albeit somewhat embryonically, from several landmark judgments and opinions of the Court of Justice emphasising the *sui generis* nature of the Community (now the EU) as a self-referential system of norms forming an integral part of the legal orders of the Member States, whilst being distinct from the international legal order.[10] Moreover, it appeared from one of the first opinions of the Court of Justice on an envisaged international agreement[11] that international commitments of the Union cannot undermine the essential mission conferred upon it by the Treaties.[12]

However, the EFTA States which negotiated the EEA did not want the Court of Justice to become the supreme judicial authority on EEA matters, to which their political and judicial bodies would be subject.[13]

B. The 'EEA Court Model' Rejected in Opinion 1/91 as Undermining the Autonomy of the EU Legal Order

The first draft EEA Agreement therefore envisaged the setting up of a specific court with jurisdiction over the whole EEA: the EEA Court, which would be ultimately

[8] See the fifteenth recital of the EEA Agreement. However, that homogeneity does not guarantee simultaneous application of internal market legislation in EFTA EEA States as it is for the EEA Joint Committee to implement such legislation in the EEA by adopting amendments to the Annexes and Protocols to the EEA Agreement. See EFTA Court, Advisory Opinion of 1 April 1998, E-3/97, *Jæger*, [1998] EFTA Ct Rep 1, para 30.

[9] S Norberg et al, *The European Economic Area: EEA Law: A Commentary on the EEA Agreement* (Stockholm, Fritzes, 1993) 104.

[10] See, in particular, the judgments of 5 February 1963, 26/62, *Van Gend & Loos* (EU:C:1963:1); of 15 July 1964; 6/64, *Costa* (EU:C:1964:66) at 594; and of 13 November 1964; 90/63 and 91/63, *Commission v Luxembourg and Belgium* (EU:C:1964:80), at 631. The Court refused in the latter judgment that Member States could invoke *exceptio non adimpleti contractus* to justify a failure to fulfil obligations resulting from Community (now Union) law. For an in-depth study of the history and scope of the autonomous EU legal order, see K Lenaerts, JA Gutierrez-Fons and S Adam, 'Exploring the Autonomy of the European Union Legal Order' (2021) 8(1) *ZaöRV* 47–87.

[11] That procedure is now set out in Art 218(11) TFEU.

[12] Opinion 1/76 (Agreement on the Establishment of a European Laying-up Fund for Inland Waterway Vessels) of 26 April 1977 (EU:C:1977:63), para 10. On the relevance of this Opinion for the scope of that autonomy, in particular the aspect of it protecting the 'essential character of the powers' that the Treaties confer upon the EU institutions, see S Adam, *La procédure d'avis devant la Cour de justice de l'Union européenne* (Brussels, Bruylant, 2011) 74 and 75.

[13] However, commitment to respect the relevant case law of the Court of Justice delivered prior to the date of signature of the EEA Agreement was never an issue, even under the first draft EEA Agreement. See Opinion 1/91 (n 5) para 8; and Art 6 of the EEA Agreement.

responsible for upholding homogeneity within the EEA. The EEA Court would have had jurisdiction to settle disputes between the Contracting Parties, to decide on actions concerning the surveillance procedure regarding the EFTA States and, in the field of competition, on appeals concerning decisions taken by the EFTA Surveillance Authority.[14]

In Opinion 1/91, the Court of Justice rejected this institutional model, which threatened the very foundations of Community integration and the autonomy of its legal order.[15] That model, coupled with the cardinal objective of homogeneity within the EEA, entailed the risk of the Court of Justice being subordinated, in its interpretation of Community law shared within the EEA, to the interpretations given to those same rules by the EEA Court.

That conclusion resulted from the combined effects of the key features of that draft.

The first part of the Opinion explains why the identical wording and content of provisions of EU law and of EEA law was not such as to ensure homogeneity. This was due to the distinct objectives pursued by the EU and by the EEA, and the distinct legal nature of those organisations.[16] The EEA merely aims at applying the rules on free trade and competition in economic and commercial relations.[17] By contrast, in the context of the Communities (now the Union), the provisions of the Treaties on free movement and competition are only means to attain the broader objectives of the economic integration within the internal market, and thus 'to contribute … to making concrete progress towards European unity'.[18] Moreover, unlike the Union, which is a new legal order distinct from the international legal order and which is based on the Treaties forming its 'constitutional charter', the EEA is 'established on the basis of an international treaty which, essentially, merely creates rights and obligations as between the Contracting Parties' and to which no sovereign powers were transferred.[19] However, it is important to observe here that these differences have not precluded the EFTA Court from adopting purposive interpretations of the EEA Agreement, such as the requirement for EFTA States to compensate damage caused to an individual by the incorrect implementation of a directive forming part of EEA law.[20]

The Court of Justice explained against that background that a large body of EEA rules would be juxtaposed to identically worded EU rules, 'which govern economic

[14] Opinion 1/91 (n 5) para 6. The draft also provided the *possibility* for the EFTA States to authorise their courts and tribunals to ask the Court of Justice for the interpretation of the agreement (Protocol 34).

[15] ibid para 71.

[16] ibid para 22.

[17] ibid para 15. That is of course without prejudice to the close cooperation developed between the EU and EFTA States beyond those (purely) economic matters, but on the basis of separate (mostly bilateral) agreements. Thus, participation of the Republic of Iceland in the Schengen *acquis* led the Court to consider that the situation of a citizen of that latter state moving to a Member State is 'objectively comparable with that of an EU citizen to whom, in accordance with Article 3(2) TEU, the Union offers an area of freedom, security and justice without internal frontiers, in which the free movement of persons is ensured'. Judgment of 2 April 2020, C-897/19 PPU *Ruska Federacija*, ECLI:EU:C:2020:262, para 58.

[18] Opinion 1/91 (n 5) paras 16–18.

[19] ibid paras 20 and 21.

[20] EFTA Court, Advisory Opinion of 2 April 1998, E-9/97 *Sveinbjörnsdóttir*, [1998] EFTA Ct Rep 95, paras 59–62. The Court reached this outcome after observing that the EEA Agreement is an 'international treaty *sui generis* which contains a distinct legal order of its own' (para 59).

and trading relations within the [EU] and [are], for the most part, fundamental provisions of the [EU] legal order'.[21] That overlap would inevitably increase over time as a result of the incorporation of new internal market EU secondary law into EEA law following the date of signature of the EEA Agreement. The EEA Court would thus have had jurisdiction to indirectly interpret a very significant body of EU law. Although that court would have had to pursue the objective of homogeneity within the EEA, the draft agreement contained no guarantee that it would comply with judgments of the Court of Justice delivered *after* signature of the agreement.[22] Moreover, whilst the draft agreement guaranteed respect of case law of the Court of Justice on EU rules corresponding to EEA rules, given *prior* to that signature, that guarantee did not unquestionably cover case law setting out the essential principles of primacy and direct effect.[23]

As a result, the Court considered not only that homogeneity could not be achieved within the EEA, but also that the system of judicial supervision envisaged was such as to 'restrict' possible interpretations of EU law corresponding to EEA law. According to the *pacta sunt servanda* principle, decisions of the EEA Court would have been binding for the EU institutions in general and for the Court of Justice in particular.[24] Thus, 'the … objective of ensuring homogeneity of the law throughout the EEA w[ould] determine not only the interpretation of the rules of the agreement itself but also the interpretation of the corresponding rules of [EU] law'.[25] That system was therefore such as to undermine the role of the Court of Justice in ensuring observance of the law in the interpretation and application of the Treaties, and hence to undermine the 'very foundations of the [Union]'.[26] In view of the significant differences in the objectives pursued by the EEA and by the EU, the fact that members of the Court of Justice would also be sitting on the envisaged EEA Court did not resolve the autonomy issue. On the contrary, a problem of judicial independence may have arisen had the judges concerned been called upon to tackle questions when sitting in cases brought before the Court of Justice after having taken part in determining those same questions as members of the EEA Court.[27]

The competence of the EEA Court to interpret the concept of 'Contracting Party' posed another threat to autonomy. The draft EEA Agreement provided that, on the EU side, that concept referred to the Union and the Member States, or the Union, or the Member States, depending on the provision of EEA law at issue and the respective competences of the EU and the Member States as a result of the Treaties. Consequently, the EEA Court, interpreting the concept of 'Contracting Party', would have ruled indirectly on the respective competences of the EU and of its Member States. This was likely to adversely affect the allocation of responsibilities defined

[21] Opinion 1/91 (n 5) paras 41–42.
[22] ibid para 26.
[23] ibid para 27.
[24] ibid para 39.
[25] ibid para 45.
[26] ibid para 46. The provision corresponding to Art 19(1) TEU was, at the material time, Art 164 of the EEC Treaty.
[27] Opinion 1/91 (n 5) para 52.

in the Treaties and to disregard the exclusive jurisdiction of the Court of Justice to decide on such issues.[28]

C. Overcoming the Obstacles: The EFTA Court and the 'Conditional' Compatibility of the Second Draft EEA Agreement

Both objections were addressed in a second draft EEA Agreement.

Giving the Court of Justice the role of an EEA 'supreme court' remained a non-starter for many negotiating parties. In order to avoid the pitfalls highlighted in Opinion 1/91, the project of a Court covering the whole of the EEA was abandoned in favour of an EFTA Court, in parallel to the Court of Justice, whose activity would be limited to the EFTA EEA States. That newly established court formed part of what is commonly referred to as the EEA's 'Two-Pillar Structure'.[29] The latter is characterised by a series of 'elaborate mechanisms'[30] designed to ensure the homogeneous interpretation and application of EEA law, whilst safeguarding the EFTA States' decision-making autonomy.[31] Within the EFTA pillar of the EEA, an EFTA Surveillance Authority was created, in charge of reviewing the implementation and application of the substantive provisions of EEA law in the EFTA EEA States and taking action against them in case of infringement.[32] In essence, that Authority exercises powers comparable to those of the European Commission in the EU pillar. The EFTA Court was granted jurisdiction to decide on infringement actions brought by the EFTA Surveillance Authority against EFTA States with regard to the implementation, application or interpretation of EEA legal rules, to settle disputes between two or more EFTA States, to give advisory opinions to courts in EFTA States on the interpretation of EEA rules, and to decide on appeals concerning decisions taken by the EFTA Surveillance Authority in the field of competition.[33] Moreover, the EEA Joint Committee was entrusted with the task of keeping 'under constant review the development of the case law of the Court of Justice … and the EFTA Court' and striving to settle disputes between the Contracting Parties concerning divergences in the interpretation of EEA law.[34]

That two-pillar structure automatically resolved the issue of a court external to the EU ruling on issues of competence of the EU and its Member States. A more delicate issue was whether the Joint Committee's competences could be exercised in a manner compatible with the objection raised in Opinion 1/91 concerning external limitations on autonomous interpretations of EU law by the Court of Justice.

[28] ibid paras 32–36.

[29] See Legal Notes by the EFTA Secretariat on the EEA Agreement – The Two-Pillar Structure – Adaptation Texts, *EFTA Bulletin*, June 2019.

[30] This expression was used by the EFTA Court itself. See EFTA Court, *Sveinbjörnsdóttir* (n 20) para 54.

[31] Van Stiphout (n 7) 433. This decision-making autonomy also explains why the EEA Agreement provides some room for negotiation at the EEA *decision-making* phase, allowing in particular EFTA States to negotiate some derogations to the EU legislation at issue if they consider, for example, that their specific concerns expressed were insufficiently taken into account in the decision-shaping phase at EU level (at 437).

[32] Article 109(1) of the EEA Agreement.

[33] Article 108(2) of the EEA Agreement and Art 34 of the Surveillance and Court Agreement.

[34] Article 105(2) of the EEA Agreement.

In Opinion 1/92, the Court of Justice observed that this new draft would not remove all risk of undermining the autonomy of the EU legal order if the Joint Committee were free to disregard the judgments of the Court of Justice, in the name of the objective of homogeneity.[35] However, the negotiation material submitted to the Court included a 'procès-verbal agréé ad article 105', which made clear that decisions taken by the Joint Committee on the basis of that provision to ensure homogeneous interpretation of EEA law could not affect the case law of the Court of Justice.[36] In the Court's view, this *procès-verbal* constituted an 'essential safeguard' for the autonomy of the Union's legal order.[37] The principle it contains therefore had to be *binding* on the Contracting Parties.[38] The Court also pointed to the fact that the revised draft EEA Agreement envisaged the situation where the Joint Committee has not succeeded in preserving the homogeneous interpretation of the EEA Agreement within two months after being alerted of a difference in the case law of the two Courts.[39] In that situation, the provision on dispute settlement may be applied.[40] If the dispute concerns the interpretation of provisions of EEA law that are identical in substance to corresponding rules of EU law, the EEA Joint Committee endeavours to settle it within three months. Failing such settlement, the Contracting Parties to the dispute may agree to request the Court of Justice to give a ruling on the interpretation of the relevant rules.[41] Although the *procès-verbal* did not formally concern that dispute settlement procedure, the principle set out in the *procès-verbal* necessarily applies to the dispute settlement procedure. This can be inferred from the express link made between Article 105(3) of the EEA Agreement and that procedure.[42] Moreover, this was the only interpretation consistent with the jurisdiction to interpret the relevant rules conferred on the Court of Justice by Article 111(3).[43]

Protocol 48 to the EEA Agreement, 'concerning Articles 105 and 111', implements those principles by stating in unambiguous – and indeed binding – terms that decisions taken by the EEA Joint Committee under those provisions 'may not affect the case law of the Court of Justice'.[44] However, this should not overshadow the importance of informal 'judicial dialogue' between the EU Courts and the EFTA Court to ensure legal homogeneity within the EEA.[45]

From a procedural point of view, this part of Opinion 1/92 was innovative in two respects.

[35] See Opinion 1/92 (n 5) paras 22 and 27.

[36] ibid para 6.

[37] ibid para 24.

[38] ibid para 25.

[39] Article 105(3) of the EEA Agreement.

[40] ibid Art 111.

[41] ibid Art 111(3). This was not the first time that an international agreement concluded by the EU provided for the possibility to refer a dispute between the Contracting Parties to the Court of Justice. See, for example, Art 25(2) of the Agreement establishing an Association between the European Economic Community and Turkey (English version available at [1977] OJ L361/29).

[42] Opinion 1/92 (n 5) paras 28 and 29.

[43] ibid para 30.

[44] [1994] OJ L1/218.

[45] See also van Stiphout (n 7) 444.

The first innovation relates to the fact that the *procès-verbal* was taken into account in the compatibility analysis, although it was formally outside the draft agreement as negotiated and its binding nature was not beyond doubt.[46] This illustrates the broad interpretation of the terms 'agreement envisaged' in what is now Article 218(11) of the Treaty on the Functioning of the European Union (TFEU). Through that broad interpretation, the Court of Justice promotes that procedure's objective of preventing difficulties – notably at a diplomatic level – which would result from declaring an agreement incompatible with the Treaties after its conclusion by the Union.[47]

A second innovation was the conditional compatibility of the draft EEA Agreement, reflected in the first paragraph of the operative part of Opinion 1/92.[48] This element paved the way for the methodological approach later used, for example, in the landmark Opinion 1/17 on the compatibility of the proposed Investor-State Dispute Settlement Mechanism between the EU and Canada, envisaged in the draft 'Comprehensive Economic and Trade Agreement' (CETA), with (inter alia) the autonomy of the EU legal order and the fundamental right of access to an independent tribunal.[49] The Court considered in that Opinion that the CETA could not be interpreted as 'permitting the Union to consent to decisions on interpretation of the CETA Joint Committee that would produce effects on the handling of disputes that have been dealt with or are pending' before the CETA Tribunal and Appellate Tribunal, as that would be incompatible with the right to an effective remedy enshrined in Article 47 of the Charter.[50] Opinion 1/92 illustrates the Court's readiness to *interpret* a draft agreement submitted to it, to the extent possible, in a manner that does not call into question its compatibility with EU primary law. This echoes a settled interpretative principle in the case law of the Court of Justice concerning the review of validity of EU acts.[51] Both Opinions 1/92 and 1/17 therefore also shed light on how guidance can be offered in an opinion of the Court of Justice as to the way in which an agreement is to be interpreted – and thus implemented – in order to fit into the EU constitutional fabric.[52]

[46] The Court thus went a step further compared to its first opinion pursuant to what is now Art 218(11) TFEU, where it considered that that provision refers to the concept of agreement 'in a general sense to indicate any undertaking entered into by entities subject to international law *which has binding force*, whatever its formal designation' (Opinion 1/75 (OECD Understanding on a Local Cost Standard) of 11 November 1975 (EU:C:1975:145), at 1360). However, Opinion 1/92 does not really depart from that approach, considering the Court's emphasis that its finding of compatibility was subject to the principle contained in the *procès-verbal* being binding for the Contracting Parties.

[47] See, for other illustrations of that broad interpretation of the term 'agreement envisaged', Opinion 2/94 (Accession of the Community to the ECHR) of 28 March 1996 (EU:C:1996:140), paras 7–12; and Opinion 1/13 (Accession of Third States to the Hague Convention) of 14 October 2014 (EU:C:2014:2303), paras 37–42. See also S Adam, 'L'examen de l'admissibilité des demandes d'avis, aux confins de l'effectivité du contrôle préventif et de l'équilibre institutionnel' (2015) 1 *Revue des affaires européennes*, 19, 20–24.

[48] In this paragraph, the Court concludes that the envisaged dispute settlement mechanism did not alter the autonomous legal order 'as long as the principle that decisions taken by the Joint Committee are not to affect the case law of the Court of Justice [would be] laid down in a form binding on the Contracting Parties'.

[49] Opinion 1/17 (EU-Canada CET Agreement), of 30 April 2019 (EU:C:2019:341) (para 237).

[50] ibid para 237.

[51] See, for example, judgment of 2 February 2021, *Consob*, C-481/19 (EU:C:2021:84), para 50 and the case law cited therein.

[52] See, to that effect, M Cremona, 'The Opinion Procedure under Article 218(11) TFEU: Reflections in the Light of Opinion 1/17' (2020) *Europe and the World, Special Issue: Reflections on Opinion 1/17 (CETA)*, available at: www.scienceopen.com/collection/Reflections-on-Opinion-1-17, 11.

In the last part of Opinion 1/92, the Court of Justice verified that the draft agreement did not alter the nature of the powers conferred upon it, which is another important aspect of autonomy, as stated above.[53] Since the various means of access to the Court of Justice provided for in the draft agreement did not distort the binding nature of its judgments, the Court declared that the second draft EEA Agreement was compatible with the Treaties. In particular, the new version of Protocol 34 thereto made it clear that the EFTA EEA States may authorise their courts to ask the Court of Justice to decide on a question of interpretation of EEA law corresponding to an EU rule. That contrasts with the former version of the agreement, which provided for the competence of the Court of Justice to 'express itself' on the interpretation of a provision of the agreement. In Opinion 1/91, the Court had found it incompatible with its judicial mission under the Treaties that the answers which it would give to the courts and tribunals in the EFTA States would be purely advisory.[54]

II. THE OPINIONS' LEGACY FOR THE EEA AND EU LEGAL ORDERS

A. Fostering the Homogeneous Interpretation and Application of EEA Law

As the two EEA Opinions themselves suggest, the autonomy of EU law implies that interpretations of the EEA Agreement or, more generally, of EEA rules corresponding to EU rules by the EFTA Court cannot be binding on the Court of Justice. However, the EEA Agreement is EU law, which means that the Court of Justice has jurisdiction to interpret it. Moreover, as the Agreement forms part of the EU legal order, the Court of Justice must respect and promote the overriding homogeneity objective that that Agreement pursues.[55]

The Court of Justice's contribution to that objective of homogeneity, which admittedly remains a 'constant challenge' within the EEA,[56] must be emphasised. It has observed that a number of provisions in the EEA Agreement aim to ensure that the interpretation of that Agreement is 'as uniform as possible throughout the EEA', so that 'the internal market established within the European Union is extended to the EFTA States'.[57] This ensures that the rules of the EEA Agreement which are identical in substance to those of the Treaties – ranging from EU antitrust rules to fundamental freedoms of the internal market – are interpreted uniformly within the Member States. This principle was established in the *Ospelt* judgment, which concerned a restriction on the free movement of capital as a result of the acquisition of agricultural land being made subject to the grant of prior administrative authorisation.[58] It has been

[53] See the case law cited in n 10 and n 2.

[54] Opinion 1/91 (n 5) para 61; and Opinion 1/92 (n 5) para 15.

[55] C Baudenbacher, 'The EFTA Court and Court of Justice of the European Union: Coming in Parts But Winning Together' in A Rosas and E Levits (eds), *The Court of Justice and the Construction of Europe: Analyses and Perspectives on Sixty Years of Case-Law* (The Hague, TMC Asser Press, 2012) 183, 187.

[56] See, to that effect, the statement made by Bernd Hammermann at the ceremony during which he took his oath as a judge of the EFTA Court on 9 April 2018 (available at: www.efta.int/EEA/news/New-EFTA-Court-Judge-constant-challenge-maintain-homogeneity-European-law-throughout-EEA-508046).

[57] Judgment in *Ruska Federacija* (n 17) para 50.

[58] Judgment of 23 September 2003, C-452/01, *Ospelt and Schlössle Weissenberg* (EU:C:2003:493), para 29.

confirmed on numerous occasions.[59] The Court of Justice thus fully endorses and promotes the homogeneity objective of the EEA Agreement, which is justified by a special relationship with the EFTA EEA States 'based on proximity, long-standing common values and European identity'.[60] It explains also why the Court of Justice has from time to time expressly referred to the EFTA Court's case law when interpreting provisions of EEA law.[61] The Court of Justice perceives the EFTA Court as an 'important and valued colleague' whose role and influence are unquestionably not limited to the national courts of the EFTA States.[62]

As already mentioned in the introduction, the EFTA Court, for its part, also promotes this homogeneity objective. This may explain, for example, why the EFTA Court has never made any distinction in its case law between the judgments of the Court of Justice delivered *before* or *after* signature of the EEA Agreement, thus *de facto* addressing a concern of the Court of Justice expressed in Opinion 1/91.[63]

However, there could be a price to pay for legal autonomy within the two pillars: the risk of divergences in the interpretation of EEA rules cannot be excluded. The 'Icesave' case, which concerned the scope of the obligations bearing on EFTA States as a result of Directive 94/19/EC of the European Parliament and of the Council, of 30 May 1994, on deposit-guarantee schemes,[64] is worth mentioning in this respect. At the material time, that directive required, in particular, the setting up of deposit-guarantee schemes covering up to ECU 20,000 in the event of deposits being unavailable.[65] ESA initiated proceedings before the EFTA Court against Iceland, as it refused to cover deposits held with branches of an Icelandic bank in two Member States following the collapse of that bank. This was in sharp contrast with measures whereby the Icelandic State had covered deposits of Icelandic savers as a result of insufficiencies of the deposit-guarantee schemes. In its judgment,[66] the EFTA Court upheld

[59] See, for example, the judgments of 11 June 2009, C-521/07, *Commission v The Netherlands* (EU:C:2009:360), para 32, of 28 October 2010; C-72/09, *Établissements Rimbaud* (EU:C:2010:645), para 20, and of 11 November 2021; C-819/19, *Stichting Cartel Compensation and Equilib Netherlands* (EU:C:2021:904), para 70.

[60] Judgment in *Ruska Federacija* (n 17) para 50.

[61] See, for example, the judgments of 26 April 2007, C-348/04, *Boehringer Ingelheim and Others* (EU:C:2007:249) para 38, referring to the EFTA Court's judgment of 8 July 2003 in Case E-3/02 *Paranova v Merck* [2003] EFTA Ct Rep 101 (paras 41–45), concerning protection of trade marks in the context of the repackaging of pharmaceutical products, and of 24 October 2013, C-22/12, *Haasová* (EU:C:2013:692), para 47, referring to the EFTA Court's judgment of 20 June 2008 in Case E-8/07 *Celina Nguyen v The Norwegian State* [2008] EFTA Ct Rep 224 (paras 26 and 27), concerning compulsory insurance against civil liability in respect of the use of motor vehicles. See also the earlier examples given by van Stiphout (n 7) 445–46.

[62] E Sharpston and M-J Clifton, 'Two EEA Courts: Unequal Balance or Fruitful Partnership?' in EFTA Court (ed), *Judicial Protection in the European Economic Area* (Frankfurt-am-Main, German Law Publishers, 2012) 185.

[63] ÓJ Einarsson, 'The Advisory Opinion Procedure and the Relationship between the EFTA Court and the Norwegian Courts: Recent Developments' (2022) 61(4) *Lov og Rett* 221. See also above, section I.B.

[64] [1994] OJ L135/5.

[65] Articles 7(1) and 10(1) of Directive 94/19. The amounts were significantly increased in the aftermath of the 2008–09 financial crisis.

[66] Judgment of 28 January 2013, E-16/11, *EFTA Surveillance Authority v Iceland* ([2013] EFTA Ct Rep 4). For an in-depth analysis of the judgment in the light of the homogeneity objective, see D Chalmers, '*Icesave* – Limited Homogeneity and Unlimited Judicial Interpretation' in EFTA Court (ed), *The EEA and the EFTA Court: Decentred Integration* (Oxford, Hart Publishing, 2014) 407–16.

in essence Iceland's position to the effect that those provisions of Directive 94/19 did not create an obligation of result for the EEA States. Departing from its traditionally teleological interpretation of EEA rules,[67] it stated in particular that that directive, at least primarily, dealt with the anticipated failure of individual banks, but not with a systemic crisis such as that which hit the Icelandic banking sector in 2008, and that it would not be appropriate to impose a level of protection which might in certain cases encourage the unsound management of credit institutions.[68] Moreover, the EFTA Court rejected the claim of discrimination, considering in essence that only action of the deposit-guarantee schemes was governed by EEA law and that, in any event, EEA States have a wide degree of discretion when making fundamental choices of economic policy in the context of a crisis.

It is unclear whether that interpretation can be reconciled with the case law of the Court of Justice, which recognised that Directive 94/19 created for depositors a *right to compensation* covering 'the repayment, by the deposit-guarantee scheme, of deposits which are unavailable to that depositor, up to the amount laid down in Article 7(1a) of the [said] directive', without excluding or restricting that right in the context of a systemic financial crisis.[69]

That said, it may also happen that the EFTA Court aligns its own case law on more recent judgments of the Court of Justice and thus restores homogeneous interpretation of EEA rules following a period of discrepancy between the two pillars. A clear example is the EFTA Court's judgment in *L'Oreal*.[70] A previous judgment of the EFTA Court regarding trade mark exhaustion interpreted the first Trade Marks Directive[71] as entailing the possibility for EFTA EEA States to provide for international exhaustion.[72] By contrast, in *Silhouette*, the Court of Justice considered that an EEA-wide exhaustion applied, meaning that that directive thus precluded 'national rules providing for exhaustion of trade-mark rights in respect of products put on the market outside the EEA under that mark by the proprietor or with his consent'.[73] The EFTA Court held in *L'Oréal* that 'the differences between the EEA Agreement and the EC Treaty with regard to trade relations with third countries d[id] not constitute compelling grounds for divergent interpretations' of the provision of the Trade Marks Directive at issue and thus aligned its case law to that of the Court of Justice.[74]

The *Icesave* and *L'Oreal* cases epitomise the difficulties – not to say the paradoxes – which may result from pursuing a common homogeneity objective in vast

[67] Chalmers (n 65) 412–13.

[68] Judgment in *EFTA Surveillance Authority v Iceland* (n 65) paras 151 and 167.

[69] See judgment of 12 October 2004, C-222/02, *Paul and Others* (EU:C:2004:606), paras 26 and 27; and judgment of 25 March 2021, C-501/18, *Balgarska Narodna Banka* (EU:C:2021:249), para 60.

[70] EFTA Court, judgment of 8 July 2008, E-9/07 and E-10/07, *L'Oréal Norge AS v Aarskog Per AS and Others and Smart Club Norge*, [2008] EFTA Ct Rep 259.

[71] First Council Directive 89/104/EEC of 21 December 1988 to approximate the laws of the Member States relating to trade marks [1989] OJ L40/1. This directive is no longer in force.

[72] EFTA Court, Advisory Opinion of 3 December 1997, E-2/97, *Mag Instrument Inc v California Trading Company Norway, Ulsteen*, [1997] EFTA Ct Rep 127.

[73] Judgment of 16 July 1998, C-355/96, *Silhouette International Schmied* (EU:C:1998:374), paras 26 and 31.

[74] See EFTA Court, *L'Oréal Norge AS v Aarskog Per AS and Others and Smart Club Norge* (n 69) para 37. On this case law, see Einarsson (n 62) 233–34.

regulatory fields, whilst taking into account the distinct nature of the EEA conceived as a less integrated area than the EU.

We will come back to this ongoing challenge in the concluding remarks.

B. The Legacy of the EEA Opinions for the EU Constitutional Fabric

Opinions 1/91 and 1/92 formed part of a series of landmark decisions in the early 1990s which established key concepts of EU constitutional law, in particular external relations law.[75] These concepts take as a starting point the 'essential characteristics' of the EU legal order, as specified in paragraph 21 of Opinion 1/91. Indeed, as the Court itself has noted,[76] this paragraph contained the seeds that would allow it to refer, in the landmark Opinion 2/13, to 'a structured network of principles, rules and mutually interdependent legal relations linking the EU and its Member States, and its Member States with each other, which are now engaged … in a "process of creating an ever closer union among the peoples of Europe"'.[77]

The central issue raised in the EEA Opinions relates to the extent to which the Union can subject itself – and by extension its institutions – to a system of judicial adjudication or a dispute settlement mechanism that is outside the EU judicial system. Opinion 1/17 sums up the Court's position of principle on that issue, referring in this respect to Opinion 1/91, but also clarifies the rationale underpinning it.[78] The dispute settlement mechanism at issue built upon the creation of CETA tribunals and, in the longer term, a multilateral investment tribunal. The Court of Justice confirmed that the EU can enter into international agreements conferring jurisdiction on courts or arbitration bodies that are outside the EU judicial system to settle disputes concerning alleged violations of that agreement by the EU or by a Member State, and therefore to entrust those courts or arbitration bodies with a competence to apply such an agreement 'as a matter of law' in order to award damages. This is not called into question by the jurisdiction of the Court of Justice to interpret such agreements as an integral part of the EU's legal order.[79] Indeed, 'the jurisdiction of the courts and tribunals specified in Article 19 of the Treaty on European Union (TEU) to interpret and apply those agreements *does not take precedence* over' jurisdiction of any of the contracting parties, 'precisely because of the reciprocal nature of international agreements and the need to maintain the powers of the Union in international relations'.[80]

[75] M Cremona, 'Opinion: European Court of Justice (ECJ)', in *Max Planck Encyclopaedia of International Procedural Law* (Oxford, Oxford University Press, 2019) para 43 (available online at: opil.ouplaw.com).

[76] Judgment of 21 December 2021, C-357/19, C-379/19, C-547/19, C-811/19 and C-840/19, *Euro Box Promotion and Others* (EU:C:2021:1034), para 247.

[77] Opinion 2/13 (Accession of the European Union to the ECHR) of 18 December 2014 (EU:C:2014:2454), paras 166 and 167. See also judgment of 24 October 2018, C-234/17, *XC and Others* (EU:C:2018:853), para 36.

[78] Opinion 1/17 (n 49).

[79] See judgment of 30 April 1974, 181/73, *Haegeman* (EU:C:1974:41), paras 3–6; and judgment of 27 February 2018, C-266/16, *Western Sahara Campaign UK* (EU:C:2018:118), para 46. However, it should be emphasised that the CETA does not have direct effect in the legal systems of the parties to it (Art 30.6.1 of the CETA).

[80] Opinion 1/17 (n 49) paras 116 and 117 (emphasis added).

Nevertheless, that 'openness' does not undermine the key lessons to be drawn from the EEA Opinions, which made clear for the very first time that such competence must be exercised in a manner that avoids any risk of undermining the EU constitutional framework.[81]

First, it is clear from those Opinions that the preservation of the autonomy of the EU legal order requires that the *essential character* of the powers of the EU and of its institutions as conceived in the Treaties remain unaltered.[82] Thus, no single alteration is incompatible with autonomy; the latter only protects the EU institutions from a fundamental alteration of the powers conferred upon them under the Treaties. This test was, for example, applied by the Court of Justice in its famous *Pringle* judgment, examining the treaty establishing a European Stability Mechanism (ESM).[83] The tasks conferred by that treaty – concluded outside the EU legal order – to the Commission, the European Central Bank (ECB) and the Court of Justice entailed no such fundamental alteration, in particular because they did not call into question the binding nature of decisions of the Court of Justice.[84]

Second, that autonomy requires that the procedures for ensuring uniform interpretation of the rules of an agreement to which the EU is a party and for resolving disputes will not have the effect of binding the EU and its institutions, in the exercise of their internal powers, to a particular interpretation of the rules of EU law referred to in that agreement.[85] In other words, 'the autonomy of the [EU] legal order would be compromised by *any extra-[EU] system* which would have the effect of binding the [EU] and its institutions to a particular interpretation of the rules of [EU] law in the exercise of their internal powers'.[86]

The EEA Opinions thus had a lasting impact on the *development of external relations* of the EU. For example, the Commission expressly stated that it had negotiated the envisaged agreement on the establishment of a European Common Aviation Area (ECAA) 'on the basis of the principles set out in *Opinion 1/92*'.[87] The purpose of the agreement was, like the EEA Agreement, to extend part of the *acquis communautaire* to third states, and ensure uniform interpretation and application of that law in the area thus created. Seised of a request for an Opinion on that draft ECAA agreement, the Court of Justice referred extensively to the EEA Opinions to conclude that the system of judicial supervision envisaged by that draft did not undermine

[81] See K Lenaerts, 'Le cadre constitutionnel de l'Union et l'autonomie fonctionnelle de son ordre juridique' in D Petrlík, M Bobek and JM Passer (eds), *Évolution des rapports entre les ordres juridiques de l'Union européenne, international et nationaux. Liber amicorum Jiří Malenovský* (Brussels, Bruylant, 2020) 297–98.

[82] Opinion 1/00 (Agreement on the establishment of a European Common Aviation Area) of 18 April 2002 (EU:C:2002:231), para 12.

[83] Judgment of 27 November 2012, C-370/12, *Pringle* (EU:C:2012:756).

[84] ibid paras 164, 165, 174 and 175. See K Lenaerts, '*Pringle* as a Landmark Judgment for the EU Constitutional Fabric' in *Pringle and Beyond: Lessons from 10 Years of ESM-Related Court Decisions* (ESM Conference, 30 June 2023) (to be published). Opinion 1/91's legacy as regards the preservation of the binding nature of the decisions adopted by the Court of Justice was already visible in the judgment of 28 March 1995, C-346/93, *Kleinwort Benson* (EU:C:1995:85), para 24.

[85] Opinion 1/91 (n 5) paras 30–35. See also Opinion 2/13 (n 76) para 184.

[86] Judgment of 12 September 2006, C-131/03 P, *Reynolds Tobacco and Others v Commission* (EU:C:2006:541), citing Opinion 1/91 in particular, para 98 (emphasis added).

[87] Cited at n 81.

the autonomy of the EU legal order. It contained safeguards 'broadly comparable' to those contained in the second version of the draft EEA Agreement examined in Opinion 1/92.[88] The mechanisms for ensuring uniform interpretation of the rules of the draft ECAA Agreement and for resolving disputes contained in that draft ensured that neither the Union nor its institutions, in the exercise of their internal powers, would be bound by a particular interpretation of the rules of EU law incorporated in the agreement.[89]

The constitutional lessons from the EEA Opinions were also useful for appraising dispute settlement mechanisms agreed upon by the Member States in Bilateral Investment Treaties (BITs). In *Achmea*,[90] the Court of Justice held in essence that the autonomy of the EU legal order precludes an international agreement entered into by the Member States removing from the jurisdiction of national courts disputes possibly involving the application and interpretation of EU law.[91] This case concerned a BIT concluded between two Member States, the Netherlands and the Slovak Republic (as a successor state to the Czech and Slovak Federative Republic). An arbitration clause entitled an investor from one of those two Member States, in the event of a dispute concerning investments in the other Member State, to bring proceedings against the latter Member State before an arbitral tribunal whose jurisdiction that Member State has undertaken to accept. The Court of Justice ruled that that arbitration clause had an adverse effect on the autonomy of the EU legal order and disregarded the prohibition for the Member States to submit their disputes concerning the interpretation or application of EU law to other methods of settlement than those set out in the Treaties.[92] This conclusion resulted, in essence, from the fact that the clause at issue involved an international commitment, on the part of Member States, to 'remove from the jurisdiction of their own courts, and hence from the [EU] system of judicial remedies … disputes which may concern the application or interpretation of EU law'.[93] Such removal 'could prevent those disputes from being resolved in a manner that ensures the full effectiveness of EU law, even though they might concern the interpretation or application of that law'.[94]

The question arose after *Achmea* as to whether the same findings would apply in relation to 'extra-EU BITs', ie, treaties entered into by a third country, on the one hand, and the EU and its Member States, on the other hand.[95] The Court of Justice addressed this question in Opinion 1/17.

[88] ibid para 38.

[89] ibid para 45.

[90] Judgment of 6 March 2018, C-284/16, *Achmea* (EU:C:2018:158).

[91] The Court of Justice fully confirmed that approach in the judgment of 2 September 2021, C-741/19, *Republic of Moldova* (EU:C:2021:655).

[92] Article 344 TFEU.

[93] Judgment in *Achmea* (n 89) para 55.

[94] ibid para 56. As a result of that judgment, 23 Member States entered into an international agreement for the termination of intra-EU BITs. See Agreement for the Termination of Bilateral Investment Treaties between the Member States of the European Union [2020] OJ L169/1.

[95] See P Koutrakos, 'The Autonomy of EU Law and International Investment Arbitration' (2019) 88(1) *Nordic Journal of International Law*, 41, 59, who correctly points out that the rationale underpinning *Achmea* does not apply to extra-EU BITs, since the Court of Justice 'places emphasis on the constitutionalised setting within which relations between Member States are regulated under EU law'.

The Court of Justice found that, just as was the case for the international court at issue in Opinion 1/09[96] and the arbitration tribunal in *Achmea*, the envisaged tribunals stood outside the EU judicial system.[97] However, the mechanism laid down in the CETA did not compromise the judicial dialogue between the Court of Justice and national courts, as the envisaged tribunals lacked jurisdiction to interpret or apply EU law *other than* that which related to the provisions of the CETA.[98] In particular, those tribunals could not determine the legality of a measure alleged to constitute a breach of the CETA under the 'domestic law of one of the Parties', including EU law (other than the CETA).[99] Moreover, questions pertaining to the interpretation or application of EU law (again, other than the CETA) were to be treated as 'a matter of fact' and the interpretation of that law made by the Court of Justice was binding upon those tribunals. Conversely, neither the Court of Justice nor national courts were to be bound by the meaning given to their own 'domestic' law by those tribunals.[100] These findings also explained why the CETA did not make any provision for the prior involvement of the Court of Justice that would permit or even oblige the envisaged tribunals to make a reference for a preliminary ruling to that Court.[101] The Court distinguished that dispute settlement mechanism, in particular, from the Unified Patent Litigation System examined in Opinion 1/09.[102] As explained above, the draft agreement creating that Unified Patent Litigation System conferred jurisdiction on an international court external to the EU judicial system to settle disputes involving individuals and to apply in that context, *as a matter of law, not only that agreement but also other EU acts or rules*. This agreement thus 'displaced' the jurisdiction of national courts on disputes concerning EU law going beyond that agreement itself. This was such as to call into question the integrity of EU law because it precluded those courts from entering into dialogue with the Court of Justice through the preliminary ruling procedure, which, as we have seen, is the 'keystone' of the EU judicial system.

The Court held moreover in Opinion 1/17 that the CETA provisions do not alter the allocation of competences resulting from the Treaties. Indeed, prior to instituting proceedings before the envisaged tribunals, a Canadian investor is required to deliver to the EU 'a notice requesting a determination of the respondent', identifying the measures in respect of which the investor intends to submit a claim. The EU is then required to inform that investor 'whether the [EU] or a Member State … [is to] be the respondent'.[103] Accordingly, it is for the EU itself to decide whether a dispute brought by a Canadian investor falls within the scope of its own competences or remains

[96] Opinion 1/09 (Agreement Creating a Unified Patent Litigation System) of 8 March 2011 (EU:C:2011:123).

[97] Opinion 1/17 (n 49) para 118.

[98] See, in this regard, C Rapoport, 'Balancing on a Tightrope: *Opinion 1/17* and the ECJ's Narrow and Tortuous Path for Compatibility of the EU's Investment Court System (ICS)' (2020) 57(6) *CML Rev*, 1725, 1749–50.

[99] Opinion 1/17 (n 49), para 121.

[100] ibid para 131.

[101] ibid para 134.

[102] ibid paras 123–25.

[103] See Art 8.21 of the CETA.

exclusively within the purview of the Member States. This distinguished the arrangements provided by the CETA from, notably, the competence of the EEA Court to rule on the concept of 'Contracting Party' under the first draft EEA Agreement or the co-defendant mechanism envisaged in the draft agreement on the Accession of the EU to the European Court of Human Rights (ECtHR) examined in Opinion 2/13, both of which implied that a judicial body other than the Court of Justice would have had the final say as to whether an alleged violation of the EEA Agreement or the ECHR was attributable to a Member State, to the EU, or to both.[104] This co-defendant mechanism could have distorted the principle of conferral, in general, and the effectiveness of Article 51(1) of the Charter, in particular.

Lastly, the mechanism laid down in the CETA does not encroach upon the prerogatives of the EU legislator: this agreement, together with its Joint Interpretation Instrument, made it clear that it was *not* for the envisaged tribunals to adjudicate on the *level of protection* of a public interest that led to the introduction by the EU legislator of regulatory restrictions in the sphere of the internal market. In the light of the principle of democracy on which the functioning of the EU is founded, as was already emphasised in *Kadi I*,[105] that was a decision for the EU legislator alone to take. This part of Opinion 1/17 confirms that representative democracy constitutes an essential 'pillar' of the EU's constitutional framework and, consequently, of the autonomy of its legal order.[106]

III. CONCLUDING REMARKS

Through Opinions 1/91 and 1/92, the legal and institutional fabrics of both the EEA and the EU have been interwoven. The threats to the autonomy of the EU legal order identified in Opinion 1/91 have been of key significance for the Court of Justice's subsequent case law. This Opinion confirmed that the EU can enter into binding international dispute-settlement mechanisms. However, such mechanisms cannot undermine the essential characteristics of EU law as a self-referential system of norms. Clear safeguards are needed in that respect, reflecting the unique role of the Court of Justice to preserve those characteristics, by ruling on the scope of EU competences and interpreting EU law. These threats to the autonomy of the EU legal order led to

[104] See Opinion 2/13 (n 76) paras 223–25. Express reference was also made to Opinion 1/91 in the judgment in *Mox-Plant* to confirm that an agreement concluded by the Member States may not *a fortiori* deprive the Court of Justice of its exclusive jurisdiction to rule on such issues concerning the allocation of competences. See judgment of 30 May 2006, *Commission v Ireland* (C-459/03, EU:C:2006:345), paras 123 and 169. See also Opinion 2/13 (n 76) para 201.

[105] Judgment of 3 September 2008, C-402/05 P and C-415/05 P, *Kadi and Al Barakaat International Foundation v Council and Commission* (EU:C:2008:461), para 303. See also, more recently, judgment of 19 December 2019, C-418/18 P, *Puppinck and Others v Commission* (EU:C:2019:1113), para 64, in which the Court dealt with a citizens' initiative within the meaning of Regulation (EU) No 211/2011 of the European Parliament and of the Council of 16 February 2011 on the citizens' initiative [2011] OJ L65/1.

[106] See also the judgment of 19 December 2019, C-502/19, *Junqueras Vies* (EU:C:2019:1115), para 63. In that judgment, the Court expressed concerns similar to those expressed in Opinion 1/17 with regard to external encroachments (although in this case by the Member States) on the functioning of the EU as a democratic political system.

a structural overhaul of the EEA's legal framework in order to ensure compatibility between the EU and the EEA legal orders, which was accepted in Opinion 1/92.

Thirty years on, one can say that there is a large degree of convergence between the two pillars of the EEA as regards interpretation of EU rules corresponding to EEA rules. This element, coupled with the smooth incorporation of EU law into the EEA Agreement, leads to the conclusion that the latter's objective of homogeneity has been achieved to a large extent. However, as we have seen, the risk of divergences is not theoretical. If that risk should materialise too frequently, this could have harmful impacts on citizens' – and businesses' – confidence in the EEA in the long term. This risk must therefore remain a point of focus. Maintaining close dialogue between our two Courts and monitoring the developments in each other's case law appears essential in that context in order to increase anticipation and foster 'mutual accommodation'.[107]

[107] Chalmers (n 65) 416.

2

Opinion 1/91 Revisited

MARC VAN DER WOUDE

THE BIRTH OF the EFTA Court was not an easy one. The initial project was a different one from the project which actually saw the light. This initial project concerned the setting up of an EEA Court, to which a Court of First Instance would be attached. It was supposed to deal with disputes between the contracting parties, infringement actions brought against the EFTA States and appeals against competition law decisions taken by the EFTA Surveillance Authority. The EEA Court would have had eight judges, including five judges from the Court of Justice of the European Union. This latter court was also supposed to play a role in the interpretation of the agreement: EFTA States could indeed authorise their courts and tribunals to ask interpretational questions to the Court of Justice. The parties to the EEA Agreement abandoned this project after the Court of Justice rendered a negative opinion on its compatibility with the EEC Treaty.

This opinion paved the way for a series of opinions and judgments concerning the compatibility of dispute settlement mechanisms set up by international agreements involving the EU. The leading criterion in the assessment of the Court of Justice concerns the specific, one may even say constitutional, nature of the European integration project. The Court of Justice does not object to international dispute settlements as regards the EU's obligations under international agreements for as long as and insofar as these mechanisms do not call into question the autonomy of the Union legal order in pursuing its unique integration objectives.

In this chapter, I will first briefly comment the Opinion of the Court of Justice in case 1/91,[1] which will be followed by a section highlighting some (but certainly not all) subsequent positions taken by the Court of Justice on international dispute settlements. After these two relatively descriptive and retrospective parts, the chapter will take a more prospective and speculative turn. The subsequent sections will deal with the question of dispute settlement mechanisms in a context of increasingly differentiated forms of integration between EU Member States as well as between these states and third states. With many new candidate countries knocking on the Union's door and with some existing members entertaining doubts on full-blown

[1] European Court of Justice, Opinion of the Court of 14 December 1991, Opinion 1/91, ECLI:EU:C:1991:490.

membership, the idea of a Union with a geometrical variety is likely to surface again. This could imply that membership may be of variable intensity and, hence, that all chapters of the future EU Treaties do not necessarily apply to all its members. The third section endeavours to make these thoughts more explicit and raises the question as to whether such forms of integration can be reconciled with the case law of the Court of Justice discussed in the two previous sections. The fourth and final section will propose a possible answer to that hypothetical question.

I. OPINION 1/91

The purpose of the judicial system set up by the EEA Agreement was to ensure an interpretation of the provisions of that agreement that would fall into line with the corresponding provisions of the EEC and for European Coal and Steel Community (ECSC) Treaties.[2] Several mechanisms were put in place to achieve this objective. In addition to the mixed composition of the EEA Court and the optional preliminary reference procedure, the Agreement explicitly provided that its provisions should be interpreted in conformity with Community law as it existed on the date of signature of the Agreement.

Before answering the question whether these measures sufficed to ensure consistent interpretation between EEA and EEC law, the Court of Justice recalled the Vienna Convention on the Law of Treaties, pursuant to which treaties must not only be interpreted on the basis of their wording, but also in the light of their objectives. In this respect the Court held that the objectives of Community law differed considerably from those pursued by the EEA Agreement. The provisions on free trade and competition were not an end in themselves, but a means to making progress towards European unity. It also underlined the specificity of the methods used in pursuing this overarching objective. Even if the EEC Treaty and the EEA Agreement are both international agreements, the former, unlike the latter, provides for a transfer of sovereign rights to intergovernmental institutions and sets up a new legal order in which individuals can directly invoke provisions of Community law that take precedence over conflicting provisions of national law. It thus constitutes the 'constitutional charter of the Community based on the rule of law'.

The Court of Justice considered that the measures foreseen by the EEA Agreement to ensure that the legal homogeneity between the two treaties did not suffice to overcome this fundamental difference. The obligation to ensure a uniform interpretation only referred to pre-existing Community law, but did not cover new developments in case law. Nor was it clear whether this obligation would extend to the principles of direct effect and primacy. Moreover, the preliminary reference procedure foreseen by the EEA Agreement was not comparable with its EEC counterpart because of its optional nature and because of the fact that the answers given by the Court of Justice would not be binding on the national courts in the EFTA States, which would have requested preliminary guidance.

[2] On Opinion 1/91, see N Jääskinen, 'The Rise and Fall of the EEA Court', ch 3 in this volume.

The Court of Justice then held that in the absence of efficient safeguards, the EEA Agreement could undermine the autonomy of the Community legal order. It referred in this respect to several factors. First, since the EEA Court had the possibility of defining the concept of 'Contracting Party' in cases brought before it, the Court would have a say in defining the respective competence of the Community and its Member States in matters covered by the EEA Agreement. Since these matters mirror those covered by the EEC, the EEA Court could therefore be called upon to take decisions on the competence of the Community and hence impinge on the exclusive jurisdiction of the Court of Justice to rule on such issues. Second, even if there is no objection to the Community concluding international agreements and submitting itself to decisions taken by a court set up by such agreements, the EEA Agreement went beyond contracting classic international obligations. This was because this agreement duplicated an essential part of the Community's rules, including its fundamental provisions. Combined with the obligation to interpret both sets of provisions in a uniform manner, the EEA Court would be competent to interpret the rules that underpin the Community legal order. Finally, these risks would not be reduced by the organic links between the Court of Justice and the EEA Court. On the contrary, the judges of the Court of Justice sitting in the EEA Court would be confronted with the sheer impossible mission of taking account of the specificities of both treaties when interpreting similar provisions.

Under these circumstances, the Court of Justice opined that the EEA Agreement set up a system of courts which conflicted with the mission conferred to the Court of Justice and with the foundations of the Community.

II. THE SUBSEQUENT CASE LAW

For the purposes of this chapter, it would be going too far to give an exhaustive overview of the case law on international dispute settlement systems. However, I dare to submit that Opinion 1/91 had a fundamental impact on that case law. The Court of Justice has indeed been very attentive in preserving the autonomy of the Union's legal order and the unique role that this jurisdiction plays in that respect. I will therefore limit myself to a few examples from recent case law.[3]

One of the main objections of the Court in Justice in Opinion 1/91 concerned the fact that the EEA Court would have jurisdiction on the division of competence between the Union and its Member States. This issue was also at the core of Case C-459/03,[4] which concerned the construction of a MOX (mixed oxide fuel) plant by the UK for the treatment of nuclear waste along the Irish Sea. Considering that this project violated the UK's obligations under an international convention against marine pollution, Ireland had initiated proceedings against the UK before an Arbitration Tribunal set up under that convention, to which both the European

[3] See for a more exhaustive overview, A Biondi and G Sangiulo (eds) 'The EU and the Rule of Law in International Economic Relations: an Agenda for an Enhanced Dialogue', Edward Elgar Publishing, 2021.

[4] Case C-459/03 *Commission of the European Communities v Ireland*, Judgment of 30 May 2006, ECLI:EU:C:2006:345.

Community and its Member States were parties. This legal action was not to the liking of the European Commission, which started treaty infringement proceedings against Ireland for having disregarded the exclusive jurisdiction of the Court of Justice to rule on environmental protection matters that Community law regulates and thus form part of the Community legal order. The Court of Justice sided with the Commission. The Community's internal dispute settlement systems take precedence over systems set up by international law when the dispute comes within the scope of Community competence.

The scope of the jurisdiction of the Court of Justice was also a bone of contention in the discussions concerning the setting up of a Unified Patent Court, to which private parties can submit their disputes on the unified European patent.[5] Interestingly, the Court of Justice paid attention not only to its own jurisdiction, but also to the competence of national courts, with whom it interacts in the context of the preliminary reference procedure. The Court of Justice recalled that international arbitration tribunals or courts are not incompatible with the autonomy of the Union legal order as such, insofar as their competence is limited to the interpretation and application of international agreements. By contrast, in the case at hand, the Unified Patent Court system was also competent to apply EU law, including in particular the Regulation on the Unified Community Patent, other intellectual property rules and competition rules. Given the exclusive nature of this competence, national courts, as ordinary Union courts, would be deprived of the possibility to refer preliminary reference questions to the Court of Justice in matters covered by that international agreement. The system underlying the Unified Patent Court thus interfered with the proper functioning of Article 267 of the Treaty on the Functioning of the European Union (TFEU).[6]

The full range of problems identified by the Court of Justice in Opinion 1/91 resurfaced in the case dealing, for the second time, with the possible accession of the Union to the European Convention on Human Rights (ECHR).[7] Before assessing the compatibility of this accession with the EU Treaties, the Court of Justice recalled the relevant provisions in those treaties and the main principles already developed in earlier cases. It underlined, in particular, that the unique and autonomous nature of the Union legal order relies on a common set of values, as enshrined in Article 2 of the Treaty on European Union (TEU) and the Charter of Fundamental Rights of the European Union, on mutual trust between the Member States and on a judicial system pivoting on Article 267 TFEU.

In its assessment, the Court of Justice repeated the presupposition that external control under an international agreement is not contrary to the EU Treaties, especially when these treaties themselves foresee such control. However, that external control cannot interfere with the internal question as to whether Member States complied with their EU obligations and in particular the Charter. The freedom of the

[5] European Court of Justice, Opinion of the Court of 8 March 2011, Opinion 1/09, ECLI:EU:C:2011:123.

[6] After a series of amendments, these problems were overcome, allowing the Unified Patent Court to start its activities on 1 June 2023.

[7] European Court of Justice, Opinion of the Court of 18 December 2014, Opinion 2/13, ECLI:EU:C:2014:2454.

contracting states under the Convention to set higher standards must be reconciled with the duties of the Member States under EU law and the Charter. The Court of Justice noted that the accession agreement did not provide for such a reconciliation mechanism. In addition, it observed that the possibility of choosing higher standards under the Convention might compromise the mutual trust upon which the Member States rely in their relations when these are governed by EU law. Nor did the accession agreement exclude the idea that, in the sphere of fundamental rights, the preliminary procedure allowing for prior consultation of the ECHR could be used to undermine the proper functioning of Article 267 TFEU.

The Court of Justice subsequently recalled the principle that, in matters governed by EU law, Member States should not submit their disputes to other judicial bodies than those foreseen by the EU Treaties. Here again, the accession agreement did not exclude the possibility that the Union or its Member States request the European Court of Human Rights (ECtHR) to rule, pursuant to Article 33 of the Convention, on violations of human rights in EU matters. Also, in proceedings before the ECtHR, that court could be called upon to define the defending parties that are (co-)responsible for a possible infringement. In certain procedural scenarios, this could lead the ECtHR to apply the EU rules governing the division of powers between the EU and its Member States. Finally, the ECHR would be competent to rule on possible human rights violations in relation to common foreign and security matters that, according to Article 40 TEU, do not fall within the jurisdiction of the Court of Justice. The control of legality would thus be placed in the hands of a jurisdiction outside the ambit of the EU.

The question of the exclusive jurisdiction of the Court of Justice to rule on EU matters also arises in cases concerning arbitration tribunals set up by bilateral investment treaties to which Member States are parties. The leading case on this issue is *Achmea*,[8] which concerned a legal claim filed by a Dutch insurance company against the Slovak Republic before an arbitration tribunal foreseen by a bilateral investment treaty concluded in 1991 between the Netherlands and Czechoslovakia. The Slovak Republic, which had in the meantime become an EU Member State, did not accept the outcome of these proceedings and contested the validity of the arbitral judgment before the German courts, which referred the matter to the Court of Justice under the preliminary reference procedure.

After having recalled the principles resulting from its previous case law and in particular Opinion 2/13,[9] the Court of Justice observed that the arbitration tribunal was called upon to apply EU law, pursuant to both the bilateral investment treaty and the law of the Member State in question of which includes EU law. It subsequently examined whether that tribunal qualified as a court within the meaning of Article 267 TFEU that could refer questions on the interpretation and validity of EU law to the Court of Justice. It concluded that this was not the case, precisely because the parties to the bilateral investment treaty had intended not to use their national courts for

[8] Judgment of 6 March 2018, Case C-284/16 *Achmea*, ECLI:EU:C:2018:158.

[9] European Court of Justice, Opinion of the Court of 18 December 2014, Opinion 2/13, ECLI:EU:C:2014:2454.

arbitrational purposes. Therefore, the arbitration tribunal could not be seen as a court of a Member State. Even if in the case at hand, the German courts were competent to verify the legality of the arbitral ruling, such judicial control is not available in all Member States. Moreover, under German law, judicial review was limited in its scope.

The Court of Justice also noted that the type of arbitration at stake in the main proceedings differed from classic commercial arbitration, because that latter type of arbitration reflects the free will of the parties, whereas the former type results from a treaty between Member States under which they decided to exclude the jurisdiction of their own courts. They therefore set up a system of dispute settlement, parallel to the public system foreseen by Article 19 TEU, in matters relating to the interpretation and application of EU law. This called into question not only the principle of mutual trust between the Member States but also the preservation of the particular nature of the law established by the Treaties, ensured by the preliminary ruling procedure provided for in Article 267 TFEU.[10]

One could reasonably infer from this brief overview that the standards for international dispute settlement systems involving the Union or its Member States are very strict. However, Opinion 1/17[11] concerning the establishment of a tribunal system by the Comprehensive Economic and Trade Agreement (CETA) concluded by the Union and its Member States with Canada shows that these standards are not unsurmountable. Under this system, investors can enforce their rights under this agreement before a tribunal and an appellate tribunal, which the parties intend to replace in the longer term by a multilateral Investment Court System. The Court of Justice held that the detailed rules underlying that system did not have adverse effects on the autonomy of the EU legal order.

Even if the Court of Justice recalled its earlier case law on the setting up of conflict settlement mechanisms outside the system foreseen by Article 19 TEU, it took a positive stand towards international tribunals. It observed that international agreements can be interpreted by the jurisdiction of both parties. Given this reciprocal nature and the need to maintain the powers of the Union in international relations, it might be preferable that international courts or tribunals interpret international agreements without those courts being subject to the interpretations of that agreement given by the jurisdictions of the parties. In order to verify whether such international court systems respect the autonomy of the EU's legal order, it developed a two-limbed test, which the CETA tribunal system successfully passed.

First, the Court of Justice noted that the tribunals would only be competent to interpret and apply the provisions of the CETA agreement[12] pursuant to the conditions laid down therein. One of these conditions explicitly precludes the tribunals from interpreting the internal law of the contracting parties and, hence, Union law. If

[10] In Case C-741/19 *République de Moldavie*, ECLI:EU:C:2021:655, the Court of Justice specified that the *Achmea* case law applies only to disputes under bilateral investment treaties involving Member States, but not necessarily to disputes between a Member State and a third state. See also point 129 of the CETA Opinion 1/17 of 30 April 2019, ECLI:EU:C:2019:341.

[11] European Court of Justice, Opinion of 30 April 2019, Opinion 1/17, ECLI:EU:C:2019:341.

[12] Comprehensive Economic and Trade Agreement (CETA) between Canada, of the one part, and the European Union and its Member States, of the other part [2017] OJ L11, 14 January, 23–1079.

necessary, they may consider that law as a matter of fact. Moreover, when a Canadian investor brings an action before the CETA tribunals, it is not for them to decide whether the defendant is the Union or its Member States and hence to rule on the division of powers under Union law. Indeed, the CETA agreement sets up a mechanism pursuant to which the Union itself identifies the defending party.

Second, the Court also considered that the CETA tribunal system did not affect the operation of the EU institutions within the EU's constitutional framework. It is true that, when they assess the merits of a claim, the tribunals may be called upon to weigh the commercial interests of the claimant against the public interests of the Union. Even so, when condemning the Union, the tribunals may only award damages. They will not have the power to annul or order the withdrawal of a Union measure. The Court of Justice also examined whether these limited powers could nevertheless have a chilling effect on the evolution of Union law to set higher levels of protection, which could harm Canadian investors. It noted that the CETA Agreement explicitly allows the contracting parties to set higher standards for the protection of public interests, as long as such standards are not applied in an arbitrary or discriminatory manner or constitute a disguised restriction on trade. The Court of Justice concluded that the discretionary powers of tribunals do not permit them to call into question the level of protection of public interest determined by the Union following a democratic process.

III. DISPUTE SETTLEMENT SYSTEMS AND DIFFERENTIATED FORMS OF INTEGRATION

It follows from the case law discussed above that there are four interacting criteria to assess whether a system of courts or tribunals set up by international agreements is compatible or not with the autonomy of the EU legal order. First, that system should not interfere with the powers of the Court of Justice to decide on the division of powers between the Union and its Member States. That power lies with the Court of Justice as the constitutional court of the Union.

Second, the Court of Justice exercises this role in close cooperation with the courts of the Member States, which collectively ensure the proper application of EU law in the EU legal order, as provided in Article 19 TEU. The preliminary reference procedure foreseen by Article 267 TFEU offers the platform for this judicial dialogue. International agreements and their conflict settlements should not interfere with the proper functioning of this unique mechanism. I note in this respect that with its gradual expansion, EU law increasingly interacts with all aspects of national law, including national constitutional law. Article 267 TFEU offers the Court of Justice and the national constitutional courts the possibility of collectively defining the division of powers between the Union and its Member States. Seen from this angle, Article 267 TFEU constitutes the constitutional anchor of the autonomy of the EU legal order.

Third, the Court of Justice has the final say on the interpretation of EU law and the validity of EU legal acts. It not only governs the proper functioning of the EU institutions, agencies and bodies, but also ensures the uniform application of EU law throughout the Union. Although the EU may enter into obligations under international law and submit itself to international dispute settlement mechanisms, such engagements should not prevent the autonomous development of EU law, as interpreted by the Court of Justice. This implies that international courts or tribunals should not interpret and apply EU law.

Fourth, the integrity of EU law relies not only on the uniform interpretation of EU law, but also on the mutual trust between Member States when they apply it. Free movement of goods, services, capital and persons in the common area implies that the Member States must be confident in the standards that they apply to each other and to their respective nationals. International agreements should not disrupt this equilibrium.

These four interrelated criteria set very high standards. They can be met, but under stringent conditions. The system of voluntary alignment set up by the current version of the EEA Agreement offers an example of how the standards can be met. This system relies on two mechanisms. As a general measure, EU law is incorporated into EEA law via consultations between, on the one hand, the EFTA States, assisted by the EFTA Secretariat, and, on the other hand, the EU represented by the Commission. As regards the EFTA Court, under a combined reading of Article 6 of the EEA Agreement and Article 3 of the Surveillance and Court Agreement, it is obliged to follow the case law of the EU Courts that pre-dated the conclusion of the EEA Agreement and to take due account of the subsequent jurisprudence.[13] The CETA agreement offers another example: it sets up international tribunals, but limits their role and powers.

The question arises as to whether these four requirements and the ad hoc solutions found to overcome them offer a long-lasting answer to the challenges posed by further European integration. The hostile world which Europe increasingly faces, especially after the Russian invasion of Ukraine, has relaunched the integration process. At least eight countries have formally applied for membership, including Ukraine, and others are likely to follow. Similarly, some states that have decided not to join the Union are keen to remain connected to the EU internal market or to specific projects, such as the Schengen area, energy networks or research programmes. This applies not only to the EFTA States and Switzerland, but also to the UK, which may be interested in revising its cooperation with the EU in the coming years. Finally, some existing Member States may reconsider their current membership and prefer less compelling alternatives.

The EU has shown a great degree of pragmatism in the past by accommodating the wishes of some of its members. It offers them flexibility to choose opt-ins or opt-outs as regards some provisions of the treaties, such as those governing the Euro currency, free movement in the Schengen area, enhanced cooperation within the meaning of Article 326 TFEU or, simply, by concluding side letters, such as Protocol 32 on Danish real estate. The Union has also been inventive in its external relations by developing bespoke arrangements with its immediate neighbours. This internal and external flexibility justifies a certain degree of optimism as regards

[13] The distinction between pre-existing and subsequent case law is not only hard to make in practice, but also complicates the obligation to ensure consistency and homogeneity between EU and EEA law. This may explain why the EFTA Court does not seem to rely on this distinction in its case law.

the integration of future members. Even so, elastic bands cannot be stretched indefinitely. Internal differentiation via opt-ins and opt-outs within the same institutional structure may not satisfy those states that do not want full membership. Conversely, external flexibility may displease those states that aspire to become full members. Finally, the incumbent Member States may consider that a candidate state qualifies for some parts of Union cooperation, but not yet for others, as illustrated by the discussions for the accession of existing Member States to the eurozone or the Schengen area.

Against this backdrop, I submit that the time may have come to redesign the structure of the EU Treaties in a manner that integrates this flexibility by defining specific consistent parts, or to use the expression used in the Maastricht Treaty – pillars – to which states can sign up. The specific form of this partial membership should not really matter, provided that it takes place within the constitutional structure of the Union and that it does not prevent further integration by the other Member States. This idea of a Europe with a geometrical variety or 'l'Europe à la carte' is far from new and has been explored by numerous authors and think tanks. It has been discarded so far for two main reasons.

First, any initiative to reopen the discussions on the treaties has been marked by the trauma of repetitive referenda held since the early 1990s in various Member States. The negative outcomes of the French and Dutch referenda on the treaty on the European Constitution in 2005, followed by the tour de force for the approval of the Lisbon Treaty, do not qualify as the most glorious moments of the European integration project. The world has been changing considerably ever since. The Union has managed to overcome various crises, including Brexit as an example of non-membership. The latest crisis triggered by Russian aggression creates a new context in which further accessions and treaty reform become unavoidable issues. Moreover, there may be one important lesson to learn from the 2005 experience. Offering the full gastronomic menu to those without the appetite was perhaps not the wisest thing to do. They might have preferred a meal 'à la carte'.

The second reason for rejecting differentiated integration models concerns practical feasibility and essentially boils down to the delicate question as to whether all members should be equally represented in the institutions of the Union, including the Court of Justice. Until now, this question has been answered positively, relying on the intergovernmental fiction that all states are equal. All Member States have their representatives within the institutions and participate fully in collegial decision making on all subject matters, including those covered by opt-outs.

Apart from the fact that it does not necessarily correspond to reality, as shown by the Eurogroup, it is no longer practicable. It is simply impossible to confer executive tasks to a collegiate body, such as the Commission, composed of 30–40 representatives. The composition of the institutions could be reconsidered to reflect not only the demographic weight of the Member States, as is currently the case under the qualified majority voting rules and the seat allocation in the Parliament, but also the subject matters to which the Member States signed up. As will be discussed below, this idea could also have its repercussions on the competencies and composition of the Court of Justice under a differentiated treaty structure.

IV. DIFFERENTIATED INTEGRATION WITHIN THE UNION JUDICIAL SYSTEM

In order to allow Member States to further differentiate their membership, the treaties could define consistent sets of rules or pillars. The internal market rules would be compulsory for all but justice and home affairs, the common currency and budgetary policy, Schengen and asylum matters, foreign policy and defence cooperation could be conceived as distinct policies in which not every Member State needs to participate, as is already the case today. Similarly, third states that do not want to join the internal market could sign up to certain sets of rules, such as those dealing with the testing of chemical substances, pharmaceuticals and foodstuffs, or participate in research programmes or networks for energy or electronic communications. Here again, such forms of specific cooperation already exist.

As with any other common project, differentiated forms of integration may give rise to legal disputes. At present, there are basically two options to deal with such disputes: either the states concerned accept the full jurisdiction of the Court of Justice or they conclude complex dispute conflict settlement mechanisms with the EU, such as those discussed in the previous sections. In other words, states are either in or out of the EU. Both options have considerable downsides. The first option implies full membership of the EU. Indeed, until now, only EU Member States are subject to the full jurisdiction of the Court of Justice. Partial membership and partial acceptance of that jurisdiction do not exist. The second option allows for partial cooperation between the EU and states that do not seek membership, but the dispute settlement systems set up under those cooperation agreements are cumbersome and difficult to put in place, as we have seen above.

Rather than imposing a choice between full membership and ad hoc agreements, finding an intermediate solution could be envisaged: states that do not seek full EU membership could choose to have their disputes settled by the EU Courts without accepting their jurisdiction in fields not covered by their cooperation agreement with the EU. The competence of the EU Courts could thus be defined in the agreement by which a state partially accedes to the EU. Alternatively, third states, which reject the idea of partial (and full) EU membership, may seek to confer jurisdiction to the Court of Justice under an arbitration clause within the meaning of Article 272 TFEU to be foreseen in the cooperation agreement they conclude with the Union for specific common rules. The acceptance of the jurisdiction of the EU Courts by a partial accession agreement or by a looser form of cooperation agreement implies that the system foreseen by Article 19 TEU would govern possible disputes involving the Union, the participating states and their natural and legal persons in the areas covered by those agreements.

This solution would have the advantage that the four problems identified in the previous sections as regards international dispute settlement involving the EU could be addressed relatively easily, at least in most cases. The option also has a serious downside, which concerns its acceptability by states that prefer to remain outside any Union structure. For some states, accepting the jurisdiction of the Court of Justice is a delicate issue. They regard that court as external to their own judicial system, hence undermining their sovereignty. It is indeed true that in areas of law governed by EU law, the Court of Justice has the final say. It is the price to pay for participating in a unique system providing peace, stability and prosperity. Pursuing common aims requires common action and hence common dispute settlement systems.

Even so, it could be possible to enhance the acceptability of the jurisdiction of the Court of Justice if judges of the participating states contributed to that jurisdiction. This is obvious for those states that participate in full to the Union project: they would have their judges in the Court of Justice, as is the case today. This is less obvious in a model of differentiated integration in which states only sign up for parts of the project. As regards this complex question, one could explore the possibility that judges of those states only sit in cases dealing with subject matters that are covered by that partial participation. These judges would deal with cases within those areas, even if these cases do not concern conflicts involving the state that designated them, but would not sit in cases in matters for which their states did not sign up. Similarly, they would sit in cases dealing with the delimitation of the subject matters of the cooperation or in fundamental cases that are relevant for all areas of the law. These cases would typically be allocated to the Grand Chamber of the Court of Justice.

For example, if this internalisation option had been followed in 1994, judges from Iceland, Norway and Liechtenstein would now be sitting as judges of the Court of Justice in cases in which EEA law and EU law coincide. This participation would not be confined to the subject matters covered by the EEA Treaty *stricto sensu*, but also extend to issues that are linked to that Treaty by additional treaties, such as the agreement of 18 May 1999 pursuant to which Norway and Iceland acceded to the Schengen area.[14] By contrast, they would not be dealing with other matters, such as most common policies. Similarly, as regards specific forms of cooperation, such as scientific programmes, various authorisation procedures or network regulation, the EU and third states could conclude international agreements of a different nature. These agreements would not only confer jurisdiction upon the Court of Justice pursuant to an arbitration clause within the meaning of Article 272 TFEU, but would also specify how judges of those states could be involved in the functioning of the EU Courts.

The direct involvement of judges in the cases covered by the subject matters governed by partial accession and specific cooperation agreements would obviously affect the functioning of the EU Courts. Having various categories of judges will certainly not simplify the management of these courts, in particular in terms of case allocation. Nor is it guaranteed that third states will accept the jurisdiction of the Court of Justice, even if they have the possibility of designating judges to the EU Courts. Even so, when weighing up these difficulties against those caused by external forms of dispute settlement, the internalisation of dispute settlement may be an avenue to explore. It may facilitate partial or gradual forms of membership of the EU or cooperation in specific technical subject matters between the EU and other European states. In the current unstable geopolitical context, the European states have an interest in focusing on solutions rather than problems.

[14] Judgment of 2 April 2020, C-897/19 *Ruska Federacija*, ECLI:EU:C:2020:262.

3

The Rise and Fall of the EEA Court Recollections of a Lost Battle in 1990–91

NIILO JÄÄSKINEN*

I. INTRODUCTION

IN A NARROW time window of less than two years, starting in June 1990, essential features of a common European legal space comprising the Communities and the States of the European Free Trade Association (EFTA) were set out. This process included two interventions by the European Court of Justice (ECJ). In December 1991, the Court delivered a negative opinion concerning the judicial mechanism envisaged for the European Economic Area (EEA) based on a joint judicial body, the EEA Court, for the Community and the EFTA States.[1] This Opinion 1/91 did not strike like lightning from a clear sky. Rumours in this direction had been circulating since April 1991.[2] In spite of this, the negative stance of the ECJ was a surprise. The European Communities (EC) and the EFTA States had invested much political capital in the EEA. The core element of this arrangement was the legal homogeneity of the EEA based on European Community law in the field of the internal market and ensured by the common EEA Court. We have since become accustomed to important international agreements of the EU being rejected by the Court of Justice of the European Union (CJEU).[3]

* The author would like to thank Dr Pekka Aalto and Mr Timothy Binham as well as the Archives Services of the Finnish Foreign Ministry for their invaluable assistance in the preparation of this chapter. However, the usual disclaimer applies.

[1] Opinion 1/91 of 14 December 1991 delivered pursuant to the second subparagraph of Article 228(1) of the Treaty – Draft Agreement between the Community, on the one hand, and the countries of the European Free Trade Association, on the other, relating to the creation of the European Economic Area, ECLI:EU:C:1991:490.

[2] These were based on the concerns expressed by members of the ECJ circulated amongst the EFTA side negotiating teams, and there was a worrying precedent in Opinion 1/76, where the ECJ found the judicial mechanism envisaged for the European laying-up fund for inland waterway vessels to be incompatible with the Treaty. See Opinion of the Court of 26 April 1977 given pursuant to Article 228 (1) of the EEC Treaty – 'Draft Agreement establishing a European laying-up fund for inland waterway vessels', ECLI:EU:C:1977:63.

[3] See Opinions 2/94 (of 28 March 1996, ECLI:EU:C:1996:140) and 2/13 (of 18 December 2014, ECLI:EU:C:2014:2454) relating to accession to the European Convention of Human Rights, and 1/09 (of 8 March 2011, ECLI:EU:C:2011:123) concerning the Draft agreement on the Creation of a unified patent litigation system – European and Community Patents Court.

As we know, the story finished with a positive outcome when the ECJ, in its subsequent Opinion 1/92 on 10 April 1992, accepted the new two-pillar judicial structure.[4] Yet, in view of the harsh words of Opinion 1/91 and of the later development of Union law towards an ever more exclusive understanding of its autonomy with regard to external dispute settlement mechanisms,[5] one might wonder how anyone could think of something as stupid as the EEA Court in the form it was planned in 1991.

Having participated in the EEA[6] process from the summer of 1989, I, for one, found the idea of a joint judicial body for the EEA both legitimate and sound, and not as an inevitable non-starter. That said, I think in retrospect that the negotiators on the Community side should have understood, based on Opinion 1/76, that the very basic idea of the EEA Court as a body being simultaneously inside and outside the ECJ would be unpalatable for that institution.

In the following, I shall describe the process in 1990 and 1991 leading up to the political solution and draft agreement on the EEA Court that was rejected in Opinion 1/91. I will not be exclusively relying on my memory, but will be building on documentation available in the archives of the Finnish Foreign Ministry (FFMA). As a junior civil servant, as I then was, I participated in this process in the EFTA Group of Legal Experts (GLE), the Negotiation Group V (NG V) on Legal and Institutional Questions, the drafting group for the EEA Agreement, and had various responsibilities relating to national preparations and implementation. Thus, this contribution to the EFTA Court thirtieth anniversary is not that of a neutral academic observer, but of a foot soldier in a campaign in which the battle was lost, but the victory was ultimately achieved. With the benefit of hindsight, the two-pillar structured EEA has been a viable solution, even if it turned out to be too ambitious for Switzerland and politically insufficient for Austria, Finland and Sweden.

II. *DRÔLE DE GUERRE* ON THE EEA JUDICIAL MECHANISM (1989 AND 1990)

The idea of an EEA started in the 1980s as a process of aiming at achieving a 'European Economic Space' (EES) by means of a structured EFTA–EC cooperation where the EFTA States[7] would speak 'with one voice' and participate in selected

[4] Opinion 1/92 of 10 April 1992, given pursuant to the second subparagraph of Article 228 (1) of the EEC Treaty – 'Draft agreement between the Community, on the one hand, and the countries of the European Free Trade Association, on the other, relating to the creation of the European Economic Area'. ECLI:EU:C:1992:189.

[5] See, for example, N Jääskinen and A Sikora, 'The Exclusive Jurisdiction of the Court of Justice of the European Union and the Unity of the EU Legal Order' in M Cremona, A Thies and R Wessel (eds), *The Exclusive Jurisdiction of the Court of Justice of the European Union and the Unity of the EU Legal Order* (Oxford, Hart Publishing, 2017) 101–11.

[6] The EEA was called the 'European Economic Space' (EES) up until the formal negotiations started in June 1990. According to Sven Norberg, who was then Director of Legal Affairs at EFTA, this purely linguistic change was due to the opinion of the then British Prime Minister Margaret Thatcher, who had expressed a preference 'for a more down-to-earth expression'. See, S Norberg, '20 Years on: Some Reflections on the European Economic Area Judicial Mechanism', in P Cardonnel, A Rosas and N Wahl (eds), *Constitutionalising the EU Judicial System: Essays in Honour of Pernilla Lindh* (Oxford, Hart Publishing, 2012) 57–76, at 61, fn 12.

[7] Austria, Finland, Iceland, Norway, Sweden, and Switzerland. Later, in 1991, Liechtenstein joined EFTA and took part in the EEA process.

fields of Community activities. This objective was already embodied in the declaration adopted by a joint EFTA–EC ministerial meeting in Luxembourg in 1984. This so-called Luxembourg process failed to achieve coherent and comprehensive results, which was a disappointment, especially to those EFTA States that considered accession to the Communities to be a politically viable option. Moreover, for all EFTA States, the emergence of the Single Market programme raised fears of marginalisation and market closure by the Communities.

This said, from the judicial point of view, the Luxembourg process featured one success, namely the Lugano Convention of 1988,[8] which created a system of recognition and enforcement of judgments in civil and commercial matters for the EFTA and the EC parallel to the Brussels Convention covering the EC Member States. Protocol 2 to the Lugano Convention included a text that was later known as the so-called Lugano formula. According to Article 1 of the Protocol: 'The courts of each Contracting State shall, when applying and interpreting the provisions of the Convention, pay due account to the principles laid down by any relevant decision delivered by courts of the other Contracting States concerning provisions of this Convention.' Furthermore, a mechanism for exchange of the relevant case law and consultation relating to its development was set out in Articles 2–4 of the Protocol. The Lugano formula was reproduced mutatis mutandis in Article 106 of the EEA Agreement and became a cornerstone of the legal homogeneity sought with the Agreement.[9]

In January 1989, the creation of an EEA received a dual political impetus from the EFTA States' urgent need to achieve as complete access as possible to the EC internal market and the endeavour of the Community to avoid, or at least to postpone, any further accessions, notably by the EFTA States. New accessions needed to wait until the Single Market programme was finalised and the process leading to the Maastricht Treaty was completed. Therefore, the proposal of Jacques Delors, the then President of the Commission, of a new form of partnership in 1989 was met with enthusiasm on the EFTA side. The basic principle of this Oslo–Brussels process was to enable, for the EFTA States, non-discriminatory and complete access to the EC internal market in exchange for their acceptance of the relevant *acquis communautaire* in its entirety, with no possibility to pick and choose.

The formal negotiations started in June 1990.[10] They were preceded by exploratory discussions that had started during the spring of 1989 and by the approval in June 1990 of the EC Council of the mandate to negotiate for the Commission as proposed by the latter institution in May 1990. The Commission thus represented

[8] The Lugano Convention of 1988 was later superseded by the Lugano Convention of 2007.

[9] See Norberg (n 6) 59–60; and S Norberg, 'The EFTA Court: One of the Two Main Components of the EEA Judicial Mechanism' in J Stuyck and A Looijestijn-Clearie (eds), *The European Economic Area EC–EFTA* (Deventer, Kluwer European Monographs, 1994) 9–32, at 20.

[10] The decision to open formal negotiations was taken by the EC-EFTA ministerial meeting of 19 December 1989, which acknowledged, among other things, the need of 'judicial monitoring' of the EEA; see https://www.cvce.eu/en/obj/joint_declaration_following_the_efta_ec_ministerial_meeting_brussels_19_december_1989-en-15be72f3-9039-4b5a-87fc-2e4a59561708.html. The EC Council authorised the opening of the negotiations only on 18 June 1990 and adopted the mandate to negotiate for the Commission; see https://archives.eui.eu/en/fonds/114557?item=EN-1760. This mandate was founded on the premise that the effects of the accord would be those of classic public international law ('de droit international public classique').

all 12 EC Member States at the negotiating table, while the state holding the presidency of EFTA represented the EFTA side. For the Community, it was an absolute prerequisite for the EEA process that the EFTA side spoke 'with one voice' so that the Commission was not bound to negotiate individually with each EFTA State. This forced the EFTA States to establish common positions, often not without great difficulties, before they were communicated to the Community side.

The issues relating to EEA Court were discussed in EFTA GLE, in the NG V, and the drafting group for the EEA Agreement. The two last mentioned groups met either in an internal EFTA formation for preparation or jointly with the EC representatives. For me, it turned out that the possibility to participate in this process as of June 1989 marked a turning point in my professional career.[11]

At the outset, it was clear that the homogeneous and dynamic EEA would need a stronger judicial backbone than the existing EFTA–EC arrangements. How this could be achieved was not obvious. Would the recently crafted Lugano formula suffice, possibly supplemented with dispute settlement by ad hoc panels such as those envisaged for the World Trade Organization? Or was something more ambitious needed? These issues were debated at the EFTA Group of Legal Experts, assisted by the young lions of the EFTA Secretariat legal affairs service. In this context, I had the privilege to get acquainted with many future colleagues such as Josef Azizi, Henrik Bull, Pernilla Lindh and Nils Wahl. Later, a special ad hoc EFTA working group for the EEA judicial body was established under the chairmanship of Leif Sevón.

The internal preparations of the EEA within EFTA structures identified the need to establish a possibility for economic operators to invoke and defend their EEA law based rights in the courts and tribunals of the EFTA States under conditions analogous with those that prevailed in the EC. This raised the constitutionally and technically difficult problem of the direct applicability and effect of EEA rules on the EFTA side as well as the need to ensure their uniform interpretation at the national level and, in the case of divergent interpretations, a binding dispute settlement mechanism.[12] Moreover, there was an urgent need to find a solution – or solutions – to the so-called *Polydor* problem. In 1982, the ECJ had come to the conclusion that in spite of the identical wording of the relevant provisions in the EEC Treaty and the free-trade agreement between Portugal and the EEC, their interpretation was not identical due to the two regimes' different policy objectives.[13]

[11] This opportunity was offered to me by my then boss Leif Sevón, later President of the EFTA Court, a judge at the ECJ and President of the Finnish Supreme Court. He was at that time the Director-General for Legislation at the Finnish Ministry of Justice, where I served as a legal adviser. Academically, I was a rarity in Finland in the 1980s because I had studied European economic law at a postgraduate level and published a book in Finnish on Community law, more precisely on the extraterritorial effects of EEC competition law.

[12] See the note by the EFTA Secretariat of 19 April 1989, Contribution to the Considerations on the Question of Surveillance and Enforcement of Treaty Obligations in EES Relations, annexed to letter R 189/89 of the same date of Georg Reisch, Secretary-General of the EFTA, to Ambassador Martin Hulid of Norway, acting as chairman of the EFTA Council. FFMA folder 37.60. 'EY/EU, EY-EFTA oikeudelliset kysymykset', subfolder 1988/4382 'Legaaliset kysymykset EY-Efta kokoukset 1989–90 (Eftan lakiasiantuntijaryhmä)'.

[13] Case 270/80 *Polydor Ltd and RSO Records Inc. v Harlequin Records Shops Ltd and Simons Records Ltd*, Judgment of the Court of 9 February 1982, ECLI:EU:C:1982:43. The relevant provisions concerned measures with equivalent effects as quantitative restrictions on imports with regard to the question of exhaustion of trade mark protection against parallel imports.

At the first formal negotiations on legal and institutional questions in July 1990, the EC's position represented by the Commission regarding the EEA judicial body was quite imprecise, whereas the EFTA team had, based on its thorough internal preparations, a relatively well-defined overview of the matter. At the 19 and 20 July 1990 EC–EFTA joint meeting of negotiating group NG V, which was dealing with these issues, the Commission reiterated its position that the EEA judicial mechanism should be integrated into the ECJ[14] and that infringement procedures in the EEA should not follow the example of the then Article 169 EC, but of Article 170 EC. In other words, the initiative in infringement procedure should remain with the contracting parties and not with an EEA surveillance mechanism. The Commission was worried about the prospect of Community law 'degenerating' into ordinary international law, which is why a solution where the EEA Court would be a 'cour plénière' was not acceptable.[15] This latter expression referred to EFTA's preferred solution, consisting of an integrated EEA Court comprising the then ECJ with its 13 judges enlarged with seven EFTA judges (ie, one judge per EFTA State) and having exclusive competence over interpretation of EEA rules, with EFTA judges also participating in the handling of pure Community law cases.

During the autumn of 1990, the EFTA ad hoc working group on the EEA judicial mechanism prepared a less ambitious model, taking into account the rather chilling feedback from the Community's chief negotiator, Director-General Jean-Louis Dewost of the Commission Legal Service. Its report was adopted by the EFTA NG V on 8 November 1990, but was not handed over to the EC negotiators. The ad hoc working group concluded that the model of a fully integrated EEA Court enabled avoiding conflicts of competences with the ECJ and eliminated the risk of divergent judgments. However, this model entailed 'serious political consequences both for the EC side and the EFTA side' because it would imply that 'EC judges could adjudicate in a dispute between two EFTA countries [and vice versa]'.[16] Thus, the model of an EEA Court legally separated from but in practice integrated into the ECJ seemed more viable. For political reasons, it was necessary that there should be one judge from each EFTA State. This solution would lead to the need to have an equal number of EC judges, notably sitting in the ECJ. Such a personal union with the ECJ was considered essential to safeguard the uniform interpretation and application of EEA rules and identical/parallel EC rules. The EEA Court was planned to have exclusive

[14] The negotiating mandate of the Commission (see n 10 above) referred at point 11 to 'un mécanisme juridictionnel. Ce dernier pourrait s'appuyer sur la Cour de Justice de Luxembourg à laquelle on pourrait adjoindre des juges des États membres de l'AELE. Cette instance serait chargée de l'interprétation des dispositions de l'accord, ainsi que du règlement des différends entre les parties'.

[15] See report (Jääskinen–Pirinen) (nd) to the Finnish Ministry of Foreign Affairs on the meetings NG V/ EFTA and NG V/ EFTA EC in Brussels on 16–18 July and 19–20 July 1990, and the annexed EC Fiche N. 2 'Procédure de surveillance et mécanisme juridictionnel', in FFMA folder 37.13 'EY_EFTA ETA HLNG NG V; Juridisia ja institutionaalisia kysymyksiä käsittelevä neuvotteluryhmä 1990/16825, 1.1.1990–30.4.1991'.

[16] See 'Draft, EFTA Negotiating group on legal and institutional questions, Ad hoc group on the EEA judicial body, Chairman's report', annexed to the report of Finland's Permanent Representation to the European Communities of 9 November 1990 (Pirinen), on the NG V/EFTA EC meeting in Brussels on 8 November 1990, in FFMA folder 37.13 'EY_EFTA ETA HLNG NG V; Juridisia ja institutionaalisia kysymyksiä käsittelevä neuvotteluryhmä 1990/16825, 1.1.1990–30.4.1991'. The text in square brackets is a handwritten addendum of unclear provenance.

competence regarding the interpretation of EEA rules and comprehensive jurisdiction relating to Contracting Party infringements and related disputes. Administratively, the EEA Court would have shared the ECJ infrastructures and facilities, except for the registry and the cabinets of the EFTA judges.

In the context of its meeting in Brussels on 13 and 14 November 1990 the following week, the EFTA NG V negotiating group held informal discussions with two Commission Legal Service representatives (Jean-Louis Dewost and Armando Toledano-Laredo). Their message was that the model based on an 'EC bis super-Community *à dix-neuf*', (ie, 12 plus seven states) was an unacceptable solution for EEA institutional structures. That said, the question of the EEA judicial mechanism would be easy to solve 'at the end of the day'. The EFTA side was told that a common court would be an ideal solution, but would be impossible for political reasons, because the Luxembourg Court was also a political institution that had promoted integration by means of its teleological interpretations, which excluded the EFTA States' participation. The EC could not accept the degeneration of the ECJ into a classic international law tribunal. However, a personal union between the ECJ and the EEA Court would be part of the solution. The future agreement needed to include political guidance for preventing *Polydor* situations, in which identically worded provisions were given different interpretations because of the different integration policy objectives of the two regimes.[17]

Despite these discussions, it seems that the EC did not have a formally approved detailed position on the EEA judicial mechanism before the early months of 1991. Thus, the handling of this set of problems constituted a kind of 'drôle de guerre' ('phoney war'), in which the EC party, like Britain and France on the Western Front from September 1939 to April 1940, avoided direct contact and confrontation, whereas there was an abundance of alternative strategies on the EFTA side.

III. TOWARDS THE ACCEPTANCE OF A JOINT EEA COURT (SPRING 1991)

If the EFTA side was frustrated with the absence of an official EC position on the EEA judicial mechanism as of July 1990, they were to become truly disappointed once they were presented with one.

Indeed, at the January 1991 meeting of NG V/EFTA EC, the Commission orally presented the EC idea of the EEA judicial mechanism taking the form of an EEA Chamber at the ECJ, consisting of five ECJ judges supplemented with two part-time EFTA judges. It was estimated that the caseload of this special chamber would be rather small – at the level of five to six cases per year – as it would only handle those interpretation differences that were not resolved by the political dispute settlement mechanism under the auspices of the 'EEA joint body'. Thus, there would be neither preliminary rulings nor infringement procedure concerning EEA rules. Uniformity of interpretation would be guaranteed by the Lugano formula, meaning that in

[17] Report to the Finnish Ministry of Justice (N Jääskinen) of 15 November 1990, NG V/EFTA meeting in Brussels on 13 and 14 November 1990, in FFMA folder 37.13 'EY_EFTA ETA HLNG NG V; Juridisia ja institutionaalisia kysymyksiä käsittelevä neuvotteluryhmä 1990/16825, 1.1.1990–30.4.1991'.

practice the EFTA was bound to follow the interpretations adopted by the ECJ. The Commission pointed out that this low-profile judicial body solution would require neither provisions on the direct effect and primacy of EEA rules nor an independent surveillance body for the EFTA pillar. On the EFTA side, the EC position was considered as an attempt to introduce a division within EFTA between the Alpine and Nordic EFTA States. The EFTA side was also shocked by the Commission's approach, which it understood as abandoning the goals of homogeneity, strong independent surveillance and unified judicial interpretation within the EEA. They were especially disappointed with the Commission's rejection of the idea of preliminary rulings. It was felt that negotiations could not be based on the EC positions. These feelings were summarised in the EFTA speaking note as follows: 'You have now presented us orally with an outline of how the Community envisages the composition, competences and functioning of the EEA judicial mechanism. Having said this, Mr Chairman, you will not be surprised if I say that we are not only surprised but also deeply concerned.'[18] My personal impression in retrospect is that the Commission needed to downplay the EEA institutional potential in order to avoid the EEA Agreement becoming a mixed agreement with the EC Member States as Contracting Parties, in addition to the European Economic Community as an international organisation.[19]

The critical negotiations on the EEA judicial mechanism led to success in the form of a joint ministerial declaration of 14 May 1991. It defined a common ground for this issue.[20] This crucial step was not easy to achieve. The long and winding road to this solution started to emerge in February 1991. Indeed, based on the documentation of the NG V level negotiations, one gets the impression of a rather confused, even chaotic process. Yet, the political stakes were quite high for the EFTA side. Sven Norberg points out that after it had become clear that the EFTA States could not expect any real influence in EC decision-making procedures, the importance of an equal footing-based judicial mechanism became even more important.[21] Meagre consolation was provided by the message conveyed by the Swiss EFTA presidency in mid-February 1991, according to which President Delors had privately assured that the EEA would not fail because of the court issue.[22]

[18] See report (Paasivirta) of 30 January 1991 to the Finnish Ministry of Foreign Affairs on the meetings NG V/EFTA and NG V/ EFTA EC in Brussels on 28–29 January 1991, and the annexed 'Elements for speaking notes on judicial body', dated 29 January 1991, in FFMA folder 37.13 'EY_EFTA ETA HLNG NG V; Juridisia ja institutionaalisia kysymyksiä käsittelevä neuvotteluryhmä 1990/16825, 1.1.1990–30.4.1991'.

[19] It seems that the definitive decision that the EEA Agreement be concluded as a mixed agreement was taken at the Committee of the Permanent Representatives of the Governments of the Member States to the European Union (COREPER) only in September 1991. See report (Paasivirta) of 20 September 1991 to the Finnish Ministry of Foreign Affairs on the meeting NG V/EFTA in Brussels on 19 September 1991, in FFMA folder 37.13 'EY_EFTA ETA HLNG NG V; Juridisia ja institutionaalisia kysymyksiä käsittelevä neuvotteluryhmä 1990/16825, 1.5.1991–31.12.1991'.

[20] According to Sven Norberg, the political compromise was found at a briefing session of 13 May 1991 between the EFTA and EC side chairs, the Austrian Wolfgang Schüssel and the Luxembourger Jacques Poos, before the ministerial meeting of 14 May 1991. See S Norberg, 'Justice in the European Economic Area: The Role of the EFTA Court' in EFTA Court (ed), *Judicial Protection in the European Economic Area* (Stuttgart, German Law Publishers, 2012) 29–52, at 37.

[21] Norberg (n 6) 61.

[22] See report (Paasivirta) of 15 February 1991 to the Finnish Ministry of Foreign Affairs on the meeting NG V/EFTA in Brussels on 12–14 February 1991, in FFMA folder 37.13 'EY_EFTA ETA HLNG NG V; Juridisia ja institutionaalisia kysymyksiä käsittelevä neuvotteluryhmä 1990/16825, 1.1.1990–30.4.1991'.

At the end of February 1991, the two sides presented their respective positions in writing, which were quite far apart. The EFTA side wanted a joint EEA Court that was legally separated but integrated into the ECJ. This could have been achieved through a personal union in which an appropriate number of EC judges sat in the EEA Court together with seven EFTA judges, ie, one judge for each EFTA State. The EEA Court would have had comprehensive and exclusive competence in EEA law, and its task would have been to ensure that the law is respected in the application and interpretation of the EEA 'Treaty'. The EEA Court would have had competence to give preliminary rulings on EEA rules, as well as for the courts of the EC Member States, whereas the ECJ would not have had the competence to issue preliminary rulings on EEA rules. For the dispute settlement, the contracting parties would have had direct access to the EEA Court without political filtering by the joint body. The EEA Court would also have had exercised legality control of EEA related EFTA decisions. Therefore, a separate EFTA Court proposed by the Commission would not have been needed, as the EEA Agreement would also have applied in intra-EFTA relations.[23]

The Commission observed that the EEA judicial mechanism should be 'aussi souple et léger que possible'. It should guarantee maximum coherence between the EEA rules and Community law, while respecting and preserving the specificity of the latter. Any differences of interpretation should primarily have been dealt with first through diplomatic means at a joint body and, if necessary, as a second step by a judicial mechanism, namely through preliminary rulings under Article 177 of the EEC Treaty delivered by a special chamber of the ECJ consisting of its five members supplemented with two EFTA judges. The judicial mechanism should have been supported by the registry and technical services of the ECJ. Otherwise, the coherence of interpretation of the EEA rules would have been ensured through the Lugano formula.[24]

In the negotiations of March and April 1991 at the NG V level, the debate travelled in different directions without any conclusive results being achieved. The parties had presented their basic positions in the form of legal provisions, EFTA in March[25] and the EC in April,[26] but new problems were introduced into the debate, especially the question of how EFTA internal competition and state aid issues should be dealt with in the EEA judicial mechanism. The solutions explored included a separate EFTA

[23] See report (Paasivirta) of 28 February 1991 to the Finnish Ministry of Foreign Affairs on the meetings NG V/EFTA and NG V/EFTA EC in Brussels on 25–26 February 1991, and the annexed EFTA position paper 'Note No. 3 In the EEA Court' of 26 February 1991 and EC position paper 'Mécanisme juridictionnel CEE/AELE, 19 février 1991' in FFMA folder 37.13 'EY_EFTA ETA HLNG NG V; Juridisia ja institutionaalisia kysymyksiä käsittelevä neuvotteluryhmä 1990/16825, 1.1.1990–30.4.1991'.

[24] ibid.

[25] See EFTA non-paper of 19 March 1991 'Rules on the EEA Court of Justice', annexed to the report (Paasivirta) of 28 March 1991 to the Finnish Ministry of Foreign Affairs on the meetings NG V/EFTA and NG V/EFTA EC in Brussels on 18–19 March 1991, in FFMA folder 37.13 'EY_EFTA ETA HLNG NG V; Juridisia ja institutionaalisia kysymyksiä käsittelevä neuvotteluryhmä 1990/16825, 1.1.1990–30.4.1991'.

[26] See EC non-paper consisting a partial English translation of the document SJ/109/01-EN, 4 March 1991, 'dispositions institutionnelles', annexed to the report (Paasivirta) of 29 April 1991 to the Finnish Ministry of Foreign Affairs on the meetings NG V/EFTA and NG V/EFTA EC in Brussels on 22–23 April 1991, in FFMA folder 37.13 'EY_EFTA ETA HLNG NG V; Juridisia ja institutionaalisia kysymyksiä käsittelevä neuvotteluryhmä 1990/16825, 1.1.1990–30.4.1991'.

Court, an EFTA Chamber of the ECJ consisting only of EFTA judges and examining, at the first instance, actions against decisions of the EFTA Surveillance Authority or an EEA Court of first instance.

The joint ministerial declaration of 14 May 1991, adopted by the ministerial meeting of 13 May 1991 between all EC Member States, the Commission and the EFTA States, was a compromise found at a higher political level.[27] The joint declaration noted that: 'The participants stressed the need to have in the European Economic Area an effective system of surveillance composed on the one hand of the Commission and on the other hand of an EFTA mechanism working in a similar way and also an independent judicial mechanism' (point 21). The principles of the independent judicial mechanism were declared to be as follows (point 22):

- nomination of seven judges from the EFTA States;
- the creation of an independent EEA Court composed of five judges from the EC Court and three of the seven EFTA judges, functionally integrated with the ECJ, which would be competent to give rulings:
  - concerning dispute settlement (including, when necessary, interpretation of the EEA rules) on request of the joint body of the contracting parties,
  - concerning disputes between the EFTA Surveillance Body and an EFTA country,
  - concerning cases brought by enterprises or states against decisions of the EFTA structure in the field of competition (including state aid);
- reinforcement of the legal homogeneity within EEA through the opening of intervention possibilities for EFTA countries before the ECJ and through a procedure inspired by that of the Lugano Convention.[28]

The compromise reflected much of the EFTA position, with one notable exception: there was no mention of the possibility for the EEA Court to deliver preliminary rulings for national courts and tribunals of the EFTA States. This issue was to be dealt with later by a separate protocol enabling the EFTA States to authorise their national courts and tribunals to ask the ECJ to express itself on the interpretation of EEA rules corresponding to EC rules.[29]

As Sven Norberg correctly points out, the compromise of May 1991 was experienced as a major breakthrough in the EEA negotiations.[30] Perhaps this general

[27] Still on 2 May 1991, the parties had limited themselves to reiterating their basic positions on EEA judicial mechanism. See the report (Paasivirta) of 3 May 1991 to the Finnish Ministry of Foreign Affairs on the meetings NG V/EFTA and NG V/EFTA EC in Brussels on 1–2 May 1991, in FFMA folder 37.13 'EY_EFTA ETA HLNG NG V; Juridisia ja institutionaalisia kysymyksiä käsittelevä neuvotteluryhmä 1990/16825, 1.5.1991–31.12.1991'.

[28] EC EFTA Ministerial Declaration of 14 May 1991, annexed to the report (Paasivirta) of 24 May 1991 to the Finnish Ministry of Foreign Affairs on the meeting NG V/EFTA in Brussels on 16 May 1991, in FFMA folder 37.13 'EY_EFTA ETA HLNG NG V; Juridisia ja institutionaalisia kysymyksiä käsittelevä neuvotteluryhmä 1990/16825, 1.5.1991–31.12.1991'.

[29] This was a political gesture that proved to be fatal for the EEA judicial mechanism as envisaged in the joint ministerial declaration, as in Opinion 1/91 the ECJ was particularly critical towards the idea of non-binding preliminary rulings.

[30] Norberg (n 6) 62.

satisfaction explains why the weak signals from the ECJ hinting at possible problems as to the acceptability of the EEA Court were not taken seriously. Indeed, President Ole Due of the ECJ had already written a letter to Director-General Jean-Louis Dewost in April 1991 expressing his concern that the judicial solution for the EEA might prove to be too ambitious and hence problematic for the ECJ,[31] and similar worries had been repeated later unofficially by the members of the Court.[32]

IV. *LES NAUFRAGÉS DU FOL ESPOIR* (AUTUMN 1991)

Les Naufragés du Fol Espoir – loosely translated as 'The Shipwreck of the Wild Hope' – was a theatrical production by the Théâtre du Soleil in Paris in 2010.[33] It is difficult to find a more accurate expression of the emotions of the EFTA side negotiators after Opinion 1/91 of the ECJ than the French title of that play.

Indeed, the May 1991 compromise had revitalised the EEA process, which had meanwhile become somewhat anaemic. In the early spring of 1991, there had been informal communications from the EC side to the effect that the EEA would be allowed to lapse, for example, by raising the level of requirements towards EFTA States to such an intolerable level that negotiations would be cut off.[34] That said, the negotiations between May and July 1991 were difficult because the ministerial declaration of 14 May had left the substance of most of the problems open and created additional problems, such as where to put the 'surplus' EFTA judges, considering that the EEA Court needed only three of seven, or the need for/utility of an EEA Court of First Instance. In the summer of 1991, the problem of adding a possibility for EFTA State courts and tribunals to seek preliminary rulings from the EC on a voluntary basis, pursuant to an optional protocol, also turned out to be a hot potato.

Despite these difficulties, a treaty text emerged in various successive versions, one of which was sent by the Commission for an opinion to the ECJ on 14 August 1991. In my recollection, during the negotiations, the EFTA side considered recourse to this procedure as a certainty, either by the Commission or by one of the EC Member States. Later, in October 1991, the EEA negotiations were formally finalised after the open fisheries issues were resolved.

[31] See the report (Paasivirta) of 16 April 1991 to the Finnish Ministry of Foreign Affairs on the meetings NG V/EFTA and NG V/EFTA EC in Brussels on 8–9 April 1991, in FFMA folder 37.13 'EY_EFTA ETA HLNG NG V; Juridisia ja institutionaalisia kysymyksiä käsittelevä neuvotteluryhmä 1990/16825, 1.1.1990–30.4.1991'.

[32] See the report (Paasivirta) of 29 April 1991 to the Finnish Ministry of Foreign Affairs on the meetings NG V/EFTA and NG V/EFTA EC in Brussels on 22–23 April 1991, in FFMA folder 37.13 'EY_EFTA ETA HLNG NG V; Juridisia ja institutionaalisia kysymyksiä käsittelevä neuvotteluryhmä 1990/16825, 1.1.1990–30.4.1991'.

[33] The play was directed by A Mnouchkine based on a text by H Cixous. It is loosely based on J Verne's posthumous novel *Les Naufragés du Jonathan* (*The Survivors of the 'Jonathan'*) published in 1909.

[34] See the report (Paasivirta) of 11 February 1991 to the Finnish Ministry of Foreign Affairs on the meetings EFTA and EFTA EC Legal experts of 6–8 February 1991, FFMA folder 37.60. 'EY/EU, EY-EFTA oikeudelliset kysymykset', subfolder 1988/4382 'Legaaliset kysymykset EY-Efta kokoukset 1991 (Eftan lakiasiantuntijaryhmä)'. At this gathering, the Commission also noted that there might be a need for an opinion of ECJ before the approval of the EEA Agreement by the Communities.

Pursuant to a version of the draft agreement dated 25 July 1991,[35] an independent EEA Court, functionally integrated with the ECJ, would be established. When sitting in plenary session, it would have consisted of five ECJ judges and, based on rotation, three judges nominated by the EFTA States. The EEA Court could also have sat in chambers of three or five judges. The presidency of the EEA Court would have rotated between the EC and EFTA judges.

The EEA Court would have been vested with three basic competences, namely the settlement of disputes between the Contracting Parties, actions concerning the surveillance procedure regarding the EFTA States and appeals against decisions in the field of competition initiated by the EFTA Surveillance Authority. The EEA Court could be seised by the Contracting Parties of the EEA Joint Committee for the settlement of disputes and by legal or natural persons appealing against decisions given by the EEA Court of First Instance[36] in the field of competition. The EFTA States were authorised to empower the EEA Court in cases where the EFTA Surveillance Authority exercised its supervisory powers. Uniformity of interpretation would have been ensured by the Lugano formula supplemented by the option for the EFTA States to empower their courts and tribunals to seek 'rulings' from the ECJ on the interpretation of the EEA Agreement and its annexes and protocols. In the final version, this was modified to the possibility to ask the ECJ 'to express itself' on 'the interpretation of an EEA rule'.

In its request for an opinion, the Commission asked the ECJ to take a stand on four questions, namely the compatibility with Opinion 1/76 of the presence of ECJ judges on the EEA Court, the compatibility with the Treaties of the possibility for EFTA States to intervene in proceedings before the ECJ, the possibility to empower courts and tribunals of the EFTA States to put questions to the ECJ on interpretation of EEA rules without amending the EEC Treaty, and the compatibility of the system of courts provided in the EEA Agreement with Article 238 of the EEC Treaty (currently Articles 217 and 218(8), second subparagraph of the Treaty on the Functioning of the European Union (TFEU)).

Despite the EEA Agreement being negotiated in English, the ECJ Opinion 1/91 was founded on an incomplete French translation that was never updated to the final mutually agreed draft. As Norberg has pointed out, the conclusion in Opinion 1/91 on the impossibility of achieving legal homogeneity between the EEA and the Community was founded on the assumption that the preamble to the EEA Agreement

[35] This version of the EEA Agreement was attached to the speech that Leif Sevón gave at the meeting of the Nordic Ministers of Justice in Bornholm of 22 and 23 August 1991, FFMA folder 37.60. 'EY/EU, EY-EFTA oikeudelliset kysymykset', subfolder 1988/4382 'Legaaliset kysymykset EY-Efta kokoukset 1991 (Eftan lakiasiantuntijaryhmä)'. The numbering of the draft agreement discussed in Opinion 1/91 does not correspond with this draft, but the provisions seem to be identical in their substance, except for details that were indicated as non-final in the July draft. The Commission asked for the opinion from the ECJ on 14 August 1991 on the basis of an incomplete draft, but sent the ECJ a non-initialled yet complete English-language draft dated 30 October 1991. See the French text of Opinion 1/91 as reproduced in the Commission document SEC 1991-2520 of 17 December 1991 (https://archives.eui.eu/en/fonds/651387?item=CEUE_SEGE-01.01.02.25-SEC(1991)2520). The English version of Opinion 1/91 is available at: https://eur-lex.europa.eu/legal-content/EN/TXT/PDF/?uri=CELEX:61991CV0001&from=EN.

[36] The EEA Court of First Instance was to be composed of three EFTA judges and two members of the EC Court of First Instance.

would have contained only a single recital, which was not correct and overlooked the fact that the negotiated preamble contained 14 other recitals, contributing to the objective of legal homogeneity in the EEA.[37]

Without going into details, it is sufficient to note that the ECJ found that '[t]he system of judicial supervision which the agreement proposes to set up is incompatible with the Treaty establishing the European Economic Community'. The presence of ECJ judges on the EEA Court was incompatible with the EEC Treaty because they would have been compelled to interpret identically worded provisions within different teleological contexts, thus possibly affecting their independence and openness in the interpretation of Community law in intra-EC situations. The competences of the EEA Court would extend to intra-EC issues in that it would be able to decide whether the relevant contracting party of the dispute was the EC or its Member States, thus contradicting the autonomy of Community law. The non-binding character of the interpretation issued by the ECJ based on requests by EFTA State courts and tribunals would dilute the nature of the preliminary references mechanism. Such existential changes to EC judicial system could not be introduced in the context of an association agreement. In sum, only the opening of the possibility of intervention by EFTA States in pending CJEU proceedings was found to be compatible with the EEC Treaty.

The EFTA NG V held an internal meeting on 16 December 1991. The general feeling appears to have been one of resignation. Opinion 1/91 was taken as a fait accompli and it was felt that the ball was now in the Commission's court. A joint judicial mechanism for the EEA was now considered a foreclosed option, but the need remained for binding judicial control, especially concerning application of the EEA competition rules on the EFTA side. Since nobody contemplated accepting the CJEU's jurisdiction in this regard, the prospect of establishing a separate EFTA Court started to appear as a more attractive option than it had during the preceding spring.[38] Hence, a new two-pillar solution embodying a separate EFTA Court was negotiated rapidly, and the compromise was finalised in February 1992.

The Commission requested anew an opinion of the CJEU, now on the revamped version of the text. After a second opinion of the CJEU,[39] the EEA Agreement was signed in Porto in May 1992, though, alas, rejected by referendum in Switzerland on 6 December 1992. Finally, the EEA Agreement entered into force on 1 January 1994 and the EFTA Court started its work.

V. SOME CONCLUDING OBSERVATIONS

The EEA process was a unique experience, not only personally, but also in the wider historical context of European integration. The process was swift in taking into account the complexity of the substance matter, the need for ample legal and political

[37] See Norberg (n 20) 44–47.

[38] See the report (Paasivirta) of 19 December 1991 to the Finnish Ministry of Foreign Affairs on the meeting of the EFTA legal experts of 16 December 1991, in FFMA folder 37.13 'EY_EFTA ETA HLNG NG V; Juridisia ja institutionaalisia kysymyksiä käsittelevä neuvotteluryhmä 1990/16825, 1.5.1991–31.12.1991'.

[39] See n 4. This is a correct reference.

imagination, and the extremely voluminous outcome of the negotiations. Like an underdog boxer in 1930s Hollywood films, the EEA stood back up after two complete knockouts in the form of Opinion 1/91 and the negative result of the Swiss referendum. The rapidity of the opinion procedure at that time is also remarkable: the ECJ adopted two opinions of major constitutional importance within six months.

As I noted at the beginning of this chapter, the idea of a joint EEA judicial body was legally, if not politically, plausible. The EEA arrangement sought legal homogeneity based on EC internal market *acquis*, and one crucial element in this was effective judicial protection of economic operators and individuals, which required uniform interpretation of the EEA rules. Unlike the ECJ supposed in Opinion 1/91, it has later proved possible to achieve legal homogeneity in the interpretation of the EEA rules, in light of the interpretation of the corresponding EU law provisions and principles, despite the integration objectives of the EEA being less ambitious than those of the EU. This is amply demonstrated by the relevant case law of both the EFTA Court and the CJEU.

However, in my opinion, Sven Norberg is right when he argues that the ECJ would have rejected the EEA Court in any case.[40] Indeed, the dual roles of those ECJ judges that would have sat at the EEA Court, and the implicit jurisdiction vested in that organ over the division of implementation and application obligations between the Community and the Member States, were understandably a constitutional anathema.[41] That said, it is to be regretted that Opinion 1/91, due to the failure of the ECJ to verify that its analysis was based on the correct version of the draft agreement, has contributed to the emergence of 'victor's historiography'. It has supported academic, judicial and political positions that have undermined the possibility of achieving a homogeneous and dynamic European Economic Area between the Union and the three EFTA States which are contracting parties to this agreement.[42]

In conclusion, the EEA Court was a noble idea, but was unrealistic in view of the basic institutional principles of the Community/Union judicial architecture. Fortunately, its demise opened the way for a less ambitious, but, perhaps, a more solid judicial solution, namely that of the EFTA Court that is now celebrating its thirtieth anniversary. With these brief recollections of its unrealised predecessor, I would like to present my congratulations to this remarkable and successful institution.

[40] Norberg (n 20) 44.
[41] See in this respect Opinion 2/13 (n 4) paras 201–14.
[42] Norberg (n 20) 46.

4

The Surveillance and Court Agreement Looking Back, Looking Ahead

BERND HAMMERMANN*

I. INTRODUCTION

On 2 May 1992, the EEA Agreement was signed in Oporto, Portugal, between the then 12 EC Member States and seven EFTA States, together with the Agreement between the EFTA States on the establishment of a Surveillance Authority and a Court of Justice (the 'Surveillance and Court Agreement' or SCA).[1] The EEA/EFTA States[2] were obliged by Article 108(2) of the EEA Agreement to establish a court of justice: the EFTA Court ('the Court').[3] The Court came into operation following the entry into force of the EEA Agreement on 1 January 1994. Three decades on since the Court's inception, it is apt to look back and to reflect upon some of the challenges that have arisen, and to make proposals in order to facilitate the Court's work for the benefit of the EEA/EFTA States, individuals and economic operators.[4]

The following discussion is divided into three sections. Section II provides an overview of the SCA, covering its contextual background and its role for the Court. Section III will look back at selected aspects of the SCA thematically and will put

* I would like to thank Michael-James Clifton and Nathalie Campbell for their support in preparation of this chapter.

1 [1994] OJ L344/1. It is worth mentioning that it took the negotiators only two months to draft the relevant provisions for the establishment of the EFTA Court. The CJEU had rejected the original idea of an EEA Court on 14 December 1991 in Opinion 1/91 ECLI:EU:C:1991:490. The negotiations were concluded on 14 February 1992; see EFTA Secretariat, *Annual Report 1992: Thirty-Second Annual Report of the European Free Trade Association* (Geneva, 1993) 25.

2 The term 'EEA/EFTA States' refers to the (at present) three EFTA States, Iceland, Liechtenstein and Norway, which are Contracting Parties to the EEA.

3 References to the EU as well as EU/Union law include references to the former EEC as well as Community law. References to EEA law/rules refer to provisions of the EEA and SCA, its Annexes and Protocols, which are applicable to the EEA/EFTA States. The provisions of the EEA constitute an integral part of EU law; see Case T-115/94 *Opel Austria GmbH v Council* ECLI:EU:T:1997:3, para 102. After a negative popular vote in 1992, Switzerland decided not to join the EEA, notwithstanding the crucial role that it played during the negotiations, due to its economic importance in Europe.

4 A preparatory committee for the EFTA Court was set up in May 1992: see [1994–95] EFTA Ct Rep 9.

forward possible areas and ideas for innovation or reform. Section IV will set out the conclusions.

II. OVERVIEW OF THE SCA AND ITS ROLE FOR THE COURT

The main agreement of the SCA consists of 55 articles and nine protocols,[5] and has been amended 30 times so far, most recently on 1 December 2020.[6] The SCA is formed of five parts. Part I sets out definitions (Article 1), states the loyalty obligation of the EEA/EFTA States (Article 2) and provides the basis for homogeneity (Article 3). Part II details the establishment of the EFTA Surveillance Authority (ESA) and outlines its tasks and powers (Articles 4–21). Part III (Articles 22–26) provides further details on these matters, including ESA's obligation to monitor the application of the EEA Agreement and the SCA by the EEA/EFTA States (Article 22). Part IV establishes the EFTA Court (Article 27) and outlines the design of the Court, its role and jurisdiction (Articles 27–41).

The jurisdiction of the EFTA Court is premised in two parts: as regards EEA/EFTA States (Article 31 – infringement proceedings against an EEA/EFTA State; Article 32 – disputes between EEA/EFTA States; and Article 34 – advisory opinions); and in relation to ESA (Articles 36, 37 and 39 – actions respectively against ESA decisions, for failure to act and for compensation for damage caused by ESA for which it has non-contractual liability).

Part V (Articles 42–53) contains general and final provisions. Critically, it provides that the Protocols and Annexes to the SCA are integral to it (Article 42) and provides that the Statute of the Court is laid down in Protocol 5 SCA and enables the Court to adopt its rules of procedure (Article 43). Further, it establishes the budgetary mechanisms for ESA and the Court (Articles 47 and 48 respectively). Provisions also set out how to modify the SCA, how an EEA/EFTA State may withdraw from the SCA or how an EFTA State may accede to the SCA (Articles 49, 50, and 51 respectively).

The SCA is supplemented by nine protocols and two annexes. Protocol 2 sets out ESA's powers and functions in the field of public procurement. Protocols 3 and 4 operate similarly as regards ESA's powers and functions in the field of state aid and competition law respectively. Protocol 5 forms the Statute of the Court. The Statute covers the Court's tasks, powers and rules of governance in 44 articles. These govern the appointment and governance of judges and the registrar, and the process for making decisions in judicial and administrative affairs, as well as the language regime for the Court and the procedures in front of the EFTA Court. Protocol 6 lays down

[5] Article 25a SCA was inserted by the Agreement amending the Agreement between the EFTA States on the Establishment of a Surveillance Authority and a Court of Justice by adding a new Art 25a and a new Protocol 8 to the Agreement of 6 October 2016. Article 44a SCA was introduced by the Agreement amending the Agreement between the EFTA States on the Establishment of a Surveillance Authority and a Court of Justice by adding Art 44a and Protocol 9 to the Agreement of 30 January 2020. Due to the non-participation of Switzerland and the accession of Liechtenstein from 1 May 1995, the SCA was accordingly revised. A consolidated version of the SCA is available at: www.efta.int/Agreement-Annexes-and-Protocols-2477.

[6] Decision amending Protocol 5 to the Agreement between the EFTA States on the Establishment of a Surveillance Authority and a Court of Justice of 1 December 2020.

provisions on the legal capacity, privileges and immunities enjoyed by ESA, with Protocol 7 setting out equivalent provisions as regards the Court. Protocols 8 and 9 were recently added to outline the functions and powers of ESA in the field of financial supervision, following the founding in the EU of the European Banking Authority (EBA), the European Insurance and Occupational Pensions Authority (EIOPA) and the European Securities and Markets Authority (ESMA), and those of ESA and the EFTA Court regarding the UK's withdrawal from the EU and separation from the EEA.[7]

As noted above, pursuant to Article 43 SCA, the EFTA Court shall adopt its rules of procedure, which must be approved by the EEA/EFTA governments. The Court's initial rules of procedure were drafted by the judges who had already been appointed from 1993 and were formally adopted during the Court's inaugural session on 4 January 1994.[8] The first significant update to the rules of procedure was only in 2021, when the rules were, in part, revised to align with those of the Court of Justice of the European Union (CJEU) insofar as they relate to the EFTA Court's structure and jurisdiction.[9] However, technological advancements had already been acted upon with the introduction of 'e-EFTA Court', which facilitates electronic filing and document service, in 2017.[10] Videoconferencing is also now possible under the new rules, with a remote oral hearing procedure being adopted in 2020. The Court adopted the possibility of holding hybrid hearings, ie, partially remote oral hearings, in February 2022, with the first hybrid hearing being held in November 2022. All public sittings have been streamed live on the Court's website since the updated rules were adopted, although the first remote and streamed hearing took place in June 2020 in Joined Cases E-11/19 and E-12/19 *Adpublisher AG v J and K*.[11]

III. SELECTED ASPECTS OF THE SCA

This section will examine certain selected aspects of the SCA thematically and will put forward possible areas and ideas for innovation or reform.[12] It will address the

[7] Protocol 8 on the functions and powers of the EFTA Surveillance Authority in the Field of Financial Supervision, 6 October 2016, and Protocol 9 on the functions and powers of the EFTA Surveillance Authority and the EFTA Court following the Withdrawal of the United Kingdom of Great Britain and Northern Ireland from the European Union and the EEA Agreement, 30 January 2020.

[8] *Thirty-Third Annual Report of the European Free Trade Association* (Geneva, 1994) 27. The judges of the EFTA Court were appointed at an EFTA ministerial meeting in Geneva in June 1993: see [1994–95] EFTA Ct Rep 9 and 172.

[9] Rules of Procedure of the EFTA Court [2021] OJ L179/13.

[10] This can be accessed at: eftacourt.int/e-eftacourt. See the Decision of the Court on the lodging and service of procedural documents by means of e-EFTACourt of 12 December 2016, which entered into force on 10 March 2017.

[11] [2021] OJ L179/13; HE Roidis-Schnorrenberg, 'Die Teilnahme an mündlichen Verhandlungen des EFTA-Gerichtshofes per Videokonferenztechnik' (2022) *Liechtensteinische Juristenzeitung* 163; MJ Clifton and C Şchiopu, 'Justice Must Also Be Seen to Be Done: Digitalisation at the EFTA Court' (2021) 63 *EU Law Live* 3 f; MJ Clifton and P Pohjankoski 'European Courts 2019–2020 Update' (2020) *International Trade Law Review* 80.

[12] For a further examination of possible reforms of the organisation and composition of the EFTA Court, see Graham Butler, ch 6 in this volume.

following issues: judicial independence, judicial appointment and the composition of the EFTA Court at large; docking; Article 34 SCA and enhanced judicial dialogue; and whether homogeneity ought to be considered vis-a-vis the Charter of Fundamental Rights of the European Union ('the Charter') and possible alternatives. In so doing, this section will seek to draw from the SCA's first 30 years in order to prepare for the next.

A. Judicial Independence, Judicial Appointment and Composition of the Court at Large

Article 30 SCA, concerning, inter alia, the appointment of judges to the EFTA Court bench, is a crucial provision ensuring judicial independence and yet has been a source of considerable tension. The issue of judges' independence was debated in *Inconsult* after a member of the EFTA Board of Auditors was found to have links to one of the parties involved in the case. However, as this member was not involved in the audit of the Court's financial statements for the year in question or subsequently, the Court concluded that there were not sufficient grounds for the judges to recuse themselves *en banc* from the case in accordance with Article 15 of the Statute.[13] Later on, significant turbulence was caused when a decision on the re-appointment of a judge was limited to three years by the governments of the EEA/EFTA States, despite the explicit wording of the relevant provision of the SCA specifying 'a term of six years'.[14] Due to the re-appointment being limited to three years, the judge's term would have concluded upon reaching the normal retirement age of 70 in his home country. This issue came to a head in *Nobile* when the composition of the EFTA Court was called into question.[15] Although it is not uncommon for judges to face age limitations, this attempt at a limited re-appointment was a substantial interference with the Court's independence. The *Nobile* decision enabled the EFTA Court to make fundamental statements on the independence of judges in response to the national court's inquiry into the legality of the EFTA Court's composition. The Court highlighted the principle of judicial independence as one of the fundamental values of the administration of justice, emphasising the necessity for judges to be both impartial and to be perceived as such. Maintaining judicial independence necessitates strict adherence to the applicable rules for judicial appointments, as outlined in Article 30 SCA. Deviation from such rules risks undermining public confidence in the Court, jeopardising its appearance of impartiality and independence.[16] Following

[13] Case E-4/09 *Inconsult* [2009–2010] EFTA Ct Rep 86, paras 8 and 9.

[14] '[Judges] shall be appointed by common accord of the Governments of the EFTA States for a term of six years.' See both the Decision of the Court and the Order of the President in Case E-21/16 *Pascal Nobile* [2017] EFTA Ct Rep 554.

[15] ibid.

[16] Reference is made to the Decision of the Court in *Nobile* (n 14) para 16. *Nobile* was referred to by the General Court in Case T-639/16 P *FV v Council* ECLI:EU:T:2018:22, para 75, as well by the European Court of Human Rights in *Guðmundur Andri Ástráðsson v Iceland* (App No 26374/18), paras 64 f.

substantial criticism, the EEA/EFTA States took a new decision and re-appointed the judge in question, in accordance with the first paragraph of Article 30 SCA, for a six-year term.[17]

Should the EEA/EFTA States wish to incorporate a general age limit for EFTA Court judges, they could adopt provisions in the SCA, such as those set out in Article 21 of the European Convention on Human Rights (ECHR), which stipulates an age limit for members of the European Court of Human Rights (ECtHR).

When appointing or re-appointing judges to the Court, another issue occasionally arises which negatively impacts the Court's work. It is the Court's practice that, when a judgment is delivered in accordance with Articles 32 and 33 of the Statute, the term of the appointment of the judges listed in the judgment should not yet have come to an end. Therefore, when the end of a judge's term of office approaches, that judge will not participate further in hearings because he or she may have left the bench before the date of delivery of the judgment. As a result of this time gap, the EFTA Court must use its ad hoc judges. At present, there are six persons serving as ad hoc judges (two nominated in respect of each state to step in for its nominated judge where that judge is prevented from, or is unable to, act in a case).[18] Especially during transitional periods when a judge is departing, it may be quite burdensome for the relevant ad hoc judges to accomplish their judicial duties for several months alongside their regular occupations.[19] Increasing the number of ad hoc judges from six to nine would ease the situation. This issue could also be addressed by including a sentence in the third paragraph of Article 5 of the Statute similar to that found in the ECHR: 'He shall, however, continue to deal with such cases as he already has under consideration.'[20]

The selection and nomination process for members of the EFTA Court, as provided for in Article 30 SCA, has also given rise to criticism when compared to the judicial nomination process at the CJEU.[21] Indeed, the strengthening of the composition of the Court was the focus of a request by the EFTA Court to the EEA/EFTA States in 2011. The proposed amendments to the SCA were summarised by the EFTA Court as follows: (i) the ability to call ad hoc judges to the bench for an Extended Court of five in particularly important cases; (ii) the establishment of an Evaluation Panel for Candidate Judges and the Advocate General, in line with Article 255 of the Treaty on the Functioning of the European Union (TFEU); and

[17] F Arnesen and HH Fredriksen, 'Preamble and Article 1 SCA' in F Arnesen, HH Fredriksen, HP Graver, O Mestad and C Vedder (eds), *Agreement on the European Economic Area: A Commentary* (Munich, Nomos, 2018) 975.

[18] Ad hoc judges are chosen from a list established by common accord by the EEA/EFTA States (fourth para of Art 30 SCA) and are appointed for a term of three years. See the online list: eftacourt.int/the-court/introduction.

[19] Ad hoc judges exercise their task at the Court part-time (fourth para of Art 30 SCA).

[20] *cf* Art 23(2) ECHR.

[21] 'The Judges shall be chosen from persons whose independence is beyond doubt and who possess the qualifications required for appointment to the highest judicial offices in their respective countries or who are jurisconsults of recognized competence.' C Baudenbacher, *Judicial Independence, Memoirs of a European Judge* (Cham, Springer, 2019) 408.

(iii) the establishment of the position of an Advocate General. The objective of this proposal was to enhance the credibility of the EFTA Court.[22] The governments of the EEA/EFTA States have never reacted to this proposal.[23]

There has been no criticism from the EU towards the Court in the past three decades.[24] The need for good governance has continued to be addressed by the Court independently, with the publication of the Code of Conduct for the Judges of the EFTA Court in January 2022 defining the obligations arising from the provisions of the Statute and of the Rules of Procedure for the Judges.[25] The appointment process for EFTA Court Members is now conducted by way of a practice of publicly advertised vacancies and candidate assessment in accordance with the rules of the relevant state of nomination. What has remained consistent since the Court's early days is its rather low staffing level. At the end of 1994, the Court listed 27 staff members, a number that has since decreased to 20 at the end of 2023. This is particularly noteworthy for an international organisation.[26]

B. Docking

Docking, as a concept, was first proposed by the EU to Switzerland in 2013.[27] Docking refers to the EFTA Court and ESA being given additional jurisdiction concerning either specific agreements ('docking of agreements'), ie, attaching them to ESA and the Court, by bringing agreements already in force in the EEA/EFTA States, or specific new agreements, under the purview of the EFTA Court, or the 'docking of countries', which entails jurisdiction in relation to non-EEA/EFTA States being attached to ESA and the EFTA Court.[28] Docking has been suggested as a governance mechanism as regards matters relating to Schengen and Dublin agreements for the EFTA States,[29] the Switzerland-EU bilateral agreements and, by Michel Barnier, as part of the Brexit process.[30] The Court was given new jurisdiction following an amendment to Protocol 9 SCA signed on 18 November 2020 (Article 2 of Protocol 9

[22] See Press Release 11/11 of 19 December 2011, 'An Extended EFTA Court? The EFTA Court Proposes Amendments to the SCA'. See also HH Fredriksen, '25 Years after Liechtenstein Saved the EFTA Court: The Case for Reform' (2020) 41 *Liechtensteinische Juristenzeitung* 50, 54.

[23] Baudenbacher (n 21) 409.

[24] See European Commission, A Review of the Functioning of the European Economic Area, SWD(2012) 425 final, p 3.

[25] See eftacourt.int/code-of-conduct.

[26] [1994–95] EFTA Ct Rep, [2022] EFTA Ct Rep 51. For a proposal to strengthen the resources of the EFTA Court, see Fredriksen (n 22) 54.

[27] C Baudenbacher, 'The Judicial Dimension of the European Neighbourhood Policy', EU Diplomacy Paper 08/2013 (Bruges, College of Europe, 2013) 3 and 22–25.

[28] MJ Clifton, 'Direct Actions: EFTA Court' *Max Planck Encyclopedia of International Procedural Law*, forthcoming.

[29] T Blanchet, 'Could Using the EFTA Surveillance and Judicial Pillar Help the Schengen Associates Deepen Their Cooperation with the EU in JHA Matters?' in C Höhn, I Saavedra and A Weyembergh (eds), *La lutte contre le terrorisme: ses acquis et ses défis/The Fight against Terrorism: Achievements and Challenges. Liber Amicorum Gilles de Kerchove* (Brussels, Bruylant, 2021) 623–38, at 635.

[30] MJ Clifton, 'Supplementary Contribution on the EFTA Court' in M Botman and J Langer (eds), National Courts and the Enforcement of EU Law: The Pivotal Role of National Courts in the EU Legal Order, The XXIX FIDE Congress in The Hague (The Hague, Eleven Publishing, 2020) 509–33, at 514–15.

to the SCA). This amendment grants powers to ESA and the EFTA Court to monitor the implementation and application of the obligations of the EEA/EFTA States to UK nationals under the EEA EFTA Separation Agreement with the UK. This is the first example of the concept of 'docking of agreements'.[31]

Importantly, the method utilised by Protocol 9 SCA may be used as a template (albeit partial, as it addresses jurisdictional matters in the EFTA pillar only) for any future docking of agreements. To that end, it may potentially be of assistance to consider possible amendments to Article 32 SCA,[32] which to date has yet to be used by the EEA/EFTA States.[33] The construction of Article 32 SCA differs considerably from the situation in EU law under Articles 259 and 273 TFEU, although it is closer in design in some respects to Article 273 TFEU. Article 32 SCA is premised, at least textually, on a dispute existing between the EFTA States regarding the *interpretation or application* of the EEA, the Agreement on a Standing Committee of the EFTA States or the SCA. In order to avoid any particular problems when the docking of an agreement or country is envisaged, Article 32 SCA may perhaps be amended so as to encompass the possibility of obtaining an opinion of the Court on such future agreements.[34]

C. Article 34 SCA and Enhanced Judicial Dialogue

Article 34 SCA has sparked intense debates in the past. Indeed, as Almestad has put it, Article 34 SCA is 'a bit difficult to grasp'.[35] The core of the discussion centres on two questions: first, whether a national judge is required to refer a question for interpretation to the EFTA Court; and, second, the binding effect of such an advisory opinion.

Article 34 SCA seeks to establish positive cooperation and judicial dialogue between the Court and national courts and tribunals in cases that require the application of EEA law. This ensures the consistent interpretation of EEA law.[36] Questions referred concerning the interpretation of EEA law by national courts enjoy a presumption of relevance in the factual and legislative context which that court is responsible for defining. The accuracy of which is not a matter for the Court to determine.[37] Even in cases where national legislation, in purely internal situations not governed by EEA

[31] MJ Clifton, 'Applying Competition Law and the View Ahead: 25 Years of the EFTA Court' in A Bugaeva (ed), *Five Years of the Treaty on the Eurasian Economic Union: The Role of the Court* (Medison, 2020) 156–57.

[32] Article 32 SCA provides that: 'The EFTA Court shall have jurisdiction in actions concerning the settlement of disputes between two or more EFTA States regarding the interpretation or application of the EEA Agreement, the Agreement on a Standing Committee of the EFTA States or the present Agreement.'

[33] See, generally, Clifton (n 28).

[34] As a further extension of Art 32 SCA, it would also be conceivable to include the possibility for the EEA/EFTA States as such to be able to request an opinion from the Court on the interpretation or application of the EEA Agreement, the Agreement on a Standing Committee of the EFTA States or the SCA.

[35] K Almestad, 'The Essentials' in EFTA Court (ed), *The EEA and the EFTA Court* (Oxford, Hart Publishing, 2014) 299–310, 307.

[36] Note for Guidance on Requests by National Courts for Advisory Opinions, eftacourt.int/the-court/guidance-for-advisory-opinion/?wpdmdl=7446&ind=1627642656131.

[37] Case E-9/22 *Verkfræðingafélag Íslands*, judgment of 19 April 2023, paras 22 and 23.

law, adopts the same or similar provisions as those adopted in EEA law, it is in the interests of the EEA to prevent future differences of interpretation. In such cases, the Court has jurisdiction. However, it is the responsibility of the national court to evaluate the exact scope of the reference to EEA law in national law.[38]

Article 34 SCA does not include an explicit requirement to refer a case to the Court or impose a formal obligation on the referring court to abide by the EFTA Court's judgment in an advisory opinion case.[39] Nevertheless, the case law of the EFTA Court has addressed, in relation to the duty of loyalty under Article 3 of the EEA Agreement and the application of fundamental rights as part of the general principles of EEA law, the obligation for courts against whose decisions there is no judicial remedy under national law to consider a referral to the EFTA Court.[40] This approach was recently reiterated in *Telenor*, where the Court held that '[t]he principle of effective judicial protection, including the right to a fair trial, which, inter alia, is enshrined in Article 6 ECHR, is a general principle of EEA law'.[41] The Court ruled in *RS* that the national judge is bound, under the principle of sincere cooperation in Article 3 EEA, to ensure the full effectiveness of EEA law when determining the dispute before him or her. It is the judge's responsibility, in particular, to secure the legal protection that individuals derive from the EEA and to make certain that those rules are fully effective.[42] This approach by the EFTA Court effectively requires the national judge to act as an EEA/EFTA judge.[43] To fulfil this duty, the national judge must apply EEA law. If the national court or tribunal is uncertain as to the correct interpretation of the relevant EEA provision, ie, 'if the legal situation lacks clarity', it is important that the national court seeks an advisory opinion from the Court.[44]

i. National Perspectives on Article 34 SCA

In this context, it is helpful to note the ruling of the Liechtenstein Constitutional Court in *StGH 2013/172*, which outlines the criteria for referral to the EFTA Court

[38] ibid para 25.

[39] P Christiansen, 'Article 34 SCA' in Arnesen et al (n 17) 1037; and G Baur, 'Preliminary Rulings in the EEA: Bridging (Institutional) Homogeneity and Procedural Autonomy by Exchange of Information' in EFTA Court (n 35) 169–86, at 177.

[40] Case E-18/11 *Irish Bank* [2012] EFTA Ct Rep 592, paras 58 and 64. Lourenço argues that the EFTA Court thus stopped only slightly short of establishing an express obligation for courts of last resort; see L Lourenço, 'European Economic Area (EEA) and European Free Trade Association (EFTA): A Successful Partnership with the EU' in RA Wessel and J Odermatt (eds), *Research Handbook on the European Union and International Organizations* (Cheltenham, Edward Elgar, 2019) 541.

[41] Case E-2/20 *Telenor ASA and Telenor Norge AS v ESA*, judgment of 5 May 2022, para 75.

[42] Case E-11/22 *RS*, judgment of 4 July 2023, paras 41 and 44. See also the eighth recital in the Preamble to the EEA: 'Convinced of the important role that individuals will play in the European Economic Area through the exercise of the rights conferred on them by this Agreement and through the judicial defence of these rights.'

[43] A Rosas, 'The National Judge as EU Judge: Some Constitutional Observations' (2014) 67 *SMU Law Review* 717, 723, with reference to CJEU Opinion 1/09 (Creation of a unified patent litigation system) ECLI:EU:C:2011:123.

[44] A request to the EFTA Court is important if the legal situation lacks clarity. Thereby, unnecessary mistakes in the interpretation and application of EEA rules are avoided. Furthermore, coherence and reciprocity in relation to rights of EEA nationals are ensured; see Case E-3/12 *Jonsson* [2013] EFTA Ct Rep 136, para 60. In this way the Court introduced its own version of an *acte clair* doctrine, which is not limited to courts of last instance: see Clifton (n 30) 519.

in Liechtenstein law.[45] The Constitutional Court held that it must refer a question on the interpretation of EEA law to the EFTA Court when the legal situation is unclear and if the legal question is relevant to the decision. If both conditions are met, then a request for referral must be granted.[46] This ruling follows the judgment of the CJEU in *CILFIT*.[47] As a result of the Constitutional Court's judgment in *StGH 2013/172*, it is widely accepted that all courts in Liechtenstein are obliged to comply with this standard.[48] The Constitutional Court has stated that judgments of the EFTA Court are binding, citing Article 7 EEA and Protocol 35 EEA (whereby EEA/EFTA States undertake to introduce, if necessary, a legal provision to the effect that in all cases of possible conflict between EEA rules and national law, the EEA rules shall prevail).[49] The Constitutional Court's interpretation of the interaction between EEA law and national law is grounded in Liechtenstein's monistic legal tradition. It diverges significantly from the dualistic approach taken by Iceland and Norway, the other two EEA/EFTA States.[50]

In Iceland and Norway, a literal interpretation of Article 34 SCA prevails. However, at least in relation to the binding effect of EFTA Court rulings, the Supreme Court of Norway has indicated an apparent acceptance of the EFTA Court as a qualified interpreter of EEA law and has held that the Court's case law must be accorded 'preeminent or significant weight'.[51]

[45] For a discussion of the situation in Liechtenstein reference is made to the chapter by Hilmar Hoch.

[46] StGH 2013/172, judgment of 7 April 2014, gerichtsentscheidungen.li/default.aspx?z=vGQ5MaIB4-1URWOuOWteIHD3SnpPu5NlrGTP2e4nFKV3RfIWY7EgBnpzopsxdmGQ33aP5yaIa-76k27b9JA7d4up-qN3bjQ2.

[47] Case 283/81 *CILFIT and Others* ECLI:EU:C:1982:335, paras 16 and 21. With reference to Case E-3/12 *Jonsson* [2013] EFTA Ct Rep 136, para 60, Baudenbacher argues that the EFTA Court did not take over the *CILFIT* criteria in relation to Art 34 SCA. Rather, in the EEA/EFTA pillar, the national judge must conclude only (but as an absolute minimum) that the legal situation is clear in order to avoid the application of Art 34 SCA; see C Baudenbacher, 'Das Vorabentscheidungsverfahren im EFTA-Pfeiler des EWR' in H Schumacher and W Zimmermann (eds), *90 Jahre Fürstlicher Oberster Gerichtshof, Festschrift für Gert Delle Karth* (Vienna, Jan Sramek Verlag, 2013) 1–22, at 20.

[48] See annotations by W Ungerank to StGH 2013/172 in LES 3/14, 148.

[49] StGH 2011/200, judgment of 7 February 2012; however, the limit to the binding effect of EEA law would be reached if EEA law were to violate the basic principles and core contents of the fundamental rights of the state constitution. Or in its original wording: '*Nach der Rechtsprechung des Staatsgerichtshofes darf EWR-Recht … nicht gegen "Grundprinzipien und Kerngehalte der Grundrechte der Landesverfassung verstossen"*.' See gerichtsentscheidungen.li/default.aspx?z=dOBLc9GibsmCNf583U7FrPoT2MZ52CN-uuoIRJJm8m6rvbKxToDQmJCkz0YXW6PqY1vseqbaRU5QaZpEpdJX6djEyLTp3ME4Wcyq6PffJGxjY-u6NsAL7tl1ftoJg8qxQDs_BDL4djQmXR6mO0eXfih-zr6qOvYA2.

[50] See Supreme Court of Norway, *National Report, Kingdom of Norway, XVI Congress of the Conference of European Constitutional Courts* (2014), 3 and 4, www.vfgh.gv.at/cms/vfgh-kongress/downloads/landesberichte/LB-Norvege-EN.pdf; and ÓÍ Hannesson, 'Advisory Opinions in the EEA: The Icelandic Supreme Court and the EFTA Court' (2018) 43 *European Law Review* 858, 863 and 873.

[51] HH Fredriksen, 'One Market, Two Courts: Legal Pluralism vs Homogeneity in the European Economic Area' (2010) 79 *Nordic Journal of International Law* 481, 488; HH Fredriksen, 'The Two EEA Courts: A Norwegian Perspective' in EFTA Court (ed), *Judicial Protection in the European Economic Area* (Stuttgart, German Law Publishing, 2012) 187–211, at 193. According to Skoghøy, in the absence of a formal binding obligation, the EFTA Court is called upon to thoroughly and convincingly reason its judgment; see JE Skoghøy, 'What Does the Supreme Court Expect from an Answer of the EFTA Court, and How Does it Deal with it Procedurally?', speech at the EFTA Seminar (2014), www.domstol.no/en/supremecourt/about/publications/articles/skoghoy/what-does-the-supreme-court-expect-from-an-answer-of-the-efta-court-and-how-does-it-deal-with-it-procedurally. A detailed examination of the Supreme Court of Norway's perspective of advisory opinions, reference is made to Ola Mestad in ch 11 of this volume.

ii. Article 34 SCA and Article 6(1) ECHR

The following section will seek to put Article 34 SCA into a new perspective 30 years after it took effect. Following the EFTA Court's judgment in *Irish Bank* in 2012, this section will consider two strands of case law from the CJEU and the ECtHR.

As noted above, the Liechtenstein Constitutional Court used the *CILFIT* criteria in order to determine the need to make a reference to the EFTA Court pursuant to Article 34 SCA. Exactly 39 years to the day after the CJEU handed down its *CILFIT* judgment, the CJEU clarified its earlier case law in *Consorzio*.[52] In this ruling, while the CJEU reiterated the *CILFIT* criteria, it tightened the obligation on national apex courts to refer, consistent with Article 267 TFEU.[53] Significantly, and of interest and importance in respect of Article 34 SCA, the CJEU held that there is an obligation on a national court or tribunal against whose decision there is no judicial remedy under national law to state the reasons for deciding that it is relieved of its obligation to make a reference to the CJEU. This obligation arises not only from Article 267 TFEU but also from the second paragraph of Article 47 of the Charter.[54] The CJEU held that:

> [T]he statement of reasons for its decision [not to refer] must show either that the question of EU law raised is irrelevant for the resolution of the dispute, or that the interpretation of the EU law provision concerned is based on the Court's case-law or, in the absence of such case-law, that the interpretation of EU law was so obvious to the national court or tribunal of last instance as to leave no scope for any reasonable doubt.[55]

The second paragraph of Article 47 of the Charter corresponds to Article 6(1) ECHR. As noted in the explanation of Article 47 of the Charter, the right to a fair hearing within the EU is not confined to disputes concerning civil law rights and obligations as in Article 6(1) ECHR.[56] This is premised on the basis that the EU is a community based on the rule of law.[57]

It must be recalled that effective judicial protection is a general principle of EEA law[58] and access to justice is an essential element of the EEA legal framework.[59] In *Irish Bank*, the EFTA Court cited the ECtHR's judgment in *Ullens de Schooten*,[60] in which the ECtHR ruled:

> In the specific context of the third paragraph of Article 234 of the Treaty establishing the European Community (Article 267 of the Treaty on the Functioning of the European

[52] Case C-561/19 *Consorzio Italian Management and Others* ECLI:EU:C:2021:799.

[53] For a review of *Consorzio Italian Management and Others*, see D Petrić, 'How to Make a Unicorn or "There Never Was an '*Acte Clair*' in EU Law": Some Remarks about Case C-561/19 *Consorzio Italian Management*' (2021) 17 *Croatian Yearbook of European Law and Policy* 307; I Maher, 'The CILFIT Criteria Clarified and Extended for National Courts of Last Resort under Article 267 TFEU' (2022) 7(1) *European Papers (European Forum)* 265; and J Claassen, 'In the Courts the CJEU Does Not Trust? The National Courts' Obligation to Refer Preliminary Questions to the CJEU after *Consorzio Italian Management*', *Verfassungsblog*, 12 October 2021, verfassungsblog.de/in-the-courts-the-cjeu-does-not-trust.

[54] Charter of Fundamental Rights of the European Union [2012] OJ C326/391.

[55] *Consorzio Italian Management and Others* (n 52) para 51.

[56] See Explanations Relating to the Charter of Fundamental Rights [2007] OJ C303/17, 30.

[57] See Case 294/83 *Parti écologiste 'Les Verts' v Parliament* ECLI:EU:C:1986:166, para 23; and C Ladenburger, Y Marinova and J Tomkin, 'Institutional Report' in *Mutual Trust, Mutual Recognition and the Rule of Law, The XXX Fide Congress in Sofia*, vol 1 (Congress Publications, 2023) 67–154, at 111.

[58] Case E-15/10 *Posten Norge* [2012] EFTA Ct Rep 246, para 86.

[59] Case E-3/11 *Sigmarsson* [2011] EFTA Ct Rep 430, para 29.

[60] *Irish Bank* (n 40) para 64; *Ullens de Schooten and Rezabek v Belgium* App Nos 3989/07 and 38353/07 (ECtHR, 20 September 2011), paras 59 and 60.

> Union), this means that national courts against whose decisions there is no remedy under national law, which refuse to refer to the Court of Justice a preliminary question on the interpretation of Community law that has been raised before them, are obliged to give reasons for their refusal in the light of the exceptions provided for in the case-law of the Court of Justice. They will thus be required, in accordance with the above-mentioned *Cilfit* case-law, to indicate the reasons why they have found that the question is irrelevant, that the European Union law provision in question has already been interpreted by the Court of Justice, or that the correct application of Community law is so obvious as to leave no scope for any reasonable doubt.[61]

In its 2021 ruling, *Bio Farmland*, the ECtHR held that:

> The Convention does not guarantee, as such, a right to have a case referred by the domestic court to the CJEU for a preliminary ruling … However, Article 6 § 1 imposes on domestic courts an obligation to give reasons, in the light of the applicable law, for any decisions in which they refuse to refer a preliminary question … The Court has deduced from this that, when it hears a complaint alleging a violation of Article 6 § 1 on this basis, its task consists in ensuring that the impugned refusal has been duly accompanied by such reasoning.[62]

Against this backdrop, it is contended that Article 34 SCA contains an obligation for national courts or tribunals of last resort to state their reasons, in accordance with Article 6(1) ECHR, should they decide not to make a possible reference to the EFTA Court, bearing in mind that the *CILFIT* criteria have been used as the benchmark by the ECtHR.[63]

The counter-argument that the *CILFIT* criteria are not applicable in the context of Article 34 SCA due to that provision's obvious difference from Article 267 TFEU (may versus shall) falls short because Article 34 SCA is a form of preliminary ruling procedure with a kind of binding effect.[64] First, the ECtHR has shown flexibility in its approach to supervisory mechanisms considering that requirements relating to the use of such mechanisms should be applied 'without excessive formalism'.[65] Second, any criticism concerning the lack of direct effect and supremacy not only disregards

[61] *Ullens de Schooten and Rezabek v Belgium* (n 60) para 62.

[62] *Bio Farmland Betriebs SRL v Romania* App No 43639/17 (ECtHR, 13 July 2021), para 49 (author's translation).

[63] For a similar view, see C Neier, 'Europäischer Menschenrechtspluralismus – die Perspektive des EGMR und die Permeabilität des EU- und EWR-Rechts' (2023) *Liechtensteinische Juristenzeitung* 193, 200. In relation to Art 6 ECHR, Temple Lang argues that the Convention establishes minimum standards for both EEA and the EU with respect to access to justice and therefore Art 6 gives an overriding right to bring arguments based on EEA law to the EFTA Court; see J Temple Lang, 'The Duty of National Courts to Provide Access to Justice in the EEA' in EFTA Court (n 51) 100–36, at 102. Provisions of the SCA are to be interpreted in the light of fundamental rights; see Case E-2/03 *Ásgeirsson* [2003] EFTA Ct Rep 185, para 23.

[64] In all EEA/EFTA States, it is generally accepted that the EFTA Court is a qualified interpreter of EEA law. Therefore, its ruling is to be followed and can only be disregarded if a national court has compelling reasons to do so; see S Magnússon, 'The Authority of the EFTA Court' in C Baudenbacher (ed), *The Handbook of EEA Law* (Cham, Springer, 2016) 139–68, 163 and 165. In addition, if a national court were to disregard a ruling of the EFTA Court, ESA could, in accordance with Art 31 SCA, initiate infringement proceedings. The subsequent verdict of the EFTA Court would be binding on the state concerned (Art 33 SCA). Clifton (n 30) 522 and 524 points to the similarities between the Art 34 SCA advisory opinion procedure and the procedure under Protocol No 16 to the ECHR for the highest national courts to request an advisory opinion from the ECtHR.

[65] *Avotiņš v Latvia* App No 17502/07 (ECtHR, 23 May 2016), para 109.

the relevant provisions in Article 7 EEA and Protocol 35 EEA,[66] but also the Court's case law in relation to the state liability of EEA/EFTA States, which leads to a similar quasi-direct effect. While the principle of state liability is common to both EU law and EEA law, it is arguably more stringent in EEA law to counter-balance the inherent weaknesses of quasi-primacy and quasi-direct effect.[67] Further, it is of dubious soundness to compare the EEA system with that of the EU, which comprises doctrines specific to itself, and to overlook the EEA system's own idiosyncrasies and *sui generis* nature. The EEA system should be evaluated in relation to the Convention system and not in terms of whether EEA law shows identical features to that of the EU.[68] Third, the national judge needs a certain yardstick by which to measure adherence to the ECHR's requirements.[69]

Furthermore, where the ECtHR provides for an obligation to state reasons for decisions refusing to make a reference for a preliminary ruling, 'especially where the applicable law allows for such a refusal only on an exceptional basis',[70] it must be understood that in such 'exceptional circumstances', the obligation to state reasons is even greater. Therefore, *Consorzio* can serve as a guideline for the national courts of EEA/EFTA States with respect to the content of a statement of reasons. In addition, it is important to recall that *RS* imposes on every national judge of an EEA/EFTA State the additional task of also acting as an EEA/EFTA judge.[71] This brings them into the sphere of Article 3 of the EEA Agreement and the principle of loyalty in order to ensure the full effectiveness of the EEA rules.[72] Failure to comply with the requirements of Article 6(1) ECHR, as well as the threat of infringement proceedings for violation of Article 3 EEA, puts national judges in a difficult position.

iii. Article 34 SCA and Bosphorus

Interestingly, the ECtHR discussed Article 34 SCA when evaluating the relationship between EEA law and the ECHR and specifically considered whether the *Bosphorus* ruling could be applied to the EEA.[73] In *Bosphorus*, the ECtHR determined that EU law's protection of fundamental rights is 'equivalent' to that of the ECHR on the basis that it protects both substantive fundamental rights *and* their procedural enforcement. Consequently, it is presumed that an EU Member State complies with

[66] P Hreinsson, 'General Principles' in Baudenbacher (n 64) 349–389, 388; Case E-9/97 *Sveinbjörnsdóttir* [1998] EFTA Ct Rep 95, para 63; and HH Fredriksen and SØ Johansen, 'The EEA Agreement as a Jack-in-the-Box in the Relationship between the CJEU and the European Court of Human Rights?' (2020) 5 *European Papers* 707, 727.

[67] S Magnússon and ÓÍ Hannesson, 'State Liability in EEA Law: Towards Parallelism or Homogeneity?' (2013) 38 *European Law Review* 167.

[68] U Lattanzi, 'The Inapplicability of the Bosphorus Presumption to the European Economic Area Agreement: A Risk for the Coherence of Legal Systems in Europe' (2023) 19 *European Constitutional Law Review* 1, 15.

[69] *CILFIT* criteria must be considered to be part of EEA law in line with Article 6 EEA; see Almestad (n 35) 308; and Magnússon (n 64) 160.

[70] *Bio Farmland Betriebs SRL v Romania* (n 62) para 49.

[71] *RS* (n 42).

[72] Franklin considers the following as possible shortcomings which would breach the duty of loyalty: the disregard for the fundamental objectives of homogeneity, reciprocity and/or the judicial defence of individual EEA rights in the specific case; see C Franklin, 'Article 3 EEA' in Arnesen et al (n 17) 195.

[73] *Bosphorus Hava Yollari Turizm Ve Ticaret Anonim Şirketi v Ireland* ECHR 2005–VI 107.

the requirement of the ECHR when it implements legal obligations stemming from its EU membership. However, such a presumption can be rebutted if, in a particular case, it is considered that the protections given by the state were manifestly deficient.[74]

In *Konkurrenten.no*, the first case for the ECtHR to rule on the EEA, the ECtHR held in an *obiter dictum* that the *Bosphorus* presumption could not be extended to the EEA.[75] According to the ECtHR, this followed from the fact that the EEA framework lacks direct effect and supremacy, and does not provide for legal instruments with the same level of protection for fundamental rights as the Convention.[76] In a second case, *Norwegian Confederation of Trade Unions*, the ECtHR had an opportunity to reassess its reasoning on the *Bosphorus* presumption and the EEA.[77]

In this second case, although the ECtHR held that the *Bosphorus* presumption could potentially apply when it comes to the implementation of EEA rules, the ECtHR dealt with the case at hand on the basis that the *Bosphorus* presumption did not apply to EEA law. It noted possible shortcomings with respect to the procedural mechanisms for ensuring the protection of fundamental rights guarantees due to the lack of binding legal effect of advisory opinions for courts in EEA/EFTA States.[78]

Not applying the *Bosphorus* presumption to the EEA, or a similar solution, could result in the ECtHR having full oversight of EU legal acts that have been incorporated into the EEA through EEA Joint Committee Decisions.[79] This would place the three EEA/EFTA States in a difficult situation due to conflicting obligations under international law stemming from both the EEA and the ECHR.[80] It is clear from the structure of the ruling in *Konkurrenten.no* that the ECtHR was concerned to ensure that it did not undermine the EEA's legal framework in the EFTA pillar.[81] Given the statement by the ECtHR in *Norwegian Confederation of Trade Unions* that it left 'it to another case, where questions in relation to the procedural mechanisms under EEA law may arise, to review this issue', this remains an open matter.[82]

It would appear clear that there is room for increased judicial dialogue. Vice-President of the Court of Justice of the European Union Antonio Tizzano, writing extra-judicially in 2019, contended that:

> [A] discussion focused on the formal and hierarchical relationship between the [Court of Justice and ECtHR] runs the risk of creating a vicious circle of difficulties, of sending

[74] ibid paras 155 and 156.

[75] *Konkurrenten.no AS v Norway* App No 47341/15 (ECtHR, 5 November 2019). See also C Neier, 'Das Verhältnis zwischen EMRK und EWR-Recht: Warum nicht eine Vermutung für die Vermutung der Konventionskonformität?'(2022) 57 *Europarecht* 213, 218.

[76] *Konkurrenten.no AS v Norway* (n 75) para 43.

[77] *Norwegian Confederation of Trade Unions (LO) and Norwegian Transport Workers' Union (NTF) v Norway* App no 45487/17 (ECtHR, 10 June 2021).

[78] ibid paras 107 and 108.

[79] Articles 92–94 EEA. See the explainer in EFTA, 'How EU law Becomes EEA Law', eealaw.efta.int.

[80] Lattanzi (n 68) 19 and 20. Lattanzi further sees the danger of strategic litigation aiming to make use of the asymmetry. Frederiksen considers that the introduction of a '*Foto-Frost* referral' (Case 314/85 *Foto-Frost* ECLI:EU:C:1987:452) from the EFTA Court to the CJEU could solve this problem; see Fredriksen (n 22) 55. However, this would, in and of itself, destabilise the two-pillar structure. Kälin refers to the Joint Declaration signed in Oporto on 2 May 1992 on the continuing applicability of existing treaties and therefore argues that the ECHR prevails over the EEA; see W Kälin, 'The EEA Agreement and the European Convention for the Protection of Human Rights' (1992) 3 *European Journal of International Law* 341, 348.

[81] Clifton (n 30) 530.

[82] *Norwegian Confederation of Trade Unions (LO) and Norwegian Transport Workers' Union (NTF) v Norway* (n 77) para 108.

> discordant or ambiguous messages to the national courts and, ultimately, of harming citizens' interests.
>
> I believe, on the contrary, that accession should allow the creation of a dynamic relationship between the court in Luxembourg and the court in Strasbourg based on co-operation and complementarity, within an integrated system of protection of fundamental rights focused on identifying the most appropriate solution for strengthening a sort of 'circular' protection. In other words, the relationship between these two courts would remain, as has been said with regard to the relationship between the EU and its Member States, 'interactive rather than hierarchical'.[83]

The circular nature of this relationship reflects the natural ebb and flow of cases in the three interconnected but distinct judicial systems. With the increased (and increasing) dialogue between the ECtHR and the EFTA Court, 'triangular dialogue'[84] has come to fruition.[85] It will be crucial to ensure that such positive dialogue is developed into enduring cooperation in order to uphold fundamental rights.[86]

D. Homogeneity and the Charter?

As is well known, the EEA Agreement, by way of Article 1(1) of the EEA Agreement, supported by the fourth and fifteenth recitals in the Preamble, endeavours to establish a dynamic and homogenous European Economic Area. To that end, Article 6 of the EEA Agreement mandates that, without prejudice to future developments of case law, any provisions of the EEA, insofar as they are identical in substance to the EU rules, must be interpreted in conformity with rulings of the CJEU given prior to the date of signature of the EEA Agreement.[87] Article 3 SCA complements Article 6 EEA and is crucial in maintaining a homogenous EEA. Article 3(1) SCA reiterates and expands the Article 6 of the EEA Agreement requirement to Protocols 1–4, as well as to the Acts listed in Annexes I and II to the SCA. The rationale for these provisions is to provide a definitive basis or starting point upon which the interpretation of EEA law can be undertaken. Article 3(2) SCA provides the basis for homogeneous interpretation. It provides that the Court 'shall pay due account to the principles laid down by the relevant rulings' by the CJEU delivered after 1 May 1992 insofar as the relevant provisions are 'identical in substance'.[88] The case law of the EFTA Court makes no

[83] A Tizzano, 'European Courts and the Protection of Fundamental Rights', in G Selvik, MJ Clifton, T Haas, L Lourenço and K Schwiesow (eds), *The Art of Judicial Reasoning: Festschrift in Honour of Carl Baudenbacher* (Cham, Springer, 2019) 23–32, at 29, referencing N MacCormick, *Questioning Sovereignty: Law, State, and Nation in the European Commonwealth* (Oxford, Oxford University Press, 1999) 118.

[84] B Hammermann, 'Mehrebenen im Grundrechtsschutz – die liechtensteinische Verfassung und der EWR' in H Hoch, C Neier and PM Schiess Rütimann (eds), *100 Jahre liechtensteinische Verfassung. Funktionen, Entwicklung und Verhältnis zu Europa* (Vaduz, Verlag der Liechtensteinischen Akademischen Gesellschaft, 2021) 291–314, at 313.

[85] Clifton (n 30) 531.

[86] B Hammermann, 'Der EFTA-Gerichtshof zwischen den Welten' in J Sild (ed), *Potenziale und Grenzen europäischer Integration* (Vienna, Jan Sramek Verlag, 2022) 15–34, at 33.

[87] P Wennerås, 'Article 6 EEA' in Arnesen et al (n 17) 210.

[88] See generally P Speitler, 'Judicial Homogeneity as a Fundamental Principle of the EEA' in C Baudenbacher (ed), *The Fundamental Principles of EEA Law: EEA-ities* (Cham, Springer, 2017) 19–34.

distinction between the approaches set out in Article 3 SCA and Article 6 of the EEA Agreement.[89]

In *Paola Piazza*, the Court pointed out that the case law of the CJEU is relevant for the interpretation of Article 40 of the EEA Agreement to the extent provided in Article 6 of the EEA Agreement and Article 3 SCA.[90] In its first-ever case, *Restamark*, the Court held that it is not required by Article 3(1) SCA to follow the reasoning of the CJEU in the interpretation of the expression 'court or tribunal'.[91] In *Scanteam AS*, the Court ruled that Article 3 SCA does not impose a duty to follow the CJEU's reasoning in interpreting the main part of the SCA.[92] The Court retains its discretion to determine the relevance of case law to the interpretation of the main part of the SCA.[93]

In general, one may say that the task of establishing and maintaining a homogeneous EEA over the past three decades has necessarily presented a challenge, but it is one that has been successfully overcome.[94]

When discussing the SCA and looking ahead, it is important to acknowledge the 'elephant in the EEA room': the Charter is not part of the EEA *acquis* and the EEA/EFTA States have not adopted it. Although the EFTA Court has made reference to the Charter in various rulings, it has never relied on it, even when an EEA/EFTA State has used it as the basis for its arguments.[95] Notwithstanding the fact that the general principles of EEA law include fundamental rights and that the provisions of the ECHR and the judgments of the ECtHR are important sources for determining the scope of these fundamental rights,[96] for the EEA/EFTA States to 'adopt' the Charter is not entirely a Potemkin argument. Certain literature has pointed to the principle of homogeneity in order to suggest that the EFTA Court should apply the Charter as is (this would, one imagines, be achieved through docking).[97] Another, perhaps more natural, option for the EEA/EFTA States could be to incorporate a tailored variant of the Charter in the SCA by way of a new Protocol 10 to the SCA.[98] Although the Court has upheld fundamental rights *ab initio*, and forthrightly too, the symbolism – at least – of the expression of fundamental rights in treaty provisions

[89] Ó Einarsson, 'Fundamental Rights in the Case Law of the EFTA Court' in JF Kjølbro, S O'Leary and M Tsirli (eds), *Liber Amicorum Robert Spanó* (The Hague, Anthemis/Eleven Publishing, 2022) 231–42, at 238.

[90] Case E-10/04 *Paola Piazza* [2005] EFTA Ct Rep 76, para 33.

[91] Case E-1/94 *Restamark* [1994–1995] EFTA Ct Rep 15, para 24. Since then, the EFTA Court has interpreted the term 'a court or tribunal' very broadly; see Clifton (n 30) 515.

[92] Case E-8/19 *Scanteam AS*, judgment of 16 July 2020, para 45.

[93] Case E-2/20 *Telenor ASA and Telenor Norge AS v ESA* (n 41) para 357. Butler voices criticism when the EFTA Court neglects the homogeneity principle with respect to EEA procedural rules; see G Butler, 'Mind the (Homogeneity) Gap: Independence of Referring Bodies requesting Advisory Opinions from the EFTA Court' (2020) 44 *Fordham International Law Journal* 307, 340.

[94] Case E-28/15 *Yankuba Jabbi* [2016] EFTA Ct Rep 575. See Wennerås (n 87) 248; and Magnússon (n 64) 156.

[95] Case E-12/10 *ESA v Republic of Iceland* [2011] EFTA Ct Rep 117, Report for the Hearing, para 125.

[96] Case E-1/20 *Kerim*, judgment of 9 February 2021, para 43, and the case law cited therein.

[97] N Wahl, 'Uncharted Waters: Reflections on the Legal Significance of the Charter under EEA Law and Judicial Cross-Fertilisation in the Field of Fundamental Rights' in EFTA Court (n 35) 281–98, at 297; and Temple Lang (n 63) 133.

[98] Fredriksen (n 22) 54 proposes an amendment to Protocol 1 EEA, thereby establishing a firm basis for the EFTA Court's approach to fundamental rights.

could be significant. This would of course be a matter for political determination by the EEA/EFTA States.

IV. CONCLUSIONS

Overall, the SCA has served the EFTA Court, the EEA/EFTA States, and individuals and economic operators well over the last 30 years. This comes as no surprise, given that the SCA is based predominantly on the comparable provisions of EU law including the Statute of the CJEU.[99] The two-pillar structure is at the very core of the EEA. The SCA has effectively served the EEA/EFTA States since its adoption in 1994 without any notable deficiencies. This chapter has examined certain selected aspects of the SCA thematically and has put forward possible areas and ideas for innovation or reform. However, to conclude the ongoing discourse surrounding Article 34 SCA and to ensure enhanced support from national courts of EEA/EFTA States, as well as bridging the widening gap between the EU legal order and EEA law, consideration may be given to revising the SCA. The EEA/EFTA States possess the autonomy to adjust or even expand the SCA. Unlike the EEA, of course, amendments to the SCA require only the consent of the three EEA/EFTA States.

For 30 years, Iceland, Liechtenstein and Norway – in a joint undertaking – have participated in the construction of a Europe based on peace, democracy, human rights and common values. Over time, as bonds have strengthened and trust has grown, so too has the complexity of the European legal space. Together with the EU Member States, the EEA/EFTA States have established a dynamic and homogeneous European Economic Area with respect to the free movement of goods, persons, services and capital based on common rules and by providing for adequate means of enforcement, including at the judicial level. This has all been achieved on the basis of equality and reciprocity based on the EEA States being convinced of the important role that individuals play through the exercise of the rights conferred on them by the EEA and the fundamental rights embedded in the general principles of EEA law, and through the judicial defence of these rights.[100] This journey continues.

[99] See Statute of the Court of Justice of the European Union, consolidated version at: curia.europa.eu/jcms/upload/docs/application/pdf/2016-08/tra-doc-en-div-c-0000-2016-201606984-05_00.pdf.

[100] See the first, second, fourth, fifth and eighth recitals in the Preamble to the EEA.

5

Could Using the EFTA Surveillance and Judicial Pillar Help the Schengen Associates Deepen their Cooperation with the EU in JHA Matters and beyond?

THÉRÈSE BLANCHET*

I. INTRODUCTION

THE FOUR 'SCHENGEN Associates' – Iceland, Liechtenstein, Norway and Switzerland (hereinafter the 'EFTA[1] States') – are, and have been for many years, the closest partners of the EU. They are treated as quasi-Member States in a number of areas.

In 2020, the sudden and serious disturbances caused by the COVID-19-related measures in the operation of free movement within the otherwise smooth European Common Area – with long queues of lorries at borders and Kafka-esque situations for citizens and businesses – brought into stark light how much unhindered movement had been taken for granted and how deep and close the relations among EU Member States, but also with the EFTA States, have become over the years.

These close relations between the EU and the EFTA States have developed in two parallel paths: the economic path, with the European Economic Area (EEA) Agreement (Iceland, Liechtenstein and Norway) and an array of several bilateral agreements (Switzerland), and the justice and home affairs (JHA) path, with the association of the four EFTA States to the Schengen area and the Dublin *acquis*.

* All views expressed in this contribution are strictly personal and do not represent the views of the Council of the European Union, or of its General Secretariat or Legal Service. This chapter is based on a speech I gave on 8 October 2019 at a Lunch-Talk organised by the EFTA Court in Luxembourg, for the preparation of which I very much thank Raphaël Meyer, Legal Adviser at the Council Legal Service, for his help. A first version of it was published in the Liber Amicorum for Gilles de Kerchove – *The Fight against Terrorism: Achievements and Challenges* – in 2021 (Brussels, Bruylant).

[1] The European Free Trade Association, established in 1960, by Austria, Denmark, Norway, Portugal, Sweden, Switzerland and the UK, later joined by Iceland, Finland and Liechtenstein. Since 1995, only four States remain in EFTA: Iceland, Liechtenstein, Norway and Switzerland.

These paths have been developed separately, with different institutional and governance mechanisms.

Given the depth of these relations, it is worth reflecting on whether one could build on the success of the governance model of the EFTA pillar within the EEA in order to help integrate and further develop the Schengen/Dublin cooperation and beyond. This cooperation has so far lived its own life, in parallel to the EEA, in relative mutual ignorance of what the other is doing.

II. THE PARALLEL PATHS: THE EEA AND SCHENGEN

The first and oldest path was taken more than 30 years ago by Iceland, Norway and (one year later) Liechtenstein through the EEA[2] which, since its entry into force on 1 January 1994, establishes what the Court of Justice of the European Union (CJEU) called 'a special relationship … which is based on proximity, long-standing common values and European identity … one of [its] principal objectives [being] to provide for the fullest possible realisation of the free movement of goods, persons, services and capital within the whole EEA, so that the internal market … is extended to the EFTA States'.[3]

Although not part of the EEA, which it rejected by referendum in December 1992, Switzerland is closely linked to the EU by an array of several agreements[4] which, for more than 20 years, have made it a very close partner of the EU in 'vast fields … prescribing specific right and obligations, analogous … to those laid down in the [Treaty on the Functioning of the European Union (TFEU)] … the objective of these agreements [being] to strengthen the economic ties between the [EU and Switzerland]'. These include an agreement which '[brings] about … free movement of persons on the basis of the rules applying in the [EU]'.[5]

The second path was taken almost 25 years ago, when in 1999, Iceland and Norway signed their association to the Schengen area, followed by Switzerland and Liechtenstein in 2004 and 2008, respectively.[6] Internal border controls on persons were lifted in 2001 for the five EU and non-EU Nordic countries (Denmark, Finland,

[2] Agreement on the European Economic Area, signed on 2 May 1992. On the EEA, see T Blanchet, R Piipponen and M Westman-Clément, *The Agreement on the European Economic Area (EEA): A Guide to the free Movement of Goods and Competition Rules* (Oxford, Clarendon Press, 1994). See also T Blanchet, 'Le succès silencieux de dix ans d'Espace économique européen: un modèle pour l'avenir avec d'autres voisins ?' in *Liber Amicorum in Honour of Sven Norberg – A European for All Seasons* (Brussels, Bruylant, 2006) 101–23.

[3] Case C-897/19 PPU *IN*, ECLI:EU:C:2020:262, Judgment of the Court of Justice (Grand Chamber) of 2 April 2020, para 50.

[4] That is, about 20 main agreements and more than 100 other agreements. See notably the first package of seven agreements signed in 1999 on free movement of persons, air transport, land transport, agricultural products, conformity assessment, public procurement and scientific cooperation ([2002] OJ L114, 30 April, p 1).

[5] Case C-656/11 *UK v Council*, ECLI:EU:C:2014:97, Judgment of the Court of Justice of 27 February 2014, paras 53 and 55.

[6] See Agreement concluded by the Council of the European Union, and the Republic of Iceland and the Kingdom of Norway concerning the latters' association with the implementation, application and development of the Schengen acquis, signed on 18 May 1999 [1999] OJ L176, 10 July, p 36; Agreement between the European Union, the European Community and the Swiss Confederation on the Swiss Confederation's

Sweden, Iceland and Norway), in 2008 for Switzerland and in 2011 for Liechtenstein. The four Schengen Associates also became part of the so-called 'Dublin *acquis*',[7] which lays down how to identify the responsible state for examining requests for asylum. The participation to this *acquis* was considered a formal precondition to the association to the Schengen area without internal border controls on persons.[8]

The reason why the EFTA States first concentrated on the EEA and the Single Market was because the Schengen adventure – which started in 1985 among its five founding states (Belgium, France, Germany, Luxembourg and the Netherlands) – was at the time a more confidential than a 'mainstream' affair on the side of the EU Treaties.[9] The Schengen *acquis* would only be integrated into the Treaties 14 years later by the Treaty of Amsterdam in 1999.[10]

At the end of the 1980s, the 'mainstream' adventure – the most urgent for the EFTA States – was, at their doorstep, the unprecedented deepening of the relations between their European neighbours which was to be brought about by the Single European Act. The EFTA States were worried about being left out in the cold by the centrifugal strength of European integration.

The EEA Agreement was negotiated and agreed when the Single European Act – which had entered into force in July 1987 – was about to deliver the 'big bang' of the completion of the Single Market scheduled to take place on 1 January 1993, with, in particular, the lifting of all internal border controls on goods. This is why the drafting of the EEA Agreement was modelled on the provisions of the EC Treaty in its post-Single European Act but pre-Maastricht version, before the so-called second (Common Foreign and Security Policy (CFSP)) and the third (JHA) pillars were integrated into the EU Treaties.

association with the implementation, application and development of the Schengen acquis, signed on 24 October 2004 [2008] OJ L 53, 27 February, p 52; and the Protocol concerning Liechtenstein added to the Agreement with Switzerland, signed on 28 February 2008 [2011] OJ L160, 18 June, p 3.

[7] Agreement between the European Community and the Republic of Iceland and the Kingdom of Norway concerning the criteria and mechanisms for establishing the State responsible for examining a request for asylum lodged in a Member State or in Iceland or Norway, signed on 19 January 2001 [2001] OJ L93, 3 April, p 40. See the same Agreement with Switzerland, signed on 26 October 2004 [2008] OJ L53, 27 February, p 5; and the Protocol concerning Liechtenstein added to the Agreement with Switzerland, signed on 28 February 2008 [2011] OJ L160, 18 June, p 39.

[8] The Dublin *acquis* was originally a chapter of the 1990 Schengen implementing Convention (Chapter 7 on responsibility for processing applications for asylum, of Title II on abolition of checks at internal borders and movement of persons). The provisions of the Schengen association agreements made participation to that *acquis* a precondition to the association of the EFTA States to the Schengen area (see Art 7 of the Iceland and Norway association agreement to Schengen, Art 15(4) of the Switzerland association agreement and Art 10(4) of the Liechtenstein Protocol).

[9] On 14 June 1985, the very same day as the Delors White Paper on the upcoming Intergovernmental Conference on the Single European Act was published, the five founding Schengen States, which were unhappy to see that the free movement of persons was the 'poor cousin' of the project, signed the Schengen Agreement (14 June 1985, 33 articles). This was deepened in 1990 by the Implementing Convention (142 articles) known as CISA – Convention Implementing the Schengen Agreement of 14 June 1985 between the Benelux States, Germany and France on the gradual abolition of checks at their common borders – which was signed on 19 June 1990. The border controls on persons were planned to be effectively lifted between the five on 1 January 1993, the same day as the lifting of internal borders for goods under the Single European Act, but this was postponed to 26 March 1995 (between the five original Schengen States as well as Spain and Portugal).

[10] On the evolution of the variable geometry in JHA, see T Blanchet, 'Justice and Home Affairs: A Laboratory for Differentiation' (2013) LXVI-3 *Brussels Journal of International Relations* 33.

The same steer that had pushed the EFTA States into wishing to integrate with the Single Market would, a few years later – after the Schengen area had become reality in March 1995 – push them towards integrating with the Schengen area.

III. TRUE FREE MOVEMENT AND COMPENSATORY MEASURES

Providing for true free movement of persons by lifting internal border controls on all persons, regardless of their nationality – in addition to the classical free movement of EU citizens and their families (the right to enter other Member States and to work and establish there) – requires moving the controls on persons from the internal borders to the common external borders, together with measures on visas, asylum and immigration, as well as police and judicial cooperation in criminal matters. This is why the 1990 Schengen implementing Convention contained about 30 articles on police and judicial cooperation in criminal matters. This is also why the Maastricht Treaty, which had deepened the four freedoms, contained the third pillar on JHA.

The logic behind these 'compensatory measures' – or 'complementary measures', as they were called in Article 17 of the first Schengen Agreement (1985) – is that law enforcement authorities and judges cannot be blocked by a border that criminals, and their activities, could freely cross.

This link is very clear in Article 3(2) of the Treaty on European Union (TEU), which, among the objectives of the EU, provides that: 'The Union shall offer its citizens an area of freedom, security and justice without internal frontiers, in which the *free movement of persons is* ensured *in conjunction with* appropriate measures with respect to external border controls, asylum, immigration and the prevention and combating of crime' (emphasis added).

This is why powerful police cooperation, law enforcement and judicial cooperation instruments have been developed in the EU. These are databases such as the Schengen Information System (SIS), the European Travel Information and Authorisation System (ETIAS), the Entry/Exit System (EES), the European asylum fingerprint database (Eurodac), the European Criminal Records Information System (ECRIS), the system of exchange of DNA, fingerprints and vehicle registration police data, known as the Prüm *acquis*, or the Passenger Name Record (PNR) system. There are also police and judicial cooperation instruments such as Europol, Eurojust, the European Arrest Warrant (EAW) and the European Investigation Order (EIO).

However, while the four Schengen Associates fully apply all the Schengen *acquis* and the complementary Dublin (and Eurodac) *acquis*, as regards other JHA matters – ie, police and judicial cooperation in criminal matters beyond the Schengen *acquis*, such as the EAW, Eurojust, Europol, the Prüm *acquis* or ECRIS – it has been much more patchy and slow.

In 2006, Norway and Iceland, on the one hand, and the EU on the other, entered into a Surrender Agreement which in substance is similar to the EAW.[11] It took

[11] Agreement between the European Union and the Republic of Iceland and the Kingdom of Norway on the surrender procedure between the Member States of the European Union and Iceland and Norway, signed on 28 June 2006 [2006] OJ L292, 21 October, p 2. It entered into force on 1 November 2019.

13 years to finally come into force in 2019. In 2009, Norway and Iceland signed, with the EU, an agreement extending to them the Prüm *acquis* and in 2019, Switzerland and Liechtenstein did the same.[12] Although some of their provisions are provisionally applicable, at the time of writing (April 2024), some of these agreements are not yet in force for all parties.

The four Schengen Associates, which are also members of EFTA, regularly express their wish to deepen their cooperation with the EU in police and judicial cooperation in criminal matters. They would like, for instance, to be more closely associated with the work of Europol and its large database.[13] There are good reasons for doing so. As we have seen above, preventing and combating crime is one of the necessary compensatory measures to the lifting of internal border controls on persons and the four Associates do apply full free movement of persons.[14] However, the Associates would need to meet higher requirements in terms of governance. The EU cannot treat a third country, even one as closely associated with it as the four Schengen Associates, better than one of its own Member States, such as Denmark. In addition, deepening cooperation in such sensitive areas needs to be accompanied by efficient governance measures which also protect the rights of the individuals, rather than dealing only with interstate disputes.

Denmark is an EU Member State that fully applies the Schengen *acquis*, as well as the Dublin and Eurodac *acquis*. As a consequence of its opt-out Protocol (No 22), it could not participate in the new Europol Regulation (2016/794)[15] and was therefore kicked out of Europol, most notably from live access to its large database. In order to minimise the effect of this, an operational agreement was concluded between Europol and Denmark and entered into force on 30 April 2017, just before the entry into force of the Europol Regulation on 1 May 2017.[16] Because Denmark is an EU and a Schengen Member State, because it is bound by the Human Rights Convention and the

[12] Agreement between the European Union and Iceland and Norway on the application of certain provisions of Council Decision 2008/615/JHA on the stepping up of cross-border cooperation, particularly in combating terrorism and cross-border crime and Council Decision 2008/616/JHA on the implementation of Decision 2008/615/JHA on the stepping up of cross-border cooperation, particularly in combating terrorism and cross-border crime, and the Annex thereto [2009] OJ L353, 31 December, p 3. It is in force for Norway since 1 December 2020, but is not yet in force in Iceland. See the same Agreement with Switzerland ([2-19] OJ L187, 12 July, p 3), which has been in force since 1 March 2023, and for Liechtenstein ([2019] OJ L184, 10 July, p 3), which is not yet in force.

[13] At the time of writing (April 2024), like other third countries, they have concluded agreements with Europol on operational and strategic cooperation (see https://www.europol.europa.eu). They also have, like others, cooperation agreements with Eurojust, but nothing more specific.

[14] In addition to Schengen, Iceland, Liechtenstein and Norway are bound by the EU *acquis* on free movement of persons through the EEA Agreement. Switzerland also applies free movement of persons through its 1999 bilateral agreement with the EU on that subject matter, one of the seven bilateral agreements which are linked by a mutual guillotine clause in the event of termination of one of them.

[15] Regulation (EU) 2016/794 of the European Parliament and of the Council of 11 May 2016 on the European Union Agency for Law Enforcement Cooperation (Europol) and replacing and repealing Council Decisions 2009/371/JHA, 2009/934/JHA, 2009/935/JHA, 2009/936/JHA and 2009/968/JHA [2016] OJ L135, 24 May, p 53.

[16] Agreement on Operational and Strategic Cooperation between the Kingdom of Denmark and the European Police Office, https://www.europol.europa.eu/cms/sites/default/files/documents/operational_agreement_europol_denmark.pdf.

Data Protection Convention No 108, because the EU Charter of Fundamental Rights applies to Denmark and because Denmark had accepted to apply the Data Protection Directive (2016/680),[17] as well as to submit to the jurisdiction of the CJEU and to the control of the European data protection supervisor, in addition to contributing to the budget of Europol, Denmark was, for all these reasons, granted preferential treatment compared to ordinary operational agreements with third countries. This consisted notably in benefiting from Danish-speaking Europol staff assigned to treat Danish requests on a 24/7 basis. The link with Schengen is such that if Denmark would leave Schengen, this very specific, and advantageous, Europol agreement would cease to apply (guillotine clause).

IV. INSTITUTIONAL AND GOVERNANCE SET-UP: THE EEA AND SCHENGEN COMPARED

Both set-ups have very specific characteristics which make them unique compared to ordinary association agreements.

A. The EEA Institutional and Governance Set-up

The EEA is based on the so-called two pillar system. This means that in addition to the usual joint bodies, such as the EEA Council and the EEA Joint Committee, where representatives of both the EU and the EFTA sides can meet and adopt decisions to operate the agreement and settle disputes (Article 111 EEA), the EFTA side had to establish its own institutional pillar, with its own bodies (Article 108 EEA): the EFTA Surveillance Authority (ESA), the EFTA Court and the Standing Committee of EFTA States.[18] While the latter is a political decision-making body similar to the EU Council, the first two exercise functions which are similar, respectively, to the EU Commission (as regards surveillance, not as an initiator of legislation – Article 109 EEA) and to the CJEU (Article 108(2) EEA).

Hence, the EFTA Court can decide on infringement actions lodged by ESA against EFTA States (Article 31 of the Surveillance and Court Agreement (SCA)), on actions for annulment against ESA decisions (Article 36), on actions for failure to act against ESA (Article 37) and on disputes between EFTA States (Article 32). Individuals can bring actions for annulment or failure to act against ESA. The EFTA Court is also competent to issue advisory opinions on the interpretation of the EEA Agreement at

[17] Directive (EU) 2016/680 of the European Parliament and of the Council of 27 April 2016 on the protection of natural persons with regard to the processing of personal data by competent authorities for the purposes of the prevention, investigation, detection or prosecution of criminal offences or the execution of criminal penalties, and on the free movement of such data, and repealing Council Framework Decision 2008/977/JHA [2016] OJ L119, 4 May, p 89.

[18] These were established by two agreements concluded between the EFTA States: an Agreement between the EFTA States on the establishment of a Surveillance Authority and a Court of Justice and an Agreement on a Standing Committee of the EFTA States, both signed on 2 May 1992, the same day as the EEA Agreement.

the request of courts or tribunals of EFTA States (Article 34), which is equivalent to the preliminary ruling procedure in the EU.

This set-up was chosen in order to allow each side to autonomously run its own matters, in particular ensuring that its respective members respect their obligations under the EEA Agreement, while at the same time, through the joint bodies, securing the dynamic taking over of the EU *acquis* into the EEA and ensuring that the agreement is implemented and interpreted in an homogeneous manner (Articles 105 and 106 EEA).[19]

This was the solution chosen to protect the EU autonomy and avoid a situation where a body external to the EU would risk dictating to the EU how to interpret provisions which are identical in substance to EU provisions or EU provisions which are made applicable to the associated partners through reference. This was all the more important since the whole logic underlying the EEA Agreement is based on the dynamic taking over of EU rules, as they develop.

As to how the three EEA EFTA States were to be associated with the decision-shaping of the EU rules, while respecting the EU decision-making autonomy, the EEA Agreement provides that the Commission should informally consult the three EFTA States upstream, when preparing future proposals, in the same way as it consults EU Member States (Article 99 EEA). In addition, EFTA experts may participate in the meetings of a number of comitology committees and other committees consulted by the Commission (Article 100 EEA). However, EFTA experts or representatives are *not* invited to attend meetings in the Council or its preparatory bodies, either formally or informally or in a back-to-back fashion.

B. The Schengen Institutional and Governance Set-up

The institutional and governance set-up provided for in the Schengen association agreements is different from other agreements and is unique when it comes to decision-shaping.

Several factors were taken into account when the set-up was being designed:

- first, the Schengen *acquis* develops through the EU decision-making procedures and, in order to preserve the EU decision-making autonomy, it is not possible to allow non-Member States to participate in the EU decision-making procedures;
- second, the Schengen area is very integrated, its *acquis* is conceived and functions as a coherent ensemble, which is to be fully accepted and applied. This has been called by Advocates General Trstenjak and Mengozzi 'the principle of integrity

[19] Compared to that of the EEA, the institutional and governance system provided for in the different bilateral agreements that Switzerland has concluded with the EU is rather deficient. This is the reason why the EU mandated that the Commission negotiate an institutional overarching agreement with Switzerland intended to remedy that. The aim of this draft institutional framework agreement, which was finalised in November 2018 but rejected by the Swiss side in May 2021, is to cover so-called market access agreements (five existing and future ones) so as to make them dynamic (adaptation to the evolution of the EU rules), ensure uniform monitoring and interpretation, and establish a more effective dispute settlement system. A two-pillar system is of course not possible in a bilateral agreement with a single partner. Following the adoption by the Council of a new negotiation mandate on 12 March 2024, the discussions between the EU and Switzerland were relaunched.

and coherence' of Schengen.[20] It is therefore not possible to pick and choose what one wants to apply or not,[21] nor would it be possible to have a situation where a regulation would take several years before being applied by the EFTA side; thus, the mechanism had to guarantee that Schengen Associates would take over the *acquis*, its amendments and the new provisions building upon that *acquis*, in a timely manner or be expelled from the Schengen area;
- third, at the same time, Schengen concerns issues that are at the core of national sovereignty, and the EFTA States would have to be closely associated with the decision-shaping.

The solution found is quite unique and specific, allowing for a close association of the four Schengen EFTA States in the decision-shaping process, a solution to which the EFTA States are, understandably, very attached.

Before a Schengen-relevant proposal is made, the Schengen association agreements provide for the participation of the four Schengen Associates in the decision-shaping through the informal, upstream consultation of experts by the Commission (eg, Article 6 of the Iceland and Norway Association Agreement). This is very similar to the shaping of EEA-relevant legislation.

The real novelty – and the significant difference compared to the EEA decision-shaping system – is that once the proposal has been formally submitted to the EU legislator, the representatives of the four Associates are closely involved in the decision-shaping through the Mixed Committee (COMIX), which meets in the Council building, with Council members and Commission representatives.[22]

In practice, when a Schengen-relevant legal act is proposed by the Commission, it is first examined by the competent Working Party of the Council (27 experts) which, back-to-back, also meets in a Mixed Committee format with the experts of the four Schengen Associates discussing the text. Once the text goes up to the Committee of Permanent Representatives (Coreper, ie, the level of ambassadors), it also meets back-to-back with the Ambassadors of the four Schengen Associates in the Mixed Committee format. The same continues once the text reaches the Council: the

[20] Opinion of 10 July 2007 by AG Trstenjak, C-77/05, *UK v Council (Frontex)*, ECLI:EU:C:2007:419, paras 111–15,; Opinion of 24 June 2010 by AG Mengozzi, C-482/08, *UK v Council (VIS)*, ECLI:EU:C:2010:366, paras 63, 64, 66 and 74,. See also Case C-482/08, *UK v Council (VIS)*, ECLI:EU:C:2010:631, para 48, judgment of the Court of Justice of 26 October 2010: 'the need for coherence of [the Schengen] acquis, and the need – where that acquis evolves – to maintain that coherence, must be taken into account'.

[21] This is the reason why, for instance, enhanced cooperation cannot apply inside the Schengen *acquis* (see exclusion of enhanced cooperation in Art 87(3), last subpara, TFEU), Schengen being already in itself a 'close cooperation' directly authorised by the Treaty (see Art 1 of Protocol 19 on the Schengen *acquis* integrated into the framework of the EU). This is also the reason why Protocol 19 reverses the logic of the opt-in/out system when it operates in the Schengen *acquis*: when it has been authorised to take part in a (coherent) part of the Schengen *acquis*, a Member State covered by an opt-in/out protocol is deemed to have opted in to acts amending or building upon the relevant Schengen *acquis* unless it actively opts out, in which case a guillotine-like system kicks in.

[22] See, for instance, the composition of the Mixed Committee as set out in Art 3 of the Iceland and Norway Association Agreement: 'representatives of the governments of Iceland and Norway, the members of the Council of the European Union … and of the Commission', which meets at three levels: experts, senior officials (ambassadors) and ministers.

ministers from the four Schengen Associates meet with their 27 EU colleagues, back-to-back with the Council meeting.

The Schengen legal act is then formally and autonomously adopted by the EU legislator (eg, Article 8(1) of the Iceland and Norway Association Agreement), but the Schengen Associates will have been closely associated throughout the process.

Once a text has been adopted on the EU side, the Schengen Associates are notified thereof, each of them having 30 days to decide whether to accept its content and implement it in their national legal order. They also have a set time to fulfil their national constitutional requirements (eg, Article 8(2) of the Iceland and Norway Association Agreement).

If the Schengen Associates accept the legal act, which so far has always been the case, all is well. If a Schengen Associate does not accept the legal act or fails to notify the fulfilment of its constitutional requirements within the set deadlines, the Schengen association agreements provide for a guillotine clause under which the agreement is to be considered terminated with respect to the Schengen Associate concerned unless the Mixed Committee, after a careful examination of ways to continue the agreement, decides otherwise within 90 days (eg, Article 8(4) of the Iceland and Norway Association Agreement).

As in the EEA, there is also a provision on uniform application and interpretation, for which the Mixed Committee should keep under constant review the development of relevant case law (eg, Article 9) and a classical dispute settlement system in the event of divergences or dispute (eg, Articles 10 and 11).

It should be noted that, by contrast, the Dublin/Eurodac association agreements do not provide for a similar decision-shaping mechanism. Their provisions provide for the same decision-shaping system as that of the EEA (upstream informal consultation of the EFTA experts on draft texts by the Commission and association to the comitology committees without back-to-back meetings in the Council building).

V. SHORTCOMINGS IN THE SCHENGEN GOVERNANCE SET-UP

The Schengen decision-shaping mechanism, through the Mixed Committee, is quite efficient, and very much to the advantage of the four Associates. However, compared to the EEA – which is also based on a system of the EFTA partners taking over large chunks of the EU *acquis* – the Schengen governance system is asymmetrically weak and underdeveloped for such an integrated and ambitious association as Schengen.

First, the interpretation/application of the Schengen *acquis* relies solely on political cooperation in the Mixed Committee. If the parties disagree as to whether the Schengen *acquis* is correctly applied, the only arbiter is the Mixed Committee, and the only sanction is the termination of the Association Agreement. Such an all-or-nothing guillotine is quite a barbaric way to deal with partners in such a sophisticated association.

Second, while for the EU side, the oversight as regards, notably, compliance with fundamental rights is ensured by the CJEU, there is no such oversight for the EFTA side, apart from the European Court of Human Rights (ECtHR) in Strasbourg. This creates imbalances which are likely to increase in the future.

Experience shows that particularly since 1 December 2014, when the CJEU became fully competent on all JHA matters – after the end of the five-year transitional period set out in the Lisbon Treaty – more and more cases of interpretation or application of the EU Schengen and JHA *acquis* have been raised in the CJEU. A similar increase in cases dealing with these issues has also taken place at the ECtHR. These have sometimes involved decisions taken by an EFTA State on the basis of the Schengen or Dublin *acquis* or EFTA nationals in EU Member States being subject to JHA decisions taken by a Member State. The same could be true of an EU national or an EFTA national subject to a Schengen or JHA decision taken in an (other) EFTA State. There is an asymmetry in such cases: while on the EU side, the matter can be brought to the CJEU by an EU national judge, the same is not true on the EFTA side, where the matter cannot be brought to the EFTA Court. The issue stops in the relevant national court system of the relevant EFTA State or may end up in the ECtHR.[23] This asymmetry is not satisfactory.

VI. TAKING ADVANTAGE OF THE SUCCESSFUL SURVEILLANCE AND JUDICIAL EFTA PILLAR

Thirty years on, the EFTA/EEA governance mechanisms have proven their worth and have allowed for a differentiated integration and close association of the EFTA/EEA States into the EU internal market. The EEA Agreement has set up a system which, at the same time:

- safeguards the sovereignty of countries who would like to remain outside the EU, whilst being closely associated with the Union;
- safeguards the integrity of the decision making and the autonomy of the EU, and hence its sovereignty;
- allows for a dynamic evolution of the rules applicable in the EEA, through an institutional mechanism to integrate the new EU rules;
- ensures that the correct application of those rules is overseen by independent institutions, under the so-called two-pillar system whereby each side relies on its own monitoring and control mechanisms (the Commission and the CJEU on the EU side and the EFTA Surveillance Authority and the EFTA Court on the EFTA side).

The Schengen association agreements do safeguard the respective autonomy and sovereignty of their respective partners and allow for a dynamic evolution of the applicable rules, but lack the last, decisive element of having a mechanism that ensures that the correct application is overseen by independent institutions and that the rights of individuals are protected in the same way as in the EU and in the EEA, with access

[23] See, for instance, Judgment of 4 November 2014 of European Court of Human Rights (Grand Chamber), *Tarakhel v Switzerland*, no 29217/12, ECLI:CE:ECHR:2014:1104JUD002921712; Judgment of 30 June 2015 of European Court of Human Rights, *AS v Switzerland*, no 39350/13, ECLI:CE:ECHR:2015:0630JUD003935013; Case C-680/17, *Sumanan Vethanayagam and Others*, ECLI:EU:C:2019:627, Judgment of the CJEU of 29 July 2019; *IN* (n 3).

to justice through preliminary ruling procedures. Given that an efficient and independent oversight is a fundamental tool in order to build and protect mutual trust, which in turn is a prerequisite to the good functioning of an area without internal border controls like Schengen, this weakness and asymmetry is susceptible to hamper improvement and further deepening of the association.

A rather simple and straightforward solution would be to resort to what has been dubbed 'EFTA-pillar docking',[24] ie, to use the time-tested mechanisms of implementation control and interpretation – ESA and the EFTA Court – as concerns EU JHA *acquis* applied or to be applied by the four EFTA Schengen Associates, including Switzerland.

The idea would not be to include the Schengen *acquis* in the EEA Agreement. The EEA would not be 'polluted' with Schengen, Dublin or other JHA matters, and the EEA and Schengen would continue their separate, parallel paths.

In practical terms, a protocol could be added to the SCA, which would provide that the ESA College would have two compositions: one with three College members for EEA matters, and one with four College members – including one member from Switzerland – for matters relating to Schengen and Dublin and, more widely, to other possible JHA matters such as the Prüm *acquis* and other future pieces of EU *acquis* (such as ECRIS, PNR or Europol).

Similarly, the EFTA Court would have two chambers: one with three judges for EEA matters, and one with four judges – including one from Switzerland – for matters relating to Schengen and Dublin and, more widely, to other JHA matters.

Homogeneity would be safeguarded in the same way as it has been under the EEA Agreement in the last 30 years.

The advantages of such a mechanism would be threefold:

- first, this would increase the confidence of the EU that the EFTA States will correctly implement the Schengen, Dublin and relevant JHA *acquis*, and it would provide for an independent assessment of this implementation, unsusceptible to political interference, which is a guarantee for the EFTA States and their citizens – this would be, more broadly, a powerful mutual trust enhancer;
- second, this would allow for an independent control of the compliance with fundamental rights in the EFTA States when they apply the Schengen, Dublin and other relevant JHA *acquis* – clearly, with the kind of databases and instruments developed in that *acquis*, this is an area where fundamental rights are at stake;
- third, it would facilitate the extension and the strengthening of the association of the EFTA States to more *acquis* in the JHA area which is intrinsically linked – as necessary compensatory measures – to the Schengen area without internal border controls on persons.

If the *acquis* in the JHA area were subject to the control of the EFTA Surveillance Authority and to the jurisdiction of the EFTA Court, it would be much easier for the EFTA States to make their case for the inclusion of those areas within the unique

[24] On this 'docking' idea, albeit in another context, see M-J Clifton, 'EEA: Another Side to Europe', European Law Reporter, 25 November 2016, https://www.monckton.com/eea-another-side-europe.

decision-shaping mechanisms foreseen for the Schengen *acquis*, namely the Mixed Committee.

Moreover, perhaps such an 'EFTA-pillar docking' avenue could be explored as a possible alternative solution in case the institutional and governance option discussed so far between the EU and Switzerland in their negotiations on making their bilateral relations more dynamic and predictable – an option that relies on an arbitration mechanism, linked to a possible interpretation of EU *acquis* rules by the CJEU – would finally not succeed.

6

Reform of the Judicial Architecture of the EFTA Pillar of the EEA

GRAHAM BUTLER*

I. INTRODUCTION

FOR 30 YEARS, the EFTA Court has fulfilled its duty in ensuring the homogenous interpretation of EU/EEA law. As the judicial institution charged in the EFTA pillar of the European Economic Area (EEA) with providing the necessary interpretation of numerous legal acts[1] in performing the judicial function in EEA law, the EFTA Court is now beyond the age of adolescence. Its rulings are in the hundreds[2] and have contributed at length towards the better understanding and application of EU/EEA law.

Mimicked in its initial design to that of something resembling the Court of Justice within the Court of Justice of the European Union (CJEU) at the time of its creation in the early 1990s, the EFTA Court, as the judicial institution of the EFTA pillar of the EEA, has largely achieved the same result of the CJEU in its judicial reasoning and judicial outcomes. In that sense, it is a job well done, on the basis that no other precedent for such a judicial body existed.

Whilst the CJEU has undergone major reforms in the last 30 years, with the institution today largely unrecognisable compared to then, the EFTA Court has, by contrast, undergone little to no change and looks much as it does today as it did in 1994 when its first members were appointed and the *Restamark* judgment was handed down.[3] This fact is even more profound when it is considered that the only fundamental changes at the EFTA Court happened after three of the then five EEA/EFTA states

* The author is grateful to Halvard Haukeland Fredriksen and Ólafur Jóhannes Einarsson for their insight and discussion. However, all views contained here remain strictly those of the author alone.

[1] For example, the EEA Agreement, the Surveillance and Court Agreement (SCA), secondary law and beyond.

[2] For the most comprehensive and most recent account of all its cases, see *Report of the EFTA Court, 2018. Book 2* (EFTA Court, 2019) 511–46. The EFTA Court's annual reports since have omitted a more up-to-date list.

[3] The EFTA Court's first ruling: Case E-1/94, *Ravintoloitsijain Liiton Kustannus Oy Restamark*, Judgment of the EFTA Court, 16 December 1994.

joined the EU, and Liechtenstein then acceded to the EEA Agreement. Therefore, since 1995, the EFTA Court has undergone no real structural reform.

In this chapter, paying homage to the EFTA Court's past and accounting for its institutional design, the discussion moves on to thinking about the *future* of the EFTA Court in light of changes on the broader horizons. With the CJEU having undergone major changes in the past 30 years, the EFTA Court will inevitably have to follow, albeit recognising that each court of law is not the master of its own destiny, but rather is nonetheless an interlocutor in the process of any such reform. Several reasoned proposals are put hence forward for the reform of the judicial architecture of the EFTA pillar of the EEA. The chapter will commence by giving an overview of the basic legal design of the judicial architecture in the EEA as envisaged by the EEA Agreement, and the subsequent Surveillance and Court Agreement (SCA) (section II). From there, the first reform proposal (section III) put forward is consideration of an expansion of the number of judgeships. The EFTA Court started its life with five judges. It was envisaged that it would have at least seven, but for most of the EFTA Court's life, from 1995 until today, it has operated with only three judges as members. The pros and cons of such a small bench are evaluated, and it is concluded that the time has come for the bench to be expanded back in time to be five members, with the possibility for the EFTA Court to sit in divisions.

The second reform proposal (section IV) put forward is the introduction of Advocates General at the EFTA Court. Here, the fact that the EFTA Court has never had Advocates General is considered a major limitation on its overall jurisprudence, and therefore misses one of the best opportunities for EEA law to be debated and better understood amongst its wider stakeholders. This is especially considered since one of the overarching reasons for the existence of the offices of Advocates General at the CJEU is the lack of dissenting opinions, which the EFTA Court also operates as its judicial policy.

The third reform proposal (section V) put forward is the formal introduction of a scrutiny panel to evaluate the credentials of nominated persons for appointment to the EFTA Court. This independent scrutiny panel, called an 'Article 30a SCA panel', would be to ensure that only suitably qualified independent persons could be appointed to the EFTA Court. This would be an equivalent body to the Article 255 of the Treaty on the Functioning of the European Union (TFEU) panel in evaluating the competence of proposed candidates for appointment to the CJEU.

It is submitted that all three reform proposals contained in this chapter, despite being considered radical to some eyes, are merely modest in nature. After all, such proposed reforms would be largely replicating the practices seen in the EU pillar of the EEA as regards the CJEU. Furthermore, it would be ensuring that the institutional design of the judiciary in the EFTA pillar of the EEA does not remain static forever more.

Achieving the proposed reforms would be rather straightforward, as all three proposals could be achieved through minor revisions to the SCA and the annexed Statute of the EFTA Court. No changes to the EEA Agreement would be necessary. Given that the SCA is an international agreement only between the three EEA/EFTA states of Iceland, Liechtenstein and Norway, it would not require the input and buy-in from the EU or its Member States. Instead, the achievement of reform of the judicial architecture of the EFTA pillar of the EEA requires relatively straightforward multilateral steps amongst the three EEA/EFTA states.

Whilst the three reasoned proposed reforms are no absolute panacea to all the potential issues arising from the judicial architecture of the EFTA pillar, they would nonetheless certainly go some way towards kickstarting changes that are needed for EEA law to withstand another 30 prosperous years. Accordingly, the annex to this chapter contains a 'blueprint', with legal text that could be used by the three EEA/EFTA states to bring about the much-needed changes to the SCA.

II. THE EEA/EFTA STATES AGREEMENT: THE SURVEILLANCE AND COURT AGREEMENT

The EEA Agreement – a mixed agreement to which the EU, its Member States, Iceland, Liechtenstein and Norway are a party – demands that an EFTA Court exist in some form. This was because the proposed 'EEA Court' was shot down by the CJEU with its immensely consequential *Opinion 1/91*.[4] Thus, a revised draft agreement was made between the parties, which received the CJEU's blessing,[5] whereby a separate judicial institution was to be established, away from the CJEU. The result was Article 108(2) EEA, which specifies, inter alia, that '[t]he EFTA States *shall establish* a court of justice (EFTA Court)' (emphasis added).

In other words, it is not the EEA Agreement that provides for that EFTA Court, but rather that the states that are to be a part of the EFTA pillar of the EEA (the EEA/EFTA States) must themselves establish an EFTA Court. Such an 'EFTA Court' would thus be an institution established under an international agreement of third states and not, formally speaking, an EFTA institution.[6]

The means by which this obligation on the EEA/EFTA states to establish an EFTA Court was manifested was the Surveillance and Court Agreement (SCA). The SCA was and continues to be the lesser-known sibling of the EEA Agreement. Following Article 108(2) EEA, the EEA's specification that they must establish a judicial body for the EFTA pillar of the EEA, the three EEA/EFTA States provided for the 'EFTA Court', in that Article 27 SCA states:

> A court of justice of the EFTA States, hereinafter referred to as the EFTA Court, is hereby established. It shall function in accordance with the provisions of this Agreement and of the EEA Agreement.

Appended as a Protocol to the SCA was Protocol 5 'on the Statute of the EFTA Court'. With Article 42 SCA stating that '[t]he Protocols … to this Agreement shall

[4] *Opinion 1/91*, EU:C:1991:490 (*EEA I*). See E Paasivirta, 'The Union's Participation in Legally Binding International Third-Party Dispute Settlement: Opinion 1/91 (EEA I) and Opinion 1/92 (EEA II)' in G Butler and RA Wessel (eds), *EU External Relations Law: The Cases in Context* (Oxford, Hart Publishing, 2022).

[5] *Opinion 1/92*, EU:C:1992:189 (*EEA II*).

[6] The membership of Switzerland of EFTA, which is *not* a signatory to the EEA Agreement, is one of the reasons why this is so. Switzerland was expected to accede to the EEA Agreement, but never did. Consequently, the name 'EFTA Court' is indeed a little bit bizarre.

form an integral part thereof', the Statute of the EFTA Court, complementing the initial text of the SCA, thus made up the corpus of law that governs the contours of the judicial architecture of the EFTA pillar of the EEA. Since its inception, the SCA has been amended by the three EEA/EFTA States on 29 occasions, none of which has entailed any substantial reforms to the EFTA Court. Steps to initiate the proposals can come from the EFTA Court or the EEA/EFTA States,[7] though for the latter's initiation right, the EFTA Court must be heard. Any decisions to amend the SCA lie with the EEA/EFTA States, acting unanimously.

III. PROPOSAL 1: MORE JUDGES IN AN EXPANDED EFTA COURT

The EFTA Court was originally conceived to have seven judges as its members upon its inception.[8] However, it first only sat with five judges from January 1994,[9] given that Liechtenstein did not ratify the EEA Agreement initially and nor did Switzerland.[10] Thereafter in January 1995, only 12 months later, having seen Austria, Finland and Sweden accede to the EU (and thus becoming EU Member States), it meant that for a period of four months in 1995, there were only two EEA/EFTA States left: Iceland and Norway. On 1 May 1995, Liechtenstein acceded to the EEA Agreement, and with that state's accession, the EFTA Court was to have three members. It has remained with three judges ever since.

There was a contingency plan in place for what to have done with the EFTA Court if Liechtenstein had not acceded to the EEA Agreement. This was to allow the two members of the EFTA Court – the only two members – to pick a third judge of their choosing, based on a list of persons drawn up and adopted by common accord of the two EEA/EFTA States.[11] Although it was highly imperfect and most problematic, the option was never needed.[12]

Today, Article 28 SCA provides that '[t]he EFTA Court shall consist of three judges',[13] with Article 29 SCA further stating that the EFTA Court's rulings 'shall

[7] See section VI below.

[8] With the envisaged EEA Agreement including seven states: Austria, Finland, Iceland, Liechtenstein, Norway, Sweden and Switzerland.

[9] With judges nominated by Austria, Finland, Iceland, Norway and Sweden.

[10] Upon the lack of accession of Liechtenstein and Switzerland, and the EEA Agreement entering into force with only five of the planned seven states acceding, it has been claimed that 'no one questioned the ability of the EFTA Court to function with five judges'. See HH Frederiksen, '25 Years after Liechtenstein Saved the EFTA Court: The Case for Reform' (2020) 41 *Liechtensteinische Juristenzeitung* 50.

[11] See Agreement between Iceland and Norway Adjusting Certain Agreements between the EFTA States, 29 December 1994. The text of the agreement is reproduced in Annex II of the Report of the EFTA Court 1 January 1994–30 June 1995.

[12] However, in the future, if one of the current three EFTA-EEA States were to ever become an EU Member State, given the current unreformed EFTA Court, this solution could very well re-appear.

[13] Contrary to the Court of Justice within the CJEU, where, rather than specifying the number of judges, it merely links the number of judges to the number of Member States. See Art 19(2) TEU, first paragraph: 'The Court of Justice shall consist of one judge from each Member State.' However, the number of judges at the General Court within the CJEU is more flexible, whereby Art 19(2) TEU, second paragraph states: 'The General Court shall include *at least one judge per Member State*' (emphasis added). Each Member State currently has the possibility to nominate two judges to the General Court.

be valid only when all its members have participated in the deliberations'. With only three judgeships at the EFTA Court, this is a small bench. Given this fact, and the necessity for all judges to sit in each case in order for a decision to be 'valid', it has thus proven necessary to have ad hoc judges as part of the judicial architecture when one of the judges of the EFTA Court cannot act for a given reason. Article 30 SCA, fourth paragraph thus provides for the possibility of ad hoc judges to sit in specific cases:

> In case one of the Judges, in the opinion of the two other Judges, is disqualified from acting in a particular case, the two other Judges shall agree on a person to replace him chosen from a list established by common accord by the Governments of the EFTA States. If they cannot agree that person shall be chosen from the list by lot by the President.

In other words, the SCA places both a floor and a ceiling on the number of judges that sit in cases: three, which the EFTA Court cannot self-expand itself in given cases to more than three by making use of the ad hoc judges. This Article 30 SCA, fourth paragraph is supplemented by Article 15, fourth paragraph of Protocol 5 to the SCA on the Statute of the EFTA Court, which provides that:

> If according to this Article a Judge shall not take part in a particular case, a person to replace him shall be chosen in accordance with Article 30, fourth paragraph, of the Agreement, among those persons on the list who have been nominated by the Government which has nominated the regular Judge who is to be replaced.

This makes one thing remarkably clear: unlike Article 30 SCA, the Statute of the EFTA Court formally links the individual judgeships on the EFTA Court to specific EEA/EFTA States. Consequent to this is that when a judge nominated to the EFTA Court by a specific state (though formally appointed by common accord of the EEA/EFTA States) is prevented from acting in a given case, the ad hoc judge to replace him or her must be one nominated by that *same EEA/EFTA State* to the list of ad hoc judges.[14]

Cumulatively, therefore, Article 30 SCA, fourth paragraph and Article 15, fourth paragraph of Protocol 5 to the SCA must be read together, meaning that a judge or ad hoc judge from each EEA/EFTA State *must* be sitting in each and every case that the EFTA Court decides. That is even though other ad hoc judges nominated by other EEA/EFTA States are equally qualified to perform the task of judging a given case in the absence of a judge of the EFTA Court.[15]

From a legal institutional perspective, this linking of judges to specific EEA/EFTA States is a considerable oversight and quite a strong departure from the practices seen at the CJEU. The evidence of specifically demanding judges from each state sit in all cases is most problematic from the perspective of judicial independence. By contrast, Article 18, fourth paragraph of the Statute of the CJEU, which is annexed to the EU

[14] For example, the judge nominated by Norway to the EFTA Court would be replaced in each case by one of the ad hoc judges nominated by Norway.

[15] It could and indeed ought to be that, whilst an ad hoc judges list is in place, it should be open to the EFTA Court to have the possibility to have any of the named persons on such a list to sit in a case, regardless of the source of their nomination.

Treaties, specifically prohibits an EU Member State from insisting that the judge that they nominated to the Court of Justice sit in specific cases:

> A party may not apply for a change in the composition of the Court or of one of its chambers on the grounds of either the nationality of a Judge or the absence from the Court or from the chamber of a Judge of the nationality of that party.[16]

What is even more remarkable about this feature of the judicial architecture of the EFTA pillar of the EEA is that the original Statute of the EFTA Court – at the time of its entering into force – did not contain such a demand. In fact, it was only added in 1996,[17] after the departure of Austria, Finland and Sweden, and after the accession of Liechtenstein.

And today, whilst Article 15, fifth paragraph of Protocol 5 to the SCA on the Statute of the EFTA Court states that '[a] party may not apply for a change in the composition of the Court on the grounds of either nationality of a Judge or the absence from the Court of a Judge of the nationality of that party' – appearing to mimic the Statute of the CJEU – it is, in effect, a redundant provision, in light of the Article 30 SCA, fourth paragraph and Article 15, fourth paragraph of Protocol 5 to the SCA, as mentioned above. The only conceivable value of the Article 15, fifth paragraph of Protocol 5 to the SCA on the Statute of the EFTA Court could be to ensure that the nationality of the members, rather than the EEA/EFTA State which nominated them, cannot be challenged.[18]

The ad hoc judges system is fundamentally flawed, as no ad hoc judge should ever be able to sit in cases at the EFTA Court.[19] Such a system has never been accepted at the CJEU, not even in the cases when, from 1952 to 1972, there was only six Member States.[20] Whilst there are good grounds as to why judges are not able to sit in all cases on the grounds of formal recusal for reasons of a conflict of interest, ill health and the like, the Court of Justice within the CJEU has always been able to adjudicate on cases from within itself. It has thus never entertained such an ad hoc system, temporarily taking in members from the outside, who have plentiful other interests and motivations.

It is thus submitted that the EFTA Court should – through the lens of reform – be able to continue to function with a sufficiently large bench of permanent members,

[16] Though it may be noted that Arts 16–17 of the Statute of the CJEU provide that the Court of Justice sits in different divisions (chambers), so that not all judges hear all the cases.

[17] Decision amending Protocol 5 to the Agreement between the EFTA States on the Establishment of a Surveillance Authority and a Court of Justice, 10 August 1996.

[18] See n 32 below regarding a national of a third state being appointed (and re-appointed on several occasions) to the EFTA Court by Liechtenstein.

[19] For an argument on what constitutes a 'tribunal' in the Nordic States within the meaning of Art 267 TFEU as per the CJEU, and Art 34 SCA as per the EFTA Court, see G Butler, 'Tribunals in the Nordic States and Referrals to the European Courts' in J Reichel and M Zamboni (eds), *Scandinavian Studies in Law: Volume 69 – Rule of Law* (Stockholm, Jure, 2023). See also G Butler, 'Mind the (Homogeneity) Gap: Independence of Referring Bodies Requesting Advisory Opinions from the EFTA Court' (2020) 44 *Fordham International Law Journal* 307. More broadly in the EU legal order, see G Butler, 'Independence of Non-judicial Bodies and Orders for a Preliminary Reference to the Court of Justice' (2020) 45 *European Law Review* 870.

[20] Rather, to ensure uneven numbers, in the earlier years, there were initially seven judges, but only six Member States. See further A Arnull, 'The Many Ages of the Court of Justice of the European Union' in C Kilpatrick and J Scott (eds), *New Legal Approaches to Studying the Court of Justice* (Oxford, Oxford University Press, 2020).

without the need for an ad hoc judges list. One only needs to account for the (in-)famous *Fosen-Linjen* cases, whereby the same underlying case made its way through the administrative and judicial system in Norway, and was referred to the EFTA Court twice, at different instances of the national judiciary. In *Fosen-Linjen I*,[21] where an advisory opinion was requested by the Frostating Court of Appeal (Frostating lagmannsrett), the EFTA Court sat with one ad hoc judge[22] and decided that a simple breach of EU law, in this case public procurement law, was itself enough for contractual liability to be established. On the case reaching the Supreme Court of Norway (Norges Høyesterett), which too made a request for an advisory opinion that became *Fosen-Linjen II*,[23] the EFTA Court sat with three entirely different members than it had in *Fosen-Linjen I*.[24] The result was that in the second judgment,[25] the EFTA Court required a sufficiently serious breach to establish contractual liability rather than a simple breach, as in the first judgment.[26]

With the actual bench of the EFTA Court spending most of its life with less than half of its envisaged membership, it is submitted that the judicial composition of the EFTA Court is no longer fit for purpose and makes it extremely vulnerable to being undermined on the basis of its small bench. With just a mere handful of legal secretaries (*référendaires*) at its disposal, whilst eminently capable, it is a monumental challenge for the EFTA Court, given the realities (not to mention the politics). It is beyond doubt that a more coherent and consistent approach to the interpretation of EU/EEA law would have been achieved in the *Fosen-Linjen* saga if there was an enlarged court, with additional judgeships, and enhanced judicial independence.

With the proposition that the bench should be expanded, the next question that naturally arises is how many judges there should be and who they should be. Given the uneven number of EEA/EFTA States,[27] the doubling of the number of judges to make it two nominated by each state would result in six members – an even number. With this being less than ideal, instead, it would be appropriate to expand the permanent judgeships from three to five, just as it once was.

A five-judge court would allow the bench to sit in two divisions (chambers), just as the CJEU used to do in its earliest days. The President would sit in both chambers, and

[21] Case E-16/16, *Fosen-Linjen AS v AtB AS*, Judgment of the EFTA Court, 31 October 2017 (hereinafter *Fosen-Linjen I*).

[22] The *Fosen-Linjen I* judgment was decided by Carl Baudenbacher (President and Judge-Rapporteur), Per Christiansen (judge) and Benedikt Bogason (ad hoc judge).

[23] Case E-7/18, *Fosen-Linjen AS, supported by Næringslivets Hovedorganisasjon (NHO) v AtB AS*, Judgment of the EFTA Court, 1 August 2019 (hereinafter *Fosen-Linjen II*).

[24] The *Fosen-Linjen II* judgment was decided by Páll Hreinsson (President and Judge-Rapporteur), Bernd Hammermann (judge) and Ola Mestad (ad hoc judge).

[25] It is not the first time that the EFTA Court has overturned itself. It has done so explicitly regarding the exhaustion of trade marks and more implicitly in its case concerning state monopolies of a commercial character. See and compare G Butler, 'Intellectual Property in the EEA' in G Butler (ed), *Research Handbook on EEA Internal Market Law* (Cheltenham, Edward Elgar, 2024); G Butler and M Meling, 'State Monopolies and the Free Movement of Goods in EEA Law: Ensuring Substantive Homogeneity at the EFTA Court' (2022) 28 *International Trade Law & Regulation* 55.

[26] For an overview of these judgments of the EFTA Court, see Albert Sanchez Graels, ch 17 in this volume.

[27] Only between 1 January 1995 and 30 April 1995 did the EFTA pillar of the EEA only have an even number of states: after the accession of Austria, Finland and Sweden to the EU, and before the accession of Liechtenstein to the EEA Agreement.

the other remaining four judges would divide into two in each chamber. Altogether, the five judges of the EFTA Court would be able to sit in a 'Full Court' formation for cases of high significance for the development of EU/EEA law,[28] as well as for its formal occasions like the swearing-in of new members or when members of the EFTA Surveillance Authority (ESA) enter into office.

The EFTA Court has not previously rejected suggestions that new judgeships should be added.[29] It is a conceivable possibility, and in 2011 it proposed that Article 28 SCA be amended and sit with ad hoc judges on a regular basis.[30] The thrust of the proposal was that its existing ad hoc judges become members of the EFTA Court, without the residence requirement at its seat of establishment. This idea, whilst merited, raises a number of issues. For example, once an ad hoc judge becomes a member of a court, they, by their very nature, can no longer be considered ad hoc. Thus, they are on the same terms as the judges who are not ad hoc. If the proposed ad hoc nature as members of the EFTA Court was proposed with budgetary considerations in mind, this is odd, given that having only partially or non-remunerated judges as members of the EFTA Court is highly problematic for inherent reasons of being susceptible to bias.

Instead, under a new five-judge system, it would preserve the existing entitlements of the EEA/EFTA States of being able to put forward one person each for appointment. For the other two judgeships, it is proposed that they would come from outside of the EFTA pillar of the EEA, through the nomination of nationals of EU Member States. This is not unprecedented, given, after all, the first judge nominated by Liechtenstein, and subsequently appointed (and re-appointed on numerous occasions) by common accord,[31] was not a national of any of the three EEA/EFTA States. At both the CJEU and the EFTA Court at present, there is no formal requirement that persons nominated and appointed to the respective courts are nationals of any state.[32] Accordingly, the expanded EFTA Court would end the use of ad hoc judges and that the remaining two judges would be nationals of EU Member States, thus

[28] The EFTA Court is of the view that an expanded EFTA Court would only sit when there is a 'public or private interest' at stake. Memorandum from the EFTA Court to the ESA/Court Committee, 'Amendments to the Agreement on the Establishment of Surveillance Authority and a Court of Justice', Ref: 20110927/3549/I, 2 October 2011, p 3.

[29] Rather, the EFTA Court has only remarked that: 'Presuming that it is unrealistic to consider increasing the number of EFTA Court judges', implying it would be responsive to such an idea. See Letter from the EFTA Court on Amendments to the SCA, Ref. 20101027/2491/O, Luxembourg, 28 October 2010, p 2 (on file with the author).

[30] Memorandum from the EFTA Court to the ESA/Court Committee (n 28).

[31] Article 30 SCA, first paragraph states, inter alia, that judges 'shall be appointed by common accord of the Governments of the EFTA[-EEA] [s]tates for a term of six years'.

[32] Carl Baudenbacher, a national of Switzerland, nominated (and multiple times renominated) by Liechtenstein to the EFTA Court remains, to the best of this author's knowledge, the only person appointed to the CJEU or the EFTA Court who was of a nationality other than that of the state which nominated a judge. This excludes the nomination and appointments to the now defunct EU Civil Service Tribunal, which, at least formally, but not practically, divorced nationality of nominees from the state of which they were a national. See G Butler, 'An Interim Post-mortem: Specialised Courts in the EU Judicial Architecture after the Civil Service Tribunal' (2020) 17 *International Organizations Law Review* 586. Outside of the EU, at the European Court of Human Rights (ECtHR), there have been several examples, both past and present, of judges being nominated and subsequently appointed as members of the ECtHR who were nationals of states other than the nominating state.

ensuring that the three EEA/EFTA States would not be able to insist on 'one of their own' filling the seats.

The proposed amendments to the SCA, to give effect to more judgeships and related matters, can be seen in the annexed 'blueprint' of this chapter.

IV. PROPOSAL 2: ADVOCATES GENERAL AT THE EFTA COURT

The second proposal that is advanced as part of reform of the judicial architecture of the EFTA pillar of the EEA is that members of the EFTA Court should not just be merely judges, but that the EFTA Court should have *other* members, Advocates General, just like the Court of Justice at the CJEU does. EEA law is very familiar with them already,[33] so their introduction at the EFTA Court would not be an unidentified flying object.

Advocates General, as a judicial office, play a crucial role in the judicial function of assisting with the interpretation and deciding of cases in the EU pillar of the EEA.[34] The literature on Advocates General is growing[35] and is very favourable towards their place within the CJEU. Despite the novelty of the Advocates General,[36] they play an important part in the broader outreach of the law that is being adjudicated upon beyond the courtroom itself.

Having Advocates General at the EFTA Court was, in fact, proposed by the EFTA Court in 2011,[37] although it left open the nuances. The EFTA Court proposed an 'EFTA Court Advocate General', which, in its view, would 'reinforce the quality of the EFTA Court decisions and enhance the credibility and authority of the … [EFTA] Court's rulings'.[38] This, it can be submitted, was the intention to have Advocates General be ad hoc in nature. This proposition of the EFTA was indeed based on past

[33] As are Advocates General of the CJEU with the case law of the EFTA Court. See C Baudenbacher, 'The EFTA Court's Relationship with the Advocates General of the European Court of Justice' in MT D'Alessio, V Kronenberger and V Placco (eds), *De Rome à Lisbonne les juridictions de l'Union européenne à la croisée des chemins: Mélanges en l'honneur de Paolo Mengozzi* (Brussels, Bruylant, 2013); C Baudenbacher, 'The EFTA Court, the ECJ, and the Latter's Advocates General – a Tale of Judicial Dialogue' in A Arnull, P Eeckhout and T Tridimas (eds), *Continuity and Change in EU Law: Essays in Honour of Sir Francis Jacobs* (Oxford, Oxford University Press, 2008).

[34] See G Butler and A Łazowski, 'Let's Take the Canvass out: Advocates General at the Court of Justice of the European Union' in G Butler and A Łazowski (eds), *Shaping EU Law the British Way: UK Advocates General at the Court of Justice of the European Union* (Oxford, Hart Publishing, 2022).

[35] See, eg, A Albors-Llorens, 'Securing Trust in the Court of Justice of the EU: The Influence of the Advocates General' (2012) 14 *Cambridge Yearbook of European Legal Studies* 509; K Borgsmidt, 'The Advocate General at the European Court of Justice: A Comparative Study' (1988) 13 *European Law Review* 106; N Burrows and R Greaves, *The Advocate General and EC Law* (Oxford, Oxford University Press, 2007); L Clément-Wilz, 'The Advocate General: A Key Actor of the Court of Justice of the European Union' (2012) 14 *Cambridge Yearbook of European Legal Studies* 587; A Dashwood, 'The Advocate General in the Court of Justice of the European Communities' (1982) 2 *Legal Studies* 202; T Tridimas, 'The Role of the Advocate General in the Development of Community Law: Some Reflections' (1997) 34 *Common Market Law Review* 1349; Butler and Łazowski (n 34).

[36] See M Bobek, 'A Fourth in the Court: Why are There Advocates General in the Court of Justice?' (2012) 14 *Cambridge Yearbook of European Legal Studies* 529.

[37] Memorandum from the EFTA Court to the ESA/Court Committee (n 28).

[38] Letter from the EFTA Court on Amendments to the SCA, Ref. 20101027/2491/O, Luxembourg, 28 October 2010, p 2 (on file with the author).

decisions of the EEA/EFTA States that were not taken, as it has been historically suggested that including Advocates General at the EFTA Court was considered on its initial establishment, but was ultimately decided against. Nor was it considered by either the EFTA Court itself in 2011, or the EEA/EFTA States in the 1990s, that a judge of the EFTA Court could act as an Advocate General in given cases, despite this possibility existing at the then Court of First Instance (now the General Court).[39]

Having two Advocates General at the EFTA Court as permanent members would significantly enhance the quality of judicial decisions emanating from the body, as the Advocates General at the Court of Justice are well known for their engagement in different sides of legal arguments, which the Court of Justice never does itself. This is not to mention that the quality of writing, given the singularity of Opinions, is much better than the judgments of the Court of Justice. As part of this proposal, the two Advocates General would be Advocates General of the EFTA Court only, and in no way would there be any overlap with Advocates General of the CJEU,[40] who cannot be shared.[41]

Indeed, it should be noted that the CJEU, in its earliest days as a small court, had two Advocates General itself.[42] Suitable candidates would thus be similar to that of judgeships – national judges, full professors of law, and the like – those who act in an independent manner, as well as having the requisite knowledge of EU/EEA law. To ensure consistency in the composition of the EFTA Court, it would be proposed that one of the two Advocates General must be a national of an EU Member State and that the upper limit would be set at two.[43]

One argument that could be advanced against the idea of installing Advocates General at the EFTA Court would be that in individual cases, it would result in an 'Opinion' of the Advocate General, as well as an 'Advisory Opinion (Judgment)' of the EFTA Court. This could, to some eyes, be viewed as two non-binding opinions emanating from the EFTA Court. Whilst a textually accurate proposition, judgments of the EFTA Court – whether they are rulings through direct actions or rulings through the request for an advisory opinion procedure – are binding because of the principle of loyalty (sincere cooperation) between the states being contracting parties to the EEA Agreement. There are corresponding and analogous provisions of

[39] Though, admittedly, it has been infrequently utilised. See D Edward, 'Reflections of a Judge Acting as Advocate General in the Court of First Instance: 1990–1992' in Butler and Łazowski (n 34).

[40] For the view that Advocates General of the CJEU could be shared with the EFTA Court, see HH Frederiksen, '25 Years after Liechtenstein Saved the EFTA Court: The Case for Reform' (2020) 41 *Liechtensteinische Juristenzeitung* 50, 55.

[41] This is because having Advocates General operating in more than one pillar would impinge upon the judicial function of Advocates General of the CJEU. Though not specifically related to Advocates General, the Court of Justice's *Opinion 1/91*, EU:C:1991:490 (*EEA I*) is evidence of the view of the CJEU that judicial resources, such as its members, cannot be shared.

[42] See A Arnull, 'The Many Ages of the Court of Justice of the European Union' in C Kilpatrick and J Scott (eds), *New Legal Approaches to Studying the Court of Justice: Revisiting Law in Context* (Oxford, Oxford University Press, 2020).

[43] Note, however, that the EU Treaties merely demand a minimum number of Advocates General, as per Art 252 TFEU, first paragraph, which is eight: 'The Court of Justice shall be assisted by eight Advocates-General. Should the Court of Justice so request, the Council, acting unanimously, may increase the number of Advocates-General.' Accordingly, there is no upper limit. The current number of Advocates General at the CJEU is 11.

Article 4(3) of the Treaty on European Union (TEU), where loyalty is found in EU law, in both the EEA Agreement and the SCA,[44] to which the EEA/EFTA States are therefore bound by the judgments of the EFTA Court. Thus, having non-binding Opinions of the Advocates General at the EFTA Court would not be an issue to cause a national court to choose 'which' ruling to follow.

The proposed amendments to the SCA, to give effect to the introduction of Advocates General and related matters, can be seen in the annexed 'blueprint' of this chapter.

V. PROPOSAL 3: SCRUTINY PANEL FOR PROPOSED APPOINTMENTS TO THE EFTA COURT

A significant development took place with the entering into force of the Treaty of Lisbon in 2009. This provided, for the first time, that candidates put forward for nomination to the CJEU – for both the Court of Justice and the General Court, and both judges and Advocates General (at the Court of Justice) alike – would be subject to a prior assessment to determine their suitability for appointment (and re-appointment) to judicial office. Article 255 TFEU states:

> A panel shall be set up in order to give an opinion on candidates' suitability to perform the duties of Judge and Advocate-General of the Court of Justice and the General Court before the governments of the Member States make the appointments referred to in Articles 253 and 254.
>
> The panel shall comprise seven persons chosen from among former members of the Court of Justice and the General Court, members of national supreme courts and lawyers of recognised competence, one of whom shall be proposed by the European Parliament. The Council shall adopt a decision establishing the panel's operating rules and a decision appointing its members. It shall act on the initiative of the President of the Court of Justice.

In other words, proposed persons for appointment to the CJEU must be predetermined by an independent body – the Article 255 TFEU panel[45] – to see whether they would be suitable for the role for which they are being proposed. Prior to 2009, any candidate put forward to be a judge or Advocate General by a Member State to the CJEU was appointed by common accord of the EU Member States,[46] without as much as a check on that individual's suitability. This resulted, on occasion, in members being appointed to both the Court of Justice and the General Court who were evidently not up to the mark of being EU judges.

[44] J Temple Lang, 'The Principle of Sincere Cooperation in EEA Law' in C Baudenbacher (ed), *The Fundamental Principles of EEA Law: EEA-ities* (New York, Springer International Publishing, 2017) 73–74.

[45] For an early evaluation, see, T Dumbrovský, B Petkova and M van der Sluis, 'Judicial Appointments: The Article 255 TFEU Advisory Panel and Selection Procedures in the Member States' (2014) 51 *Common Market Law Review* 455. For its latest activity report, see 'Seventh Activity Report of the Panel Provided for by Article 255 of the Treaty on the Functioning of the European Union' (Publications Office of the European Union, 2022).

[46] In line with Art 253 TFEU.

The intended high standard of persons to become members of the CJEU is also seen, in part, regarding the EFTA Court. Article 30 SCA, first paragraph demands some standards, in that:

> The Judges shall be chosen from persons whose independence is beyond doubt and who possess the qualifications required for appointment to the highest judicial offices in their respective countries or who are jurisconsults of recogni[s]ed competence. They shall be appointed by common accord of the Governments of the EFTA States for a term of six years.[47]

Whilst the SCA was equivalent to the EU Treaties at the time of the adoption of the SCA, the EU Treaties have moved on following reforms. The SCA does not provide, at present, for an analogous 'Article 255 TFEU panel', and thus the EFTA pillar of the EEA has no safeguard mechanisms to ensure that a person who does not possess the requisite capabilities, such as that of independence and knowledge of EU/EEA law, does not become a member of the EFTA Court.

The EFTA Court itself proposed an equivalent Article 255 TFEU panel in 2011. Here, the EFTA Court suggested that Article 30 SCA, first paragraph, the equivalent of Article 253 TFEU for the CJEU, be amended to state that members of the EFTA Court 'shall be appointed by common accord of the Governments of the EFTA States for a term of six years, after consultation of the panel provided for in Article [30a SCA]'.

With that proposed change came a new supplementing provision to regulate the terms of the new 'Article 30a SCA panel' to account for the modalities of the EFTA pillar. It wished for a former member of the EFTA Court to chair the panel, with a former member of the CJEU also being nominated, as well as the inclusion of '[j]urisconsults of recognised competence, i.e. University Professors of Law'.[48]

The inclusion of an 'Article 30a SCA panel' would certainly better secure the independence of the EFTA Court and simultaneously boost its credibility in being analogous to the procedures that apply with regard to the CJEU. Remarkably, a recent Activity Report of the Article 255 TFEU panel as regards the CJEU showed that almost one in four persons put forward by the Member States for appointment to either the Court of Justice or the General Court within the CJEU has had a negative opinion rendered against them, determining them unsuitable for office.[49] This reform is all the more urgent given the prevailing rule of law problems in Europe,[50] which, in turn, result in national proceedings whereby EU Member States' CJEU nomination

[47] What a jurisconsult is must be given an autonomous definition as a matter of EEA law, is not subject to qualification by national law and should not be in any way equated with qualification for national judicial office.

[48] Memorandum from the EFTA Court to the ESA/Court Committee (n 28) 5.

[49] 'Seventh Activity Report of the Panel Provided for by Article 255 of the Treaty on the Functioning of the European Union' (n 45) 9. Whilst in 2020, only 73 per cent of candidates were deemed qualified, the more alarming statistic is that in 2011, only 67 per cent of candidates put forward by EU Member States were qualified. This raises the odd question of how many members of the CJEU appointed prior to 2009 were actually deemed suitable for office(!).

[50] Which, it is argued, the Nordic States are not immune from. See G Butler, 'The European Rule of Law Standard, the Nordic States, and EU Law' in A Bakardjieva Engelbrekt, A Moberg and J Nergelius (eds), *Rule of Law in the EU: 30 Years after the Fall of the Berlin Wall* (Oxford, Hart Publishing, 2021).

procedures are coming under increased scrutiny.[51] This is the case without even going into the details surrounding an attempt of the EEA/EFTA States to re-appoint a judge for only half a mandate, in violation of the SCA.[52]

Thus, the proposal for an 'Article 30a SCA panel' is sound, though slightly different from the EFTA Court's 2011 vision that if the rule of law and judicial independence is going to be on the overall agenda of the EU for many years to come, then action too has to be taken as regards the judicial institution of the EFTA pillar of the EEA.[53] With proposals 1 and 2 seeking an increase in the size of the EFTA Court – from three judges to five, and the introduction of two Advocates General – there would be a need for checks to be put in place to ensure that the seven members of the EFTA Court in the future would be sufficiently qualified and independent to hold such important offices.

The proposed amendments to the SCA, to give effect to the introduction of an Article 30a SCA panel and related matters, can be seen in the annexed 'blueprint' of this chapter.

VI. CONCLUSION

The EEA Agreement is one of the EU's most comprehensive and sophisticated international agreements.[54] As a prime example of how EU external relations can work,[55] the institutional framework around it must stay in touch with the times, in that homogeneity is an evolving matter. The EFTA Court cannot continue to operate like it is 1995, when *(What's the Story) Morning Glory?* was a new chart-topping album by Oasis, President Mitterrand was just about to hand over power to President Chirac in France, and the Yugoslav Wars were still ongoing. Evidently, the world is very different in 2024.

There are aspects of the EFTA Court's early developments in the mid-1990s that were absolutely right in hindsight: the moving of its initial seat from Geneva to a permanent home in Luxembourg;[56] the regular formal and informal communications

[51] See, eg, Case C-119/23, *Virgilijus Valančius v Lithuania*, pending, in relation to a judge of the General Court seeking re-appointment challenging the validity of the national measures which, he argues, are not in compliance with EU primary law.

[52] For history on issues related to judicial appointments at the EFTA Court, see AF Tatham, 'Reappointment to International Courts and the Case of the EFTA Court' (2021) 20 *Law & Practice of International Courts and Tribunals* 119.

[53] For a critique of the weaknesses regarding the design of the appointment and composition of the CJEU in the EU pillar of the EEA and how there can be further improvements, see D Kochenov and G Butler, 'Independence of the Court of Justice of the European Union: Unchecked Member States Power after the Sharpston Affair' (2021) 27 *European Law Journal* 262.

[54] From an external relations perspective, see E Neframi, 'The EEA Agreement from the Perspective of the European Union's External Action' in T Gunnarsson and others (eds), *Afmælisrit – Páll Hreinsson sextugur* (Reykjavík, Fons Juris, 2023).

[55] Of all the leading cases relating to EU external relations, in real terms, very few have related specifically to the EEA Agreement. See Butler and Wessel (n 4).

[56] Note, however, this was not strictly a decision of the EFTA Court. Rather, Article 45 SCA states, 'The seat of the … EFTA Court … shall be determined by common accord of the Governments of the EFTA States'.

that the EFTA Court has had with the CJEU to foster judicial dialogue; and the bringing about of both substantive and procedural homogeneity of EU/EEA law for the EFTA pillar. But reform of the judicial architecture has, for some reason, not been seen as a priority.

In 2010, the EFTA Court warned the EEA/EFTA States that, with an evolving primary law framework for the CJEU, under which substantial reforms were suggested, and with nothing being undertaken as regards the EFTA Court, this constituted '[a] shortcoming' of the EEA legal order and that consequences will come, in that it will 'have implications for homogeneity as well as equality and reciprocity of rights and obligations and thereby to negatively affect the good functioning of the EEA as a whole'.[57]

The evident fear of the EFTA Court – reading between the lines – is that one day it could find the CJEU seeing to it that the EEA Agreement was, in practice, seeking different objectives or was trying to achieve a different purpose. In other words, there could be a risk that the EEA Agreement could be *Polydor*'d.[58] Homogeneity is always at risk.[59] Whilst nothing of the sort has occurred to date,[60] thus far, the EEA/EFTA States have, shamefully, ignored the EFTA Court's warning. Given that CJEU reform was again on the table at the time of writing this chapter, with the proposed transfer of some references for a preliminary ruling from the Court of Justice to the General Court, it is time that EEA/EFTA States listened to the EFTA Court's (and this chapter's) warning and acted. This is exactly why the annexed blueprint to this chapter should be given serious consideration by the EEA/EFTA States – or, again, for the EFTA Court to formally communicate to the EEA/EFTA States the need for reform like it has previously, preferably endorsing the exact text of the annexed blueprint.

This chapter argued that: first, the number of judgeships at the EFTA Court should be expanded to five; second, there should be two Advocates General at the EFTA Court; and, third, an equivalent scrutiny panel should be established to ensure the competence and independence of members of the EFTA Court. None of the proposed changes involves amendments to the EEA Agreement – a mixed agreement – ratified by the EU, all its Member States and the three EEA/EFTA States. Rather, it merely involves changes to the SCA, which is a multilateral agreement of just the three EEA/EFTA States, and makes it practicably easier to reform, without opening the larger and more substantial question of how a reformed EEA Agreement would look.

What underpins all three proposals that have been put forward in this chapter is that of strengthening the rule of law and judicial independence. Small multinational courts can be weak, especially when parties know exactly which judges will hear and

[57] Letter from the EFTA Court on Amendments to the SCA, Ref. 20101027/2491/O, Luxembourg, 28 October 2010, p 1 (on file with the author).

[58] Case 270/80, *Polydor Limited and RSO Records Inc. v Harlequin Records Shops Limited and Simons Records Limited*, EU:C:1982:43. See J Klabbers, 'The Purpose of International Agreements and Their Direct Effect: Polydor' in Butler and Wessel (n 4).

[59] See HP Graver, 'The EFTA Court and the Court of Justice of the EC: Legal Homogeneity at Stake?' in P Müller-Graff and E Selvig (eds), *EEA-EU Relations* (Berlin, Berliner Wissenschafts-Verlag, 1999).

[60] See eg, the very 'homogeneous' view of the two pillars of the EEA in Case C-897/19 PPU, *Russian Federation v IN*, EU:C:2020:262. See also C Hillion and HH Fredriksen, 'The "Special Relationship" between the EU and the EEA EFTA States: Free Movement of EEA Citizens in an Extended Area of Freedom, Security and Justice: *Ruska Federacija v. IN*' (2021) 58 *Common Market Law Review* 851.

deliver rulings given to them.[61] Whilst the EFTA Court has lasted for much of its life in a manner which was not originally intended, and that it has made it to the age of 30,[62] such a success does not necessarily mean the status quo will suffice for it to reach the age of 60.[63] Rather, genuine reform of the EFTA Court has to happen sooner or later.

However, the textual amendments to the SCA that are needed for the three proposals are no panacea. They are put forward without addressing many of the other deficiencies as regards the judicial architecture of the EFTA pillar of the EEA. Further reforms could be considered, such as obligations placed upon national courts at final instances, or those who make decisions to which an appeal does not lie, to make requests for advisory opinions;[64] not allowing higher instance national courts to restrict requests for advisory opinions sent by lower instance national courts;[65] and the need to provide the EFTA Court with the necessary jurisdiction to interpret other EU/EEA-related international agreements of the EEA/EFTA States, such as those relating to Schengen, Lugano and surrender arrangements, among others.

As was mentioned at the outset of this chapter, the three proposals, interrelated with one another, are modest in nature. The title of this chapter has been 'Reform of the Judicial Architecture of the EFTA Pillar of the EEA', and not 'Reform of the EFTA Court'. The latter name would imply that it would be up to the EFTA Court itself to reform from within. However, reform entails a constellation of actors – namely, the three EEA/EFTA States – to undertake the necessary amendments to the SCA. Amendments to the SCA can be initiated by the EEA/EFTA States[66] and, furthermore, Article 44 of Protocol 5 to the SCA on the Statute of the EFTA Court provides

[61] By contrast, a national court in an EU Member State that makes a request for a preliminary ruling will not know which judges will hear the case, or whether its case will be dealt with by a small three-judge chamber or a 'Full Court' (27 judges) formation.

[62] The EFTA Court was given a good health check at the ages of 10 and 20. See C Baudenbacher, P Tresselt and T Örlygsson (eds), *The EFTA Court: Ten Years on* (Oxford, Hart Publishing, 2005); EFTA Court (ed), *The EEA and the EFTA Court: Decentred Integration* (Oxford, Hart Publishing, 2014).

[63] The EFTA Court's founding members have written extensively and will make a lasting contribution to understanding the judicial body well into the future. See, eg, S Norberg, 'Justice in the European Economic Area: The Role of the EFTA Court' in EFTA Court (ed), *Judicial Protection in the European Economic Area* (Stuttgart, German Law Publishers, 2012); L Sevón, 'The ECJ, the EFTA Court and the National Courts of the EFTA Countries' in P Lødrup et al (eds), *Rettsteori og rettsliv: Festskrift til Carsten Smith* (Oslo, Universitetsforlaget, 2002); T Vilhjálmsson, 'EFTA-domstolen' in P Lødrup et al (eds), *Rettsteori og rettsliv: Festskrift til Carsten Smith* (Oslo, Universitetsforlaget, 2002).

[64] As specified for courts and tribunal in EU Member States in Art 267, third paragraph TFEU.

[65] Article 34, third paragraph SCA, which provides that '[a]n EFTA State may in its internal legislation limit the right to request such an advisory opinion to courts and tribunals against whose decisions there is no judicial remedy under national law' and is highly problematic, and should be removed from the SCA. See G Butler, 'Lower Instance National Courts and Tribunals in Member States and Their Judicial Dialogue with the Court of Justice of the European Union' (2021) 4 *Nordic Journal of European Law* 19; G Butler and J Cotter, 'Just Say No! Appeals against Orders for a Preliminary Reference' (2020) 26 *European Public Law* 615.

[66] See Arts 49 SCA and 50(3) SCA. Article 49 SCA: 'The Governments of the EFTA States may, unless otherwise provided in this Agreement, on a proposal from or after hearing the EFTA Surveillance Authority, by common accord amend the main Agreement as well as Protocols 1 to 4 and 6 to 9. Such an amendment shall be submitted to the EFTA States for acceptance and shall enter into force provided it is approved by all EFTA States. Instruments of acceptance shall be deposited with the Government of Sweden which shall notify all other EFTA States.' Article 50(3) SCA: 'The Governments of the remaining EFTA States shall, by common accord, decide on the necessary amendments to be made to the present Agreement.'

that '[t]he … EFTA States may, on a proposal from or after hearing the Court, by common accord amend this Statute'.

This means that the EEA/EFTA States *or* the EFTA Court itself may propose such amendments.[67] The EFTA Court did so in 2011, but the EEA/EFTA States did not act. The time has come for the EFTA Court to push the EEA/EFTA States again with new proposals.

ANNEX: BLUEPRINT

Amendments to the SCA

Article 28 SCA (Current)

> 'The EFTA Court shall consist of three judges.'

Article 28 SCA (Proposed)

> 'The EFTA Court shall consist of seven members. There shall be five judges, at least two of whom must be nationals of EU Member States. The EFTA Court shall be assisted by two Advocates General, at least one of whom must be a national of an EU Member State.
>
> It shall be the duty of the Advocate General, acting with complete impartiality and independence, to make, in open court, reasoned submissions on cases which, in accordance with the Statute, require his involvement.'

Article 29 SCA (Current)

> 'Decisions of the Court shall be valid only when all its members are sitting in the deliberations.'

Article 29 SCA (Proposed)

> 'The Court shall sit either as a Regular Court, consisting of three Judges, or as a Full Court, consisting of five Judges. Decisions of the Regular Court shall only be valid when three Judges are sitting in the deliberations. Decisions of the Full Court shall only be valid when five Judges are sitting in the deliberations.
>
> The Court may choose to sit as a Full Court where it considers a case to involve particular public or private interest. For all other matters the Court shall sit as a Regular Court.'

[67] The CJEU has similar powers with respect to proposing changes to its Statute. See Art 281 TFEU: 'The Statute of the Court of Justice of the European Union shall be laid down in a separate Protocol. The European Parliament and the Council, acting in accordance with the ordinary legislative procedure, may amend the provisions of the Statute, with the exception of Title I and Article 64. The European Parliament and the Council shall act either *at the request of the Court of Justice* and after consultation of the Commission, or on a proposal from the Commission *and after consultation of the Court of Justice*' (emphasis added).

Article 30 SCA (Current)

'The Judges shall be chosen from persons whose independence is beyond doubt and who possess the qualifications required for appointment to the highest judicial offices in their respective countries or who are jurisconsults of recognized competence. They shall be appointed by common accord of the Governments of the EFTA States for a term of six years.

Retiring Judges shall be eligible for reappointment.

The Judges shall elect the President of the EFTA Court from among their number for a term of three years. He may be re-elected.

In case one of the Judges, in the opinion of the two other Judges, is disqualified from acting in a particular case, the two other Judges shall agree on a person to replace him chosen from a list established by common accord by the Governments of the EFTA States. If they cannot agree that person shall be chosen from the list by lot by the President. With regard to a Judge chosen in this way the rules applicable to regular Judges shall apply mutatis mutandis. In any case Article 4, second paragraph, and Article 13, of Protocol 5 shall not apply.'

Article 30 SCA (Proposed)

'The Judges and Advocates General shall be chosen from persons whose independence is beyond doubt and who possess the qualifications required for appointment to the highest judicial offices in their respective countries or who are jurisconsults of recognised competence. They shall be appointed by common accord of the Governments of the EFTA States for a term of six years, after consultation of the panel provided for in Article 30a'.

Retiring Judges and Advocates General shall be eligible for re-appointment.

The Judges shall elect the President of the EFTA Court from among their number for a term of three years. He may be re-elected.

The Advocates General shall elect a First Advocate General of the EFTA Court from among their number for a term of three years. He may be re-elected.

In case one of the Judges, in the opinion of the other Judges, is disqualified from acting in a particular case, the other Judges shall agree that a case be decided by the Regular Court.'

Article 30a SCA (New Article)

'A panel shall be set up in order to give an opinion on candidates' suitability to perform the duties of a Judge or Advocate General of the Court before the Governments of the Member States make the appointments referred to in Article 30.

The panel shall comprise five persons: one chosen from among former members of the Court who shall also be Chairman, one from among the former members of the Court of Justice of the European Union, one university professor of law in an EU Member State, one university professor of law in an EFTA State, and one other jurisconsult of recognised competence. The EFTA States shall adopt a decision establishing the panel's operating rules and a decision appointing its members as well as their remuneration. It shall act on the initiative of the President of the Court.'

Amendments to Protocol 5 of the SCA on the Statute of the EFTA Court

Article 2 (Current)

'Before taking up his duties each Judge shall, in open court, take an oath to perform his duties impartially and conscientiously and to preserve the secrecy of the deliberations of the Court.'

Article 2 (Proposed)

'Before taking up his duties each Judge and Advocate General shall, in open court, take an oath to perform his duties impartially and conscientiously and to preserve the secrecy of the deliberations of the Court.'

Article 4, First Paragraph (Current)

'The Judges may not hold any political or administrative office.'

Article 4, First Paragraph (Proposed)

'The Judges and Advocates General may not hold any political or administrative office.'

Article 5 (Current)

'Apart from normal replacement, or death, the duties of a Judge shall end when he resigns.

Where a Judge resigns, his letter of resignation shall be addressed to the President of the Court for transmission to the Governments of the EFTA States. Upon this notification a vacancy shall arise on the bench.

Save where Article 6 applies, a Judge shall continue to hold office until his successor takes up his duties.'

Article 5 (Proposed)

'Apart from normal replacement, or death, the duties of a Judge or Advocate General shall end when he resigns.

Where a Judge or Advocate General resigns, his letter of resignation shall be addressed to the President of the Court for transmission to the Governments of the EFTA States. Upon this notification a vacancy shall arise on the bench.

Save where Article 6 applies, a Judge or Advocate General shall continue to hold office until his successor takes up his duties.'

Article 6 (Current)

'A Judge may be deprived of his office or of his right to a pension or other benefits in its stead only if, in the unanimous opinion of the Court in plenary, he no longer fulfils the requisite conditions or meets the obligations arising from his office.

The Judge concerned shall not take part in any such deliberations.'

Article 6 (Proposed)

'A Judge or Advocate General may be deprived of his office or of his right to a pension or other benefits in its stead only if, in the unanimous opinion of the Court in plenary, he no longer fulfils the requisite conditions or meets the obligations arising from his office.

The Judge or Advocate General concerned shall not take part in any such deliberations.'

Article 7 (Current)

'A Judge who is to replace a member of the Court whose term of office has not expired shall be appointed for the remainder of his predecessor's term.'

Article 7 (Proposed)

'A Judge or Advocate General who is to replace a member of the Court whose term of office has not expired shall be appointed for the remainder of his predecessor's term.'

Article 13 (Current)

'The Judges and the Registrar shall be required to reside at the place where the Court has its seat.'

Article 13 (Proposed)

'The Judges, Advocates General, and the Registrar shall be required to reside at the place where the Court has its seat.'

Article 15 (Current)

'No Judge may take part in the disposal of a case in which he has previously taken part as agent or adviser or has acted for one of the parties, or in which he has been called upon to pronounce as a member of a court or tribunal, of a commission of inquiry or in any other capacity.

If, for some special reason, any Judge considers that he should not take part in the judgment or examination of a particular case, he shall so inform the President of the Court. If, for some reason, the President considers that any Judge should not sit in a particular case, he shall notify him accordingly.

Any difficulty arising as to the application of this Article shall be settled according to the fourth paragraph of Article 30 of this Agreement.

If according to this Article a Judge shall not take part in a particular case, a person to replace him shall be chosen in accordance with Article 30, fourth paragraph, of the Agreement, among those persons on the list who have been nominated by the Government which has nominated the regular Judge who is to be replaced.

A party may not apply for a change in the composition of the Court on the grounds of either nationality of a Judge or the absence from the Court of a Judge of the nationality of that party.'

Article 15 (Proposed)

'No Judge or Advocate General may take part in the disposal of a case in which he has previously taken part as agent or adviser or has acted for one of the parties, or in which he has been called upon to pronounce as a member of a court or tribunal, of a commission of inquiry or in any other capacity.

If, for some special reason, any Judge or Advocate General considers that he should not take part in the judgment or examination of a particular case, he shall so inform the President of the Court. If, for some reason, the President considers that any Judge or Advocate General should not sit in a particular case, he shall notify him accordingly.

Any difficulty arising as to the application of this Article shall be settled by the President of the Court.

A party may not apply for a change in the composition of the Court on the grounds of either nationality of a Judge or Advocate General, or the absence from the Court of a Judge or Advocate General of the nationality of that party.'

Article 32a (New, Proposed)

'Opinions of the Advocate General shall state the reasons on which they are based. They shall contain the name of the Advocate General.'

7

Principled Reasoning in the EFTA Court

MICHAEL REIERTSEN

I. INTRODUCTION

THE MOST ESSENTIAL task of any court is to provide reasons for their binding decisions and judgments.[1] Indeed, providing reasons is an essential part of legal culture.[2] It is a necessary condition for rationality and a prerequisite for being able to understand legal decisions.[3] Yet, how judges provide reasons may be affected by a number of factors, such as the jurisdiction and functions of the relevant court, and the institutional legal framework under which that court operates.[4] Thus, because, for example, the EFTA Court, the Court of Justice of the European Union (CJEU), the European Court of Human Rights (ECtHR) and domestic apex courts have different jurisdictions and functions, and operate under different institutional legal frameworks, the manner in which they reason and justify may vary.

With principled reasoning in this context, I mean reasoning with a character and form capable of influencing future situations and cases, not connected to the specific facts of the case at hand. Further, when courts (or any other individual or institution) provide reasons, they must, to some degree, generalise. In this sense, reasons are propositions that contain a greater generality than the conclusions which they underpin. Principled reasoning is therefore perhaps best contrasted with the other end of

[1] The framework which I present in section II and apply in section III below, in order to illustrate how courts tend to provide principled reasoning, builds on the framework developed in M Reiertsen, *Effective Domestic Remedies and the European Court of Human Rights: Applications of the European Convention on Human Rights Article 13* (Cambridge, Cambridge University Press, 2022), in particular at 291–99. The analysis reflects my personal view and should not be understood to reflect the views of the EFTA Court. I am greatly indebted to my trainee in the EFTA Court, Per Silnes Tandberg, for his most valuable contribution to the research process, in particular the research of case law from the EFTA Court.

[2] See, for example, F Schauer, 'Giving Reasons' (1995) 47 *Stanford Law Review* 633.

[3] See, for example, Opinion no 11 (2008) on the Consultative Council of European Judges (CCJE) to the attention of the Committee of Ministers of the Council of Europe on the quality of judicial decisions, para 32.

[4] On factors that may influence the reasoning of courts, see, more generally, JE Pedersen, *Begrunnelse av rettsavgjørelser* (Oslo, Universitetsforlaget, 2016).

the scale, namely particularity or the concrete facts of the case.[5] In short, at one end of the scale, there is generality, expressed through general and abstract reasoning, and at the other end of the scale, there is pure particularity expressed through the concrete facts of the case. General and abstract reasoning clearly has the potential to influence future situations and cases not connected to the case at hand. Fact-based reasoning, on the other hand, does not have this potential.

Between the extremes of generality and particularity, it is possible to identify many forms and combinations of reasoning and ways in which judges may try to limit the consequences of a case. Yet, in the following section II I present: (1) the basic arguments which are usually cited for and against principled reasoning; and (2) a succinct framework for describing how courts may provide such reasoning (or not). In section III, I apply this framework on the case law of the EFTA Court and illustrate how the Court, since its birth on 1 January 1994, has been principled (or not). In Section IV, I conclude with some evaluative remarks.

II. TO BE OR NOT TO BE PRINCIPLED?

Predictability is often cited as the main advantage of principled reasoning in the sense that it establishes general rules which may be followed in the future.[6] It is also claimed that principled reasoning reduces the likelihood of arbitrary and discriminatory court decisions, and to demonstrate to the parties that they have been heard, thereby contributing to a more willing acceptance of the decision.[7]

The major disadvantage of principled reasoning is that, through the force of precedent, it may (unduly) bind future authority. This affects both the authority of courts and legislators, and is connected to democratic concerns and perceptions of what courts and legislators should be able to decide on. The danger of unduly binding future authority arises because the reasoning must build on the imperfect material in the case at hand and because it is difficult to foresee the future and the scenarios to which the general rule and reasoning may be applied.[8]

On the other hand, fact-based reasoning, or case-by-case-based reasoning, offers less predictability for future cases, at least outside the scope of the case at hand, but provides flexibility since it does not bind authority to the same extent.[9] At a federal and international level, fact-based reasoning further runs the risk of undermining unity, since differences may develop between states, at least to the extent that the rules in question remain unclear.[10]

[5] *cf* Schauer (n 2) 638 and 641.

[6] See, for example, A Scalia, 'The Rule of Law as a Law of Rules' (1989) 56(4) *University of Chicago Law Review* 1175, at 1179; and DA Strauss, 'On the Origin of Rules (With Apologies to Darwin): A Comment to Antonin Scalia's "The Rule of Law as a Law of Rules"' (2008) 75 *University of Chicago Law Review* 997, at 998. However, it should be noted that Scalia and Strauss strongly disagree as to how judges should be principled.

[7] See, for example, Scalia (n 6) 1178; and the Grand Chamber judgment of the ECtHR 16 November 2010, *Taxquet v Belgium* (App No 926/05) paras 90 and 91.

[8] See, for example, F Schauer, 'Do Cases Make Bad Law?' (2006) 73 University of Chicago Law Review 883, at 897; and Strauss (n 6) 1003.

[9] See, for example, Scalia (n 6) 1177.

[10] See, for example, ibid 1179.

Moreover, principled reasoning may be performed in different ways. A rough distinction may be made between reasoning which develops clearly defined rules that are limited to a specific area or subject matter, in contrast to reasoning which develops broad principles, which in a general and overarching manner may be applied to several areas or subject matters.[11] The debate as to where to draw the line between such approaches and forms of reasoning has been central in both national and international systems of law.[12]

My definition of principled reasoning above draws no firm line between fact-based reasoning and reasoning that develops strict rules or principled standards; instead, the boundaries are fluid and fluctuating. Further, a judgment containing more general principled reasoning may be followed up by judgments that specifically regulate different areas of the general rule (and reasoning), and, on the other hand, several cases with fact-based reasoning and/or strict rules may pave the way for principled standards. In this sense, the relationship between principled standards, strict rules and fact-based approaches may be perceived as fluctuations on a vertical line stretching from pure generality to pure particularity, for which the approaches, over time, may be both descending (starting from generality) and ascending (starting from particularity).[13] That said, the approach of developing clearly defined rules remains closer to the purely fact-based approach, whereas the principled standard approach is closer to an extreme version of generality.

Based on this, a succinct framework for describing how courts reason and develop precedent could be as follows:

(1) general principled reasoning, through which a court develops broad principles and rules which could be applied to and give guidance to a number of different future scenarios and cases;
(2) concrete principled reasoning, through which a court develops strict (concrete) rules with clear and limited boundaries; and
(3) case-by-case reasoning, through which the court limits the reasoning and the scope of the rule to the specific facts of the case at hand.

The primary tool which courts have at their disposal to develop (or not develop) precedent and principled reasoning is their legal method. The EFTA Court generally applies the same method of interpretation as the CJEU, but with a few twists of its own, which are connected to its specific jurisdiction and institutional framework.[14]

However, the tool, as such, is not the decisive factor as to whether courts actually are more or less principled, or not principled at all. Indeed, the starting point for any legal analysis is always the legal framework which the court has jurisdiction

[11] See, for example, Schauer (n 8); and J Greene, 'The Rule of Law as a Law of Standards' (2011) 99 *Georgetown Law Journal* 1289.

[12] In the US, for example, on the one hand, Scalia (n 6), and, on the other hand, Strauss (n 6); and in Europe, for example, on the one hand, J Habermas, *Between Facts and Norms*, W Rehg (trans) (Cambridge, MA: MIT Press, 1996) and, on the other hand, R Alexy, *A Theory of Constitutional Rights*, J Rivers (trans) (Oxford, Oxford University Press, 2002).

[13] *cf* M Koskenniemi, *From Apology to Utopia* (Cambridge, Cambridge University Press, 1988).

[14] See, for example, OJ Einarsson, 'The View from the EFTA Court' in C Butler (ed), *Research Handbook on EEA Internal Market Law* (Cheltenham, Edward Elgar, 2024).

to interpret. It is this legal framework, most notably the wording of the rules which are at stake in a specific case, that form the starting point for any legal analysis. What the correct starting point is may of course be contested. However, generally the starting point is clear. And this starting point may, depending on the circumstances, provide a larger or smaller legitimate penumbra under which principled reasoning may or may not be developed. Accordingly, the possibility to provide principled reasoning is above all present in cases where the starting point is either not clear or not really regulated by the legislator, or for which there are conflicting provisions at the same level, or where the provisions at stake are more or less open-ended, and for which there is no previous precedent setting out clear boundaries.[15]

III. PRINCIPLED REASONING IN THE EFTA COURT

A. Introduction

As of 1 January 2024, the Court had received 355 cases, of which 173 were requests for advisory opinions and 182 direct action cases. These 355 cases form the basis of the analyses given below. However, the analyses should not be seen as an exhaustive account of how the Court has been principled (or not), but as illustrative examples. Further, the depth of the analyses is not an indication of the extent to which, and how, the Court has been principled (or not). On the contrary, even though the analyses show that most of the case law has been concrete principled and/or case-by-case-based, I have primarily attached weight to describing when and how the Court has engaged in general principled reasoning. Moreover, this must be accompanied by the warning that any classification is subjective and that the boundaries between the categories, as described in the previous section, are fluid.

The purpose of this partly selective focus is to allow me to conclude in section IV with some evaluative remarks on the basis of, inter alia, that which is not there – why has the general principled reasoning of the Court been limited, both in numbers and substance?

B. General Principled Reasoning

i. State Liability

The clearest example of general principled reasoning in the Court's case law is the seminal judgment of 10 December 1998 in *Sveinbjörnsdóttir*,[16] in which the Court established a general principle of state liability for violations of EEA law. The heading of the extensive justification for this principle, commencing in paragraph 44 of the judgment, is illustrative: 'The existence of State liability as a matter of principle'.

[15] *cf*, for example, Reiertsen (n 1) 18–23, specifically with regard to the case law of the ECtHR.
[16] Case E-9/97 *Sveinbjörnsdóttir* [1998] EFTA Ct Rep 95.

At the outset, it should be noted that the prime reason as to why the Court was in a position to develop such a general principle was that the EEA Agreement contained no explicit provisions on state liability. The question was therefore whether such a state obligation was to be derived from the stated purposes and the legal structure of the EEA Agreement.[17] In response to this question, the Court concluded that the objectives of homogeneity and equal treatment and opportunities were so strongly expressed in the EEA Agreement that the EFTA States were obliged to provide compensation for loss and damage caused to an individual by incorrect implementation of a directive.[18] The Court also developed the conditions for state liability taking the case law of the CJEU as a starting point, most notably in *Francovich and Others*.[19] This illustrates a more general point in the case law of the EFTA Court, namely that the Court has been more prone to engage in general principled reasoning when it has found support in the case law of the CJEU. This is certainly not surprising, given that the EEA Agreement constitutes an extension of the internal market.[20]

Although the introduction of the doctrine of state liability was controversial, the reasoning of the EFTA Court was able to convince domestic courts, which, again, has proved to be pivotal for the implementation and effectiveness of EEA law in national law.[21]

The reasoning in *Sveinbjörnsdóttir* has been concretised in a string of later judgments, primarily through concrete principled reasoning in specific areas.[22]

ii. The Concept of a Court or a Tribunal in Article 34 of the Surveillance and Court Agreement

The first paragraph of Article 34 of the Surveillance and Court Agreement (SCA) provides that the EFTA Court has jurisdiction to give advisory opinions on the interpretation of the EEA Agreement. The second paragraph of the same Article provides that 'any court or tribunal in an EFTA State' may request the EFTA Court to give such an opinion.

In its very first judgment, delivered on 16 December 1994 in *Restamark*,[23] the Court was given the opportunity to consider how the terms 'court' and 'tribunal' should be construed. The Court answered in a general principled manner. Indeed, it started out by proclaiming that the expression 'court or tribunal' had to be given its own interpretation.[24] In this interpretation, it was not decisive how the body was defined

[17] ibid para 47.

[18] ibid para 60.

[19] Joined Cases C-6/90 and C-9/90 *Francovich and Others*, ECLI:EU:C:1991:428, [1991] ECR I-5357.

[20] See, for example, the judgment of 23 September 2003 in Case C-452/01 *Ospelt*, ECLI:EU:C:2003:493, [2003] ECR I-9743, para 29.

[21] See, for example, HH Fredriksen, 'The EFTA Court and the Principle of State Liability: Protecting the Jewel in the Crown', in EFTA Court (ed), *The EEA and the EFTA Court* (Oxford, Hart Publishing, 2014); and, for examples from the Norwegian Supreme Court, the judgment in Rt 2005 s 1365 *Finanger II* and from the Icelandic Supreme Court, the judgment in H 236/1999.

[22] See, for example, Case E-4/01 *Karlsson* [2002] EFTA Ct Rep 240; Case E-8/07 *Nguyen* [2008] EFTA Ct Rep 224; Case E-2/10 *Kolbeinsson* [2009–2010] EFTA Ct Rep 234; Case E-7/12 *DB Schenker II* [2013] EFTA Ct Rep 356; and Case E-19/14 *ESA v The Kingdom of Norway* [2015] EFTA Ct Rep 300.

[23] Case E-1/94 *Restamark* [1994–1995] EFTA Ct Rep 15.

[24] ibid, para 24.

under national rules. Furthermore, even though the reasoning of the CJEU in relation to the same expression in Article 177 EC was relevant, the Court was not required by Article 3(1) SCA to follow that reasoning when interpreting the main part of that Agreement. Still, the Court took the same criteria as the CJEU as a starting point, namely whether the body had been established by law, had a permanent existence, exercised binding jurisdiction, was bound by rules of adversary procedure, applied rules of law and was independent. However, the Court added that the purpose of Article 34 SCA was to establish cooperation between the Court and the courts and tribunals in the EFTA States. Indeed, it was intended as a means for ensuring a uniform interpretation of the EEA Agreement and to provide assistance to the courts and tribunals in the EFTA States in cases in which they had to apply provisions of the EEA Agreement. That purpose also had to be taken into account when interpreting the expression 'court or tribunal'. In the judgment of 16 July 2020 in *Scanteam*,[25] the Court confirmed that this purpose may lead to different interpretations of the concept of a court or tribunal within EU and EEA law.[26]

The reasoning from *Restamark* has survived the test of time remarkably well. Indeed, even though the Court has dealt with the concept of a court or tribunal in a string of later cases, it has only to a very limited extent been necessary to supplement the *Restamark* reasoning with more concrete principled reasoning.[27] However, in two cases, the Court has adapted and nuanced the precedent. In the judgment of 15 December 2011 in *Dr A*,[28] the Court expanded on what it means for a court to be independent, and in the judgment of 9 May 2014 in *Hellenic Capital Markets Commission*,[29] it clarified that a body exercising several function may be classified as a court or tribunal only when it is performing judicial functions.

iii. Admissibility in Advisory Opinion Cases

Connected to the concept of a court or tribunal in Article 34 SCA is the question of who is to decide when it is 'necessary' to ask the Court for an advisory opinion. This is not a question of minor importance. Indeed, if the Court were to construe the term strictly, many cases would be declared inadmissible. However, already in *Samuelsson*,[30] the Court stated, in a general manner, that it was primarily for the referring court to assess what it considered necessary to enable it to give judgment. This was soon followed up thereafter in *Nille*.[31] In both cases, the Court set out a wide margin of appreciation for domestic courts to refer questions to it.

[25] Case E-8/19 *Scanteam* [2020] OJ C374/47.

[26] ibid, in particular paras 46 and 47.

[27] See, for example, Joined Cases E-8/94 and E-9/94 *Mattel/Lego* [1994–95] EFTA Ct Rep 113; Case E-4/04 *Pedicel* [2005] EFTA Ct Rep 1; Case E-4/09 *Inconsult* [2009–2010] EFTA Ct Rep 86; Joined Cases E-3/13 and E-20/13 *Fred Olsen and Others* [2014] EFTA Ct Rep 400; Joined Cases E-26/15 and E-27/15 *Criminal Proceedings against B and B* [2016] EFTA Ct Rep 740; Case E-5/16 *Municipality of Oslo* [2017] EFTA Ct Rep 52; and *Scanteam* (n 25).

[28] Case E-1/11 *Dr A* [2011] EFTA Ct Rep 484.

[29] Case E-23/13 *Hellenic Capital Markets Commission* [2014] EFTA Ct Rep 88.

[30] Case E-1/95 *Samuelsson* [1994–95] EFTA Ct Rep 145.

[31] Case E-5/96 *Nille* [1997] EFTA Ct Rep 30.

In later cases, it has narrowed down this starting point through concrete principled reasoning,[32] but it has also confirmed a wide margin, even in cases in which this was not obvious.[33]

iv. No Primacy and Direct Effect as in EU Law

The fact that EEA law does not contain requirements of primacy and direct effect similar to those that exist under EU law is a major difference between EEA and EU law. In *Restamark* and *Sveinbjörnsdóttir*, the Court had briefly implied that this could be a question which might be dealt with differently under EEA and EU law.[34] However, it was not until the judgment of 22 February 2002 in *Einarsson*[35] that the Court, in a general and overarching manner, concluded that EEA law contained no such requirements, at least in the manner that they are understood under EU law. This was done with a specific reference to Article 7 EEA and Protocol 35 of the EEA Agreement, which led to the conclusion that only implemented EEA law should prevail over national law.[36]

However, this difference between EU and EEA law should not be exaggerated, not least because the Court had already established the principle of state liability in *Sveinbjörnsdóttir*, but also because the Court, soon thereafter, in the judgment of 20 May 2002 in *Karlsson*,[37] established a principle of EEA conform interpretation of domestic legislation with EEA law which had not been implemented. Still, it was not until the judgment of 3 October 2007 in *Criminal Proceedings against A*[38] that the Court, in a general and overarching manner, firmly established the scope of the principle. Indeed, with reference to the Court's judgments in *Sveinbjörnsdottir* and *Karlsson*, it pointed to the objective of homogeneity and underlined that the EEA Agreement was an international treaty *sui generis* that contains a distinct legal order of its own and that the depth of integration of the EEA Agreement was less far-reaching than under the EC Treaty, even though the scope and objective of the EEA Agreement went beyond what is usual for an agreement under public international law. Further, Article 7 and Protocol 35 EEA were specific mechanisms to achieve these objectives. On this basis, the Court concluded that national courts were bound to interpret national law as far as possible in conformity with EEA law and 'apply

[32] See, for example, Case E-10/04 *Piazza* [2005] EFTA Ct Rep 76 (hypothetical questions) and Case E-13/11 *Granville Establishment* [2012] EFTA Ct Rep 400 (not provided with sufficient information to answer questions properly).

[33] See, for example, Case E-6/01 *CIBA* [2002] EFTA Ct Rep 281 (possible to ask again); Case E-17/11 *Aresbank* [2012] EFTA Ct Rep 916; and Case E-19/16 *Thue* [2017] EFTA Ct Rep 880 (possible to ask questions concerning EEA law in cases connected to national legislation regulating purely internal aspects).

[34] See, in particular, *Restamark* (n 23) para 77; and *Sveinbjörnsdóttir* (n 16) para 63.

[35] Case E-1/01 *Einarsson* [2002] EFTA Ct Rep 1.

[36] ibid, in particular paras 51–55. That said, this requirement has been understood and interpreted strictly by the Court; see, for example, the judgment of 4 July 2023 in Case E-11/22 *RS* [2023] OJ C365, 19 October 2023, para 50.

[37] *Karlsson* (n 22).

[38] Case E-1/07 *Criminal Proceedings against A* [2007] EFTA Ct Rep 246.

the interpretative methods recognised by national law as far as possible in order to achieve the result sought by the relevant EEA rule'.[39]

v. The Objective of Homogeneity

The objective of homogeneity is a general principle guiding any interpretation of EEA law. Indeed, already in *Restamark*, the Court underlined that when interpreting the EEA Agreement, it must be borne in mind that the objective of the Contracting Parties was to create a dynamic and homogeneous EEA. This was done by referring, inter alia, to several recitals in the Preamble to and Article 6 of the EEA Agreement as well as Article 3(2) SCA. In this sense, it was neither surprising nor controversial that the Court underlined this objective. The interesting aspect, in this context, is that the Court did so in an overarching and general manner, without formulating any limitations. Thus, the scope of the principle of homogeneity was, from the outset, wide and potentially far-reaching.

Similar statements have been reiterated in many cases and have paved the way for a principle of procedural homogeneity.[40] However, over time, the Court has, through concrete principled reasoning, also limited the scope of the principle of homogeneity. In the judgment of 3 December 1997 in *Maglite*,[41] for example, the Court emphasised that the objective of homogeneity does not require similar rules between EU and EEA law in all circumstances as there may be relevant differences between the two pillars.[42] Yet, already in the judgment of 10 December 1998 in *Rainford-Towning*,[43] the Court took a step back by underlining that the objective of homogeneity, as the clear starting point, demands an equal interpretation.[44] That said, the Court still examines whether there are differences in scope and purpose between EU law and EEA law that constitute 'compelling grounds' for a divergent interpretation.[45]

vi. National Procedural Autonomy

In a similar manner to the CJEU, the Court developed a principle of procedural autonomy in the judgment of 13 June 2013 in *Koch and Others*.[46] The Court stated, in a general and overarching manner, that in the absence of EEA rules it is for the

[39] ibid, in particular paras 37–39. These statements have been repeated in a string of later judgments; see, for example, Joined Cases E-9/07 and E-10/07 *L'Oréal* [2008] OJ C275/20, para 22; Case E-18/11 *Irish Bank* [2012] EFTA Ct Rep 592, paras 121 ff; and Case E-15/12 *Wahl* [2013] EFTA Ct Rep 534, para 54.

[40] See, for example, *Restamark* (n 23) para 24; Case E-2/94 *Scottish Salmon Growers* [1994–95] EFTA Ct Rep 59, para 11; Case E-2/02 *Bellona* [2003] EFTA Ct Rep 52, paras 39–40; Joined Cases E-5/04, E-6/04 and E-7/04 *Fesil and Finnfjord* [2005] EFTA Ct Rep 117, para 53; Case E-5/07 *Private Barnehagers Landsforbund* [2008] EFTA Ct Rep 62, para 47; Case E-13/10 *Aleris* [2011] EFTA Ct Rep 3, para 24; and Case E-15/10 *Posten Norge* [2012] EFTA Ct Rep 246, para 110.

[41] Case E-2/97 *Maglite* [1997] EFTA Ct Rep 127.

[42] In this book, Einarsson notes that *Maglite* seems to be the odd one out in the EFTA Court's case law, whereas Rognstad examines the limits of homogeneity in the field of intellectual property.

[43] Case E-3/98 *Rainford-Towning* [1998] EFTA Ct Rep 205.

[44] Similarly, but slightly more concretely, the judgment of 24 January 2003 in Case E-1/02 *ESA v Norway* [2003] EFTA Ct Rep 1, para 45.

[45] See, for example, the judgment of 8 July 2008 in *L'Oréal* (n 39) paras 29–31.

[46] Case E-11/12 *Koch and Others* [2013] EFTA Ct Rep 272.

domestic legal system of each EEA State to designate the courts and tribunals having jurisdiction and to lay down the detailed procedural rules governing actions for safeguarding rights which EFTA and EU citizens and economic operators derive from EEA law, provided, first, that such rules are no less favourable than those governing similar domestic actions (the principle of equivalence) and, second, that they do not render practically impossible or excessively difficult the exercise of rights conferred by EEA law (the principle of effectiveness).[47] Thereafter, the Court, in a general manner, and with reference to case law from the CJEU, specified the content of the principles of equivalence and effectiveness.

vii. The EFTA Surveillance Authority's Duty to State the Reasons on which its Decisions are Based

According to Article 16 SCA, the EFTA Surveillance Authority (ESA) 'shall state the reasons on which its decisions are based'. In its judgment of 21 March 1995 in *Scottish Salmon Growers*, the second case to be handled by the Court, it stated, in a general and overarching manner, that this provision implied that anyone concerned by ESA's decisions must be able to assess, on the basis of what is communicated to them in writing, why the decision has been taken, how ESA has applied the EEA Agreement and the SCA, and whether or not there are grounds to seek judicial review. This requires an appropriate explanation of the considerations which led ESA to adopt the decision. A decision by ESA must therefore 'set out, in a concise but clear and relevant manner, the principal issues of law and fact upon which it is based and which are necessary in order that the reasoning which led the Authority to its decision may be understood'.[48] The Court added that this conclusion was in accordance with general principles of law and in line with the relevant principles developed by the CJEU.[49]

viii. Human Rights

The EEA Agreement contains no express catalogue of human rights, such as the European Convention on Human Rights (ECHR) and the EU Charter of Fundamental Rights. In fact, the only reference to human rights in the main part of the EEA Agreement is to be found in the first recital of the Preamble, which states that the Contracting Parties are convinced that the EEA will contribute 'to the construction of a Europe based on peace, democracy and human rights'. It should thus come as

[47] ibid para 121. Similar statements have been repeated in a string of later cases. See, for example, Case E-7/13 *Creditinfo Lánstraust* [2013] EFTA Ct Rep 970, para 45; Case E-24/13 *Casino Admiral* [2014] EFTA Ct Rep 732, para 69; Case E-16/16 *Fosen-Linjen* [2017] EFTA Ct Rep 617, para 70; Case E-6/17 *Fjarskipti* [2018] EFTA Ct Rep 78, para 31; Case E-10/17 *Nye Kystlink* [2018] EFTA Ct Rep 292, paras 110 and 111; Joined Cases E-11/19 and E-12/19 *Adpublisher* [2021] OJ C113/9, para 58; Case E-13/20 *O v Arbeids- og velferdsdirektoratet* [2021] OJ C417/25, para 64; and *RS* (n 36) para 55.

[48] See *Scottish Salmon Growers* (n 40) para 26.

[49] This reasoning has been referred to and applied in several later cases. See, for example, *Fesil and Finnfjord* (n 40); Joined Cases E-6/10 and E-7/10 *Reassur* [2010] OJ C237/19; Joined Cases E-17/10 and E-6/11 *Liechtenstein and VTM v ESA* [2012] EFTA Ct Rep 114; and Case E-10/11 *Hurtigruten* [2012] EFTA Ct Rep 758.

no surprise that the relationship between the freedoms flowing directly from the EEA Agreement and human rights is an area where the Court has applied a cautious step-by-step approach towards more general principled reasoning.[50]

The first time that the Court referred to human rights was the judgment of 12 June 1998 in *TV 1000*,[51] in which it referred to the ECtHR's judgment in *Handyside*[52] as an argument supporting that a restriction on EEA rights was following a legitimate aim.[53] In the judgment of 19 June 2003 in *Bellona*, the Court held that even though the idea of human rights inspires the increased significance of the judicial function and calls for widening the avenues of access to justice, it did not find it necessary to pursue the issue any further in the case at hand.[54]

In the judgment of 12 December 2003 in *Ásgeirsson*,[55] the Court, for the first time, engaged in more principled reasoning by holding that the EEA Agreement and the SCA, more generally, were 'to be interpreted in the light of fundamental rights' and that the provisions of the ECHR and the judgments of the ECtHR 'are important sources for determining the scope of these rights'.[56]

In the judgment of 18 April 2012 in *Posten Norge*, the Court took a further step by referring to the principle of effective judicial protection, including the right to a fair trial enshrined in Article 6(1) ECHR, as a general principle of EEA law. The Court added that the principle was now also enshrined in Article 47 of the EU Charter of Fundamental Rights.[57] Previously, in its judgment of 26 July 2011 in *Clauder*,[58] it had said more or less the same with regard to the right to respect for private and family life in Article 8(1) ECHR and Article 7 of the EU Charter of Fundamental Rights.[59]

However, the real breakthrough came with the judgment of 9 July 2014 in *Fred. Olsen and Others*, in which the Court extended its previous statements to human rights more generally. Indeed, all provisions in the EEA Agreement and the SCA were 'to be interpreted in the light of fundamental rights' and the provisions of the ECHR and the judgments of the ECtHR were, more generally, cited as 'important sources for determining the scope of these fundamental rights'.[60] And, most importantly, this implied that 'the national rules in question may fall under the exceptions provided for *only if they are compatible with fundamental rights*' (emphasis added).[61] In the judgment of 19 April 2016 in *Holship*,[62] the Court confirmed that fundamental rights form part of the unwritten principles of EEA law.[63]

[50] See, for example, R Spano, 'The EFTA Court and Fundamental Rights' (2017) 13(3) *European Constitutional Law Review* 475; and OJ Einarsson, 'Fundamental Rights in the Case Law of the EFTA Court' in JF Kjølbro, S O'Leary and M Tsirli (eds), *Liber Amicorum Robert Spano* (The Hague, Eleven International, 2022) 231–42.

[51] Case E-8/97 *TV 1000* [1998] EFTA Ct Rep 68.

[52] ECtHR, plenary judgment 7 December 1976, *Handyside v UK* (App No 5493/72).

[53] See *TV 1000* (n 51) para 26.

[54] See *Bellona* (n 40) para 37.

[55] Case E-2/03 *Ásgeirsson* [2003] EFTA Ct Rep 185.

[56] ibid para 23. Similar statements were repeated in Case E-12/10 *ESA v Island* [2011] EFTA Ct Rep 117, para 60.

[57] See *Posten Norge* (n 40) para 86.

[58] Case E-4/11 *Clauder* [2011] EFTA Ct Rep 216.

[59] ibid para 49.

[60] See *Fred Olsen and Others* (n 27) para 224.

[61] ibid para 226.

[62] Case E-14/15 *Holship* [2016] EFTA Ct Rep 240.

[63] ibid para 123.

The Court has thus made it clear that it is effectively protecting not only economic freedoms, but also human rights. That said, in advisory opinion cases, the Court generally leaves it in the hands of domestic courts to ensure that the interpretation and application of acts incorporated into the EEA Agreement do not result in a conflict with fundamental rights protected by EEA law.[64]

ix. *Abuse of Rights*

In something of a contrast with private parties invoking human rights stand the arguments from states that private parties are attempting to circumvent national legislation by abusing their rights under the EEA Agreement, in particular the right to free movement. Also in this regard, the Court has applied a step-by-step approach towards a more general principled reasoning.

In *Mattel/Lego*, the Court dealt with the issue very concretely and held that although the attitude of the private party, from a national perspective, could be viewed as a circumvention of national law, it was, from an EEA context, a logical and necessary consequence of the main principles of the directive in question.[65]

In the judgment of 3 October 2012 in *Arcade Drilling*,[66] the Court considered the issue in a concrete principled manner by limiting its reasoning to an issue of abuse in the form of 'tax avoidance'. In this regard, it held that 'an EEA State is entitled to take measures designed to prevent certain companies established in that State from attempting, under cover of the rights created by the EEA Agreement, from improperly circumventing their national legislation, or to prevent these companies from improperly or fraudulently taking advantage of provisions of EEA law'.[67] Therefore, for the purposes 'of preventing tax avoidance', a national measure restricting freedom of establishment may be justified when 'it specifically targets artificial arrangements designed to circumvent the legislation of the EEA State concerned'.[68] For this line of reasoning, the Court found explicit support in the case law of the CJEU.

In the judgment of 13 September 2017 in *Yara*,[69] the Court provided more general principled reasoning with explicit reference to the general principle in EU law on the abuse of rights. Indeed, it repeated that EEA States remain free to enact rules which have the objective of precluding wholly artificial arrangements leading to tax avoidance, but added, more generally, that this was 'a corollary of the prohibition of abuse of rights, an essential feature of EEA law, which aims, inter alia, at preventing companies established in an EEA State from attempting, under cover of the rights created by the EEA Agreement, to circumvent their national legislation, or improperly or fraudulently take advantage of provisions of EEA law'.[70]

[64] See, for example, ibid para 123; the judgment of 9 February 2021 in Case E-1/20 *Kerim* [2021] OJ C245/19, para 43; the judgment of 21 April 2021 in Case E-2/20 *UNE v L* [2021] OJ C324/29, para 50.

[65] See *Mattel/Lego* (n 27) para 48.

[66] Case E-15/11 *Arcade Drilling* [2012] EFTA Ct Rep 676.

[67] ibid para 87.

[68] ibid para 89. Similarly, see *Fred Olsen and Others* (n 27) paras 164 ff.

[69] Case E-15/16 *Yara* [2017] EFTA Ct Rep 434.

[70] ibid para 49.

Thereafter, in the judgment of 13 May 2020 in *Campbell*,[71] the Court has clarified that the principle of abuse of rights applies under Directive 2004/38[72] concerning the right to move and reside freely within the territory of the EEA, referring in particular to Article 35 of the Directive.[73] In the judgment of 5 May 2021 in *Criminal Proceedings against* N,[74] it was further clarified that the principle applies in the area of social security benefits.[75]

C. Concrete Principled Reasoning

One of the many important areas in which the Court has been concretely principled is the scope of the precautionary principle, in particular in cases where public health is invoked as a ground for limiting EEA rights. In the judgment of 5 April 2001 in *Kellogg's*,[76] the Court considered whether the risk for public health could justify a limitation on the free movement of goods in the specific area of foodstuff treatment. Although the Court underlined some general elements of a precautionary principle, it limited the scope by setting out specifically how it was to be applied in this area.[77] This concrete principled reasoning was considered convincing by the CJEU, which in the judgment of 23 September 2003 in *Commission v Denmark* cited extensively from the judgment of the Court.[78] Similarly, in the judgment of 25 February 2005 in *Pedicel*, the EFTA Court limited the reasoning to the extent to which EEA States could invoke public health in order to restrict advertising of alcoholic beverages.[79] Further, in the judgment of 14 July 2017 in *ESA v The Kingdom of Norway*, the Court's reasoning was limited to the risk for public health caused by chemical substances as regulated by the Regulation (EC) No 1907/2006[80] (the REACH Regulation).[81]

The scope of Directive 2004/38/EC (the Citizenship Directive), in an EEA context, is another area in which the Court has provided important concrete principled

[71] Case E-4/19 *Campbell* [2020] OJ C283/3.

[72] Directive 2004/38/EC of the European Parliament and of the Council of 29 April 2004 on the right of citizens of the Union and their family members to move and reside freely within the territory of the Member States amending Regulation (EEC) No 1612/68 and repealing Directives 64/221/EEC, 68/360/EEC, 72/194/EEC, 73/148/EEC, 75/34/EEC, 75/35/EEC, 90/364/EEC, 90/365/EEC and 93/96/EEC [2004] OJ L158/77.

[73] See *Campbell* (n 71) paras 69–71. See also *Kerim* (n 64) paras 35–39.

[74] Case E-8/20 *Criminal Proceedings against* N [2021] OJ C324/31.

[75] ibid, in particular para 97.

[76] Case E-3/00 *Kellogg's* [2000–01] EFTA Ct Rep 73.

[77] ibid, in particular paras 26–30.

[78] Case C-192/01 *Commission v Denmark*, ECLI:EU:C:2003:492, [2003] ECR I-9693, in particular paras 47 ff.

[79] See *Pedicel* (n 27), in particular paras 59 and 60. See also the judgment of 12 September 2011 in Case E-16/10 *Philip Morris* [2011] EFTA Ct Rep 330 para 72, as regards tobacco advertisements and public health, although the Court never used the term 'precautionary principle' in its reasoning.

[80] Regulation (EC) No 1907/2006 of the European Parliament and of the Council of 18 December 2006 concerning the Registration, Evaluation, Authorisation and Restriction of Chemicals (REACH), establishing a European Chemicals Agency, amending Directive 199/45/EC and repealing Council Regulation (EEC) No 793/93 and Commission Regulation (EC) No 1488/94 as well as Council Directive 76/769/EEC and Commission Directives 91/155/EEC, 93/67/EEC, 93/105/EEC and 200/21/EC [2006] OJ L396/1.

[81] See Case E-9/16 *ESA v The Kingdom of Norway* [2017] OJ C413/08, in particular paras 77 and 78.

reasoning.[82] Indeed, the scope of this Directive has proved to be particularly problematic in an EEA context. This is due not least to the fact that the EEA Agreement has no parallel to Articles 20 and 21 TFEU on EU citizenship, and because the EEA Joint Committee did not really address this when incorporating the Directive into the EEA Agreement.[83] The consequence is that the Directive may, in some instances, have to be construed differently in an EEA context.[84] In this most delicate landscape, it should come as no surprise that the EFTA Court has navigated in a cautious concretely principled manner.[85]

Further, with regard to the applicability of the EEA Agreement to different products, the Court has set out concrete principled reasoning by limiting the effects of the judgments to the specific products in question.[86] This is not surprising, considering that the goods encompassed by the EEA Agreement are listed in a detailed manner in a harmonised system according to Article 8(3) of the EEA Agreement.

The Court's reasoning concerning the aims which may justify restrictions on fundamental EEA rights and freedoms has also typically been concretely principled. This is not surprising, considering the many different areas in which restrictions may be justified. Indeed, what may serve as a legitimate aim in one context may not necessarily be legitimate in another.[87]

A specific aspect of much of the Court's concrete principled reasoning, which deserves particular mention, is the many examples of cases where the Court slightly nudges or clarifies case law from the CJEU. One example is the judgment of 25 September 1996 in *Eidesund*,[88] which concerned the interpretation of the concept of transfer of an undertaking in Article 1(1) of Directive 77/187/EEC.[89] At the time of the judgment, there was no explicit judgment from the CJEU on the issue of what could be considered a 'transfer' with regard to catering services/contracts. After a thorough analysis of the case law of the CJEU, the Court concluded in a concretely principled manner on the specific situation of catering contracts.[90]

[82] See *Clauder* (n 58); *Wahl* (n 39); Case E-26/13 *Gunnarsson* [2014] EFTA Ct Rep 254; Case E-28/15 *Jabbi* [2016] EFTA Ct Rep 575; Case E-2/19 *D and E* [2020] OJ C40/33; Case E-4/19 *Campbell* (n 71); *Kerim* (n 64); *UNE v L* (n 64); Case E-16/20 *Q and Others* [2022] OJ C69/11.

[83] See the Decision of the EEA Joint Committee of 7 September 2007 (No 158/2007) [2008] OJ L124/20.

[84] See, for example, the judgment in *Campbell* (n 71) para 57.

[85] However, in *Jabbi* (n 82) paras 49–67, the reasoning concerning the significance of the right to free movement of persons and its link to the internal market was of a more general character than in the subsequent judgment in *Campbell* (n 71), even though both judgments examined the same provisions of the Directive.

[86] See, for example, *Restamark* (n 23) (whisky and wine); Case E-6/96 *Wilhelmsen* [1997] EFTA Ct Rep 53 (beer); Case E-9/00 *ESA v The Kingdom of Norway* [2002] EFTA Ct Rep 72 (alcopops); Case E-17/15 *Ferskar kjötvörur* [2016] EFTA Ct Rep 4 (raw meat); Case E-1/16 *Synnøve Finden* [2016] EFTA Ct Rep 931 (milk products).

[87] See, as one of many examples, the judgment of 12 December 2003 in Case E-1/03 *ESA v Iceland* [2003] EFTA Ct Rep 143 (whether possible public interest aims may justify a restriction on Article 36 EEA – freedom of services – in the field of air passenger tax).

[88] Case E-2/95 *Eidesund* [1995–1996] EFTA Ct Rep 1.

[89] Council Directive 77/187/EEC of 14 February 1977 on the approximation of the laws of the Member States relating to the safeguarding of employees' rights in the event of transfers of undertakings businesses or parts of businesses [1977] OJ L61/26.

[90] See *Eidesund* (n 88) para 45. This line of reasoning was confirmed in Cases E-3/95 *Langeland* [1995–96] EFTA Ct Rep 36 and E-2/96 *Ulstein* [1995–1996] EFTA Ct Rep 65 and by the CJEU in Case C-13/95 *Süxen*, ECLI:EU:C:1997:141, [1997] ECR I-1259.

D. Case-by-Case Reasoning

Much of the case law of the EFTA Court contains case-by-case reasoning in which the scope and consequences are limited to the specific facts of the case at hand, often (but not always) by referring to case law of the CJEU which has dealt with more or less similar questions. This should by no means be understood as meaning that this case law is not important; indeed, many of these cases have had significant consequences for individuals and domestic legal systems.

This line of reasoning is, for example, visible in the many social security cases which the Court has received in recent years, not least concerning the scope of Regulation 883/2004/EC[91] on the coordination of social security systems in cases concerning whether specific benefits, in specific countries, are covered by the Regulation.[92] This is not surprising, for several reasons, not least the fact that the Regulation contains detailed provisions on the various benefits, the substantial case law from the CJEU in the area, and the many differences between the social security systems of EEA States.

Similarly, cases concerning Directives which provide for total harmonisation have often been decided with case-by-case reasoning. This is neither surprising, since such Directives usually contain detailed rules which are supplemented by substantial case law from the CJEU.[93]

Another area in which the reasoning of the Court, to a large extent, has been case-by-case-based relates to the many state aid and competition cases in which the validity of ESA's decision is contested. Indeed, in these cases the applicable legal principles are mostly already clarified through extensive case law from the CJEU so that the controversy is, mostly, connected to the assessment of facts.[94]

Case-by-case reasoning is also prevalent in the many cases concerning failure to implement Regulations and Directives within the time limits set in accordance with Articles 7 and 13 of the EEA Agreement.[95]

A specific aspect of case-by-case reasoning is the situation in which the result of the case clearly follows from a comparison with the facts in a previous case from the Court or the CJEU. A recent example is the judgment of 19 October 2023 in *Amann*.[96]

[91] Regulation (EC) No 883/2004 of the European Parliament and of the Council of 29 April 2004 on the coordination of social security systems [2004] OJ L166/1.

[92] See, for example, *Criminal Proceedings against N* (n 74) paras 49–60 (sickness benefit within the meaning of point (a) of Art 3(1) of Regulation 883/2004) and the judgment of 29 July 2022 in Case E-2/22 *A v The Labour and Welfare Directorate* [2023] OJ C29/42, paras 31–48 (family benefit within the meaning of point (j) of Art 3(1) of the Regulation). See, in a similar vein, the judgment of 13 December 2019 in Case E-1/18 *ESA v the Kingdom of Norway* [2020] OJ C90, 19 March 2020 which concerned the question of whether Norwegian conditions for granting parental leave constituted employment and working conditions within the meaning of Art 14(1)(c) of Directive 2006/54/EC (the Equal Treatment Directive).

[93] See, for example, the judgment of 16 July 2012 in Case E-9/11 *ESA v The Kingdom of Norway* [2012] EFTA Ct Rep 442, para 72, with regard to Directive 2004/39/EC on markets and financial instruments (MiFiD); and the judgment of 14 November 2017 in Joined Cases E-2/17 and E-3/17 [2017] EFTA Ct Rep 727, paras 64–67, regarding veterinary checks according to Directive 89/662/EEC.

[94] See, for example, from the field of state aid, *Hurtigruten* (n 49); Case E-9/19 *Abelia* [2021]; and Case E-1/22 *Standard Wool* [2023].

[95] See, for example, Case E-7/97 *ESA v The Kingdom of Norway* [1998] EFTA Ct Rep 62; Case E-2/99 *ESA v The Kingdom of Norway* [2000–01] EFTA Ct Rep 1; Case E-6/06 *ESA v The Principality of Lichtenstein* [2007] EFTA Ct Rep 238; Case E-3/07 *ESA v Iceland* [2007] EFTA Ct Rep 356.

[96] Case E-14/22 *Amann* [2023] OJ C158/8, in particular para 39.

IV. CONCLUSION

Some might find it surprising that the case law of the Court does not contain more general principled reasoning, not least considering that the fundamental freedoms in the main part of the EEA Agreement are formulated in a general and open-ended manner. However, when the Court started its work on 1 January 1994 some 30 years ago, the CJEU had already developed ample general and overarching reasoning concerning these freedoms. In addition, newer regulations and directives tend to be of a detailed character, supported by case law of the CJEU, which similarly paves way for concrete principled or case-by-case reasoning from the EFTA Court. In addition, because of, inter alia, the objective of homogeneity, it is necessary for the Court to more generally attach considerable weight to the case law of the CJEU, which, for obvious reasons, is significantly greater in numbers than that of the EFTA Court. The jurisdictions, functions and different institutional legal framework under which the EFTA Court and the CJEU operate therefore clearly affect the extent to which, and how, the Courts may provide principled reasoning. In particular, for the substantive content of EEA law, it is fair to say that it is primarily the CJEU that has provided predictability through general principled reasoning, whereas the EFTA Court, in many areas, has provided concrete principled and case-by-case reasoning of significant importance.

Consequently, the EFTA Court has primarily provided general principled reasoning in areas of law which are specific to EEA law, most notably substantive principles such as state liability, no direct effect and the principle of homogeneity, but also procedural issues which are specific to EEA law, such as the concept of a court or a tribunal in Article 34 SCA, admissibility in advisory opinion cases and ESA's duty to state the reasons on which its decisions are based.

An area in which the EFTA Court has been principled in a general manner, but which still retains a number of unanswered questions, is how EEA law and human rights law are to be brought into conformity. It still remains to be solved, for example, whether and, if so, to what extent other human rights than those included in the ECHR – for example, in the EU Charter of Fundamental Rights – may be considered part of the fundamental principles of EEA law. It also remains to be seen whether the EFTA Court will embrace the distinction between the essence of fundamental rights and balancing as a method advocated by the CJEU,[97] give preference to the method of interpretation of the ECtHR,[98] or proceed as it has done in advisory opinion cases so far by leaving it in the hands of domestic courts to ensure that the interpretation and application of economic EEA rights do not result in a conflict with fundamental human rights protected by EEA law.

[97] See, for example, K Lenaerts, 'Limits on Limitations: The Essence of Fundamental Rights in the EU' (2019) 20(6) *German Law Journal* 779.

[98] See, for example, ECtHR, *LO and NTF v Norway*, 10 June 2021 (App No 45487/17), para 118.

The EFTA Court and Supreme Courts of the EFTA States

8

The Liechtenstein Constitutional Court and the Primacy of EEA Law

HILMAR HOCH

I. INTRODUCTION

Accession to the Agreement on the European Economic Area (EEA)[1] was a turning point for Liechtenstein in economic, political and legal terms. Although Liechtenstein was already familiar with the need to adopt foreign law by virtue of the 1923 Customs Union Treaty with Switzerland[2] – so, here too, an anniversary – the multilateral EEA represents a different dimension with a far greater dynamic than previously encountered in connection with the Customs Union Treaty.[3] This chapter deals with a crucial legal aspect of Liechtenstein's accession to the EEA, namely the recognition and enforcement of the primacy of EEA law over domestic law and the central role played by the Liechtenstein Constitutional Court (Staatsgerichtshof (StGH)) in this regard.

II. THE PRIMACY OF EEA LAW

A. The Principle: Primacy of EEA Law

Pursuant to Article 7 of the EEA Agreement, legal acts referred to in the annexes to the Agreement or in decisions of the EEA Joint Committee are binding on the

[1] Agreement on the European Economic Area of 2 May 1992, Liechtenstein Law Gazette (LGBl) 1995 No 68.

[2] Treaty of 29 March 1923 between Switzerland and Liechtenstein concerning the accession of the Principality of Liechtenstein to the Swiss customs territory (Zollanschlussvertrag (ZV)), LGBl 1923 No 24. Previously, Liechtenstein had already been connected to the Austro-Hungarian Empire by the Customs Treaty of 1852; see G Baur, 'Dynamische Rechtsübernahme im EWR und der durch die Landesverfassung vorgegebene Rahmen' in H Hoch, C Neier and PM Schiess Rütimann (eds), *100 Jahre liechtensteinische Verfassung* (Schaan, Verlag der Liechtensteinischen Akademischen Gesellschaft, 2021) 315, 317 with further references.

[3] The difference is particularly due to the sheer extent of the EEA law to be adopted. However, from the perspective of the loss of sovereignty, Liechtenstein's link through the Customs Union Treaty is even closer due to the automatic adoption of law in accordance with Art 4 ZV (in contrast to 'mere' dynamic adoption in accordance with Arts 102 and 103 EEA); see Baur (n 2) 321f.

contracting parties and must be transposed into domestic law. Thus, Article 7 EEA presupposes, at least implicitly, the primacy of transposed EEA law over the domestic law of the EEA/EFTA States. Indeed, it is undisputed that transposed EEA law takes precedence over domestic laws.[4] However, the relationship between the EEA Agreement and national constitutional law is controversial. In the other two EEA/EFTA States, Norway and Iceland, national constitutional law takes precedence over any EEA law.[5] In contrast, the Liechtenstein Constitutional Court, in line with the view taken by commentators in the Liechtenstein legal literature, has always qualified the EEA Agreement as amending the Liechtenstein Constitution, like the European Convention on Human Rights (ECHR).[6] Hence, according to StGH case law, EEA fundamental freedoms can be invoked by way of individual constitutional complaints in the same way as domestic fundamental rights.[7] However, to date, this case law has not had an explicit constitutional basis, nor has this new review power of the Liechtenstein Constitutional Court even been provided for in legislation. In contrast, following Liechtenstein's accession to the ECHR in 1982 and to the International Covenant on Civil and Political Rights (ICCPR) in 1999, corresponding amendments to the Constitutional Court Act were made.[8] Nevertheless, in the legal literature, criticisms have been repeatedly voiced that these additional legal competences for the Liechtenstein Constitutional Court in relation to the ECHR and the ICCPR lack a constitutional basis. Therefore, it is all the more surprising that the analogous case law of the Liechtenstein Constitutional Court concerning EEA law hardly met with any criticism of that kind, even though not even a basis in legislation had been created for the review power.[9]

Contrary to the view taken by some legal commentators,[10] the Liechtenstein Constitutional Court has also never questioned the fact that the primacy of EEA law

[4] See also Protocol 35 to the EEA Agreement. Due to Liechtenstein's adherence to the doctrine of monism in international law (see the text to n 22 below), the Liechtenstein Constitutional Court does not clearly distinguish in its case law on the primacy of EEA law whether or not the relevant EEA legislation has been transposed into national law.

[5] See P Bussjäger and C Frommelt, 'Europäische Regulierung und nationale Souveränität. Praxisfragen zur Übernahme europäischen Rechts ausserhalb der EU' (2017) *Liechtensteinische Juristen-Zeitung* 40, 42.

[6] First in StGH 1998/2, LES 1999, 169 (171 para 1.4); see also StGH 2006/94 [2.1] (www.gerichtsentscheide.li) and B Hammermann, 'Mehrebenen im Grundrechtsschutz – die liechtensteinischen Verfassung und der EWR' in Hoch, Neier and Schiess Rütimann (n 2) 291, 294. In the legal literature, commentators sometimes accord EEA law constitutional rank; see P Bussjäger, 'Einführende Bemerkungen zur liechtensteinischen Verfassung' in Liechtenstein-Institut (ed), *Kommentar zur liechtensteinischen Verfassung* (Bendern, Liechtenstein Institut, 2016) para 156.

[7] StGH 1998/2, LES 1999, 169 (171 para 1.4); for the effects of the constitution amending character of the EEA Agreement on the judicial review powers of the Liechtenstein Constitutional Court, see section III.B below.

[8] See the respective amendments of Art 15(2) pursuant to LGBl 1982/057 and LGBl 1999/046.

[9] See, however, A Kley, 'Die Beziehungen zwischen dem Liechtensteinischen Staatsgerichtshof und den übrigen einzelstaatlichen Rechtsetzungsorganen, einschliesslich der diesbezüglichen Interferenz des Handelns der europäischen Rechtsprechungsorgane' (2004) *Europäische Grundrechte-Zeitschrift* 43, 56. But Kley also primarily only criticises the lack of a legal basis; see also Hammermann (n 6) 294.

[10] See the references in C Baudenbacher, 'Das Vorabentscheidungsverfahren im EFTA-Pfeiler des EWR' in H Schumacher and W Zimmermann (eds), *Festschrift für Gert Delle Karth – 90 Jahre Fürstlicher Oberster Gerichtshof* (Vienna, Jan Sramek Verlag, 2013) 1, 4f; C Baudenbacher, 'Reciprocity' in C Baudenbacher (ed), *The Fundamental Principles of EEA Law* (Cham, Springer, 2017) 44, 51f.

includes the case law of the EFTA Court. Accordingly, the Liechtenstein Constitutional Court considers not only the opinions of the EFTA Court as binding for the domestic proceedings concerned, but also that the case law of the EFTA Court must generally be respected as part of EEA law.[11]

B. The Liechtenstein Constitutional Court's Reservation to the Primacy of EEA Law

However, the Liechtenstein Constitutional Court has formulated a reservation to the primacy of EEA law. Accordingly, it would exceptionally carry out a review of EEA law if a violation of 'fundamental principles and core contents of the fundamental rights of the national constitution' were suspected.[12] In doing so, the Liechtenstein Constitutional Court relied on a reservation that the Swiss Federal Council had formulated in the *travaux préparatoires* for Switzerland's accession to the EEA, which was subsequently rejected in a referendum. The wording of the Swiss and Liechtenstein reservations closely follows that of the German Federal Constitutional Court's reservation in relation to EU law.[13] The EEA reservation formulated by the Liechtenstein Constitutional Court was thus embedded in similar and also rather vague reservations expressed not only by courts in Germany, but also in numerous other EU Member States.[14] In the leading case StGH 1998/061, the Liechtenstein Constitutional Court already emphasised that this reservation would hardly ever be applied, especially since the need to protect fundamental rights is also recognised by EEA law.[15] Nonetheless, this ruling of the Liechtenstein Constitutional Court has given rise to a discussion as to whether this reservation can be qualified as a barrier to material constitutional amendments at the domestic level, for if domestic fundamental values are to be considered as barriers to EEA law, they must also be taken into account for constitutional amendments.[16]

[11] StGH 2013/044 [3.4.2]; StGH 2011/200 [3.2] (both www.gerichtsentscheide.li); H Wille, *Die liechtensteinische Staatsordnung: Verfassungsgeschichtliche Grundlagen und oberste Organe* (Schaan, Verlag der Liechtensteinischen Akademischen Gesellschaft, 2015) 704, fn 565.

[12] See especially StGH 1998/061, LES 2001, 126 (130, para 3.1), available at: www.gerichtsentscheide.li and excerpted in *Schweizerisches Zentralblatt für Staats- und Verwaltungsrecht* 1999, 585; see also StGH 2021/099 [2.3]; StGH 2021/030 [2.4.2]; StGH 2006/094 [2.1] (all www.gerichtsentscheide.li); H Hoch, 'Grundprinzipien und Kerngehalte der Grundrechte der Landesverfassung' in Hoch, Neier and Schiess Rütimann (n 2) 51, 53f with further references to case law.

[13] BVerfGE 73, 339 (*Solange II*): 'protection of fundamental rights that the Basic Law regards as indispensable', 'essential content of fundamental rights'; BVerfGE 123, 267 (Lisbon): 'inalienable core content of the constitutional identity of the Basic Law'.

[14] See Hoch (n 12) 55f with numerous references.

[15] First recital in the preamble to the EEA Agreement; StGH 1998/061, LES 2001, 126 (130 para 3.1).

[16] See on this discussion Hoch (n 12) 57. Although the reservation formulated by the Swiss Federal Council in its governmental message (Botschaft) on Switzerland's EEA accession was deprived of its intended purpose, as mentioned above, due to Switzerland's non-accession to the EEA, this reservation was referred to – as was the case in Liechtenstein, albeit 20 years later – in the context of the discussion on barriers to material constitutional amendments. See Hoch (n 12) 70 with further references.

C. The Constitutional Revision of 2003

In 2003, a constitutional revision came into force in Liechtenstein,[17] which – at least based on its wording – had far-reaching consequences for the position of EEA law in the domestic hierarchy of norms. According to the revised version of Article 104(2) of the Liechtenstein Constitution (Landesverfassung (LV)), the Liechtenstein Constitutional Court now has the additional competence to examine the constitutionality of international treaties, so that consequently international law now only has subconstitutional rank. Nevertheless, the Liechtenstein Constitutional Court has maintained its previous case law, according to which both constitutional and international fundamental rights can be invoked in individual complaint procedures and thus international fundamental rights have de facto constitutional rank as well.

In reaching this conclusion, the Liechtenstein Constitutional Court relied on the fact that in the new (recast) Constitutional Court Act (Staatsgerichtshofgesetz (StGHG)), enacted in the same year as the constitutional revision (2003), several new individual rights anchored in international treaties were added as protected rights.[18] Furthermore, the Liechtenstein Constitutional Court took account of the fact that the new Constitutional Court Act had been passed by the parliament and approved by the prince only a few months after the constitutional revision. Accordingly, 'the legislative author of the constitutional revision and of the new Constitutional Court Act are identical, so that it cannot be presumed that the provision in the Constitutional Court Act [which confirms the equivalence of constitutional and international human rights] contradicts the will of the constitutional legislator'.[19] Thus, the Liechtenstein Constitutional Court was able to temper the primacy of the Constitution over international law, provided for in the wording of Article 104(2) LV. However, with regard to EEA law, there was an additional problem, namely that the provisions of the Constitutional Court Act did not reflect the Liechtenstein Constitutional Court's equal treatment of EEA fundamental freedoms and national fundamental rights. To that extent, the Liechtenstein Constitutional Court relied on the government's argument in the *travaux préparatoires* for the new Constitutional Court Act: namely, that it was the government's intention that the new Constitutional Court Act should not affect previous Liechtenstein Constitutional Court practice regarding EEA fundamental freedoms.[20] Thus, the Liechtenstein Constitutional Court was able to preserve its case law on the primacy of EEA law, notwithstanding the constitutional revision of 2003 – albeit with reasoning that was doctrinally somewhat 'rough'.[21]

[17] LGBl 2003 No 186.

[18] See Art 15(2) StGHG (LGBl 2004 No 32). These treaties are the two conventions against racial and gender discrimination; the Convention against Torture, and the Convention on the Rights of the Child.

[19] StGH 2004/045 [2.1]; StGH 2005/089 [4] (both www.gerichtsentscheide.li); see P Schiess, *Die Stellung der EMRK in Liechtenstein* (Bendern, Liechtenstein-Institut, 2019) 31; Wille (n 11) 422; TM Wille, *Liechtensteinisches Verfassungsprozessrecht* (Schaan, Verlag der Liechtensteinischen Akademischen Gesellschaft, 2007) 69.

[20] See Stellungnahme der Regierung (Government Statement) of 4 November 2003 (BuA No 95/2003) 16f.

[21] See StGH 2006/094 [2.1] (www.gerichtsentscheide.li); *cf* Hoch (n 12) 82f, especially fn 123.

D. Case Law of the Liechtenstein Constitutional Court on the National Implementation of the Primacy of EEA Law

As already mentioned, the fact that the primacy of EEA law over national law is largely recognised in Liechtenstein does not determine how EEA law is actually applied. According to scholarly writing and case law, Liechtenstein adheres to monism in international law.[22] Accordingly, for international law, and therefore also for EEA provisions, no act of implementation into national law is required if a provision is directly applicable (ie, 'self-executing' norms). Nonetheless, Article 7 EEA requires that EEA norms be formally incorporated into Liechtenstein's legal system in accordance with the procedure laid down in this provision. In this regard, the EEA (and even less so the EU) bodies do not have any autonomous legislative powers vis-a-vis the EEA/EFTA States.[23]

Overall, Liechtenstein hardly faces any constitutional problems in enforcing the precedence of EEA law over national law – unlike the two other EEA/EFTA States, Norway and Iceland, which maintain a dualist approach to international law.[24] However, a controversy also arose in Liechtenstein in connection with the question – in the light of the power of the Liechtenstein Constitutional Court to review the legality of legislation – of how to deal with domestic legislation that violates EEA law. Furthermore, in its recent judgment in *RS*, the EFTA Court held that the Liechtenstein Constitutional Court's exercise of its power of judicial review had violated EEA law.[25] These issues are discussed in more detail below.

III. THE POWER OF THE LIECHTENSTEIN CONSTITUTIONAL COURT TO REVIEW THE LEGALITY OF LEGISLATION AND THE PRECEDENCE OF EEA LAW

A. Controversy over Domestic Provisions that Violate EEA Law

The trigger for this controversy was a 2006 ruling of the Liechtenstein Administrative Court (Verwaltungsgerichtshof (VGH)). In this ruling, the Liechtenstein Administrative Court relied on an EEC directive that was directly applicable under Liechtenstein's monistic approach and the court disregarded a Liechtenstein statutory provision that contravened it.[26] From the perspective of EEA law, this is permissible because directly applicable EEA law displaces conflicting national law without further ado. However, a controversy arose among legal scholars as to whether this approach was permissible in the light of the Liechtenstein Constitutional Court's function to review the legality

[22] See, eg, StGH 2013/196 [2.2.1] (www.gerichtsentscheide.li) with further references.

[23] See StGH Opinion 1995/014, LES 1996, 119 (122f para. 2.1); P Bussjäger, 'Kommentar zu Art. 8 LV' in Liechtenstein-Institut (n 6) para 108; C Frommelt, 'Liechtenstein and the EEA' in F Arnesen, HH Fredriksen, HP Graver, O Mestad and C Vedder (eds), *Agreement on the European Economic Area: A Commentary* (Baden-Baden, Nomos, 2018) 35, 46, para 38; Hammermann (n 6) 294; Baudenbacher, 'Reciprocity' (n 10) 44; Bussjäger and Frommelt (n 5) 40f.

[24] See Bussjäger and Frommelt (n 5) 40f.

[25] Case E-11/22 *RS*.

[26] VGH 2005/94, LES 2006, 300 para 29.

of legislation or, more fundamentally, whether national law could play a role in this context at all. The following section first presents the function of the Liechtenstein Constitutional Court to review the legality of legislation and its role in ensuring the precedence of EEA law, before addressing the question of how properly to deal with a domestic legal rule which violates EEA law.

B. The Power of the Liechtenstein Constitutional Court to Review the Legality of Legislation

The Liechtenstein Constitutional Court[27] is a specialised constitutional court modelled on the Austrian Constitutional Court.[28] In accordance with the Austrian model of constitutional jurisdiction, which was significantly shaped by Hans Kelsen, the Liechtenstein Constitutional Court has a monopoly on reviewing the legality of legislation (concentrated constitutional jurisdiction). In contrast, constitutional courts established in an earlier era, starting with the US Supreme Court and later the Swiss Federal Court, have additional functions as the final instances in ordinary matters; moreover, in those jurisdictions, lower courts are also authorised to review the legality of legislation (so-called diffuse constitutional jurisdiction). Finally, what is characteristic of the Kelsenian constitutional court is the fact that, due to its competence not only to determine the unconstitutionality of laws, but also to formally repeal them, it becomes an actual 'negative legislator'.[29]

The Liechtenstein Constitutional Court has, pursuant to Article 104(2) LV, a comprehensive abstract and concrete function to review the legality of legislation: from the outset, this function has pertained not only to laws, but also to ordinances (Articles 18 and 20 StGHG).[30] In individual complaint proceedings the Liechtenstein Constitutional Court can examine *ex officio* a provision that is relevant to the decision in the specific case, but such examination can also be 'suggested' by the parties to the proceedings. A concrete review of legality can also be initiated by a court through the staying of proceedings and referring a provision that it has to apply to the Liechtenstein Constitutional Court for a review of its constitutionality (Articles 18(1)(b) and (c), 20(1)(a) and (b), and 22(1) StGHG). A request for an abstract review of the legality of laws can be made at any time by the government or a municipality (Article18(1)(a) StGHG) and in relation to ordinances by 100 listed voters within one month of the date of publication in the Legal Gazette (Article 20(1)(c) StGHG).[31] The Liechtenstein

[27] The Liechtenstein Constitutional Court consists of five regular and five substitute judges. One regular and one substitute judge traditionally have Swiss and Austrian nationality, respectively. The Constitutional Court has been in continuous operation since 1926; see H Hoch, 'Verfassungsgerichtsbarkeit im Kleinstaat – das Beispiel Liechtenstein' (2021) *Zeitschrift für öffentliches Recht* 1219, 1223f with further references.

[28] See A Gamper, 'Constitutional Borrowing from Austria? Einflüsse des B-VG auf ausländische Verfassungen' (2020) *Zeitschrift für öffentliches Recht* 99, 115f.

[29] See Hoch (n 27) 1227 with further references.

[30] Although the Constitutional Court has also had the power to review the constitutionality of treaties since the revisions of the Constitution in 2003 and of the Constitutional Court Act in 2004 (Art 22 StGHG), as was mentioned earlier, this has not affected the Constitutional Court's case law on the precedence of EEA law.

[31] See Hoch (n 27) 1224 for more details.

Constitutional Court may defer the operative date of the annulment of an unconstitutional provision by up to one year (Articles 19(3), 21(3) and 23(2) StGHG).

However, the Liechtenstein Constitutional Court's monopoly on judicial review does not mean that ordinary courts and public authorities are not allowed to examine the constitutionality of provisions they apply. In fact, they are obliged to do so since all state action is bound by the Constitution.[32] From this obligation, the requirement arises to interpret provisions that are to be applied in a specific case in compliance with the Constitution.[33] However, if such a constitutionally compliant interpretation is not possible, a provision cannot simply be ignored, as would be possible in all instances in a system of diffuse constitutional jurisdiction. Instead, the seemingly unconstitutional provision to be applied in the specific case must be submitted to the Liechtenstein Constitutional Court for a review of its constitutionality and, if necessary, for its repeal.[34] Conversely, courts and public authorities entitled to submit a provision for review are not permitted to apply a provision and dispense with a submission to the Liechtenstein Constitutional Court where they have serious doubts as to the provision's constitutionality. In such a case, too, there is an obligation to submit.[35] Failure to do so could violate the guarantee of a lawful judge pursuant to Article 33 LV (or of Article 6(1) ECHR).[36]

These remarks show that, upon closer examination, the Liechtenstein Constitutional Court's judicial review monopoly is limited to a monopoly on the annulment of provisions. Other courts may and should examine the constitutionality of the provisions that they apply, but only the Liechtenstein Constitutional Court may annul them.

C. Is the Annulment of a Domestic Provision that Violates EEA Law itself a Violation of EEA Law?

We must now return to the aforementioned controversy of whether the Liechtenstein Constitutional Court may annul domestic provisions that contradict EEA law.

[32] See StGH 2021/099 [4.2] (www.gerichtsentscheide.li).

[33] TM Wille, 'Verfassungs- und Grundrechtsauslegung in der Rechtsprechung des Staatsgerichtshofes' in Liechtenstein-Institut (ed), *Beiträge zum liechtensteinischen Recht aus nationaler und internationaler Perspektive. Festschrift zum 70. Geburtstag von Herbert Wille* (Schaan, Verlag der Liechtensteinischen Akademischen Gesellschaft, 2014) 131, 170ff.

[34] As mentioned above, public authorities only have a limited right to submit provisions for review. In the absence of such a right, public authorities must therefore apply an unconstitutional provision if it cannot be interpreted in a constitutionally compliant manner. The affected party then has no choice but to go through the court system until a competent court submits the provision to the Liechtenstein Constitutional Court for review. And if this does not happen in the ordinary court system, the affected party can still bring an individual complaint to the Liechtenstein Constitutional Court and initiate a review of legality.

[35] StGH 1995/020, LES 1997, 30 (39, para 6); also StGH 1996/36, LES 1997, 211 (216, para 9). These decisions relate to the provisions of the old Constitutional Court Act (LGBl 1925 No 8). As the wording of the relevant provisions – Arts 24(1) and 28(2) of the old Constitutional Court Act – did not provide for an obligation to submit, this expansive case law was criticised by commentators. The new Constitutional Court Act no longer contains such judicial discretion and is therefore more aligned with the case law; see Wille (n 19) 171f with further references.

[36] This is the view of the EFTA Court concerning its own referral procedure set out in Case E-18/11 *Irish Bank Resolution Corporation Ltd v Kaupþing hf* [2012] EFTA Ct Rep 592 [64]; see P Christiansen, 'Article 34 Advisory Opinion' in Arnesen et al (n 23) 1032, 1037, para 19.

As already noted, commentators in the legal literature and the Liechtenstein Constitutional Court agree that the EEA Agreement has a 'constitution changing and supplementing character'. And as the EEA Agreement is considered to be on the same level as the Constitution, established case law implies that the compatibility of domestic laws and ordinances with EEA law can also be challenged by means of judicial review proceedings before the Liechtenstein Constitutional Court.[37]

However, this competence asserted by the Liechtenstein Constitutional Court to review the conformity of domestic provisions with EEA law, and in particular the associated competence to repeal such provisions, was called into question by some commentators in the legal literature following the VGH 2005/94 ruling. This was based on the argument that the direct applicability of suitable EEA law left no room for proceedings before the Constitutional Court for a review of legality.[38] The Constitutional Court countered this in its StGH 2006/94 ruling, holding that it was not apparent 'to what extent it should be a violation of EEA law to formally remove provisions contrary to EEA law from the national legal order – even if this is not strictly necessary to enforce the precedence of EEA law'.[39] In this connection, the EFTA Court has ruled that the question of whether the national provision is repealed or displaced by EEA law is to be answered not by EEA law, but by the national legal order.[40]

In its StGH 2006/94 ruling, the Liechtenstein Constitutional Court repealed a provision of the Civil Procedure Code (Zivilprozessordnung (ZPO)) concerning security for costs as contrary to EEA law. It justified the formal setting aside of the domestic provision, first, on account of legal certainty considerations and, second, by the finding that:

> Without a formal setting aside the relevant ZPO provisions would continue to apply, apart from third-country nationals, also to Liechtenstein nationals with a foreign residence, so that they would be disadvantaged compared to EEA foreigners. Admittedly, such so-called

[37] See StGH 1996/34, LES 1998, 74 (80). This pre-existing case law has been upheld although it was only confirmed for ordinances (but not for laws) in Art 20(1) StGHG. Pursuant to this new provision, ordinances can be reviewed by the Liechtenstein Constitutional Court for their 'treaty conformity', therefore including conformity with EEA law; see A Batliner, 'Die Anwendung des EWR-Rechts durch liechtensteinische Gerichte – Erfahrungen eines Richters' (2004) *Liechtensteinische Juristen-Zeitung* 139, 141.

[38] P Bussjäger, 'Rechtsfragen des Vorrangs und der Anwendbarkeit von EWR-Recht in Liechtenstein' (2006) *Liechtensteinische Juristen-Zeitung* 140, 145.

[39] StGH 2006/94 [3] (www.gerichtsentscheide.li), referring to H Wille, 'Das Abkommen über den Europäischen Wirtschaftsraum und seine Auswirkungen auf das liechtensteinische Verfassungs- und Verwaltungsrecht' in T Bruha, ZT Pállinger and R Quaderer (eds), *Liechtenstein – 10 Jahre im EWR, Bilanz, Herausforderungen, Perspektiven* (Schaan, Verlag der Liechtensteinischen Akademischen Gesellschaft, 2005) 108, 132; see also Wille (n 11) 704 ff.

[40] See Hammermann (n 6) 304 referring to the judgment in Case E-4/01 *Karl K. Karlsson hf v Iceland* [2002] EFTA Ct Rep 240 [28]. Neither in this nor in any other case has the EFTA Court made reference to Case 106/77 *Amministrazione delle Finanze dello Stato v Simmenthal SpA* ECLI:EU:C:1978:49, [1978] ECR 629 (*Simmenthal II*), where the CJEU decided that a national constitutional review procedure must not hinder the precedence of EU law. Indeed it is questionable whether *Simmenthal II* could at all be relevant in the EEA setting; however, see G Baur, 'Kohärente Interpretationsmethoden als Instrument europarechtskonformer Rechtsanwendung – eine rechtspolitische Skizze' in Liechtenstein-Institut (ed), *25 Jahre Liechtenstein-Institut (1986–2011)* (Schaan, Verlag der Liechtensteinischen Akademischen Gesellschaft, 2011) 47, 54f. But even beyond *Simmenthal II* national judicial review procedure can conflict with EEA law, as the recent judgment in Case E-11/22 shows (see section III.B below, last para).

discrimination against nationals does not fall within the scope of Article 4 EEA, as this provision is intended only to prevent discrimination against EEA foreigners. In the light of the equality principle of the Constitution, however, such discrimination against nationals is indeed problematic.[41]

The problem of discrimination against nationals was overlooked when it was argued by commentators in the legal literature[42] that the formal abolition of domestic laws that violate EEA law would overshoot the mark, as EEA law only required non-application to EEA nationals.[43]

In summary, it is clear that the Liechtenstein Constitutional Court may annul domestic laws that violate EEA law without, in so doing, in itself violating EEA law. As already mentioned, the Liechtenstein Constitutional Court has a monopoly on the annulment of unconstitutional domestic laws. It remains to be examined below whether, due to this monopoly, the Liechtenstein Constitutional Court is not only permitted but also required to annul such laws.

D. The Liechtenstein Constitutional Court's Monopoly on the Annulment of Laws and the Precedence of EEA Law

Neither in the StGH 2006/094 ruling nor in a subsequent judgment has the Liechtenstein Constitutional Court had to reach a finding on whether domestic laws that violate EEA law must be annulled by the Constitutional Court.

In fact, Liechtenstein's courts have always directly addressed the EFTA Court on the question of the compatibility of a Liechtenstein provision with EEA law. Likewise, domestic legal norms recognised by the EFTA Court as violating EEA law have not been submitted to the Liechtenstein Constitutional Court for formal annulment.[44] However, as mentioned earlier, in its ruling in VGH 2005/94, the Administrative Court simply did not apply a statutory provision it deemed – even without referral to the EFTA Court – to be obviously in violation of EEA law in the specific case. However, Herbert Wille has strongly criticised this legal position. He argues that, due to the Liechtenstein Constitutional Court's monopoly on the annulment of legislation, domestic laws that violate EEA law cannot just be ignored, but must be formally

[41] StGH 2006/94 [3] (www.gerichtsentscheide.li), with reference to A Schäfer, 'Die Prozesskostensicherheit – Eine Diskriminierung' (2006) *Liechtensteinische Juristen-Zeitung* 17, 23.

[42] Bussjäger (n 38) 145.

[43] See also StGH 2016/066 [4.3]; StGH 2011/155 [3.4]; and StGH 2009/145 [5] (all at www.gerichtsentscheide.li) on the unlawfulness of discrimination against nationals.

[44] It is not surprising that this has not been necessary so far for the parties to the proceedings. It is irrelevant for the parties whether a domestic rule recognised as being contrary to EEA law by the EFTA Court is also formally annulled by the Liechtenstein Constitutional Court or not. Even a party disadvantaged by the finding of the EFTA Court has no interest in bringing such a case before the Liechtenstein Constitutional Court, as the latter would have no other option but to annul the relevant provision due to the precedence of EEA law (including the case law of the EFTA Court; see the text to n 11 above; see also Wille (n 11) 705). But in its ruling in StGH 2013/196 [2.4.2] (www.gerichtsentscheide.li), the Liechtenstein Constitutional Court also calls upon the legislator, in the interests of legal certainty, to formally annul or amend at the first opportunity domestic provisions from which it must be derogated as a result of directly applicable EEA law.

annulled by the Constitutional Court. Even if the EFTA Court has determined the incompatibility of a national provision with EEA law in an advisory opinion, this incompatibility with EEA law corresponds to the unconstitutionality of the provision, meaning that the domestic court 'must proceed in the same way as with the unconstitutionality of a comparable provision of domestic law. Therefore, there is an obligation to submit [the provision to the Constitutional Court for review]'.[45] Herbert Wille's analysis is convincing. First, under EEA law, as already mentioned, the decision on whether a national provision is repealed or displaced by EEA law is left to national law. In addition, only formally repealed provisions of national law are removed from the national legal order; accordingly, only then may they no longer be applied. Apart from the legislator (and, in the case of ordinances, the government), the Constitutional Court is the only authority with the power to repeal domestic norms. According to the leading decision of the Liechtenstein Constitutional Court (StGH 2006/94), considerations of legal certainty and, depending on the circumstances, the avoidance of discrimination against nationals also speak in favour of formal annulment.

But even if the formal annulment of a national provision contrary to EEA law is basically a matter of domestic law, in so doing, the Liechtenstein Constitutional Court nonetheless recently came into conflict with EEA law. In its StGH 2019/095 ruling, the Liechtenstein Constitutional Court annulled a Liechtenstein tax law provision which infringed the freedom of movement for workers (Article 28(2) EEA); however, the date on which the annulment became operative was deferred by one year pursuant to Article 19(3) StGHG. The Liechtenstein Constitutional Court reasoned that the annulment required action by the legislature to avoid legal uncertainty and results that were questionable from the perspective of legal policy, including considerable losses in tax revenue.[46] When in a different case the Administrative Court had to apply the annulled tax provision as the deferral period had not yet expired, it made a referral to the EFTA Court for an advisory opinion. In its judgment in *RS*, the latter confirmed that in exceptional cases, for reasons of legal certainty, EEA States may temporarily maintain the effects of a national rule that is contrary to EEA law. But the EFTA Court held that in the case at hand, a 'mere reference to the budgetary and administrative problems' arising from the immediate annulment of the contested provision was not sufficient to establish overriding considerations of legal certainty. Therefore, the Administrative Court had to grant an effective remedy, including the repayment with interest of any taxes already paid in breach of EEA law. If that was not possible, state liability could be invoked.[47]

[45] Wille (n 11) 704f. It has been argued that since such an advisory opinion from the EFTA Court was binding upon (and hence the relevant domestic provision had to be ignored by) the national courts, the requirement that the provision be decisive in the case at hand was not met and, consequently, the Liechtenstein Constitutional Court had no power of review and could not repeal that provision (see V Morat, 'Das EWR-Recht als Teil der liechtensteinischen Rechtsordnung', Arbeitspapiere Liechtenstein-Institut No 79 (Bendern, Liechtenstein-Institut, 2023) 62. In contrast, the Constitutional Court has emphasised the necessity to repeal any national provision that violates EEA law, especially in light of considerations of legal certainty, and hence that the requirement for the provision to be decisive is fulfilled (see StGH 2019/095 [1.2.1f] (www.gerichtsentscheide.li)).

[46] StGH 2019/095 [5] (www.gerichtsentscheide.li).

[47] Case E-11/22 *RS v Steuerverwaltung des Fürstentums Liechtenstein*, 4 July 2023, [46f], [59]. The EFTA Court further emphasised in recital 44 that an unconditional and sufficiently precise EEA rule which has

IV. REFERRAL TO THE EFTA COURT

A. Is there an Obligation to Refer?

Unlike the provision concerning references to the European Court of Justice (Article 267 TFEU), the third paragraph of Article 34 of the Surveillance and Court Agreement (SCA) allows for the right of referral to the EFTA Court to be limited to the final national instance. However, none of the three EEA/EFTA States has made use of this possibility.[48] Due to the Liechtenstein Constitutional Court's monopoly on the annulment of legislation, it would have been appropriate for Liechtenstein to restrict the right to refer accordingly. This would have allowed the Liechtenstein Constitutional Court to better enforce its monopoly on the annulment of legislation. However, unlike the rule for EU Member States set out in the third paragraph of Article 267 TFEU, the wording of the third paragraph of Article 34 SCA does not impose an obligation on final national courts of the EEA/EFTA States to refer to the EFTA Court national provisions that are potentially incompatible with EEA law. However, in its judgments in *Irish Bank* and *Jonsson*, the EFTA Court postulated, based on the loyalty principle under Article 3 EEA, a 'quasi-obligation' for the final national instances to refer if the legal situation is 'unclear'.[49]

The question of whether there is an obligation to refer a case to the EFTA Court arises in a similar way to the corresponding question in domestic proceedings. The Liechtenstein Constitutional Court has postulated a referral obligation 'in the case of serious doubts' as to the constitutionality of a domestic provision, going beyond the wording of the old Constitutional Court Act.[50] Against this background, it was by no means surprising that the Liechtenstein Constitutional Court did not reject the approach taken by the EFTA Court in its *Irish Bank* ruling. In the leading case (StGH 2013/172), the Liechtenstein Constitutional Court held as follows in relation to its own obligation to refer to the EFTA Court: 'The Constitutional Court, as a court within the meaning of Article 34 paragraph 2 [SCA], refers a question on the interpretation of EEA law to the EFTA Court for a preliminary ruling or for the preparation of an opinion if the legal situation is unclear.' Where, in addition, the legal question at issue is decisive in the complaint case at hand, 'the application of the complainant for referral and subsequently for suspension of the individual complaint proceedings in question must be granted'.[51] From the StGH 2013/172 ruling, it is not evident whether this

been duly incorporated into national law 'must be fully and uniformly applied in all the EFTA States from the day on which the respective legal act is made part of the EEA Agreement'. However, this consideration does not seem to prohibit a lower court from submitting a national provision contrary to EEA law to the Liechtenstein Constitutional Court for formal annulment. From the viewpoint of EEA law, it seems essential that such a provision be not applied. Whether the provision is also formally annulled or not is a matter of domestic law (see n 40 above).

[48] See Christiansen (n 36) 1036f, para 18.

[49] *Irish Bank* (n 36) [57f]; and Case E-3/12 *Staten v/Arbeidsdepartementet v Stig Arne Jonsson* [2013] EFTA Ct Rep 138 [60]. See also Baudenbacher, 'Reciprocity' (n 10) 57, subheading 'Irish Bank and Jonsson: A Quasi-obligation to Refer'.

[50] See n 34 above.

[51] StGH 2013/172 [2.1] (www.gerichtsentscheide.li = LES 2014, 148).

obligation to refer only affects last instance courts or courts of all instances.[52] On the one hand, in its StGH 2013/172 ruling, the Liechtenstein Constitutional Court cited the *Jonsson* decision of the EFTA Court, which had been handed down shortly beforehand; on the other hand, the Constitutional Court did not refer to the third paragraph of Article 34 SCA, which concerns only supreme instances, but to the second paragraph of this provision, which provides for the right to refer for all national court instances.

What is evident is the following. According to the view presented here, as argued for by Herbert Wille, Liechtenstein national courts must, if the EEA law conformity of a domestic provision is questionable, either refer the matter to the EFTA Court or to the Liechtenstein Constitutional Court. For if a court does not refer the question to the EFTA Court, it must, in light of the Liechtenstein Constitutional Court's case law on the domestic obligation to refer, submit the question to the Constitutional Court, since the question of EEA law conformity is equivalent to the question of constitutional conformity. In the case of any doubt concerning the conformity with EEA law, the Constitutional Court, as a national court of last instance, is in any case obliged to refer the matter to the EFTA Court, provided that it does not immediately annul the domestic provision as incompatible with EEA law. And even if, upon a referral by a lower court, the EFTA Court has qualified the domestic provision as incompatible with EEA law, the lower court must, according to the view advanced here, still turn to the Constitutional Court for the formal annulment of the provision.

B. Referral Practice

Until today, a total of 45 referrals from Liechtenstein courts have been made to the EFTA Court.[53] While the Administrative Court made its first referrals to the EFTA Court as early as 1998 and the Princely Court of Liechtenstein (Landgericht) did so in 2004, the Liechtenstein Constitutional Court only initiated its first reference in the context of StGH 2013/044.[54] Since then, the Constitutional Court has submitted just one further reference to the EFTA Court.[55]

However, the Liechtenstein Constitutional Court never justified this rather restrained practice of referral by arguing that there was no obligation to refer.[56] Furthermore, the Liechtenstein Constitutional Court was hardly deterred from making referrals to the EFTA Court by political or other extraneous motives, as has been partly surmised of the Norwegian and Icelandic Supreme Courts.[57] Nor is it apparent

[52] See W Ungerank, 'Anmerkung zu StGH 2013/172' (2014) *Liechtensteinische Entscheidsammlung* 149.

[53] Requests for advisory opinion submitted before 1 February 2024.

[54] Decision to refer of 8 November 2013; Case E-24/13 *Casino Admiral AG v Wolfgang Egger* [2014] EFTA Ct Rep 732; see also StGH 2013/044 [14f] in the section 'Facts' (Sachverhalt) (www.gerichtsentscheide.li).

[55] Decision to refer of 20 January 2015 in StGH 2014/57; Case E-3/15 *Liechtensteinische Gesellschaft für Umweltschutz v Gemeinde Vaduz* [2015] EFTA Ct Rep 512.

[56] Ungerank (n 52) 149.

[57] Baudenbacher, 'Vorabentscheidungsverfahren' (n 10) 21.

that the first reference procedure initiated by the Liechtenstein Constitutional Court was prompted by the stricter case law of the EFTA Court on referral, even though the relevant rulings in *Irish Bank* and *Jonsson* had been delivered shortly beforehand. In any event, neither in the decision to refer nor in the ensuing StGH 2013/044 ruling is there a reference to this case law. As already mentioned, it was not until its StGH 2013/172 ruling that the Liechtenstein Constitutional Court referred to this new case law of the EFTA Court, which it took note of approvingly without further ado.[58]

As an alternative to referring to the EFTA Court, the Liechtenstein Constitutional Court does not hesitate to annul domestic provisions that appear obviously contrary to EEA law without referring them to the EFTA Court for review, as it did in the aforementioned StGH 2006/94 ruling.[59]

While it cannot be assumed that the Liechtenstein Constitutional Court will refer to the EFTA Court significantly more often in the future than it has done thus far, it stated in the StGH 2013/172 ruling that it will do so in accordance with the *Irish Bank* case law of the EFTA Court whenever it has doubts about the EEA legality either of a decision submitted to it for review or of the domestic provision underlying that decision.

V. OUTLOOK

On the occasion of the thirtieth anniversary of the EFTA Court, the following conclusions can be drawn. The Liechtenstein Constitutional Court has recognised the primacy of EEA law, including the case law of the EFTA Court, over domestic law from the outset to just about the greatest extent possible. In line with the EFTA Court, it has postulated an obligation, at least for Liechtenstein courts of last instance, to refer 'unclear' cases. Accordingly, it has also made its own referrals to the EFTA Court. In addition, the Liechtenstein Constitutional Court declares domestic provisions void without referring them to the EFTA Court if they appear obviously contrary to EEA law and therefore must also be considered unconstitutional. If the EFTA Court considers provisions of Liechtenstein law submitted to it by other Liechtenstein courts to be contrary to EEA law, according to the view expressed here, a referral to the Liechtenstein Constitutional Court would still have to be made, so that the latter can annul the provision in question and thus eliminate any possible discrimination against nationals and, in any event, establish legal certainty. However, this is a question of domestic law, which does not call into question the primacy of EEA law and of the case law of the EFTA Court.

[58] StGH 2013/172 [2.1], [2.3.9] (www.gerichtsentscheide.li). Ironically, this leading judgment of the Liechtenstein Constitutional Court on the obligation to refer was delivered in a case where, due to the fact that the provision was not decisive to the ruling, no referral was made to the EFTA Court.

[59] See the text to n 41 above.

9

The EFTA Court and the Supreme Court of Iceland

BENEDIKT BOGASON AND ÞORGEIR ÖRLYGSSON

I. INTRODUCTION

THE AGREEMENT ON the European Economic Area ('the EEA Agreement'), which was signed in Oporto, Portugal on 2 May 1992, came into effect on 1 January 1994. Iceland's membership of the agreement opened a new chapter for the country and ushered in significant changes in all parts of society. It is clear that the access that Iceland gained to the internal market of the EU through its membership of the agreement has promoted economic prosperity and wellbeing in the country during the 30 years since the agreement took effect.

The EFTA Court was established in accordance with Article 108(2) of the EEA Agreement. The Court functions under the Agreement between the EFTA States on the Establishment of a Surveillance Authority and a Court of Justice, which was signed in conjunction with the EEA Agreement. Its responsibilities include the adjudication of cases brought by the EFTA Surveillance Authority against EFTA States for failure to fulfil their obligations under the EEA Agreement as regards the implementation, application, and interpretation of the EEA Agreement (see Article 31) and the giving of advisory opinions to EFTA States on the interpretation of the EEA Agreement (see Article 34).

This chapter will examine the impact that the EFTA Court has had on the case law of Iceland's Supreme Court through its advisory opinions over the three decades during which the EFTA Court has been functioning. This will be done by considering the most important cases that have been examined by the two courts and assessing the significance they have had for the evolution of the EEA Agreement and its application in Iceland. Before turning to the cases themselves, it will be useful to give a brief account of the main aim of the EEA Agreement: the creation of a dynamic and homogeneous European Economic Area.

It may be mentioned here that there has been a great deal of contact between the EFTA Court and the Supreme Court of Iceland in view of the number of Icelandic Supreme Court judges who have sat on the EFTA Court bench. Þór Vilhjálmsson was the first of these, following a long period of service in the Supreme Court. He was succeeded by one of the authors of this chapter, Þorgeir Örlygsson, who, after leaving the EFTA Court in 2011, became a Supreme Court Judge and was President of the Court from 2017 to 2020. His seat on the EFTA Court was taken by Páll Hreinsson, who is still serving at the time of writing; he was a Supreme Court Judge from 2007 to 2011. The other author of this chapter, Benedikt Bogason, has been on the bench of the Supreme Court since 2012 and has been its President since 2020; from 2007 to 2022, he was an ad hoc judge at the EFTA Court and sat there on a number of cases. Finally, Ása Ólafsdóttir, a Supreme Court Judge, has been an ad hoc judge at the EFTA Court since 2013 and has sat there on several cases.

II. HOMOGENEITY

The preamble to the EEA Agreement states that the contracting parties have the objective of establishing a dynamic and homogeneous European Economic Area, based on common rules and equal conditions of competition, and providing for the adequate means of enforcement including at the judicial level, and achieved on the basis of equality and reciprocity and of an overall balance of benefits, rights and obligations for the contracting parties. Article 1(1) of the EEA Agreement also states that the aim of the agreement is 'to promote a continuous and balanced strengthening of trade and economic relations between the Contracting Parties with equal conditions of competition, and the respect of the same rules, with a view to creating a homogeneous European Economic Area'.

The requirement of homogeneity throughout the EEA means that the rules of the EEA Agreement must be interpreted and applied in the same way in all the Member States. This is expressed, for example, in the preamble to the agreement, which states that:

> [I]n full deference to the independence of the courts, the objective of the Contracting Parties is to arrive at, and maintain, a uniform interpretation and application of this Agreement and those provisions of Community legislation which are substantially reproduced in this Agreement and to arrive at an equal treatment of individuals and economic operators as regards the four freedoms and the conditions of competition.

As can be seen from the foregoing paragraphs, the EEA Agreement allows for the independence of the judiciaries of the Member States, while at the same time emphasising the need for uniform interpretation and application of the agreement so as to secure the goal of homogeneity. In this, the Member States have to tread a fine line between respecting the independence of their courts and fulfilling their obligations under the agreement. Naturally, the courts in the Member States have an important role in reconciling and coordinating potentially opposing points of view. It is extremely important that, in striving to observe this obligation, the courts seek guidance in the form of advisory opinions from the EFTA Court on the interpretation of the applicable rules of the EEA Agreement so as to have the best possible foundation on which to base their judgments. As has been stated above, the aim of this chapter is to examine how this process has worked in Iceland by considering the most important cases that have been examined both by the EFTA Court and the Supreme Court.

III. THE MOST SALIENT CASES

A. *Erla María Sveinbjörnsdóttir*

The first Icelandic case in which an advisory opinion was sought from the EFTA Court was *Erla María Sveinbjörnsdóttir* (E).[1] E had worked for a limited liability company which was taken into receivership in 1995. The receiver refused to recognise E's wage claim as a priority claim against the estate on the grounds that she was the sister of one of the principal owners of the company. Consequently, the Wage Guarantee Fund (Insolvencies) rejected E's demand for payment from the fund, referring, among other things, to the requirement in the act on the fund that a wage claim must be recognised as a priority claim in order for the fund to become liable for its payment. E then brought an action against Iceland for compensation on the grounds that it had not correctly harmonised domestic legislation with Council Directive 80/987/EEC on the approximation of the laws of the Member States relating to the protection of employees in the event of the insolvency of their employer, as this had been adopted in the EEA Agreement.

In its examination of the case, the district court put two questions to the EFTA Court. The first was whether Directive 80/987/EEC was to be interpreted as precluding that, under domestic legislation, an employee could be denied wage payments from a public wage guarantee fund due to his or her family relationship with a person owning a large share in a company when the employee held a claim against that company's insolvency estate for unpaid wages. In the event that the answer to this was in the negative, then the second question was whether the state would be liable to pay compensation where it had failed, in view of its membership of the EEA Agreement, to amend domestic legislation in such a way as to ensure that the employee was entitled to wage payments.

Regarding the first question, the EFTA Court, in its advisory opinion of 10 December 1998, concluded that the Directive must be interpreted as precluding Iceland from maintaining a provision of national law, according to which, in the case of a sibling relationship between an employee of an insolvent company and an owner of a large share in the company, the employee was excluded from the guarantee provided for in Article 3 of the Directive on the basis of that family relationship.

Regarding the second question, the EFTA Court noted that there was no explicit provision in EEA law establishing a basis for public liability on account of incorrect adaptation of national legislation and, consequently, it was necessary to consider whether such liability could be derived from the stated purposes and the legal structure of the EEA Agreement. Citing the scope of the agreement and its objective of homogeneity, and the methods of achieving it in accordance with Article 1 of the EEA Agreement, the court noted that the provisions of the agreement were, to a great extent, intended for the benefit of individuals and economic operators throughout the European Economic Area. Consequently, the functioning of the agreement depended on those individuals and economic operators being able to rely on the rights intended

[1] Case E-9/97 *Erla María Sveinbjörnsdóttir v The Government of Iceland.*

for their benefit. In the light of these considerations, the court concluded that the EEA Agreement was an international treaty *sui generis* which contained a legal order of its own, its scope and objective going beyond what was usual for an agreement under public international law. Finally, the court referred to Article 3 of the EEA Agreement, under which the contracting parties were required to take all appropriate measures, whether general or particular, to ensure fulfilment of their obligations under the agreement; this meant that they had a duty to make good loss or damage resulting from the incorrect implementation of directives integrated into the agreement. The court took the view that the obligation to provide for compensation was a principle of the EEA Agreement, and consequently that national legislation implementing the main part of the agreement was to be interpreted as also comprising the principle of state liability.

Having established this position, the EFTA Court set out three conditions for state liability in circumstances of this type: first, that the directive in question must be intended to confer rights on individuals, the content of which can be identified on the basis of its provisions; second, that the breach on the part of the state concerned must be sufficiently serious; and, third, that there must be a causal link between the breach of the state's obligation and the loss and damage suffered by the injured parties. The court took the view that the first of these conditions appeared to be fulfilled in the case, leaving it to the national courts to assess whether the same applied to the other two.[2]

In its judgment of 16 December 1999,[3] the Supreme Court accepted that the state bore compensatory liability towards E and she was awarded compensation. The Court noted that in interpreting the EEA Agreement, it was obliged to take account of the advisory opinion from the EFTA Court and deviations therefrom should be based on compelling grounds. It considered that there was a discrepancy between the Directive and Iceland's national legislation, the consequences of which were serious in E's case. Regarding state liability, the Court noted that under Iceland's Constitution, it was for the country's courts to rule on whether there were sufficient grounds in Icelandic law for compensatory liability. Next, the Court referred to the objective stated in the preamble to the EEA Agreement, ie, the establishment of a homogeneous European Economic Area based on common and harmonised rules that were to be interpreted consistently. Article 3 of the EEA Agreement constituted an obligation on the contracting parties to take all appropriate measures, whether general or particular, to ensure fulfilment of the obligations arising out of the agreement. Thus, Iceland had undertaken, under Article 7 of the EEA Agreement, to align Icelandic legislation with Directive 80/987/EEC so as to bring about consistency between Icelandic provisions and those of the Directive. Such alignment was to have guaranteed individuals' entitlement to payments from the Wage Guarantee Fund in the event of insolvency of their employer, and the court considered it clear that E would have received payments from the fund if the correct adaptation of legislation had been made.

[2] This judgment and state liability under the EEA Agreement has been extensively examined by commentators. For an excellent account, see, eg, HH Fredriksen, 'The EFTA Court and the Principle of State Liability: Protecting the Jewel in Crown' in C Baudenbacher (ed), *The EEA and the EFTA Court: Decentred Integration* (Oxford, Hart Publishing, 2014).

[3] Case No 236/1999.

Referring to Article 7 of and Protocol 35 to the EEA Agreement, the Supreme Court ruled that the agreement did not involve a delegation of legislative power. On the other hand, the main part of the agreement had the force of law in Iceland, and it was logical 'that the legislation implementing the main part of the agreement should be interpreted in such a way that the individual could demand that statutes be interpreted in conformity with EEA rules. If this were not done successfully, then it followed from that legislation, and the general principles and objectives of the EEA Agreement, that the state would bear compensatory liability under Icelandic law'. Thus, there was a sufficient legal basis for state liability in the event of inadequate implementation of the directive. The Court ruled that as Iceland had substantially failed to fulfil its obligation of guaranteeing E her entitlements from the Wage Guarantee Fund (Insolvency) in accordance with the Directive, it bore compensatory liability towards her for this error, this liability being subject to the general rules on state liability for damages.

Under the Supreme Court's conclusion, state liability followed from the legislation implementing the EEA Agreement in Iceland. Interpretation of the EEA Agreement was unavoidable for the resolution of the case. In this, the Supreme Court relied on the advisory opinion from the EFTA Court, observing the different roles of each of the two courts and the position of the Icelandic judiciary under the country's constitution. There is no doubt that the advisory opinion from the EFTA Court and the Supreme Court's judgment in the case were of fundamental significance for the application of the EEA Agreement and the development of cooperation based on the agreement.

B. *Fagtún ehf*

The first time an advisory opinion was obtained from the EFTA Court at the initiative of the Supreme Court was in the interesting case *Fagtún ehf*.[4] In this case, a company had submitted a tender for the supply and installation of roof elements as part of the construction of a secondary school; this was based on using roof elements from Norway. However, the works contract presented by the school's construction committee, acting on behalf of the authorities, provided for the roof elements to be produced in Iceland. In view of this, an advisory opinion was sought from the EFTA Court as to whether this requirement in the works contract was in violation of Articles 4 and 11 of the EEA Agreement.

In its advisory opinion of 12 May 1999, the EFTA Court ruled that the aforementioned requirement in the works contract had an effect equivalent to a quantitative restriction, which was prohibited under Article 11 of the EEA Agreement. In addition, the Court ruled that such a measure could not be justified on the grounds of protection of the health and life of humans under Article 13 of the EEA Agreement. In this context, the Court underlined that the measure led to overt discrimination.

[4] Case E-5/98 *Fagtún ehf*.

The Supreme Court, in its judgment of 18 November 1999 in Case No 169/1998, noted, with reference to Article 1 of Act 21/1994 on the Obtaining of Advisory Opinions from the EFTA Court on the Interpretation of the Agreement on the European Economic Area, that the EFTA Court's opinions were not binding in Icelandic law. The Court stated that the authorisation that the Icelandic judiciary had to seek such opinions was provided so as to promote consistency and homogeneity in the interpretation of the EEA Agreement, and thus the uniform application of the agreement throughout the EEA, which was one of the main objectives of the Agreement, as was stated, for example, in the preamble and was set out in further detail in Article 3 of the Agreement. It was also noted that Iceland had undertaken to take all appropriate measures to promote these aims. It followed from this that the Icelandic judiciary should take account of advisory opinions from the EFTA Court when interpreting the substance of the EEA Agreement. The Court considered that nothing had been revealed that would entail deviation from the EFTA Court's advisory opinion regarding the substance of Article 11 of the EEA Agreement. On this basis, the Supreme Court found that the requirement in the works contract that roof elements were to be produced in Iceland was at variance with the EEA Agreement and was, as a consequence, unlawful. As a result of this requirement, Fagtún ehf lost the contract, something which the Court considered was the fault of the school's building committee. Thus, the appropriate public authorities were considered as being liable, in accordance with the ordinary rules on compensatory liability, for loss and damage that could be attributed to the fact that no contract was made with Fagtún ehf.

With its finding in this case, in the early days of the EEA Agreement, the Supreme Court gave an unequivocal indication of the influence that conclusions from the EFTA Court had on the Icelandic judiciary, and the Icelandic courts appear to have followed this lead ever since. Broadly, the Supreme Court's judgment showed that the judiciary was obliged to take account of advisory opinions from the EFTA Court regarding the interpretation of the EEA Agreement, though without excluding the possibility that they could deviate from them in exceptional cases. However, no description was given of circumstances in which deviation from an advisory opinion might be considered. It is interesting to compare this approach with the one adopted by the Supreme Court of Norway in *Finanger*, in which it concluded that an advisory opinion should be followed unless weighty and compelling reasons are present.[5] Although the Icelandic judgment is less detailed than the Norwegian one, it may be assumed that both Supreme Courts share a similar understanding of the circumstances under which an advisory opinion may be deviated from.

C. *Hörður Einarsson*

Any discussion of the impact of advisory opinions from the EFTA Court on the case law of the Supreme Court of Iceland must include *Hörður Einarsson* (H).[6] One of

[5] HR-2000-1811.
[6] Case E-1/01 *Hörður Einarsson*.

the points that arose in this case was the question of which legislation should prevail when provisions in national law were at variance with those of the EEA Agreement. The circumstances of the case were that H was ordered to pay value-added tax (VAT) at a rate of 24.5 per cent on the customs value of books in English which he imported from Britain, while the rate of VAT on Icelandic books was 14 per cent. H argued that this discrimination was at variance with Article 14 of the EEA Agreement and demanded reimbursement of the difference. In light of this, an advisory opinion was sought from the EFTA Court as to whether it was compatible with the EEA Agreement to impose a higher rate of VAT on foreign-language books than on books in Icelandic. The Court was also asked whether the agreement, or other rules derived from it, contained provisions on the rules to be applied in the event of inconsistencies between the rules of national legislation and those following from the EEA Agreement.

In its advisory opinion of 22 February 2002, the EFTA Court's main conclusion was that the power of an EEA State to levy VAT did not exclude the application of EEA rules. It also considered it incompatible with Article 14 of the EEA Agreement if a national provision of an EEA State provided that books in the language of that state were to be subject to a lower rate of VAT than books in foreign languages. Such a national provision could not be justified, the Court ruled, on grounds relating to the public interest of enhancing the position of the national language. Finally, it ruled that when a provision of national law was incompatible with Article 14 of the EEA Agreement and that article had been implemented in national law, this gave rise to a situation which was governed by the undertaking assumed by the EFTA States under Protocol 35 to the EEA Agreement, the premise of which was that the implemented EEA rule was to prevail.

In its judgment of 15 May 2003 in Case No 477/2002, the Supreme Court again noted, as it had in its previous judgments, that the Icelandic judiciary was to take account of advisory opinions from the EFTA Court when interpreting the EEA Agreement, unless particular circumstances militated against this, even though these opinions were not binding in Icelandic law. The Supreme Court noted, as the EFTA Court had done in its advisory opinion, that the general objective of Article 14 of the EEA Agreement was to ensure the free movement of goods under normal conditions of competition between EEA Member States by preventing all protective measures resulting from internal taxation constituting discrimination against products of other contracting parties and to ensure that internal taxation did not distort competition between domestic and imported products.

In the closing section of its judgment, the Supreme Court referred to the fact that the main text of the EEA Agreement had been implemented in Iceland under Article 2 of Act 2/1993. It also noted that Article 3 of the same Act provided that laws and regulations were to be interpreted, to the extent appropriate, in accordance with the EEA Agreement and rules based thereon. The Court took the view that it could be concluded from the notes accompanying Article 2 of the Act, when it was presented as a bill, that this article had been intended to meet the requirement of Protocol 35 to the EEA Agreement. The notes also stated that Article 3 meant that domestic legislation based on the EEA Agreement would normally be interpreted as special provisions vis-a-vis incompatible legislation of a later date in such a way that, in the event of conflict between them, the later provisions would not prevail over them unless the legislator stated particularly that this was to be the case. In light of this, the court regarded Article 14 of the EEA Agreement as prevailing over the Value-Added Tax Act. Following the implementation of the EEA Agreement, it was therefore unlawful to discriminate between books in Icelandic and books in other languages when levying VAT.

This judgment is notable because the Supreme Court interpreted Article 3 of Act 2/1993 in the same way as the EFTA Court interpreted Protocol 35 to the EEA Agreement. In this, the Supreme Court went further than was provided for in the actual wording of Article 3 of the Act, basing its interpretation on the notes to the draft article which allowed for the precedence of EEA rules. On the other hand, the text of the article, as enacted, contains no such provision, an issue to which we will return below.

D. *Þór Kolbeinsson*

One of the more important cases in which an advisory opinion has been sought from the EFTA Court is *Þór Kolbeinsson* (Þ).[7] The circumstances here were that Þ had been involved in a work-related accident while stepping between floor joists in the course of his work on the construction of a shopping centre. He lost his footing and fell five metres from a dividing ceiling onto a concrete floor. He sustained physical injury for which he sought compensation, but the claim he brought against his employer and his insurer was rejected by the Supreme Court in its judgment of 20 December 2005 in Case No 246/2005. The Supreme Court observed that Þ was a qualified master carpenter with extensive experience of work of this type and that he was fully familiar with the circumstances. He therefore should have known what measures should have been taken under these circumstances and should have been aware of the danger involved in moving about in the area in the way that he did. The Court did not consider that the employer should have given Þ any special instructions or guidance on these matters; in the light of the facts of the case, it instead considered that it lay within Þ's sphere of responsibilities to react to the situation. Thus, the Court concluded, the accident could not be attributed to circumstances for which the employer was responsible.

Following this judgment, Þ brought an action against Iceland for compensation on the grounds that the resolution of his case against his employer indicated that the state had not fulfilled its obligation under the EEA Agreement to implement certain directives in Icelandic law. In connection with this case, an advisory opinion was sought from the EFTA Court as to whether it was compatible with Council Directive 89/391/EEC, on the introduction of measures to encourage improvements in the safety and health of workers at work, and with Council Directive 92/57/EEC, on the implementation of minimum safety and health requirements at temporary or mobile construction sites, that a worker was made liable for loss or injury that he himself incurred through his own contributory negligence in a work-related accident when

[7] Case E-2/10 *Þór Kolbeinsson*.

it was established that the employer had not, on his own initiative, complied with the rules on safety and conditions in the workplace. If this was at variance with the directives, then an opinion was also requested as to whether the state bore compensatory liability towards the employee due to these directives not having been correctly implemented in Icelandic law.

In its advisory opinion of 10 December 2010 in Case E-2/10, the EFTA Court's conclusion was that except in exceptional circumstances, it was not compatible with the aforementioned directives to hold a worker liable under national tort law for all, or the greater share, of the losses suffered as the result of an accident at work due to his own contributory negligence when it had been established that the employer had not, on his own initiative, complied with rules regarding safety and conditions in the workplace. The Court took the view that exceptional circumstances might exist where the employee had caused the accident wilfully or by acting with gross negligence. However, even in such circumstances, a complete denial of compensation would be disproportionate and not in compliance with the directives, except in extreme cases of the employee being substantially more to blame for the accident than his employer. Regarding state liability, the Court considered that an EEA State could be held liable for a breach of the rule on contributory negligence inherent in the directives referred to. Such liability depended on the breach being considered sufficiently serious. The Court ruled that it was for the national court to decide, in accordance with settled case law on state liability for breaches of EEA law, whether this condition was fulfilled in the case before it.

In its judgment of 21 February 2013 in Case No 532/2012, the Supreme Court took the view that, irrespective of whether the directives had set limits to the reduction or waiving of compensation that the employee might be made to suffer in circumstances such as these due to his own contributory negligence and of what those limits might be, it could not regard the condition of sufficient seriousness in the state's failure to meet its obligations as having been met. For this reason, the Court did not accept that Þ was able to demand compensation from the state due to the inadequate implementation of the directives in Icelandic law.

Although the Supreme Court's judgment in this case did not address the question of whether implementation of the directives regarding the employee's own contributory negligence had been adequate, it should be mentioned that prior to both the delivery of this judgment and the EFTA Court's delivery of its advisory opinion, the Tort Damages Act, No 50/1993, was amended by Act No 124/2009 in order to strengthen the legal standing of employees who suffered physical injury at work. Under the amendment, the employee's entitlement to damages was not reduced due to his own negligence unless he had played a part, through gross negligence or by intention, in the occurrence of the accident. Thus, a legislative amendment had already been made, which resulted in Icelandic legislation being made compatible with the directives, even though this aim was not stated in the notes to the accompanying bill of law.

It may be mentioned that in 2022, Þ applied for the re-examination of the case described above (Case No 246/2005) which had been concluded by the Supreme Court's judgment of 20 December 2005. The EFTA Court's advisory opinion was cited as one of the grounds for this application. The court dealing with applications for re-examination ruled on the application on 30 January 2023 in Case No 16/2022, rejecting it. In the reasoning for this decision, the Court noted that the advisory opinion from the EFTA Court concerned Þ's action against Iceland for inadequate implementation of EEA rules, and not the case he brought against his employer and insurer. Consequently, Þ could not have the case re-examined on this basis.

E. *Jan Anfinn Wahl*

The case of *Jan Anfinn Wahl* (J),[8] involving a Norwegian citizen, concerned the right of nationals of EEA States to move freely throughout the EEA. The circumstances were that customs officers searching J's luggage when he arrived in Iceland on 5 February 2010 found clothing marked with the insignia of the Hell's Angels Motorcycle Club and he was quickly expelled from the country by order of the Immigration Agency. When questioned, J admitted to membership of the organisation and that the one of the purposes of his visit was to make contact with a motorcycle club in Iceland that had applied for affiliation and was later granted it at the suggestion of the Norwegian chapter. After questioning, J was held in a prison cell and deported the following day. He lodged an appeal against his deportation with the Ministry of Justice, which upheld the Immigration Agency's decision in its ruling of 16 June 2010. J then brought an action against Iceland for damages for non-financial loss.

After the pleading of the case on 5 November 2012, the Court asked the parties whether they thought there was reason to seek an advisory opinion from the EFTA Court on the matters at issue. The parties saw no reason to take the initiative on such a move, but had no objection to it being done. The Supreme Court then took the decision to seek an advisory opinion on its own initiative regarding specific points; these concerned, in particular, the interpretation of Directive 2004/38/EC on the right of citizens of the Union and their family members to move and reside freely within the territory of the Member States.

The EFTA Court delivered its advisory opinion on 22 July 2013 in Case E-15/12. Among other things, this stated that under Article 27 of Directive 2004/38/EC, it was sufficient for an EEA State to decide not to grant an individual, who was a national of another EEA State, leave to enter its territory on grounds of public policy and/or public security only upon a danger assessment. This could apply if the assessment concerned the role of the individual in the accession of a new chapter to an organisation of which the individual was a member, and it concluded that the organisation was associated with organised crime and that where such an organisation had managed to establish itself, organised crime had increased. The opinion went on to state that such an assessment must be based exclusively on the personal conduct of the individual concerned, which must then represent a genuine, present and sufficiently serious threat to one of the fundamental interests of society, and that the restriction of the right must be proportionate. On the other hand, it was up to the national court to decide whether these requirements were met, taking account of the relevant matters

[8] Case E-15/12 *Jan Anfinn Wahl*.

of fact and law. The EFTA Court also took the view that an EEA State could not be obliged to declare an organisation, and membership thereof, unlawful before denying a member of that organisation who was a national of another EEA State leave to enter its territory under Article 27 of the Directive if such a measure was thought appropriate in the circumstances. However, the EEA State must have clearly defined its standpoint as regards the activities of the organisation and, considering the activities to be a threat to public policy and/or public security, it must have taken administrative measures to counteract those activities. Finally, the opinion stated that the national authorities must ensure that there was sufficient evidence to conclude that the individual concerned was likely to engage in personal conduct that represented a genuine, present and sufficiently serious threat affecting one of the fundamental interests of society. It was for the national court to determine, in compliance with the principles of equivalence and effectiveness, whether this was the case.

In its judgment of 17 October 2013 in Case No 191/2012, the Supreme Court found that the Icelandic government had defined its standpoint as regards the Hell's Angels Motorcycle Club in a clear manner and taken measures to counter them, considering the organisation as posing a threat to public policy and public security. The Court also considered that by means of the hazard assessment by the National Commissioner of Police, the report on the search of J's luggage and the questioning of J by the police, the Icelandic authorities had ensured that sufficient evidence was available in order to assess whether J engaged in, or was likely to engage in, activities that could be regarded as threatening the fundamental interests of Icelandic society. The Court considered that J had, through his participation in the motorcycle club, identified himself with its objectives and intentions, thus exhibiting personal conduct involving, or being likely to involve, a genuine, present and serious threat to the fundamental interests of Icelandic society in maintaining public policy and defending public security. The Court considered that the decision to expel J from Iceland had sufficient basis in law and that the conditions stated in law for such a decision, taken in the light of Iceland's international obligations, had been met. Thus, J's claim for damages for non-financial loss was not considered.

This Supreme Court judgment is a clear example of the resolution of a case that is based on an advisory opinion from the EFTA Court. This was important here because the case involved the fundamental principle of the EEA Agreement of freedom of movement for nationals of EEA States throughout the EEA.

F. *Atli Gunnarsson*

Finally, we turn to *Atli Gunnarsson* (A).[9] The circumstances here were that A and his wife were domiciled in Denmark, but paid tax on disability benefits from the Icelandic Social Insurance Administration and on benefits from two Icelandic pension funds. The couple apparently had no other sources of income. In accordance with the then valid Income Tax Act, No 90/2003, A's personal tax credit was deducted

[9] Case E-26/13 *The Icelandic State v Atli Gunnarsson*.

from his tax; on the other hand, he had no chance of using his wife's personal tax credit for a deduction because the couple were not domiciled in Iceland. A considered that the provision in the law on this point was at variance with Article 28 of the EEA Agreement, providing for the free movement of workers throughout the EEA, and of Article 7 of Directive 2004/38/EC, on the right of citizens of the Union and their family members to move and reside freely within the territories of the Member States. On this basis, A brought a case against Iceland, demanding that the decision of the Director of Internal Revenue, denying him the right to use his wife's personal tax credit, be set aside and that he be reimbursed the excess sums he had paid in tax. accordingly.

After the pleading of the case in the Supreme Court on 14 November 2013, the Court asked the parties whether there was reason to seek an advisory opinion from the EFTA Court on the matter at issue. The parties saw no reason to take the initiative on such a move, but had no objection to it being done. Following this, the Supreme Court decided on its own initiative to seek an advisory opinion from the EFTA Court on specific points involving, in particular, the interpretation of the rules of EEA law which had a bearing on the case.

The EFTA Court submitted its advisory opinion on 27 June 2014 in Case E-26/13. Its conclusion was that it was compatible neither with Article 1 of Directive 90/365/EEC, on the right of residence for employees and self-employed persons who have ceased their occupational activity, nor with Article 7(1)(b) and (d) of Directive 2004/38/EC, on the right of citizens of the Union and their family members to move and reside freely within the territories of the Member States, that an EEA state did not give spouses who had moved to another EEA state the option of pooling their personal tax credits in connection with the assessment of income tax, whereas they would be entitled to pool their personal tax credits if they lived in the home state, in a situation where one of them received a pension from the home state and that pension constituted all or nearly all of that person's income, while the other spouse had no income.

In its judgment of 2 October 2014 in Case No 92/2013, the Supreme Court found that whereas the EFTA Court had, on the basis of legal interpretation, concluded in its advisory opinion that provisions in Iceland's Income Tax Act were at variance with those of Directives 90/365/EEC and 2004/38/EC, it should be noted that the provisions of the Income Tax Act had not been amended when these directives were implemented. Despite the provision in Article 3 of the EEA Act, No 2/1993 that laws were to be interpreted in conformity with the EEA Agreement, the Supreme Court considered that the Directorate of Internal Revenue, when interpreting the law, was not permitted to completely ignore the clear and unequivocal provisions of the tax legislation. For this reason, there was no basis in law for A to have his wife's personal tax credit taken into account in his tax assessment, and so his demand to have the decision to reject his claim to this effect set aside was dismissed. The Court also rejected his demand for damages on the grounds that Iceland bore liability due to its failure to implement EEA rules correctly, as it considered the violation of EEA law not sufficiently serious as to meet the liability requirement.

It was while this case was under consideration by the district court that the appropriate amendments were made to the tax legislation by Act No 165/2020, thus securing conformity of the law with the EEA Agreement on this point. These amendments were enacted as a response to infringement proceedings ESA had initiated against Iceland.

The Supreme Court's judgment on this case can be seen as sounding a different tone from the one it adopted in *Hörður Einarsson*:[10] in that case, the court took the view that a specific provision in the EEA Agreement had the status of a special rule vis-a-vis the tax legislation and so prevailed over it.

IV. CONCLUSIONS

Descriptions have been given above of six court cases involving interpretation of the EEA Agreement which have been examined by the EFTA Court and the Icelandic Supreme Court. A considerably larger number of such cases have arisen, but not all can be included in an chapter of this length.

The Icelandic courts have generally complied with advisory opinions from the EFTA Court, and collaboration and cooperation between the judiciary and the EFTA Court has been very smooth. In this, the tone was set early on, in the Supreme Court's judgment in *Erla María Sveinbjörnsdóttir*,[11] where the Court noted that when interpreting the EEA Agreement, it was to take account of advisory opinions from the EFTA Court. The Supreme Court confirmed this position in *Fagtún ehf*[12] and *Hörður Einarsson*, stating that even though the EFTA Court's opinions were not binding, the Icelandic judiciary should take account of them when interpreting the substance of the EEA Agreement unless there were special reasons not to do so.

Nevertheless, there is no avoiding the fact that some uncertainty has emerged in Icelandic case law in instances of conflict between provisions implementing obligations under the EEA Agreement, on the one hand, and incompatible provisions of domestic legislation, on the other. This is illustrated in the Supreme Court's approaches in *Hörður Einarsson* and *Atli Gunnarsson*,[13] which were described above.

In its advisory opinion in *Hörður Einarsson*,[14] the EFTA Court pointed out that where a provision in national legislation was incompatible with Article 14 of the EEA Agreement, that article having been implemented in the state's legal order, this gave rise to a situation involving the obligations of the EFTA States under Protocol 35 to the EEA Agreement: the protocol was based on the principle that EEA legislation that had been implemented in the domestic legal order was to prevail. The Supreme Court's judgment is interesting in that it interpreted Article 3 of the EEA Act, No 2/1993 in the same way as the EFTA Court interpreted Protocol 35 to the EEA Agreement. In this, the Supreme Court actually went further than the wording of Article 3 of the Act entails, invoking what was stated in the explanatory notes to the draft of that Act regarding the prevalence of EEA rules. No such instruction is expressed in the text of the provision itself.

[10] *Hörður Einarsson* (n 6).
[11] *Erla María Sveinbjörnsdóttir* (n 1).
[12] *Fagtún ehf* (n 4).
[13] *Atli Gunnarsson* (n 9).
[14] *Hörður Einarsson* (n 6).

In *Atli Gunnarsson*,[15] on the other hand, the Supreme Court took the view that whereas the EFTA Court had found, in its advisory opinion, that provisions in Iceland's Income Tax Act were incompatible with those of Directives 90/365/EEC and 2004/38/EC, it should be noted that the provisions of the Act had not been amended when the directives were implemented. Even though Article 3 of Act No 2/1993 prescribed that legislation was to be interpreted in conformity with the EEA Agreement, the Supreme Court considered that the Directorate of Internal Revenue had not been free, in interpreting the law, to ignore the clear and unequivocal provisions of the Income Tax Act. Consequently, there was no authorisation in law for pooling the couple's personal tax credits when assessing A's tax, so his demand to have the decision rejecting his request to have this set aside was dismissed. The Supreme Court's position in this case was rather different from the one it adopted in *Hörður Einarsson*.

Protocol 35 to the EEA Agreement states that for cases of possible conflicts between implemented EEA rules and other statutory provisions, the EFTA states undertake to introduce, if necessary, a statutory provision to the effect that EEA rules prevail in these cases. From the notes to the bill which was passed as Act No 2/1993, it is clear that Article 3 of the Act was intended to meet the requirement laid down in Protocol 35; Article 3 of the Act states that laws and regulations are to be interpreted, to the extent appropriate, in accordance with the EEA Agreement and rules based thereon. In other words, the rule was implemented as one of legal interpretation and not as a priority rule.

The question of whether, with Article 3 of Act No 2/1993, Iceland adequately implemented Protocol 35 to the EEA Agreement has been examined by scholars over the past few decades. Examples of this are the articles by Ólafur Jóhannes Einarsson,[16] Margrét Einarsdóttir,[17] Gunnar Þór Pétursson[18] and two articles by Margrét Einarsdóttir and Stefán Már Stefánsson.[19]

All the authors of these articles share the view that Article 3 of Act No 2/1993 fails to meet the obligation undertaken by Iceland under Protocol 35 to the EEA Agreement as it has been interpreted by the EFTA Court. The same view has been expressed in a case yet to be resolved which has been brought by the EFTA Surveillance Authority (ESA) for a breach of the agreement, both in a letter of formal notice of 13 December 2017, setting out ESA's formal observations regarding Iceland's implementation of Protocol 35, and in its reasoned opinion of 30 September 2020. At the time of writing, the next step in this case is expected to be the bringing of an action by ESA before the EFTA Court. Such an action would seek confirmation by the court of Iceland's breach of its obligations under the EEA Agreement by it having failed to implement Protocol 35 to the agreement in a satisfactory manner. It should also be mentioned that Norway, Sweden and Finland, which were originally members of the

[15] *Atli Gunnarsson* (n 9).

[16] OJ Einarsson, 'Bókun 35 og staða EES-samningsins að íslenskum rétti' (2007) *Tímarit lögfræðinga* 371.

[17] M Einarsdóttir, 'Forgangsáhrif EES-réttar í íslenskum rétti' (2014) *Tímarit Lögréttu* 75.

[18] GT Pétursson, 'Forgangur EES-reglna. Hvað er að frétta af bókun 35?' (2017) *Afmælisrit Davíðs Þórs Björgvinssonar* 201.

[19] M Einarsdóttir and SM Stefánsson, 'Beiting innleiddra EES-reglna í íslenskum rétti í ljósi bókunar 35' (2020) *Hæstiréttur í hundrað ár – ritgerðir* 341.

EEA Agreement, implemented Protocol 35 differently, clearly stating that EEA rules were to take precedence in the event of conflict between them and other domestic legislation.

Our view is that in light of the uncertainty that has arisen regarding whether Iceland implemented Protocol 35 to the EEA Agreement in an adequate manner, and inconsistencies in the case law of the Icelandic judiciary regarding this, it is important that the Icelandic legislator resolves the issue and enacts a clear and unambiguous provisions on the matter, respecting the undertaking laid down in Protocol 35 EEA.

10

The Supreme Court of Norway and the EFTA Court through 30 Years

TORIL MARIE ØIE AND HENRIK BULL*

I. INTRODUCTION

IT IS GENERALLY accepted that one of the most important developments in law in the last few decades has been the internationalisation of legal sources. No longer do international rules almost exclusively regulate the relationship between states; they also regulate the relationship between the state and its own citizens and enterprises, and to some extent also between private entities. This means that national courts must take them into account to a much larger extent than they have previously been accustomed to doing. By extending a large part of the EU's internal market law to Norway, Iceland and Liechtenstein (the EEA/EFTA States), the EEA Agreement – EEA law – is by far the most important development in this regard for these three states. By limiting the states' right to regulate economic activity, EEA law also poses new challenges for national courts with regard to what was previously thought of as 'political' rather than 'legal' questions and considerations.

The internationalisation of legal sources is not limited to the impact of the provisions of the various international instruments as such. Some of these instruments establish their own bodies that interpret the instruments, sometimes in the form of purely advisory bodies,[1] but also – and more pertinent to the topic of this chapter – as regular international courts with varying powers, such as the European Court of Human Rights (ECtHR), the Court of Justice of the European Union (CJEU) and, as the youngest of these three courts, the EFTA Court. The relevance, and relative weight compared to other sources, of decisions by such bodies is also a question that national courts have to deal with, both from a principled and a more practical point of view.

The growing importance of human rights for EU law and EEA law also means that the ECtHR on the one hand, and the CJEU and the EFTA Court on the other hand

* The authors thank law clerk Fredrik Lilleby for his invaluable help in preparing this chapter.

[1] For instance, the Human Rights Committee established by the International Covenant on Civil and Political Rights, or the Committee on the Rights of the Child established by the Convention of the Rights of the Child.

may, directly or indirectly, come to address the same questions. This poses particular problems to national courts.

The possibility to refer questions of interpretation of EEA law to the EFTA Court in cases pending before national courts provides a forum for dialogue that is unique, even compared to the parallel system of preliminary rulings within the EU system. All national courts may ask the EFTA Court for guidance on the interpretation of EEA law. However, this dialogue has a special significance for national supreme courts, whose most important task is to provide guidance to other courts within the national judicial system. It is this dialogue that we will seek to explore in this chapter.

II. ADVISORY OPINIONS AS A 'PARTNER-LIKE' RELATIONSHIP

According to Article 34 of the Agreement between the EFTA States on the Establishment of a Surveillance Authority and a Court of Justice (SCA), any 'court or tribunal' in an EEA/EFTA State may request the EFTA Court to give an advisory opinion on the interpretation of the EEA Agreement if such interpretation is necessary to enable that national court or tribunal to give judgment in a case pending before it.[2] This means that, unlike the situation in the EU, there is no obligation on national courts of last resort to make a reference to the EFTA Court. As the EFTA Court pointed out in *Irish Bank Resolution Corporation Ltd*, this in turn means that the relationship between the EFTA Court and national courts of last resort is 'more partner-like'.[3] However, the EFTA Court then went on to point out that when considering whether to refer a question to the EFTA Court, national courts of last resort must take account of the duty of loyal cooperation as laid down in Article 3 EEA.

Furthermore, and again unlike the system in the EU, the EFTA Court gives 'advisory opinions' rather than binding judgments to national courts. This also makes the system 'more partner-like' by opening a possibility of dialogue between the EFTA Court and national courts. As we shall see in section VI below, this dialogue often centres on the understanding of CJEU case law.

III. WHEN TO ASK? THE DISTINCTION BETWEEN INTERPRETATION AND APPLICATION

In Norwegian law, the possibility to ask the EFTA Court for advice is provided for in section 51a of the Courts of Justice Act.[4] Unlike the situation in Iceland described

[2] Article 34 allows the EFTA-EEA States to limit the right to request advisory opinions to courts and tribunals against whose decisions there is no judicial remedy. However, none of the EFTA-EEA States has done so, although Norway has barred its 'conciliation boards' (*forliksråd*) from requesting advisory opinions. These boards consist of laypeople. As the name suggests, their principal task is to facilitate amicable solutions to small-claims legal disputes between private parties, but they may also render judgment in such cases, provided they do not raise any complicated legal issues, typically non-disputed money claims. This means that such claims may become enforceable through a cost-efficient procedure and without burdening the regular courts.

[3] Case E-18/11 *Irish Bank Resolution Corporation Ltd*, para 57.

[4] Lov 13 august 1915 nr 5 om domstolene, with later amendments.

in *Irish Bank Resolution Corporation Ltd*,[5] a decision to ask, not to ask or how to ask may not be appealed. There is no requirement to give reasons for the decision. However, if the parties, or one of them, have argued in favour of submitting questions to the EFTA Court, it would often be natural for the court to give reasons for a decision not to do so. One example of the Supreme Court giving reasons for not asking is found in the *Gaming Machines* case, where the Appeals Selection Committee stated that the limits to regulating the market for games of chance had been clarified through rather extensive case law from the CJEU, and that concrete application of that case law to the factual and legal issues of the case at hand was a task for the national court.[6]

This distinction between interpretation on a more general level and concrete application plays an important role in Norwegian procedural law, as appellate rulings by the courts of appeal on orders and decisions by district courts may only be appealed on a point of law to the Supreme Court provided that the appeal concerns the general interpretation of a written rule.[7] In other words, the role of the Supreme Court is to safeguard the correct application of the law on a general level, not to substitute the view of lower courts with that of its own on the consequences of a correct interpretation for a concrete set of factual circumstances. For Norwegian courts, particularly the Supreme Court, it is natural to see the task of the EFTA Court in giving advisory opinions in the same light. This is even more so because the EFTA Court cannot rule on the evidence or the correct meaning of national law when dealing with a request for an advisory opinion, and it may have to give its advisory opinion at a stage of the case where the national court is yet to rule on evidence and national law. Thus, an advisory opinion that is too closely tied to the specifics of the case, as they seem to be at the time of the referral to the EFTA Court, may turn out to be less helpful than the EFTA Court intended.

On the other hand, an advisory opinion that is too general and abstract may also turn out to be less helpful than anticipated. Often, there is no clear dividing line between general interpretation and concrete application. Further, it may be that the description of the facts of the case and of national law provided by the national court – which are not necessarily either unclear or in dispute – demonstrates to the EFTA Court that the national court may make good use of an answer

[5] Case E-18/11 *Irish Bank Resolution Corporation Ltd*, paras 36–38.

[6] HR-2005-1630-U. From 2016, the traditional mode of referring to judgments by the Supreme Court underwent a change as the paper-based publication Norsk Retstidend (Rt) was discontinued at the end of 2015. From 2016, referrals are made to the Supreme Court's own decision numbers: 'HR-[year]-[number]-[either "A" for judgments by the Supreme Court, or "U" for decisions by the Supreme Court's Appeals Selection Committee, which also rules on certain others matters than leave to appeal, or "F" for decisions by the a single justice]'. For judgments and decisions prior to 2016, referrals are to 'Rt-[year]-[page]' if published in Norsk Retstidend; if not, as with HR-2005-1630-U, the decision number is used. Some Supreme Court judgments have become known under a specific name; in which case this name is used. Other judgments are simply referred to by the decision number or Rt-citation. The decision number, given after judgment has been rendered or the decision made, is not the same as the case number attributed to each case as the appeals are communicated to the Supreme Court by the courts of appeal.

[7] See § 30-3, first paragraph and § 30-6 litra c of the Dispute Act (lov 17 Juni 2005 nr 90 om mekling og rettergang i sivile tvister (tvisteloven)) and Section 388, first paragraph No. 3 of the Criminal Procedure Act (lov 22 mai 1981 nr 25 om rettergangsmåten i straffesaker (Straffeprosessloven)).

that is more detailed than the one envisaged by the national court when making the request.[8]

When a case reaches the Supreme Court, one should think that these problems do not play a role. When selecting judgments for further consideration, the Appeals Selection Committee of the Supreme Court will look for judgments that raise unsolved questions of interpretation of a general interest, rather than judgments where the parties still disagree on the facts of the case or the concrete application of the law. However, the correct general interpretation of national law may well depend on a rather concrete application of EEA law. Typically, one plausible interpretation of national law may raise an issue of proportionality of a restriction on free movement that another plausible interpretation will not. Even though it is well known on a general level how to apply the EEA principle of proportionality, it may be desirable in some cases to get the view of the EFTA Court on the consequences of the principle for a particular rule of national law.

A case in point is *Criminal Proceedings against* N (*NAV I*).[9] For years, persons who had been receiving work-assessment allowance (*arbeidsavklaringspenger*) from the Norwegian Labour and Welfare Administration (NAV) while going abroad without having received an exemption from the obligation to stay in Norway while receiving such an allowance had been convicted of fraud, often receiving a prison sentence. It was clear that the legislature, the Storting, wanted such punishment for violating this 'presence requirement'. In 2019, it came to light that this practice may be contrary to EEA law, in particular the rules on free movement of services and of persons. The defendants themselves, the defence lawyers, the Public Prosecution Service and the courts – or the legislature – had not spotted this problem. At one point within NAV, there were seemingly doubts as to whether the situation was compatible with EEA law, although no action was taken. This 'NAV affair' led to much national debate and soul-searching, where opinions differed on whether the practice really was contrary to EEA law.[10] Earlier convictions were reopened, among them a judgment by the Supreme Court in which only the sentencing, not the conviction as such, had been appealed.[11] On reopening, it was clear that the Supreme Court would also consider the lawfulness of the conviction. In such a case, whatever the conclusion would be, it would gain in authority by being based on an advisory opinion by the EFTA Court. The Supreme Court put several questions to the EFTA Court, among them questions that clearly invited the EFTA Court to conclude on the proportionality of the practice, an invitation to which the EFTA Court responded.[12] In its grand chamber judgment, the Supreme Court accepted the view of the EFTA Court.[13]

[8] On this issue, which the CJEU must also deal with, see a more detailed analysis by OJ Einarsson, 'The Advisory Opinion Procedure and the Relationship between the EFTA Court and the Norwegian Courts: Recent Developments' (2022) *Lov og Rett* 221, in particular 236–38.

[9] Case E-8/20 *Criminal Proceedings against N*.

[10] See the report of the commission of enquiry, *NOU 2020: 9 Blindsonen*, with summary in English in Chapter 3.

[11] Case HR-2017-560-A. For the Supreme Court, the question of principle at that time was whether, in deciding on the correct punishment, account should be taken of the likelihood of getting an exemption from the presence requirement had the person in question applied for it before going abroad.

[12] See the advisory opinion in *Criminal Proceedings against* N (n 9) paras 42 and 107–28.

[13] HR-2021-1453-S at paras 174–84.

In section V, we will revert to the Supreme Court's view of the relevance and weight of advisory opinions. First, we will consider the actual use of the possibility to ask the EFTA Court for guidance on EEA law.

IV. THE SUPREME COURT'S OWN REFERRALS TO THE EFTA COURT

Between 1994 (when the EEA Agreement entered into force) and 2015, the Supreme Court only used the possibility to pose questions to the EFTA Court three times. However, in one of those cases, Rt-1998-330, the request ended up being withdrawn before the EFTA Court had delivered an advisory opinion. This case concerned security for litigation costs. The appeal to the Supreme Court was withdrawn and, consequently, so was the request for an advisory opinion.[14]

The two cases that the Supreme Court did decide after having received advisory opinions in this period were *Finanger I*[15] on motor vehicle insurance and *Paranova*[16] on parallel import of pharmaceuticals. However, the picture would be incomplete without pointing out that the Supreme Court in this period also decided four cases where lower courts had received advisory opinions from the EFTA Court. These were two cases, *Stavanger Catering*[17] and *Bardufoss Flyservice*,[18] respectively, on transfer of undertakings, *Pedicel*[19] on the Norwegian ban on advertisements for alcoholic beverages and *STX*[20] on the posting of workers.

In the same period, it is possible to identify four cases in which requests by one or both parties to the case to submit questions to the EFTA Court were rejected: Rt-2005-1365 (state liability for breach of EEA law), Rt-2007-1003 (state monopoly on gaming machines; the decision not to submit, HR-2005-1630-U, is mentioned above), Rt-2008-354 (motor vehicle insurance and reduction of damages due to own fault by the injured party) and Rt-2010-1500 (state liability for taxes imposed in violation of EEA law). In all four cases, the distinction between general interpretation and concrete application seems to have been an important factor in deciding not to submit.[21]

In a further nine cases in this period, the Supreme Court expressed some doubt with regard to the application of EEA law, without the parties having requested that the EFTA Court be asked for guidance or the Supreme Court doing so of its own motion.[22] In part, this is probably a reflection of the Supreme Court in this period seeing it as mainly up to the parties to take the initiative for questions to be put to the

[14] Rt-1998-330; Case E-5/97 *European Navigation Inc and Star Forsikring AS (uoa)*.

[15] Rt-2000-1811.

[16] Rt-2004-834.

[17] Rt-1997-1965.

[18] Rt-2010-330.

[19] Rt-2009-839.

[20] Rt-2013-258.

[21] For a more detailed analysis, see H Bull, 'Høyesteretts bruk av EU- og EØS-rett' in T Schei, JEA Skoghøy and TM Øie (eds), *Lov Sannhet Rett – Norges Høyesterett 200 år* (Oslo, Universitetsforlaget, 2015) 383–86.

[22] Rt-1999-393, Rt-1999-569, Rt-1999-579, Rt-2001-1390, Rt-2002-391, Rt-2005-1601, Rt-2006-1473, Rt-2012-686 and Rt-2012-761.

EFTA Court, but also in part the reluctance in referring the concrete application of EEA law to the EFTA Court, or the Supreme Court ending up with conclusions that did not really challenge EEA law.[23]

From 2015 until the autumn of 2023, the frequency of referrals to the EFTA Court by the Supreme Court has increased. During this period, the Supreme Court submitted questions in 10 cases, seven of which have already led to judgments, one of which was discontinued due to the appeal being withdrawn and two of which in the autumn of 2023 are still pending.

The seven cases are *Holship* (plenary judgment concerning the legality of a boycott action by dock workers and the right of establishment under EEA law),[24] *Ski Taxi SA* (joint bids for public procurement contracts as a possible restriction on competition),[25] *Thue* (the concept of 'working time' in Directive 2003/88/EC),[26] *Fosen-Linjen II* (the impact of EEA law on national rules on liability for breach of public procurement law),[27] *Kerim* (on the criteria for marriage of convenience in Directive 2004/38/EC),[28] *NAV I* (the compatibility with EEA law of a requirement not to leave Norway without permission while receiving a work assessment allowance, mentioned above in section III)[29] and *Norep* (the understanding of 'commercial agent' in Norwegian law based on Directive 86/653/EEC).[30]

In an eighth case, *Campbell*, the case before the Supreme Court was discontinued due to the appeal being withdrawn.[31] At that point, the EFTA Court had already delivered its advisory opinion to the Supreme Court.[32] The case concerned the derived right of residence in Norway for a third-country national married to a Norwegian national after the couple had been residents of Sweden. It must be understood in conjunction with *Jabbi*[33] before the EFTA Court. We will comment further on these two cases in section VII below.

The two cases that are still pending in the autumn of 2023 are both criminal cases. One concerns COVID-19 restrictions and free movement, and the other revisits the question of derived rights of entry and stay for non-EEA nationals married to EEA nationals, this time as a possible barrier to sanctioning a violation of an expulsion order issued against the non-EEA national.[34]

[23] For further analysis, see Bull (n 21) 387–91.

[24] HR-2016-2554-P; Case E-14/15 *Holship Norge AS v Norsk Transportarbeiderforbund.*

[25] HR-2017-1229-A *Ski Taxi*; Case E-3/16 *Ski Taxi SA, Follo Taxi SA og Ski Follo Taxidrift AS v Staten v/Konkurransetilsynet.*

[26] HR-2018-1036-A; Case E-19/16 *Thorbjørn Selstad Thue v The Norwegian Government.*

[27] HR-2019-1801-A; Case E-7/18 *Fosen-Linjen AS supported by the Confederation of Norwegian Enterprise (Næringslivets Hovedorganisasjon) v AtB AS.* The Frostating Court of Appeal had asked the EFTA Court for guidance in the same case, and the answer of the EFTA Court in Case E-16/16 had generated a debate on whether the answer of the EFTA Court in that case was in line with CJEU case law on this question; see section VI below.

[28] HR-2021-1435-A; Case E-1/20 *Kerim v The Norwegian Government, Represented by the Immigration Appeals Board.*

[29] HR-2021-1453-S; *Criminal Proceedings against N* (n 9).

[30] HR-2022-728-A; Case E-2/21 *Norep AS v Haugen Gruppen AS.*

[31] HR-2020-1146-F.

[32] Case E-4/19 *Campbell v The Norwegian Government, Represented by the Immigration Appeals Board (Utlendingsnemnda – UNE).*

[33] Case E-28/15 *Yankuba Jabbi v The Norwegian Government Represented by the Immigration Appeals Board.*

[34] Case E-5/23 *LDL v Påtalemyndigheten*; Case E-6/23 *MH v Påtalemyndigheten.*

Since 2015, the Supreme Court has also delivered two judgments in which lower courts had already asked the EFTA Court for guidance: first, *Yara* on Norwegian rules on intra-group contributions and the right of establishment,[35] where the EFTA Court had rendered an advisory opinion in the same case; and, second, *NAV II* and *NAV III*, where the advisory opinions concerned two other cases raising the same question of EEA law.[36] Like *NAV I*, the latter judgment of the Supreme Court concerned the presence requirement under Norwegian national insurance law, but this time tied to a different type of benefits, namely unemployment benefits. For this type of benefit, the EFTA Court found that Regulation 883/2004[37] did indeed allow for a presence requirement in the situation obtaining in those two cases.[38] This case and its relationship to *NAV I*[39] is discussed in more detail in section VI below.

In the period after 2015, there seem to be two cases in which the Supreme Court has rejected requests by one of the parties to submit questions to the EFTA Court. These are *CHC Helikopter Service*[40] on the criteria for calculating seniority in connection with workforce reduction, and *ISS Facility Services*[41] on the transfer of undertakings. It seems that the Supreme Court found the general interpretation of relevant EEA law to be sufficiently clarified through CJEU case law.

One may ask what the reasons are for this apparent shift in frequency of requests after 2015. We would caution against making too much out of this. Some of it may simply be the result of coincidence. Relevant cases do not necessarily come at regular intervals.

However, it seems to be a more general trend that it takes some time from new international instruments having been acceded to for their impact on national law to be fully understood by the courts. A case in point is the European Convention on Human Rights (ECHR).[42] Norway acceded to the Convention in 1953. Nevertheless, it was only in the 1990s that it became part of everyday life in Norwegian courts, with a particular impact on criminal procedural law.[43] It is not unreasonable to assume that EEA law has been going through a similar development. As new international rules gradually have more impact on lower courts, the rules will also play a more prominent role for the Supreme Court.

It may be that a few high-profile cases have contributed to increasing the awareness both of parties and courts of EEA law. As already mentioned, the *Holship* case

[35] HR-2019-140-A; Case E-15/16 *Yara International ASA v The Norwegian Government*.

[36] HR-2023-301-A; Case E-13/20 *O v The Norwegian Government Represented by the Labour and Welfare Directorate (Arbeids- og velferdsdirektoratet)* on questions posed by Norwegian National Insurance Court; and Case E-15/20 *Criminal Proceedings against A* on questions posed by the Borgarting Court of Appeal (whose judgment was not appealed to the Supreme Court), both delivered by the EFTA Court on 30 June 2021.

[37] Regulation (EC) No 883/2004 of the European Parliament and of the Council of 29 April 2004 on the coordination of social security systems [2004] OJL166, p 1.

[38] *O v The Norwegian Government* (n 36) and *Criminal Proceedings against A* (n 36), which were delivered on the same day.

[39] HR-2021-1453-S and *Criminal Proceedings against N* (n 9) before the EFTA Court.

[40] HR-2017-1943-A.

[41] HR-2020-1339-A.

[42] Convention for the Protection of Human Rights and Fundamental Freedoms, signed on 4 November 1950.

[43] E Møse, 'Den internasjonale rettens innflytelse i Norge – EMK og andre menneskerettskonvensjoner' in Schei, Skoghøy and Øie (n 21) 324–27.

ended up as a plenary case before the Supreme Court. This made it necessary for the Supreme Court to go into sensitive questions of workers' right to organise. The 'NAV affair' demonstrated the indirect but very real impact that EEA law may have on criminal law and brought home to the courts the importance of verifying whether EEA law may be relevant, even if the parties themselves have not identified any EEA law issue.

V. THE 'ADVISORY' NATURE OF ADVISORY OPINIONS

In the plenary judgment reported in *Finanger I*,[44] the Supreme Court, for the first time, had occasion to comment on the advisory opinions being advisory rather than, as in the EU, judgments that are binding on the requesting national court. On p 1820 of Rt-2000, the Court states that since the opinion was advisory, the Supreme Court had the power and the obligation to decide whether the Supreme Court's judgment should be based on the opinion. For constitutional reasons, the Supreme Court could hardly have taken another view: without a basis in legislation, it could not have declared itself formally bound by a decision that expressly was 'advisory'.[45] However, it went on to state that advisory opinions must be accorded 'significant weight'. This, in the opinion of the Court, followed from the very fact that an EFTA Court had been set up with the task of rendering advisory opinions and that the Norwegian legislature, the Storting, had assumed that the advisory opinions be treated in this way. The Supreme Court also pointed to the expertise of the EFTA Court in a field of law governed by its own legal method, and to the procedure giving EFTA and EU institutions the possibility to submit written observations and make oral submissions.

This view was upheld in *Holship*, where, at paragraph 77, the Supreme Court stated the following:

> In their interpretation of EEA law, however, national courts shall attach considerable importance to the opinions of the EFTA Court concerning the interpretation of EEA law. The purpose of the EFTA Court is, according to the preamble of the Surveillance and Court Agreement, among other things, to 'arrive at and maintain a uniform interpretation and application of the EEA Agreement and those provisions of the Community legislation which are substantially reproduced in that Agreement and to arrive at an equal treatment of individuals and economic operators as regards the four freedoms and the conditions of competition'. The EFTA state's courts must therefore normally apply the EFTA Court's interpretation of EEA law, and cannot disregard an advisory opinion by the EFTA Court unless 'special circumstances' so indicate, cf. Rt-2013-258, paragraphs 93–94, with reference to the plenary judgment of Rt-2000-1811 p. 1820. In order for the EFTA Court to fulfil its intended purpose, the court's interpretation of EEA law cannot normally be disregarded unless there are weighty and compelling reasons for doing so.[46]

[44] Rt-2000-1811.

[45] *Finanger I* was a split decision, but the majority and the minority agreed on this. The dissent concerned another issue.

[46] Also, *Holship* was a split decision, but not on this point.

The reference to 'special circumstances' and Rt-2013-258 concerns the *STX* case on the posting of workers, the only judgment in which the Supreme Court has demonstrated a willingness to disagree with the opinion of the EFTA Court so far. However, as the Supreme Court saw it, this was not decisive for the outcome of the case, and the disagreement turned on how best to understand relevant CJEU case law – the judgment does not demonstrate any willingness to depart from the principle of EU/EEA homogeneity and insist on the Supreme Court's own understanding of EEA law. Rather, as we shall see in section VI, the Supreme Court did not seem convinced that the EFTA Court's understanding of the relevant CJEU case law was on point.

However, the advisory nature of the opinions does mean that the Supreme Court may find it appropriate to give reasons for its acceptance of the interpretation given by the EFTA Court, even if no one has argued against it. Thus, in *Norep*,[47] mentioned above, the justice writing the lead opinion stated the following at paragraphs 47 and 48 after having cited the passage from *Holship* quoted above:

> In other words, an advisory opinion from the EFTA Court may only be disregarded if there are compelling reasons for doing so.
>
> I cannot see that such reasons have been demonstrated in the case at hand. The EFTA Court's statement is clear and builds on a number of sources of EU law. The statement is particularly supported by the ECJ's judgment of 4 June 2020 in Case C-828/18 *Trendsetteuse*.

In *NAV I*,[48] the Supreme Court also found it appropriate to discuss EEA law at some length rather than simply point to the conclusions of the EFTA Court, even though it did not disagree with the EFTA Court, and nor did the prosecution or counsel for the defence. This must be explained by the fact that the conclusions of the EFTA Court meant that Norwegian provisions on national insurance fraud could not be given the intended scope of application, and that different opinions had been voiced in the public debate on whether the presence requirement was compatible with EEA law.

With the opinions of the EFTA Court being advisory, there is also no need to distinguish between opinions rendered in the case at hand and opinions rendered in other cases. The latter carry the same weight as the former insofar as they concern the relevant question. The Supreme Court made this clear in *NAV II*, where, as was pointed out in section IV above, it relied on two advisory opinions by the EFTA Court concerning other cases, but the same question.[49]

VI. THE ADVISORY OPINION VERSUS CJEU CASE LAW

It follows from Article 6 EEA and Article 3 SCA that the case law of the CJEU is of paramount importance when interpreting EEA law. This is also clear from the EFTA

[47] HR-2022-728-A.

[48] HR-2021-1453-S.

[49] HR-2023-301-A, *O v The Norwegian Government* (n 36) and *Criminal Proceedings against A* (n 36) on questions by the Borgarting Court of Appeal. The Norwegian National Insurance Court does not handle criminal cases, so the case before it concerned a claim for refund of unemployment benefits received while abroad. However, the EEA law issue was the same.

Court's own case law. In practice, the EFTA Court has not distinguished between CJEU judgments rendered before and after the signing of the EEA Agreement, as the wording of Article 6 EEA and Article 3 SCA may suggest. Making a distinction on this point would have jeopardised the attainment of homogeneity between EU and EEA law. The Supreme Court of Norway has followed the same line.

However, the case law of the CJEU, as with all case law, is not necessarily unambiguous and completely stable. Opinions may differ on how to apply it to questions and situations that are slightly on the side of what the CJEU has dealt with thus far. On the one hand, this is precisely why an advisory opinion from the EFTA Court may be useful. On the other hand, this may also lead to a discussion on whether the CJEU would agree with the EFTA Court had the same questions been put to the CJEU. When the opinion of the EFTA Court has been challenged before the Supreme Court, and other Norwegian courts, the argument has mostly been that either the EFTA Court has overlooked or misinterpreted relevant CJEU judgments, or that the CJEU has handed down a conflicting judgment after the advisory opinion was issued.

The Supreme Court has treated such situations as a potential 'special circumstance' in which CJEU case law could give 'compelling reasons' to depart from the view of the EFTA Court.

The argument that the advisory opinion of the EFTA Court conflicted with a new judgment from the CJEU was heard in the plenary judgment reported in *Finanger I*[50] on the understanding of the motor insurance directives. The Supreme Court found it necessary to discuss the question in some detail but concluded that the new CJEU judgment did not constitute grounds for departing from the opinion of the EFTA Court.

A new example is *NAV II*.[51] As previously mentioned, this case concerned the presence requirement under Norwegian national insurance law, for being entitled to unemployment benefits. In *O v The Norwegian Government*[52] and *Criminal Proceedings against P*,[53] the EFTA Court had found that, unlike the work assessment allowance it had dealt with in *Criminal Proceedings against N*,[54] which had been found to fall under the provisions on sickness benefits in Regulation 883/2004,[55] unemployment benefits were regulated by Regulation in such a way as to exclude the application of the general principles on free movement as additional grounds for having the right to continue receiving them during temporary stays in other EEA States as long as the unemployed person was still under an obligation to be available for work. Before the case was pleaded before the Supreme Court, the EFTA Court's view was criticised by some scholars for not being in harmony with CJEU case law,[56] and counsel for the defence made the same argument before the Supreme Court. The

[50] Rt-2000-1811.

[51] HR-2023-301-A.

[52] *O v The Norwegian Government* (n 36).

[53] *Criminal Proceedings against A* (n 36), delivered on the same day as *O v The Norwegian Government* (n 36).

[54] *Criminal Proceedings against N* (n 9).

[55] Regulation (EC) No 883/2004 (n 37) 1.

[56] T. Bekkedal and MT Andenæs, 'Er mottakere av dagpenger beskyttet av EØS-avtalens grunnleggende rett til fri bevegelighet?' (2022) *Lov og Rett* 145.

Supreme Court followed the view of the EFTA Court, which had expressly dealt with the CJEU judgments in question.[57] This meant that in the case at hand, the presence requirement could be upheld, even as a basis for criminal liability. However, it did discuss the relevant CJEU case law in detail before it concluded that this case law did not provide 'sufficiently clear grounds to depart from the understanding of the EFTA Court'.[58] In a separate concurring opinion, one justice found reason to explain that even if the critics were right, and the case fell to be examined under the general rules of free movement of services, as had been the case for the work assessment allowance, the Norwegian presence requirement for unemployment benefits, in his view, was a legitimate and proportionate restriction on free movement. The very detailed discussion in *NAV II* should probably be understood against the background of this being a criminal case, and the difference between the view of the EFTA Court and the view of the critics meant the difference between conviction and acquittal.

As previously mentioned, *STX*[59] on the posting of workers is the only example of a Supreme Court judgment signalling disagreement with the opinion of the EFTA Court so far. In this case, there were no CJEU judgments that directly dealt with the same questions that the EFTA Court had answered. The Supreme Court seems to have found the view of the EFTA Court hard to reconcile with the wording of the directive in question and was not convinced that the CJEU judgments to which the EFTA Court had referred really could be interpreted in the way in which the EFTA Court had done.

It has been debated whether the Supreme Court should have stayed the proceedings and asked the EFTA Court for a new advisory opinion in a request where it explained its doubts rather than proceeding to signal this to the EFTA Court directly in the judgment. It may be that the Supreme Court did not see the need for a new advisory opinion because, in its view, the disagreement was not on a point that really decided the outcome of the case.

In a later case, the Supreme Court took the opportunity to ask again when there had been a discussion on whether the EFTA Court's opinion was in harmony with CJEU case law. *Fosen* concerned liability for the contracting authority after a public tender competition for new car ferries had been cancelled due to error in the competition base. In an advisory opinion to the Frostating Court of Appeal,[60] the EFTA Court seemed to conclude that EU and EEA law demanded strict liability. A debate arose as to whether the EFTA Court had interpreted CJEU case law correctly, centring on the relationship between the judgments in *Strabag*,[61] which could be interpreted to require strict liability, and *Combinatie Spijker*,[62] which was based on the concept of a 'sufficiently serious' breach. In its judgment, the Frostating Court of Appeal voiced its doubts about the EFTA Court's conclusion on this point, but found that in any case,

[57] Case C-406/04 *Gérald De Cuyper v Office national de l'emploi*, ECLI:EU:C:2006:49; C-228/07 *Jörn Petersen v Landesgeschäftsstelle des Arbeitsmarktservice Niederösterreich*, ECLI:EU:C:2008:494.

[58] Paragraph 116 of the judgment in HR-2023-301-A (n 51).

[59] Rt-2013-258.

[60] HR-2023-301-A; Case E-16/16 *Fosen-Linjen AS v AtB AS*.

[61] Case C-314/09 *Strabag and Others* ECLI:EU:C:2010:567.

[62] Case C-568/08 *Combinatie Spijker and Others*, ECLI:EU:C:2010:751.

there was not a sufficient causal link between the breach and the loss of the positive contract interest.

When the case reached the Supreme Court, the Court requested a new advisory opinion, citing new judgments of the CJEU as one reason why the EFTA Court might wish to reconsider its view on liability. In its advisory opinion in *Fosen-Linjen AS*,[63] the EFTA Court, where incidentally two of the three judges had not participated in the previous case, now concluded that liability could be made contingent on a 'sufficiently serious' breach of EEA law, and the Supreme Court endorsed this view.[64]

The *Fosen* cases are a good example of the 'partner-like' relationship between the EFTA Court and national courts.

VII. THE MEANING OF 'HOMOGENEITY'

Another area where the Supreme Court has engaged in a partner-like dialogue with the EFTA Court concerns the meaning of 'homogeneity' between EU law and EEA law. Does it mean homogeneous results even if a homogeneous understanding of the relevant legal sources suggests otherwise, or does it mean homogeneous understanding of the legal sources even if it leads to heterogeneous results?

This may seem like an odd question: a homogeneous understanding of legal sources is the best guarantee for homogeneous results. The problem nevertheless arises in areas where EU law has moved on from EEA law, and the CJEU bases its interpretation of provisions that form part both of EU law and EEA law on legal sources that are part only of EU law, not EEA law.

So far, this question has presented itself in the area of free movement of persons. Directive 2004/38/EC on free movement of persons[65] forms part of the EEA Agreement. Building on a previous generation of directives that were also part of the EEA Agreement,[66] the Directive extends a right to free movement, on certain conditions, beyond workers and self-employed persons, to groups that are not economically active, such as students and pensioners. According to the CJEU, the directive does not give a third-country national married to an EU Member State national a derived right to settle with his or her spouse in the home state of the EU Member State national after the latter has exercised his or her right to free movement by residing, with the third-country national, in another EU Member State. However, according to the

[63] Case E-7/18 *Fosen-Linjen AS Supported by the Confederation of Norwegian Enterprise (Næringslivets Hovedorganisasjon) v AtB AS.*

[64] On these judgments of the EFTA Court, see A Sanchez-Graells, 'The *Fosen-Linjen* Saga: Not So Simple after All?', ch 18 in this volume.

[65] Directive 2004/38/EC of the European Parliament and of the Council of 29 April 2004 on the right of citizens of the Union and their family members to move and reside freely within the territory of the Member States amending Regulation (EEC) No 1612/68 and repealing Directives 64/221/EEC, 68/360/EEC, 72/194/EEC, 73/148/EEC, 75/34/EEC, 75/35/EEC, 90/364/EEC, 90/365/EEC and 93/96/EEC [2004] OJL158, p 77.

[66] Directive 90/364/EEC on the right of residence, Directive 90/365/EEC on the right of residence for employees and self-employed persons who have ceased their occupational activity and Directive 93/96/EEC on the right of residence for students.

CJEU, an analogous right does exist by virtue of Article 21(1) of the Treaty on the Functioning of the European Union (TFEU) on free movement for Union citizens.[67]

This question does not arise when the EU Member State citizen has resided, together with the third-country spouse, in another EU Member State as an employed or self-employed person. In that case, it follows from the general rules on free movement of workers and the right of establishment that are part of both TFEU and the EEA Agreement that both may settle in the home country of the EU Member State national, provided certain conditions are fulfilled.[68] This means that the principle that the CJEU has established based on Union citizenship has limited practical importance.

There is no EEA equivalent to Union citizenship. This concept entered EU law after the EEA Agreement had been negotiated. In light of the more limited objectives of the EEA Agreement compared to that of the EU, it is in any case not obvious that a parallel concept of 'EEA citizenship' would have been included in the EEA Agreement.

This leaves a potential gap between EU law and EEA law. Even if it has limited practical importance, it is of course quite decisive for those individuals that risk falling into the gap.

In *Jabbi*,[69] the EFTA Court, in an advisory opinion to the Oslo District Court, closed the gap by coming to the conclusion that Directive 2004/38 as part of the EEA Agreement did indeed establish a derived right for third-country nationals to settle in the home country of their EEA State national spouse after the couple had lived together in another EEA State. In its judgment,[70] the Borgarting Court of Appeal remarked that it saw a 'certain tension' between CJEU case law and the opinion of the EFTA Court, but found that the conditions that had to be fulfilled according to the EFTA Court were in any case not fulfilled. Leave to appeal was denied by the Appeals Selection Committee of the Supreme Court.[71]

Another case raising the same question, *Campbell*, did reach the Supreme Court. In the oral hearing, the attorney representing the state invited the Supreme Court to reject the view of the EFTA Court in *Jabbi* as not consistent with the principle of homogeneity. This principle, it was argued, meant that in this case there was indeed a different outcome in EU law and EEA law. The Supreme Court stayed the proceedings and asked the EFTA Court for a new advisory opinion, again citing new case law from the CJEU in which the CJEU had confirmed its view that Directive 2004/38 on its own did not provide a derived right of residence for third-country spouses. In its response, in *Campbell*,[72] the EFTA Court held on to its view in *Jabbi*, but elaborated on its reasoning. It pointed out, among other things, that since no parallel to

[67] Case C-456/12 *O v Minister voor Immigratie, Integratie en Asiel and Minister voor – 10 – Immigratie, Integratie en Asiel v B.*, ECLU:EU:C 2014:135. One could perhaps ask whether the CJEU would have found such a right in the directive had there been no Art 21 TFEU on the right of free movement for EU citizens.

[68] See, for instance, Case C-291/05 *Minister voor Vreemdelingenzaken en Integratie v RNG Eind*, ECLI:EU:C:2007:771.

[69] *Yankuba Jabbi v The Norwegian Government* (n 33).

[70] LB-2017-98329-2 *A mot staten ved Utlendingsnemnda*.

[71] HR-2018-1711-U.

[72] *Campbell v The Norwegian Government* (n 32).

Article 21 TFEU exists in EEA law, the Directive must be interpreted differently in the EEA than in an EU context in order to realise the objective of the Directive, namely, above all, to facilitate and strengthen the exercise of the primary and individual right to move and reside freely within the territory of the EEA States.[73]

Before the Supreme Court could hold its second oral hearing, which this time was to take place before the grand chamber, Ms Campbell withdrew her appeal. The Supreme Court never got to continue its dialogue with the EFTA Court on this issue.

VIII. A DIALOGUE ALSO WITH THE ECtHR

In *Holship*,[74] on the legality of a boycott action by dock workers, it was argued before the Supreme Court that if EEA law prevented the boycott action from going ahead, EEA law would conflict with the freedom of association under Article 11 ECHR.[75] One could see this as a question of whether the boycott action, as an exercise of freedom of association, constituted a legitimate, including proportionate, restriction on free movement.[76] In its advisory opinion, the EFTA Court had very strongly suggested that the boycott in question could not otherwise be deemed to pursue an aim that could legitimately justify a restriction on free movement. Alternatively, one could see this as a question of whether declaring the boycott unlawful in the interest of free movement fulfilled the criteria, including proportionality, for restricting the freedom of association. In practice, the application of the principle of proportionality under both EU/EEA law and Article 11 ECHR was the central question under both approaches.[77] The Supreme Court[78] based itself on the pragmatic assumption that in conducting this test on the issue at hand, the CJEU, the EFTA Court, the ECtHR and the Norwegian Supreme Court would come to the same conclusions.[79] The Supreme Court then conducted the proportionality test from the starting point of EEA law.[80]

The case was brought before the ECtHR, which accepted the view of the Supreme Court that there was no violation of Article 11 ECHR.[81] In that sense, the Supreme Court's pragmatic approach to the proportionality test was proven right. However, as a matter of principle, the ECtHR did remark that from its perspective, the EEA

[73] Paragraph 57 of the advisory opinion.

[74] *Holship* (n 24).

[75] Convention for the Protection of Human Rights and Fundamental Freedoms.

[76] See paras 125–27 of the advisory opinion.

[77] For a more in-depth discussion, see TM Øie and H Bull, 'Fundamental Rights and Fundamental Law: The 2014 Revision of the Norwegian Constitution' in G Selvik, M-J Clifton, T Haas, L Lourenço and K Schwiesow (eds), *The Art of Judicial Reasoning: Festschrift in Honour of Carl Baudenbacher* (Cham, Springer, 2019).

[78] This was a split decision. The position of the minority meant that it did not have an opinion on this question.

[79] *Holship* (n 24) para 86. An English translation of the judgment is to be found on the website of the Supreme Court of Norway.

[80] ibid paras 110 et seq. The Supreme Court then avoided having to give a definitive answer to the question of whether the protection of freedom of association under Art 11 ECHR extended to boycott actions. This was also in dispute, and, at the time, there was no clear answer in the ECtHR case law.

[81] *Norwegian Confederation of Trade Unions (LO) and Norwegian Transport Workers Union (NTF) v Norway*, App No 45487/17.

freedom of establishment was not a counterbalancing fundamental right to freedom of association, but rather one element, albeit an important one, to be taken into consideration in the assessment of proportionality under Article 11, paragraph 2 ECHR on the criteria for legitimate restrictions on the freedom of association.[82]

It is logical that a court, whether national or international, considers its own legal system to be the starting point for legal reasoning. However, this means that national courts must balance potentially conflicting international instruments, each with its own international court. National courts may find it hard to satisfy all of them. With different starting points in EU law, EEA law and human rights law, there is no guarantee that the result will always be the same.

Probably, the remark by the ECtHR should be seen as part of a dialogue not only with the Norwegian Supreme Court and the EFTA Court, but also – and perhaps most importantly – with the CJEU. The judgments of the CJEU in *Viking Line*[83] and *Laval*[84] concerning industrial action and the principles of free movement were central to the *Holship* case. In its judgments in these cases, the CJEU recognised the right to collective action as a fundamental right under EU law, and then, after observing that this right may be made subject to certain restrictions,[85] went on to discuss whether, in the cases at hand, it constituted legitimate grounds for accepting proportionate restrictions on free movement.[86] The EU as such is not party to the ECHR, but discussions on its accession are ongoing. It is tempting to think that in *Holship*, the ECtHR took the opportunity to send a signal to the CJEU that under the ECHR, the approach to balancing EU and ECtHR rights is different from that applied by the CJEU in *Viking Line* and *Laval*.

IX. CONCLUDING REMARKS

Since 1994, the relationship between the Norwegian Supreme Court and the EFTA Court has developed and intensified. The number of requests for advisory opinions has increased. This development seems to continue, with two requests having been made in 2023. High-profile cases in the last 10 years or so, most notably *Holship* and the two NAV cases, have alerted Norwegian courts to the impact of EEA law.

The Supreme Court has introduced measures to better identify possible EEA law issues that the parties may not have seen themselves as the appeals are prepared for consideration by the Appeals Selection Committee. One can also see a tendency to

[82] *Holship* (n 24) para 118.

[83] Case C-438/05 *International Transport Workers' Federation and Finnish Seamen's Union v Viking Line ABP and OÜ Viking Line Eesti*, ECLI:EU:C:2007:292.

[84] Case C-341/05 *Laval un Partneri Ltd v Svenska Byggnadsarbetareförbundet, Svenska Byggnadsarbetareförbundets avd 1, Byggettan, Svenska Elektrikerförbundet, Svenska Elektrikerförbundet*, ECLI:EU:C:2007:809.

[85] *Viking Line* (n 83) para 77, referring to para 74 of Case C-112/00 *Schmidberger*, *Laval* (n 84).

[86] *Viking Line* (n 83) paras 78 et seq; *Laval* (n 84) paras 94 et seq. It seems that in *Viking Line*, the CJEU treated the right to take collection action mostly as a means of attaining a wider aim of protection of workers and not really as part of a right to assembly as a fundamental right and legitimate aim in itself.

ask the EFTA Court for advice in cases where the parties themselves have not asked for it, as in *Ski Taxi*.[87]

The close connection of EEA law to EU law, but also, as demonstrated by *Holship*, to human rights law poses challenges to national courts and the EFTA Court alike. The willingness of the EFTA Court to engage in dialogue with national supreme courts is the best guarantee for a continued fruitful development of both EEA law and national law.

[87] HR-2017-1229-A.

11

EFTA Court Decisions as a Source of Law in Norway

OLA MESTAD

I. INTRODUCTION

What importance do EFTA Court decisions have in Norway as a source of law? This question has been responded to several times by the Norwegian Supreme Court in slightly different ways. The phrasing of the answer has developed somewhat since 1994 when the EEA Agreement came into force. This chapter sets out to discuss how the Norwegian Supreme Court approaches EFTA Court judgments in cases where EEA law questions are involved – and what it does not say.[1]

The leading case today is the *NAV* case from July 2021, which the Supreme Court, sitting in Grand Chamber, decided unanimously. An advisory opinion from the EFTA Court had been asked for and given to the Supreme Court (*Criminal Proceedings against N*).[2] The case concerned whether the Norwegian statutory rule requiring recipients of work assessment allowance ('arbeidsavklaringspenger') to stay in Norway to receive the benefit was a violation of EEA law, which the EFTA Court and the Supreme Court found to be the case.[3]

The Supreme Court set out its opinion on the use of EFTA Court judgments, which will be examined in section III below.

Section II will recall the legal background of the system behind EFTA Court decisions and their role in EEA law. Section IV will study the historical development of the Supreme Court's approach to EFTA Court judgments from the 1990s until the *NAV* case, examining the different ways in which the Supreme Court has expressed itself and the extent to which it has followed the EFTA Court.

[1] Special thanks to Professor Dr Matthias Ruffert for excellent working conditions at the Walter Hallstein-Institut für Europäisches Verfassungsrecht, Humboldt-Universität zu Berlin in the autumn of 2023 and to Ólafur J Einarsson for valuable comments to the draft version of this chapter.

[2] Case E-8/20 *Criminal Proceedings against N*, judgment of 5 May 2021.

[3] HR-2021-1453-S *NAV*. An unofficial English translation of the judgment is available at: www.domstol.no/globalassets/upload/hret/decisions-in-english-translation/hr-2021-1453-s.pdf.

Special importance should be given to what the Supreme Court has stated when sitting in plenary session (all judges) and Grand Chamber (13 out of 21 judges). Section V analyses the development after the *NAV* case. In section VI, we will discuss the relationship between the interpretation and application of EEA law. In section VII, we will examine more closely the content of the Supreme Court's dictum stating the rule that 'the EFTA Court's interpretation of EEA law may not be challenged without "weighty and compelling reasons"'[4] (in Norwegian: 'gode og tungtveiende grunner for det').[5] Section VIII addresses the relationship between the facts of an EFTA Court case and the impact it has in Norwegian law, while section IX adds a discussion on the subsequent use of observations submitted to the EFTA Court and section X draws some conclusions.

What sort of reasons might be 'weighty and compelling'? We will examine what the area of application is for this rule. In the *NAV* case, as well as in several other cases, the Supreme Court itself had asked the EFTA Court for an opinion. Does the same rule apply with respect to other judgments of the EFTA Court – for example, when the judgment is rendered in another case, or where the opinion of the EFTA Court is expressed in a case against one of the EEA EFTA States, or in a case against the EFTA Surveillance Authority (ESA)? Is the application by the Norwegian courts of EFTA Court decisions different from their direct application of decisions from the Court of Justice of the European Union (CJEU) itself? And what about the different parts of an EFTA Court judgment: statements about law, statements about facts, and in between, the application of the law in the assessment of the final outcome of a case.[6]

II. THE LEGAL FRAMEWORK

The legal basis for the advisory opinion of the EFTA Court is the first paragraph of Article 34 of the Agreement between EFTA States on the Establishment of a Surveillance Authority and a Court of Justice (SCA). The wording is as follows: 'The EFTA Court shall have jurisdiction to give advisory opinions on the interpretation of the EEA Agreement.' What is important here is the concept of *interpretation*. Part IV of the SCA also lays down other provisions conferring jurisdictions on the EFTA Court; for the purposes of this chapter, Article 31 SCA concerning infringement proceedings is of relevance, as will be set out below. The advisory opinion procedure

[4] ibid para 65.

[5] Literally, this means 'good and heavy weighing reasons'.

[6] For a general study of the Norwegian Supreme Court's relationship with EU and EEA law, see H Bull, 'Høyesteretts bruk av EU- og EØS-rett' in G Bergby et al (eds), *Lov, sannhet, rett* (Oslo, Universitetsforlaget, 2015) 358–92 – on the application of EFTA Court decisions, see 368–73. For another broad type of study, see HH Fredriksen, EU/EØS-rett i norske domstoler, *Rapport # 3 til Europautredningen*, 2011, studying different aspects of the use of EEA law and EU law in the Norwegian legal system, and with some comments of the effect of EFTA Court decisions at 81–83. See also a shorter but updated presentation of the effect of EFTA Court decisions: F Arnesen et al, *Oversikt over EØS-retten* (Oslo, Universitetsforlaget, 2022) 519–22; and for a somewhat more reluctant analysis of any special effects of EFTA Court decisions, see HH Fredriksen and G Mathisen, *EØS-rett* (Bergen, Fagbokforlaget, 2022) 377–81.

is closely related to the EU law system of preliminary references in accordance with Article 267 of the Treaty on the Functioning of the European Union (TFEU). However, such rulings in the EU law system are binding on the national court which asks for the ruling.[7]

The overarching principle of Norwegian courts' application of EFTA Court decisions, and EEA law in general, is the principle of homogeneity based on express provisions of the EEA Agreement and the SCA, Article 6 EEA and Article 3(2) SCA, as well as considerations of loyalty as laid down under Article 3 EEA.[8]

III. THE *NAV* CASE

The *NAV* case was decided by the Supreme Court in Grand Chamber in July 2021 and the decision was unanimous. As mentioned in section I above, this is the most recent of the Grand Chamber and plenary cases of the Norwegian Supreme Court with respect to EEA law. At issue was whether it was a violation of EEA law that the Norwegian statutory rule required recipients of the work assessment allowance ('arbeidsavklaringspenger') to stay in Norway to receive the benefit (with some exceptions). In translation, the rule was worded: 'It is a condition for the entitlement to work assessment allowance that the member stays in Norway.'[9]

The Supreme Court unanimously found that this was a violation. In 2017, the recipient of the allowance had been sentenced by the Supreme Court itself to 75 days of imprisonment for social security fraud because he had not informed the Labour and Welfare Administration that he had been abroad. Following a lengthy discussion in Norway about the content of EEA law in this respect, the criminal case was later reopened because of the possible violation of EEA law. In the new case, he was acquitted.

In the case, the EFTA Court, after being asked by the Supreme Court itself, had given a judgment on the 16 questions that the Supreme Court had asked (*Criminal Proceedings against N*). Even if the opinion of the EFTA Court is advisory according to Article 34 SCA, the Supreme Court reiterated that the rule is that 'the EFTA Court's interpretation of EEA law may not be challenged without "weighty and compelling reasons"'.[10]

Because the person had been convicted for receiving benefits both before and after 1 June 2012, the case concerned two different questions of EEA law: one with respect to Articles 7 and 21 of Regulation (EC) No 883/2004 on social security coordination,

[7] See P Christiansen, 'Commentary on Article 34' in F Arnesen et al (eds), *Agreement on the European Economic Area: A Commentary* (Baden-Baden, Nomos, 2018) and M Broberg and N Fenger, *Preliminary References to the European Court of Justice*, 3rd edn (Oxford, Oxford University Press, 2021), which has a separate section on the EFTA system and does some comparison of the two systems at 8–14. See also OJ Einarsson, 'The Advisory Opinion Procedure and the Relationship between the EFTA Court and the Norwegian Courts: Recent Developments' (2022) *Lov og Rett* 221, at 223–26.

[8] See the interesting reflections on how the principle of homogeneity has been developed under the EEA Agreement in P Wennerås, 'Commentary on Article 6' in Arnesen et al (n 7).

[9] Section 11-3, sub-s 1 of the National Insurance Act (LOV-1997-02-28-19).

[10] *NAV* (n 3) para 65.

which was incorporated into the EEA Agreement from 1 June 2012; and the other with respect to the earlier period, which was assessed in relation to Article 36 EEA on the freedom to provide services.

On the effect of a judgment by the EFTA Court, the Supreme Court started out by referring to the jurisdiction of the EFTA Court to give advisory opinions set out in the first paragraph of Article 34 SCA.[11] Then it continued:

(64) The EFTA Court's opinions are not formally binding. The national court must therefore independently decide on the interpretation and application of EEA law in the individual case. However, when interpreting EEA law, the national court must 'attach considerable importance to the opinions of the EFTA Court concerning the interpretation of EEA law' see the Supreme Court judgment HR-2016-2554-P *Holship* paragraph 77. The following is specified in the same paragraph:

> In their interpretation of EEA law, however, national courts shall attach considerable importance to the opinions of the EFTA Court concerning the interpretation of EEA law. The purpose of the EFTA Court is, according to the preamble of the Surveillance and Court Agreement, among other things, to 'arrive at and maintain a uniform interpretation and application of the EEA Agreement and those provisions of the Community legislation which are substantially reproduced in that Agreement and to arrive at an equal treatment of individuals and economic operators as regards the four freedoms and the conditions of competition'. The EFTA state's courts must therefore normally apply the EFTA Court's interpretation of EEA law, and cannot disregard an advisory opinion by the EFTA Court unless 'special circumstances' so indicate, *cf* Rt-2013-258 [*STX*], paragraphs 93–94, with reference to the plenary judgment of Rt-2000-1811 [*Finanger I*] page 1820. In order for the EFTA Court to fulfil its intended purpose, the court's interpretation of EEA law cannot normally be disregarded unless there are weighty and compelling reasons for doing so.[12]

(65) In other words, the EFTA Court's interpretation of EEA law may not be challenged [better: 'deviated from'] without 'weighty and compelling reasons'.[13] With regard to the further distribution of jurisdiction between the EFTA Court and the national court, the following is set out in paragraph 78:

> The EFTA Court has jurisdiction to give advisory opinions on the interpretation of EEA law, *cf* Article 34, paragraph 1, of the Surveillance and Court Agreement. The assessment of evidence falls under the jurisdiction of the courts of each EFTA State. The same normally applies to the application of the law to the facts, but there is no clear distinction here. How far the EFTA Court will go in describing EEA law in minute detail, will, among other things, depend on the questions posed by the EFTA State's court and the level of detail included in the request.

(66) Many EEA rules are by nature approximate or appear as general principles. For instance, when interpreting and applying the basic freedoms in the main part of the EEA Agreement, one must assess whether the restrictions are suitable, necessary and proportionate. The EFTA Court's task is thus to give specifying guidelines

[11] ibid para 63.

[12] See HR-2016-2554-P *Holship*, para 77.

[13] In Norwegian: 'EFTA-domstolens forståelse av EØS-retten kan altså ikke fravikes uten at det foreligger "gode og tungtveiende grunner for det".'

> for the application of the EEA rule, and to clarify which aspects should be emphasised. The findings of fact and the individual decision whether a national provision or regulation is compatible with EEA law, are assigned to the national court. To the extent the EFTA Court has carried out more specific assessments, for instance based on the questions referred by the national court, this may be of help to the national court. However, such statements considered in isolation carry less weight than direct statements from the Court regarding the interpretation of EEA law. This follows already from the fact that the EFTA Court, in interpretation cases referred by national courts, considers neither the facts of the case nor the content of the national legislation.

As is apparent, the Supreme Court quotes the plenary case *Holship*,[14] from 2016, which in turn quotes the *STX* case from 2013,[15] which then again in the quote refers to the plenary case *Finanger I* from 2000.[16] This looks like a line of precedent, leaving aside the question of whether it is reasonable to say that a theory of precedent also applies to methodological questions and not only to issues of substantive law. This requires a further examination of the historical development of the Supreme Court's reasoning on this question.

IV. THE DEVELOPMENT OF SUPREME COURT GUIDANCE ON EFTA COURT DECISIONS BEFORE THE *NAV* CASE

A. From *Eidesund* to *Finanger II*

The first judgments of the EFTA Court were handed down in 1994. Since then, the Norwegian Supreme Court has pronounced its opinion on the application of EFTA Court decisions in several cases and in somewhat different ways.

The first Supreme Court case is the *Eidesund* case from 1997.[17] This was an ordinary Supreme Court case decided by five judges. The EFTA Court had given an advisory opinion in *Eidesund*[18] after this had been requested by Gulating Court of Appeal. The case concerned the interpretation of the Directive on Transfer of Undertakings.[19]

With respect to the effect of EFTA Court and CJEU decisions, the Supreme Court stated that the CJEU 'has in a line of cases given its opinion on the more precise content of the directive and there are also several opinions by the EFTA Court'.[20] Then, the Supreme Court gave a few statements on the source of law impact of the decisions. First, it quoted Article 6 EEA and Article 3(2) SCA (referred to above).

[14] *Holship* (n 12).

[15] Rt-2013-258 *STX*.

[16] Rt-2000-1811 *Finanger I*.

[17] Rt 1997 p 1965 *Eidesund*.

[18] Case E-2/95 *Eidesund* [1995–96] EFTA Ct Rep 1.

[19] Council Directive 77/187/EEC on the approximation of the laws of the Member States relating to the safeguarding of employees' rights in the event of transfers of undertakings, businesses or parts of businesses [1977] OJ L61/26.

[20] *Eidesund* (n 17) 1970 (author's translation).

To this, it added that the distinction between previous and subsequent CJEU decisions was not of significance in the case at hand.

The two provisions cited by the Supreme Court are, as we have seen in section II above, the two most important binding provisions on homogeneity between EU law and EEA law with respect to the relevant areas. Thereafter, with respect to EFTA Court decisions, the Supreme Court briefly stated that the statements by the EFTA Court are 'advisory', referring to Article 34 SCA. Nothing more was said about the effect of EFTA Court decisions. However, in its final decision in the case, the Supreme Court found in line with the EFTA Court decision as well as CJEU decisions.[21] In this case, it may appear as if the Supreme Court did not distinguish between the weight allocated to EFTA Court cases and CJEU cases.

This brief treatment changed with the first plenary case on EEA law in the Supreme Court, the *Finanger I* case.[22] The Supreme Court itself had asked the EFTA Court whether the Norwegian legislation on motor vehicle insurance was, on one specific point, in violation of the relevant EEA directives. The EFTA Court found this to be the case in its opinion in *Finanger*.[23]

With respect to the effect of the EFTA Court decision, the justice delivering judgment on behalf of the majority in the Supreme Court, also with full support on this point from the minority, stated:

> The EFTA Court's opinion is of an advisory nature, *cf* Article 34 of the Surveillance and Court Agreement between EFTA and the Norwegian State. This means that the Supreme Court has the authority and duty to consider independently whether and to what extent the Supreme Court's decision should be based on this opinion.
>
> Nevertheless, I find that significant importance ['vesentlig vekt'] must be attributed to the opinion. This follows in my view from the fact that the EFTA States, in accordance with Article 108(2) of the EEA Agreement, upon entering into the Surveillance and Court Agreement found reason to establish this court, one of the reasons being the need to reach and maintain uniformity in the interpretation and application of the EEA Agreement. Real reasons also support this assumption.[24]

The majority in the Supreme Court reasoned as follows. The legal method ('rettskildebruken') applied in EEA law may deviate from the national legal method. This should allow the EFTA Court with its special knowledge to render judgments with significant authority. In this connection, the Supreme Court points to the procedure before the EFTA Court that gives the EEA States (EFTA and EU) as well as ESA and the European Commission the opportunity to give their views on the questions raised. Finally, the Supreme Court refers to the opinion of the Norwegian government, given when the EEA Agreement was presented to the Norwegian Parliament for ratification, according to which it must be assumed 'that the national court will base its decision on the opinion of the EFTA Court when applying Norwegian rules of law on issues covered by the provisions of the EEA Agreement'.[25]

[21] Referring to the EFTA Court decision at 1971–75.
[22] *Finanger I* (n 16) 1811.
[23] Case E-1/99 *Finanger* [1999] EFTA Ct Rep 119.
[24] *Finanger I* (n 16) 1820. This translation is taken from the English translation in *STX* (n 15) para 93.
[25] Quote taken from Storting proposition no 100 (1991–92) 33 (author's translation).

On these matters, the minority of the Court was in complete agreement with the majority, stating that the opinion of the EFTA Court 'must be given significant weight for the reasons [the majority spokesman] mentions'.[26]

When read against the statements in the *Eidesund* case, it seems clear that the Supreme Court now gives more weight to EFTA Court decisions. They are special.

On the substance, the Supreme Court, both the majority as well as the minority, agreed with the EFTA Court that the Norwegian motor vehicle insurance rule in question violated the relevant motor vehicle insurance directives. The disagreement between the majority and the minority concerned what the consequence of this should be under Norwegian law. That does not interest us here.

The statements in *Finanger I* were explicitly followed in *Paranova*, where the Supreme Court had asked the EFTA Court for its advisory opinion on a question about parallel imports.[27] The Supreme Court followed the opinion of the EFTA Court.[28] It also added some remarks about the effect of EFTA Court decisions. First, it referred to the general remarks given in the *Finanger I* case (quoted above).[29] Then the justice delivering the Supreme Court's judgment added:

> In my opinion, much is needed, to make the Supreme Court deviate from what the [EFTA] Court says about the understanding of the EEA law provisions, and especially so in a field like the one at hand, where the EU/EEA law is specialised and developed.[30]

If there is any change in the tone from the *Finanger I* case to this ruling, it is that even more weight should be put on EFTA Court decisions, at least in specialised fields of the law. However, the Court added that it was the task of the EFTA Court to interpret EEA law, not to assess evidence and undertake the specific application of the law to the facts, as the EFTA Court itself had also stated in its opinion.

In another case from the same year, *Volvoimport*, about protection of trade marks, the Supreme Court simply referred to what had been stated in the *Paranova* case, and also quoted part of what had been said by the EFTA Court in that case.[31]

The *Finanger* case complex came before the Supreme Court again, also this time as a plenary case, in *Finanger II*.[32] Now it concerned state liability for the wrongful implementation of the motor vehicle insurance directives. The full Supreme Court found that there was a principle of state liability in EEA law and basically agreed on the content of the principle. However, with respect to the application of the principle, there were differing opinions. The majority of nine judges found the state liable for the wrongful implementation of the directives, while four judges dissented. The Supreme Court had decided not to ask the EFTA Court for its opinion, but relied

[26] *Finanger I* (n 16) 1835. Norwegian original: 'må tillegges betydelig vekt av de grunner han nevner'.

[27] Rt 2004 p 904 *Paranova*. No translation of the Supreme Court judgment is available. Case E-3/02 *Paranova* [2003] EFTA Ct Rep 101.

[28] *Paranova* (n 27) paras 65 and 66.

[29] *Finanger I* (n 16) 1820.

[30] Rt 2004 p 904, para 67 (author's translation). In Norwegian: 'Etter min mening skal det meget til for at Høyesterett skal fravike det domstolen uttaler om forståelsen av de EØS-rettslige bestemmelsene, og ganske særlig på et område som det foreliggende, hvor EU/EØS-retten er spesialisert og utviklet.'

[31] Rt 2004 p 1474 *Volvoimport*, paras 39 and 40.

[32] Rt 2005 p 1365 *Finanger II*. An unofficial English translation of the judgment is available at: www.domstol.no/globalassets/upload/hret/decisions-in-english-translation/hr-2005-1690-p.pdf.

heavily on previous EFTA Court decisions, as well as on CJEU decisions. The EFTA Court advisory opinions were the well-known rulings in *Sveinbjörnsdóttir*[33] and *Karlsson*,[34] both given in response to requests for advisory opinion from courts in Iceland.

With respect to the effect of advisory opinions from the EFTA Court, the Supreme Court referred[35] in some detail to what had been stated in *Finanger I*.[36] The spokeswoman for the majority stated that she found 'the argumentation of the EFTA Court in favour of state liability convincing, with its emphasis on the basic considerations of homogeneity, equal treatment of individuals/legal persons and protection of their activities'.[37] She also added that there is an underlying assumption of liability in the EEA Agreement and that this is covered under section 1 of the Norwegian EEA Act. She mentioned that the Norwegian government was of the same opinion and that the Supreme Court of Iceland had come to the same result in its judgment in the *Sveinbjörnsdóttir* case.

No distinction was made by the Supreme Court between the emphasis on advisory opinions given in the case at hand and other advisory opinions given by the EFTA Court.

B. From *Gaming Machines* to *Non-economic Loss*

The weight granted to a different type of decision by the EFTA Court, a judgment in infringement proceedings under Article 31 SCA, was considered in the *Gaming Machines* case.[38] The Supreme Court had to decide a case concerning the Norwegian legislation giving a monopoly to the state-owned undertaking Norsk Tipping AS to operate gaming machines in Norway. The case is also often called the *Norsk Tipping* case, even though that enterprise was not a party to the case.

Before the Supreme Court, the parties to the case were, on the one hand, an association of lottery and gaming machine owners and, on the other hand, the Norwegian government. *ESA v Norway*[39] was closely related and had been decided by the EFTA Court earlier in the same year. In infringement proceedings, the EFTA Court renders binding judgments and also has full jurisdiction with respect to the facts. One question before the Supreme Court was what effect such a decision should have on the Supreme Court case. It was obvious that the case would be relevant because the planned hearing, in plenary session, of the Supreme Court had been stayed due to the upcoming case in Luxembourg.[40]

After the EFTA Court had found in favour of the Norwegian government, the Supreme Court decided, after all, to hear the case in an ordinary sitting of five

[33] Case E-9/97 *Sveinbjörnsdóttir* [1998] EFTA Ct Rep 95.
[34] Case E-4/01 *Karlsson* [2002] EFTA Ct Rep 240.
[35] *Finanger II* (n 32) para 51.
[36] *Finanger I* (n 16) 1820.
[37] *Finanger II* (n 32) para 52.
[38] Rt 2007 p 1003 *Gaming Machines*. No translation of the Supreme Court judgment is available.
[39] Case E-1/06 *ESA v Norway* [2007] EFTA Ct Rep 8.
[40] On this, see *Gaming Machines* (n 38) paras 39 and 40.

justices.[41] The Supreme Court unanimously found in favour of the government. In this, it relied heavily on the judgment of the EFTA Court.

On the effect of the EFTA Court judgment, the Supreme Court started out by stating that such a judgment must be given 'substantial weight' (in Norwegian: 'betydelig vekt'). Then the spokesman added 'in particular when [the EFTA Court] has handled all sides of a case which later shall be decided nationally'. In this respect, he also referred to what had been stated on behalf of the full Supreme Court in the *Finanger I* plenary case, also clarifying that this had been an advisory opinion case, not an infringement proceedings. He further quoted the specific reasoning given by the Supreme Court in that case, which have been quoted above here.[42]

The spokesperson stated that it was irrelevant that the organisation that was now the only party to the appeal had not been a party to the case before the EFTA Court. The organisation had complained to ESA and its views had been made known.

Then the judge on behalf of the Norwegian Supreme Court developed the reasoning further with respect to infringement cases under Article 31 SCA where the EFTA Court has full jurisdiction:

> It is self-evident that the EFTA Court's general understanding of EEA law must have great persuasive force (in Norwegian: 'stor gjennomslagskraft') in Norwegian courts. The same applies to the EFTA Court's specific application of the law in an infringement case. There is not the same reason to allocate the EFTA Court's assessment of the facts independent significance. In the case at hand, however, it is first and foremost a question of applying the law to the facts, not assessment of evidence in the narrow sense of the word.[43]

The case was then unanimously decided in line with the judgment of the EFTA Court and with several references to that judgment.

In *Pedicel*, a 2009 case on the prohibition of alcohol advertisement,[44] the Supreme Court followed closely the advisory opinion of the EFTA Court in *Pedicel*.[45] With respect to the effect of EFTA Court decisions, the Supreme Court only referred briefly to the *Finanger I* case, stating that even if the opinion of the EFTA Court is not binding for the Supreme Court, it must be 'allocated substantial weight'.[46]

In a case on state liability for illegally charged corporate tax, the state was found not to be liable under the principle of state liability because the EEA law at the time of the payment of the taxes had not been sufficiently clear to induce liability,[47] The Supreme Court referred to the EFTA Court decisions in *Sveinbjörnsdóttir* and *Karlsson* as well as the Supreme Court's own decision in *Finanger II*,[48] and applied the criteria therein. It did not address the weight attached to decisions by the EFTA Court or others.

[41] See ibid para 48.
[42] See ibid para 79.
[43] ibid para 81 (author's translation).
[44] Rt 2009 p 839 *Pedicel*.
[45] Case E-4/04 Pedicel [2005] EFTA Ct Rep 1.
[46] *Pedicel* (n 44) para 7.
[47] Rt 2010 p 1500 *Edquist*, para 114.
[48] ibid paras 90 and 91.

In *Non-economic Loss*,[49] a case on state liability concerning redress for non-economic loss under the insurance directives, the question was how far back in time the state's duty to compensate for wrongful implementation of the motor insurance directives would go. The Norwegian government had already accepted the outcome of *Nguyen*[50] and paid compensation. This new case concerned losses going further back. The Supreme Court found that the legal situation had been clear enough after the 1996 judgment of the CJEU in *Bernáldez*.[51] Accordingly, the Court referred to and discussed both decisions by the EFTA Court, the CJEU and itself, but did not pronounce specifically on the weight attached to the different decisions.

C. The *STX* Case

The much-discussed judgment in *STX*[52] concerned the validity of provisions on working conditions included in the Regulation concerning partial general application of the Engineering Industry Agreement to the maritime construction industry.[53] The case was decided by the Supreme Court in an ordinary sitting of five justices, two of whom, however, were the President of the Court at the time, Justice Schei, and the subsequent President, Justice Øie. The main question was whether the application of the provisions on working conditions constituted a violation of Article 36 EEA on the freedom to provide services and Article 3 of the Posting of Workers Directive.[54] The Norwegian courts found the provisions of the regulation to be valid. Before the hearing in the Court of Appeal, that court asked the EFTA Court for an advisory opinion, which was given.[55] The EFTA Court found that some of the provisions of the Norwegian regulation were in violation of the Directive. The Supreme Court did not accept that conclusion.

On the effect of EFTA Court decisions, the Supreme Court started out by quoting the plenary decision on that matter in the *Finanger I* case.[56] Then the justice delivering the Supreme Court judgment stated:

> Consequently, I find that the Supreme Court shall not accept the EFTA Court's opinion without due examination; it has the authority as well as the duty to consider independently whether and to what extent this is warranted. In this light, I cannot see that the Supreme Court is formally prevented from relying on a different opinion (in Norwegian: 'avvikende syn'). However, because significant importance must obviously be attributed to

[49] (Rt 2012 p 1793 *Non-economic Loss*.

[50] Case E-8/07 *Nguyen* [2008] EFTA Ct Rep 224.

[51] Case C-129/94 *Ruiz Bernáldez* ECLI:EU:C:1996:143.

[52] *STX* (n 15).

[53] An unofficial English translation of the judgment is available at: www.domstol.no/en/supremecourt/rulings/2013/translated/validity-of-provisions-in-concerning-partial-general-application-of-the-engineering-industry-agreement-to-the-maritime-construction-industry.

[54] Directive 96/71/EC of the European Parliament and of the Council concerning the posting of workers in the framework of the provision of services [1997] OJ L18/1.

[55] Case E-2/11 *STX* [2012] EFTA Ct Rep 4.

[56] *STX* (n 15) para 93.

> the opinion, special reasons (in Norwegian: 'særlige grunner') would be required for the Supreme Court to diverge.[57]

Then the Court unanimously diverged from parts of the opinion of the EFTA Court, partly through its reading of CJEU case law and partly through its assessment of what restrictions with respect to Article 36 EEA were allowed because they 'pursue a public interest objective and their application is not disproportionate',[58] as was found with respect to the out-of-town allowance.

It is also interesting to note that the question of directly interpreting the Directive to include the out-of-town allowance was avoided by the Supreme Court,[59] apparently out of respect for the EFTA Court judgment.

The most striking feature of the statement about EFTA Court decisions is the emphasis on the Supreme Court's *duty* to consider the EFTA Court's opinion independently. This could be read as signalling a more critical stance to the EFTA Court's decisions.

D. The *Holship* Case

The plenary judgment most extensively quoted by the Supreme Court in the *NAV* case, as we have seen above in section 3, is the plenary judgment in *Holship*,[60] which was decided by a majority of 10 judges to seven.

The case concerned the legality of a boycott. The Holship company wanted to undertake loading and unloading services at a seaport, but was not willing to enter into a collective agreement containing a priority of engagement clause, reserving loading and unloading work for dockworkers associated with the Administration Office for Dock Work in the harbour of Drammen. The boycott was intended to make the company accept this agreement. The lower courts had both accepted the boycott as legal.

Before deciding the case, the Supreme Court asked the EFTA Court for an advisory opinion and decided to hear the case in a plenary session. The EFTA Court delivered its advisory opinion in *Holship Norge*.[61] For the Supreme Court, the questions to be heard were the issue of whether the collective agreement exemption under competition law could be applied in this case and whether the boycott was unlawful in light of the right to freedom of establishment in Article 31 EEA, as well as Article 101 of the Norwegian Constitution and Article 11 of the European Convention on Human Rights.[62]

On the effect of EFTA Court decisions, the majority of the Supreme Court stated that 'the EFTA Court's opinions on the interpretation of the EEA Agreement are not binding for national courts, but rather "advisory"'. The conclusion drawn from this

[57] ibid para 94.
[58] ibid para 105.
[59] See ibid para 103.
[60] *Holship* (n 12).
[61] Case E-14/15 *Holship Norge* [2016] EFTA Ct Rep 240.
[62] *Holship*,(n 12) para 24.

was 'that the courts of the EFTA States must independently consider how to interpret and apply EEA law'.[63] Then the Court stated what has been fully quoted in the *NAV* case referred to above (see the quotation in section III).[64]

Also, the minority of the Supreme Court addressed the issue of the effect of EFTA Court decisions. The justice delivering the minority opinion stated that as regards 'the advisory opinion of the EFTA Court, I refer to the review of the Supreme Court's previous conclusions, as described by the justice delivering the leading opinion of the court: the national court must independently consider how to interpret and apply EEA law'.

The justice went on to say that the national court 'shall, however, attach considerable importance to the opinions of the EFTA Court concerning the interpretation of EEA law. Only when special circumstances so indicate, can the Court's interpretation be disregarded'. She also referred to the EFTA Court's opinion,[65] where it stated that the advisory opinion procedure 'is an instrument of cooperation between the EFTA Court and the national courts'.[66] She explained the allocation of tasks as follows:

> It is the function of the EFTA Court to provide the national court with guidelines[67] for the interpretation of EEA law that are required for the decision of the matter before it. It is for the national court to examine and evaluate evidence and to make factual findings, and then apply EEA law to the facts of the case.

She went on to draw the following methodological conclusion from this division of tasks:

> From this, I conclude that if the national court finds that the actual circumstances of the case differ from those considered by the EFTA Court in its opinion in relevant ways, the national court may arrive at a different conclusion than the EFTA Court. In the present case, this is relevant.[68]

For the minority, the purpose of the collective agreement was decisive both with respect to the competition law exception for collective labour agreements as well as in relation to freedom of establishment. After having referred to parts of the examination conducted by the EFTA Court in relation to the framework agreement in dispute, the minority concluded on the facts as follows:

> In my view, this must be based on a misinterpretation of the circumstances of the present case, which is relevant for the consideration of the purpose of the collective agreement.[69]

[63] ibid para 76.

[64] ibid paras 77 and 78.

[65] *Holship Norge* (n 61) EFTA Court's opinion at para 37.

[66] *Holship* (n 12) para 142.

[67] The use of the term 'guidelines' is a somewhat misleading translation of the Norwegian text: 'veiledning om tolkningen av de EØS-bestemmelser som er relevante for avgjørelsen av den verserende saken'. Guidance would be a more appropriate translation.

[68] *Holship* (n 12) para 143. In Norwegian: 'Jeg utleder av dette at dersom den nasjonale domstolen finner at de faktiske omstendigheter på relevante måter avviker fra de EFTA-domstolen legger til grunn for sine vurderinger, vil den nasjonale domstolen kunne komme til et annet resultat enn EFTA-domstolen. I saken her har det betydning.'

[69] ibid para 151. On this point, the English translation is not pertinent. The word 'misinterpretation' is somewhat unfortunate. The original Norwegian wording is: 'Jeg kan ikke skjønne annet enn at det her

Such techniques have also been applied by some other Supreme Courts when they were not pleased about an answer from the CJEU.[70] For the purposes of this chapter, we do not need to examine the substantive conclusions of the majority and the minority, but point simply to the methodological consideration that if the EFTA Court has misrepresented relevant facts, it may be appropriate to deviate from its conclusions.

E. From the *Working Time* Case to *Proforma Marriage*

In the *Working Time* case,[71] the Supreme Court had asked the EFTA Court for an advisory opinion given in *Thue*[72] on the interpretation of Directive 2003/88/EC of the European Parliament and of the Council concerning certain aspects of the organisation of working time.[73] Here, the Supreme Court followed the EFTA Court's opinion. With respect to the methodological issue, it simply referred to what the Supreme Court had held in the *Holship* judgment.[74]

In 2019, the Supreme Court handed down its judgment in *Yara*, which demonstrated a disagreement between some justices of the Court with respect to the degree of how precisely an advisory opinion of the EFTA Court should be followed. The whole Court found that a final loss giving a right to a tax deduction for a group contribution to a foreign subsidiary had not been demonstrated. The majority of three justices, however, did not form a firm opinion on the conditions for tax deduction, while the minority of two justices stated that the ′ final loss exception is established, and later specified, in several ECJ rulings. In accordance with the EFTA Court′s judgment, the exception also applies under the EEA Agreement. In such a situation, I find that Norwegian courts are bound by the *limitation* given to the exception therein′ (emphasis in the original).[75] The same year, the Supreme Court decided the *Fosen-Linjen* case, where the EFTA Court had twice been asked its opinion.[76] The EFTA Court was asked, first, by the Court of Appeal and, second, by the Supreme Court itself.[77] The Supreme Court explained why it had asked the EFTA Court again in the following manner:

> Because, among other things, the Court of Appeal did not follow the EFTA Court's opinion in *Fosen I* on the issue of basis of liability, the Supreme Court asked on 19 November 2018 for clarification and amplification, or possibly a reconsideration, from the EFTA Court.[78]

The case concerned liability for errors in public procurement. Basically, the Supreme Court followed the second opinion with respect to the basis of liability. However, no

foreligger uriktige oppfatninger [wrong understandings] om de faktiske forholdene som har betydning for vurderingen av formålet med tariffavtalen.'

[70] See J Krommendijk, 'Between Interpretation and Application of EU Law: Case-Tailored CJEU Judgments in the Preliminary Ruling Procedure' (2023) 6(3) *Nordic Journal of European Law* 1, at 23.

[71] Case HR-2018-1036 *Working Time*.

[72] Case E-19/16 *Thue and the Norwegian Police Federation* [2017] EFTA Ct Rep 880.

[73] Directive 2003/88/EC of the European Parliament and of the Council concerning certain aspects of the organisation of working time [2003] OJ L299/9.

[74] See *Working Time* (n 71) paras 63 and 64, citing *Holship* (n 12) paras 76–78.

[75] HR-2019-140 *Yara* paras 122 and 128; and E-15/16 *Yara International ASA* [2017] EFTA Ct Rep 432.

[76] HR-2019-1801-A *Fosen-Linjen*.

[77] See Case E-16/16 *Fosen-Linjen* [2017] EFTA Ct Rep 617 (*Fosen I*) and Case E-7/18 *Fosen-Linjen*, judgment of 1 August 2019 (*Fosen II*).

[78] *Working Time* (n 71) para 33.

comment was given by the Supreme Court on the significance of the two opinions or on any methodological questions.[79]

The *Proforma Marriage* case[80] concerned the question of whether a marriage had been entered into in order to obtain a residence permit. The Supreme Court had asked the EFTA Court for an advisory opinion in *Kerim*.[81] With respect to effect of the advisory opinion, the Supreme Court referred to the *Holship* judgment.[82] The parties before the Supreme Court also agreed on the opinion given by the EFTA Court and the Supreme Court based its reasoning in relation to EEA law 'directly' on that opinion.[83]

V. SUPREME COURT DECISIONS AFTER THE *NAV* CASE: THE *UNEMPLOYMENT ALLOWANCES* CASE

After the *NAV* case was decided in 2021, as discussed in section III above, there have been two interesting decisions. One is *Commercial Agents* and the other is *Unemployment Allowances*, which is a part of the *NAV* case complex.[84]

The judgment in *Commercial Agents* referred to and followed the methodology of the *Holship* case.[85] The Supreme Court had asked the EFTA Court for an advisory opinion in *Norep*.[86]

On the issue of whether there were any 'weighty and compelling reasons' for not following the advisory opinion, the justice delivering the Supreme Court judgment stated: 'I cannot see that such reasons have been demonstrated in the case at hand'.[87] This is a somewhat surprising statement as it appears that it had not even been argued by the parties that this was the case. However, the justice giving the judgment of the court continued:

> The statement [by the EFTA Court] is particularly supported by the CJEU's judgment of 4 June 2020 in Case C-828/18 *Trendsetteuse*. There, the CJEU sets out that a commercial agent's tasks include bringing the principal new customers and increasing the volume of business with existing customers, and that this can be accomplished by providing information and advice, as well as through discussions. There is no requirement on the commercial agent to take and forward orders.[88]

Why the Court referred to and commented upon the relationship to the *Trendsetteuse* case is somewhat surprising. In the EFTA Court's opinion, the *Trendsetteuse* case is central and is referenced 11 times. In the Supreme Court's judgment, it looks as if it is correcting the EFTA Court. However, it may also be read as simply reinforcing how obvious the answer to the question was, since the two lower Norwegian courts had

[79] For an account of these judgments see A Sanchez-Graells, ch 18 in this volume.

[80] HR-2021-1435-A *Proforma Marriage*.

[81] Case E-1/20 *Kerim*, judgment of 9 February 2021.

[82] *Holship* (n 12) paras 76–78.

[83] *Proforma Marriage* (n 80) para 42.

[84] HR-2022-728-A *Commercial Agents*; HR-2023-301-A *Unemployment Allowances*.

[85] An unofficial English translation of the judgment is available at: www.domstol.no/en/supremecourt/rulings/rulings-2022/supreme-court-civil-cases/HR-2022-728-A.

[86] Case E-2/21 *Norep*, judgment of 14 December 2021.

[87] HR-2022-728-A *Commercial Agents* (n 84) para 48.

[88] ibid.

both come to a different interpretation of the Norwegian Agency Act which implemented the relevant directive.

It may also be surprising that in the *Commercial Agents* case, the Supreme Court referred to the methodological remarks made in the *Holship* case instead of those in the *NAV* case, since the judgment in the *Commercial Agents* case was pronounced nine months after the *NAV* judgment.[89] However, this may be because of the relationship between a plenary case (the *Holship* case) and a Grand Chamber case (the *NAV* case).

After the *NAV* case, there has been one more methodologically important Supreme Court case: *Unemployment Allowances*.[90] In this case, two decisions of the EFTA Court were examined by the Supreme Court. The Supreme Court had not itself asked the EFTA Court in this specific case, but relied on two EFTA Court decisions[91] given in related cases. Both of these concerned parallel questions about unemployment allowances and the two advisory opinions had been coordinated by the EFTA Court and were rendered simultaneously.

The Supreme Court case concerned a recipient of unemployment benefits. The man involved had periodically stayed in Sweden despite the requirement of stay in Norway in section 4-2 of the National Insurance Act and without notifying NAV. During these stays, he had received a significant amount in unemployment benefits. He was sentenced by the Court of Appeal to suspended imprisonment of 60 days for fraud.[92] The Supreme Court unanimously found, as had the Court of Appeal, that the stay requirement in section 4-2 of the National Insurance Act was compatible with EEA law.

Great emphasis was placed on the advisory opinions from the EFTA Court, including the conclusion that the Member States are free to lay down a stay requirement in cases other than those regulated in Articles 64–65a of the Social Security Regulation. The EFTA Court had considered that these rules constituted harmonisation and that, accordingly, the EEA Agreement's basic rules on free movement were thus not applicable.

The basic difference between the *NAV* case from 2021 and this case is that the latter concerned daily unemployment benefits, while the *NAV* case concerned the work assessment allowance, which for the purposes of the Social Security Regulation is classified as a sickness benefit. As outlined above, the EFTA Court held that the rules of the Regulation were different as regards the exportability of these two types of benefits.

On the effect of EFTA Court decisions, the Supreme Court referred to the *NAV* case and requoted the quote from the *Holship* case.[93] This was summed up to the effect that the EFTA Court's understanding of EEA law cannot be deviated from unless there are 'good and heavy weighing reasons for it'.[94]

[89] The *NAV* judgment was given on 2 July 2021, while the *Commercial Agents* judgment was given on 7 April 2022.

[90] *Unemployment Allowances* (n 84).

[91] Case E-13/20 O, judgment of 30 June 2021; Case E-15/20 *Criminal Proceedings against P*, judgment of 30 June 2021.

[92] Section 271; *cf* s 270, sub-s 1(2) of the Penal Code of 1902.

[93] *Unemployment Allowances* (n 84) para 74, referring to *NAV* (n 3) paras 63–66 and *Holship* (n 12) para 77.

[94] Or 'weighty and compelling reasons'. *Unemployment Allowances* (n 84) para 75.

The Supreme Court went on to address the relevance of the fact that the advisory opinions had been given in cases other than the case at hand, and stated:

> It is insignificant that the advisory opinions the EFTA Court has given in Cases E-13/20 and E-15/20 have not been obtained directly in connection with the case at hand, as long as the questions are the same. Further, the requests concern pure questions of interpretation, and the distribution of competences between the EFTA Court and the national court addressed in the *Holship* judgment paragraph 78, does not raise any problems.[95]

The defence lawyer in the case had precisely addressed the questions of 'weighty and compelling reasons' to convince the Supreme Court not to follow the EFTA Court. The Supreme Court summarised these arguments as a question of the wording of the relevant article of the EEA Regulation and of the overall purpose of increasing free movement of persons by coordinating the national insurance systems. Also, the prosecution phrased its arguments along the same lines, but, of course, with the opposite outcome to that intended.

The Supreme Court unanimously found that the requirement of staying in the state of residence was not a violation of EEA law. The reasons presented by the defence for deviating from the EFTA Court's opinion relied in particular on two CJEU decisions, which the Supreme Court discussed extensively before the arguments were dismissed.[96]

One of the justices gave a separate opinion on one question. In the advisory opinions, the EFTA Court had decided not to assess the requirement for a benefit recipient to stay in Norway in light of Article 36 EEA on free movement of services. The majority of the Supreme Court (four justices) followed this.[97] The fifth justice agreed with the majority in the result and on all but one point, where he apparently assessed the requirement to stay in Norway as if he were assessing it as a restriction under Article 36 EEA.

The fifth justice started his reasoning by addressing the weight that should be given to opinions of the EFTA Court:

> Given the substantial weight that shall be given to opinions of the EFTA Court, I, however, agree with the justice giving the opinion for the majority ['førstvoterende'], that it is here not sufficient reason to deviate from the interpretation of the EFTA Court. But contrary to what she has done, I do not – in the lack of deeper analysis, that the EFTA Court has not had opportunity to undertake – form a position on whether Article 36 of the EEA Agreement does apply or not. For me that is not necessary.[98]

Then he continued with a hypothetical analysis with respect to Article 36 EEA: '*If* the case of A (the defendant) should be assessed under Article 36 of the EEA Agreement',

[95] ibid para 76 (author's translation).

[96] See ibid paras 100–18. In a recent article, the authors criticise the Supreme Court for uncritically following the opinion of the EFTA Court. Although referring to the requirement of weighty and compelling reasons for deviating from the EFTA Court, the authors do not discuss what that requirement implies in a situation such as the one in the *Unemployment Allowances* case. To me, it seems as if they assume that another understanding of the same EU/EEA sources as those that the EFTA Court had examined would be sufficient. See Ø Bø and LK Furuholmen, 'Høyesteretts dom i dagpengesaken – en vurdering av begrunnelsen for ikke å fravike EFTA-domstolens tolkning av trygdeforordningen' (2023) 58 *Jussens Venner* 304, especially at 306, where the requirement is given a brief and flexible interpretation.

[97] See ibid paras 98 and 116.

[98] ibid para 140 (author's translation).

he found that a restriction would exist.[99] However, this restriction would be justified because it was legitimate, suitable and necessary, especially because of the purpose of getting persons on unemployment benefits back to work.

What is interesting here is that the justice took an opportunity to give an analysis of how the question should be solved under the primary rules of the EEA Agreement without expressly doing so. Further, he reinforced the deference that the national courts should give to opinions of the EFTA Court. An interesting question is what would have been done if the justice had held the opinion that the restriction was not justified. Would he then still have followed the EFTA Court's opinion?

VI. THE MAIN PRINCIPLES TODAY

From the *Eidesund* case of 1997 until today, the principles governing EFTA Court decisions as a source of law have changed. However, the principles appear to have been fairly stable since the *Holship* case in 2016.

As is clear from the *NAV* case, it is the phrasing of the weight allocated to EFTA Court opinions, as set out in the plenary decision in the *Holship* case with the addition of the distinctions set out in the *NAV* case,[100] that are today's basic principles on the effects of EFTA Court judgments in Norwegian law.

In the *NAV* case, the Supreme Court distinguished between four different aspects of an EFTA Court decision. First came the pure interpretation of EEA law. The starting point is that with respect to the interpretation of EEA law or 'the EEA Agreement' as is stated in Article 34 SCA, the courts should follow that. It should not be deviated from without 'weighty and compelling reasons'.[101]

Next came situations with EEA rules that are discretionary 'or appear as general principles'. As an example, the Supreme Court mentioned that in the case 'when interpreting and applying the basic freedoms in the main part of the EEA Agreement, one must assess whether the restrictions are suitable, necessary and proportionate'. In these situations, the task of the EFTA Court is to give 'specifying guidelines for the application of the EEA rule, and to clarify which aspects should be emphasised'.[102] As I understand the Supreme Court, in these situations, it is not the task of the EFTA Court to reach a conclusion on the application of the EEA rule, but to give precise guidelines. This must be understood as also being covered by the concept of interpretation as set out in Article 34 SCA. It appears that the Supreme Court assumes that these guidelines should be given the same weight as when the EFTA Court gives an interpretation of a provision that has a more clear-cut rule character. This manner of understanding is in line with what the Supreme Court itself does under national law in some cases where it only pronounces itself on the interpretation of legal provisions

[99] ibid para 141.

[100] *NAV* (n 3) para 66.

[101] In Norwegian: 'EFTA-domstolens forståelse av EØS-retten kan altså ikke fravikes uten at det foreligger "gode og tungtveiende grunner for det".' ibid para 65.

[102] In Norwegian: 'Mange EØS-rettslige regler er etter sin art skjønnsmessige eller har karakter av generelle prinsipper. Ved tolkningen og anvendelsen av de grunnleggende frihetene i EØS-avtalens hoveddel

and leaves it for the court against whose decision an appeal has been brought to undertake the concrete application of the rule.

Third came the findings of fact. In all cases heard by the EFTA Court, also in advisory opinions, there is a set of facts more or less clearly explained by the requesting court and in the submissions to the EFTA Court. To decide on the facts is the task of the national court.

Fourth came the decision on 'whether a national provision or regulation is compatible with EEA law'. That is also for the national court to decide.

With respect to these last two categories, the Supreme Court stated as follows in the *NAV* case: 'To the extent the EFTA Court has carried out more specific assessments, for instance based on the questions referred by the national court, this may be of help to the national court.' This 'help' could be useful. But the Supreme Court went on to say that 'such statements considered in isolation carry less weight than direct statements from the Court regarding the interpretation of EEA law'.[103] However, what is interesting here is that such statements are also given some weight by the Supreme Court. To me it is rather unclear what this means. Under the system of allocation of competences between the EFTA Court and national courts, it should formally carry no weight since it is part of what is allocated to the national courts. However, it may have been said by the Supreme Court because all assistance may be useful.[104]

The most important issue then is to discuss more thoroughly what the weighty and compelling reasons are that may lead Norwegian courts to deviate from the interpretation that the EFTA Court has reached. This is the subject of the next section.

VII. WEIGHTY AND COMPELLING REASONS: WHAT ARE THEY?

As was explained in section II above, homogeneity between the core parts of EU law and EEA law is the overarching goal for interpretations in those areas that are covered by the same rules, excluding questions where the EEA Agreement deviates from EU law. That should be, and is, decisive for the weight to be allocated to EFTA Court decisions.

A starting point for the principle is that older Norwegian case law – traditional precedents – are not relevant for the Norwegian courts if the EFTA Court has found that the EEA rule is different from the rule expressed in such cases. This is of course striking in the *NAV* case itself, which set aside a provision of the law as well as judgments applying it.

The typical situation when a Norwegian court, and especially the Supreme Court, has requested an advisory opinion from the EFTA Court, is that the EFTA Court judgment represents the latest case law on the question. This implies that it does give the best and most up-to-date advice on the questions raised in the request. One reason

står eksempelvis vurderinger av om restriksjoner er egnede, nødvendige og forholdsmessige, sentralt. Oppgaven for EFTA-domstolen vil da være å gi presiserende retningslinjer for anvendelsen av den EØS-rettslige regelen, og herunder klargjøre hvilke momenter som skal inngå og vektlegges' ibid para 66.

[103] *NAV* (n 3) para 6.

[104] Also, with respect to EU law, there is an ongoing discussion on where to draw the line between interpretation and application of the law; see M Broberg and N Fenger, 'European Court of Justice versus Member

to deviate from this is that the CJEU has given a judgment with a different interpretation *after* the EFTA Court decision was issued. In such cases, there is good reason to deviate from the EFTA Court decision for reasons of homogeneity. The well-known dynamic character of EU law and its somewhat open character make this situation possible. The EFTA Court itself has stated that it will adjust its own case law to align with that of the CJEU unless there are compelling grounds specific to EEA law which would justify deviating from the interpretation of the CJEU.[105] The task for a lawyer arguing in front of the Supreme Court would be to show that the more recent CJEU case law really is different with respect to the interpretation.

Another situation is where a party to a case has an opinion of CJEU case law or secondary legislation that is different from what the EFTA Court has found, based on the same sources. This type of case is, in my opinion, at the core of what the Supreme Court's principle intends to solve. One example is the *Unemployment Allowances* case, where the private party argued for a different understanding of the wording of the social security regulation as well as for a different effect of an underlying principle compared to that of the EFTA Court. The Supreme Court took this seriously and examined the arguments put forward by the private party, but reached a conclusion in line with that of the EFTA Court.[106]

Another means of handling such an issue where the Supreme Court itself really is in doubt is to send a new request to the EFTA Court. This was the case in *Fosen-Linjen*, where Frostating Court of Appeal did not follow the advisory opinion of the EFTA Court in *Fosen I* because it did not agree with its interpretation of the relevant rules and considered that weighty and compelling reasons within the meaning of the Supreme Court's case law were present. The judgment of the Court of Appeal also referred to an article by two law professors who had been very critical of the decision of the EFTA Court in *Fosen I*.[107] The new request resulted in the advisory opinion in *Fosen II*, which the Supreme Court followed with respect to the question of the basis of liability.[108]

In Norwegian law, and, especially, in Norwegian legal method, it is usual to emphasise the importance of considerations of equity in the resolution of legal questions after the 'harder' sources have been examined. This is often called applying *reelle hensyn*, what we would call here equitable considerations. In EU and EEA legal method, this is not a general category, even if principles related to EEA law such as the principle of effectiveness exist. One consequence that the principle of 'weighty and compelling reasons' must imply with respect to adjudication by Norwegian courts is that the application of equitable considerations is basically excluded from the assessment of a case after the EFTA Court has given its opinion. Regardless of whether the

State Courts: Who Decides What? Preliminary Rulings Concerning the Application of EU Law in the Main Proceedings' (2022) 4 *Yearbook on Procedural Law of the Court of Justice of the European Union* 27. See further the comment in Einarsson (n 7) 244.

[105] On how the EFTA Court has dealt with conflicting case law, see Einarsson (n 7) 233–36.

[106] See *Unemployment Allowances* (n 84), especially paras 81–86.

[107] See the Court of Appeal case LF-2015-187242, in Norwegian only, which discussed openly whether to follow the EFTA Court; and F Arnesen and HH Fredriksen, 'Erstatningsansvar ved brudd på anskaffelsesreglene – etter EFTA-domstolenses tolkningsuttalelse i Fosen-Linjen' (2017) *Tidsskrift for forretningsjus* 169, https://doi.org/10.18261/issn.0809-9510-2017-03-04-01.

[108] See section IV.E above. The author took part in the *Fosen II* case as an ad hoc judge of the EFTA Court.

judge would have liked to arrive at a different interpretation because it was more just or balanced, this is barred in such cases.

However, underlying equitable considerations may of course to some degree guide the national court's emphasis on how to understand the facts of a case and thereby take the case out of the ambit of the principle of weighty and compelling reasons.

Whether the use of EFTA Court decisions concerns advisory opinions or direct action cases relating to issues other than those in the case at hand, for the Norwegian Supreme Court, this does not seem to make any difference with respect to the weight allocated to the judgment. This is explicitly said in the *Unemployment Allowances* case.[109]

VIII. THE FACTS OF A CASE AND EFTA COURT DECISIONS

According to the first paragraph of Article 34 SCA, the subject on which the EFTA Court gives advice in advisory opinions is the '*interpretation* of the EEA Agreement' (emphasis added). As has often been said by the EFTA Court, it is for the national court to ascertain the facts and to apply the law to the facts. However, in its advice on how to request an advisory opinion, the EFTA Court suggests that the request should include, among other things, 'a statement of the facts which are essential for a full understanding of the legal significance of the main proceedings'.[110] That means that the EFTA Court will have a set of facts as a basis for its reasoning and interpretation. If these facts turn out to be partly misstated or misunderstood, this may be relevant for the application of the EFTA Court judgment.[111]

This has also been relevant for the Norwegian Supreme Court. This can be seen from the minority's reasoning in the *Holship* case where it discussed the understanding of the facts of a case. The spokesperson explained the allocation of tasks between the EFTA Court and the national court as follows:

> It is the function of the EFTA Court to provide the national court with guidelines[112] for the interpretation of EEA law that are required for the decision of the matter before it. It is for the national court to examine and evaluate evidence and to make factual findings, and then apply EEA law to the facts of the case.[113]

She drew the following methodological conclusion from this division of tasks:

> From this, I conclude that if the national court finds that the actual circumstances of the case differ from those considered by the EFTA Court in its opinion in relevant ways, the

[109] *Unemployment Allowances* (n 84) para 76.

[110] The EFTA Court's Note for guidance on requests by national courts for advisory opinions is available at: eftacourt.int/the-court/guidance-for-advisory-opinion/?wpdmdl=7446&ind=1627642656131.

[111] Similar questions arise with respect to preliminary rulings of the CJEU; see Broberg and Fenger (n 7) 402–04.

[112] The use of the term 'guidelines' is a somewhat misleading translation of the Norwegian text: 'veiledning om tolkningen av de EØS-bestemmelser som er relevante for avgjørelsen av den verserende saken'. 'Guidance' would be better word.

[113] *Holship* (n 12) para 142.

> national court may arrive at a different conclusion than the EFTA Court. In the present case, this is relevant.[114]

After having referred to parts of the examination of the framework agreement in dispute conducted by the EFTA Court, the minority concluded on the facts as follows:

> In my view, this must be based on a misinterpretation of the circumstances of the present case, which is relevant for the consideration of the purpose of the collective agreement.[115]

This use of a misunderstanding of the facts of a case is perfectly loyal to the system of advisory opinions. However, one may speculate that the minority of the Supreme Court did not find the outcome of the EFTA Court judgment to be in line with equitable considerations and was looking for a way to come to another conclusion without being disloyal or subverting the system of advisory opinions.

In direct action cases, the situation is somewhat special, as can be seen from the *Gaming Machines* case. The Supreme Court started out by saying that 'the EFTA Court's general understanding of EEA law must have great persuasive force in Norwegian courts'. Then the Supreme Court stated that the 'same applies to the EFTA Court's specific application of the law in an infringement case. And this is different from the situation in advisory opinion cases. However, with respect to the facts, the Supreme Court said, as a matter of principle, that there 'is not the same reason to allocate the EFTA Court's assessment of the facts independent significance'. Yet, this was not relevant in the case at hand, since it was 'first and foremost a question of applying the law to the facts, not assessment of evidence in the narrow sense of the word'.[116]

IX. LATER USE OF OBSERVATIONS SUBMITTED IN EFTA COURT CASES

A special question relating to the use of EFTA Court decisions is whether one, in later proceedings, may make use of written observations submitted to the EFTA Court in earlier cases. As outlined above, the EFTA Court invites the European Commission, ESA and the 30 EEA States to submit written and oral observations, as well as the parties to the main proceedings. ESA and the European Commission invariably submit both written and oral observations and participation from some EEA States is quite frequent.

In the *STX* case, such observations were used as arguments and referred to by the Supreme Court. The unanimous Supreme Court referred to the observations submitted to the EFTA Court from the European Commission, ESA and the governments of Belgium, Poland, Sweden and Iceland. As is evident, this included EU Member States as well as EEA/EFTA States. The Supreme Court stated that:

> All of these observations – except the one from Iceland, which failed to answer the question directly – argue that Article 3(1) of the Directive is an exhaustive provision where 'there is

[114] ibid para 143.
[115] ibid para 151.
[116] *Gaming Machines* (n 38) para 81 (author's translation).

> no room for a separate evaluation of the compatibility of those provisions with Article 36 EEA', as expressed by the [European] Commission with reference to *Laval*, paragraphs 80–81.[117]

This could give support for not undertaking an examination of the case under Article 36 EEA. However, the Supreme Court did not form a final conclusion on this question since, instead, it chose to assess the question of whether the national provision was compatible with Article 36 EEA on the free movement of services, even if there were 'many indications that any benefits considered to constitute minimum rates of pay in the sense of the Directive, need not also be examined for compatibility with Article 36 of the EEA Agreement'.[118]

In any case, the reference to such materials demonstrates that the Supreme Court considers them relevant in the assessment of an EFTA Court advisory opinion. In my opinion, this is sensible. However, any relevance granted to these observations must respect the EFTA Court's authoritative interpretation of EEA law in the event of the Court having reached a different conclusion from that of the Commission or ESA. One could nevertheless envisage them being used to argue that the EFTA Court's interpretation is not in line with the case law of the CJEU.[119]

Often, the observations from the Commission and ESA are well researched and well argued.[120] Both institutions have a thorough knowledge of EU and EEA law. The Commission, in particular, often also has a deep knowledge of the development of secondary legislation and can explain this to the EFTA Court. However, readers of these observations should not plainly accept what those institutions say because they may both have an agenda with respect to developing EU and EEA law further in a particular direction. This may also be done through the EFTA Court. Sometimes too, the analysis of the law on behalf of different governments can be useful.

Are the observations sources of law? Not in any strict sense of that concept. They are expressions of *opinio juris*, somewhat like legal writings. However, they are different from them in the sense that they have been written with the specific questions of the case in mind and are based on explanations of the facts of the case given by the court asking for an advisory opinion or by the parties to a case. That could make the analyses even more pertinent than general legal treatises or articles.

All written observations in advisory opinion cases lodged after 1 January 2021 have been published on the EFTA Court's website after the judgment in the case has been delivered. This makes them easily available. Previously, the Report for the Hearing would contain many of the arguments from the written observations, but since 2020 the Report has, in advisory opinion cases, been reduced to presenting the case and the different proposed answers to the questions posed by the referring court.

My prediction is that, normally, the observations will not provide much material to challenge the judgments of the EFTA Court. However, for users of EFTA

[117] ibid para 102.
[118] ibid para 103.
[119] *cf* the discussion in section VII above.
[120] For the sake of completeness, it should be noted that it is far from the case that the Commission and ESA always speak with one voice – for example, in *Unemployment Allowances* (n 84), they advocated different interpretations of the Social Security Regulation.

Court decisions, it may also be valuable to gain insights into what had actually been presented to the Court. This may sometimes also demonstrate that the Court has had knowledge of considerations and opinions that those criticising a judgment may not be aware of.

X. CONCLUSIONS

The Norwegian Supreme Court has now established a fairly stable set of principles for the use of EFTA Court judgments as a source of law. This is summed up in sections VI and VII above. The advisory opinions are not formally binding, but they usually decide the outcome of a case. This is the logical conclusion under the homogeneity principle of the EEA Agreement.

The principle is also efficient. The theory of sources of law that was developed in the early nineteenth century had at its core the idea that what one could refer to and examine in a court case should be restricted. One should not quote the Bible and the philosophers from antiquity any longer. The principle of relevance became narrower. The situation regarding the application of EU law, and by implication also EEA law, is somewhat similar. For national administrations, EU and EEA law is, to a large degree, a question of interpreting legislation, which is often very detailed. For the courts, it is different. For them, EU law is mainly case law and there is an abundance of this, which might even be contradictory.

Under the institutional set-up of the EFTA pillar, the EFTA Court is the court specialised in EEA law. Moreover, the Court's procedure allows all EEA States and, importantly, ESA and the European Commission to submit observations, Accordingly, this ensures that the relevant case law has been identified, sorted and evaluated, and the same goes for the relevant provisions of EEA law. It is then the task of the EFTA Court to assess that case law and adjudicate on the relevant issues of EEA law. Furthermore, the case law is presented in relation to the questions asked in the request from a national court, or precise questions in direct action cases. The fact that the judgments are based on facts and specific questions raised increases the value of the judgments. This applies, in particular, with respect to requests in cases that are to be decided by the national courts. However, in other cases, it also gives the user of the EFTA Court judgments a taste of what the case really is about. And as long as a case is raised from the same country or from a country with a similar court system and society, this makes the judgments even easier to understand and apply.

The Interpretation and Application of Internal Market Law

12

Dynamism, Homogeneity and Byzantine Structures

A Reassessment of Integration in the EEA

MARISE CREMONA

I. INTRODUCTION

WRITING ABOUT THE fledgling EEA 30 years ago, in the wake of the two famous Opinions of the Court of Justice,[1] I was sceptical both about its ability to achieve its objective of establishing 'a dynamic and homogeneous European Economic Area … on the basis of equality and reciprocity'[2] and its longer-term prospects.[3] Time has certainly proven me overpessimistic: while several of the original EFTA States have moved across to EU membership, the EEA has proved remarkably resilient and adaptive.[4] It is not only a core element of the EU's relationship with its neighbours; the EEA is an important integration project in its own right, which is paradigmatic of the possibilities (and constraints) of 'integration without (EU) membership',[5] helping us to define what that membership means.[6]

In this short chapter, I would like to return to my 1994 assessment from the perspective of 2023, reflecting on the problems identified then and on subsequent

[1] Opinion 1/91, EU:C:1991:490; Opinion 1/92, EU:C:1992:189.

[2] Agreement on the European Economic Area [1994] OJ L1/3, recital 4.

[3] M Cremona, 'The "Dynamic and Homogeneous" EEA: Byzantine Structures and Variable Geometry' (1994) 19(5) *European Law Review* 508.

[4] See, eg, HH Fredriksen and CNK Franklin, 'Of Pragmatism and Principles: The EEA Agreement 20 Years on' (2015) 52(3) *Common Market Law Review* 629; HH Fredriksen, 'The European Economic Area' in P Craig and R Schütze (eds), *Oxford Principles of European Union Law, Volume II: Internal Market* (Oxford, Oxford University Press, forthcoming).

[5] See, eg, M Öberg, *The Boundaries of the EU Internal Market: Participation without Membership* (Cambridge, Cambridge University Press, 2020); A Petti, *EU Neighbourhood Law: Wider Europe and the Extended EU's Legal Space* (Oxford, Hart Publishing, forthcoming, 2024); M Cremona and A Petti, 'Extending the Internal Market through EU Trade Agreements' in Craig and Schütze (n 4).

[6] M Cremona and N Nic Shuibhne, 'Integration, Membership, and the EU Neighbourhood' (2022) 59 *Common Market Law Review* 155.

legal developments: how have the key concepts of homogeneity and dynamism evolved over three decades, and what should we make of the undoubtedly 'Byzantine structures' of integration created in 1994 to satisfy the concerns of the EFTA and EU negotiators and the Court of Justice of the European Union (CJEU)?

II. HOMOGENEITY AND EQUALITY IN THE EEA LEGAL ORDER

The creation of 'a homogeneous European Economic Area' is identified as an objective of the EEA in both the Preamble to the Agreement and in its Article 1. Homogeneity is defined in terms of establishing and maintaining 'a uniform interpretation and application' of the EEA and 'those provisions of [Union] legislation which are substantially reproduced' in the EEA – primarily, of course, those reflecting the 'four freedoms' of the internal market. How was this aim of homogeneity approached in the initial years? At the centre of the Court of Justice's discussion of homogeneity in Opinion 1/91 were two concerns. First, the Court questioned whether it would be possible to achieve real homogeneity, given what it regarded as fundamentally different characteristics of the EU Treaty and the EEA. It was in this Opinion that for the first time the Court referred to the EU Treaties as 'the constitutional charter of a Community based on the rule of law' in which economic integration is not an end in itself, but part of broader project of European unity.[7] The EEA in contrast was characterised as an international treaty which 'merely creates rights and obligations as between the Contracting Parties and provides for no transfer of sovereign rights to the inter-governmental institutions which it sets up'.[8] Referring to the so-called '*Polydor* principle',[9] as well as the Vienna Convention on the Law of Treaties, the Court recalled that it cannot be assumed that even identically worded provisions will be interpreted the same way, since treaty interpretation depends on the objectives of the instrument and the context of the specific provision.[10] The Court was also sceptical about the ability of Article 6 EEA to deliver full homogeneity of interpretation,[11] first, because it does not apply to future CJEU judgments[12] and, second, as a result of the lack of clarity over whether Article 6 EEA is intended to apply to the CJEU case law on direct effect and primacy. Indeed, the implication of Protocol 35 is that the primacy of EEA law was to be achieved via national legislation in the EFTA States, not via judgments of the CJEU, and the wording of Article 7 EEA likewise suggests that EEA law is to be given effect within the EFTA States by means of domestic legislation. The Court's conclusion in Opinion 1/91 was that 'Article 6 as such cannot

[7] Opinion 1/91(n 1) para 21.

[8] ibid para 20.

[9] Derived from Case 270/80 *Polydor*, EU:C:1982:43.

[10] 'The fact that the provisions of the agreement and the corresponding Community provisions are identically worded does not mean that they must necessarily be interpreted identically. An international treaty is to be interpreted not only on the basis of its wording, but also in the light of its objectives.' Opinion 1/91 (n 1) para 14.

[11] Article 6 EEA provides that the provisions of the EEA which are 'identical in substance' to the corresponding rules of the EU Treaties and EU secondary legislation should be 'interpreted in conformity with the relevant rulings' of the CJEU given prior to the date of signature of the EEA.

[12] However, Art 3(2) of the Agreement establishing the EFTA Court and Surveillance Authority does require the EFTA Court to take 'due account' of 'relevant rulings' of the CJEU.

secure the objective of homogeneity of the law throughout the EEA, either as regards the past or for the future', and that the divergencies in the aims and context of the EEA and the EU Treaties 'stand in the way' of the objective of homogeneity in the interpretation and application of the EEA.[13]

This assessment did not in itself call into question the compatibility of the draft EEA agreement with EU law. However, the Court's second homogeneity-related concern necessitated amendments to be made to the EEA before it could come into force.[14] The Court required that the modalities used in the original draft agreement to ensure homogeneity should not threaten the principle of autonomy.[15] While this was not the first time that the Court had referred to the autonomy of the Community/Union system,[16] this Opinion, with its detailed examination of the proposed joint Court and its role in interpreting the agreement, including the delicate question of allocation of competences between the Community and its Member States as Contracting Parties to this mixed agreement, firmly established the contours of the principle, and especially the concept of judicial autonomy based on the exclusive jurisdiction of the CJEU under what is now Article 344 of the Treaty on the Functioning of the European Union (TFEU). In this Opinion and Opinion 1/92 on the revised EEA, the Court laid the foundations for what has become a substantial case law on the constraints imposed by the principle of autonomy in external relations and, in particular, on the establishment of external dispute settlement mechanisms.[17]

What do we Make of these Arguments 30 Years Later?

Let us look first at the principle of autonomy. First, the Court's ruling that it was not per se incompatible with the Treaties for the EU to conclude an agreement with third states establishing institutions with binding dispute settlement powers is an important statement of principle from the perspective of the international 'actorness' of the EU,[18] although of course it immediately raises questions as to the conditions under which such arrangements would be compatible with EU law.[19] Aspects of the

[13] Opinion 1/91 (n 1) paras 28–29.

[14] Under what is now Art 218(11) TFEU.

[15] See Opinion 1/91 (n 1) para 30. As I put it in 1994, 'the autonomy of the Community legislative system has been preserved at the risk of a distortion of homogeneity'. Cremona (n 3) 517.

[16] See, eg, Opinion 1/76, EU:C:1977:63.

[17] See E Paasivirta, 'The Union's Participation in Legally Binding International Third-Party Dispute Settlement: Opinion 1/91 (EEA I) and Opinion 1/92 (EEA II)' in G Butler and RA Wessel (eds), *EU External Relations Law: The Cases in Context* (Oxford, Hart Publishing, 2022).

[18] 'An international agreement providing for such a system of courts is in principle compatible with Community law. The Community's competence in the field of international relations and its capacity to conclude international agreements necessarily entails the power to submit to the decisions of a court which is created or designated by such an agreement as regards the interpretation and application of its provisions.' Opinion 1/91 (n 1) para 40. It is significant that the Court here bases its finding on what it sees as necessary for the Union to exercise its capacity as an international actor. For more recent reiterations, see Opinion 2/13, EU:C:2014:2454, para 182; Opinion 1/17, EU:C:2019:341, para 106.

[19] B de Witte, 'A Selfish Court? The Court of Justice and the Design of International Dispute Settlement Beyond the European Union' in M Cremona and A Thies (eds), *The European Court of Justice and External Relations Law: Constitutional Challenges* (Oxford, Hart Publishing, 2014).

ruling which related directly to the form of court structure and its role in the draft EEA agreement have proved relevant to the future planning of dispute settlement structures – in particular, the need to ensure that such external courts or tribunals are not put in a position in which they need to determine the respective competences of the EU and its Member States (an issue of special relevance for mixed agreements),[20] and the need to ensure that the exclusive jurisdiction of the CJEU over the interpretation of EU law is preserved.[21] This latter requirement has led to a certain ambiguity over the status of the international agreement in question: while for the purposes of establishing the interpretational jurisdiction of the CJEU itself, it is regarded as 'an integral part of EU law',[22] it may – despite the exclusive jurisdiction of the CJEU over questions of EU law – be interpreted authoritatively by the court or tribunal established by the agreement.[23]

In the EEA Opinions, the principle of autonomy was closely linked to the homogeneity objective. The Court emphasised the particularity of the EEA in carrying over many provisions of EU law with the express intention of establishing a homogeneous interpretation and application of this EEA law. The proposal to create a joint court also underlined the very close nature of the integration envisioned. The Court's Opinion was designed to ensure, despite this strong integration objective, the distinctiveness and separateness of the EU legal order. Thus, it has been regarded as effectively setting limits to the degree of integration possible between the EU and third countries. The EEA has worked remarkably well as a result of what Halvard Haukeland Fredriksen has called the pragmatism of both the EFTA State Parties to the Agreement, and the EU,[24] their willingness to live with the constraints demanded on both sides, with all the democratic and efficiency challenges they pose.[25]

However, the last 30 years have shown that the autonomy concerns of the Court were not specific to the EEA model, but were more general in nature. The principle of autonomy has become an important principle in structuring EU external relations,[26] in so doing articulating the 'essential characteristics' of the EU's constitutional order.[27] Relevant not only in cases of very close integration such as that

[20] See eg, Opinion 2/13 (n 18) paras 215–35.

[21] See eg, ibid paras 201–14; Opinion 1/17 (n 18) para 118.

[22] Case 181/73 *Haegeman*, EU:C:1974:41, paras 3–5.

[23] Opinion 1/17 (n 18) para 118.

[24] Fredriksen (n 4); Fredriksen and Franklin (n 4).

[25] C Frommelt, 'Institutional Challenges for External Differentiated Integration: The Case of the EEA', Working Paper, EUI RSCAS, 2020/65.

[26] De Witte (n 19); J-W van Rossem, 'The Autonomy of EU Law: More is Less?' in RA Wessel and S Blockmans (eds), *Between Autonomy and Dependence: The EU Legal Order under the Influence of International Organisations* (The Hague, TMC Asser Press, 2013); C Contartese, 'The Autonomy of the EU Legal Order in the ECJ's External Relations Case Law: From the "Essential" to the "Specific Characteristics" of the Union and Back Again' (2017) 54 *Common Market Law Review* 1627; M Klamert, 'The Autonomy of the EU (and of EU Law): Through the Kaleidoscope' (2017) 42 *Common Market Law Review* 815; J Odermatt, 'When a Fence Becomes a Cage: The Principle of Autonomy in EU External Relations Law' in M Cremona (ed), *Structural Principles in EU External Relations Law* (Oxford, Hart Publishing, 2018); K Lenaerts, 'The Autonomy of European Union Law' (2019) I *Post di Aisdue*, https://www.aisdue.eu/wp-content/uploads/2019/04/001C_Lenaerts.pdf.

[27] M Cremona, 'Structural Principles and Their Role in EU External Relations Law' in Cremona (n 26); Opinion 1/17 (n 18) paras 109–11.

represented by the EEA, autonomy has emerged as a concern in the context of multilateral conventions,[28] sectoral agreements such as that establishing the European and Community Patents Court,[29] and the Energy Charter Treaty,[30] as well as bilateral investment treaties and free trade agreements.[31] We have seen that institutional closeness does not mitigate autonomy concerns – rather, the contrary. The emphasis in recent agreements (and case law) has been on the institutional and legal distinctness of the international regime and the autonomous EU legal order,[32] with the incidental effect of drawing attention to the uniqueness of the EEA.

Let us now turn to one aspect of that uniqueness: the objective of homogeneity. Here, the last 30 years have seen some striking developments. Despite the *Polydor* principle and the different objectives of the EEA and the EU, to which the CJEU had drawn attention, when specific provisions came before the courts, it was generally found that there was no good reason to interpret them differently and that Article 6 EEA required the courts to follow prior CJEU case law.[33] Indeed as the CJEU said in *Ospelt*, 'several provisions of the [EEA] are intended to ensure as uniform an interpretation as possible thereof throughout the EEA … It is for the Court, in that context, to ensure that the rules of the EEA Agreement which are identical in substance to those of the Treaty are interpreted uniformly within the Member States'.[34] The EFTA Court has also established a presumption that, in the absence of specific circumstances justifying a different interpretation, 'homogeneity should prevail' and, as Einarsson has pointed out, it is very rare for this presumption to be rebutted.[35]

Beyond the interpretation of specific provisions, over the last 30 years, the EFTA Court has overseen the emergence of a 'distinct legal order' founded on the EEA Agreement.[36] The EEA legal order is distinct from EU law; it includes the principle of state liability,[37] and the principle of conforming interpretation,[38] but has adopted its own distinct approach to the question of direct effect. The EEA does not require that its provisions or annexes have direct effect, and despite a somewhat puzzling

[28] Case C-459/03 *Commission v Ireland*, EU:C:2006:345 (*Mox Plant*); Opinion 2/13 (n 18).

[29] Opinion 1/09, EU:C:2011:123.

[30] Case C-741/19 *Republic of Moldova v Komstroy LLC*, EU:C:2021:655.

[31] Case C-284/16 *Achmea*, EU:C:2018:158; Opinion 1/17 (n 18).

[32] See, eg, Opinion 1/17 (n 18) Case C-66/18 *Commission v Hungary (GATS)*, EU:C:2020:792; the EU-UK Trade and Cooperation Agreement.

[33] For an early example, see Case T-115/94 *Opel Austria GmbH v Council*, EU:T:1997:3.

[34] Case C-452/01 *Margarethe Ospelt* EU:C:2003:493, para 29.

[35] Case E-3/98 *Rainford-Towning*, [1998] EFTA Ct Rep 205, para 21; Case E-1/03 *EFTA Surveillance Authority v Iceland* [2003] EFTA Ct Rep 143, para 27. See further ÓJ Einarsson, 'The Advisory Opinion Procedure and the Relationship between the EFTA Court and the Norwegian Courts: Recent Developments' (2022) 61 *Lov og Rett* 221, at 232.

[36] The phrase used in Case E-9/97 *Sveinbjörnsdóttir v Iceland* [1998] EFTA Ct Rep 95, para 59. The discussion in the following paragraphs is drawn from M Cremona, 'Extending the Reach of EU Law: The EU as an International Legal Actor' in M Cremona and J Scott (eds), *EU Law beyond EU Borders: The Extraterritorial Reach of EU Law* (Oxford, Oxford University Press, 2019).

[37] *Sveinbjörnsdóttir* (n 36) paras 46–63, referring to Joined Cases C-6/90 and C-9/90 *Andrea Francovich and Danila Bonifaci and Others v Italian Republic*, EU:C:1991:428.

[38] Case E-4/01 *Karlsson v Iceland* [2002] EFTA Ct Rep. 240, para 28.

comment by the CJEU on the legal effect of EU Regulations in the EEA[39] the EFTA Court has maintained this position.[40] The legal boundary remains clear, as does the institutional boundary. Just as the EU's own requirements of autonomy would not allow the legal boundary to shift in the sense of accepting an external input into law-making structures, the EEA was deliberately shaped to accommodate the EFTA States' concerns about sovereignty.

Central to this EEA legal order is the objective of ensuring equality of treatment of individuals and economic operators throughout the EEA. The Preamble to the EEA agreement expressly links homogeneity and equality,[41] and we can, I think, see within the EEA legal order an emphasis on equality of individual rights within a broader legal space rather than legal homogeneity.

Let us look at a couple of examples from the EFTA Court and the CJEU. The EFTA Court's approach to treaty interpretation has been influenced by the need, where possible, to ensure equality of rights between EU and EFTA nationals. In *Sveinbjörnsdóttir*, for example, the EFTA Court held that the doctrine of state liability applies in the EEA context. The EFTA Court affirmed both the existence of an EEA legal order and the importance of equality of rights in that order, linked to the homogeneity objective:

> The Court finds that the homogeneity objective and the objective of establishing the right of individuals and economic operators to equal treatment and equal opportunities are so strongly expressed in the EEA Agreement that the EFTA States must be obliged to provide for compensation for loss and damage caused to an individual by incorrect implementation of a directive.[42]

Even more striking, perhaps, is the way in which the EFTA Court has responded to changes in EU primary law, which have not been reflected in amendments to the EEA Agreement. The most important of these changes for the EEA are the Charter of Fundamental Rights and the creation of EU citizenship, especially given the latter's close connection to free movement of persons. Interestingly, the relevance of the Charter to the interpretation of EEA law has not assumed great significance before the EFTA Court.[43] When Directive 2004/38 (the so-called 'Citizens' Rights Directive') was incorporated into the EEA Annexes, the Joint Committee adopted a declaration affirming that EU citizenship 'has no equivalent' in the EEA. This has posed a

[39] In Case C-431/11 *UK v Council*, EU:C:2013:589, paras 53–54, the CJEU appeared to say that under Art 7 EEA, an EU regulation takes effect within the EEA without the need for implementation, an interpretation counter to that taken by the EFTA Court in, eg, *Karlsson v Iceland* (n 38) para 28.

[40] Case E-15/14 *EFTA Surveillance Authority v Iceland* [2015] EFTA Ct Rep 40, paras 31–32. See further T Bekkedal, 'Understanding the Nature of the EEA Agreement: On the Direct Applicability of Regulations' (2020) 57 *Common Market Law Review* 773.

[41] EEA Preamble, recital 15: 'Whereas, in full deference to the independence of the courts, the objective of the Contracting Parties is to arrive at, and maintain, a uniform interpretation and application of this Agreement and those provisions of Community legislation which are substantially reproduced in this Agreement and to arrive at an equal treatment of individuals and economic operators as regards the four freedoms and the conditions of competition.'

[42] *Sveinbjörnsdóttir* (n 36) para 60.

[43] For an exception, see Case E-10/14 *Deveci* [2014] EFTA Ct Rep 1364, para 64, in which the EFTA Court, in the context of the Transfer of Undertakings Directive, 'found no reason' to address Art 16 of the Charter, while expressing the view that 'freedom to conduct a business lies … at the heart of the EEA Agreement and must be recognised in accordance with EEA law and national law and practices'.

challenge to the EFTA Court in its attempts to interpret the Directive for the EEA in the light of EU case law, and the EFTA Court has shown remarkable ingenuity in managing to maintain homogeneity.[44] For example, in *Gunnarsson*, the EFTA Court held that Article 7 of Directive 2004/38 (on the right of residence) can be interpreted to impose obligations on a home state,[45] despite the fact that in similar cases the CJEU has applied the EU Treaty provisions on citizenship – Articles 20 and 21 TFEU, which of course do not exist in the EEA Agreement – rather than the Directive.[46] This result was confirmed in both *Jabbi*[47] and *Campbell*,[48] in which the EFTA Court interpreted Directive 2004/38 so as to achieve equality of rights (in these cases derived rights for third-country national family members) within the EEA, which in CJEU case law have been based on the citizenship provisions of the EU Treaties (in particular Article 21 TFEU). The EFTA Court in *Campbell* explained its approach to its interpretation clearly:

> [T]he Court's interpretation of the Directive must take into account the context in which the Directive is situated in EEA law and the manner in which this context differs from the EU pillar. In the context of EEA law, the fact that no parallel to Article 21 TFEU exists in EEA law entails that the Directive must be interpreted differently in the EEA, in order to realize the objective of the Directive, which is, above all, to facilitate and strengthen the exercise of the primary and individual right to move and reside freely within the territory of the EEA States.[49]

As Franklin and Fredriksen point out,[50] the EFTA Court's statement in *Campbell* that 'freedom of movement for workers represents a specific expression of the general right to move and reside freely within the EEA'[51] reflects CJEU rulings.[52] Within the EU legal order, the source of the 'general right' of free movement is found in Articles 20 and 21 TFEU, the citizenship provisions of the EU Treaties; Franklin and Fredriksen suggest that the EFTA Court may be prepared to identify such a 'general right' as an unwritten principle of EEA law.[53]

Gunnarsson, *Jabbi* and *Campbell* demonstrate the distinction between homogeneous interpretation of a specific piece of legislation (Directive 2004/38) and homogeneity of result, in terms of individual rights. In these cases, the EFTA Court, in what Christa Tobler has called 'a very particular understanding of homogeneity',[54] preferred the latter over the former.

[44] Fredriksen (n 4).

[45] Case E-26/13 *Gunnarsson* [2014] EFTA Ct Rep 254, paras 77–81.

[46] See, eg, Case C-224/02 *Pusa*, EU:C:2004:273.

[47] Case E-28/15 *Yankuba Jabbi v The Norwegian Government, Represented by the Immigration Appeals Board* [2016] EFTA Ct Rep 575.

[48] Case E-4/19 *Campbell v The Norwegian Government, Represented by the Immigration Appeals Board*.

[49] ibid paras 56–57.

[50] CNK Franklin and HH Fredriksen, 'Differentiated Citizenship in the European Economic Area' in D Thym and D Kostakopoulou (eds), *Research Handbook on Union Citizenship* (Cheltenham, Edward Elgar, 2021).

[51] *Campbell* (n 48) para 48.

[52] See, eg, Case C-233/12 *Gardella*, EU:C:2013:449, para 38.

[53] Franklin and Fredriksen (n 50) 298.

[54] C Tobler, 'Free Movement of Persons in the EU v in the EEA: Of Effect-Related Homogeneity and a Reversed Polydor Principle' in N Cambien, D Kochenov and E Muir (eds), *European Citizenship under*

What about the CJEU? Two recent judgments echo the EFTA Court's concern for equality of treatment as well as strikingly illustrating the degree to which the EEA creates an integrated legal space. In *UK v Council*, the Court had to decide the correct legal basis in the EU Treaties for a Council decision on the position to be taken by the EU within the EEA Joint Committee concerning an amendment to one of the EEA Annexes, bringing it into line with amended EU legislation on coordination of social security for migrant workers. The Court rejected the possible legal bases of Article 79(2)(b) TFEU, which concerns the rights of third-country nationals residing legally in a Member State,[55] and Article 217 TFEU, which is the legal basis for the EEA itself. Instead, it agreed with the Commission and the Council on the choice of Article 48 TFEU, on social security for migrant workers within the EU, as the appropriate legal basis. In doing so, it contrasted the EU's immigration policy with the EEA agreement, which – it stressed – ensured free movement for EU nationals in the EFTA States as well as vice versa:

> [The adopted decision is a measure] by which the law governing the EU internal market is to be extended as far as possible to the EEA, with the result that nationals of the EEA States concerned benefit from the free movement of persons under the same social conditions as EU citizens. Were it not for the amendment contemplated by the contested decision, free movement of persons could not be exercised within the EEA under the same social conditions as within the European Union, which would undoubtedly undermine the development of the association and the realisation of the objectives pursued by the EEA Agreement.[56]

Here, the Court is not simply stressing the need to amend the EEA Annexes to ensure a dynamic homogeneity between EU and EEA law; it is emphasising the equality between EEA/EFTA nationals and EU citizens – their 'essentially identical' right of free movement[57] – which render it appropriate to use the same legal basis. The EEA, for the EU, is close to being seen as an extension of the internal rather than external policy:

> [I]t is only in the sphere of the internal policies and actions of the European Union or of the external actions relating to third countries which can be placed on the same footing as Member States of the European Union … that Article 48 TFEU empowers the European Union to adopt measures in this area.[58]

In *Ruska Federacija v IN*,[59] the EU Court of Justice took a significant further step in establishing the principle of equality throughout the EEA and its conception of the EEA legal order. Within the EU, of course, free movement has become entwined with both citizenship and the Area of Freedom, Security and Justice (AFSJ), which

Stress (Leiden, Brill, 2020) 492. Tobler argues that this may be thought of as a 'reverse *Polydor* principle': different contexts leading to different interpretations of the same text.

[55] Article 79(2)(b) TFEU was the legal basis for Regulation 1231/2010 [2010] OJ L 344/1, which extends EU social security regulations to third-country nationals who are legally resident within the EU.

[56] *UK v Council* (n 39) paras 58–59.

[57] ibid para 51. Similar phrasing is routinely used: see, eg, Case C-39/10 *Commission v Estonia*, EU:C:2012:282, para 67, where the phrase used is 'substantially identical'.

[58] Case C-81/13 *UK v Council*, EU:C:2014:2449, para 59, distinguishing the Association Agreement with Turkey.

[59] Case C-897/19 PPU *Ruska Federacija v IN*, EU:C:2020:262.

do not form part of the EEA Agreement as such. Nonetheless, in the context of an extradition request from Russia respecting a Russian-Icelandic dual national on holiday in Croatia, the Court applied the reasoning it had previously developed in *Petruhhin* with respect to the extradition of EU citizens exercising their rights of free movement.[60] It drew on the network of agreements concluded between the EU and EFTA States alongside the EEA, including those extending the Schengen *acquis* and the surrender procedure of the European Arrest Warrant to Iceland and Norway.[61] The Court was able to argue – despite the fact that the EEA Agreement itself has not been amended, and in striking contrast to the rather reductive view expressed in Opinion 1/91 – that Iceland has 'a special relationship with the European Union which goes beyond economic and commercial cooperation' and which is 'based on proximity, long-standing common values and European identity'.[62] The point of connection with EEA law for the Icelandic national in *Ruska Federacija v IN* was the fact that he was a recipient of services in an EU Member State.[63] Building on this, the Court went on to declare the 'objectively comparable' status of EU citizens and nationals of EFTA EEA States in terms which are striking in terms of referring to both citizenship and the AFSJ as the legal context of free movement of persons:

> It is appropriate to add that not only the fact that the person concerned has the status as a national of an EFTA State, which is a party to the EEA Agreement, but also the fact that that State implements and applies the Schengen *acquis*, renders the situation of that person objectively comparable with that of an EU citizen to whom, in accordance with Article 3(2) TEU, the Union offers an area of freedom, security and justice without internal frontiers, in which the free movement of persons is ensured.[64]

Both the EFTA Court and the CJEU have therefore found ways to bridge the gap between the two EEA pillars,[65] the EFTA Court through creative interpretation of implemented secondary legislation and the CJEU emphasising the 'essentially identical' nature of the rights established within the EEA and the 'objectively comparable' status of EFTA/EEA nationals and EU citizens. Certainly, both Courts use homogeneity as a starting point in their reasoning; however, as we have seen, homogeneity as to the substance of individual rights has proved to carry more weight than the formal homogeneity of interpretation or questioning the precise scope of Article 6 EEA.

These cases – especially the CJEU judgments – also demonstrate the place of the EEA Agreement as part of a broader relationship of integration between the EFTA and EU Member States, and it is to this point that we will now turn.

[60] Case C-182/15 *Petruhhin*, EU:C:2016:630.

[61] Agreement between the European Union and the Republic of Iceland and the Kingdom of Norway concerning the latters' association with the implementation, application and development of the Schengen acquis [1999] OJ L176/36; Agreement between the European Union and the Republic of Iceland and the Kingdom of Norway on the surrender procedure between the Member States of the European Union and Iceland and Norway [2006] OJ L292/2.

[62] *Ruska Federacija v IN* (n 59) paras 44 and 50.

[63] ibid para 52; the Court relied on Case 186/87 *Cowan*, EU:C:1989:47.

[64] *Ruska Federacija v IN* (n 59) para 58.

[65] *Jabbi* (n 47) para 62.

III. DYNAMISM AND INTEGRATION IN THE EU NEIGHBOURHOOD

The European Economic Area envisaged in the EEA Agreement is 'dynamic' as well as homogeneous; political and legal mechanisms were put in place to ensure the continued alignment of EEA and EU law. This is a key characteristic of EEA integration, and although it has been remarkably successful, it is characterised by elements of ambiguity. Exploring the nature of dynamism in the EEA throws light on the nature of the EU's integration relationships within its neighbourhood.

Scholars have highlighted a number of features of this dynamism.[66] First, the mechanisms established in the EEA Agreement lack reciprocity: the EFTA States' input into new EU legislative proposals, while not negligible, is not on a level with that of EU Member States and EU structures do not allow for full participation of third countries in EU legislative institutions. Second, the Agreement lacks any methodology (short of formal EEA revision) to ensure dynamism in case of changes to EU primary law, and this is not only a matter of the EU developing new fields of integration which the EEA does not share, such as the Economic and Monetary Union; as the case law on free movement of persons illustrates, changes to primary law also impact secondary law forming part of the EEA legal order. Third, the changing nature of EU governance, such as the widespread 'agencification' of EU regulation, poses challenges in terms of maintaining the effectiveness of the EEA's institutional structures of integration.[67] Fourth, as EU law becomes more complex and interconnected (the policy fields of environmental law and energy law, to give an example), the challenge of assessing the 'EEA relevance' of new measures becomes ever more difficult. The management of dynamism through an intergovernmental process in the EEA Joint Committee has, on the one hand, led to a tendency to resolve difficulties through extended negotiation and delay rather than the use of Article 102 EEA or a formal veto and, on the other hand, has demonstrated the remarkable resilience of the EEA, given how dramatically the EU has changed over the last 30 years.[68]

However, in addition to these features, we can see the 'dynamism' of the EEA from a different perspective: that of the broader context of a relationship based on integration. The EU's relations with its neighbours – not least its EFTA neighbours – are integration-based.[69] While external relationships based on integration are certainly not limited to the EU's neighbourhood, we may say that there is a constitutional expectation, reflected in Article 8 of the Treaty on European Union (TEU), that neighbourly relations will be integration-based.[70] The UK's insistence on a post-withdrawal

[66] See, eg, Fredriksen and Franklin (n 4); Fredriksen (n 4).

[67] T Bekkedal, 'Third State Participation in EU Agencies: Exploring the EEA Precedent' (2019) 56 *Common Market Law Review* 381.

[68] Fredriksen (n 4).

[69] Cremona and Nic Shuibhne (n 6). See also S Blockmans and A Lazowski (eds), *The European Union and its Neighbours: A Legal Appraisal of the EU's Policies of Stabilisation, Partnership and Integration* (The Hague, TMC Asser Press, 2006); S Gstöhl and D Phinnemore (eds), *The Proliferation of Privileged Partnerships between the European Union and its Neighbours* (Abingdon, Routledge, 2019).

[70] Article 8 TEU mandates the EU to 'develop a special relationship with neighbouring countries, aiming to establish an area of prosperity and good neighbourliness, founded on the values of the Union and characterised by close and peaceful relations based on cooperation'. Alongside the EEA, we may point to the

relation that was transactional rather than integrational in character, while at the same time pressing for some more integrational elements (such as measures relating to the area of freedom, security and justice), as well as making the negotiation more complicated, forced the EU to more closely define what it expected of its neighbourhood relationships, and the dividing line between members and non-members.[71]

What then do we mean by an integration-based external relationship? Two dimensions are especially relevant for our discussion of the EEA. First, integration-based relations are conceived as long-term commitments with the potential for development. Second, while integration-based relations will have a formal agreement at their core – normally an Association Agreement (the legal basis of the EEA) – that agreement will typically operate within a policy framework establishing a broader field of cooperation, with more or less formal elements, including additional agreements and possibly financial instruments, with these different elements evolving over time.

We can, I think, see the commitment to the creation of a 'dynamic' EEA in the light of both these characteristics of an integration-based relationship. The ability of the EEA to adjust to developments in EU integration (while not necessarily incorporating them per se), and the importance the CJEU has attached to the network of relations between the EU and EFTA partners (as in *Ruska Federacija v IN*) support this understanding of dynamism in the context of the EEA. Indeed, Rye makes a persuasive argument that the EEA is best seen as one stage in an ongoing two-way process of integration between the EU and EFTA States:

> There is a connection between the 1972/73 bilateral free trade agreements, the 1984 Luxembourg Declaration, the 1992 EEA Agreement, and the 1995 enlargement. These events were not simply responses to isolated challenges of the time, but key moments in a gradually more comprehensive integration process. Not only did they formalise the cooperation between the EFTA countries and the EC that had already begun, but they also paved the way for further integration in that they included gradually more ambitious aims for future cooperation.[72]

The reference in this passage to the 1995 enlargement leads us to question the relationship between such integration-based relationships – integration as a foreign policy objective of the EU – and EU membership.[73] To what extent does the kind of integration exemplified by the EEA inevitably tend towards EU accession? There is clearly a tension here; the very longevity of the EEA, its success as a form of integration without membership, and the challenges it poses reflect the challenge the EU faces in developing an integration-based policy which is 'neither one of absorption

Stabilisation and Association Agreements with the countries of the Western Balkans, and the European Neighbourhood Policy, including the Deep and Comprehensive Free Trade Agreements concluded with Ukraine, Moldova and Georgia.

[71] M Cremona, 'EU External Action: Learning from Brexit', https://cadmus.eui.eu/bitstream/handle/1814/75187/EU_Learning_Brexit_Cremona_Art_2022.pdf?sequence=1&isAllowed=y, 251.

[72] L Rye, 'Integration from the Outside: The EC and EFTA from 1960 to the 1995 Enlargement' in HA Ikonomou, H Andry and R Byberg (eds), *European Enlargement across Rounds and beyond Borders* (Abingdon, Routledge, 2017).

[73] See further M Cremona, 'Enlargement as Foreign Policy: A Research Agenda' in Ikonomou, Andry and Byberg (n 72).

(through accession) nor one of dominance through satellite forming'.[74] With this in mind, let us briefly address two aspects of the way in which the EEA has evolved as an integration agreement.

The first is the question of reciprocity. Reciprocity appears in the EEA's Preamble, linked to equality and 'an overall balance of benefits, rights and obligations' for the Contracting Parties. What is its significance in the context of an agreement which creates what the CJEU has called 'special relations of integration' with the EU? In such agreements, the Court has in fact been relaxed about how reciprocity in implementation is achieved. For example, it has been prepared to interpret an agreement as capable of creating directly effective rights within the EU, despite the agreement's lack of substantive reciprocity and without looking for reciprocity in the method of implementation. In the early case of *Bresciani*, for example, the Court held that it was no bar to direct effect that the respective obligations of the EC and the Yaoundé partners were not fully reciprocal.[75] Provisions of the Yaoundé Convention relating to the abolition of customs duties and charges of equivalent effect created directly effective rights because under those provisions, 'the Community undertook precisely the same obligation towards the Associated States to abolish charges having equivalent effect as, in the Treaty, the Member States assumed towards each other'.[76] And in *Kupferberg*, the Court held that for the Community to interpret a free trade agreement with Portugal as capable of direct effect, although Portugal may not grant such rights, 'is not in itself such as to constitute a lack of reciprocity in the implementation of the agreement'.[77] In contrast, where the agreement is not integrational but transactional in nature – as with the World Trade Organization, for example, or the recent free trade agreement with Canada (CETA) – the Court has emphasised reciprocity in the context of implementation and enforcement.[78] From this perspective, then, we can better understand the nature of reciprocity in the EEA, which is more concerned with equality of treatment;[79] the absence of direct effect within the EFTA EEA States does not – as in *Kupferberg* – constitute a lack of reciprocity.

Second, let us return briefly to the principle of autonomy. If that principle is concerned with safeguarding the distinctiveness of the EU legal order with respect to international law, then by its nature, it sets limits to the degree of integration that may be achieved within a dynamic integrative framework such as the EEA. 'Integration through law' may have an external dimension, forming part of the EU's external

[74] Cremona (n 3), citing Spinner, in M Robinson and J Findlater (eds), *Creating a European Economic Space: Legal Aspects of EC-EFTA Relations* (Dublin, Irish Centre for European Law, 1990).

[75] Case 87/75 *Bresciani*, EU:C:1976:18, paras 22–23: 'the Convention was not concluded in order to ensure equality in the obligations which the Community assumes with regard to the Associated States, but in order to promote their development in accordance with the aim of the first Convention annexed to the Treaty. This imbalance between the obligations assumed by the Community towards the Associated States, which is inherent in the special nature of the Convention, does not prevent recognition by the Community that some of its provisions have a direct effect'.

[76] ibid para 25.

[77] Case 104/81 *Kupferberg*, EU:C:1982:362, para 18.

[78] Case C-149/96 *Portugal v Council*, EU:C:1999:574, paras 42–47; Opinion 1/17 (n 18) para 117 and *cf* also para 77.

[79] *UK v Council* (n 39) para 55.

policy, but the external does not thereby become internal.[80] This of course works in both directions: the EFTA EEA States also have their autonomy/sovereignty concerns. The complexity of EEA 'two pillar' institutional relations, the 'Byzantine structures' that I referred to in 1994, is a natural consequence of this. In the case of a transactional agreement such as the CETA, the autonomy-driven separation between the EU legal order and the CETA treaty regime operates within the framework of international law; as the Court pointed out in Opinion 1/17, the 'need to maintain the powers of the EU in international relations' requires the EU to be able to enter into this kind of agreement and establish institutions which 'stand outside the EU system'. In the case of the EEA, on the other hand, while the two-pillar structure preserves an institutional separation, the aim is one of deep integration and the creation of a distinct EEA legal order, with its own structural principles.

It is perhaps no coincidence that the CJEU has matured its jurisprudence on the principle of autonomy since 2016. While the UK experience as a Member State demonstrated that internal differentiation within a membership framework[81] gives rise to its own 'Byzantine' complexity, one impact of the UK's decision to withdraw from the EU has been to provoke a clearer definition of the limits of integration without membership and to sharpen, both politically and legally, the distinction between membership and non-membership. The enormous complexity of the attempt in the Northern Ireland Protocol – for good political and legal reasons – to bridge that distinction, while satisfying both the EU's autonomy and the UK's sovereignty concerns, bears witness to just how difficult this is.

IV. CONCLUSION

In this short reflection, I have returned to my 1994 analysis of the aim to create a 'dynamic and homogeneous' EEA and the 'Byzantine structures' that this aim, when faced with the need to comply with the principle of autonomy, entailed. We have seen that the principle of autonomy is not only triggered by the far-reaching homogeneity envisaged in the EEA, but has also become a central tenet of EU external relations, helping to define the relationship between the EU and international law. However, it is in the context of deeply integrated relationships such as the EEA that autonomy plays a role in determining the limits to integration and renders a highly complex institutional structure inevitable. Homogeneity, in the context of the EEA, has developed a specific orientation, centred on equality of rights operating within the EEA legal space, even at the expense of the homogeneous interpretation of secondary legislation. The EFTA Court has striven to produce homogeneity of result, and the CJEU, taking account of the network of relations linking the EFTA and EU Member States, has declared the position of EFTA/EEA nationals to be 'objectively comparable' to EU citizens. Turning to the 'dynamic' aspect of the EEA, the argument has been made that this dynamism is best understood in the context of its integration-based

[80] Cremona (n 36).

[81] An idea floated in Cremona (n 3).

character. The EU's integration-based agreements are anchored in a wider context of cooperation and are conceived as long-term projects capable of evolution. The EEA has shown itself capable of such development, even without formal changes to the EEA Agreement itself. At the same time, the EEA also demonstrates the challenges faced by the EU and its neighbourhood partners in attempting to achieve such close (and evolving) integration while safeguarding autonomy and sovereignty.

13

The Liechtenstein EEA Coordination Unit and the EFTA Court

ANDREA ENTNER-KOCH AND ROMINA SCHOBEL

SINCE THE VERY first Liechtenstein case before the EFTA Court (*Herbert Rainford-Towning*),[1] a close relationship has been established between the EFTA Court and the EEA Coordination Unit, which represents the Liechtenstein government in proceedings before the EFTA Court. This chapter mainly focuses on this long-lasting relationship between the EFTA Court and the EEA Coordination Unit. Furthermore, some particularly important EFTA Court judgments concerning Liechtenstein from the last 10 years[2] will be presented. Some general remarks on the role of the EEA Coordination Unit are also given as an introduction.

I. THE ROLE OF THE EEA COORDINATION UNIT

On 1 May 1995, the Principality of Liechtenstein became a full participant in the EEA. Shortly thereafter, in July 1995, the Liechtenstein government established the EEA Coordination Unit, reporting directly to the Prime Minister. The EEA Coordination Unit acts as the central contact and coordination office between the national authorities and the EFTA Institutions. The following tasks have, among others, been assigned to the EEA Coordination Unit with regard to the EEA Agreement:

- coordinating the incorporation of EEA-relevant EU legal acts;
- coordinating the national implementation of incorporated EU legal acts;
- advising the Liechtenstein government and the offices of the national administration on EEA-related matters;
- acting as Liechtenstein's SOLVIT Centre and as the National Internal Market Information Coordinator (NIMIC) of the Internal Market Information (IMI) System;

[1] Case E-3/98 *Herbert Rainford-Towning* [1998] EFTA Ct Rep 205.
[2] From 1 January 2013 until 31 October 2023.

- representing the Liechtenstein government in infringement proceedings initiated by the EFTA Surveillance Authority (ESA);
- representing the Liechtenstein government before the EFTA Court and the Court of Justice of the European Union (CJEU).

In its role of acting as a representative of the Liechtenstein government before the EFTA Court and the CJEU, the EEA Coordination Unit prepares written and oral statements, and participates in hearings before these European Courts on behalf of the Liechtenstein government.

The EEA Coordination Unit represents Liechtenstein in Liechtenstein cases pending before the EFTA Court (requests for advisory opinions by Liechtenstein courts and actions for infringement brought by ESA) as well as in cases of particular significance to Liechtenstein. In cases before the CJEU, the EEA Coordination Unit represents Liechtenstein in those cases of particular significance to Liechtenstein or the EEA in general.

II. LIECHTENSTEIN CASES BEFORE THE EFTA COURT

Since its establishment in 1994, the EFTA Court has delivered a number of important judgments concerning Liechtenstein. In this chapter we focus on some of the particularly important judgments that the EFTA Court has issued over the last 10 years,[3] which have either led to changes in Liechtenstein law or have provided important guidelines on the interpretation of EEA law.

These judgments were either based on requests for an advisory opinion by the Liechtenstein courts or actions for infringement brought by ESA. Over the last 10 years, the EFTA Court delivered 27 judgments[4] in cases where the Liechtenstein courts have requested an advisory opinion from the EFTA Court, and seven judgments[5] in cases where ESA brought an action for infringement against Liechtenstein before the EFTA Court. Of these seven infringement proceedings, three concerned the interpretation or application of EEA law and four concerned the late implementation of EEA law.

In the view of the Liechtenstein government, the EFTA Court has succeeded in being the guardian of a well-functioning, dynamic and homogeneous EEA. This trust and respect in the EFTA Court is also reflected by the high number of requests for advisory opinions made by the Liechtenstein courts in the last 10 years alone.

[3] From 1 January 2013 until 31 October 2023. Between 1 January 2023 and 1 November 2023, the Beschwerdekommission der Finanzmarktaufsicht has requested an advisory opinion from the EFTA Court in two more cases (Case E-2/23 *A Ltd v Finanzmarktaufsicht* and Case E-10/23 *X v Finanzmarktaufsicht*). A judgment in E-2/23 was delivered on 25 January 2024.

[4] Since 1995 the Liechtenstein courts have asked the EFTA Court for an advisory opinion in 36 cases. Joined cases have been counted as one.

[5] Since 1995, ESA has brought an action for infringement against Liechtenstein before the EFTA Court in 19 cases. Eleven of these cases concerned the interpretation or application of EEA law, six concerned the late implementation of EEA law and two were actions for annulment of a decision of ESA by Liechtenstein. Joined cases have been counted as one.

Liechtenstein courts	**Requests for an advisory opinion**[6]
Beschwerdekommission für Verwaltungsangelegenheiten	1
Beschwerdekommission der Finanzmarktaufsicht	2[7]
Fürstliches Landgericht	5
Fürstliches Obergericht	10
Fürstlicher Oberster Gerichtshof	3
Verwaltungsgerichtshof des Fürstentums Liechtenstein	4
Staatsgerichtshof des Fürstentums Liechtenstein	2
Total	**27**

According to Article 34 of the Agreement between the EFTA States on the Establishment of a Surveillance Authority and a Court of Justice (hereinafter the Surveillance and Court Agreement), only courts or tribunals in an EEA/EFTA State are entitled to refer questions on the interpretation of the EEA Agreement to the EFTA Court. In *Inconsult Anstalt*,[8] the EFTA Court noted that a number of factors have to be considered when deciding if a referring body qualifies as a court or tribunal within the meaning of Article 34 of the Surveillance and Court Agreement. These include whether the referring body is established by law, has a permanent existence, exercises binding jurisdiction, applies rules of law and is independent, and, as the case may be, whether its procedure is *inter partes* and similar to the procedure in court. In its judgment in *Inconsult Anstalt*, the EFTA Court qualified the Beschwerdekommission der Finanzmarktaufsicht as a court or tribunal within the meaning of Article 34 of the Surveillance and Court Agreement.

This qualification of the Beschwerdekommission der Finanzmarktaufsicht and consequently the Beschwerdekommission für Verwaltungsangelegenheiten as courts and tribunals, and their recognition as independent decision-making bodies by the EFTA Court as a European court, was important for Liechtenstein.

A. Social Security

In the area of social security, the EFTA Court provided clarity and legal certainty with its interpretations of Regulation 883/2004[9] as well as Regulation 987/2009.[10]

[6] Requests where a judgment was adopted between 1 January 2013 and 31 October 2023. Joined cases have been counted as one. Between 1 January 2023 and 1 November 2023, the Beschwerdekommission der Finanzmarktaufsicht has requested an advisory opinion from the EFTA Court in two more cases (Case E-2/23 *A Ltd v Finanzmarktaufsicht* and Case E-10/23 *X v Finanzmarktaufsicht*). A judgment in E-2/23 was delivered 25 January 2024. The Verwaltungsgerichtshof des Fürstentums Liechtenstein requested an advisory opinion in Case E-1/24 *TC* on 3 January 2024.

[7] In one case, the Beschwerdekommission der Finanzmarktaufsicht withdrew the request for an advisory opinion (Case E-6/20 *Pintail AG v Finanzmarktaufsicht*).

[8] Case E-4/09 *Inconsult Anstalt v Finanzmarktaufsicht*, [2009–10] EFTA Ct Rep 86.

[9] Regulation (EC) No 883/2004 of the European Parliament and of the Council of 29 April 2004 on the coordination of social security systems [2004] OJ L166, 30 April, p 1.

[10] Regulation (EC) No 987/2009 of the European Parliament and of the Council of 16 September 2009 laying down the procedure for implementing Regulation (EC) No 883/2004 on the coordination of social security systems [2009] OJ L284, 30 October, p 1.

In a judgment delivered at the beginning of 2023, the EFTA Court answered questions concerning the personal scope of Regulation 883/2004 and whether an EEA national must also be resident in an EEA State to fall within the personal scope of that Regulation. The EFTA Court found in its judgment in *Christian Maitz*[11] that, in addition to being a national of an EEA State and being subject to the legislation of one or more EEA States, Article 2(1) of Regulation 883/2004 does not require a person to be resident in an EEA State. In addition, the EFTA Court found that, to produce legal effect, an attestation of the competent institution of the EEA State stating that its legislation is applicable pursuant to Regulation 883/2004 must not necessarily be issued by means of form PDA1.

Further important clarification was given by the EFTA Court in *ISTM International Shipping & Trucking Management GmbH*[12] when determining that the mere presence of a registered office of an undertaking does not suffice for the purposes of Article 13(1)(b) of Regulation 883/2004, read in conjunction with Article 14(5a) of Regulation 987/2009. Article 13(1)(b) of Regulation 883/2004 specifies that the legislation of the EEA State in which the registered office or place of business of the undertaking or employer is situated is applicable if the person does not pursue a substantial part of their activities in their EEA State of residence and if the person normally pursues an activity as an employed person in two or more EEA States. According to Article 14(5a) of Regulation 987/2009, the 'registered office or place of business' is where the essential decisions of the undertaking must be adopted and the functions of its central administration must be carried out. To determine where the essential decisions are adopted and the functions of the central administration are carried out, a series of factors must be taken into account. This is in line with the interpretation by the Administrative Commission for the Coordination of Social Security Systems (hereinafter 'the Administrative Commission') as set out in its Practical guide on the applicable legislation in the European Union, the European Economic Area and in Switzerland (hereinafter 'the Practical Guide') and also by the CJEU. Concerning the Practical Guide, the EFTA Court noted that it is neither legally binding nor enforceable, but is a useful tool for the interpretation of Regulation 883/2004 and Regulation 987/2009.

In *C v Concordia Schweizerische Kranken- und Unfallversicherung*,[13] the EFTA Court held that according to Article 24(1) of Regulation 883/2004, if a pensioner is not entitled to benefits in kind in their EEA State of residence because the benefits do not fall within the scope of the national social security system, that pensioner is entitled to benefits in kind on behalf of the competent institution in the EEA State under whose legislation the pension is paid.

[11] Case E-5/22 *Christian Maitz v Liechtensteinische Alters- und Hinterlassenenversicherung, Liechtensteinische Invalidenversicherung and Liechtensteinische Familienausgleichskasse*.

[12] Case E-1/21 *ISTM International Shipping & Trucking Management GmbH v Liechtensteinische Alters- und Hinterlassenenversicherung, Liechtensteinische Invalidenversicherung, and Liechtensteinische Familienausgleichskasse*.

[13] Case E-2/18 *C v Concordia Schweizerische Kranken- und Unfallversicherung AG, Landesvertretung Liechtenstein*.

Furthermore, within a short period of time, the EFTA Court was asked twice by the Fürstliche Obergericht for an advisory opinion concerning the interpretation of Article 87(2) of Regulation 987/2009. According to Article 87(2) of Regulation 987/2009, the social security institution of the place of stay or residence will forward a report to the debtor institution that requested the medical examination. These findings of the institution of the place of stay or residence are binding for the debtor institution. In *Abuelo Insua Juan Bautista*,[14] the EFTA Court was asked whether the findings according to Article 87(2) of Regulation 987/2009 are also binding for the recipients of benefits and prohibit the recipient from challenging those findings in the procedure before the debtor institutions. The EFTA Court declared that the recipient or claimant of benefits is not prevented from challenging those findings in an administrative procedure. In *Walter Waller*,[15] the EFTA Court determined that Article 87(2) of Regulation 987/2009 prohibits the debtor institution from challenging the medical findings of the institution of the place of stay or residence in the administrative procedure. The binding nature of the aforementioned Article 87(2) applies in court proceedings following from an administrative proceeding before the debtor institution in circumstances such as those in the main proceeding of the underlying national case.

B. Financial Services and Solvency II

Pursuant to the EEA Agreement, the EEA/EFTA States are fully integrated into the EU's internal market for financial services. Hence, an effective and homogeneous application of common rules and supervision throughout the EEA is of great interest both to the EU and to the EEA/EFTA States. Accordingly, numerous requests for an advisory opinion concerning the interpretation of various financial services acts have been submitted to the EFTA Court by the Liechtenstein courts.

Over the last 10 years, no fewer than four requests for an advisory opinion concerned the interpretation of Directive 2009/138/EC (hereinafter 'Solvency II').[16]

With the request for an advisory opinion in *Gable Insurance AG in Konkurs*[17] concerning the winding-up of an insurance undertaking, the Fürstliche Landgericht called for clarification on the interpretation of Solvency II and in particular the definition of 'insurance claims'. The insolvency proceedings concerned Gable Insurance AG in Konkurs, a Liechtenstein insurance undertaking entitled to market non-life insurance products. Due to the fact that Gable Insurance AG pursued its business in several European countries and marketed around 50 different non-life insurance products, it was a large and complex insolvency. In its judgment, the EFTA Court clarified that a claim is an 'insurance claim' if it is based on an insured event which

[14] Case E-13/15 *Abuelo Insua Juan Bautista v Liechtensteinische Invalidenversicherung* [2015] EFTA Ct Rep 720.

[15] Case E-24/15 *Walter Waller v Liechtensteinische Invalidenversicherung* [2016] EFTA Ct Rep 527.

[16] Directive 2009/138/EC of the European Parliament and of the Council of 25 November 2009 on the taking-up and pursuit of the business of insurance and reinsurance [2009] OJ L335, 17 December, p 1.

[17] Case E-3/19 *Gable Insurance AG in Konkurs* (*Gable I*).

occurred before the cancellation of an insurance contract. However, the scope of an insurance claim cannot be limited to claims that have arisen, been lodged or admitted before the opening of the winding-up procedure if the claim cannot yet be fully determined. It is for the national legislator to set further conditions and rules on the lodging, verification and admission of claims. Claims for repayment of premiums due to a termination of an insurance contract which takes place after the opening of the winding-up procedure will not be considered as insurance claims within the meaning of Article 268(1)(g) of Solvency II.

In *SMA SA and Société Mutuelle d'Assurance du Bâtiment et des Travaux Publics Liechtenstein*,[18] the Fürstlicher Oberster Gerichtshof asked whether in particular Articles 27 and 28 of Solvency II, and its predecessor Directives, are to be interpreted as granting rights to creditors of a supervised direct insurance undertaking who are not policy holders, insured persons or beneficiaries, or another party to an insurance contract, and who have no direct right of action against an insurance undertaking, which can be the basis for liability claims towards the competent supervisory authority. Two French insurance companies brought an action against the Finanzmarktaufsicht Liechtenstein alleging that the Finanzmarktaufsicht failed to fulfil its supervisory obligations and was ultimately responsible for losses incurred by the French insurance companies as a result of the insolvency of Gable Insurance AG. According to the EFTA Court's ruling, Solvency II does not aim to provide assurance against insolvency or the liquidation of insurance companies, and it does not offer protection to economic operators against losses resulting from the insolvency of insurance companies. Due to the fact that neither Solvency II nor its predecessor Directives confer any express rights on economic operators such as the French insurance companies, the Directives do not give rise to state liability claims against the competent supervisory authority.

Additionally, in *Pascal Nobile v DAS Rechtsschutz-Versicherungs AG*,[19] the EFTA Court was asked to give an advisory opinion concerning the interpretation of Article 201(1)(a) of Solvency II concerning the free choice of lawyer. The EFTA Court held that Article 201(1)(a) of Solvency II precludes a legal expense insurance contract to release the insurance company from its obligations if the insured person mandates an attorney without the consent of the company, at a point in time when the insured person would be entitled to make a claim under the contract.

C. The Free Movement of Persons

A specific sectoral adaptation to Annexes V and VIII to the EEA Agreement applies to Liechtenstein in the field of the free movement of persons, also covering Directive 2004/38/EC.[20] According to this sectoral adaptation, Liechtenstein is entitled to

[18] Case E-5/20 *SMA SA and Société Mutuelle d'Assurance du Bâtiment et des Travaux Publics Liechtenstein* (*Gable II*).

[19] Case E-21/16 *Pascal Nobile v DAS Rechtsschutz-Versicherungs AG* [2017] EFTA Ct Rep 554.

[20] Directive 2004/38/EC of the European Parliament and of the Council of 29 April 2004 on the right of citizens of the Union and their family members to move and reside freely within the territory of the Member States [2004] OJ L158, 30 April, p 77.

maintain a system of prior authorisation for the taking up of residence and to set annual quantitative limits in line with the sectoral adaption.

In its judgment in *D and E*,[21] the EFTA Court acknowledged the sectoral adaptation to Annexes V and VIII of the EEA Agreement and the fact that Liechtenstein is not obliged to grant residence permits to EEA nationals outside the sectoral adaptation. However, the EFTA Court also held that the sectoral adaptation does not deprive family members of EEA nationals who hold a valid residence permit and reside in Liechtenstein of the right to accompany or join the EEA national in Liechtenstein on the basis of Article 7(1)(d) of Directive 2004/38/EC, even if the EEA national's residence permit in Liechtenstein does not fall within the quota system set up according to the sectoral adaptations.

Referring to the EFTA Court judgment, the Verwaltungsgerichtshof des Fürstentums Liechtenstein decided that the Personenfreizügigkeitsgesetz[22] and Directive 2004/38/EC were to be applied to the case in hand, and referred the case back to the Migration and Passport Office for assessment as to whether the requirements for family reunification were fulfilled according to the Personenfreizügigkeitsgesetz.

D. Right of Access to a Judicial Review Procedure and the Effect of EEA Law in National Legal Orders

The EFTA Court also provided clarification in the area of environmental protection. With its judgment in *Liechtensteinische Gesellschaft für Umweltschutz*,[23] the Court held that it is not compatible with Article 11 of the Environmental Impact Assessment Directive[24] to defer the clarification of issues essential to decision making with regard to the environmental impact to subsequent authorisation procedures in which non-governmental groups promoting environmental protection do not have access to judicial review.

The Staatsgerichtshof des Fürstentums Liechtenstein also enquired about the effect of EEA law in national legal orders or, more precisely, whether the provisions concerning the Environmental Impact Assessment procedure of the Environmental Impact Assessment Directive at issue have direct effect, even though the Environmental Impact Assessment Directive was only implemented into Liechtenstein law after the completion of the respective procedure. The EFTA Court concluded that EEA law does not require that non-implemented EEA acts and rules be directly relied upon before national courts. Nevertheless, it can be derived from EEA law that, when interpreting national legislation rules, the national court is obliged to apply, as far as

[21] Case E-2/19 *D and E*.

[22] Gesetz vom 20 November 2009 über die Freizügigkeit für EWR- und Schweizer Staatsangehörige (Personenfreizügigkeitsgesetz) LGBl-Nr 2009.348.

[23] Case E-3/15 *Liechtensteinische Gesellschaft für Umweltschutz v Gemeinde Vaduz* [2015] EFTA Ct Rep 512.

[24] Directive 2011/92/EU of the European Parliament and of the Council of 13 December 2011 on the assessment of the effects of certain public and private projects on the environment [2012] OJ L26, 28 January, p 1.

possible, the methods of interpretation recognised by national law in order to achieve the result sought by the Environmental Impact Assessment Directive.

E. The Freedom of Establishment and to Provide Services and the Obligation of Transparency

The former Liechtenstein Geldspielgesetz[25] was passed on 30 June 2010 and entered into force on 1 January 2011. It regulated all commercial or publicly operated games of chance and skill for money or other monetary benefits, in particular the licensing and operation of casinos, as well as the licensing and operation of lotteries, betting, games of skill and online gaming. A concession from the government is required to operate a casino and to organise online gambling. At the time, the Liechtenstein government limited the number of concessions for casinos to one and opened a tender procedure for the award of a casino licence on 1 February 2011. Two applications were received as part of this tender process. On 31 January 2012, the Liechtenstein government granted the concession to operate a casino to Casino Vaduzerhof AG and rejected the application from Casino Admiral AG. In the subsequent legal dispute, which lasted several years, the matter was twice referred to the Verwaltungsgerichtshof des Fürstentums Liechtenstein, twice to the Staatsgerichtshof des Fürstentums Liechtenstein and once to the EFTA Court.

As there was no pertinent case law of the EFTA Court or the CJEU which provided an answer to the question whether the tender procedure for the casino concession infringed EEA law requirements, in particular Articles 31 and 36 of the EEA Agreement, the Staatsgerichtshof des Fürstentums Liechtenstein asked the EFTA Court for its interpretation. In its judgment in *Casino Admiral AG*,[26] the EFTA Court concluded that in the absence of relevant EEA provisions, national authorities must respect the fundamental rules of EEA law when awarding service concessions. This does not preclude the national authority from attaching relative weighting to the award criteria. However, the national authority is obliged to comply with the obligation of transparency. In instances where there is a breach of the transparency obligation in relation to the award of a service concession, it is not automatically required for national authorities to terminate a contract or for national courts to invalidate an award decision. However, it is important to ensure that effects contrary to Articles 31 and 36 of the EEA Agreement do not subsist and that the public interest objective of good administration is adequately reflected in the award of concessions, so that awards can be made in a way that is non-arbitrary and non-discriminatory.

Subsequently, with its judgment of 16 December 2014,[27] the Staatsgerichtshof des Fürstentums Liechtenstein terminated the concessions procedure without the award of a casino concession. This concluded the concession procedure for a casino, as there was no obligation for the Liechtenstein government to conduct a new award procedure – in particular, there was no legal entitlement to the award of a concession.

[25] Liechtenstein Geldspielgesetz (GSG) vom 30 Juni 2010 (Geldspielgesetz) LGBl-Nr 2010.235.
[26] Case E-24/13 *Casino Admiral AG v Wolfgang Egger* [2014] EFTA Ct Rep 732.
[27] StGH 2013/44.

F. Lawyers' Freedom to Provide Cross-Border Services

In December 2022, a total of 234 lawyers were registered in the Liechtenstein register for lawyers and 67 European lawyers were registered in the Liechtenstein register for European lawyers. In proportion to the size of the market and the lawyers registered, the percentage of European lawyers registered in Liechtenstein is one of the highest in the EEA.

Accordingly, the Fürstliche Landgericht asked the EFTA Court for interpretation of Directive 77/249/EEC[28] However, in its judgment in *Metacom AG*,[29] the EFTA Court first had to answer the question as to whether a lawyer bringing proceedings in an EEA State other than the one in which they are established can rely on the provisions of Directive 77/249/EEC in a case in which they are representing themself rather than providing legal services for a client. The EFTA Court noted that the lawyer may rely on Directive 77/249/EEC insofar as they are acting in a professional capacity and the national order of the host EEA State foresees that a lawyer may represent themself in legal proceedings.

Furthermore, the EFTA Court was asked whether the notification obligation according to Article 59 of the Rechtsanwaltsgesetz[30] is in line with Directive 77/249/EEC, to what extent a late notification affects the possibility of claiming the domestic lawyers' tariff and whether the obligation to notify must be pointed out by the national court. The EFTA Court found that the obligation to notify provided for in Article 59 of the Rechtsanwaltsgesetz had to be considered a measure restricting the freedom to provide cross-border services, which went beyond Article 7 of Directive 77/249/EC. A breach of the notification obligation according to Article 59 of the Rechtsanwaltsgesetz may not be considered a condition for the possibility of the cross-border lawyer to claim the domestic lawyers' tariff.

In line with the judgment of the EFTA Court, the respective article of the Rechtsanwaltsgesetz was adapted to be in line with Directive 77/279/EC and the freedom to provide cross-border services.

In 2022 the EFTA Court was asked twice for its opinion in cases concerning lawyers established in Liechtenstein.

First, the Verwaltungsgerichtshof des Fürstentums Liechtenstein asked the EFTA Court whether a national provision, according to which a lawyer, who normally practises their profession in an EEA State other than the one in which they obtained their qualification, is not authorised to be appointed as a legal aid lawyer, legal aid defence counsel or public defender, compatible with Directive 98/5/EC.[31]

In its judgment in *Maximilian Maier*,[32] the EFTA Court held that Directive 98/5/EC should be understood as prohibiting a national rule that restricts the

[28] Council Directive 77/249/EEC of 22 March 1977 to facilitate the effective exercise by lawyers of freedom to provide services [1977] OJ L78, 26 March, p 17.

[29] Case E-6/13 *Metacom AG* [2013] EFTA Ct Rep 856.

[30] Rechtsanwaltsgesetz (RAG) vom 8. November 2013, LGBl-Nr 2013.415.

[31] Directive 98/5/EC of the European Parliament and of the Council of 16 February 1998 to facilitate practice of the profession of lawyer on a permanent basis in a Member State other than that in which the qualification was obtained [1998] OJ L77, 14 March, p 36.

[32] Case E-12/22 *Maximilian Maier*.

appointment of a lawyer, practising their profession on a continuous basis in an EEA State under their home-country professional title, from serving as a legal aid lawyer, legal aid defence counsel or public defender. Accordingly, the EFTA Court confirmed that the exceptions outlined in Article 5(2) and 5(3) of Directive 98/5/EC provide exhaustive exceptions.

Shortly afterwards, in *Alexander Amann*,[33] the EFTA Court was asked by the Fürstliche Obergericht whether the Services Directive[34] precludes provisions prohibiting proactive advertisement by lawyers, where the lawyers offer their services in certain situations to selected (groups of) people who have not themselves expressed an interest in those services.

The EFTA Court concluded that Article 24(1) of the Services Directive should be understood as prohibiting provisions, which generally forbid members of a regulated profession, such as lawyers, from conducting proactive advertising when offering their services to specific (groups of) individuals who have not indicated an interest in those services themselves. However, the EFTA Court also emphasised that reaching this conclusion did not automatically mean that other regulations relating to focused proactive advertising by lawyers would be considered a total prohibition under Article 24(1) of the Services Directive.

G. Prior Authorisation Schemes for Establishment and Cross-Border Services

In 2015, ESA brought an action under the second paragraph of Article 31 of the Surveillance and Court Agreement, claiming that Liechtenstein breached its obligations arising from the Services Directive by maintaining in force national rules on prior authorisation schemes for undertakings willing to establish themselves and/or to provide cross-border services in Liechtenstein.

In its subsequent judgment in *EFTA Surveillance Authority v the Principality of Liechtenstein*,[35] the EFTA Court found that in particular Articles 7 and 21 of the Gewerbegesetz[36] were in breach of the Services Directive as well as the freedom of establishment and free movement of services. The EFTA Court further elaborated that retrospective control would be equally effective as the Liechtenstein prior authorisation scheme. Therefore, according to the EFTA Court, Article 7 of the Gewerbegesetz violates Article 9 of the Services Directive. With regard to the cross-border provision of services pursuant to Article 21 of the Gewerbegesetz, the EFTA Court found that the said provision could not stand up to the proportionality test, as less restrictive measures could have been adopted to achieve the desired objective. Therefore, Article 21 of the Gewerbegesetz infringed Article 16 of the Services Directive.

In addition, the EFTA Court declared that by imposing conditions that are not clear and unambiguous for granting prior authorisation, and by failing to ensure that

[33] Case C-14/22 *Alexander Amann*.

[34] Directive 2006/123/EC of the European Parliament and of the Council of 12 December 2006 on services in the internal market [2006] OJ L376, 27 December, p 36.

[35] Case E-19/15 *EFTA Surveillance Authority v the Principality of Liechtenstein* [2016] EFTA Ct Rep 437.

[36] Gewerbegesetz (GewG) vom 30. September 2020, LGBl-Nr 2020.415.

these conditions do not duplicate requirements and controls which are equivalent or essentially comparable to those the service provider must already fulfil according to the national law in another EEA State, Liechtenstein was in breach of the Services Directive.

Following the judgment of the EFTA Court, the Gewerbegesetz was changed and adapted accordingly.

III. CONCLUSION

Liechtenstein welcomes the institutional set-up of the EEA and highly respects the institutions of the EEA, in particular ESA and the EFTA Court. These institutions have proven to be independent and effective in enforcing EEA law. Liechtenstein especially regards the surveillance carried out by ESA and the EFTA Court as a key element in strengthening confidence in the EEA.

In cases where the EFTA Court did not agree with Liechtenstein's arguments, Liechtenstein has always endeavoured to take the necessary measures to implement the judgment within a reasonable time, as provided for in the Surveillance and Court Agreement. This may well explain that while EFTA Court judgments are extensively debated in Liechtenstein, there is never any (long-lasting) resistance to taking the legislative or administrative measures necessary to comply with those judgments, even if it means that a cherished provision is to be abolished or an established practice is to be changed.

14

Maglite, L'Oreal *and* RAAP

Making Sense of Third-Country Regulation of Intellectual Property Rights in the EEA

OLE-ANDREAS ROGNSTAD*

I. INTRODUCTION

INTELLECTUAL PROPERTY (IP) law has traditionally been one of the fields of law that produces the highest number of cases before the Court of Justice of the European Union (CJEU). Although the trend may vary a little from year to year, statistics show that over the years 2018–22, there were 349 new cases in this field brought before the CJEU, which ranks it second in all fields, only superseded by the broad category of 'freedom, security and justice'.[1] Along with the numerous legislative instruments produced in the IP field over the years, most of them classified as 'EEA relevant' and included in Annex XVII to the EEA Agreement, this also shows the importance of intellectual property in the EEA.

However, this importance is not reflected in the number of cases brought before the EFTA Court, which is still comparatively very low.[2] There may be several reasons for this, but among the few cases that have been brought before the Court, there are two landmark cases where the principally important question of the relevance of the EU's third-country policy for the EEA Agreement has come to a head – in the *Maglite*

* This chapter is based on the following article: OA Rognstad, 'EØS-avtalens homogenitetsmål og tredjelandsregulering – særlig i lys av EU-domstolens dom i sak C-265/19 RAAP' (2024) 63 *Lov og Rett* no 5.

[1] See 'Statistics Concerning the Judicial Activity of the Court of Justice', *Court of Justice of the European Union Annual Report 2022*, available at: curia.europa.eu/jcms/upload/docs/application/pdf/2023-03/stats_cour_2022_en.pdf.

[2] See OA Rognstad, 'Intellectual Property Law' in C Baudenbacher (ed), *The Handbook of EEA Law* (Cham, Springer, 2016) 703–20; and OA Rognstad, 'Article 65(2)' in F Arnesen et al (eds), *Agreement on the European Economic Area: A Commentary* (Munich/Oxford/Baden-Baden, Beck/Hart Publishing/Nomos, 2018) 641–58.

and *L'Oreal* cases about exhaustion of trade mark rights.[3] Given the increased importance of the topic, also beyond the IP field, the celebration of the thirtieth anniversary of the EFTA Court seems like a good opportunity to address the continued relevance of these two cases.

Moreover, a relatively recent ruling of the CJEU in the *RAAP* case, decided in September 2020, has raised the question whether a provision that, according to the CJEU, confers IP rights not only on right holders associated with the EEA but also all right holders irrespective of their nationality, applies homogeneously in the EEA.[4] We will come back to the further facts of the case, and the legal questions it involved, in section V below. Here, in the introduction, it suffices to say that the core problem to be addressed in light of the *RAAP* case is whether this case demonstrates the limits of the homogeneity principle under the EEA Agreement that the EFTA Court signalled in its *Maglite* decision 26 years ago.

Even though the *RAAP* case did not concern the interpretation of the EEA Agreement as such, my belief is that the CJEU ruling represents a situation where homogeneity must yield due to differences between the EU and EEA regarding third-country relations. This was what the EFTA Court in *Maglite* held on the question of whether Article 7(1) of the 1989 Trade Mark Directive[5] prohibited the EEA/EFTA States from having rules on international exhaustion of trade mark rights. However, 10 years later, in *L'Oreal*, the Court came to the conclusion that there were not 'compelling grounds' for deviating from the principle of homogeneity regarding exhaustion in third-country relations as the CJEU had in the meantime ruled contrary to the result in *Maglite*. The claim made here is that even though the *L'Oreal* position is understandable and may be defended, the *RAAP* situation is an example of there being such 'compelling grounds'. Thus, there is a line from the reasoning in *Maglite* via the ruling in *L'Oreal* – diverging in terms of the result but not necessarily inconsistent – to the question of how to handle the *RAAP* situation under the EEA Agreement. The keywords in this respect are the preservation of the Contracting Parties' autonomy in third-country relations. The keywords imply that the findings may have repercussions beyond the field of IP, but the analysis as such is limited to the three IP cases already mentioned. In the following, the line between the three cases will be outlined (sections II–V) before drawing a few conclusions at the end (section VI).

II. *MAGLITE*: EMPHASISING THE IMPACT OF DIFFERENCES IN THIRD-COUNTRY REGULATION IN THE EU AND THE EEA

The *Maglite* case[6] concerned parallel imports of flashlights under the trade mark Maglite produced in the US and imported from there to Norway. The trade mark

[3] Case E-2/97 *Mag Instrument Inc* [1997] EFTA Ct Rep 127; and Joined Cases E-9/07 and E-10/07 *L'Oréal Norge AS* [2008] EFTA Ct Rep 259.

[4] Case C-265/19 *Recorded Artists Actors Performers Ltd* ECLI:EU:C:2020:677 (*RAAP*).

[5] First Council Directive 89/104/EEC to approximate the laws of the Member States relating to trade marks [1989] OJ L40/1. The same provision is now found in Art 15(1) of Directive (EU) 2015/2436 of the European Parliament and of the Council to approximate the laws of the Member States relating to trade marks [2015] OJ L336/1.

[6] *Maglite* (n 3).

owner, Mag Instrument Inc, opposed the importation, referring to Article 7(1) of the 1989 Trade Mark Directive.[7] At the time of the case, it was disputed whether this provision was to be interpreted as a rule of mandatory EU/EEA exhaustion, implying not only the positive consequence from its wording (that trade mark rights are exhausted through bringing the trade marked goods onto the market in the EU/EEA with the trade mark holder's consent) but also the negative (that the rights were *not* exhausted by the marketing of the products outside the EU/EEA). If so, the trade mark holder, like Mag Instruments Inc, could oppose the parallel imports of goods imported from countries outside the EEA, like the US. At the time that the *Maglite* case was brought before the EFTA Court, a case concerning the same subject matter was pending before the CJEU;[8] however, the EFTA Court had the chance to give its ruling first. The reasoning of the EFTA Court must be considered against this backdrop.

The EFTA Court came to the conclusion that the Trade Mark Directive interpreted in an *EEA context* did not prevent the EEA/EFTA States from retaining rules on international exhaustion of trade mark law. The Court followed two different lines of reasoning in this respect. First, it held that the principle of international exhaustion, implying that parallel imports from third countries were permitted, was in accordance with free trade and competition interests, and thus was also in the interests of consumers. Moreover, such a principle also corresponded with the essential function of a trade mark as a guarantee of origin for the products. According to the EFTA Court, the wording of the Trade Mark Directive did not provide an answer to the question of whether international exhaustion could be maintained. The Court also explicitly observed that, at the time of the ruling, the CJEU had not yet decided on the matter. Given these circumstances, the EFTA Court found that Article 2(1) of Protocol 28 to the EEA Agreement, which provides for the same exhaustion in the EEA as in the EU, was 'not relevant to answer the question whether these States may still provide for a general principle of international exhaustion'.[9] Second, the EFTA Court highlighted the differences between the EU rules and the EEA rules regarding third-country relations. Using formulations such as 'Unlike the EC Treaty' and 'differences between the Community and the EEA',[10] and also specifying that it was the EEA/EFTA States which, in light of the EFTA Court's considerations, would have the freedom to decide whether they wished to introduce or maintain the principle of international exhaustion,[11] the EFTA Court seemed to pave the way for an EEA-specific interpretation of Article 7(1) of the 1989 Trade Mark Directive, irrespective of how the CJEU might interpret the same provision in an EU context. The fact that in the *L'Oreal* decision, the Court did not follow up on this is a different matter, to which we will return in the next section.

The EFTA Court's EEA-specific arguments in Maglite may be divided into three, although they remain closely connected to each other. First, the Court emphasised that the EEA Agreement, unlike the EC Treaty (now the Treaty on the Functioning of the

[7] *L'Oréal* (n 3).
[8] Case C-355/96 *Silhouette International* ECLI:EU:C:1998:374.
[9] *Maglite* (n 3) paras 19–21.
[10] ibid paras 25 and 26.
[11] ibid para 28.

European Union (TFEU)), does not establish a customs union, but a free trade area. This had to be reflected, the Court held, in the application of the principle of exhaustion of trade mark rights. The Court here referred to the limitation on the application of the free movement of goods rules laid down in Articles 11–13 EEA (corresponding to Articles 34–36 TFEU) that follows from Article 8(2) EEA, deciding that the provisions only apply to goods originating in the EEA. Obviously with reference to the fact that the exhaustion principle originally was developed on the basis of the free movement of goods rules,[12] the Court noted that the goods in question were manufactured in the US and consequently concluded that these were not subject to the free movement of goods rules in the EEA, in contrast to the situation in the EU.[13]

The reasoning of the Court must be seen against the background of the pleadings from, inter alia, the European Commission in the case to the effect that the functioning of the internal market dictated the result of a mandatory rule on EEA exhaustion. If the individual EEA States were free to decide on international exhaustion, so the argument went, the situation could arise that goods could be parallel imported into one state but not another, which could create disparities in the internal market.[14] The Court's finding that the principle of free movement of goods did not apply, in any event, to goods from third countries was meant to reject the relevance of these pleadings. As argued elsewhere, the reasoning of the Court was questionable because the basis for the exhaustion principle in this case was not the free movement of goods, but the Trade Mark Directive, and because the IP provisions of the EEA Agreement apply to 'all products' pursuant to Article 65(2) EEA.[15] This seems to be the reason why the EFTA Court did not reiterate these limitations in the *L'Oreal* case, to which we will return in the next section.

Second, the EFTA Court referred to the fact that the EEA Agreement does not entail a common commercial policy towards third countries, again unlike the EU (citing Article 113 of the EC Treaty, now Article 207 TFEU).[16] What can be deduced from this reference is that this difference may justify different interpretations of EU and EEA rules. However, it is debatable whether this argument hit the target in the case at hand, since the Treaty basis for the adoption of the Trade Mark Directive was the internal market competence (now Article 114 TFEU) and not the common commercial policy.[17] At the time of the EFTA Court's opinion in *Maglite*, the area of intellectual property law fell altogether outside the common commercial policy,[18] but this was amended with the Lisbon Treaty.[19] The EU's stance on having mandatory

[12] See, eg, Case 15/74 *Centrafarm v Sterling* ECLI:EU:C:1974:114; Case 16/74 *Centrafarm v Winthrop* ECLI:EU:C:1974:115; and Case 102/77 *Hoffmann-La Roche & Co AG* ECLI:EU:C:1978:108.

[13] *Maglite* (n 3) paras 25 and 26.

[14] ibid para 24.

[15] See OA Rognstad, 'The Conflict between Internal Market and Third Country Policy Considerations in the EEA. *Maglite* vs *Silhouette*' in PC Müller-Graff and E Selvig (eds), *EEA-EU Relations* (Berlin, Verlag, 1999) 137–38. See also Rognstad, 'Intellectual Property Law' (n 2) 710.

[16] *Maglite* (n 3) para 27.

[17] See Rognstad (n 15) 138–40; Rognstad, 'Intellectual Property Law' (n 2) 709.

[18] Opinion 1/94 *Competence of the Community to conclude international agreements concerning services and the protection of intellectual property – Article 228 (6) of the EC Treaty* ECLI:EU:C:1994:384.

[19] See Art 207(1) TFEU, which includes the 'commercial aspects of intellectual property'. In Case C-414/11 *Daiichi Sankyo* ECLI:EU:C:2013:520 the CJEU confirmed that TRIPS falls within the scope

rules on EEA-wide exhaustion still has no connection with the common trade policy. This is underscored by the fact that both the Agreement on Trade-Related Aspects of Intellectual Property Rights (TRIPS) and the WIPO Conventions on copyright and related right, to which we will return later on, grant the contracting parties freedom to regulate the exhaustion issue.[20] In *Silhouette*, when the CJEU confirmed for the first time that Article 7(1) of the 1989 Trade Mark Directive provided for a rule of mandatory EEA-wide exhaustion, the Court emphasised, after having rejected arguments by the Swedish government that the Directive could not regulate relations between Member States and non-EU countries since it was based on the internal market competence, that the exhaustion provided for in the Directive could be extended by the EU entering into international agreements.[21] Thus, it is clear from that judgment that a mandatory rule on EEA-wide exhaustion is intended to safeguard equal market conditions in the EU for goods parallel imported from third countries, to the benefit of the internal market,[22] and not to affect external trade policy as such.

Closely connected to this, the EFTA Court's third EEA-specific argument in favour of allowing international exhaustion of trade-marked goods in the EFTA States was that these states had not transferred their respective treaty-making competence to any kind of supranational organ. The EFTA Court here referred to Articles 5 and 6 of Protocol 28 to the EEA Agreement as the basis for the Contracting Parties' freedom to enter into treaties and agreements with third countries in the IP field. These provisions establish an obligation on the Contracting Parties to adhere to various multilateral conventions (Article 5) and to improve the IP regime established by the EEA Agreement considering the negotiations of the WTO Agreement in the so-called Uruguay Round (which in 1994 resulted in the TRIPs Agreement). It is not entirely clear what the EFTA Court intended to demonstrate through these references, but the provisions may be said to confirm that it is up to the individual Contracting Parties to undertake such obligations. It is somewhat surprising that, in this context, the Court did not refer to Recital 16 of the EEA Agreement, which explicitly and directly addresses the Contracting Parties' autonomy regarding external treaty competences: 'this Agreement does not restrict the decision-making autonomy or the treaty-making power of the Contracting Parties, subject to the provisions of this Agreement and the limitations set by public international law'. In any case, it seems as though the EFTA Court in *Maglite* was of the opinion that a rule on mandatory EEA-wide exhaustion, derived from Article 7(1) of the 1989 Trade Mark Directive, would restrict 'the treaty-making power of the EFTA States' in that such an interpretation of the Directive would 'impose restraints on the EFTA States in their third-country trade relations'.[23] However, that this would be the result is not obvious, given the CJEU's finding in

of the common commercial policy; see further B Gotsova, 'The Gordian Knot of European Union Competence: Commercial Aspects of Intellectual Property after the Judgment in Case C-414/11 *Daiichi Sankyo*' (2014) 15 *German Law Journal* 511.

[20] TRIPs, Art 6; WIPO Copyright Treaty (WCT), Art 6(2); WIPO Performances and Phonograms Treaty (WPPT), Arts 8(2) and 12(2).

[21] *Silhouette* (n 8) para 30.

[22] ibid para 27.

[23] *Maglite* (n 3) para 27.

Silhouette that the EU maintained its freedom to extend exhaustion to third countries.[24] Whether the EEA/EFTA States have a corresponding freedom after *Silhouette* will be discussed in the following sections against the backdrop of the subsequent *L'Oreal* ruling of the EFTA Court.

III. *L'OREAL*: EMPHASISING COMPELLING GROUNDS FOR DEVIATION, BUT PRIORITISING HOMOGENEITY

Just over a decade after the EFTA Court's advisory opinion in *Maglite*, the question of whether the Trade Mark Directive required EEA-wide exhaustion of trade mark rights in an EEA context came up again before the Court in another case concerning parallel imports (this time of cosmetic products) from the US – the *L'Oreal* case. The legal background was now somewhat different, as the CJEU had decided in the meantime that the Directive had to be interpreted in this way in an EU context.[25] As in *Maglite* the EFTA Court had emphasised so strongly the third-country aspects and the special features of the EEA Agreement, it was uncertain what the outcome of the new proceedings would be. This time the Court came to the opposite conclusion, ruling in favour of mandatory EEA-wide exhaustion.

In its reasoning, the Court emphasised that the main object of the EEA Agreement is to create a homogeneous EEA and that homogeneous interpretation and application of common rules is essential for the effective functioning of the internal market within the EEA.[26] The EFTA Court referred both to Article 3(2) of the EFTA Surveillance and Court Agreement (SCA), which contains an obligation for the EFTA Court to 'pay due account to the principles laid down by the relevant rulings' of the CJEU even when given after the date of signature of the EEA Agreement, and the above-mentioned provision in Article 2(1) of Protocol 28 EEA on the harmonisation of the exhaustion of IP rights as two instruments to secure homogeneous interpretation in this case. The Court noted that neither of these provisions explicitly addresses the situation where the EFTA Court has ruled on an issue first and the CJEU has subsequently come to a different conclusion. However, the Court stated, the consequences for the internal market would be the same in this situation as in the situation where the EFTA Court has ruled on an issue first and the CJEU were subsequently to come to a different conclusion. According to the EFTA Court, this called for 'an interpretation of EEA law in line with new case law of the CJEU regardless of whether the EFTA Court has previously ruled on the question'.[27] The statements emphasise the importance of homogeneity under the EEA Agreement and imply the refusal of any suggestion that the EFTA Court may, or should, follow a different 'policy line' in internal market issues.[28] This is underscored by the fact that even though the EFTA

[24] *Silhouette* (n 8) para 30.

[25] *Silhouette* (n 8); and Case C-173/98 *Sebago Inc* ECLI:EU:C:1999:347, the latter concerning parallel imports of non-EEA originating goods.

[26] *L'Oreal* (n 3) paras 27–30 and 37.

[27] ibid para 29.

[28] See C Baudenbacher, 'Between Homogeneity and Independence: The Legal Position of the EFTA Court in the European Economic Area' (1997) 3 *Columbia Journal of European Law* 169, 202–08. See

Court held that its own reference to free trade and free competition in the interests of the consumer and the CJEU's emphasis on the importance of uniform market conditions in the internal market 'were equally valid in a Community law context and an EEA law context', homogeneity tipped the scale in favour of the latter.[29]

What is of particular interest in this context is the EFTA Court's handling of the differences in scope between EU law and EEA law that were strongly emphasised in *Maglite*. After having underscored the importance of homogeneity under the EEA Agreement, the EFTA Court stated that it needed to be considered whether these differences 'nevertheless constitute compelling grounds for divergent interpretations of Article 7(1) [of the 1989 Trade Mark Directive]'.[30] The formulation implies a requirement of 'compelling grounds' for deviating from the homogeneity principle on the basis of differences in scope between EU and EEA law.

In short, the EFTA Court found that there were no such 'compelling grounds' in this case, despite the Court's emphasis on the different scope in *Maglite*. First, the EFTA Court addressed the arguments concerning trade relations with third countries. Here, the Norwegian and Icelandic governments had asserted at the oral hearing that it is unusual for their agreements with third countries to include clauses concerning exhaustion of intellectual property rights, and that it was therefore more important in practice to be able to decide on the exhaustion regime vis-a-vis third countries purely as a matter of domestic law. The Court noted, to this effect, that the present case did not 'concern a situation in which the EFTA State in question has entered into an agreement with a third State on exhaustion of trade mark rights', but solely whether 'the Trade Mark Directive should be interpreted as not restricting the EFTA States in their freedom to provide for international exhaustion of trade mark rights, as a unilateral measure, in relation to goods originating from outside the EEA'.[31] This seems on the face of it a retraction from the argument that a rule on mandatory EEA-wide exhaustion restricted the EEA/EFTA States in their third-country relations.

Second, the EFTA Court also seemed to retract from the argument that the rule of exhaustion of trade mark rights under the EEA Agreement only applies to goods originating from the EEA. The Court remarked that the provisions contained in Protocol 28 and Annex XVII to the Agreement 'shall apply to all products … unless otherwise specified'. The Court added that neither these provisions nor the intellectual property provision in Article 65(2) EEA 'make a reservation against rules providing for mandatory EEA-wide exhaustion of rights relating to goods originating from outside the EEA'. On the contrary, the Court referred to Article 2(1) of Protocol 28 EEA, stating that 'the Contracting Parties shall provide for such exhaustion of intellectual property rights as laid down in Community law', allowing for 'the incorporation into

also C Baudenbacher, *Restoring the Balance in the European Economic Area* (Luxembourg, European Law Reporter, 2021) 72, who criticises the *L'Oreal* ruling of the EFTA Court on the ground, among other things, that 'an element of the Scandinavian free trade tradition had been eliminated in favour of protectionism inspired by the southern (Catholic!) Member States of the EU, something that is at the expense of Norwegian consumers'. However, the question of why national (or regional) interests should be prioritised in *this context* specifically remains unanswered.

[29] *L'Oreal* (n 3) para 30.

[30] ibid para 31.

[31] ibid para 32.

Annex XVII of legal acts providing for mandatory EEA-wide exhaustion of rights, regardless of the origin of the goods to which the rights relate'.[32] It added that even in situations where the wording of exhaustion provisions in IP directives expressly provided rules on mandatory exhaustion – for example, Article 4(2) of the Copyright Directive[33] – the decision of the EEA Joint Committee contained no EEA-specific adaptations.[34] The arguments here were quite different from those in *Maglite*.

Third, the Court emphasised that the interpretation of Article 2(1) of Protocol 28 EEA in *Maglite* was linked to the fact that at the time of delivery of that decision, the CJEU had not yet ruled on the issue of mandatory EEA-wide exhaustion. Hence, *Maglite* was built on the premise that 'to date', there was no case law of the CJEU which ruled out international exhaustion of rights. It should be noted that the Court's interpretation of that provision was questionable even at the time of the *Maglite* ruling,[35] but the Court nevertheless found support for its conclusion that 'it is clear that the EEA Agreement foresees the possibility of mandatory EEA-wide exhaustion of intellectual property rights, also in relation to goods originating from outside the EEA'.[36] In any case, the changed position of the EFTA Court can both be explained by the fact that the CJEU had decided on mandatory EEA exhaustion of trade mark rights in the meantime, and that the EFTA Court reconsidered the relevance of the differences in third-country regulation between the EU and the EEA for the issue in question.

IV. RECONCILING *MAGLITE* AND *L'OREAL*

Nevertheless, despite the differences in reasoning between *Maglite* and *L'Oreal*, the statements in these rulings can be reconciled on several levels. Even though the EFTA Court put emphasis on homogeneity in *L'Oreal*, the ruling cannot be understood as a general rejection of the idea that differences in the regulation of third-country relations in the EU and the EEA may constitute 'compelling reasons' for interpreting an EEA provision differently from an identical EU rule. On the contrary, the rationale in *Maglite* that the lack of a customs union and a common trade policy in the EEA may provide a basis for different interpretation of similar rules is not contradicted by *L'Oreal*. What is contradicted is only their concrete relevance to the issue of mandatory EEA-wide exhaustion. This applies both for the argument that the exhaustion principle does not apply to goods originating from third countries[37] and that a rule on mandatory EEA exhaustion would restrict the EFTA States in their third-country relations.

[32] ibid para 33.

[33] Directive 2001/29/EC of the European Parliament and of the Council on the harmonisation of certain aspects of copyright and related rights in the information society [2001] OJ L167/10.

[34] *L'Oreal* (n 3) para 34.

[35] See Rognstad (n 15) 138.

[36] *L'Oreal* (n 3) para 36.

[37] See T Blanchet, R Piipponen and M Westman-Clément, *The Agreement on the European Economic Area (EEA): A Guide to the Free Movement of Goods and Competition Rules* (Oxford, Clarendon Press, 1994) 43, who claim that: 'Although it was discussed during the negotiations whether in particular the rules

At the same time, the Court's observation in *L'Oreal* that the case did not 'concern a situation in which the EFTA State in question has entered into an agreement with a third State on exhaustion of trade mark rights'[38] may be understood as maintaining that the EEA/EFTA States should retain their freedom to enter into international agreements on international exhaustion. This understanding brings coherence between *Maglite* and *L'Oreal* at some level. Moreover, it corresponds with the position of the CJEU on the relationship between the Trade Mark Directive and the EU external treaty competence. In *Silhouette*, the CJEU maintained that 'the [EU] authorities could always extend the exhaustion provided for by Article 7 [of the Trade Mark Directive] to products put on the market in non-member countries by entering into international agreements in that sphere, as was done in the context of the EEA Agreement'.[39] A parallel interpretation in the EEA context would imply that the EFTA States could also extend exhaustion by way of international agreements. Only such an interpretation would comply with the statement in Recital 16 EEA that the Agreement does not restrict the treaty-making power of the Contracting Parties. Moreover, it is supported by the principle of reciprocity that the EFTA Court has derived from Recital 4 EEA.[40] A different solution would imply an imbalance in the third-country policy of the Contracting Parties if the internal market policy were to allow the EU to enter freely into agreements with third countries, but prevent the EEA/EFTA States from doing the same. Such a solution would, as the EFTA Court emphasised in *Maglite*, conflict with the main purpose of the EEA Agreement – that is, to expand the internal market to the EEA without at the same time implying the establishment of a customs union and a common commercial policy. Hence, the differences between the EU and the EEA Agreement may imply EEA-specific interpretations of equally or similarly formulated rules, and consequently a deviation from the homogeneity principle. Both *Maglite* and *L'Oreal* support this finding – the latter by way of a reference to 'compelling grounds'.[41]

On the face of it, it may seem odd that an EEA/EFTA State may enter into a free trade agreement to deviate from the principle of mandatory EEA-wide exhaustion without having the competence to decide this on its own. However, the anomaly can be explained by the principle of homogeneity justifying an equal scope of IP rights in the EEA, but not a restriction on the freedom to enter into agreements with third countries in a situation where the EU has retained that freedom. If exhaustion is extended by the EU or the EEA/EFTA States entering into such agreements, there is an obligation under Article 7 of Protocol 28 EEA for the Contracting Parties to keep each other informed 'in the context of work within the framework of international

pertaining to technical barriers to trade (TBTs), or on exhaustion of intellectual property rights, should be limited to originating products, the negotiators voluntarily made them applicable to non-originating products.'

[38] *L'Oreal* (n 3) para 32.

[39] *Silhouette* (n 8) para 30.

[40] See, eg, Case E-12/13 *ESA v Iceland* [2014] EFTA Ct Rep 58, para 68.

[41] *L'Oreal* (n 3) para 31. For an example of the EFTA Court holding that the context of the EEA Agreement justifies adopting a different interpretation than the CJEU, see Case E-4/19 *Campbell*, paras 55–58. For a further examination, see OJ Einarsson, 'The Advisory Opinion Procedure and the Relationship between the EFTA Court and the Norwegian Courts: Recent Developments' (2022) *Lov og Rett* 232–35.

organizations and within the context of agreements dealing with intellectual property'. Thus, homogeneity and internal market considerations may be safeguarded by way of coordinating external agreements in the IP field.

V. *RAAP*: DEMONSTRATING COMPELLING GROUNDS FOR DEVIATION FROM HOMOGENEITY?

A. The *RAAP* Case and the EEA Legal Problems it Raises

The *RAAP* case[42] concerned the interpretation of Article 8(2) of the Rental and Lending Directive[43] (RLD), which is included in Annex XVII to the EEA Agreement. The provision establishes that performing artists and phonogram producers are entitled to remuneration for the communication to the public of their performances, without specifying which performers and producers are subject to the entitlement. The case before the CJEU arose because of Irish copyright rules deciding that only performers who were citizens of, resident in or participated in recordings made in an EEA State would be granted remuneration under this provision. This meant, among other things, that US artists did not receive remuneration for the communication to the public of their recordings.[44] The CJEU (Grand Chamber) found that this restriction contravened Article 8(2) RLD, and the grounds of the judgment indicate that remuneration must be given to all artists (and producers) regardless of their nationality, ie, also all artists (and producers) of third-country origin, until the EU legislature has decided otherwise.[45] As the case concerned the obligation of an EU Member State – Ireland – it does not follow from the judgment that the EEA/EFTA States have the same obligations under the EEA Agreement. This depends on the scope of homogeneity, discussed above regarding the *Maglite* and *L'Oreal* decisions of the EFTA Court on exhaustion of trade mark rights. The question that will be raised here is whether the *RAAP* case represents an example of the limits of homogeneity in third-country relations.

An important backdrop for the CJEU's interpretation of Article 8(2) RLD was the 1996 WIPO Performances and Phonograms Treaty (WPPT). In contrast to its 'sister convention', the Rome Convention of 1961, on which the WPPT is based,[46] both the

[42] *RAAP* (n 4).

[43] Directive 2006/115/EC of the European Parliament and of the Council on rental right and lending right and on certain rights related to copyright in the field of intellectual property [2006] OJ L376/28.

[44] On the further facts of the case, see OA Rognstad, 'The *RAAP* Decision of the CJEU: What Happened to Reciprocity?' in M Rosenmeier et al (eds), *Festskrift til Jørgen Blomqvist* (Copenhagen, Ex Tuto, 2021) 527–30; and OA Rognstad, 'Performing Artists' Right to Remuneration: On the Junction of External Treaty Competence, Material Reciprocity and Fundamental Rights: *RAAP*' (2021) 58 *Common Market Law Review* 1523, 1527–29. See also M Ficsor, 'RAAP: The Obvious, the Missing, the Regrettable and the Desirable', available at: www.copyrightseesaw.net/uploads/raap-v-ppi-what-is-obvious-what-is-not-what-seems-missing.docx, 5 f.

[45] See *RAAP* (n 4) para 88.

[46] See further J Blomqvist and M Rosenmeier, 'International Protection of Performers in the EU: Points of Attachment and National Treatment vs Material Reciprocity after the RAAP Decision by the CJEU' (2021) 269 *Revue internationale du droit d'auteur*, 33–39.

EU and the US have acceded to the WPPT. As the EU itself, and not only its Member States, is party to the WPPT, it is therefore an integral part of EU law[47] and is central to the interpretation of Article 8(2) RLD in *RAAP*.[48] In particular, the CJEU in its interpretation placed considerable weight on the principle of national treatment codified in Article 4(1) WPPT in combination with the remuneration right for performers and phonogram producers provided for in Article 15(1) WPPT. Hence, it referred to Article 4(1) WPPT when concluding that the phrase 'relevant performers' in Article 8(2) RLD could not be limited to performing artists with a connection to the EEA.

Although national treatment is the main rule under the WPPT, Article 4(2) provides for an exception in relation to the remuneration right for performers and phonogram producers which is linked to the opt-out mechanism in Article 15(3). According to the latter provision, a Contracting Party may make a reservation against the obligation to pay remuneration for public communication of sound recordings provided that the reservation is notified to the WIPO's Directorate General. Most importantly, the US has made a reservation for essential kinds of communication to the public, including performance of sound recordings in public places such as restaurants and shops, which is due to restrictions inherent in US copyright law. As a consequence of the opt-out possibility provided for in Article 15(3) WPPT, Article 4(2) WPPT states that the obligation to accord national treatment provided for in Article 4(1) 'does not apply to the extent that another Contracting Party makes use of the reservations permitted by Article 15(3) of this Treaty'. This expresses, in fact, a principle of *material reciprocity* instead of national treatment, ie, that performers and phonogram producers are entitled to the rights they are granted in their home country, but not the same rights as the host state grants its own nationals. When answering the first two questions referred by the Irish court – to what extent must Article 8 of the Directive be interpreted in light of the requirement for 'national treatment' under Article 4 WPPT, and whether a Member State has discretion to prescribe criteria for determining which performers qualify as 'relevant performers' under Article 8(2) RLD – the Court referred exclusively to Articles 4(1) and 15(1) WPPT, and not to Articles 4(2) and 15(3) WPPT.[49] The relevance of Article 15(3) WPPT was discussed by the Court, instead, in relation to the third question raised by the Irish court – namely, what discretion the EU Member States have to respond to reservations entered by a Contracting Party under Article 15(3).

In short, the CJEU concluded that reservations made under Article 15(3) WPPT do not lead to limitations on the remuneration right provided for in Article 8(2) RLD, but that limitations may be introduced by the EU legislature. In other words, the principle of material reciprocity does not apply to the remuneration right as the law now stands. On the contrary, the grounds of *RAAP* go far, indicating that all performers and producers who take part in a sound recording are entitled to remuneration, irrespective of their nationality, until the EU legislature has decided otherwise. In this

[47] *RAAP* (n 4) para 61.

[48] ibid paras 63–65.

[49] See my criticism of this in Rognstad, 'The *RAAP* Decision of the CJEU' (n 44) 532–33, and even more targeted in Rognstad, 'Performing Artists' Right to Remuneration' (n 44) 1535–38.

context, it is the Court's detailed reasoning that is of interest, as it has a bearing on whether Article 8(2) RLD must be interpreted homogeneously in the EEA. In other words, the question that will be discussed in the next section is whether the EEA/EFTA States are also prevented from applying the principle of material reciprocity to the right of remuneration. The question is of special interest for Norway where a bill confirming the principle was launched prior to the *RAAP* ruling and recently renewed, despite the ruling, on the premise that the ruling is not relevant to the EEA.[50]

In *RAAP*, the CJEU recognises that the fact European artists and producers do not receive remuneration for the public performance and transmission of sound recordings in a third country prejudices their interest in being treated on an equal footing with nationals of that third country. Consequently, the Court held that 'the need to safeguard fair conditions of involvement in the recorded music business constitutes an objective in the public interest capable of justifying a limitation of the right related to copyright provided for in Article 8(2) [RLD]'.[51]

However, when the Court did not land on that solution, but concluded that Article 15(3) WPPT was without significance for the interpretation of Article 8(2) RLD, it was on the basis that the right to remuneration is protected as an intellectual property right under Article 17(2) of the Charter of Fundamental Rights of the European Union (CFREU). Consequently, it followed from Article 52(1) CFREU that any limitation on the exercise of a right relating to copyright, such as the right to remuneration, must be provided for by law, which implies that the legal basis for the limitation must be clearly and precisely stated.[52] In the opinion of the CJEU:

> The mere existence of a reservation duly notified in accordance with Article 15(3) of the WPPT does not fulfil that requirement, because such a reservation does not enable nationals of the third State in question to ascertain in precisely what way their [remuneration right] would, consequently, be limited in the European Union.[53]

Thus, Article 15(3) WPPT could not have the effect of limiting the remuneration right pursuant to Article 8(2) RLD.

The further conclusions that the CJEU drew from its reasoning attracted much interest for the consequences of the Grand Chamber ruling in the EEA context. First, the CJEU maintained that:

> Since Article 8(2) [RLD] is a harmonised rule, it is for the EU legislature alone and not the national legislatures to determine whether the [remuneration right] should be limited in respect of the nationals of third States and, if so, to define that limitation clearly and precisely.[54]

The Court noted in this respect that neither Article 8(2) RLD nor any other EU provision contains a limitation of this kind. Second, the CJEU emphasised that the EU has exclusive external competence pursuant to Article 3(2) TFEU to negotiate new reciprocal commitments with third countries, within the framework of WPPT or outside it. This is since any agreement in this regard would be liable to alter the

[50] *cf* bill of 6 December 2019, www.regjeringen.no/contentassets/8ab9b07a35514e6fbba69253b79dc8a6/horingsnotat-091219-final---oppdatert.pdf; and bill of 22 November 2023, www.regjeringen.no/contentassets/449f5b4495644cf2af1df7680d1649e5/horingsnotat-221123.pdf.

[51] *RAAP* (n 4) paras 83 and 84.

[52] ibid paras 85 and 86.

[53] ibid para 87.

[54] ibid para 88.

scope of Article 8(2) RLD, as a common EU rule, as the subject matter covered by such agreement would coincide fully with the identical subject matter covered by Article 8(2) RLD. With reference to its earlier case law – reflecting the so-called ERTA doctrine[55] – the Court confirms that the EU has the exclusive external competence referred to in Article 3(2) TFEU in situations where there is such full coincidence.[56]

The latter arguments are EU-specific, concerning special circumstances linked to the EU's exclusive external competence, which has no counterpart under the EEA Agreement. Combined with the fact that the CJEU in RAAP judgment supports its interpretation on a treaty the EU has entered into in the exercise of its external treaty competence, the question of whether Article 8(2) RLD must be interpreted in the same way in an EEA context is subject to discussion. The EFTA Court's rulings in *Maglite* and *L'Oreal* are highly relevant in this respect, and we will return to the observations made in sections II–IV for the following discussion about the relevance of *RAAP* in an EEA context, before raising the issue of homogeneity in third-country relations to a more general level in the concluding section VI.

B. The *RAAP* Case in an EEA Context in the Light of *Maglite* and *L'Oreal*

As follows from the discussion in section IV above, it can be deduced from both the *Maglite* and *L'Oreal* rulings of the EFTA Court that the mandatory EEA exhaustion provided for in the Trade Mark Directive would not prevent the EEA/EFTA States from entering into deviating agreements with third countries. This understanding is supported by the fact that the CJEU made it possible for the EU to enter into agreements with third countries on international exhaustion, of which the EEA Agreement itself was an example. Thus, a parallel interpretation of the Trade Mark Directive in an EEA context, in line with the statements in *Maglite* and *L'Oreal*, implies that the EEA/EFTA States have also such freedom, even if deviations both on the EU side and on the EFTA side may imply certain distortions in the EEA market. Nevertheless, this was not the result in *L'Oreal* because, as was highlighted by the EFTA Court, the case did not concern agreements with third countries, but, rather, only the question of whether the EEA/EFTA States could *unilaterally* deviate from mandatory EEA-wide exhaustion. Consequently, the regulation of third-country relations did not represent a compelling ground for deviating from a homogeneous interpretation of the Trade Mark Directive. The question that may be raised with regard to the *RAAP* case is whether *this case* represents a situation where there are 'compelling grounds' for deviating from a homogeneous interpretation of an EU/EEA rule (Article 8(2) RLD).

The legal situation regarding the EEA/EFTA States of Norway and Iceland is different from that in the EU and its Member States, since Norway and Iceland have not yet acceded to the WPPT[57] – only to its predecessor, the Rome Convention.[58] As

[55] Following the ruling in Case 22/70 *Commission v Council (European Agreement on Road Transport)* ECLI:EU:C:1971:32.

[56] *RAAP* (n 4) para 90 with further references.

[57] However, Liechtenstein acceded to the WPPT in 2007.

[58] In Norway, the recent bill for the amendment of the Copyright Act of 22 November 2023 (see n 50 above) proposes the accession of Norway to the WIPO Conventions of 1996, the WCT and the WPPT, and

the EEA/EFTA States are not members of the EU, they are also not bound by the EU's accession to the WPPT. Admittedly, even the Rome Convention has rules on remuneration for performers and phonogram producers, but since the US has not acceded to the Rome Convention, the Convention's principle of national treatment does not apply to recordings with the necessary attachment to the US. This is of great practical importance since many recordings have US origins.

A homogeneous interpretation of Article 8(2) RLD will, in practice, result in 'impose[d] restraints on the EFTA States in their third-country trade relations', to quote the EFTA Court in *Maglite*.[59] However, the situation is different from that in *Maglite* and *L'Oreal*, since a homogeneous interpretation *will* indeed impose restrictions on the EFTA States' freedom to enter into agreements with third countries, contrary to the finding of the EFTA Court in *L'Oreal*. To take the WPPT, which was central to the *RAAP* ruling, as an example: if Norway accedes to the Convention, which has been proposed in the latest bill to amend the Norwegian Copyright Act,[60] an interpretation of Article 8(2) RLD in accordance with *RAAP* will imply that Norway cannot make use of the material reciprocity that Article 4(2) WPPT allows for. This means, in practice, that Norway, as an EEA State, will be dependent on the EU rules, including the EU exclusive external competence, and will only be able to apply the principle of material reciprocity towards nationals of third countries to the extent that this is provided for at the EU level. This is arguably, on the face of it, in conflict with the premise laid down in Recital 16 of the EEA Agreement that the EEA Agreement does not restrict the treaty-making power of the Contracting Parties. It clearly follows from *RAAP* that the EU external competence is not restricted in this respect. If the EU were to enter into new reciprocity agreements with third countries, the EEA/EFTA states are obviously not bound by them, and homogeneity would not be achieved in any case. This is more than a hypothetical possibility and shows the limits of the homogeneity principle.[61] The question is therefore whether Article 8(2) RLD provides a basis for limiting the *EFTA States'* treaty-making competence. As the statement in Recital 16, to the effect that treaty-making power is not restricted, is expressed as being subject to the 'provisions of this Agreement', it remains to be seen whether Article 8(2) RLD, interpreted in accordance with the homogeneity principle, can be considered such a 'provision'.

An argument that has been put forward in this context is that the CJEU's interpretation is in accordance with the wording of Article 8(2) RLD, and that it is not certain that the CJEU would have interpreted the provision differently if it were not for the EU's exclusive treaty competence in the area.[62] However, what actually follows from the wording is debatable at the very least. In *RAAP*, the CJEU emphasised that Article 8(2) RLD 'does not expressly state whether the words "relevant performers" [in the provision] refer solely to performers who are nationals of a State in which that directive applies or whether they equally refer to performers who are nationals of another State'.[63] Instead, the Court

hence to apply material reciprocity to the remuneration right set out in Art 21 of the Norwegian Copyright Act in accordance with Art 4(2) WPPT, on the ground that *RAAP* does not apply to the EEA.

[59] *Maglite* (n 3) para. 27.

[60] See n 50.

[61] *RAAP* (n 4) para 89.

[62] *cf* HH Fredriksen and G Mathisen, *EØS-rett*, 4th edn (Bergen, Fagbokforlaget, 2022) 363.

[63] *RAAP* (n 4) para 49.

makes a contextual interpretation, drawing heavily on the WPPT, as part of the EU legal order, and its rule on national treatment in Article 4(1) WPPT, to establish that the right to remuneration cannot be limited to performers with the necessary points of attachment to the EEA. On the other hand, in the same context, the CJEU fails to take account of the *limitation* to national treatment inherent in Article 4(2) WPPT, confirming the principle of material reciprocity. The significance of this provision is only discussed under the (third) question of whether EU Member States can limit the right to remuneration under Article 8(2) RLD in accordance with the right to make reservations under Article 15(3) WPPT.[64] It is from that perspective that the Court drew on Article 52(1) CFREU and noted that a reservation made in accordance with Article 15(3) WPPT does not satisfy the requirement that the limitation of a fundamental right must be clear and precise. As I have explained elsewhere, there is much to be said about this line of reasoning.[65] Had the Court instead started by finding that the WPPT does not impose on the EU a duty of national treatment – only a duty of material reciprocity – at least the starting point for the CJEU's assessment would have been different.[66] However, it appears quite clear that the Court's overall reasoning is aimed at the conclusion that the EU has exclusive regulatory and external treaty competence with regard to determining limitations on the scope of Article 8(2) RLD, and that this competence has not yet been utilised.[67] In any case, the CJEU's interpretation is mainly based on a treaty that is part of the EU's internal law as a result of the fact that the EU has exercised its external treaty competence, and which is thus also not covered by the EEA Agreement.

Against this background, it is far from a given that the expression 'relevant performers and producers' should be interpreted in the same way in an EEA context as in the EU context. On the contrary, it can be argued that the expression must be limited to performers and producers from (or with the necessary points of attachment to) EEA States, in accordance with the non-discrimination rule in Article 4 of the EEA Agreement. The reason is that a different interpretation will inevitably limit the freedom of EFTA States to enter into deviating agreements with third countries, contrary to what can be inferred from the *Maglite* and *L'Oreal* decisions. In the *RAAP* situation, an interpretation that only limits states' unilateral measures and not their treaty competence, as emphasised by the EFTA Court in *L'Oreal* concerning the non-exhaustion of trade mark rights, is not relevant.[68] An interpretation of Article 8(2) RLD in an EEA context that only obliges states to interpret the expression 'relevant performers and producers' in accordance

[64] See n 49.

[65] See Rognstad, 'The *RAAP* Decision of the CJEU' (n 44) 533–36; and Rognstad, 'Performing Artists' Right to Remuneration' (n 44) 1538–40.

[66] See 'Comment of the European Copyright Society on the Impact and Consequences of the CJEU Decision in C-265/19 (*RAAP*)', available at: europeancopyrightsocietydotorg.files.wordpress.com/2022/05/comment-of-the-european-copyright-society-on-the-impact-and-consequences-of-the-cjeu-decision-in-c-265.19-raap-1.pdf, 5–7, where it is argued that the question of the protection of IP rights under Art 17(2) CFREU should be decided concretely and not *in abstracto*. See also OA Rognstad, 'Repercussions of the *RAAP* Judgment: Some Introductory Remarks' (2022) *Nordiskt Immateriellt Rättsskydd* 517, 521–22.

[67] See *RAAP* (n 4) paras 88–89.

[68] See n 38.

with the non-discrimination rule in Article 4 EEA appears from that perspective as plausible.

Such an interpretation by no means implies that the interpretation of EEA law is unaffected by the EU's international obligations and agreements with third countries. To take the WPPT and the corresponding WIPO Copyright Treaty (WCT) of 1996 as an example, it is obvious that these conventions have strongly influenced the content of the Directive on copyright and related rights in the information society (hereinafter 'the Infosoc Directive').[69] As this Directive is included in Annex XVII to the EEA Agreement, it is equally obvious that its substantive provisions, as a main rule, will have to be interpreted homogeneously with the EEA Agreement, irrespective of whether or not the EEA/EFTA States have acceded to the conventions. What the solution to limit the scope of the expression 'relevant performers and producers' in an EEA context entails is that the principle of homogeneity, without further support, cannot justify an interpretation of an EEA provision that deprives the EEA/EFTA States of their freedom to enter into agreements with third countries regarding who is entitled to the rights and obligations that follow from the provision in a situation where the EU (or its Member States) has retained its freedom in this respect. As mentioned above (see section IV), the principle of reciprocity underpins this understanding.[70]

As follows from Recital 16 of the EEA Agreement, a deviation from this point of departure may follow from the EEA provisions themselves. Had Article 8(2) RLD expressly established that all performers and producers are entitled to remuneration, without any adjustments to the provision from the EEA Joint Committee, the situation would have been different. In other words, the EEA Agreement does not prevent the Contracting Parties (EFTA States and the EU and its Member States) from limiting their external treaty competence. However, there is a need for specific reference points supporting this result beyond the general homogeneity aim. A CJEU judgment which states that a particular result does not follow from the wording, but from a contextual interpretation, of conventions entered into by the EU, and in which the EU's exclusive external competence is an important element for justifying that result, constitutes a weak basis for limiting the external treaty competence of the EEA/EFTA States. In line with the assumptions of the EFTA Court in *Maglite* and *L'Oreal*, the differences in scope between the EU and the EEA Agreement may lead to different interpretations of equally formulated rules where such differences constitute 'compelling grounds' for the different interpretation. It also follows, expressly from *Maglite* and implicitly from *L'Oreal*, that consideration of the Contracting Parties' external competence constitutes such compelling ground. The fact that an EU regulation in the copyright field which regulates the relationship between the EU and third

[69] Directive 2001/29/EC (n 33). See Art 3 on the communication to the public, which must be considered as a mere implementation of Art 8 WCT and Arts 10 and 14 WPPT.

[70] See n 40. On this principle, see, eg, C Baudenbacher, 'The EFTA Court: Structure and Tasks' in Baudenbacher (n 2) 145; P Hreinsson, 'General Principles and Prohibition of Discrimination on Grounds of Nationality' in Baudenbacher (n 2) 354–55; and C Baudenbacher, 'Reciprocity' in C Baudenbacher (ed), *The Fundamental Principles of EEA Law* (Cham, Springer, 2017) 35–71.

countries has been kept outside the EEA Agreement, due to a lack of EEA relevance, provides some further support for this approach applicable to the *RAAP* situation.[71]

Nevertheless, the question may be raised as to whether there are decisive arguments in favour of a homogeneous interpretation of the term 'relevant performers and producers' in Article 8(2) RLD in an EEA context. One possible argument is the consideration of the fundamental rights that the CJEU highlighted in *RAAP*. Again, the contexts are arguably different in the EU and the EEA. As already pointed out, the CJEU interpreted the term in light of the national treatment rule in the WPPT, which does not form part of the EEA Agreement. Against that backdrop, a limitation on the right to remuneration was considered a limitation to the performers' (and producers') IP right, regarded as a fundamental right pursuant to Article 17(2) CFREU, and consequently subject to the limitations provided for in Article 52(1) CFREU. Irrespective of my own opinion that this approach to Article 17 CFREU is highly questionable,[72] the perspective changes if Article 8(2) RLD in the EEA context is interpreted as to not oblige national treatment beyond the non-discrimination principle enshrined in Article 4 EEA. In that case, performers and producers attached to third countries do not have any rights in relation to communication to the public in the EEA/EFTA States, as the rights must be determined at a national level in accordance with the states' international obligations. If the EEA/EFTA States in such a situation refrain from granting rights to third-country performers or producers – for example, on the ground of international conventions, there will be no interference with established IP rights and consequently no limitation of fundamental rights neither under the EU Charter nor under the EEA Agreement.[73]

An interpretation of the expression 'relevant performers and producers' in Article 8(2) RLD in an EEA context which is limited to performers and producers with the necessary attachment to the EEA, in accordance with the non-discrimination principle in Article 4 EEA, implies a parallel – instead of a homogeneous – interpretation with the EU rule. This means, in practice, that the EFTA States are put in the same position as the EU with regard to the freedom both to determine the provision's scope in third-country relations and to enter into agreements – for example, on material reciprocity – with non-EEA countries. This interpretation should imply that any limitations prescribed for at the EU level as a result of the CJEU ruling in *RAAP*[74]

[71] *cf* the fact that Regulation (EU) 2017/1563 of the European Parliament and of the Council on the cross-border exchange between the Union and third countries of accessible format copies of certain works and other subject matter protected by copyright and related rights for the benefit of persons who are blind, visually impaired or otherwise print-disabled [2017] OJ L242/1 is held to fall outside the EEA Agreement due to a lack of EEA relevance because the EEA Agreement regulates the relationship between the EU and third countries. See the Norwegian government's comments, available at: www.regjeringen.no/no/sub/eosnotatbasen/notatene/2017/juni/marrakechtraktat-direktivet/id2556741.

[72] See Rognstad (n 66). In my opinion, the CJEU should have decided on the significance of the limitation to the obligation of national treatment in Art 4(2) WPPT for the interpretation of Art 8(2) RLD before raising any question about the relevance of Art 17(2) CFREU.

[73] *cf*, eg, Case C-283/11 *Sky Österreich* ECLI:EU:C:2013:28, para 34. The EFTA Court has recognised that fundamental rights form part of the general principles of EEA; see, eg, Case E-1/20 *Kerim*, para 43. This includes the right to property as protected under Art 1 of Protocol 1 of the European Convention on Human Rights, *cf* Joined Cases E-3/13 and E-20/13 *Fred Olsen*, paras 228–29.

[74] See the consultation by the European Commission on the conditions for the remuneration of music performers and record producers from third countries for recorded music played in the EU:

are not to be considered as EEA-relevant. At the same time, the provision of the mutual information rule regarding 'the context of agreements dealing with intellectual property' set out in Article 7 of Protocol 28 to the EEA also applies to this situation, with a view to possible coordinated solutions in order to safeguard homogeneity in this manner. The interpretation advocated here is in accordance with the EFTA Court rulings in *Maglite* and *L'Oreal*.

VI. CONCLUSION AND OUTLOOK

To conclude on the basis of the above discussion, differences in third-country regulation in the EU and the EEA can lead to parallel rather than homogeneous interpretations of identically formulated EU and EEA rules. The CJEU decision in *RAAP* is an example of a case where the legal sources, including the EFTA Court rulings in *Maglite* and *L'Oreal*, point in the direction of such a parallel interpretation. The result of the parallel interpretation of the term 'relevant performers and producers' in Article 8(2) RLD is that both the EU and the EEA/EFTA States retain their competence to decide, within the framework of their international obligations, which performers and producers from third countries shall be entitled to remuneration pursuant to the provision. A similar approach is also viable if the *RAAP* rationale is applied to copyright rules other than the remuneration right of performers and phonogram producers.[75]

In *RAAP*, the CJEU resolved the issue of the EU's regulatory and external treaty competence in the area of performers' and producers' right to remuneration by interpreting the expression 'relevant performers and producers' so that it includes all performers and producers, regardless of their nationality,[76] even though there were several possible alternative interpretations.[77] Here, the Court relies on a rule of national treatment that is laid down in EU internal law (WPPT), but which is not included the EEA Agreement. At the same time, it left it to the EU legislature to limit the scope of the provision either through legislation, within the framework of the EU's international obligations, or by entering into new reciprocity agreements with third countries. A parallel interpretation of Article 8(2) RLD in the EEA context, which gives the EEA/EFTA States the corresponding freedom to enter into agreements with third countries regarding the territorial scope of the remuneration right, would mean that the expression 'relevant performers and producers' in that context means performers and producers with the necessary points of attachment to the EEA as follows from the non-discrimination rule in Article 4 EEA. It is clear that Article 4

digital-strategy.ec.europa.eu/en/consultations/targeted-consultation-conditions-remuneration-music-performers-and-record-producers-third-non-eu.

[75] See, eg, Case C-227/23 *Kwantum Nederland*, request for a preliminary ruling from the Supreme Court of the Netherlands regarding material reciprocity for copyright protection of applied art. See also on this question Blomqvist and Rosenmeier (n 46) 59–61.

[76] However, this interpretation is not incontestable. An alternative interpretation is that the remuneration right in Art 8(2) RLD applies to nationals of WPPT states; see further Rognstad, 'The *RAAP* Decision of the CJEU' (n 44) 537 and Rognstad, 'Performing Artists Right to Remuneration' (n 44) 1537–38.

[77] See Rognstad (n 66) 518–20, identifying four possible alternative interpretations.

EEA must be interpreted homogeneously with Article 18 TFEU and must imply that the right to remuneration be granted to EU nationals.[78] However, the EEA Agreement entails no corresponding rules on national treatment of third-country nationals, and putting the EEA/EFTA States and the EU (by virtue of having exclusive regulatory and external treaty competence in the field) on an equal footing under the EEA Agreement will imply that the EEA obligations do not extend beyond that. The EU Member States are certainly bound by the interpretation of Article 8(2) RLD in an EU context. Thus, the consequences of the Directive's provisions being interpreted differently in an EEA context is that the EEA/EFTA States remain free to determine the scope of third-country nationals' right to remuneration.

Two underlying considerations dictate a parallel instead of a homogeneous interpretation in situations such as *RAAP*: the Contracting Parties' autonomy in third-country relations, and the reciprocity consideration. The former is reflected in Recital 16 of the Preamble to the EEA Agreement, stating that the EEA Agreement does not restrict the decision-making autonomy or the treaty-making power of the Contracting Parties beyond what follows from the EEA Agreement itself and limits set by public international law. The reciprocity consideration, or principle, is reflected in Recital 4 of the Preamble, and has often been cited in support of the fact that the Contracting Parties must, to the greatest extent possible, ensure that EEA nationals receive the same rights in each of the EEA pillars.[79] In this respect, the principle of homogeneity and the reciprocity principle go hand in hand. However, the reference to equality and reciprocity in Recital 4 should also imply that the EEA/EFTA States should have the same opportunity as the other Contracting Parties – ie, the EU in areas where it has the exclusive competence to act under EU law – to decide the extent of third-country nationals' rights. However, this implies that the principle of reciprocity may also lead to non-homogeneous solutions, due to differences in the regulation of third-state relations in the EU and the EEA. In this sense, the principle has a wider scope than just being 'the twin maxim to the principle of homogeneity'.[80]

The above findings do not imply that the EEA Agreement cannot restrict the Contracting Parties' external treaty competence, for example, acts of secondary law which expressly provide for such a restriction have been incorporated into the EEA Agreement without special EEA adjustments. What the discussion above has sought to prove is that the homogeneity principle is not in itself a sufficient basis for such restrictions. Support for this is found in the *Maglite* and *L'Oreal* rulings of the EFTA Court, in that there will be 'compelling grounds' for deviating from the principle in situations where a homogeneous interpretation of a provision would put restrictions on the freedom of the EEA/EFTA States to enter into agreements with third countries on the scope of third-country nationals' rights in situations where the EU has a corresponding freedom. Although both existing case law and the example highlighted here of the existence of such 'compelling grounds' relate to the field of IP law, these findings are believed to also have a general bearing beyond the IP field. In other words, there are reasons for adopting the same approach to other types of legal relationships.

[78] See Joined Cases C-92/92 and C-326/92 *Phil Collins and Others* ECLI:EU:C:1993:847.

[79] See the references in n 70.

[80] The expression cited is taken from Baudenbacher, 'Reciprocity' (n 70) 35.

However, on this point, it must cautioned against drawing too far-reaching a conclusion from a statement that the EFTA Court has made in a few cases, which in essence provides that the EEA/EFTA States cannot make the rights conferred by EEA law subject to the provisions of another international agreement.[81] Although the correctness of the statement is not disputed as such, this chapter demonstrates that the very question of the scope of 'rights conferred by EEA law' cannot always be determined without reference to the relationship with other international agreements.[82] The problem with the above statement is that it postulates a tension between 'rights conferred by EEA law' and 'agreements with other states', without going into the grounds for the rights being conferred by EEA law. *RAAP* represents a good example here. If Article 8(2) RLD were to be interpreted homogenously with *RAAP* in an EEA context, without taking account of the treaty-making autonomy of the Contracting Parties, the application of the above statement of the EFTA Court would mean that the interpretation is unaffected by agreements that the EEA/EFTA States have entered (or will enter) into. Yet, as highlighted above, the content of the EEA rules in situations like *RAAP* cannot be determined without taking into consideration the significance of the third-country aspect.

In other words, when it comes to the question of *which* rights can be derived from the EEA Agreement, account must be taken of the freedom of the Contracting Parties to enter into agreements with third countries. At the same time, the views explained above imply that this freedom does not prevent the EEA rules from *placing* restrictions on the content of agreements with third countries. However, such restrictions should not solely be derived from a homogeneous interpretation of equally formulated EU rules, in situations where the EU is not equally restricted in its third country relations. An opposite solution would mean that the external competence of the EEA/EFTA States is restricted without the EEA rules providing a sufficient basis for it. The *RAAP* ruling is an example of where the line must be drawn.

[81] See Case E-5/22 *Christian Maitz*, paras 45-48, with reference to similar statements in Case E-1/04 *Fokus Bank* [2004] EFTA Ct Rep 11, para 31 and Case E-14/15 *Holship Norge* [2016] EFTA Ct Rep 240, para 128.

[82] *cf* H Bull, 'Article 40', in Arnesen et al (n 2) 479–80, who observes that the position of the EFTA Court in Case E-1/04 *Fokus Bank* implying that bilateral tax agreements with other Member States have no impact on the interpretation of Article 40 EEA on free movement of capital 'sits uncomfortably besides the ECJ's judgment i.a. in Case C-487/08 *Commission v Spain*' and that 'it may reasonably be expected that the EFTA Court, following the principle of homogeneity as applied in … *L'Oreal*, will follow the ECJ's view'.

15

Two Tales, One Outcome? The Principle of Proportionality in the Case Law of the EFTA Court

GUNNAR THOR PETURSSON

I. INTRODUCTION

ALTHOUGH THE PRINCIPLE of proportionality appears regularly in the case law of the Court of Justice of the European Union[1] – and now with an explicit reference in the Treaties and the Charter of Fundamental Rights of the European Union, as will be discussed, its background and scope remains somewhat elusive. The reasons for this may be numerous, but the lack of direct reference in the founding treaties, and lack of substantive content, play a role. Similarly, the EEA Agreement, which was signed in 1992, and entered into force in 1994, contains no direct reference to a principle of proportionality, but, as will be discussed, the principle holds a firm place in the case law of the EFTA Court as well.

In this chapter, the principle of proportionality will be analysed, with a focus on the case law of the EFTA Court, and, as appropriate, compared to the approach of the Court of Justice. The comparative angle is the case law on free movement, but a fully fledged comparative analysis covering all fields of EU and EEA law would not be relevant due to certain substantive and institutional differences between the EEA Agreement and the EU Treaties, as will be explained later on.

Taking into account the similarities and differences of these two interlinked regimes, the EU and the EEA, in the following sections I will analyse and compare the application of the principle of proportionality before these two European courts, starting from its origins in the case law of the Court of Justice, and the uncertain background, and from there will move on to give an analysis and comparison of the case law of the EFTA Court on the free movement principles from various angles. As will be demonstrated, this is a field where the proportionality principle has flourished in both courts, even if it lacks a specific treaty/agreement base, and additional honing of its different elements and stages continues to this day.

[1] Hereinafter referred to as 'the Court of Justice'.

II. THE ORIGIN AND EMERGENCE OF THE PRINCIPLE OF PROPORTIONALITY IN EU LAW

Historically, the notion of proportionality can be traced back to ancient times and is encapsulated in the Greek dictum 'pan metron ariston', which roughly translates as all things are good in moderation.[2] Furthermore, as Barak has pointed out in his in-depth analysis of the principle of proportionality in its constitutional and comparative context, the notion of proportionality has inspired thinkers throughout history, and ideas of proportionality may also be found in the old Hebrew culture, as reflected in the 'eye for an eye' reference in the Exodus as a measured response.[3]

In modern times, the proportionality principle is mainly seen as playing a key role in protecting the individual vis-a-vis the state and its regulatory intervention. The main tenets of the proportionality principle can be found in virtually all effective systems of constitutional justice in the world, except the US.[4] This has often been a gradual development – the result of a doctrinal construction that has subsequently emerged as an unwritten general principle of law, mainly through judicial recognition and choice. In Europe, Germany has been held to be the legal system that first developed the principle, moving from being an administrative principle and subsequently becoming recognised as a principle holding a constitutional status, as confirmed by the German Constitutional Court in 1969.[5] The emergence and development of the proportionality principle in German constitutional law has had a significant influence on the Court of Justice, particularly when initially adopting the principle.[6]

As mentioned above, the principle of proportionality is, first and foremost a legal construction and a methodological tool and conventionally that is held to have four elements:[7]

- First, to verify that the (contested) measure pursues *a legitimate objective*.[8]
- Second, that the measure is *suitable/appropriate* in order to achieve the pursued objective.

[2] T Tridimas, *The General Principles of EU Law*, 2nd edn (Oxford, Oxford University Press, 2006) 136.

[3] A Barak, *Proportionality: Constitutional Rights and Their Limitations* (Cambridge, Cambridge University Press, 2012) 175.

[4] A Sweet and J Mathews, 'Proportionality Balancing and Global Constitutionalism' (2008) 47 *Columbia Journal of Transnational Law* 72, 75.

[5] Judgment of 15 December 1969, Case 19 BVerfGE 342; see D Grimm, 'Proportionality in Canadian and German Constitutional Jurisprudence' (2007) 57 *University of Toronto Law Journal* 383, 385. See also Barak (n 3) 10.

[6] FG Jacobs, 'Recent Developments in the Principle of Proportionality in European Community Law' in E Ellis (ed), *The Principle of Proportionality in the Laws of Europe* (Oxford, Hart Publishing, 1999) 1–2. Sweet and Mathews (n 4) 144 have also traced the origins and inspirations of the use of the principle by the Court of Justice down to the purely personal level, ie, to two of its justices: Hans Kutcher, who was formerly a judge at the German Federal Constitutional Court, and Pierre Pescatore, who left a professorship to become a judge at the Court of Justice and who wrote about the principle in 1970.

[7] B Pirker, *Proportionality Analysis and Models of Judicial Review* (Groeningen, Europa Law Publsishing, 2013) 15; Barak (n 3) 131.

[8] In EU and EEA law, this first element of verifying legitimate interests has indeed been considered separately from the core proportionality analysis. This approach is also seen in the case law of the European Court of Human Rights and in dispute resolution in the WTO framework; see Sweet and Mathews (n 4) 76.

- Third, that the measure is *necessary* in order to achieve the legitimate aim and that a less restrictive alternative is not available.
- Fourth, and finally, proportionality *stricto sensu*, or proportionality which is in essence a test of balancing/weighing different and even, as the case may be, hierarchically equal legitimate interests.

The nature of proportionality *stricto sensu*, and the distinction between that level and the *necessity* test, is a thorny issue, as will be discussed below. In the view of Robert Alexy, who has analysed proportionality assessment as practised by the German Constitutional Court in detail, the fourth level of the proportionality principle – proportionality *stricto sensu* – is a matter of balancing interests. Therefore, Alexy refers to this as the *law of balancing*, which he summarises as follows:

> The greater the degree of non-satisfaction of, or detriment to, one right or principle the greater must be the importance of satisfying the other.[9]

Even if in EU law, the principle of proportionality has mostly been developed in the context of the free movement case law of the Court of Justice, its origins may be traced back to cases and questions concerning the *validity* of EC secondary norms.

In the European Communities at the time, traces or elements of the proportionality principle are seen in one of the first cases of the Court of Justice. In the *Fédéchar* case,[10] which was decided in 1955 and concerned the annulment of a decision adopted by the High Authority of the European Coal and Steel Community, the Court held that:

> [I]n accordance with a generally-accepted rule of law such an indirect reaction by the High Authority to illegal action on the part of the undertakings must be in *proportion* to the scale of that action. (Emphasis added)[11]

The acceptance of ideas of proportionality seems to have been taken on without any detailed explanation or reflection in the early cases.[12] However, when specific questions came from the German courts, where fundamental rights, as protected in the German Constitution, formed the core of the preliminary reference, the Advocate General (AG) in the case, AG Dutheillet de Lamothe, started to reflect on the origins and nature of the principle of proportionality. This all happened in the well-known *Internationale Handelsgesellschaft* case,[13] in which AG Dutheillet de Lamothe considered the sources of the proportionality principle in (then) Community law and thus its force in application 'against a measure issued by the Community authorities'.[14] From several alternatives, the AG suggested that the principle was to be found in an express and very clear provision of the Treaty, namely, Article 40(3) EEC (now Article 40(2) of the Treaty on the Functioning of the European Union

[9] R Alexy, 'On Balancing and Subsumption: A Structural Comparison' (2003) 16 *Ratio Juris* 433, 437.

[10] Case 8/55 *Fédération Charbonnière de Belgique v High Authority of the European Coal and Steel Community* ECLI:EU:C:1956:11.

[11] ibid 299.

[12] See also Case 19/61 *Mannesmann AG v High Authority of the European Coal and Steel Community* ECLI:EU:C:1962:31.

[13] Case 11/70 *Internationale Handelsgesellschaft mbH* ECLI:EU:C:1970:114.

[14] ibid, Opinion of AG Dutheillet de Lamothe, ECLI:EU:C:1970:100, p 1146.

(TFEU)), from which it follows that the common organisation of the agricultural market may include only those measures required to attain the objectives set out in Article 39 EEC (now Article 39 TFEU).[15] Francis G Jacobs, former AG of the Court, has in academic writings referred to *Internationale Handelsgesellschaft* as the case where the proportionality principle emerged as a general principle of law. Even if he did not agree with AG Dutheillet de Lamothe's ideas, in particular as regards Article 40(3) EEC sufficing as the source of the principle, he argued that the Court and the AG in the case were responding to concerns in German legal circles that the principles of fundamental rights, and the principle of proportionality, were not given full effect in (then) Community law.[16]

The ruling of the Court of Justice in the *Internationale Handelsgesellschaft* case is of course of high importance in the sense that the Court of Justice in this case recognised fundamental rights as forming 'an integral part of the general principles of law protected by the Court of Justice'.[17] However, it is less certain to what extent the Court followed the suggestions of AG Dutheillet de Lamothe in recognising the proportionality principle as a Community law (general) principle of law. Schwarze has, for example, argued that the Court adopted the solution proposed by AG Dutheillet de Lamothe, although he points out that the Court of Justice not only applied the *necessity* test, which is the only test explicitly stated in Article 40(3) EEC, but also referred to the *appropriateness* of the measure and how this affected the process of weighing up the interests involved (proportionality *stricto sensu*).[18] However, Jacobs has maintained that the Court, perhaps rightly, preferred to treat proportionality as a 'general principle of law', in a similar way to how it had acknowledged the same in terms of fundamental rights in this case.[19]

Despite this, the Court of Justice eventually firmly positioned the principle of proportionality among the general principles of (then) Community law in the *Schräder* case, which also originated from Germany,[20] holding that:

> [T]he principle of proportionality is *one of the general principles of Community law*. By virtue of that principle, measures imposing financial charges on economic operators are lawful provided that the measures are appropriate and necessary for meeting the objectives legitimately pursued by the legislation in question. Of course, when there is a choice between several appropriate measures, *the least onerous measure must be used* and the charges imposed must not be *disproportionate* to the aims pursued. (Emphasis added)[21]

In the *Fedesa* case,[22] the Court further elaborated on the essentials of the proportionality principle as a general principle of Community (at the time) law, highlighting its three elements:

> The Court has consistently held that the principle of proportionality is one of the general principles of Community law. By virtue of that principle, the lawfulness of the prohibition

[15] ibid 1147.

[16] Jacobs (n 6) 2. Other AGs had also previously discussed the idea of the principle of proportionality in EC law, such as AG Karl Roemer in Case 31/59 *Acciaieria e Tubificio di Brescia* ECLI:EU:C:1960:3, 88–89.

[17] *Internationale Handelsgesellschaft* (n 13) para 4.

[18] J Schwarze, *European Administrative Law* (London, Sweet & Maxwell, 2006) 713–14.

[19] Jacobs (n 6) 2.

[20] Case 265/87 *Schräder* ECLI:EU:C:1989:303.

[21] ibid para 21.

[22] Case C-331/88 *Fedesa and Others* ECLI:EU:C:1990:391.

> of an economic activity is subject to the condition that the prohibitory measures are *appropriate* and *necessary* in order to achieve the objectives legitimately pursued by the legislation in question; when there is *a choice* between several appropriate measures recourse must be had to the *least onerous*, and the disadvantages caused must not be disproportionate to the aims pursued. (Emphasis added)[23]

It is important to note that the above-mentioned cases are preliminary ruling cases, often also involving questions on the *validity* of EC/EU secondary law, not least in the light of fundamental rights.

The principle of proportionality subsequently emerged in the field of free movement, also through a line of preliminary ruling cases. This is a field where the proportionality principle has flourished and is now an essential feature in any analysis of potential justification of measures restrictive of free movement principles.

In *Cassis de Dijon*,[24] the Court of Justice introduced the *mandatory requirements* as potential grounds of justification, while at the same time indicating that they would have to meet conditions of the proportionality principle:

> In the absence of common rules ... obstacles to movement within the Community resulting from disparities between the national laws relating to the marketing of [a product] must be accepted in so far as those provisions may be recognized as being *necessary* in order to satisfy *mandatory requirements* relating in particular to the effectiveness of fiscal supervision, the protection of public health, the fairness of commercial transactions and the defence of the consumer. (Emphasis added)[25]

Subsequently, in the *Rau* case,[26] which was decided shortly after *Cassis de Dijon*, the Court of Justice clarified the 'necessity test' and held that:

> It is also necessary for such rules to *be proportionate to the aim in view*. If a Member State has a choice between various measures to attain the same objective it should choose the means which *least restricts* the free movement of goods. (Emphasis added)[27]

In *Sandoz*, the Court of Justice finally referred to the proportionality principle as a 'principle' in the context of free movement case law and held that it 'underlies the last sentence of Article 36 of the Treaty'.[28]

III. THE PRINCIPLE OF PROPORTIONALITY IN THE FREE MOVEMENT CASE LAW OF THE EFTA COURT

A. The Origins

As mentioned above, the EEA Agreement includes no reference to the principle of proportionality. However, already in its first case, *Restamark*, the EFTA Court relied

[23] ibid para 13.
[24] Case 120/78 *Rewe-Zentral* (*Cassis de Dijon*) ECLI:EU:C:1979:42.
[25] ibid para 8.
[26] Case 261/81 *Walter Rau* ECLI:EU:C:1982:382.
[27] ibid para 12. Subsequently, a similar approach was confirmed by the Court of Justice to also apply outside the field of free movement of goods. See Case C-76/90 *Säger* ECLI:EU:C:1991:331, para 15; and Case C-55/94 *Gebhard* ECLI:EU:C:1995:411.
[28] Case 174/82 *Sandoz* ECLI:EU:C:1983:213, para 18.

on and made a reference to proportionality as a 'principle', without much hesitation it appears. The case was an advisory opinion request from the Appeals Committee at the Finnish Board of Customs and concerned rules relating to the Finnish alcohol monopoly and their compatibility with Articles 11 and 16 EEA. The EFTA Court held the state monopoly's import licensing rules to be a restriction within the meaning of Article 11 EEA, and therefore considered the potential justification of the rules on public health grounds under Article 13 EEA. In that context, the EFTA Court stated as follows:

> However, according to the second sentence of Article 13 EEA, prohibitions or restrictions must not constitute a means of arbitrary discrimination or a disguised restriction on trade between the Contracting Parties. The *principle of proportionality*, which *underlies* the second sentence of Article 13 EEA, requires that the power of the Contracting Parties to prohibit imports from other Contracting Parties should be restricted to that which is *necessary* to attain the legitimate aim of protecting health. (Emphasis added)[29]

Furthermore, in this case, the EFTA Court cited case law of the Court of Justice, with a reference to Article 6 EEA, when emphasising that, as a derogation, Article 13 EEA needs to be interpreted strictly, and emphasised that the burden of proof regarding the proportionality of the restrictive measure is laid on the state responsible for the restriction.[30]

It is noteworthy that in the above-cited paragraph, the EFTA Court used, without hesitation, the term 'principle', and at the same time was positioning the principle within the remits of the second sentence of Article 13 EEA. However, that was in line with the case law of the Court of Justice at the time and the wording seemingly inspired by *Sandoz*. However, there is no reference to the Court of Justice's case law specifically concerning the principle of proportionality in the field of free movement. In a way, this approach stands out, both in terms of finding a ground for the proportionality principle in a specific provision of the EEA Agreement itself and for the lack of reference to the Court of Justice's case law in support of the scope or ambit of the principle (or status as a principle), which could have been expected.

However, and as will be further demonstrated below, in its subsequent case law the EFTA Court has very diligently cited the case law of the Court of Justice and has followed closely the evolution and development of the principle of proportionality, in particular in the context of the free movement principles.

Already in *Restamark*, although not in the context of application of the principle of proportionality, the EFTA Court cited and relied on both the foundational principles laid down by the Court of Justice in *Dassonville* and *Cassis de Djion*.[31] A summary of the EFTA Court's approach and understanding of the proportionality principle may be found in *Pedicel*,[32] where the Court described the principle of

[29] Case E-1/94 *Restamark* [1994–95] EFTA Ct Rep 15, para 58. See also a reference to the principle in Case E-1/95 *Samuelsson* [1994–95] EFTA Ct Rep 145, para 31, even if in a materially different context.

[30] *Restamark* (n 29) paras 56 and 60.

[31] ibid paras 47 and 51.

[32] Case E-4/04 *Pedicel* [1995] EFTA Ct Rep 1.

proportionality and its role when reviewing measures restricting free movement in the following way:

> Under the proportionality principle, the measure chosen by an EEA Contracting Party must be proportionate to the aim pursued. It must be established that measures taken are suited to achieve the objective sought, and that the same objective may not be as effectively achieved by measures which are less restrictive of intra-EEA trade.[33]

The EFTA Court has even taken this a step further, emphasising that a measure that is restrictive of the fundamental freedoms must, in terms of its proportionality, satisfy the conditions laid down in the case law of *both* the EFTA Court and the Court of Justice.[34]

B. The Margin of Discretion

It is clear that states will, in certain circumstances, be granted a wide margin of discretion when it comes to a judicial review of public policy choices, for example, the level of the public health protection offered, or for the protection of other deep or sensitive national interests. However, in the context of the free movement principles/ case law, this discretion is controlled primarily through the principle of proportionality. The depth and intensity of the proportionality analysis may vary, depending on the circumstances of the case, the interests involved and/or invoked, and even the procedural ground on which they are based.

For example, public policy, public security and public order interests have traditionally been associated in the case law of the Court of Justice with a margin of discretion granted to the state. In the foundational case *Van Duyn*,[35] which concerned the refusal of leave to enter the UK due to Ms Van Duyn's relationship with the Church of Scientology, the Court of Justice held that:

> [T]he particular circumstances justifying recourse to the concept of public policy may vary from one country to another and from one period to another, and it is therefore necessary in this matter to allow the competent national authorities *an area of discretion* [Fr. *une marge d'appreciation*] within the limits imposed by the Treaty. (Emphasis added)[36]

However, in that case, and in numerous subsequent cases concerning public policy issues, the Court of Justice has nonetheless emphasised that the concept of public policy in the context of EU law should be interpreted *strictly* and that its scope cannot be determined *unilaterally* by the states without being subject to *control* by the institutions of the EU, and not relied upon unless there is a genuine, present and sufficiently serious threat to a fundamental interest of society.[37]

[33] ibid para 56.

[34] See Case E-1/06 *ESA v Norway* (*Gaming Machines*) [2007] EFTA Ct Rep 8, paras 29 and 31; and Case E-3/06 *Ladbrokes* [2007] EFTA Ct Rep 86, para 42.

[35] Case 41/74 *Van Duyn* ECLI:EU:C:1974:133. See the different view taken by AG Mayras in his Opinion in *Van Duyn* ECLI:EU:C:1974:123, 1357, who felt that it was not possible to deduce from the Treaty of Rome a Community concept of public security and the concept to remain national.

[36] ibid para 18.

[37] See to that effect Case C-54/99 *Église de scientologie* EU:C:2000:124, para 17; and, more recently, Case C-78/18 *Commission v Hungary* EU:C:2020:476, para 91.

The EFTA Court has followed a similar approach in this type of case, as can be seen in the *Wahl* case,[38] where it used a similar methodology as that employed by the Court of Justice and cited several cases from the Court of Justice in that context,[39] including *Van Duyn*. Despite the institutional 'concept control' and a general strict interpretation of derogations, a margin of discretion being afforded to the state may nonetheless be warranted, as is also acknowledged in the *Wahl* case.[40]

Likewise, states may be allowed a margin of discretion when it comes to determining the level of protection in cases relating to public health interests and the choice of acceptable risk levels. Here, the EFTA Court has also followed the approach of the Court of Justice[41] and has acknowledged that it is for the EEA States, within the limits imposed by the EEA Agreement, to decide on the acceptable level of protection they wish to assure and the way in which to reach that level.[42] As indicated above, the proportionality principle plays a specific and key role in these circumstances, that is, when the balance between important public policy issues and the interest of free movement of goods must be determined. As the EFTA Court held in *Philip Morris*:[43]

> [A]n assessment of whether the principle of proportionality has been observed in the field of public health must take account of the fact that an EEA State has the power to determine the *degree of protection* that it wishes to afford to public health and the way in which that protection is to be achieved. As EEA States are allowed *a certain margin of discretion* in this regard, protection may vary from one EEA State to another. Consequently, the fact that one EEA State imposes less strict rules than another does not mean that the latter's rules are disproportionate. (Emphasis added)[44]

However, in this case, and in comparable circumstances, the national restrictive measures are not sheltered from a proportionality analysis, despite the 'certain' margin. In *Philip Morris*, prompted by the questions from the national court, the EFTA Court provided a detailed answer in terms of the *suitability* and *necessity* of the national measures, in light of the public health grounds provided for in Article 13 of the EEA Agreement.

Various other interests and circumstances may justify a margin to the state, which may be reflected in the proportionality analysis. Likewise, this does not automatically mean that the margin of discretion is unlimited and the proportionality analysis us weak. In fact, the circumstances of the case may call for a thorough proportionality analysis, as the EFTA Court pointed out in *Ladbrokes*[45] in the context of the public policy choices for gaming:

> Moral, religious and cultural factors, as well as the morally and financially harmful consequences for the individual and for society associated with gaming, may serve to justify *a*

[38] Case E-15/12 *Wahl* [2013] EFTA Ct Rep 534.

[39] ibid para 83.

[40] See, eg, ibid paras 100–02.

[41] See, eg, Case C-141/07 *Commission v Germany* ECLI:EU:C:2008:492, para 51; and Case C-169/07 *Hartlauer* ECLI:EU:C:2009:141, paras 29–32. Concerning the level of protection and margin of discretion, see also Case C-108/09 *Ker-Optika* ECLI:EU:C:2010:725, in particular paras 58 and 75.

[42] See, eg, *Pedicel* (n 32) para 55; and Case E-16/10 *Philip Morris* [2011] EFTA Ct Rep 330, para 77.

[43] *Philip Morris* (n 42).

[44] ibid para 80.

[45] *Ladbrokes* (n 34).

> *margin of discretion* for the national authorities, sufficient to enable them to determine what is required in order to ensure consumer protection and the preservation of public order. The EEA Contracting Parties are free to set the objectives of their policy on gaming and, where appropriate, to define in detail the level of protection sought. (Emphasis added)[46]

In relation to the arguments of the Norwegian state in that case that judicial review of national restrictions on the provision of gaming should be limited and that the courts ought to assess the *necessity* of the measures only where there are reasons to believe that the rules in question are in fact discriminatory or protectionist, the EFTA Court firmly stated that:

> Even though the Contracting Parties do have *discretion* in setting the level of protection in the field of gambling, this does not mean that the measures are sheltered from judicial review as to their necessity. (Emphasis added)[47]

C. Additional Elements of the Proportionality Principle

In recent years, additional elements have been making their way into the proportionality test in the case law of the Court of Justice, particularly in the field of free movement.[48]

First, *procedural requirements*, which remain closely related to the concepts of legal certainty and transparency, have been introduced, with which restrictive measures must comply in order to be considered proportionate.[49] In the case law of the Court of Justice, the proportionality test, in this respect, has been developed under the case law of free movement of goods, not least in relation to various licensing schemes and as regards access to justice (judicial review). Licensing schemes need to be transparent; decisions based on rules of law, reasoned and subject to review

The first example is the well-known *Reinheitsgebot* case.[50] Interestingly, the Court of Justice held that 'by virtue of the principle of proportionality, traders must also be able to apply [for the use of additives], under a procedure which is easily accessible to them and can be concluded within a reasonable time'. Furthermore, the Court has held that a trader should be able to challenge before courts an unjustified refusal to grant authorisations.[51] A similar approach may be found concerning the other freedoms, for example, in the case of *Topfit and Biffi*,[52] where the Court of Justice had to

[46] ibid para 42.

[47] ibid para 55.

[48] See further, GT Petursson and X Groussot, 'Balancing as a Judicial Methodology of EU Constitutional Adjudication' in S de Vries, X Groussot and GT Petursson (eds), *Balancing Fundamental Rights with the EU Treaty Freedoms: The European Court of Justice as 'Tightrope' Walker* (Utrecht, Eleven Law Publishing, 2012).

[49] Catherine Barnard has referred to this development as the *proceduralisation of proportionality*; see C Barnard, *The Substantive Law of the EU*, 6th edn (Oxford, Oxford University Press, 2019) 188–90.

[50] Case 178/84 *Commission v Germany (Reinheitsgebot)* ECLI:EU:C:1987:126. See also the case law on state monopolies, which was foundational in this context: Case C-189/95 *Franzén* ECLI:EU:C:1997:504, paras 44 and 51; and Case C-438/02 *Hanner* ECLI:EU:C:2005:332, paras 38–39.

[51] See also Case C-95/01 *Greenham and Able* ECLI:EU:C:2004:71, paras 35 and 50.

[52] Case C-22/18 *Topfit and Biffi* ECLI:EU:C:2019:497.

assess the legality of a prior authorisation scheme of a sports association in the light of EU law.

The EFTA Court has followed a similar approach and has confirmed that in order for a restriction on the fundamental freedoms to be justified, the principle of *legal certainty* must be complied with.[53] The EFTA Court has emphasised that 'a system of prior administrative approval must be based, as a general rule, on objective, non-discriminatory criteria which are known in advance to the undertakings concerned' and that all persons affected by a restrictive measure of that type 'must have a legal remedy available to them'.[54] In the *NAV* case,[55] the EFTA Court held that a system of prior authorisation, such as the one at issue, was disproportionate and that it had not been demonstrated that a less restrictive scheme, such as a system of *prior notification*, would not have been sufficient. The EFTA Court emphasised that:

> With respect to the principle of proportionality, it is necessary that any condition, such as a system of prior authorisation, may be justified with regard to the overriding considerations mentioned above, that it does not exceed what is objectively necessary for that purpose and that the same result cannot be achieved by *less restrictive rules*. (Emphasis added)[56]

The *precautionary principle* is also of relevance in this context, but it has been developed, particularly in the field of free movement of goods, in cases where uncertainty exists in terms of the scientific evidence for the public health risk at stake.[57] States are allowed, in these circumstances and in accordance with the precautionary principle, to take protective measures without having to wait until the reality and seriousness of those risks are fully demonstrated.[58] In fact, the EFTA Court was instrumental in developing the application of the precautionary principle in EU/EEA law. In *Kellogg's* the EFTA Court, in a novel judgment, rendered operational the idea that had been presented by the Court of Justice in *Sandoz* and advanced the understanding and rationale for using the principle.[59] The EFTA Court held that:

> EEA law in this area may be summarised as follows. In the absence of harmonisation of rules, when there is uncertainty as to the current state of scientific research, it is for the Contracting Parties to decide what degree of protection of human health they intend to assure, having regard to the fundamental requirements of EEA law, notably, the free movement of goods within the European Economic Area. This means that a risk management decision rests with each Contracting Party. It is within the discretion of the Contracting Party to make a policy decision as to what level of risk it considers appropriate. Under those conditions, a Contracting Party may invoke the precautionary principle, according to which it is sufficient to show that there is relevant scientific uncertainty with regard to the

[53] See, eg, Case E-1/04 *Fokus Bank* [2004] EFTA Ct Rep 11, para 37; and Case E-9/11 *ESA v Norway* [2012] EFTA Ct Rep 442, para 99.

[54] *ESA v Norway* (n 53) paras 99–100.

[55] Case E-8/20 *Criminal Proceedings against* N, judgment of 5 May 2021.

[56] ibid para 118.

[57] The principle emerged first in the case law of the Court of Justice in Case 174/82 *Sandoz* ECLI:EU:C:1983:213, para 16. See also, eg, Case C-192/01 *Commission v Denmark* ECLI:EU:C:2003:492; and Case C-24/00 *Commission v France* ECLI:EU:C:2004:70.

[58] See, eg, *Commission v Denmark* (n 57) para 49.

[59] A Alemanno, 'The Precautionary Principle' in C Baudenbacher (ed), *Handbook of EEA Law* (Cham, Springer, 2015) 844–45.

risk in question. That measure of discretion must, however, be exercised subject to judicial review.[60]

It is precisely through this 'judicial review' where the proportionality principle becomes the key, including specific *procedural requirements*. As the EFTA Court explained in *Kellogg's*, the measures taken by the state 'must be based on scientific evidence; they must be *proportionate*, *non-discriminatory*, *transparent* and *consistent* with similar measures already taken' (emphasis added).[61] Furthermore, even if the level of protection chosen by the state should not be questioned, 'the principle of proportionality must be respected'.[62] In the *Kellogg's* case the EFTA Court emphasised that states must run 'a comprehensive evaluation of the risk to health based on the most recent scientific information'.[63] In the case at hand, the Norwegian authorities failed to demonstrate that such a comprehensive risk assessment had taken place under the procedure for marketing of fortified foodstuffs.[64] In fact, in a number of cases before the Court of Justice, where the precautionary principle has been invoked and accepted, states have failed to fulfil the procedural requirements of the proportionality principle.[65]

Second, under the suitability (appropriateness) part of the proportionality test, the Court of Justice has developed the so-called *consistency test*.[66] The basis for this is found in case law relating to free movement of services, the so-called *gambling cases*. Since *Gambelli*, a Member State can rely on a national interest, such as consumer protection and the prevention of fraud, inasmuch as it serves to limit betting activities in a 'consistent and systematic manner'.[67] The test of consistency has now also clearly found its way into the case law on the freedom of establishment,[68] free movement of workers,[69] free movement of capital[70] and free movement of goods.[71] In these cases the requirements of consistency may call for detailed evidence to support the appropriateness of the measures, for example, specific evidence, including detailed analysis supported by figures and solid and consistent data.[72]

[60] Case E-3/00 *ESA v Norway* (*Kellogg's*) [2000–2001] EFTA Ct Rep 73, para 25.

[61] ibid para 26.

[62] ibid para 27.

[63] ibid para 30.

[64] ibid paras 36–38. The precautionary principle was further developed by the EFTA Court in *Philip Morris* (n 42) paras 83–84. In a more recent line of cases, where there is 'scientific uncertainty' as to the actual effects of the restrictive measures, the Court of Justice has emphasised the need for a detailed proportionality analysis by the national courts; see Case C-333/14 *Scotch Whisky Association* ECLI:EU:C:2015:845, paras 64–65.

[65] See, eg, Case C-192/01 *Commission v Denmark* ECLI:EU:C:2003:492; Case C-24/00 *Commission v France* ECLI:EU:C:2004:70; Case C-41/02 *Commission v The Netherlands* ECLI:EU:C:2004:762; and Case C-338/08 *Commission v France* ECLI:EU:C:2010:364.

[66] As regards the application of the consistency test, see also the chapter by Halvard Haukeland Fredriksen and Christian Franklin, ch 17 in this volume.

[67] Case C-243/01 *Gambelli* ECLI:EU:C:2003:597, para 63. For more on this and on the consistency test in general, see G Mathisen, 'Consistency and Coherence as Conditions for Justifications of Member State Measures Restricting Free Movement' (2010) 47 *Common Market Law Review* 1021.

[68] See, eg, Case C-500/06 *Corporación Dermoestética* ECLI:EU:C:2008:421; and *Hartlauer* (n 41) paras 29–32 and 55.

[69] Case C-651/16 *DW* ECLI:EU:C:2018:162, para 34.

[70] See, eg, Case C-78/18 *Commission v Hungary* ECLI:EU:C:2020:476, para 76.

[71] *Commission v Germany* (n 41) para 56. See more recently *Scotch Whisky Association* (n 64) paras 37–38 and 53.

[72] See, eg, *DW* (n 69) para 34.

The EFTA Court first clearly applied the *consistency test* in its *Gaming Machines* case and subsequently in the *Ladbrokes* case, both of which concerned gambling (services and establishment), although traces of the test may also be found in the *Kellogg's* case.[73]

In more recent case law of the EFTA Court, the consistency test is very visible as can be seen for example in *Kristoffersen*[74] and *Netfonds*.[75] As was mentioned in the context of *procedural requirements*, in the *NAV* case[76] the EFTA Court analysed the Norwegian prior approval system for receipt of social security benefits while the recipient was temporarily abroad. In this judgment, the EFTA Court added in this same context the elements conventionally found in the *consistency test* and held that:

> It has not been demonstrated why less restrictive measures, such as *a prior notification system*, would not be sufficient, whilst minimising the restriction upon the free movement of services. In any event, the reasons invoked by an EEA State by way of justification must be accompanied by *appropriate evidence* or by an analysis of the *appropriateness* and proportionality of the measure adopted by that State and *by specific evidence* substantiating its arguments. Such an objective, detailed analysis, *supported by figures* if necessary, must be capable of demonstrating, with *solid and consistent data*, that there are genuine risks to the attainment of the stated objectives. (Emphasis added)[77]

D. Fundamental Rights

The Court of Justice has long accepted that fundamental rights play an important role when it comes to the question of acceptable limitations to the principles of free movement. The existence of fundamental rights within the framework for limitations of free movement principles has a real and significant effect on the important balancing of the rights and principles, steered by the proportionality principle.

The *ERT* case is the first case where fundamental rights played a key role in the context of the assessment of acceptable justifications in the field of free movement. In the case at hand, the Court of Justice held that when Member States relied on the EC Treaty to justify national rules that restricted the fundamental freedoms (*in casu* the freedom to provide services and Greek rules relating to television broadcasting), those national rules 'must be interpreted in the light of the general principles of law and in particular of fundamental rights' and were only to be allowed as a justified restriction if 'compatible with fundamental rights'.[78] This may be called the 'additional hurdle' approach, ie, the restrictive measures also have to comply with fundamental rights in order to be deemed acceptable grounds of justification. In subsequent case law, the

[73] See *Gaming Machines* (n 34) para 43; and *Ladbrokes* (n 34) paras 52–53.

[74] Case E-8/17 *Kristoffersen* [2018] EFTA Ct Rep 383, paras 118ff.

[75] Case E-8/16 *Netfonds* [2017] EFTA Ct Rep 163, paras 117ff. It is interesting that the EFTA Court, in this context, places the evaluation under a specific heading of 'Suitability/consistency' and in doing so diverges from the approach taken by the Court of Justice.

[76] *Criminal Proceedings against N* (n 55).

[77] ibid para 119.

[78] Case C-260/89 *ERT* ECLI:EU:C:1991:254, para 43. This case is symbolic for this type of case.

Court of Justice has also confirmed that the Member States could also, as a mandatory requirement (citing *Cassis de Dijon*), rely on fundamental rights as the very basis on which the justification for restrictive national measures could be built.[79]

From 2009, the Charter of Fundamental Rights of the European Union (hereinafter 'the EU Charter') became a legally binding instrument in EU law. For limitations on fundamental rights in EU law, Article 52(1) of the EU Charter is central, since it serves as the core 'analytical framework' in terms of limitations of fundamental rights under the Charter within 'the scope of Union law' (see Article 51(1) of the EU Charter).[80] As a specific limitation clause, Article 52(1) is to be applied 'horizontally' across the EU Charter, to all Charter rights which are subject to limitation (non-absolute rights).[81]

Article 52(1) of the EU Charter stipulates as follows:

> Any limitation on the exercise of the rights and freedoms recognised by this Charter must be provided for by law and respect the essence of those rights and freedoms. Subject to the principle of proportionality, limitations may be made only if they are necessary and genuinely meet objectives of general interest recognised by the Union or the need to protect the rights and freedoms of others.

As can be seen here, Article 52(1) of the EU Charter specifically refers to the principle of proportionality. In the context of the free movement principles and the EU Charter (the *ERT* situation), the Court of Justice has now explained that when Member States rely on the exceptions provided for by EU law in order to justify restrictions to a fundamental freedom guaranteed by the Treaty, this must be regarded as 'implementing Union law' within the meaning of Article 51(1) of the EU Charter.[82]

Furthermore, as already held in *ERT*, a restriction on free movement is only justified if it is also compatible with fundamental rights. The Court of Justice has explained that in that context, the restrictive measures must be examined 'in the light of both of the exceptions thus provided for by the Treaty and the Court's case law, on the one hand, and of the fundamental rights guaranteed by the Charter, on the other hand'.[83]

The roots of the EFTA Court's fundamental rights jurisdiction lie in the *TV 1000* case,[84] where the EFTA Court cited the *Handyside* judgment of the European Court of Human Rights,[85] and in the *Bellona* case,[86] which concerned access to justice (locus

[79] See Case C-368/95 *Familiapress* ECLI:EU:C:1997:325; and Case C-112/00 *Schmidberger* ECLI:EU:C:2003:333.

[80] See further C-617/10 *Åkerberg Fransson* ECLI:EU:C:2013:105, paras 17–22.

[81] See further GT Petursson, 'A New Framework for Limitation of Fundamental Rights in EU Law?' in A Engel, X Groussot and GT Petursson (eds), *New Directions in Digitalisation: Perspectives from EU Competition Law and the Charter of Fundamental Rights* (Dordrecht, Springer, forthcoming, 2024).

[82] Case C-201/15 *AGET Iraklis* ECLI:EU:C:2016:972, para 64, Case C-235/17 *Commission v Hungary (Rights of Usufruct over Agricultural Land)* ECLI:EU:C:2019:432, paras 64 and 65; and *Commission v Hungary* (n 70) para 101.

[83] See *AGET Iraklis* (n 82) para 65; and *Commission v Hungary* (n 82) para 66. Article 52(2) of the EU Charter may also come into play in this context; see Case C-233/12 *Gardella* ECLI:EU:C:2013:449.

[84] Case E-8/97 *TV 1000* [1998] EFTA Ct Rep 68.

[85] ibid para 26.

[86] Case E-2/02 *Bellona v ESA* [2003] EFTA Ct Rep 52.

standi). The EFTA Court has held that the provisions of the EEA Agreement as well as the procedural provisions of the Surveillance and Court Agreement (SCA) are to be interpreted in the light of fundamental rights[87] and that, in essence, 'the fundamental rights guaranteed in the legal order of the EEA Agreement are applicable in all situations governed by EEA law'.[88] Furthermore, in *Holship*, the EFTA Court stated that fundamental rights 'form part of the unwritten principles of EEA law'.[89]

In the context of the interpretation and application of EEA secondary law, the EFTA Court in *Kerim* emphasised that 'the EEA States, in particular their courts, must not only interpret their national law in a manner consistent with EEA law but are also under an obligation to ensure that the interpretation and application of acts incorporated into the EEA Agreement does not result in a conflict with fundamental rights protected by EEA law'.[90]

As for fundamental rights, in the context of the free movement provisions, the EFTA Court has followed the *ERT* line of case law of the Court of Justice. In *Olsen*[91] (concerning *the right of establishment* and *the free movement of capital*), the EFTA Court held that national restrictive measures could *only* be compatible with EEA law *as long as they were also* compatible with fundamental rights, which was similar to what the Court of Justice maintained in *ERT*.[92] The EFTA Court then held further:

> For such an interference to be compatible with fundamental rights under the EEA Agreement, it must be provided for by law and respect the essence of the right to property. Moreover, the interference can only be made if it is necessary and genuinely meets the objectives of general interest recognised by EEA law or the need to protect the rights and freedoms of others.[93]

While the EU Charter is not a legally binding part of EEA law,[94] it is clear that this paragraph of the EFTA Court's ruling in *Olsen* is inspired by Article 52(1) of the EU

[87] See, eg, Case E-2/03 *Ásgeir L Ásgeirsson* [2003] EFTA Ct Rep 185, para 23.

[88] Joined Cases E-3/13 and E-20/13 *Olsen* [2014] EFTA Ct Rep 400, paras 225–27.

[89] Case E-14/15 *Holship Norge* [2016] EFTA Ct Rep 240, para 123. In *Kerim*, the EFTA Court used the term 'general principles of EEA law' to describe the same: Case E-1/20 *Kerim*, judgment of 9 February 2021, para 43.

[90] *Kerim* (n 89) para 43. See also (even if not as firm a holding) Case E-28/15 *Jabbi* [2016] EFTA Ct Rep 575, para 81.

[91] See also Case E-10/04 *Piazza* [2005] EFTA Ct Rep 76, where the EFTA Court held that fundamental rights (the good functioning of the civil justice system), as public policy arguments, were the very grounds on which the derogation from the free movement principle could be based, much like the Court of Justice had held in *Familiapress* and *Schmidberger*.

[92] *Olsen* (n 88) para 227. It is also noteworthy that here the EFTA Court cites the Court of Justice's ruling in *Pfleger* 'by analogy', but in that case the Court of Justice cited the EU Charter, while not considering it necessary to undertake a 'separate examination' of the fundamental rights at issue, since the restrictions were otherwise held to be disproportionate (Case C-390/12 *Pfleger* ECLI:EU:C:2014:281, paras 36 and 59–60).

[93] *Olsen* (n 88) para 230.

[94] The EU Charter has been an issue in several cases before the EFTA Court. In Case E-4/11 *Clauder* [2011] EFTA Ct Rep 216, the Court held that Art 8 of the European Convention on Human Rights (ECHR) contains 'the same right' as Art 7 of the EU Charter, and in Case E-15/10 *Posten Norge* [2012] EFTA Ct Rep 246, the Court referred to Art 47 of the EU Charter as being comparable to Art 6 ECHR concerning the right to effective judicial protection. However, in Case E-10/14 *Deveci and Others* [2014] EFTA Ct Rep 1364, the Court explicitly held that there was 'no reason' to address Art 16 of the EU Charter ('freedom to conduct a business') finding that: 'The freedom to conduct a business lies … at the heart of the EEA Agreement and must be recognised in accordance with EEA law and national law and practices' (para 64). See also Joined Cases E-11/19 and E-12/19 *Adpublisher*, judgment of 10 December 2020, para 50.

Charter and the limitation framework of the EU Charter, while omitting, in this paragraph, a direct reference to the term 'principle of proportionality'.

E. Which Court?

An important and underlying question in each case where the proportionality principle is being invoked is which court should undertake the proportionality analysis? In simple terms, it may be held that the procedural circumstances of the case play the most important role in that context. In *infringement proceedings* under Article 31 SCA, which concern a potential breach of the fundamental free movement provisions, such as Article 11 EEA, it is for the EFTA Court to complete the assessment of the proportionality of the restrictive measure in the context of the interests invoked.[95] A binding final ruling needs to be given and the EFTA Court needs to realise the balancing inherent in the proportionality principle, to the extent necessary. However, when it comes to *advisory opinion* cases under Article 34 SCA, the EFTA Court is providing guidance to the national referring court, which finally needs to resolve the case at a national level, based on the ascertained facts and appropriately undertake the proportionality analysis.[96]

In general terms, both the Court of Justice and the EFTA Court have laid down the basic approach in this context of dialogic and cooperative process that is the preliminary ruling/advisory opinion procedure. This is very much based on the 'better placed' argument – that is, that the national court is better placed to complete the proportionality analysis.

In the *Gourmet* case,[97] the Court of Justice held that:

> [T]he decision as to whether the prohibition on advertising at issue in the main proceedings is proportionate, and *in particular* as to whether the objective sought might be achieved *by less extensive prohibitions or restrictions or by prohibitions or restrictions having less effect on intra-Community trade*, calls for an analysis of the circumstances of law and of fact which characterise the situation in the Member State concerned, which the national court is in *a better position* than the Court of Justice to carry out. (Emphasis added)[98]

Similarly, in the *Visnapuu* case[99] the Court of Justice held:

> In the present case, the review of the proportionality and necessity of the measures in question calls for an analysis of the circumstances of law and of fact which characterise *the situation in Finland*, which the national court is in *a better position* than the Court of Justice to carry out. Accordingly, it is for the national court to verify, on the basis of all the matters of law and fact before it, whether the prior authorisation system at issue in the main proceedings is such as to achieve the objective of the protection of health and public

[95] As it is for the Court of Justice under Art 258 TFEU.

[96] A similar position applies under Art 267 TFEU in relation to the preliminary ruling procedure before the Court of Justice, albeit that there is an important distinction in relation to the issue of 'validity' of acts, which does not form part of Art 34 SCA.

[97] Case C-405/98 *Gourmet* ECLI:EU:C:2001:135.

[98] ibid para 33.

[99] Case C-198/14 *Visnapuu* ECLI:EU:C:2015:751. See also Case C-434/04 *Ahokainen and Leppik* ECLI:EU:C:2006:609, paras 37–38.

> policy, and whether that objective can be achieved with at least an equivalent level of effectiveness *by less restrictive methods.* (Emphasis added)[100]

A similar approach has been followed by the EFTA Court. In the *Pedicel* case,[101] the EFTA Court held that:

> As the application of the proportionality test calls for an analysis of the circumstances of law and of fact which characterise the situation in the EEA Contracting Party concerned, *the national court is in a better position* than the Court to undertake it ... The Court can only give general guidance as to which elements are to be taken into account. The national court will have to take into account the availability of *means less restrictive* on intra-EEA trade as compared to a general prohibition of advertisements for alcoholic beverages, provided that such means are equally effective in attaining the legitimate objective of Norwegian alcohol policy. (Emphasis added)[102]

In *Philip Morris*, the EFTA Court further held that:[103]

> As regards the further assessment of whether *measures less restrictive* than the visual display ban could ensure a similar result, it is appropriate *to leave this to the national court* to decide on the basis of all the matters of law and fact before it. Review of proportionality and of the effectiveness of the measures taken relies on findings of fact which the referring court is in a *better position* than the Court to make. (Emphasis added)[104]

It appears from these findings that the focus of the assessment to be undertaken by the national court may also concern the elements which characterise the last prong of the proportionality principle, that is, proportionality *stricto sensu*. In that context, given that the elements of *suitability* and *necessity* are satisfied, the focus is on whether the objective can be achieved nonetheless by a less disruptive measure. This was apparent in *Philip Morris*, where the EFTA Court held that it was appropriate to leave the final assessment of proportionality of the national measure to the national court, on the basis of all the matters of law and fact before it, since that court was 'in a better position' to make that assessment than the EFTA Court.[105] At the same time, the EFTA Court has highlighted the nature of the cooperation between courts – that is, the advisory opinion process – and stated:

> In this regard, it should be recalled that in proceedings under Article 34 [SCA] which is based on a clear separation of functions between the Court and the national courts, it is for the national court to ascertain the facts which have given rise to the dispute and to establish the consequences that they have for the judgment which it is required to deliver.[106]

However, the assessment of the suitability/appropriateness and necessity is often de facto completed by both the Court of Justice and the EFTA Court in the preliminary

[100] *Visnapuu* (n 99) para 119.
[101] *Pedicel* (n 32).
[102] ibid paras 57–58.
[103] *Philip Morris* (n 42).
[104] ibid para 86, also citing similar case law from the Court of Justice.
[105] ibid.
[106] ibid para 87. See similar views expressed in Case E-2/12 *HOB vín* [2012] EFTA Ct Rep 1092, para 38. See also Case E-18/11 *Irish Bank* [2012] EFTA Ct Rep 592, para 53, where the EFTA Court held that Art 34 SCA provides for a *special means of judicial cooperation.*

ruling/advisory opinion proceedings, and in reality, as regards that aspect of the proportionality analysis, little discretion is left to the national court.[107] In that light, there would be no need to undertake *stricto sensu* assessment if the measure would otherwise have been held either not suitable/appropriate or necessary. However, even if not itself undertaking a clear proportionality analysis *stricto sensu*, the EFTA Court has in its advisory opinions given, at times, clear instructions to the national court as to what factors have to be considered in that context.[108]

The Court of Justice rarely enters into a clear proportionality analysis *stricto sensu* in preliminary ruling procedures in 'classic' free movement cases.[109] However, proportionality *stricto sensu* becomes relevant, in particular, in cases involving fundamental rights and questions concerning the *validity* of EU norms in light of those fundamental rights, where the Court of Justice is the only court competent to give a final ruling. In the *Sky Österreich* case,[110] which involved questions regarding the compatibility of provisions of Directive 2010/13/EU (the Audiovisual Media Services Directive)[111] in light of the freedom to conduct a business protected by Article 16 of the EU Charter and the 'fair balance' between these provisions, the Court of Justice emphasised that:

> Where several rights and fundamental freedoms protected by the European Union legal order are at issue, the assessment of the possible disproportionate nature of a provision of European Union law must be carried out with a view to *reconciling* the requirements of the protection of those different rights and freedoms and *a fair balance* between them. (Emphasis added)[112]

The Court of Justice finally concluded that the provision of EU secondary law was valid, but, for example, in *Volker und Markus Schecke and Eifert*,[113] the Court annulled provisions of EU secondary law, with a reference to the EU Charter.[114]

[107] The author has examined this in detail, analysing more than 200 cases. See GT Petursson, 'The Proportionality Principle as a Tool for Disintegration in EU Law – of Balancing and Coherence in the Light of the Fundamental Freedoms' (Dr Juris thesis, Faculty of Law, University of Lund, 2014) which demonstrates that in the majority of preliminary ruling cases concerning free movement, the ECJ de facto exhausts the proportionality analysis. Similar trends may be detected in the case law of the EFTA Court, which often de facto completes the proportionality analysis by holding a measure disproportionate for not complying with either suitability/appropriateness or necessity in advisory opinion proceedings. See, eg, the rulings in Case E-3/98 *Rainford-Towning* [1998] EFTA Ct Rep 205; Case E-4/00 *Brändle* [2000–01] EFTA Ct Rep 123; Case E-2/01 *Pucher* [2002] EFTA Ct Rep 44; *Piazza* (n 91); Case E-2/11 *STX* [2012] EFTA Ct Rep 4; Case E-15/11 *Arcade Drilling* [2012] EFTA Ct Rep 676; and *Netfonds* (n 75).

[108] See, eg, *Pedicel* (n 32) paras 58–69; and Case E-5/10 *Kottke* [2009–2010] EFTA Ct Rep 320, paras 47–50.

[109] However, see *Schmidberger* (n 79) paras 81–93, where the Court of Justice entered into a detailed (*stricto sensu*) proportionality analysis, evaluating the restrictive national measures not only in the light of free movement, but also in the light of fundamental rights – here Art 10 ECHR – eventually concluding that the national authorities 'were reasonably entitled, having regard to the wide discretion which must be accorded to them in the matter, to consider that the legitimate aim of that demonstration could not be achieved in the present case by measures less restrictive of intra-Community trade' (para 93).

[110] Case C-283/11 *Sky Österreich* ECLI:EU:C:2013:28.

[111] Directive 2010/13/EU of the European Parliament and of the Council on the coordination of certain provisions laid down by law, regulation or administrative action in Member States concerning the provision of audiovisual media services (Audiovisual Media Services Directive) [2010] OJ L95/1.

[112] *Sky Österreich* (n 110) para 60.

[113] Joined Cases C-92/09 and C-93/09 *Volker und Markus Schecke and Eifert* ECLI:EU:C:2010:662.

[114] ibid para 77. Similarly, in Case C-236/09 *Test-Achats* ECLI:EU:C:2011:100 a provision in Directive 2004/113 was deemed to be incompatible with Arts 21 and 23 of the EU Charter. For more recent examples, see Joined Cases C-37/20 and C-601/20 *Luxembourg Business Registers* ECLI:EU:C:2022:912; and Case C-694/20 *Orde van Vlaamse Balies and Others* ECLI:EU:C:2022:963.

Similarly, in categories of cases concerning the interpretation and application of EU secondary law at the national level in light of fundamental rights,[115] the Court of Justice has emphasised that:

> Where several fundamental rights and principles enshrined in the Treaties are at issue, such as, in the present case, the right guaranteed in Article 10 of the Charter and animal welfare enshrined in Article 13 TFEU, the assessment of observance of the principle of proportionality must be carried out in accordance with the need to *reconcile* the requirements of the protection of those various rights and principles at issue, striking *a fair balance* between them. (Emphasis added)[116]

In these circumstances, the Court of Justice may enter into a detailed proportionality analysis, fully realising the balancing test, in order to verify the compatibility of the national implementing measure with EU secondary law, as interpreted and applied in the light of fundamental rights.[117]

IV. CONCLUSIONS

The principle of proportionality has evolved over the past few decades and has gradually taken on new and different dimensions – not least in order to secure important procedural guarantees and requirements of consistency and sufficient evidence in decision making and policy choices. In that sense, the proportionality analysis may become rather strict. At the same time, it is clear that the application of the proportionality principle also brings forward the classic questions regarding how far courts, in general, should go in re-evaluating (reviewing) the assessment of the democratically elected when it comes to public policy choices, involving sensitive national interests. Closely related to those questions is also the debate on the division of tasks, and the 'better placed' approach, in the procedure for preliminary rulings/advisory opinions, that is, the relationship between the Court of Justice/EFTA Court and the national judiciary.

The comparative analysis offered here has focused on the case law relating to the free movement principles, which are equally found both in the EU Treaties and the EEA Agreement and are 'identical in substance'.[118] The EEA Agreement in its recitals reaffirms 'the special relationship between the European Union, its Member States and the EFTA States, which is based on proximity, long-standing common values and European identity'.[119] For both the Court of Justice and the EFTA Court, it is therefore important to ensure that the interpretation of the EEA Agreement 'is as uniform as possible throughout the EEA'.[120]

[115] A good summary of the meaning and scope of this as a general principle of interpretation can be found in Case C-817/19 *Ligue des droits humains* ECLI:EU:C:2022:491, paras 86–87.

[116] Case C-336/19 *Centraal Israëlitisch Consistorie van België and Others* ECLI:EU:C:2020:1031, para 65. See also Case C-128/22 *Nordic Info* ECLI:EU:C:2023:951, paras 92–97.

[117] See, eg, *Centraal Israëlitisch Consistorie van België and Others* (n 116) paras 66–80.

[118] See, to that effect, Case C-897/19 PPU *Ruska Federacija (I.N.)* ECLI:EU:C:2020:262, para 50, and Case C-452/01 *Ospelt and Schlössle Weissenberg* ECLI:EU:C:2003:493, para 29.

[119] Case C-897/19 PPU *Ruska Federacija (I.N.)*, para 50.

[120] ibid.

It is clear from the above that the EFTA Court has held this obligation of 'uniform interpretation' in high regard and has diligently both cited and followed the Court of Justice's use of the proportionality principle in cases concerning the free movement principles. Moreover, the EFTA Court has gone so far as to hold explicitly that a measure restrictive of the fundamental freedoms must, in terms of its proportionality, satisfy the conditions laid down in the case law of *both* the EFTA Court and the Court of Justice.

While the origins and basis of the proportionality principle were initially somewhat unclear, the principle has become an essential feature of both EU and EEA law, and has an established status as a general principle of law. It is an important methodological tool that has the ability to bring to the fore all the necessary elements in the sensitive task of balancing rules and principles that need to be reconciled.

16

On the Margins

The Case Law of the EFTA Court Regarding the Scope of the EEA Agreement

ÓLAFUR JÓHANNES EINARSSON

I. INTRODUCTION

IN EU LAW, litigation about the scope of the competences granted to the Union and the dividing line between the competences of the Union and its Member States is an issue of significant political sensitivity. The Court of Justice of the European Union (CJEU), as Joseph Weiler has put it, disposes of *judicial Kompetenz-Kompetenz*: the competence to declare or determine the limits of the Union's competences.[1] Under EEA law, the stakes are not equally high; however, despite this, the question of the EEA Agreement's scope has at times been fiercely debated before the EFTA Court. This has generated some interesting case law, which only to a limited extent has a counterpart under EU law. In this book, which has been published to celebrate 30 years of EEA Agreement and the EFTA Court, it is appropriate to examine this case law.

This chapter will start by setting out the relevant provisions of the EEA Agreement governing its scope. Moreover, it will briefly examine how the EFTA Court has dealt with situations in which one of the fundamental freedoms collide with a provision of law in an area outside the Agreement's scope, such as taxation. The focus will then turn to the main topic of the chapter, namely an analysis of the case law of the EFTA Court concerning the scope of the EEA Agreement. First, the product scope as laid down in the Article 8(3) EEA Agreement will be analysed as well as its impact on the Main Part of the Agreement and incorporated secondary legislation. Second, the case law concerning rules of origin will be examined. Third, the geographical scope of the

[1] JHH Weiler, *The Constitution of Europe 'Do the New Clothes Have an Emperor' and Other Essays on European Integration* (Cambridge, Cambridge University Press, 1999) 288.

Agreement will be scrutinised, focusing on *Scanteam*, a relatively recent judgment in which the issue was explored. Finally, the chapter will conclude with a more generalised examination of the EFTA Court's approach to issues concerning the scope of the EEA Agreement.

II. PROVISIONS CONCERNING THE SCOPE OF THE EEA

Article 1(1) EEA sets out the aim of the Agreement, which is to promote a continuous and balanced strengthening of trade and economic relations between the Contracting Parties with equal conditions of competition, and the respect of the same rules, with a view to creating a homogeneous EEA. The EFTA Court has relied on this provision as a basis for the principle of homogeneity in several judgments.[2]

Following on from the Agreement's objective, which is essentially to include the EEA/EFTA States in the EU internal market, Article 1(2) EEA lays down its material scope and thus the extent of their participation therein. The provision provides that the Agreement shall entail: (a) the free movement of goods; (b) the free movement of persons; (c) the free movement of services; (d) the free movement of capital; (e) the setting up of a system ensuring that competition is not distorted and that the rules thereon are equally respected; as well as (f) closer cooperation in other fields, such as research and development, the environment, education and social policy.[3] It is appropriate to emphasise that the wording of Article 1(2) EEA is open-ended and, accordingly, on its own Article 1(2) places little limitations on the Contracting Parties' ability to extend the scope of the Agreement by decisions of the EEA Joint Committee.[4] Article 98 EEA provides the Joint Committee with the competence to amend the annexes and certain protocols, and thus incorporate new acts into the annexes of the EEA Agreement. Significant examples thereof include the transformation of Annex I on Veterinary and Phytosanitary Matters and the Incorporation of the EU Emissions Trading Scheme into the Agreement. The effects of the incorporation of the veterinary *acquis* will be examined further in the analysis of the EFTA Court's case law regarding the product scope in section IV.B below.

Article 118 EEA contains an evolutionary clause providing for the possibility of developing 'the relations established by this Agreement by extending them to fields not covered thereby'.[5] A provision such as this one is a familiar feature of the EU's external agreements. The Contracting Parties have never made use of this article and

[2] F Arnesen and HH Fredriksen, 'Preamble' in F Arnesen et al (eds), *The Agreement on the European Economic Area: A Commentary* (Munich/Oxford/Baden-Baden, CH Beck/Hart Publishing/Nomos Universitetsforlaget, 2018) 175.

[3] The EFTA Court rarely refers directly to this article; however, *Jabbi* is an example thereof. In *Jabbi*, the Court cited the Article to underline the importance of free movement of persons under the EEA Agreement and that it has been present as a main objective of the EEA from the very beginning: Case E-28/15 *Jabbi*, para 59.

[4] Arnesen and Fredriksen (n 2) 175.

[5] It is interesting to note that from the beginning it was recognised that the fields covered by the EEA Agreement were in constant development within the Community and this dynamic aspect had been fully taken over by the EEA. Accordingly, the scope of the Agreement was considered to be quite extensive. See S Norberg et al, *EEA Law a Commentary on the EEA Agreement* (Stockholm, Fritzes, 1993) 294.

are perhaps not likely to do so in the immediate future. This may be explained by several reasons, such as that the procedure is cumbersome, as the resulting agreement requires ratification by all Contracting Parties in accordance with their national procedures. Importantly, the competence of the Joint Committee provides a less demanding means of broadening the cooperation between EEA States, and this has certainly also played a role.[6] Moreover, it is worth observing that the EFTA States, both individually and together, have entered into several agreements with the EU outside the framework of the EEA. The most prominent example is undoubtedly the Schengen *acquis*, which the EFTA States have agreed to implement and to apply.[7] The Court of Justice of the European Union (CJEU) has made it clear that these agreements and the EEA must be understood as a single system, involving systemic integration and providing for a comprehensive relationship between the EFTA States and the EU.[8]

III. OUTSIDE THE SCOPE – BUT …

It was not long until the EFTA Court was called on to rule on the interaction between national law in a field outside the scope of the Agreement, as defined in Article 1(2) EEA, *in casu* tax law, in a case concerning one of the fundamental provisions of the main part of the Agreement. The Court observed that, as a general rule, an EEA/EFTA State's tax system would not be covered by the EEA Agreement. However, the operation of such a system might generate consequences that would bring it within the scope of application of Article 61(1) EEA. This conclusion followed from established CJEU case law, providing that the fiscal nature of a measure does not shield it from the application of what is now Article 107 of the Treaty on the Functioning of the European Union (TFEU). The definition of a measure as state aid is based on its effects rather than its causes and aims.[9] Subsequently, the EFTA Court made similar findings in relation to the fundamental freedoms.[10] As an example, in the *Passenger Tax* case it stated that 'as a general rule, the tax system of an EEA/EFTA State is not covered by the EEA Agreement. The EEA/EFTA States must, however, exercise their taxation power consistently with EEA law'.[11] Similarly, even if criminal law falls outside the scope of the EEA Agreement, the imposition of penalties for breaches relating to EEA law must respect the general principles of the Agreement.[12]

In this context, the so-called *Hjemfall* case is also of interest. The case concerned the difference in treatment between privately and publicly owned hydropower

[6] C Hillion, 'Article 118' in Arnesen et al (n 2) 905.

[7] Agreement concluded by the Council of the European Union and the Republic of Iceland and the Kingdom of Norway concerning the latters' association with the implementation, application and development of the Schengen acquis [1999] OJ L176, 18 May, p 36. Liechtenstein subsequently concluded its own agreement regarding Schengen and became a member at the end of 2011.

[8] Case C-897/19 *Ruska Federaja* EU:C:2020:262, para 58. As regards the Agreement on the surrender procedure between the Member States of the European Union and Iceland and Norway, see also Case C-488/19 *JR* EU:C:2021:206.

[9] Case E-6/98 *Norway v ESA*, para 34.

[10] Case E-1/01 *Einarsson*, para 17; E-1/04 *Fokus Bank*, para 17.

[11] Case E-1/03 *ESA v Iceland*, para 26.

[12] Case E-15/20 *Criminal Proceedings against P*, paras 56–58.

undertakings in Norway. The Norwegian government claimed that due to the fundamental differences between EEA law on the one hand and EU law on the other, Article 125 EEA on the systems of property ownership should be interpreted differently from its EU counterpart, Article 345 TFEU.[13] The EFTA Court categorically rejected this contention, relying heavily on the rebuttable presumption it had established that identically worded provisions of EEA and EU law are to be given the same interpretation. The Court's case law has demonstrated that the threshold for rebutting that presumption is high.[14] However, in rejecting the arguments to that effect, the Court provided interesting observations regarding the Agreement's scope.

In *Hjemfall*, Iceland and Norway claimed that subjecting the contested rules to the provisions of the Agreement would contradict their understanding of its scope, as expressed during the negotiations of the Agreement and subsequent parliamentary ratification. Norway stressed that such arguments had particular relevance when interpreting and defining the articles concerning the outer limits of the EEA Agreement, and that uniform interpretation was more important in relation to substantive provisions.[15] The EFTA Court was unmoved, and denied that such unilateral understandings of the Agreement could constitute compelling reasons for deviating from homogeneous interpretation.[16] The Court also rejected the notion that the management of natural energy resources fell outside the scope of the Agreement. It considered that this was not supported by the Agreement's text and, on the contrary, as Article 73(1)(c) EEA made clear, environmental actions should pursue the objective of ensuring a prudent and rational utilisation of natural resources.[17]

The EFTA Court's conclusion in these cases is fully in line with consistent case law from the CJEU and does not call for a detailed examination for the purposes of this chapter. However, it is worth noting that the EFTA Court has rigorously applied the rebuttable presumption regarding the interpretation of identical provisions, which is clearly applicable to provisions regarding the Agreement's limits. *Hjemfall* demonstrates that the Court does not accept that a different interpretative method is to be applied to questions regarding the limits of the Agreement than that which is applicable in other contexts.

IV. PRODUCT SCOPE

A. *Pedicel*

Article 8 EEA establishes the free movement of goods for the purposes of the Agreement. However, paragraph 3 of that Article also limits the scope of the Agreement, which has been the subject of considerable litigation. As these limitations have no counterpart in EU law, there is no corresponding case law from the CJEU,

[13] Case E-2/06 *ESA v Norway*, paras 58–63.

[14] ÓJ Einarsson, 'The View from the EFTA Court' in G Butler (ed), *Research Handbook on EEA Internal Market Law* (Cheltenham, Edward Elgar, 2023).

[15] *ESA v Norway* (n 13), report for the hearing, para 49.

[16] ibid para 59.

[17] ibid para 60.

which makes these cases particularly interesting. It follows from Article 8(3) EEA that the Agreement shall apply only to: (a) products falling within Chapters 25–97 of the Harmonized Commodity Description and Coding System, excluding the products listed in Protocol 2; and (b) products specified in Protocol 3, subject to the specific arrangements set out therein. Effectively, this means that most agricultural and fisheries products fall outside the product scope of the Agreement. The question is to what extent this exclusion has spill-over effects to other parts of the EEA Agreement.

In *Pedicel*, which concerned the Norwegian ban on alcohol advertising, the EFTA Court had to resolve this question. The Court concluded that, based on Article 8(3) EEA, wine did not fall within the scope of Article 11 on the prohibition of quantitative restrictions and measures having an equivalent effect (Article 34 TFEU). It was noted that the underlying reason for excluding products from the scope of the EEA Agreement must be that the EEA States wished to maintain the freedom to decide on their respective regulations, unaffected by the rules of the EEA Agreement, unless otherwise agreed.[18] These findings were confirmed and elaborated upon in *Synnøve Finden* concerning state aid in the dairy sector. The Court observed that the exclusion set out in Article 8(3) EEA was not limited to the free movement of goods, as the article referred to the products falling outside the scope of application of 'the provisions of this Agreement'. According to the Court, this was indicative of the intention of the Contracting Parties for those products to fall outside the scope of the EEA Agreement entirely, and not only with respect to the rules on free movement of goods. Such goods could only come within the Agreement if a specific legal basis in EEA law was present.[19] It is difficult to argue against this conclusion of the Court, which is firmly grounded in the wording of Article 8(3) EEA.

In *Pedicel*, the Court also had to examine the claim that Article 18 EEA regarding 'other technical barriers to trade' should be interpreted as encompassing the same types of restrictions as Article 11 EEA. This was rejected by the Court: first, with reference to the different wording of the two Articles; and, second, noting that the objective of Article 18 EEA was not to bypass the Agreement's product scope. Interestingly, however, the Court found it necessary to add the obiter dictum that Article 8(3) EEA should not be subject to dynamic interpretation.[20] On the basis of these statements, attempts have been made to construe a general approach to the interpretation of the scope of the Agreement. This will be examined in the final section of this chapter.

Interestingly, the CJEU had already examined the compatibility of restrictions on advertising not only from the perspective of the free movement of goods, but also the free movement of services.[21] Thus, in *Pedicel*, the EFTA Court had to resolve the question as to whether advertising services promoting the sale of wine were excluded from the scope of Article 36 EEA (free provision of services) since, according to Article 8(3) EEA, wine is excluded from the product scope of the Agreement. As referred to above, the Court concluded, in line with the wording of Article 8(3) EEA, that wine

[18] Case E-4/04 *Pedicel*, paras 23–25.
[19] Case E-1/16 *Synnøve Finden*, para 57.
[20] *Pedicel* (n 18) paras 27–28.
[21] Case C-405/98 *Gourmet International Products* EU:C:2001:135.

fell outside the scope of the Agreement. The EFTA Court further declared that the service offered by Pedicel AS was 'inseparably' linked to the sale of wine and, for that reason, did not fall under Article 36 EEA. It was argued by the Commission that the EFTA Court should base itself on the position taken by the CJEU concerning corresponding EU rules. On this point, the Court stated: 'Article 8(3) has no counterpart in Community law. In light of this difference in scope, the case law of the Court of Justice of the European Communities referred to by the Commission is not relevant as regards the question of interpretation of Articles 8(3) and 36 EEA in the case at issue.'[22]

The result of *Pedicel* is that the exclusion laid down in Article 8(3) EEA is also applicable to services inseparably linked to the sale of wine. *Pedicel* represented a rare case in which two fundamental freedoms, namely goods and services, were simultaneously applicable. However, *Synnøve Finden* made it clear that these findings were not limited to that situation. The EFTA Court concluded that a subsidy for distribution of products was not within the state aid rules in Article 61 EEA if it was inseparably linked to trade in products outside the Agreement. On the facts of that case, it was clear that a volume-based distribution support was inseparably connected to trade in the products.[23]

The question whether the logic underlying *Pedicel* is also applicable to other fundamental freedoms has not been litigated before the EFTA Court. The author has previously maintained that such an extension is doubtful, as a matter of principle, and, moreover, is of limited practical relevance.[24] On the other hand, Finn Arnesen has maintained, with reference to *Pedicel* and *Synnøve Finden*, that homogeneity-based arguments carry little weight when examining the material scope of the Agreement. He claims that not only services inseparably linked to trade in products outside the scope of the Agreement, but also the EEA States' regulation of other issues might fall outside its scope.[25] The Norwegian Supreme Court relied, inter alia, on Arnesen's writings when concluding that restriction on reindeer grazing, imposed on Swedish Sami, fell outside the scope of Article 31 EEA (the right of establishment) based on *Pedicel*.[26] The circumstances of that case were, admittedly, quite particular. However, whether the EFTA Court would have been satisfied that the condition of inseparability was fulfilled is an open question. Arnesen has floated the idea that *Pedicel* could be interpreted as allowing the EEA States to reserve to their own nationals the right to provide veterinary services to, for example, slaughterhouses and farms.[27] Even assuming that the condition of being inseparably linked to production in goods would be fulfilled, which would seem far from obvious, given, for example, the animal welfare aspects of such services, such an interpretation is too far-reaching. It disregards the fact that veterinarians are covered by the Directive on the Recognition of Professional

[22] *Pedicel* (n 18) paras 34 and 39.

[23] *Synnøve Finden* (n 19) paras 57-60.

[24] ÓJ Einarsson, 'Article 36' in Arnesen et al (n 2) 457.

[25] F Arnesen, 'Homogeneity and Disparity' in S Lorenzmeier et al (eds), *Recht und Realität Festschrift for Christoph Vedder* (Baden-Baden, Nomos, 2017) 260.

[26] HR-2021-1429-A.

[27] F Arnesen, 'Homogeneity and Disparity' in *Recht und Realität Festschrift for Christoph Vedder* (n 25) 261.

Qualifications and are thus not regulated differently from other regulated professions at the EEA level. Finally, it should not be overlooked that *Pedicel* makes it clear that the EFTA Court wished to avoid that the exception that it carved out in that case should be interpreted expansively in other contexts.[28]

B. Product Scope Exclusion and Secondary Legislation

As we have seen, the exclusion laid down in Article 8(3) EEA has also had an impact on the definition of the scope of other articles of the Main Part of the Agreement. However, was that conclusion also transposable to secondary legislation incorporated into the EEA? This was one of the issues examined in *Ferskar kjötvörur*, where the question was whether the Icelandic licensing system for the import of fresh meat from other EEA States was compatible with EEA law. Iceland claimed that since the products fell outside the scope of Agreement, it followed from Article 8 EEA that it enjoyed discretion to enact rules free from the constraints of the Agreement. The Court rejected that contention.[29]

According to Article 17 EEA, Annex I to the Agreement 'contains specific provisions and arrangements concerning veterinary and phytosanitary matters'. By decision of the EEA Joint Committee No 69/98, this Annex was completely revised. Under the terms of that decision, the acts in the Annex only applied to Iceland when specifically stated. This changed with the adoption of several Joint Committee Decisions in 2007. By these decisions, the new food and feed safety legislation of the EU was incorporated into the EEA Agreement and the broad exemptions Iceland had previously enjoyed were abolished.[30] It should not be overlooked that this Annex to the Agreement is voluminous and provides for a detailed regulation of agricultural and fisheries products.

In *Ferskar kjötvörur*, the EFTA Court noted that this extension of the scope of the Agreement was intended to further a continuous and balanced strengthening of trade and economic relations between the EEA States in a homogeneous and a dynamic EEA. The Court continued by noting that in the incorporation of this legislation into the EEA, certain adaptations had been made with regard to Iceland, including in particular that provisions concerning live animals were excluded. From this, the Court concluded that the acts contained in Annex I applied fully to Iceland in the absence of adaptions providing for an exemption thereto.[31] As no such adaptation was present in the case at hand, Directive 89/665/EEC was considered to be fully applicable. The CJEU had already concluded that a Swedish notification scheme was incompatible with the Directive and, a fortiori, the same conclusion was applicable to the Icelandic licensing system.[32] The judgment clearly reveals that the EFTA Court found no reason to deviate from a homogeneous interpretation of the Directive in the EEA context.

[28] Einarsson (n 24) 456.
[29] Case E-17/15 *Ferskar kjötvörur*, paras 42–49.
[30] See Decision Nos 133/2007, 134/2007 and 137/2007.
[31] For a similar conclusion regarding Annex II, see Case E-2/12 *HOB-vín*, para 46.
[32] Case C-111/03 *Commission v Sweden* EU:C:2005:619.

The EFTA Court's conclusion entails that once the EEA States have agreed to incorporate acts into the Agreement that go beyond the product scope as defined in Article 8 EEA, the limitations laid down therein are no longer relevant. This is logical, as interpreting Article 8 in such a way that it also has an impact on the interpretation of the acts incorporated, in the absence of any provisions to that effect in the decisions of the EEA Joint Committee, would have made their application difficult and jeopardised the objective of the incorporation. The result of the Court's approach is that it is for the Contracting Parties in the Joint Committee, when incorporating the acts into the Agreement, to decide to what extent the regulatory freedom that is afforded by the limitations on product scope is to be carried over to the secondary legislation. This was explicitly stated by the EFTA Court when the same issue arose in the context of infringement proceedings against Iceland. There it remarked that 'Iceland has committed itself to not impose technical barriers to the import of agricultural products when they satisfy the relevant EEA legislation'.[33]

These judgments of the EFTA Court were criticised as examples of judicial activism and in effect altering the text of the Agreement.[34] The reasons for this criticism were, inter alia, that the Court did not allow Iceland to have recourse to the public interest justifications in Article 13 EEA (equivalent to Article 36 TFEU). The Court had rejected this argument, as the Directive constituted exhaustive harmonisation and, accordingly, such a justification was precluded. The Court's critics alleged that this was in disregard of Article 18 EEA, which provided for the applicability of Article 13 EEA. This criticism overlooks the fact that Article 18 EEA and, by extension, Article 13 EEA are only applicable to other technical barriers to trade, ie, not to the secondary legislation incorporated into the Annexes. Justification under Article 13 EEA is thus available both to restrictions under Article 11 EEA (products within the scope of Article 8(3)) and other technical barriers to trade under Article 18 EEA (products outside the scope of Article 8(3)). Accordingly, the EFTA Court's approach to the non-applicability of Article 13 EEA had solid support both in the wording and context of Article 18 EEA.[35]

V. RULES OF ORIGIN AND THIRD STATES

Having examined the EFTA Court's case law regarding the product scope of the Agreement, it is interesting to compare it with the Court's case law regarding another limitation to its scope, namely concerning the rules of origin. Article 8(2) EEA states that, unless otherwise specified, Articles 10–15, 19, 20 and 25–27 shall apply only to products originating in the Contracting Parties. The wording of this Article thus differs in an important respect from Article 8(3) EEA as, in contrast to the latter, it lists the provisions of the Agreement affected by this exclusion.

[33] Joined Cases E-2-3/17 *ESA v Iceland*, para 70.

[34] EG Gunnarsson and SM Stefánsson 'EFTA-dómstóllinn í ljósi lýðræðishalla', https://ulfljotur.com/2018/04/10/efta-domstollinn-i-ljosi-lydraedishalla.

[35] ÓJ Einarsson 'Á rökum reistur – dómur EFTA-dómstólsins í máli nr. E-17/15 (Ferskar kjötvörur gegn íslenska ríkinu' (2017) *Tímarit lögfræðinga* 184.

The rules of origin played an important role in the Court's judgment in *Maglite*, in which it had to rule on whether the Trade Marks Directive provided for an EEA-wide or international exhaustion of trade mark rights. The Court opted for the latter, observing that the EEA was a free trade area and not a customs union, and that the EEA did not entail a common commercial policy. In a similar vein, and interestingly for the present purposes, it also noted that according to Article 8 EEA, the free movement of goods under Articles 11–13 EEA applied only to goods originating in the EEA. This was in contrast to the situation under EU law, under which a product is in free circulation once it has been lawfully placed on the market in a Member State. In the context of the EEA, this applied only in relation to products originating in the EEA.[36] However, In *Silhouette*, the CJEU interpreted the Directive as providing for EEA-wide exhaustion, a conclusion which *Sebago* made clear was equally applicable to products originating outside the EEA.[37] These diverging interpretations by the CJEU and the EFTA Court resulted in the latter being asked again how to resolve the issue of exhaustion. The result was that in *L'Oreal* the EFTA Court adjusted its conclusion to align it with that of the CJEU.[38] The question as to whether the EFTA Court was right to change its interpretation has been discussed many times and views differ.[39] This discussion will not be repeated here; rather, the emphasis will be on the EFTA Court's examination as to whether any compelling grounds existed for maintaining a different interpretation under EEA law. However, it is worth underlining that the judgment in *L'Oreal* sets out detailed reasons for why no such compelling grounds existed.

The EFTA Court turned its attention to Article 65(2) EEA, which states that 'Protocol 28 and Annex XVII contain specific provisions and arrangements concerning intellectual, industrial and commercial property, which, unless otherwise specified, *shall apply to all products and services*' (emphasis added). Accordingly, this provision provides for a different regime regarding the rules of origin than the general rule laid down in Article 8(2) EEA, as intellectual property rights are covered by the EEA Agreement irrespective of their origin, unless there is a particular specification to the contrary. Therefore, the Court concluded that Article 65(2) EEA did not call for a reservation against rules providing for mandatory EEA-wide exhaustion of rights relating to goods originating from outside the EEA. The same applied to Protocol 28 and Annex XVII to the EEA Agreement concerning intellectual property rights. The Court noted that according to Article 2(1) of Protocol 28, 'the Contracting Parties shall provide for such exhaustion of intellectual property rights as laid down in Community law'. This was, the Court stated, the basis for the incorporation into Annex XVII to the EEA Agreement of legal acts providing for mandatory EEA-wide exhaustion of rights, regardless of the origin of the goods. The Court added that this

[36] Case E-2/97 *Mag Instruments Inc*, particularly paras 25–28.

[37] Case C-355/96 *Silhouette* EU:C:1998:374, paras 25–30; Case C-173/98 *Sebago* EU:C:1999:347.

[38] Joined Cases E-9/07 and E-10/07 *L'Oreal Norge*.

[39] For an examination of the EFTA Court's approach to diverging case law, see ÓJ Einarsson, 'The Advisory Opinion Procedure and the Relationship between the EFTA Court and the Norwegian Courts: Recent Developments (2022) *Lov og Rett* 232.

interpretation of the provisions was reflected in the fact that directives with a clear wording to this effect have been incorporated into the Agreement.[40]

As may be gathered from this brief description, the EFTA Court's conclusion that no specific compelling grounds of EEA law justified a different interpretation of the Trade Marks Directive is based primarily on the wording of the provisions of the Agreement setting out its scope vis-a-vis intellectual property rights. Since they provide for a deviation from the general rules of origin, as set out in Article 8(2) EEA, the differentiation made in *Maglite* between EU law, on the one hand, and EEA law, on the other hand, is not very convincing. Remarkably, Article 65(2) EEA was not referred to at all in the Court's reasoning in this judgment, which seems to suggest that it was simply overlooked.[41] Moreover, as noted by Rognstad, the references in *Maglite* to the EEA not being a customs union, and the common commercial policy not being part of the Agreement, seem misplaced. Exhaustion regulates the scope of trade mark rights and is thus of limited relevance to the notion of a customs union. Similarly, the legal basis of the Trade Marks Directive was (primarily) the general provision on the internal market, ie, Article 114 TFEU, and not Article 207 TFEU regarding the common commercial policy, to whose predecessor the EFTA Court had referred.[42] Accordingly, the elements relied upon by the EFTA Court to underline the specific EEA law context are misguided. However, this is not to say that there may not be instances in which there may be differences between the EEA/EFTA States and the EU Member States when it comes to intellectual property rights and relations to third countries.[43]

Given that the only other judgment of the EFTA Court concerning the rules of origin, *Ásgeirsson*, concerns quite technical issues regarding the scope of Protocol 9 EEA on fishery products and what constitutes processing under the rules, it is difficult to compare the Court's handling of these rules. *L'Oreal* shows the Court being attentive to the specific regime of the rules of origin regarding intellectual property rights. In contrast, *Maglite* appears to be the 'odd' one out in the EFTA Court's case law, as the emphasis is very much on the difference between EU and EEA law, although, as set out above, the differentiation is far from convincing. The judgment in *Maglite* is also the only judgment of the EFTA Court to rely on the conclusion of CJEU in Opinion 1/91,[44] in which the original draft of the EEA Agreement was rejected as incompatible with Community law.

VI. GEOGRAPHICAL SCOPE

One of the most contentious areas of the scope of the EEA Agreement has been its geographical reach. Article 126 EEA defines its geographical area as covering the

[40] Joined Cases E-9 and E-10/07 *L'Oreal Norge*, paras 33–37.

[41] OA Rognstad, 'Intellectual Property Law' in C Baudenbacher (ed), *The Handbook of EEA Law* (Dordrecht, Springer, 2016) 710; OA Rognstad, ch 14 in this volume.

[42] ibid 709.

[43] OA Rognstad, 'Performing Artists' Right to Remuneration – on the Junction of External Treaty Competence, National Treatment, Material Reciprocity and Fundamental Rights: RAAP' (2021) 58 *CMLR*, 1523, 1540–43.

[44] European Court of Justice, Opinion of the Court of 14 December 1991, Opinion 1/91, ECLI:EU:C:1991:490.

territory of application of the EU Treaties (under the conditions laid down therein) and the territories of Iceland, Liechtenstein and Norway. The Norwegian government has always claimed that the concept of territory in the Article should be interpreted in line with international law, with the result that the exclusive economic zone and the continental shelf are outside the scope of the EEA Agreement. Although the issue has been the subject of disputes between the EFTA Surveillance Authority and Norway several times, these cases were always settled without the EFTA Court being called upon to provide a definitive ruling. It was not until *Scanteam* that the Court was required to examine this question.[45]

The case turned on whether procurement by an embassy in a third country is subject to the Public Procurement Directive 2014/24/EU, incorporated into Annex XVI EEA. The Procurement Directive does not contain any provisions concerning its geographical scope and, consequently, the EFTA Court found that the scope was the same as that of the main part of the Agreement. Relying on established case law of the CJEU, the Court held that the geographical scope of the Agreement did not prevent EEA law from having effects outside the territory of the EEA.

The EFTA Court noted that in the field of competition law, the CJEU had interpreted Articles 53 and 54 EEA as being applicable to conduct adopted outside of the EEA, which would have foreseeable, immediate and substantial effects within the EEA. The Court also relied on established CJEU case law, providing that EU law applies to all legal relationships insofar as they can be located within the territory of the EU either by reason of the place they are entered into or the place where they take effect. In the same vein, the CJEU has held that EU law may apply to professional activities pursued outside the territory of the EU as long as the employment relationship retains a sufficiently close link thereto. Importantly, what the CJEU is interpreting is not the provisions governing the geographical scope of the Treaties (currently Article 52 of the Treaty on European Union (TEU) and Article 355 TFEU), but rather the substantive rules.[46] To ensure their effectiveness, they are considered to be applicable as long as there is a sufficient link to EU law.

The EFTA Court adopted the same methodology in the context of the public procurement rules, concluding that procurement conducted outside the territory of the EEA is within the scope of EEA law if it is sufficiently closely linked to the EEA. The Court explained in some detail the criteria to be taken into account in that context, which need not be examined further here.[47]

Having reached this conclusion, the Court stated that: 'The Norwegian Government has argued that the territorial scope of the EEA Agreement differs between EFTA States and EU Member States due to the wording of Article 126 EEA. As the Court has already found that the Directive applies if the procurement at issue is sufficiently closely linked to the EEA, there is no reason to examine Article 126 EEA'.[48] These words might be taken as meaning that no examination of Article 126

[45] Case E-8/19 *Scanteam*, paras 65–73. For a thorough examination of this case and the geographical scope of EEA law, see HH Fredriksen, 'The Geographical Reach of EEA Law after Scanteam' in T Gunnarsson et al (ed), *Afmælisrit Páll Hreinsson* (Reykjavik, Fons Juris, 2023) 263–80.

[46] Fredriksen (n 45) 276.

[47] *Scanteam* (n 45) paras 68–69.

[48] *Scanteam* (n 45) para 73.

EEA had taken place in this judgment. The author submits that such a reading of this paragraph is not fully accurate and overlooks the preceding conclusion of the Court. As noted above, the EFTA Court correctly, and on the basis of homogeneity, applied the same effectiveness-based interpretation to the procurement rules as the CJEU had done vis-a-vis the free movement and competition provisions.

As Professor Fredriksen notes, the CJEU has applied two distinct approaches to the geographical reach of EU law: (1) the effect-related approach, adopted by the EFTA Court, which examines whether the activities under examination have a sufficiently close link to the EU; and (2) the sovereign rights approach, which extends the territory of the Union to include, for example, the exclusive economic zone and the continental shelf.[49] Thus, it would be logical to interpret the statement above, about an examination of Article 126 EEA not being needed, as the EFTA Court reserving judgment on whether the second approach is also applicable in the context of the EEA. Given the emphasis on homogeneity in *Scanteam*, it must be regarded as being likely that the EFTA Court would reach that conclusion should that question come before it. However, and perhaps more importantly, the EFTA Court's adoption of the effect-based approach considerably limits the practical relevance of whether the more principled approach is also transposable to EEA law.

VII. INTERPRETATION OF PROVISIONS REGARDING THE SCOPE OF THE AGREEMENT

This section will attempt to draw some lines together and explore whether the EFTA Court has applied a particular approach to the interpretation of the scope of the Agreement. Following on from the principle of homogeneity, and in particular Article 6 EEA and Article 3 of the Surveillance and Court Agreement (SCA), the EFTA Court generally applies the same interpretative methods as the CJEU.[50]

As was noted above, in *Pedicel* the Court gave, by way of an obiter dictum, a statement concerning dynamic interpretation in the context of the product scope of the Agreement, which warrants a closer examination. The Court stated as follows:

> The Contracting Parties are pursuing the objective of creating a dynamic and homogeneous European Economic Area. This fundamental goal, which is laid down, inter alia, in the fourth and fifteenth recitals of the Preamble to the EEA Agreement, may make a dynamic interpretation of EEA law necessary. That is, however, not so with regard to Article 8(3) EEA. The Court cannot hold that Article 11 EEA applies to trade in wine *since this would amount to extending the scope of the Agreement.*[51] (Emphasis added)

This paragraph has served as a basis for maintaining that provisions of EEA law setting out the borders of the EEA Agreement – borders that are different from those under EU law – are not to be interpreted dynamically or homogeneously.[52] This argument has, for example, been made in *D and E* regarding the interpretation of

[49] Fredriksen (n 45) 267.
[50] Einarsson (n 14).
[51] *Pedicel* (n 18) para 28.
[52] Case E-2/19 *D and E*, para 46 RfH.

the so-called sectoral adaptations for Liechtenstein in the field of free movement of persons. According to these adaptations, Liechtenstein is allowed to maintain a quota of residence permits granted to other EEA nationals.[53] The EFTA Court did not explicitly deal with the argument in its judgment; however, it seems clear that the Court does not subscribe to it. The Court concluded that once Liechtenstein had unilaterally decided to grant an EEA national a residence permit outside the quota system, it could not rely on that system to deny him reunification with a family member. The Court stated that to create two separate classes of EEA nationals residing in Liechtenstein based on the nature of their residence permits would require a clear legal basis in the sectoral adaptations, which was not present.[54]

Thus, the Court did not accept that the sectoral adaptations could implicitly limit the rights of EEA nationals lawfully residing in Liechtenstein, as such a conclusion would reduce the effectiveness of EEA law rights granted to those persons. If Liechtenstein wanted to be allowed to impose further restrictions on those rights, such restrictions would have to be laid down explicitly and, by extension, be agreed upon by all Contracting Parties. However, it should be underlined that the EFTA Court's interpretation, whilst safeguarding the effectiveness of free movement rights, is safely anchored in the text of the adaptions.[55]

In this context, it has been asserted that the EFTA Court's approach in its case law regarding the Citizenship Directive – for example, *Jabbi* – sits rather uncomfortably with the cited statement from *Pedicel*.[56] This line of case law has been criticised for entailing an extension of the scope of the EEA Agreement to include free movement rights for non-economically active persons.[57] Before examining that claim, it is appropriate to note that a considerable amount of ink has been spilled to analyse these cases, and opinions on the Court's approach are divided.[58] The author believes that the Court's dynamic interpretation of Article 7 of the Citizenship Directive to also encompass obligations placed on the home state of EEA nationals is well grounded in the principle of homogeneity and effectiveness.[59]

However, this is not the place to repeat that discussion, but rather to examine whether it is accurate to claim that the EFTA Court has extended the scope of the Agreement in the judgments in question. To answer that question, it is necessary to start by looking at the state of the law at the time of the entry into force of the EEA Agreement. In *Gunnarsson*, the EFTA Court examined the predecessors of the Citizenship Directive: Directives 90/364/EC, 90/365/EC and 90/366/EC.[60] As explained

[53] Decision of the EEA Joint Committee No 191/1999.

[54] *D and E* (n 52) paras 55–57.

[55] Einarsson (n 14).

[56] HH Fredriksen, 'EEA Law in and beyond the Text of the Main Part of the EEA Agreement' in Arnesen et al (n 2) 134.

[57] P Wennerås, 'Article 6' in Arnesen et al (n 2) 242–45; SM Stefánsson and M Einarsdóttir, 'Um valdmörk og valdheimildir stofnana Evrópusambandsins og Evrópska efnahagssvæðis' (2018) *Tímarit lögfræðinga* 381–83.

[58] HH Fredriksen and C Franklin, 'Differentiated Citizenship in the European Economic Area' in D Kostakopoulou and D Thym (eds), *European Union Citizenship Law and Policy* (Cheltenham, Edward Elgar, 2022) 297–319.

[59] Einarsson (n 14).

[60] Case E-26/13 *Atli Gunnarsson*, paras 73–79.

by the Court, these Directives provided for residence rights for non-economically active persons, retired persons and students. The legal basis for these Directives was the residual competence laid down in Article 235 EC (Article 352 TFEU) and the recitals make clear that they were adopted in relation to the free movement of persons and the completion of the internal market.[61] Accordingly, the free movement of non-economically active persons was covered by EU law before the creation of the citizenship provisions of the Treaty, which were the result of changes made by the Treaty of Maastricht. Importantly, these rights were reflected in the EEA Agreement from the beginning and, accordingly, were not the creation of the EFTA Court following the entry into force of the Citizenship Directive. The Court's dynamic interpretation has undoubtedly rendered these rights more effective and there is space for diverging views concerning whether the Court's interpretation was correct. However, to criticise the Court for extending the personal scope of the Agreement would seem to be off the mark, as those non-economically active persons were within its scope from the start. It may certainly be noted that these rights were granted towards the host state rather than the home state, unlike the interpretation adopted by EFTA Court. However, the Court treated the free movement of non-economically active persons in an analogous manner to the free movement provisions, under which there is settled case law that they also encompass exit restrictions enacted by the home state.[62]

In its pleadings in *Campbell*, the Norwegian government was also highly critical of the EFTA Court's approach in *Jabbi*. It went as far as stating that the concept of homogeneity underlying the conclusion in *Jabbi* went against the rule of law. For the present purposes, the most significant part of the government's objections is as follows:

> Homogeneity 'in result', on the other hand, would entail that the judiciary engages in homogenous law making, by bridging legal differences in the two systems. This conflicts with the principle of separation of powers, *including the prerogative of the Contracting Parties under Article 118 EEA to extend the scope of the EEA Agreement*. It follows from settled case law that this falls outside the realm of the judicial function and the EFTA Court has repeatedly dismissed the relevance of acts not incorporated in the EEA.[63] (Emphasis added)

As has been discussed above, the EFTA Court did not extend the personal scope of the Agreement; rather, it enhanced the rights of non-economically active persons who were already within the scope of the Agreement. It would thus seem quite far-fetched to claim that the EFTA Court disregarded Article 118 EEA, which, as outlined above, covers the extension of the Agreement. In this context, it is interesting to note that the joint declaration which accompanied the decision of the EEA Joint Committee, incorporating the Citizenship Directive, did contain a reference to Article 118 EEA. After having noted the derived rights enjoyed by third-country family members, the declaration reads: 'This is without prejudice to Art 118 of the EEA Agreement and the future development of independent rights of third country nationals which do

[61] C Neier, 'The Right to Come Home – within or outside the Scope of the EEA Agreement?', https://www.efta-studies.org/post/the-right-to-come-home.

[62] *Atli Gunnarsson* (n 60) para 77.

[63] Case E-4/19 *Campbell*, written observations of the Norwegian government, para 63.

not fall within the scope of the EEA Agreement.' Accordingly, it would seem that the Contracting Parties themselves considered that recourse to Article 118 EEA would be appropriate if they intended to grant third-country nationals other rights than those deriving from being a family member of an EEA national.

The quoted observations of the Norwegian government also referred to case law of the EFTA Court dismissing the relevance of acts not incorporated into the EEA Agreement, inferring that the approach adopted in these cases differed from that in *Jabbi*. Therefore, it is appropriate to examine this issue further and explain why these cases are not comparable to those under the Citizenship Directive. Early on, in *Jæger*, the EFTA Court had to tackle the significance of a relevant piece of Community law not yet being incorporated into the EEA Agreement.[64] It was submitted that the Court should, based on the principle of homogeneity, consider a block exemption regulation on motor vehicle distribution applicable to the EEA as well. The Court categorically rejected that invitation and stated that it was for the Joint Committee, acting under Article 102 EEA, to ensure 'as closely as possible' simultaneous application of new legislation. This approach has been confirmed more recently, for example, in *Fjarskipti*, in which the Court found that the provisions of the Damages Directive, which had not been incorporated into the EEA, were not applicable to the dispute at hand. Exceptions could only be made if the provisions of the Directive were regarded to represent a codification of case law resulting from the application of the competition rules of the Agreement.[65]

The question of how to deal with issues where provisions of the TFEU, which do not have a direct counterpart under the Main Part of the EEA Agreement, has also surfaced before the EFTA Court. In *Einarsson*, the EFTA Court concluded that the discrimination made under Icelandic tax law between books in Icelandic and books in other languages was in breach of Article 14 EEA (equivalent to Article 110 TFEU). The Icelandic government had sought to justify the different tax rates with reference to the Contracting Parties' joint declaration on cultural affairs. The Court did not find that these formulations could form a basis for a derogation from Article 14 EEA. Interestingly, it was also alleged that the joint declaration corresponded to the objectives of Article 151(4) EC and that this provision, introduced by the Treaty of Amsterdam, might be relied on by analogy. The EFTA Court rejected that contention, stating that 'it would not be a proper exercise of the judicial function to seek to extend the scope of application of the EEA Agreement on that basis'.[66] As commentators have noted, it would have been impossible for the EFTA Court to reach a different conclusion as there was no basis in the Agreement for considering a provision similar to Article 151(4) EC to be applicable as a matter of EEA law.[67] *Einarsson*

[64] Case E-3/97 *Jan and Kristian Jæger AS*, para 30.

[65] Case E-6/17 *Fjarskipti*, para 44.

[66] *Einarsson* (n 10) paras 44–45. For similar considerations concerning equal treatment, see Case E-1/02 *ESA v Norway*, para 55: 'As to the Defendant's submissions to the effect that Article 141(4) EC and the new Directive 2002/73/EC of 23 September 2002 amending Directive 76/207/EEC should apply to the present case by analogy, the Court observes that these provisions have not been made part of EEA law. They therefore do not provide a legal basis to decide the present application either directly or by analogy.'

[67] N Fenger, 'Limits to a Dynamic Homogeneity between EC Law and EEA Law' in N Fenger at al (eds), *Festskrift Claus Gulman* (Copenhagen, Forlaget Thomson, 2006) 147.

is distinguishable from the Citizenship Directive cases, as there the Court was essentially faced with the question as to whether to interpret a new provision into EEA law. In contrast, the citizenship cases turned on an interpretation of the Directive in the EEA context and whether a dynamic interpretation imposing obligations on the home states was possible. The two situations might perhaps be regarded as being comparable had the EFTA Court been invited to find a basis in EEA law for the political rights associated with EU citizenship.

VIII. CONCLUDING REMARKS

As the examination of the EFTA Court's case law carried out in this chapter has demonstrated, the Court has tackled interesting issues concerning the scope of the EEA Agreement, which do not have a direct parallel under EU law. The most noteworthy examples of this case law are perhaps *Pedicel*, concerning the extent of the exclusion of certain products from the Agreement, and *Maglite*, subsequently overturned by *L'Oreal*, regarding the exhaustion of trade marks and the special rules of origin for intellectual property rights. The chapter has also demonstrated that the interpretative approach of the EFTA Court to these questions has been comparable with the one the Court generally adopts and, accordingly, homogeneity has continuously played a key role in the Court's judgments.

17

The NAV Case in the EFTA Court and the Supreme Court of Norway

HALVARD HAUKELAND FREDRIKSEN AND CHRISTIAN NK FRANKLIN

I. INTRODUCTION

IN THE NOW 30-year history of the EFTA Court, its relationship to the courts of last instance of the EFTA Member States of the European Economic Area (EEA) has fluctuated from rather troubled to quite close.[1] As far as the relationship between the EFTA Court and the Supreme Court of Norway is concerned, the last 10 years have seen a most welcome improvement.[2] At the time of the EFTA Court's twentieth anniversary in 2014, the relationship could only be described as chilly, with a dry spell of more than 10 years since the last referral of a case from the Supreme Court being topped by the (in)famous refusal in 2013 to follow the advisory opinion in the *STX* case without giving the EFTA Court the opportunity to express its view on novel arguments that the Supreme Court found to be convincing.[3] Ten years later, the Supreme Court has sent 11 cases to the EFTA Court – a much higher number than, for example, that of the referrals from the Supreme Court of Denmark to the Court of Justice of the European Union (CJEU) in the same period.[4] What is more, the Justices in Oslo have demonstrated in *Fosen-Linjen* and again in *Campbell* that in cases where they are not convinced by the reasoning of the EFTA Court, they will – 'in the interests of dialogue' – ask the EFTA Court for 'clarification and amplification, or possibly even reconsideration' before rendering their own judgment – a welcome change of course from *STX*.[5] To its credit, the EFTA Court has welcomed

[1] See, eg, HH Fredriksen and C Franklin, 'Of Pragmatism and Principles: The EEA Agreement 20 Years on' (2015) 52 *Common Market Law Review* 629, 671 ff.

[2] As noted with satisfaction by the Registrar of the EFTA Court; see ÓJ Einarsson, 'The Advisory Opinion Procedure and the Relationship between the EFTA Court and the Norwegian Courts: Recent Developments', (2022) 61 *Lov og Rett* 221, 245.

[3] Fredriksen and Franklin (n 1) 671 and 674, with further references.

[4] According to the CJEU's InfoCuria database, as at October 2023, the Supreme Court of Denmark has only sent five requests for preliminary rulings from the CJEU since 2013.

[5] See Case E-7/18 *Fosen-Linjen AS v AtB AS (Fosen-Linjen II)*, judgment of 1 August 2019, paras 37–38, presenting the request of the national court; and Case E-4/19 *Campbell v Norway*, Report for the Hearing, para 4, detailing the referring court's concerns.

these 'rematches' by reiterating that it is 'important that questions on the interpretation of the EEA Agreement are referred to the Court under the procedure provided for in Article 34 SCA if the legal situation lacks clarity' and stating that all it takes for a new request to be admissible is for the national court to submit 'new considerations which might lead to a different answer to a question submitted earlier'.[6] The EFTA Court's preparedness to let itself be convinced by such new considerations was demonstrated by the reconsideration of *Fosen-Linjen I* in *Fosen-Linjen II*.[7] However, as proved by *Campbell*, the EFTA Court will stand its ground if it considers the new considerations unconvincing, even if they are brought forward by the Supreme Court.[8]

A manifestation of the improved relationship between the Supreme Court of Norway and the EFTA Court is the judicial clearing-up of the Norwegian social security scandal, dubbed (rightly or wrongly) by many as the so-called *NAV* scandal, which shook the Norwegian legal community to its core when it was revealed in the autumn of 2019.[9] For reasons that have (and perhaps may) never fully been understood, the Norwegian Labour and Welfare Administration (NAV) considered EEA-based exportability of sickness benefits in cash to be limited to cases where the recipient transferred his or her residence to another EEA State, thus excluding all other shorter stays abroad (holidays, weekend trips etc). The misinterpretation of the 2004 Social Security Regulation,[10] as well as the failure to consider other parts of EEA law, affected mainly (although not exclusively) Norwegian nationals who had never exercised their EEA rights, for example, to work or study in another EEA State, and whose cases were therefore (wrongfully) not classified as EEA cases to be considered by the EEA law specialists within NAV. The recipients of these benefits were met with hefty (and often ruinous) reimbursement claims in cases where the authorities revealed that they had stayed in other EEA States whilst receiving benefits. More than 40 cases resulted in criminal convictions for social security fraud, including 36 cases of imprisonment.

In this contribution to the EFTA Court's thirtieth anniversary, we will analyse in some detail the Supreme Court's referral of the *NAV* case to the EFTA Court, the EFTA Court's answers to the many questions put to it, and the Supreme Court's final judgment in the case.[11] Our aim is not only to document the case as such, but also to

[6] Case E-7/18 *Fosen-Linjen II*, paras 48–49.

[7] See further A Sanchez-Graells, ch 18 in this volume.

[8] Case E-4/19 *Campbell*, judgment of 13 May 2020, para 58.

[9] For an overview in the English language, see the summary provided by the investigative committee appointed by the government in Chapter 3 of its final report: NOU 2020:9 *Blindsonen – Gransking av feilpraktiseringen av folketrygdlovens oppholdskrav ved reiser i EØS-området*, 26–29, available at: www.regjeringen.no/no/dokumenter/nou-2020-9.

[10] Regulation (EC) No 883/2004 of the European Parliament and of the Council of 29 April 2004 on the coordination of social security systems [2004] OJ L166/1, which was incorporated into the EEA Agreement by Decision of the EEA Joint Committee No 76/2011 of 1 July 2011 [2011] OJ L262/33. It entered into force on 1 June 2012 and is referred to at point 1 of Annex VI (Social Security) to the EEA Agreement.

[11] Case E-8/20 *Criminal Proceedings against N*, judgment of 5 May 2021, and HR-2021-1453-S *The Public Prosecution Authority against A*, respectively. An English translation of the Supreme Court's judgment is available at: www.domstol.no/en/supremecourt/rulings/2021/supreme-court-criminal-cases/hr-2021-1453-s. For some reason, the defendant was anonymised as *N* in the EFTA Court and as *A* in the Supreme Court. We will simply refer to the case as the *NAV* case in the following.

explain why we consider it a manifestation of a closer relationship between the EFTA Court and the Supreme Court of Norway.[12]

II. THE IMPLICATION OF THE SUPREME COURT IN THE *NAV* SCANDAL AND THE DECISION TO REFER THE CASE TO THE EFTA COURT

In an intriguing twist, the Supreme Court itself was implicated in the *NAV* scandal as it had passed final judgment in one of the cases.[13] True enough, the question whether EEA law hindered the conviction for social security fraud of a man who had failed to inform NAV that he had spent several short-term stays in Italy whilst receiving a work assessment allowance was not an issue before the Supreme Court. However, as was subsequently acknowledged by the Supreme Court itself, any court passing sentence in a criminal case has an *ex officio* responsibility to ensure that there is a legal basis for the judgment (*iura novit curia*).[14] Although the Supreme Court's role in causing the scandal was limited, it was significant as a matter of principle and attracted the attention of both the media and the investigative committee appointed by the government.[15]

The Supreme Court's complicity in the scandal had implications for the subsequent involvement of the EFTA Court. Under the Norwegian Criminal Procedure Act, the reopening of a criminal case by the independent Criminal Cases Review Commission will send the case back to the same level in the court hierarchy where final judgment was passed.[16] Thus, when the *NAV* case decided by the Supreme Court was reopened, it was sent directly to the Supreme Court. This enabled the Supreme Court to move quickly, without having to wait for one of the cases in the NAV complex to make its way through the court hierarchy. Indeed, it took only three-and-a-half months from when the case was reopened until a long and detailed request for an advisory opinion was sent, suggesting that the decision to involve the EFTA Court was taken more or less immediately after the reopening. The Supreme Court did not explain in any detail why it found it appropriate to refer the case to the EFTA Court, but it did state that the Social Security Regulations (both the 'new' one from 2004 and the 'old' one from 1971)[17] as well as other relevant EEA rules 'on certain

[12] For the sake of good order, attention is drawn to the fact that both authors of this chapter were involved in the attempts to rights the wrongs in the *NAV* cases – Fredriksen as chair of the law commission that reviewed the EEA compatibility of the National Insurance Act and proposed numerous legislative amendments (NOU 2021:8 *Trygd over landegrensene*) and Franklin as special advisor to the Acting Director General of Public Prosecution as well as co-author of a report commissioned by NAV (I Ikdahl, C Franklin and M Hennig, *Ikke stykkevis og delt – rapport om Arbeids- og velferdsetatens EØS-rettslige forpliktelser*, 2020).

[13] HR-2017-560-A.

[14] HR-2021-1453-S, para 191.

[15] As to the latter, see the investigative committee report, NOU 2020:9 *Blindsonen* 28 (English summary) and, in more detail, 182 ff (in Norwegian only).

[16] Criminal Procedure Act of 22 May 1981 No 25, s 400.

[17] Regulation (EEC) No 1408/71 of the Council of 14 June 1971 on the application of social security schemes to employed persons, to self-employed persons and to members of their families moving within the Community [1971] OJ Spec Ed (II) 416, which was part of Annex VI (Social Security) to the EEA Agreement from its entry into force.

points raises interpretative doubts', and later in the request added that clarification could only be achieved through the courts 'and preferably after interpretive opinions have been obtained from the EFTA Court on how EEA law should be understood'.[18] Whether the Supreme Court's own role in the case contributed to the decision – its first ever request in a criminal case – remains uncertain. But it would certainly have seemed rather striking if the Supreme Court had decided *not* to turn to the EFTA Court in this particular case.

The result was in any event a wide-ranging request that included not only the 1971 and the 2004 Social Security Regulations, but also Article 28 EEA on the free movement of workers, Article 36 EEA on the free movement of services and the Citizenship Directive.[19] However, the EFTA Court found that the 1971 Regulation, which remains applicable to facts occurring before 1 June 2012, only covers exportability of sickness benefits in cases where the recipient transferred his or her *residence* to another EEA State.[20] Furthermore, the EFTA Court saw no reason to deal with Article 28 EEA, as the description of the facts provided by the Supreme Court contained nothing to suggest that the freedom of movement for workers was relevant in the case.[21] Further still, as a result of the interpretation of the 2004 Social Security Regulation and Article 36 EEA, the EFTA Court decided to leave the question concerning the interpretation of the Citizenship Directive for another day.[22] Accordingly, we will focus on the 2004 Social Security Regulation and Article 36 EEA in the following section.

III. THE 2004 SOCIAL SECURITY REGULATION

Since 1 June 2012, the exportability within the EEA of sickness benefits in cash has been regulated by the 2004 Social Security Regulation. This is the date on which the Regulation entered into force in the EEA, some two years after its entry into force in the EU.[23]

The questions put to the EFTA Court concerning the 2004 Regulation all concerned the interpretation of Article 21(1) of that Regulation, which states that an insured person (and members of his or her family) residing or staying in a Member State other than the competent Member State shall be entitled to cash benefits provided by the competent institution in accordance with the legislation it applies.

[18] Request from the Supreme Court of Norway for an advisory opinion from the EFTA Court, 30 June 2020, 1 and 9 (our translations).

[19] Directive 2004/38/EC of the European Parliament and of the Council of 29 April 2004 on the right of citizens of the Union and their family members to move and reside freely within the territory of the Member States [2004] OJ L158/77. The Directive was incorporated into the EEA Agreement by Decision of the EEA Joint Committee No 158/2007 of 7 December 2007 [2008] OJ L124/20, which adapted and added it at point 3 of Annex VIII, and points 1 and 2 of Annex V. The decision entered into force on 1 March 2009.

[20] Case E-8/20 *N*, para 67.

[21] ibid para 74. It was left to the Supreme Court to determine whether the facts of the case nevertheless made Art 28 EEA applicable, but the Supreme Court saw no need for this as Art 28 EEA was presumed to offer little in addition to Art 36 EEA; see HR-2021-1453-S, para 184. As will be explained in section IV.A below, the defence counsels' invocation of Art 28 EEA was misguided and could have harmed their client's case considerably if it had been picked up by the courts.

[22] *N* (n 20) para 130.

[23] It entered into force in the EU on 1 May 2010.

A. Whether Article 21(1) Encompasses Short-Term Stays in Other EEA States

The Norwegian Labour and Welfare Administration had originally understood the term 'staying' in Article 21 of the 2004 Regulation as not including short-term stays. The reason for this at first sight somewhat strained view was the specific definition of 'stay' in Article 1(k) of the Regulation. In the English version, 'stay' is defined as 'temporary residence'. The Norwegian version of the Regulation used similar language, defining 'stay' as 'midlertidig bosted'. The use of the term 'bosted' ('residence') in this definition caused NAV to believe that short-term stays were excluded. However, a teleological interpretation of Article 21 clearly suggested that the terms 'residing' and 'staying' in Article 21(1) together cover all forms of presence or residence in another EEA State. Other language versions of Article 1(k) of the Regulation confirmed this, including the Danish ('midlertidigt ophold'), French ('séjour temporaire') and German ('vorübergehenden Aufenthalt') texts.[24] As NAV itself had come to the conclusion that its original understanding of Article 21 was wrong and that this view was shared by the Norwegian government, the EFTA Surveillance Authority (ESA) and the European Commission, there was little reason for the EFTA Court to elaborate on the rather unfortunate Norwegian version of the text. Accordingly, the EFTA Court simply stated that the juxtaposition of the terms 'residing' and 'staying' in the wording of Article 21(1), as well as the definition of 'stay' in Article 1(k) ('temporary residence'), makes it clear that the term 'staying' in Article 21(1) must be understood as including short-term stays in another EEA State.[25] However, a somewhat regrettable result of this approach is that the Norwegian version of the Advisory Opinion reads less well on this point. Even if the literal interpretation of 'temporary residence' in the English text is as straightforward as suggested by the EFTA Court, it is rather forced to consider it 'clear' that the Norwegian term 'midlertidig bosted' covered short-term stays.[26] In our opinion, it would have been better to explain to readers of the Norwegian version that other language versions as well as a systematic and teleological interpretation were decisive. It is telling that Norway subsequently, as part of the clearing-up after the *NAV* scandal, considered it necessary to correct the Norwegian definition of 'stay' in Article 1(k) from temporary 'bosted' ('residence') to temporary 'opphold' ('stay').[27]

Given the fact that the interpretation of the term 'staying' in Article 21 was no longer in dispute, the Supreme Court nevertheless endorsed the EFTA Court's view without further ado.[28]

[24] However, the Swedish text is similar to the (then) Norwegian version, defining 'stay' as 'tillfällig bosättning'. The EFTA Court's reference to not only the Danish, French and German but also the Swedish text (*N* (n 20) para 133) in support of its interpretation of Art 21 is therefore not quite convincing.

[25] *N* (n 20) para 133.

[26] As neither the English nor the Norwegian version of Art 21 was called into question by the EFTA Court, neither appears in the other language version of the advisory opinion. This leaves the rather odd impression in the English version that the Court considered, eg, the Danish and Swedish texts, but not the Norwegian one, and the equally odd impression in the Norwegian version that that Court failed to consider the English text.

[27] See the Norwegian version of the EEA Supplement to the Official Journal of the European Union No 23/2022 p 728, available at: www.efta.int/publications/eea-supplements/supplements-2022-no.

[28] HR-2021-1453-S, para 117.

B. Whether Article 21(1) is Limited to Situations where a Medical Diagnosis is Given During a Stay in Another EEA State

An arguably rather more complicated question is whether Article 21(1) was intended by the EU legislator to cover only situations where the medical condition giving rise to sickness benefits in cash from the competent state appears during a stay in another EEA State. This question was raised by the Supreme Court as the result of an article written by a former member of that court, who argued that an interpretation of Article 21(1) in light of the subsequent paragraphs of that provision as well as the associated provisions of the 2009 Implementing Regulation,[29] and (some of) the predecessors of Article 21(1) in the 1971 Regulation,[30] suggested an answer in the affirmative.[31] However, before the EFTA Court, all the participants to the proceedings agreed that Article 21(1) also covers situations where the medical condition giving rise to sickness benefits in cash from the competent state is recognised by the competent institution before departure. The EFTA Court thus confined itself to stating that it saw no basis in the wording of Article 21 for limiting its applicability to situations where a medical diagnosis is given during a stay in an EEA State other than the competent EEA State, and that there was nothing to suggest that the provision ought to be interpreted in any other way.[32]

The Supreme Court of Norway took note of the EFTA Court's answer and endorsed it without further ado.[33]

Whether the interpretation of Article 21(1) on this point is really so straightforward might be questioned,[34] yet the practical importance of the issue seems limited. In light of the general aim of the 2004 Regulation as a means to contribute to the free movement of persons within the EEA,[35] a narrow interpretation of Article 21(1) is only tenable if combined with a broad interpretation of Article 7 on the waiving of residence rules, so that the right to go to another EEA State for a shorter stay without losing sickness benefits in cash already granted is covered by the latter.[36] Interestingly, the EFTA Court later in its Advisory Opinion reasoned in favour of such an interpretation of Article 7, holding that a requirement of continuous physical presence in the competent EEA State, which excludes entitlement to sickness benefits during short stays abroad, is significantly more restrictive than a residence requirement and

[29] Articles 27 and 28 of Regulation (EC) No 987/2009 of the European Parliament and of the Council of 16 September 2009 laying down the procedure for implementing Regulation (EC) No 883/2004 on the coordination of social security systems [2009] OJ L284/1, which was incorporated into the EEA Agreement by Decision of the EEA Joint Committee No 76/2011 of 1 July 2011 [2011] OJ L262/33. It entered into force on 1 June 2012, and is referred to at point 1 of Annex VI (Social Security) to the EEA Agreement.

[30] Articles 19 and 22(1)(a).

[31] KA Utgård, 'Trygdesaka – ein gjennomgang av dei grunnleggande rettsreglane', www.Rett24.no (19 February 2020).

[32] *N* (n 20) para 136.

[33] HR-2021-1453-S, para 119.

[34] See the analysis of the law commission that reviewed the EEA compatibility of the National Insurance Act in NOU 2021:8, pp 70–71.

[35] As highlighted by the EFTA Court in N (n 20) para 46.

[36] This was overlooked by Utgård (n 31), who argued for a narrow interpretation of Art 21(1) *and* a literal interpretation of Art 7, confining the latter to cases where a recipient of a sickness benefit in cash moves to reside in another EEA State.

therefore caught by Article 7.[37] If this interpretation of Article 7 is accepted, then it might be possible to argue that Article 21(1) ought to be understood as a specific provision for situations where the medical condition giving rise to sickness benefits in cash arises during a stay in another EEA State. However, rather than elaborate on the relationship between Articles 7 and 21(1), the EFTA Court opted for a belt-and-braces approach, essentially merging the two provisions into one. According to the EFTA Court, the right to go to another EEA State for a shorter stay without losing sickness benefits in cash already granted can be derived from both Article 7 and Article 21(1).[38]

The Supreme Court followed this up in its final judgment by referring to both Articles 7 and 21(1) when endorsing the EFTA Court's view that an insured person cannot be denied a work assessment allowance for the sole reason that he or she is residing or staying in another EEA State.[39]

C. Whether the Reference in Article 21(1) to the Legislation of the Competent EEA State Allows for National Restrictions on the Exportability of Sickness Benefits

The final question from the Supreme Court concerning the 2004 Regulation was whether the reference in Article 21(1) to the social security legislation of the competent EEA State[40] allows that state to: (i) limit the exportability to a maximum of four weeks per year; (ii) require any stay in other EEA States to be compatible with activity obligations and not to impede follow-up and control by the competent institution; and (iii) require the person concerned to obtain authorisation in advance. The essence of this question is whether Article 21(1) adds anything to the in any event applicable main rules on the free movement of persons in the EEA. Does Article 21(1) per se prevent requirements in national social security law that apply to the right to retain cash benefits while staying in another EEA State, or might such requirements be justified if they pursue a legitimate aim in accordance with the general EEA law principle of proportionality?

This question had been addressed by the investigative committee which was established by the government in the autumn of 2019. In its first report, issued in March 2020, the committee held that Article 21(1) cannot be understood as merely a reference back to the in any event applicable main rules on the free movement of persons in the EEA – Article 21(1) is an independent basis for an individual right to retain

[37] *N* (n 20) para 139. This broad interpretation of Art 7 of the 2004 Regulation does not sit easily with the EFTA Court's literal interpretation of the transfer of residence requirement in Art 22(1)(b) of the 1971 Regulation; see paras 66–67. However, the latter provision requires authorisation by the competent state, so the Court's conclusion that it was inapplicable in the case at hand nevertheless seems sound.

[38] Even though the EFTA Court rather curiously did not return to Art 7 after para 139, the conclusions drawn from Art 7 in that paragraph and the subsequent conclusions as to the interpretation of Art 21 appear to concur, see the analysis of the law commission that reviewed the EEA compatibility of the National Insurance Act in NOU 2021:8, pp 71–72.

[39] HR-2021-1453-S, paras 135 and 140.

[40] Article 21(1) requires the competent institution to provide cash benefits 'in accordance with the legislation it applies', ie, with the social security legislation of the competent EEA State.

sickness benefits in cash while staying in another EEA State.[41] However, when it came to the content of this right, the committee was of the opinion that restrictions put upon that right might be justified in accordance with the general principles of EEA law as long as the restrictions are not imposed solely because the recipient was staying in another EEA State.[42] This led the committee to conclude that Article 21(1) allows for a prior authorisation scheme based on the need to control that the recipients fulfil all activity obligations and do not engage in undeclared work whilst abroad, but only if the scheme is limited to stays 'of a certain duration'.[43]

The EFTA Court saw this differently. In line with the pleadings of ESA and the European Commission, but contrary to those of the Norwegian government, the EFTA Court held that Article 21(1) does not provide a basis for derogating from the right to retain social security benefits when going to another EEA State.[44] According to the EFTA Court, a teleological interpretation of Article 21(1) requires a distinction to be drawn between 'the criteria for entitlement' to the sickness benefit in question and 'further conditions'[45] – whilst the former is left to national law (within the general limits of the general principles of EEA free movement law),[46] the latter is quite simply prohibited.[47]

As national social security law typically does not distinguish between 'criteria for entitlement' to a sickness benefit and 'further conditions' (for entitlement to the same benefit), the distinction introduced by the EFTA Court might at first seem strained. When read in light of the Court's earlier interpretation of Article 7 as well as the example given of one such 'further condition', namely a requirement of physical presence on the territory of the competent EEA State,[48] it becomes clear that the distinction is between *general* criteria/conditions for entitlement and any *special criteria/conditions directly linked to the fact that the recipient stays, or wants to stay, in another EEA State*. Thus, as suggested by the law commission that reviewed the EEA compatibility of the National Insurance Act,[49] and subsequently confirmed by the Supreme Court, the EFTA Court's interpretation of Article 21(1) does not preclude general criteria for entitlement in national law that indirectly restrict free movement, such as activity obligations or control measures requiring physical presence at a given place at a given time (for example, the local doctor or the local NAV office). As noted by the Supreme Court, Article 21(1) 'only' precludes 'special conditions connected to the right to retain cash benefits while staying in another EEA State'.[50]

However, as all the conditions at issue in the *NAV* case were linked to stays abroad and thus fell into the category of 'further conditions' prohibited by Article 21(1), the EFTA Court concluded that no further assessment of those conditions under

[41] Investigative committee report NOU 2020:9, s 4.2.3.
[42] ibid s 4.2.6.
[43] ibid s 7.2.
[44] *N* (n 20) para 143.
[45] ibid.
[46] ibid para 142.
[47] ibid paras 147–48.
[48] ibid para 143.
[49] NOU 2021:8, s 2.4.4.
[50] HR-2021-1453-S, paras 139 and 143.

other provisions of EEA law was necessary: not only the four-week limit but also the requirement of any stay in other EEA States to be compatible with activity obligations and the related authorisation scheme were deemed incompatible with the Regulation.

The EFTA Court's interpretation of Article 21(1) comes across as rather strict on this point, particularly as it effectively precludes a control regime adapted to the undeniable differences in the social security authorities' control possibilities at home and abroad.[51] However, before the Supreme Court, the Norwegian government accepted the stance taken by the EFTA Court. The Supreme Court saw no reason to disagree, thereby confirming an interpretation of Article 21(1) that essentially equates stays in the competent EEA State and in all other EEA States for the purpose of entitlement to sickness benefits.

IV. ARTICLE 36 EEA AND THE RIGHT TO RECEIVE SERVICES IN OTHER EEA STATES

A. The Choice between Article 36 EEA and Other Possible Legal Bases

Before the entry into force within the EEA of the 2004 Regulation (1 June 2012), a right to retain sickness benefits in cash during stays abroad had to be based on more general EEA rules on free movement as the EFTA Court (as already mentioned) found that the 1971 Social Security Regulation only covers exportability of sickness benefits in cases where the recipient transferred his or her *residence* to another EEA State.[52]

For workers whose employment in the competent EEA State fell within the scope of Article 28 EEA, this provision provides an obvious first choice as a legal basis for a right to retain sickness benefits in cash during stays in other EEA States. Due to the cross-border requirement of Article 28 EEA, most workers in this category will be nationals of EEA States other than the competent EEA State, ie, 'EEA foreigners'. A typical example will be a worker from another EEA State who falls ill and who wants to spend time with his or her family in this other EEA State (or another EEA State) while recuperating. Article 28 EEA undoubtedly provides such a right. This also appears to have been understood all along by the Norwegian Labour and Welfare Administration (or at least by the EEA law specialists in the NAV international department)[53] – the *NAV* scandal primarily concerned Norwegian citizens whose employment in Norway was not covered by Article 28 EEA and who could not therefore fall back on this provision when NAV failed to recognise their rights under the 2004 Regulation.[54]

[51] As highlighted by the investigative committee; see NOU 2020:9, Annex II, s 7.2.

[52] Ssee section II above.

[53] This department was responsible for EEA matters until it was closed down in 2016 as part of a reorganisation of NAV.

[54] There are cases in the NAV complex involving workers from other EEA States too, but here the problem seems to have been a failure by individual case handlers to identify the EEA dimension of the case and not a systemic failure by NAV to recognise that Art 28 EEA gives rise to a right to retain sickness benefits in cash during stays abroad.

The case brought before the EFTA Court was a typical case of a Norwegian national who had never made use of his right to seek work in another EEA State before he fell ill. Before the Supreme Court as well as before the EFTA Court, the defence counsels nevertheless argued that Article 28 EEA was applicable because their client had later, whilst receiving sickness benefits from NAV, allegedly worked remotely in at least some of the periods that he stayed in Italy.[55] Luckily for the defendant, this line of argument was not picked up by either court. If the defendant had indeed worked whilst staying in Italy, not only Article 28 EEA but also the choice-of-law rules of the Social Security Regulations would have been triggered, the latter making Italy the competent state and leaving the defendant without any claim for sickness benefits from Norway.[56]

For recipients of sickness benefits who cannot invoke Article 28 EEA, the Citizenship Directive might provide a possible legal basis for a right to retain the benefits during stays abroad. Arguably, Article 4 on the right of exit and/or Article 6 on right of residence for up to three months give rise to a general right to move freely within the EEA which can also be invoked against a home state whose national social security law hinders the right to leave it for shorter stays in other EEA States.[57] The Directive entered into force in the EEA on 1 March 2009, thus covering about three years more than the 2004 Social Security Regulation. For cases extending further back, it might be supplemented by a general, unwritten EEA law principle of free movement for all EEA citizens, whose existence was suggested by the EFTA Court in *Campbell* and reiterated in *L*, but whose status and reach remains unclear.[58]

However, as already identified in section II above, the EFTA Court decided to leave the question concerning the interpretation of the Citizenship Directive for another day, focusing instead on Article 36 EEA and the right enshrined in this provision to go to other EEA States in order to receive services there. This prioritising of the possible legal bases was in line with that of the investigative committee as well as the Supreme Court in its referral of the case. It had the advantage of exceeding the temporal limit of the Citizenship Directive and allowed for an early endorsement of the CJEU's judgment in *IN*, where the CJEU confirmed that Article 36 EEA is to be interpreted in line with Article 56 TFEU and therefore offers citizens of the EEA/EFTA States the same protection as recipients of services in EU Member States as Union citizens.[59]

Still, the decision to rely on Article 36 EEA in the *NAV* case required a rather liberal approach to the notion of a service recipient. In the case before the EFTA Court, the defendant could reasonably be considered as a recipient of tourist services,[60] but in

[55] See *N* (n 20) para 74, and HR-2021-1453-S, para 44.

[56] Based on the information provided by the Supreme Court in para 9 of its final judgment, it appears that the 'work' done by the defendant was part of a work fitness programme under the auspices of NAV. Who the employer was, if any, remains unclear.

[57] The question was raised by the investigative committee, but no answer was provided; see NOU 2020:9, Annex II, s 1.2.4.

[58] Case E-4/19 *Campbell*, para 48; and Case E-2/20 *L*, para 24. See further C Franklin and HH Fredriksen, 'Differentiated Citizenship in the European Economic Area' in D Kostakopoulou and D Thym (eds), *European Citizenship Law and Policy* (Cheltenham, Edward Elgar, 2022) 297–319, at 298f.

[59] Case C-897/19 *IN* ECLI:EU:C:2020:262, paras 52–53.

[60] Through acquaintances, the defendant and his spouse were offered the use of a house in Italy and, during the material time, they had a total of 14 three and four-week stays there; see *N* (n 20) para 33.

several of the other cases in the NAV complex, the motivation for the stays in other EEA States was quite simply to visit family or friends. The EFTA Court was probably aware of this as it established a presumption that a person who for whatever reason travels to another EEA State will in fact receive services there, and that this is sufficient to be covered by Article 36 EEA.[61] Thus, it is not required that the decision to go to another EEA State is motivated by an interest in a specific service provided there.[62] Arguably, this presumption establishes Article 36 EEA as a legal basis for a general right to free movement, possibly equalling that of Article 20(2)(a) TFEU. Potential critics of this interpretation of Article 36 EEA will nevertheless have to take into account the ease of justifying a stay in any given EEA State with an alleged interest in a particular service offered there. Thus, the practical significance of a less liberal approach to Article 36 EEA appears limited.

The Supreme Court noted that the interpretation prescribed by the EFTA Court entails a wide application of the rules on the freedom to provide services, but accepted this without further ado.[63]

B. The Existence of Restrictions on the Freedom to Receive Services

The question whether the conditions for the exportability of sickness benefits in cash established by section 11-3 of the National Insurance Act constituted restrictions on the freedom to receive services was rather straightforward.[64] As noted by the EFTA Court, a condition limiting the duration of stays abroad constitutes, by its very essence, a restriction on the freedom to receive services abroad because it is liable to render the provision of services between EEA States more difficult than within the home state.[65] Furthermore, the EFTA Court considered it clear that a system of prior authorisation represents an additional burden for individuals wishing to stay in another EEA State compared to those staying in Norway, and that the condition that the stay abroad had to be compatible with the planned activity and possibility of control by Norwegian authorities, by its very nature, severely limited the possibility to go to another EEA State to obtain services there.[66] The EFTA Court quite rightly also gave short shrift here to the Norwegian authorities' argument based on *Commission v Spain*, which seemed rather irrelevant in the case at hand.[67]

The Supreme Court took note of the EFTA Court's view and simply stated that it was 'clear' that section 11-3 of the National Insurance Act constituted restrictions on the freedom to receive services in another EEA State.[68]

[61] ibid para 77.

[62] For a sceptical view of such an approach and of the view that the right to free movement and residence ought to be limited to receipt of specific services, see, eg, F Wollenschläger, 'A New Fundamental Freedom beyond Market Integration: Union Citizenship and its Dynamics for Shifting the Economic Paradigm of European Integration' (2011) 17 *European Law Journal* 1, 11.

[63] HR-2021-1453-S, paras 164–65.

[64] The conditions are set out in section III.C above.

[65] *N* (n 20) para 85.

[66] ibid para 86.

[67] ibid paras 88–89, with reference to Case C-211/08 *Commission v Spain* ECLI:EU:C:2010:340.

[68] HR-2021-1453-S, paras 166–68.

C. Whether the Restrictions could be Justified

i. Legitimate Objectives: The Objective of Re-integrating Recipients of Sickness Benefits into the Labour Market in Particular

The Norwegian authorities claimed that there were four potential public interest objectives which could justify the restrictions on Article 36 EEA: avoiding the risk of seriously undermining the financial balance of the Norwegian social security system; avoiding the risk of abuse of sickness benefits; the need to monitor compliance with the conditions for said benefits; and re-integration of recipients of sickness benefits into the labour market.[69] The first three of these were accepted as legitimate aims without further ado, but apparently not the final one. Although 'encouragement of recruitment' was accepted as a legitimate aim of EEA States' social or employment policy in principle,[70] the EFTA Court emphasised that sickness benefits (as understood under the Social Security Regulations) are health-related benefits and 'cannot be considered to be primarily instruments of national employment policy designed to improve opportunities for entering the labour market'.[71] This led the EFTA Court to conclude that 'considerations devised to fit the specific purposes of the employment policy of re-integrating persons into the labour market cannot justify the restriction in question'.[72]

If interpreted to suggest that the objective of re-integration into the labour market can never justify restrictions on free movement rights for recipients of sickness benefits, the implications for national social security law would be rather dramatic.[73] Indeed, the whole point of the activity obligations placed on the recipients of sickness benefits is to re-integrate them into the labour market as soon as possible, and it is rather inevitable that activity obligations can and often will limit the recipients' free movement rights. There was therefore much to suggest that the EFTA Court's statements were made with the specific restrictions in section 11-3 of the National Insurance Act in mind, given the reference in the last part of paragraph 106 to 'the restriction in question' as well as the otherwise somewhat confusing references to the proportionality test (suitability) in the preceding paragraphs.

The Supreme Court was clearly aware of this matter, as this part of the EFTA Court's answers to the Supreme Court had raised some eyebrows in the Norwegian legal community.[74] It therefore chose to focus on the EFTA Court's more general acceptance of 'encouragement of recruitment' as a legitimate aim of EEA States' social or employment policy instead, and then used this to interpret the less fortunate wording later on in the Opinion in the narrower way in which the EFTA Court surely intended.[75] In apparent deviation from the Advisory Opinion, the Supreme

[69] N (n 20) para 96.

[70] ibid para 98.

[71] ibid para 105.

[72] ibid para 106.

[73] See SB Tronsmoen, '- I ytterste konsekvens avliver EFTA-domstolen arbeidslinja', *Advokatbladet.no* (21 May 2021).

[74] ibid; and see the discussion in NOU 2021:9, s 2.4.4.

[75] See HR-2021-1453-S, paras 172–73.

Court held that integration into the labour market was a legitimate objective to also be considered with regard to the specific restrictions in section 11-3 of the National Insurance Act, but then simply concluded that it had not been satisfactorily demonstrated that it was with a view to obtaining employment that the recipient had to be physically present in Norway.[76]

ii. Proportionality

The EFTA Court proceeded to examine each of the three exceptions to the prohibition on export of sickness benefits under the National Insurance Act in turn and in light of the otherwise legitimate objectives, finding them all to fail to fulfil the requirements of the proportionality principle. The four-weeks-per-annum time limit for stays abroad was deemed both unsuitable and unnecessary in order to monitor compliance with the conditions for retaining the sickness benefits in question, since no comparable limitations applied for travel and stays within Norway and less restrictive means (a general control system or individual activity plans) could equally achieve this aim.[77] The same applied as far as the prior authorisation requirement was concerned, as it did not apply to travel within Norway (where unilateral reporting to NAV every 14 days sufficed) and less restrictive alternatives (prior notification schemes) seemed to be available.[78] Concerning the activity and control conditions, in something of a more *obiter* fashion, the EFTA Court concluded that these must also be deemed both unsuitable and unnecessary for countering the risk of beneficiaries falling ill when travelling to other EEA States and thereby preserving the financial balance of the Norwegian social security system.[79] There was simply no evidence put forward concerning the costs attached to this risk, and a different and less restrictive requirement of notification every second week applied for travel within Norway. In common with its assessment of each of the three exceptions, the EFTA Court seemed to emphasise a lack of persuasive evidence (or in parts a complete lack of argumentation whatsoever) on the part of Norwegian authorities backing up their arguments.

The EFTA Court's approach to the proportionality principle left very little for the Supreme Court to do. This may go some way towards explaining the Supreme Court's emphasis in its decision on the fact that statements in an Advisory Opinion from the EFTA Court on 'more specific assessments' carry less weight than statements regarding the interpretation of EEA law.[80] Notwithstanding this general, principled declaration, the Supreme Court chose not to follow up with an independent, in-depth review of the EFTA Court's proportionality assessment in this case, endorsing the EFTA Court's findings in whole.[81]

[76] ibid para 180.
[77] *N* (n 20) paras 107–13.
[78] ibid paras 114–20.
[79] ibid paras 121–28.
[80] HR-2021-1453-S, para 66.
[81] ibid paras 176–81.

V. A CLOSER LOOK AT THE EFTA COURT'S APPROACH TO THE CONSISTENCY REQUIREMENT

Looking more closely at the EFTA Court's approach to the proportionality principle, the consistency requirement (ie, that the national measures must genuinely pursue their stated, legitimate aims in a consistent and systematic manner) takes centre stage. Consistency requirements are of course nothing new in the context of proportionality assessments, and frequently appear in the judgments of the CJEU and the EFTA Court,[82] most often in assessments as to the suitability of a given national measure, but also at times in connection with their alleged necessity. The EFTA Court's opinion in the *NAV* case nevertheless sheds light on how the consistency requirement has developed over the years, exposing not only where it seems to have originated from, but also how certain internal market rules continue to converge.

In order to understand these developments, it is important to recall the different ways in which consistency arguments are used. First, where inconsistencies or contradictions exist between the national measures and other national rules or practices, which serve to undermine the very legitimacy of the aim itself, such measures may be deemed both inconsistent and unsystematic (with emphasis particularly on the latter) and therefore as unsuitable.[83]

Second, and more relevant in the NAV context, inconsistencies may also be used to show that a given national measure will not in fact be able to achieve the alleged legitimate aim behind it.[84] In other words, the inconsistency exists between the means and the ends, with the result that the measure cannot be deemed as an effective way to achieve its goal.[85] In such cases, consistency arguments arguably seem to offer little more than support to that which could already be drawn from a classic application of the suitability test (ie, determination as to the appropriateness of a given measure to achieve its goal). Consistency in this second context was indirectly touched upon in the *NAV* case. There, it was applied to evaluate the Norwegian authorities' claim that the activity and control conditions, operationalised through a system of prior authorisation for travel to other EEA States, was suitable and necessary in order to mitigate the risk of undermining the financial stability of the Norwegian social security system. This risk would otherwise follow from having to cover the costs of sickness benefit recipients needing medical treatment whilst abroad. As the EFTA Court held, the Norwegian authorities failed to present any persuasive argument or evidence that the financial viability of the wealthy Norwegian state's social security system was in fact at risk of being seriously undermined by the potential costs.[86]

[82] For case law examples, see, eg, GT Petursson, *The Proportionality Principle as a Tool for Disintegration in EU Law – of Balancing and Coherence in the Light of the Fundamental Freedoms* (Lund, Lund University, 2014) 161.

[83] See, eg, Case C-333/14 *Scotch Whisky Association and Others* ECLI:EU:C:2015:845, paras 37–38; and Case E-3/06 *Ladbrokes* [2007] EFTA Ct Rep 86, para 51.

[84] See, eg, Case C-153/08 *Commission v Spain* ECLI:EU:C:2009:618, para 42; and Case C-169/08 *Presidente del Consiglio dei Ministri* ECLI:EU:C:2009:709, paras 43–45.

[85] D Chalmers, G Davies and G Monti, *European Union Law*, 4th edn (Cambridge, Cambridge University Press, 2019) 834–35.

[86] N (n 20) para 125.

Implicitly, the point seemed to be (at least in part) that the national measure would not be capable of effectively achieving such a goal.

Third, consistency arguments may be used to expose and prevent various forms of unequal treatment on grounds other than nationality.[87] Herein lies the real added value of the development of consistency as a central facet of the proportionality test, as also illustrated in the *NAV* case itself – where it is relied upon in this manner in several places: first, in finding the four-week time limit unsuitable to achieve the aim of monitoring compliance, since no similar limitation applied as far as travel within Norway was concerned;[88] second, in finding the prior authorisation requirement unsuitable to achieve the same end, given that – again – no such requirement was imposed for travel within Norway;[89] and, third, regarding the activity and control conditions, that these must be regarded as unsuitable and unnecessary given that travelling to another EEA State posed no exceptional or additional risk of becoming sick compared to travelling within Norway.[90] To put it another way, the situations of a beneficiary travelling to another EEA State and another travelling within Norway being deemed comparable, such unequal treatment is deemed an inconsistency in itself, rendering the measure(s) in question *potentially* unsuitable to attaining the legitimate aim allegedly behind it.

It is important to note that the unequal treatment referred to here is clearly not based on nationality, but rather on other grounds or parameters.[91] This is not surprising, since otherwise it would in certain cases be impossible for a Member State to justify a breach – the justification stage would be rendered entirely redundant. Member States found in breach of free movement rules due to direct or indirect discrimination at the prior stage of investigation would otherwise automatically fail in any attempt at justification. And as we know, the CJEU has (on rare occasions) also found even directly discriminatory breaches to be justified.[92]

Whilst the three different ways in which consistency arguments may be used present nothing new in themselves, the use of the third dimension exposes another significant EU and EEA legal development in itself connected to theories of convergence between the four freedoms more generally.[93] And identifying where this aspect of the consistency requirement stems from may in turn inform us further as to how it works today.

Whilst the first express mention of the 'consistent and systematic' requirement appears to have been in the CJEU's decision in *Gambelli*,[94] Mathisen has traced the

[87] See, eg, Case C-500/06 *Corporación Dermoestética* ECLI:EU:C:2008:421, para 39; and Case C-169/07 *Hartlauer* ECLI:EU:C:2009:141, paras 54–60.

[88] *N* (n 20) para 109.

[89] ibid para 117.

[90] ibid para 126.

[91] See, eg, Case C-137/09 *Josemans* ECLI:EU:C:2010:774, para 76: 'it is important to point out that the discriminatory nature of the rules at issue in the main proceedings does not, on its own, mean that the way in which they pursue the intended objective is inconsistent'.

[92] See, eg, Case 4/75 *Rewe-Zentralfinanz* ECLI:EU:C:1975:98; and Case C-141/07 *Commission v Germany* ECLI:EU:C:2008:492.

[93] Generally concerning convergence theories, see, eg, H Toner, 'Non-discriminatory Obstacles to the Exercise of Treaty Rights: Articles 39, 43, 49 and 18' (2004) 23 *Yearbook of European Law* 275; and A Tryfonidou, 'Further Steps on the Road to Convergence Among the Market Freedoms' (2010) 35 *European Law Review* 36.

[94] Case C-243/01 *Gambelli* ECLI:EU:C:2003:597, para 67.

presence of (implicit) consistency requirements in CJEU case law all the way back to the 1980s.[95] However, having seen above how the third dimension of consistency operates, the consistency requirement might even be claimed to have originated even further back in EU history – in what are today's Articles 36 and 54 TFEU, concerning the free movement of goods and capital. As we know, Article 36 TFEU was not 'new' as such when introduced by the Treaty of Rome, being largely a copy of Article XX of the General Agreement on Tariffs and Trade (GATT) 1947 (often referred to as the 'chapeau' provision),[96] which itself was modelled on the International Convention for the Abolition of Import and Export Prohibitions and Restrictions of 1927(!).[97]

As we recall, after listing the many express derogations to restrictions on the free movement of goods, the second sentence of Article 36 TFEU provides that such restrictions shall not in any event 'constitute a means of *arbitrary discrimination or a disguised restriction* on trade between Member States' (emphasis added).[98] Article 65(3) TFEU identically provides that any derogating measures covered by the two preceding paragraphs shall not constitute a means of *arbitrary discrimination or a disguised restriction* on the free movement of capital and payments. The provisions on workers, services and establishment contain no similar requirements. However, looking at how Articles 36 and 65(3) TFEU have been interpreted and applied in practice, there seems little doubt that the CJEU and the EFTA Court have sought to close this gap by incorporating the arbitrary discrimination/disguised restriction requirement into the proportionality test, which naturally applies universally to all of the four freedoms.[99] Indeed, the CJEU has even indicated the link as much in its case law, stating how the proportionality principle constitutes the basis for the arbitrary discrimination/disguised restriction test in Article 36 TFEU.[100] The link becomes even clearer bearing

[95] G Mathisen, 'Consistency and Coherence as Conditions for Justification of Member State Measures Restricting Free Movement' (2010) 47 *Common Market Law Review* 1021, 1029. Langer and Sauter for their part have contended that its use stretches back a few years further, to CJEU case law on taxation issues from the 1990s; see J Langer and W Sauter, 'The Consistency Requirement in EU Law' (2017) 27 *Columbia Journal of European Law* 39, 53.

[96] See, eg, S Enchelmaier, 'Art. 36 TFEU: General', in P Oliver (ed), *Oliver on Free Movement of Goods in the European Union*, 5th edn (Oxford, Hart Publishing, 2010) 215, 222.

[97] The chapeau itself provides for a two-tier, cumulative test – first providing for several general exceptions, and second subjecting reliance on these to a requirement that such measures 'are not applied in a manner which would constitute a means of arbitrary or unjustifiable discrimination between countries where the same conditions prevail, or a disguised restriction on international trade'.

[98] The second sentence of Art 36 TFEU is reproduced verbatim in Art 13 EEA.

[99] As can be seen, eg, in cases such as Case C-55/94 *Gebhard* ECLI:EU:C:1995:411, para 37 (establishment), Case C-338/04 *Placanica* ECLI:EU:C:2007:133, para 49 (services) and Case C-42/07 *Liga Portuguesa*, ECLI:EU:C:2009:519, para 60 (services), where the CJEU appears to require that the national measures are 'non-discriminatory' as a separate heading under the justification assessment. All three cases concerned mandatory/public interest requirements, as opposed to express derogations.

[100] See, eg, Case 174/82 *Sandoz* ECLI:EU:C:1983:213, para 18. Emiliou therefore contends that since the arbitrary discrimination/disguised restriction test under Art 36 TFEU and the proportionality test overlap to a significant extent, they should not therefore be viewed in isolation; see N Emiliou, *The Principle of Proportionality in European Law: A Comparative Study* (Dordrecht, Kluwer, 1996) 259. Interestingly, the link between the prohibition against arbitrary discrimination/disguised restrictions set out in Art 36 TFEU and consistency requirements was raised a few years earlier in Case 34/79 *Henn and Darby* ECLI:EU:C:1979:295. The appellants in the case argued that since stricter rules existed for imports than those which applied internally, 'no consistent policy of public morality' could be said to exist, thus constituting arbitrary discrimination under today's Art 36 TFEU. The CJEU disagreed and deemed the UK authorities' reliance on the derogations to be genuine.

in mind the aim of the arbitrary discrimination/disguised restriction test, which according to the CJEU is designed to prevent the derogations mentioned in the first sentence of Article 36 'from being diverted from their proper purpose and used in such a way as to either create discrimination in respect of goods originating in other Member States or indirectly protecting certain national products'.[101] The consistency requirement, as part and parcel of the principle of proportionality, naturally has the same objective of filtering out unmeritorious claims in view. There is also an uncanny resemblance between the situations where arbitrary discrimination or a disguised restriction in trade has been considered to exist, and those deemed by the CJEU or the EFTA Court to constitute inconsistencies born out of unequal treatment.[102] Simply put, it seems as though the majority of (if not all) national measures deemed to fall foul of the second sentence of Articles 36 and 65(3) TFEU by the CJEU in the past could be dealt with as an issue of (in)consistency under the proportionality assessment today. This much seems apparent from the fact that in quite a few recent cases where Article 36 or 65 derogations have been relied upon, the CJEU makes no mention of the express prohibition against arbitrary discrimination/disguised restrictions whatsoever, simply applying the consistency requirement in its place.[103]

However, the introduction and development of the consistency requirement not only broadens the scope of equal treatment assessments under the TFEU and Main Part of the EEA Agreement. It also both alters and strengthens the suitability strand of the proportionality test, which has changed rather dramatically from one based solely on the relationship between the means and ends in terms of adequateness or appropriateness, by taking on an additional requirement of equal treatment on grounds other than nationality. The consistency requirement also amplifies the more traditional, classic 'means and ends' suitability test, too. Traditionally, little seems to have been required before a state could maintain that a given measure was suitable for attaining an (at least in principle) accepted legitimate aim. Showing how a measure pursues its aim in a consistent and systematic fashion may arguably lend a robustness to proving the effectiveness of the measure in question.

Integrating the arbitrary discrimination/disguised restriction requirement into the proportionality test has in turn also had the effect of extending their remit beyond the express derogations set out in Articles 36 and 65(3) TFEU. As part of the general proportionality assessment, the consistency requirement will naturally also apply in

[101] See, eg, cases such as Case 34/79 *Henn and Darby* ECLI:EU:C:1979:295, para 21; Case C-170/04 *Rosengren and Others* ECLI:EU:C:2007:313, paras 41–42; Case C-434/04 *Ahokainen and Leppik* ECLI:EU:C:2006:609, paras 29–30; and Case C-198/14 *Visnapuu* ECLI:EU:C:2015:751, paras 123–29. Therefore, this was aptly described as a 'notwithstanding' requirement; see, eg, LW Gormley, *EU Law of Free Movement of Goods and Customs Union* (Oxford, Oxford University Press, 2009) 502.

[102] *cf* the findings of the EFTA Court set out above with, eg, Case 53/76 *Bouhelier* ECLI:EU:C:1977:17, para 15, where the CJEU found a French measure requiring quality certificates for watches due for export to constitute arbitrary discrimination, since no similar requirement was imposed on watches destined for the domestic French market. Similarly, in Case 152/78 *Commission v France* ECLI:EU:C:1980:187, para 18, French advertising restrictions on alcoholic beverages were deemed to constitute arbitrary discrimination as they affected imported alcoholic goods more heavily than (at least certain) domestically produced alcoholic drinks.

[103] See, eg, Case C-161/09 *Kakavetsos-Fragkopoulos* ECLI:EU:C:2011:110; Case C-648/18 *ANRE* ECLI:EU:C:2020:723; and Case C-663/18 *Criminal Proceedings against B S and C A* ECLI:EU:C:2020:938.

situations where the court-made mandatory/public interest requirements are relied upon to justify restrictions on the free movement of goods and capital.

It has been said that the introduction of consistency generally makes it easier to justify a restriction.[104] Had the test merely centred on the objective element of whether an inconsistency is present or not, this would undoubtedly be true. Yet the test also contains a subjective element. Just as with Articles 36 and 65(3) TFEU, which require the unequal treatment or restriction to be *arbitrary or disguised*, the condition that the unequal treatment or restriction is *genuine* involves a rather clear value judgment to be made by the court assessing the justification alleged by the Member State in question.[105] This may obviously prove a delicate issue, as it requires the court to look behind the reasons provided and question the state's intentions and whether it believes these to be true or not. And the very finding of a breach of the proportionality principle owing to an inconsistency, with no less than three examples of this in the *NAV* case, implies that the state in question has acted disingenuously, even if this is not explicitly stated in the judgment or opinion itself.

Tied in with the subjective element, there are also certain interesting points to note concerning the burden of proof in the *NAV* case. As we know, the burden naturally rests with the EEA States, and the amount of evidence required may varies quite considerably from one case to another – from almost nothing to a rather strict burden.[106] In cases where a state has been accused of pursuing an otherwise legitimate objective in an inconsistent or unsystematic manner, this has seldom been linked to a very strict burden of proof by the EFTA Court[107] – and quite rightly so in our view, since not every inconsistency can or should lead to a finding of disproportionality. To put it another way, the existence of an inconsistency is a necessary yet insufficient element in itself in finding a measure disproportionate. Whether it should be deemed so hinges on the genuine nature of the state's action. Furthermore, as stated by the CJEU in several cases, social policy – including social security – is still merely subject to coordinating EU competence and rules.[108] The fact that EEA States therefore still enjoy a wide discretion in exercising their powers in this field seems at times to be also reflected in a rather 'light' application of the proportionality principle.[109] The

[104] Mathisen (n 95) 1047.

[105] As pointed out by Gormley ((n 101) 505), as far as the second sentence of Art 36 TFEU is concerned, the use of the word arbitrary 'is, however, not superfluous and is probably meant to indicate that different treatment may in some circumstances be justified. … Overall, that second sentence acts as something of an "emergency brake" means of ensuring that the [express derogations in] the first sentence of [Art 36 TFEU] is not misused'.

[106] See, eg, T Tridimas, 'The Principle of Proportionality' in R Schütze and T Tridimas (eds), *Oxford Principles of European Union Law – Volume I: The European Legal Order* (Oxford, Oxford University Press, 2018).

[107] See, eg, Case E-3/06 *Ladbrokes* [2007] EFTA Ct Rep 86; Case E-8/16 *Netfonds* [2017] EFTA Ct Rep 163; Case E-8/17 *Kristoffersen* [2018] EFTA Ct Rep 383; and Case E-9/20 *ESA v Norway (Corporate Officers)*, judgment of 15 July 2021.

[108] That coordinating rules in this field may also have certain de facto harmonising effects has been pointed out by several writers and seems beyond doubt (see, eg, F Marhold, 'Modernisation of European Coordination of Sickness Benefits' (2009) 9 *European Journal of Social Security* 119, 127–29), although exactly how and why would certainly be deserving of further research and analysis.

[109] See, eg, the Grand Chamber ruling in Case C-213/05 *Geven* ECLI:EU:C:2007:438, paras 27–29, where the CJEU required the national authorities merely to show that they were reasonably entitled(!) to consider

NAV case thus seems to represent something of an anomaly in this respect, in several places demanding a very high evidentiary burden on the part of the state in seeking to show that its measures were consistent and systematic, and hence both suitable and necessary. The reasons invoked had to be accompanied 'by specific evidence substantiating its arguments. Such an objective, detailed analysis, supported by figures, if necessary, must be capable of demonstrating, with solid and consistent data, that there are genuine risks to the attainment of the stated objectives'.[110] The level and clarity of guidance provided on this point is commendable, and no doubt of great value more generally for national courts and authorities when seeking to decide cases at final instance. The EFTA Court's opinion also leaves little doubt as to its implied judgment over the disingenuous nature of the Norwegian state's actions. Given that the Norwegian authorities themselves publicly had admitted a wrongdoing to begin with, the fact that much would be asked of them in terms of evidence to the contrary in justifying their measures seems only natural. The very high evidentiary burden imposed in this case nevertheless warrants a small note of caution moving forward. It is important to remember that the *NAV* case is a rather exceptional case of EEA malpractice in itself. The evidence threshold should therefore not automatically be set too high simply because an inconsistency seems present in a case, but only where the genuine manner in which the objective seems to have been pursued can be called into question. In other words, the evidentiary burden should – in our view – be clearly linked to the determination of the subjective element of the consistency test. This may provide even greater clarity to national courts and authorities in applying the proportionality principle in cases, whilst also avoiding tipping the important balance that should and must exist between restrictions and justifications too far for the future.

VI. OUTLOOK

The *NAV* scandal resulted in much soul-searching in the Norwegian legal community, including in the Supreme Court. In an unprecedented move, the final acquittal of the defendant in the case discussed in this chapter was accompanied by an apology from the Supreme Court for the failure to discover the violation of his free movement rights when first hearing his case in 2017.[111] Furthermore, the Supreme Court's guidelines to lawyers appearing before it, as well as the guidelines to the Court's own clerks, have been updated to prevent similar mistakes in future cases.

However, for the EFTA Court, the *NAV* case offered an opportunity to further strengthen its relationship with Norwegian courts both generally and with the Supreme Court more particularly. This was an opportunity which the EFTA Court

that the measure in question was suitable and necessary. See further S O'Leary, 'Developing an Ever Closer Union between the Peoples of Europe? A Reappraisal of the Case Law of the Court of Justice on the Free Movement of Persons and EU Citizenship' (2008) 27 *Yearbook of European Law* 167, 188. Other cases from the field of social security where similarly light proportionality assessments were made include, eg, Case C-406/04 *De Cuyper* ECLI:EU:C:2006:491; see M Cousins, 'Citizenship, Residence and Social Security' (2007) 32 *European Law Review* 386, 393.

[110] *N* (n 20) para 119, repeated in similar terms in paras 95 and 125.

[111] HR-2021-1453-S, para 191.

seized, delivering its detailed answers to (most of) the many questions put by the Supreme Court in roughly 10 months.[112] This again allowed the Supreme Court to render final judgment in the case only two months later, on the basis of grounds largely only echoing those provided by the EFTA Court. The Supreme Court's introductory note that statements in an Advisory Opinion from the EFTA Court on 'more specific assessments' carry less weight than statements regarding the interpretation of EEA law comes across as merely a friendly reminder. And on the points in the Advisory Opinion which were not perhaps as clear as they ought to have been – concerning the distinction between 'criteria for entitlement' for a sickness benefit and 'further conditions in the application of Article 21(1) of the 2004 Regulation (see section III.C above), and the acknowledgement of re-integration of recipients of sickness benefits into the labour market as a legitimate aim under Article 36 EEA (see section IV.C.i) – the Supreme Court opted for unassertive clarification in line with the presumed intentions of the EFTA Court. It thus seems justified to claim, as the EFTA Court's President indeed has, that the *NAV* case demonstrates the 'close partnership' that now exists between the EFTA Court and Norwegian courts.[113]

The same conclusion may also be drawn when looking at the assessment of the justifications provided in the case. The requirement to genuinely pursue the accepted aim(s) in a consistent and systematic manner clearly played a central role in the EFTA Court's Advisory Opinion. The impact and increased use of consistency requirements in proportionality assessments – which has had the effect of extending two black-letter requirements related to goods and capital under the TFEU to all of the four freedoms under EU and EEA law – is rather astonishing and shows how important continued guidance and judicial dialogue remains, even concerning fundamental aspects of EEA law. The development of the consistency requirement itself does not of course help judges avoid having to make discretionary, value-based decisions on policy choices made by national authorities in the EEA States in the future. But if used properly and explained clearly to the national courts – as the EFTA Court has endeavoured to do in the *NAV* case – it may well prove of some assistance in packaging such decisions into somewhat more palatable and diplomatic terms, and with a clearer signal to national authorities as to what levels of proof may be required in a given situation to dispel any concerns the CJEU and/or the EFTA Court might have.

[112] In comparison, the average time taken by the CJEU to deal with requests for preliminary rulings was 17.3 months in 2022 (CJEU, Annual Report 2022, p 27).

[113] P Hreinsson, 'The EFTA Court – Past, Present, Future' (2023) 62 *Lov og Rett* 77–78, 78.

18

The Fosen-Linjen *Saga*
Not So Simple after All?

ALBERT SANCHEZ-GRAELLS[1]

> … altogether, our case law is more market oriented than the ECJ's. And more fact- and effect-based.
>
> – Professor Dr Dr hc Carl Baudenbacher[2]
> EFTA Court President (15 January 2003–31 December 2017)

I. THE *FOSEN-LINJEN* SAGA AS A TORTUOUS PATH TOWARDS THE EU LAW CANON

On 31 October 2016,[3] the EFTA Court received a request for an advisory opinion from the Norwegian Frostating Court of Appeal on the interpretation of the Remedies Directive[4] as it applied to a claim for damages arising from a breach of the applicable procurement rules. The request included several questions and subquestions, and was premised on the referring Court's difficulty in

[1] This chapter builds on previous analysis in my blog https://www.howtocrackanut.com (9 and 29 November 2017) and the following articles: A Sanchez-Graells, 'You Can't Be Serious: Critical Reflections on the Liability Threshold for Damages Claims for Breach of EU Public Procurement Law after the EFTA Court's *Fosen-Linjen* Opinion' (2018) 1(1) *Nordic Journal of European Law* 1; A Sanchez-Graells, 'Liability Threshold for Damages in Public Procurement: The EFTA Court's *Fosen-Linjen* Saga' (2019) 70(4) *Northern Ireland Legal Quarterly* 511; and A Sanchez-Graells, 'The EFTA Court's *Fosen-Linjen* Saga on Procurement Damages: A There and Back Again Walk' (2019) 14(4) *European Procurement & Public Private Partnership Law Review* 248. The interested reader will find additional analyses in the special issue in which the latter is included, comprising discussion by Dag Sørlie Lund on the way in which the Norwegian Supreme Court decided the underlying case.

[2] Speech to the Law Society, Competition Section, Annual Dinner, London, 22 November 2017, https://communities.lawsociety.org.uk/Uploads/m/r/w/baudenbacher-speech-competition-section-annual-dinner.pdf.

[3] Case E-16/16 *Fosen-Linjen AS v AtB AS*, para 36 (hereinafter '*Fosen-Linjen I*').

[4] Directive 89/665/EEC on the coordination of the laws, regulations and administrative provisions relating to the application of review procedures to the award of public supply and public works contracts [1989] OJ L395/33, as amended by Directive 92/50/EEC [1992] OJ L209/1 and by Directive 2007/66/EC [2007] OJ L335/31 (hereinafter the 'Remedies Directive').

reconciling the judgments of the Court of Justice of the European Union (CJEU) in *Commission v Portugal*[5] and *Strabag*,[6] on the one hand, with *Spijker*,[7] on the other.

Such stated difficulty concerned the debated relationship between the Remedies Directive and the general doctrine of state liability.[8] In particular, it concerned whether the Remedies Directive is placed within a single system of state liability under EU law, on which it builds[9] ('unitary thesis') or whether it is outside the general system and rather creates a self-standing liability regime ('separation thesis'). The core of the debate stems from the fact that, while the doctrine of state liability imposes a threshold of 'sufficiently serious' breach of EU law as a condition for liability,[10] the Remedies Directive requires Member States to implement review procedures, including provisions to 'award damages to persons harmed by *an infringement*' (emphasis added).[11] Under the unitary thesis, the requirement of 'sufficiently serious' breach would be embedded in the assessment of the relevant infringement triggering liability in damages, whereas the separation thesis would facilitate making damages available for any type of infringement.

Interestingly, this was explicitly addressed by the CJEU in *Spijker*, when it stated that Article 2(1)(c) of the Remedies Directive:

> [*G*]*ives concrete expression to the principle of State liability* for loss and damage caused to individuals as a result of breaches of EU law for which the State can be held responsible.[12]
>
> … as regards state liability for damage caused to individuals by infringements of EU law for which the state may be held responsible, *the individuals harmed have a right to redress where* the rule of EU law which has been infringed is intended to confer rights on them, *the breach of that rule is sufficiently serious*, and there is a direct causal link between the breach and the loss or damage sustained by the individuals. In the absence of any provision of EU law in that area, *it is for the internal legal order of each member state, once those conditions have been complied with, to determine the criteria on the basis of which the damage arising from an infringement of EU law on the award of public contracts must be determined* and estimated, provided the principles of equivalence and effectiveness are complied with.[13] (Emphasis added)

[5] Case C-275/03 *Commission v Portugal* EU:C:2004:632.

[6] Case C-314/09 *Strabag and Others* EU:C:2010:567.

[7] Case C-568/08 *Combinatie Spijker and Others* EU:C:2010:751.

[8] For an overview, see R Caranta, 'Damages in EU Public Procurement Law: *Fosen-Linjen* Hardly the Last Chapter' (2019) 14(4) *European Procurement & Public Private Partnership Law Review* 214, 217–20. See also S Treumer, 'Enforcement of the EU Public Procurement Rules: The State of Law and Current Issues' in S Treumer and F Lichère (eds), *Enforcement of the EU Public Procurement Rules* (Copenhagen, DJØF, 2011) 17, 37–39; and R Caranta, 'Many Different Paths, But are They All Leading to Effectiveness?' in S Treumer and F Lichère (eds), *Enforcement of the EU Public Procurement Rules* (Copenhagen, DJØF, 2011) 53, 71.

[9] For a related discussion, see S Weatherill, 'EU Law on Public Procurement: Internal Market Law Made Better' in X Groussot, J Hettne and S Bogojevic (eds), *Law and Discretion in EU Public Procurement* (Oxford, Hart Publishing, 2019) 21.

[10] This is clear from textbook accounts; see M Bobek, 'The Effects of EU Law in the National Legal Systems' in C Barnard and S Peers (eds), *European Union Law*, 4th edn (Oxford, Oxford University Press, 2023) 151, 185–86.

[11] Article 2(1)(c) of the Remedies Directive.

[12] *Spijker* (n 7) para 87.

[13] ibid para 92.

In my view, this quote provides a perfect example of the unitary thesis, and the CJEU dispelled any doubts as to the relationship between the general principle of state liability and its expression in the Remedies Directive. However, perhaps surprisingly, *Spijker* was not (immediately) universally seen as having settled the issue of the interaction between the grounds for actions for damages under the Remedies Directive and the state liability doctrine. Indeed, although it is arguable that *Spijker* had settled the question in 2010, it was still disputed in academic debates when the request for an advisory opinion reached the EFTA Court.[14]

The EFTA Court thus had an opportunity to revisit the issue and put forward its view on the state of EEA/EU procurement law. By chance, the UK Supreme Court faced the same issue at around the same time.[15] It is thus interesting to contrast the approaches of both courts.

By 2019, both the UK Supreme Court and the EFTA Court had reached the same conclusion: ie, that the CJEU had confirmed the unitary thesis in *Spijker*, and therefore the relevant threshold to qualify as infringement for the purposes of Article 2(1)(c) of the Remedies Directive for damages under that Directive is that of a 'serious breach' of a procurement rule.[16] However, both courts reached the same destination through very different paths.

The UK Supreme Court took a shortcut. In a straightforward judgment, and as a matter of the *acte clair* doctrine,[17] it appreciated no difficulties in reconciling the existing CJEU case law under the unitary thesis.[18] The UK Supreme Court emphasised that, in its view, there was 'very clear authority of the Court of Justice confirming that the liability of a contracting authority under the Remedies Directive for the breach of the [public procurement rules] is assimilated to that of the state or of a public body for which the state is responsible'.[19]

In contrast, the EFTA Court embarked on a much more tortuous path. First, at the end of 2017 in *Fosen-Linjen I*, it took the opposite view and (roughly) following a separation thesis[20] found that a '*simple breach* of public procurement law is in itself sufficient to trigger the liability of the contracting authority to compensate the person harmed for the damage incurred, pursuant to Article 2(1)(c) of the Remedies Directive' (emphasis added).[21] However, after the Frostating Court of

[14] See H Schebesta, *Damages in EU Public Procurement Law* (Heidelberg, Springer, 2016) 65–71.

[15] In the appeal against *Energysolutions EU Ltd v Nuclear Decommissioning Authority* (2015) EWCA Civ 1262.

[16] This is the rather uncontroversial view on the EU law 'canon'; see C Ginter and MA Simovart, 'Art 2 of Directive 89/665/EC' in M Steinicke and P Vesterdorf (eds), *Brussels Commentary on EU Public Procurement Law* (Oxford, Hart Publishing, 2018) 1408–10.

[17] The relevance of the explicit invocation of the *acte clair* doctrine is that the UK Supreme Court may have incurred state liability itself if it had incorrectly found no issue and thus unjustifiably withheld a request for a preliminary reference to the ECJ; see Case C-224/01 *Köbler* EU:C:2003:513, and Case C-173/03 *Traghetti del Mediterraneo* EU:C:2006:391. See M Broberg and N Fenger, *Broberg and Fenger on Preliminary References to the European Court of Justice*, 3rd edn (Oxford, Oxford University Press, 2021) 239–40.

[18] *Nuclear Decommissioning Authority v EnergySolutions EU Ltd (now ATK Energy Ltd)* (2017) UKSC 34 per Lord Mance, at [25].

[19] ibid at [25].

[20] For a more detailed discussion, see A Sanchez-Graells, 'You Can't Be Serious' (n 1) 11.

[21] *Fosen-Linjen I* (n 3) para 82.

Appeal considered that the 'judgment in *Fosen-Linjen I* "does not appear to be clearly correct" on this point',[22] it decided not to follow it, and saw its ruling appealed to the Norwegian Supreme Court; the latter decided to send a new request for an advisory opinion on the interpretation of the Remedies Directive in order to allow the EFTA Court to reconsider its approach – which it did, in August 2019. In *Fosen-Linjen II*, the EFTA Court performed a U-turn, adopted the unitary thesis[23] and found that Article 2(1)(c) of the Remedies Directive 'does not require that *any breach* of the rules governing public procurement in itself is sufficient to award damages' (emphasis added).[24]

This roundabout route is interesting because it does not derive from a misunderstanding of EU law, but from judicial activism seeking to change the rules on procurement damages under EEA (and EU) law.

II. *FOSEN-LINJEN I* AS JUDICIAL ACTIVISM

This claim that *Fosen-Linjen I* was an exercise in excessive judicial activism is supported in both external and internal considerations. Interestingly, the *Fosen-Linjen I* judgment of the EFTA Court came at the end of October 2017,[25] more than six months after the UK Supreme Court's decision.[26] Thus, there would have been ample opportunity for the EFTA Court to consider the arguments of the UK Supreme Court's view that the CJEU had settled the issue in *Spijker*, not least because the same arguments had been put to the EFTA Court by the Norwegian government.[27] However, there is no trace of the UK's antecedent in *Fosen-Linjen I*, despite the then EFTA Court's President's undoubted familiarity with it.[28]

Moreover, *Fosen-Linjen I* could have been decided without addressing the overarching relationship between the Remedies Directive and the state liability doctrine. The relevant questions by the Frostating Court of Appeal sought clarification on whether liability under the Remedies Directive was conditional on the contracting authority: (a) having deviated markedly from a justifiable course of action; (b) having incurred a material error that justified a finding of culpability under a general assessment; or (c) having incurred an inexcusable 'material, gross and obvious error' (question 1), or whether liability could be triggered under a test of 'sufficiently qualified breach'

[22] Case E-7/18 *Fosen-Linjen AS, supported by Næringslivets Hovedorganisasjon (NHO) v AtB AS*, para 32 (hereinafter '*Fosen-Linjen II*').

[23] Almost implicitly, but uncontrovertibly; see ibid para 117.

[24] ibid para 121. It should be stressed that the full finding is that Art 2(1)(c) of the Remedies Directive 'does not require that any breach of the rules governing public procurement in itself is sufficient to award damages *for the loss of profit*', which could raise the question whether the EFTA Court considered that *Fosen-Linjen I* applies in other types of damages claims. I think that would be an untenable position, but the analysis of that specific aspect of the *Fosen-Linjen* saga is relatively speculative and exceeds the possibilities of this contribution.

[25] *Fosen-Linjen I* (n 3).

[26] *Nuclear Decommissioning Authority* (n 18).

[27] *Fosen-Linjen I* (n 3) para 54.

[28] See n 2 above at section IV, para 5, where then President Baudenbacher stressed that '*Fosen-Linjen* puts the EFTA Court at variance with the UK Supreme Court's *EnergySolutions v NDA* judgment …'.

where the contracting authority was left with no discretion as to how to interpret or apply the infringed substantive rule (question 2).[29] The EFTA Court decided to group these two questions and address them together.[30] This was determinative of the outcome – ie, the finding that any breach of the EU public procurement rules can trigger liability in damages.

Had the EFTA Court addressed the questions sequentially, and inverting their order, it would have been possible to establish that a breach of a substantive provision, for which interpretation and application the contracting authority has no discretion, constitutes a 'sufficiently serious breach' of EU/EEA procurement law triggering liability (if all other requirements are met),[31] which would have rendered the other issues surrounding the interpretation of the requirement of sufficient seriousness moot and unnecessary in this case. By not doing so and seeking to address the more general issue, the EFTA Court actively sought an opportunity to reinterpret EEA/EU law, despite *Spijker*.

Although the EFTA Court eventually backtracked and re-aligned EEA law with EU law in *Fosen-Linjen II*, there are two aspects of the attempt at the re-regulation of procurement damages in *Fosen-Linjen I* that are worth exploring in more detail. First, *Fosen-Linjen I* took issue with the minimum harmonisation in the Remedies Directive. Second, *Fosen-Linjen I* sought to push for a much more extensive use of (some types of) damages as a mechanism for the private enforcement of procurement law, albeit in an internally contradictory manner. Both the issue of minimum versus maximum harmonisation and the role of damages awards would be relevant to a review of the Remedies Directive. The remainder of this chapter thus focuses on these two issues and their implications in turn, and extracts some conclusions for a long-overdue review of the Remedies Directive.[32]

III. MINIMUM VERSUS MAXIMUM HARMONISATION OF REMEDIES IN THE *FOSEN-LINJEN* SAGA

A first strand of the judicial activism in *Fosen-Linjen I* concerned an overt attempt to use the Remedies Directive to (further) level the playing field across the EEA/EU by creating equal conditions for economic operators to access procurement remedies. This required the EFTA Court to sidestep the fact that the Remedies Directive is a minimum harmonisation instrument that sets the basic elements of the effective and equivalent remedies that Member States must regulate for, in accordance with the peculiarities of their own domestic systems. This characterisation of the Remedies Directive is uncontroversial.[33] Following the logic of minimum harmonisation, it is

[29] *Fosen-Linjen I* (n 3) para 36.

[30] ibid paras 46–48.

[31] See Case C-118/00 *Larsy* EU:C:2001:368, paras 39 ff.

[32] For which there are many reasons. See, eg, A Sanchez-Graells, '"If it Ain't Broke, Don't Fix it"? EU Requirements of Administrative Oversight and Judicial Protection for Public Contracts' in S Torricelli and L Folliot-Lalliot (eds), *Oversight and Challenges of Public Contracts* (Brussels, Bruylant, 2018) 495–534.

[33] See, eg, Report by the European Commission on the effectiveness of the Remedies Directive concerning review procedures in the area of public procurement, COM (2017) 28 final at 4.

possible for Member States to facilitate the existence of two potential tiers of remedies: a lower or more basic EU tier (subject, inter alia, to the threshold of 'sufficiently serious breach') and a higher or more protective domestic tier (subject, for example, to a trigger for 'any infringement'). This higher or more protective tier may or may not exist depending on the policy orientation of each EEA/EU State, but it cannot be conceptualised as a requirement of EEA/EU public procurement law arising from the Remedies Directive.

In stark contrast to this approach, in *Fosen-Linjen I*, the EFTA Court considered that a 'requirement that only a breach of a certain gravity may give rise to damages could also run contrary to the *objective of creating equal conditions for the remedies available in the context of public procurement*' (emphasis added).[34] In stressing the need for 'equal conditions', the EFTA Court sought to configure the Remedies Directive as an instrument of maximum harmonisation. The EFTA Court had derived this objective in an earlier passage, where it stressed that a:

> [F]undamental objective of the Remedies Directive is to create the framework conditions under which tenderers can seek remedies in the context of public procurement procedures, *in a way that is as uniform as possible* for all undertakings active on the internal market. Thereby, as is also apparent from the third and fourth recitals to the Remedies Directive, *equal conditions shall be secured* [sic]. (Emphasis added)[35]

This was a clear judicial excess. The Remedies Directive cannot reasonably be considered an instrument of maximum harmonisation (ie, a tool that sets a ceiling, or even a common core of protections that must be uniformly provided in all EEA States) in the way that the EFTA Court initially did. This is particularly clear from recital (6) of the Remedies Directive, according to which 'it is necessary to ensure that *adequate procedures* exist in all the Member States to permit the setting aside of decisions taken unlawfully and compensation of persons harmed by an infringement' (emphasis added)[36] – which the EFTA Court acknowledged,[37] but then largely ignored in *Fosen-Linjen I*.

Conversely, in *Fosen-Linjen II*, the EFTA Court returned to the orthodoxy of considering the Remedies Directive as an instrument of minimum harmonisation, stressing that:

> As set out in the sixth recital of the Remedies Directive, one of the aims of the Directive is to *ensure that adequate procedures exist* in all the Member States to permit the setting aside of decisions taken unlawfully and compensation of persons harmed by an infringement. *Adequate review procedures, as formulated in the directive, must not necessarily be homogenous or identical*, they must merely satisfy minimum conditions, which are required by the Directive in order to ensure compliance with EEA law. It follows that *the Remedies Directive is an instrument of minimum harmonisation*. (Emphasis added)[38]

Despite the clear position that the Remedies Directive is an instrument of minimum harmonisation, it is interesting to dig a bit deeper into the reasons given in

[34] *Fosen-Linjen I* (n 3) para 78.
[35] ibid para 67.
[36] Note that adequate procedures are not necessarily homogeneous or identical procedures.
[37] *Fosen-Linjen I* (n 3) para 3.
[38] *Fosen-Linjen II* (n 22) para 109.

Fosen-Linjen I against such a regulatory approach. In that regard, the EFTA Court stressed that under a minimum harmonisation framework:

> Depending on the circumstances, a breach of the same provision of EEA public procurement [law] could lead to liability in one EEA State while not giving rise to damages in another EEA State. In such circumstances, economic operators would encounter substantial difficulties in assessing the potential liability of contracting authorities in different EEA States.[39]

This is a feature of the current system that relates not only to the minimum harmonisation of the Directive, but also to the (limited) general constraints resulting from the principles of equivalence and effectiveness in the design of domestic remedies in relation with those aspects where the Member States retain procedural autonomy. A finding that the available remedies were significantly different across the EEA/EU could prompt a reconsideration of whether the Remedies Directive should be revised to create an entirely homogeneous system across the EEA/EU by means of maximum harmonisation (or a Regulation). However, variation at the national level did not seem to carry any weight in the Commission's most recent review of the effectiveness of the Remedies Directive,[40] which makes this prospect unlikely. I will return to this issue in the conclusion.

IV. THE ROLE OF DAMAGES IN PROMOTING COMPLIANCE WITH EEA/EU PROCUREMENT LAW

A second strand of the judicial activism in *Fosen-Linjen I* concerned an attempt at increasing the availability of (some types of) damages to discipline the behaviour of the contracting authorities and to promote compliance with EEA/EU procurement law. Indeed, one of the most remarkable normative aspects on which the EFTA Court built its *Fosen-Linjen I* judgment concerns the incentives that different liability thresholds and requirements create for contracting authorities and economic operators. In that regard, the EFTA Court seemed to adopt two contradictory normative standpoints in dealing with the twin question of the threshold for liability and the causality requirement, which are indivisibly interlinked in its overall finding that a '*simple breach of public procurement law is in itself sufficient* to trigger the liability … *provided* that the other conditions for the award of damages are met, including, in particular, *the condition of a causal link*' (emphasis added).[41] The contradiction is as follows.

On the one hand, the EFTA Court considered that a simple infringement of EU/EEA public procurement rules must suffice to trigger liability because:

> [D]amages seek to achieve a three-fold objective: to compensate for any losses suffered; to restore confidence in the effectiveness of the applicable legal framework; and *to deter*

[39] *Fosen-Linjen I* (n 3) para 78.
[40] COM (2017) 28 final (n 33) 4.
[41] *Fosen-Linjen I* (n 3) para 82.

> *contracting authorities from acting in such a manner, which will improve future compliance with the applicable rules. Liability through damages may also provide a strong incentive for diligence in the preparation of the tender procedure, which will, ultimately, prevent the waste of resources and compel the contracting authority to evaluate the particular market's features. Were liability to be excluded, this may lead to a lack of restraint of the contracting authority*. (Emphasis added)[42]

Thus, in this part of the *Fosen-Linjen I* judgment, the EFTA Court considered a high likelihood of liability in damages a proper incentive for adequate diligence and decision making on the part of the contracting authority.

Conversely, when assessing the causality requirements for the recognition of a right to damages compensation,[43] the EFTA Court stressed that:

> [T]here must be a balance between the different interests at stake. While liability of the contracting authority for any errors committed promotes, in principle, the overall compliance with the applicable legal framework, *exaggerated liability of the contracting authority could lead to excessive avoidance costs, reduce the flexibility of the applicable framework and may even lead to the unjust enrichment of an unsuccessful tenderer. Furthermore, excessive liability may provide an incentive for a contracting authority to complete award procedures, that were evidently unlawful, or impinge upon the freedom to contract.* (Emphasis added)[44]

This led the EFTA Court to establish different tests in relation to claims in damages seeking compensation for bidding costs (negative interest) and loss of profit (positive interest),[45] with the latter rather explicitly considered a potential source of exaggerated or excessive liability. Whereas the EFTA Court advocated for a weak causation analysis for bidding cost claims,[46] it created a test that would almost always exclude causation where the claim of lost profits was based on a breach of EEA/EU procurement law that could not be reasonably remedied other than 'by cancelling a tender procedure and conducting it anew'[47] – with the logical implication that, in the counterfactual situation of a procedural or substantive defect being susceptible of correction in different ways, the test would arguably also exclude positive damage compensation, except where a contracting authority had (recalcitrantly) decided not to implement the correction (for example, by backtracking on the procedure and amending the relevant intermediate decision).

Overall, the EFTA Court's complex approach clearly indicates that it considered that the existence of liability (or rather the claimable *quantum*) needed to be constrained or modulated, even where access to remedies is seen as a positive regulatory tool. In *Fosen-Linjen I* the EFTA Court seemed to want to do so by establishing a complicated approach to causality requirements that would distinguish between those applicable to claims for negative and positive damages (ie, bid costs and loss of profits). This may have been justified due to the peculiarities of the Norwegian

[42] ibid para 76.
[43] In the context of the fourth question referred by the Norwegian court; ibid para 36.
[44] ibid para 101.
[45] ibid paras 100–07.
[46] ibid para 102.
[47] ibid para 106.

tort law system, but it is difficult to square with the general mechanism of liability in damages under EU law. Moreover, the EFTA Court had already shown some inconsistency when establishing that 'a claim for damages can only succeed if certain other conditions are fulfilled, such as the condition that *there must be a sufficient causal link* between the infringement committed and the damage incurred' (emphasis added)[48] – which, however, is not equally reflected in the wording of its general finding, which only makes reference to 'the condition of a causal link'.[49] What the EFTA Court intended with the qualifier of 'sufficient' causal link, and how this results in a functional approach that materially differs from the requirement of a 'sufficiently serious' rather than a 'simple' breach, is left unexplained.

The approach (implicitly) followed by the EFTA Court in *Fosen-Linjen I* would not have been better than the alternative approach of closely sticking to a requirement for a sufficiently serious breach of EU/EEA public procurement rules. Not even if a combination of low liability threshold (simple breach) and high causality requirements ('sufficient causality') could lead to the same practical results as a requirement for a 'sufficiently serious breach'. With simple causation analysis, the EFTA Court's approach would have created legal uncertainty and more scope for divergence across EU/EEA jurisdictions (with which it had taken issue; see section III above), not least because causation is within the remit of domestic law. In addition, it would have precluded one of the mechanisms built into EU law – in particular, the doctrine of state liability – to mitigate its effects. Under EU law, a proportionate application of the state liability doctrine is done by requiring both sufficient seriousness of the breach and direct causality in the creation of the recoverable damage. By suppressing the first proportionality requirement, *Fosen-Linjen I* would have placed all pressure on the causality mechanism, which can also have distortive effects if, for example, existing causality tests need to be adapted to compensate for the suppression of the requirement of 'sufficiently serious' breach. In other words, if lowering the threshold of a qualifying breach results in a modification of the causality analysis, as implicitly advanced in the (*obiter*) requirement for the causal link to be 'sufficient' (rather than, more simply, 'direct'). More importantly, this approach could have created a wave of litigation based on any (minimal, formal or irrelevant) errors in the conduct of procurement procedures in an attempt to test the boundaries of the trigger for liability in damages – at the very least in relation to claims for reimbursement of bidding costs.

On the whole, it is preferable to stick to the general framework of the state liability doctrine as specified in the Remedies Directive. Therefore, the approach followed by the EFTA Court in *Fosen-Linjen II* is preferable, although there are some lingering questions on the extent to which the interpretation of the causality requirement in *Fosen-Linjen I* still holds and how it interacts with the more general position on the need for a serious breach of EEA/EU procurement law. In that regard, it is worth stressing that *Fosen-Linjen I* made the above-mentioned distinction between the causation analysis in relation to claims in damages seeking compensation for negative

[48] ibid para 81.
[49] ibid para 82.

and positive interests *as a matter of EEA/EU law*,[50] whereas *Fosen-Linjen II* simply stressed that, as a matter of EU/EEA law, the existence of liability is premised not only on the existence of a sufficiently serious breach, but also of 'a *direct causal link* between the breach of the obligation resting on the state and the damage sustained by the injured party' (emphasis added).[51] It can be argued that, in its return to the EU law canon, *Fosen-Linjen II* deactivated the interpretation in *Fosen-Linjen I* and devolved the issue of causation to the domestic domain, with subjection only to the general requirements of the principles of effectiveness[52] and equivalence. However, given that *Fosen-Linjen II* did not explicitly disavow or retract *Fosen-Linjen I*, further issues can arise down the line. Be that as it may, the issue of the proper role of damage compensation could feature in a future revision of the Remedies Directive. I will return to this in the concluding section below.

V. CONCLUSIONS

Having a major supranational court perform such a U-turn as the EFTA Court did in the *Fosen-Linjen* saga is a rare occurrence. As an outsider, it is hard to assess the extent to which the *Fosen-Linjen* saga may have damaged or improved the reputation of the EFTA Court. In my view, while *Fosen-Linjen I* was an excessive exercise in judicial activism that could have undermined the credibility of the Court, the fact that – with the aid of the creative approach of the Norwegian Supreme Court finding a way to send a second request for an advisory opinion – the EFTA Court (albeit with a different composition) found a way to correct at least the most direct affront to the principle of uniform interpretation and the goal of legal homogeneity that *Fosen-Linjen I* had created in sidelining the CJEU's *Spijker* judgment speaks volumes about its institutional commitment to sincere cooperation and judicial dialogue, and should be a boon to its international standing and reputation going forward.

More generally, in relation to the substance of the legal dispute, the *Fosen-Linjen* saga offers some opportunity to reconsider some aspects of the Remedies Directive in a future (long-overdue) review. First, the choice of instrument could be revisited. A minimum harmonisation directive may fall short of creating a homogeneous system of procurement remedies across the EEA/EU, as the EFTA Court, in *Fosen-Linjen I*, gingerly disliked. However, the alternative of a maximum harmonisation directive, or even the adoption of a regulation, would not necessarily be preferable, especially as the remedy of damages is concerned, as sectoral EU economic law using damages to boost its private enforcement generates significant legal issues at the domestic level.[53] It may seem that a preferable approach would be to retain the choice of instrument,

[50] ibid paras 100–07.

[51] *Fosen-Linjen II* (n 22) para 117.

[52] ibid para 117.

[53] For a discussion in the context of competition law, see O Odudu and A Sanchez-Graells, 'The Interface of EU and National Tort Law: Competition Law' in P Giliker (ed), *Research Handbook on EU Tort Law* (Cheltenham, Edward Elgar, 2017) 154–83, as well as the rest of the contributions to that volume in relation to other areas of EU law.

but to consider raising the level of the minimum harmonisation, as well as widening the set of issues covered by the Directive. Second, and in that connection, the possibility of establishing two tiers of claimable damages should be assessed in detail. In ways not too dissimilar from how it featured in *Fosen-Linjen I*, the potential need to facilitate access to reimbursement of bidding costs at a lower threshold of 'impropriety' or 'illegality' in the conduct of procurement procedures than for other types of (more substantial) financial compensation – or to cap the latter to avoid 'excessive' or 'exaggerated' liability – has been evidenced in other contexts of procurement regulation discussion, such as the current process of revision of the UK domestic rules post-Brexit. It may be that such a change could create a moderate incentive for more private enforcement of the EEA/EU procurement rules without opening the floodgates of relatively speculative litigation seeking lost profits.

However, it seems that one of the crucial issues that a review of the Remedies Directive should address is the balance between public and private enforcement of EEA/EU public procurement rules. In line with the programmatic goals of the judicial activist intervention in *Fosen-Linjen I*, there are growing calls for the review of EEA/EU procurement law to facilitate private enforcement, but for very different reasons – for example, while the EFTA Court in *Fosen-Linjen I* could be charged with having tried to create a more 'market-oriented' (or business-friendly) case law than the CJEU did in *Spijker*, other recent calls are concerned with the promotion of sustainable procurement.[54] This could, for example, lead well-meaning courts to 'creatively review' the rules on active standing to find ways to overcome the constraints in Article 1(3) of the Remedies Directive. However, such intervention would be as much an instance of excessive judicial activism as *Fosen-Linjen I* was. Regardless of the normative background or justification for a change of current EEA/EU procurement law, legal reform cannot be attained through the courts. This clearly emerges from the *Fosen-Linjen II* judgment and its very intentional return to the EU law canon with minimalistic aspirations.

On the whole, there is plenty to reflect on in terms of the way in which the *Fosen-Linjen* saga unfolded, both in the detail of the specific issues of procurement regulation it raises, and the broader themes of the role and position of the EFTA Court, and the CJEU as well. In my view, it is certainly a remarkable set of judgments of the EFTA Court in its first 30 years. May many more come.

[54] See R Caranta, 'Opening the Doors to Civil Society Litigation in Public Contracts' (*REALaw.blog*, 1 November 2022), https://realaw.blog/?p=1909.

19

Taking Procedures Seriously

The Case Law of the EFTA Court in the Field of State Aid

GJERMUND MATHISEN*

I. A RETROSPECTIVE

STATE AID LAW is a field where rather a lot can turn on procedure, and on administrative procedure in particular. That is not unique to this field, nor is it a surprising feature of the law. It might even appear a somewhat tedious aspect to state aid control. Be that as it may, I would advise that taking procedures seriously is a good rule of life – or certainly if life is being a state aid lawyer. What is more, I would argue that a good share of the EFTA Court's case law in this field may usefully be viewed through the lens of taking procedures seriously and discussed in that particular light.

That said, there is of course more to the EFTA Court's case law than procedure. It has substance and it has depth, and it remains thus, even if the number of judgments continues to be limited, as is expected in an EFTA pillar of three states. From the Court's case law in the field of state aid, we have learned about issues ranging from the notion of state aid to recovery and the scope of the EEA Agreement. So, after 30 years of the EFTA Court as a state aid court, a case law retrospective seems in order or even called for. Whilst the most recent judgments are often the ones we discuss the most, on occasion it may indeed be fitting to also go back and bring older judgments to the fore again. And what is 30 years if not an occasion?

Wanting to curate this retrospective of sorts and wanting to put some particular focus on taking procedures seriously, one is faced very early on with the question of which works (or EFTA Court decisions) to include and which to exclude. I shall not spill much ink explaining my 'artistic choices' in this respect other than to say that I will not be dwelling on decisions that – while relating to state aid cases – deal exclusively with *Court* procedures (such as dismissing an application as inadmissible).

* Thanks to Luna Henry for valuable feedback.

In presenting the cases that I have selected, I have decided not to opt for any strict chronology; rather, old and new will be juxtaposed and compared. However, we shall start our tour at the beginning.

II. THE BEGINNING: REASONS, PLEASE!

In any good retrospective, there is a place for an artist's (or in this case a court's) early work. And even if somehow on the margins, this early work touched on state aid.[1] The second case (yes, already the second case) lodged at the Court, *Scottish Salmon Growers*, sprung out of the EFTA Surveillance Authority (ESA)'s handling of a complaint regarding state aid.[2] In February 1994, a complaint had been lodged with ESA by the Scottish Salmon Growers Association against alleged state aid within the Norwegian fish farming industry. The complaint was dismissed the following month, as ESA found it lacked the competence to assess state aid measures in the fisheries sector.[3] The applicant challenged ESA's decision to dismiss their complaint.

ESA's quick decision in March 1994 must be seen against the legal background that Article 4(1) of Protocol 9 to the EEA Agreement contains special rules on trade in fish and other marine products, including on aid granted through state resources to the fisheries sector. Moreover, in Protocol 26 to the EEA Agreement on the powers and functions of ESA in the field of state aid, Article 1 outlines the state aid rules for which the Authority shall have surveillance powers, without including the provisions in Protocol 9.[4]

With its judgment of 21 March 1995, the Court annulled ESA's decision for infringement of an essential procedural requirement: the duty to state reasons. In hindsight – and is that not what a retrospective is about? – this might seem obvious. The only reasoning in the half-page Decision was the one sentence: 'The relevant provisions of the Agreement on the European Economic Area do not confer upon the Surveillance Authority the competence to assess State aid to fisheries'(!) Yet, at the time, ESA argued forcefully before the Court that the decision was 'sufficiently reasoned'.[5]

Having had the Court send the complaint back for reconsideration, ESA proceeded, after a more in-depth assessment, to confirm its earlier decision.[6]

[1] Some elements in the following draw on G Mathisen, 'State Aid Control in the EEA. Whence? Hence? A Look at 25 Years and Counting' (2020) *Beiheft 1 Europarecht* 313.

[2] Case E-2/94 *Scottish Salmon Growers Association Ltd v EFTA Surveillance Authority* [1994–95] EFTA Ct Rep 59. The Court's very first case, Case E-1/94 1994 *Ravintoloitsijain Liiton Kustannus Oy Restamark* [1994–95] EFTA Ct Rep 15, lodged at the Court just one day earlier on 27 April 1994, was a request for an Advisory Opinion, from the Appeals Committee at the Finnish Board of Customs concerning the Finnish state monopoly on the commercial import of alcohol. And so it was that the EFTA Court could get to work in the spring of 1994 with a good deal of salmon, a fair amount of Italian red wine and a couple of cases of whisky.

[3] ESA Document No 207152 of 24 March 1994.

[4] See further below regarding Case E-12/16 *Marine Harvest ASA v EFTA Surveillance Authority* [2017] EFTA Ct Rep 807.

[5] See the Report for the Hearing, para C.4, p 11.

[6] Decision No 195/96/COL.

Again, ESA maintained that state aid in the fisheries sector could not be controlled by ESA under the EEA Agreement, but only by the Contracting Parties themselves. But this time, now taking procedures seriously, the Decision came in at 14 pages, offering extensive reasoning. Since then, ESA has only once lost a state aid case at the EFTA Court for lack of reasoning, and then only in part.[7] The Court has instead been more preoccupied with another procedural issue: the initiation of the formal investigation procedure by ESA.

III. THE COURT'S RALLYING CRY: INVESTIGATE!

The Court wants ESA to open formal investigations in state aid cases. The Court very much wants that – to the point where one could almost imagine a caricature (though obviously a most respectful one) with the Court striking its gavel and ordering that ESA: 'Investigate!'

What is it in the case law that might lead someone to see the Court's work in this way? Well, for one thing there is ESA losing, and losing badly, on most occasions when it has been challenged for not initiating the formal investigation procedure. Looking at the Court's case law in retrospect, one can see this already from the early years, at least by squinting – as a keen student of the Court's early work might want to do. The judgment in *Husbanken II*[8] is complex, and admittedly ESA did not lose the case because it failed to initiate the formal investigation procedure. The applicant had complained to ESA about the framework conditions for the Norwegian State Housing Bank, but ESA essentially found this existing aid compatible and closed the case without further action. The Court also concurred with ESA that the aid at issue constituted existing aid. Therefore, the issue was whether to propose appropriate measures.[9] The Court held that ESA enjoyed 'broad discretion' in 'the prescribed review of existing aid'.[10] However, the Court still annulled ESA's Decision, not because the Court was able to conclude that ESA's conclusions were substantively wrong, but because ESA in its Decision 'did not go into depth' and failed to carry out 'complex analyses and assessments which the Court cannot carry out but which must be done by the EFTA Surveillance Authority'.[11] It only

[7] Jinx. The case at issue was Case E-14/10, *Konkurrenten.no AS v EFTA Surveillance Authority* [2011] EFTA Ct Rep 266('*Konkurrenten I (Oslo Sporveier)*'), which will be further elaborated upon below. In one other case, though, ESA had a close shave. See Case E-6/98 *The Kingdom of Norway v EFTA Surveillance Authority* [1999] EFTA Ct Rep 74, ('*Social Security Contributions*'), para 70: 'The Court does not find that there are sufficient grounds for annulling the Decision for lack of reasoning covering factors other than those warranting the granting of regional transport aid but emphasises that it is the obligation of the EFTA Surveillance Authority, in considering a revised system of regional aid, to consider all aspects of the matter.' The case concerned the validity of proposed appropriate measures in an existing aid case (regionally differentiated social security contributions).

[8] Case E-4/97 *Norwegian Bankers' Association v EFTA Surveillance Authority* [1999] EFTA Ct Rep 1 ('*Husbanken II*'). Note that there was no separate *Husbanken I* case, but the name *Husbanken I* has been used to refer to the Court's separate Decision on admissibility, of 12 June 1998, in the same case.

[9] ibid paras 19–37 of the judgment.

[10] ibid para 36.

[11] ibid paras 68 and 70.

takes a little bit of squinting to see that the Court wanted ESA to investigate, and to investigate thoroughly. And if confirmation were needed, the Court provided it in its observations on the applicant's plea of insufficient reasoning. Here, the Court noted that it was annulling the decision 'on the basis of the arguments … which are, in part, closely linked to the arguments concerning the statement of reasons' and so it was 'not necessary to deal further with whether the reasoning is sufficient'.[12] Seeing this, a critic might propose that the Court preferred to order that ESA carry out a thorough investigation rather than 'just' annulling the Decision on reasons, which would leave ESA free to re-adopt the Decision with additional reasoning added.[13]

Much the same can be seen more than 23 years later, reading the Court's judgment in *Sýn*.[14] The applicant challenged ESA's refusal to initiate a formal investigation into alleged unlawful aid to the company Farice for investment into a submarine telecommunications cable from Iceland to Europe. Reading the judgment, one could be forgiven for thinking that the Court wanted ESA to initiate the formal investigation procedure so much that the Court *almost* seems to imagine sufficient reasoning in order to be able to review whether the procedure should have been opened.[15] However, this is not a criticism of the Court's approach, and it is not quite what the Court actually does. Rather, the Court explains its approach (and explains it well) by stating that 'if the assessment carried out by ESA during the preliminary examination is insufficient or incomplete, this constitutes evidence of the existence of serious difficulties'.[16] The line between insufficient or incomplete assessment and insufficient reasoning is blurry, and it is an entirely justifiable judicial choice to draw the line such that insufficient reasoning takes a less prominent place as a ground for annulment.[17] In *Sýn*, the Court very clearly does just that by drawing on arguments that the applicant had only made in support of its plea of insufficient reasoning in order to examine the applicant's plea of failure to initiate the formal investigation procedure.[18] By way of an example, the Court finds that:

> Even though ESA states in the contested decision that it would apply the guidelines by analogy, where relevant, the reasoning in the contested decision leaves little, if any, trace

[12] ibid para 71.

[13] After *Husbanken II*, ESA investigated, but still wound up finding the aid at issue to be (existing aid) compatible with the functioning of the EEA Agreement; see ESA's Decision No 121/00/COL. Indeed, in no case has the formal investigation procedure initiated after the Court's annulment of the initial decision led to any material change that favoured the applicant. See further Mathisen (n 1) 319.

[14] Case E-4/21 *Sýn hf v EFTA Surveillance Authority*.

[15] Your author is painfully aware that as ESA's Director of State Aid at the time, he bore responsibility for any shortcomings (in the reasoning or otherwise) in the Decision at issue.

[16] *Sýn* (n 14) para 59 of the judgment, with reference to Case E-9/19 *Abelia and WTW v EFTA Surveillance Authority*, para 82, which in turn refers to Case E-1/13 *Míla I*, para 91, which refers to Case E-1/12 *Den norske forleggerforening*, para 107, which in turn refers to Case T-304/08 *Smurfit Kappa Group* ECLI:EU:T:2012:351, para 81.

[17] It also appears consistent with more recent case law at the EU Courts; see, eg, Case T-167/19 *Tempus Energy Germany GmbH and T Energy Sweden AB v Commission*, EU:T:2021:645, para 51, and the case law cited therein: 'It is for the applicant to prove the existence of serious difficulties or doubts. It may do so by reference to a body of consistent evidence, in particular, by claiming and establishing that the examination carried out by the Commission during the preliminary examination procedure was insufficient or incomplete.'

[18] *Sýn* (n 14) paras 69 et seq of the judgment.

of the principles in the guidelines actually being applied. This is an indication that ESA's preliminary examination was incomplete.[19]

On this basis, the Court in *Sýn* annulled ESA's decision for failure to initiate the formal investigation procedure and dispensed with considering the applicant's plea of insufficient reasoning.[20]

Between *Husbanken II* and *Sýn*, there are a number of other judgments where ESA lost a challenge because it failed to initiate the formal investigation procedure. ESA lost the case outright on this basis in *HFF*,[21] *Den norske forleggerforening*[22] and *Míla I*.[23] Also in these cases, one can see that the Court draws on arguments that could have been assessed as pertaining to a lack of reasoning in its assessment of whether ESA failed to open a formal investigation.[24] *Kimek Offshore* is much the same,[25] with the one distinction that ESA's Decision was only annulled in part.

The odd case out, at first glance, is *Konkurrenten I (Oslo Sporveier)*,[26] where ESA did lose the case, but only in part on the basis that it had failed to open a formal investigation. Other parts of ESA's Decision were annulled for a breach of the duty to state reasons. Here, the Court underlined that 'an absence of or inadequate statement of reasons constitutes an infringement of an essential procedural requirement'.[27] And the Court found that because 'the grounds of the contested decision did not make it clear how and for what reasons ESA' arrived at its conclusions, 'the Court is not in a position to address' the plea that ESA failed to open a formal investigation.[28] These findings should, however, be seen in the light that the main issue here was whether to categorise the aid in question as existing aid or new aid. If aid must indeed be categorised as existing aid, a different procedure applies. Thus, it is logical, as long as it is not in a position to decide whether the aid is new or existing, for the Court rather to focus on reasons.

Yet, where ESA has been challenged for decisions adopted after having carried out a formal investigation procedure, ESA has not lost a single case.[29] Four of these

[19] ibid para 75.

[20] ibid para 79.

[21] Case E-9/04 *The Bankers' and Securities Dealers' Association of Iceland v EFTA Surveillance Authority* [2006] EFTA Ct Rep 42 ('*HFF*'). This case concerned the operation of the publicly owned Icelandic Housing Financing Fund.

[22] This case concerned alleged aid to Nasjonal Digital Læringsarena, an entity set up by Norwegian municipalities in order to purchase digital learning material with a view to publishing it on the internet free of charge.

[23] This case concerned alleged aid through the subsidised lease of optical fibres in Iceland previously operated on behalf of the North Atlantic Treaty Organization (NATO).

[24] Perhaps the clearest examples can be seen in *Den norske forleggerforening* (n 22) paras 127 and 134, and *Míla I* (n 22) paras 100–01 and 104.

[25] Case E-23/14 *Kimek Offshore AS v EFTA Surveillance Authority* [2015] EFTA Ct Rep 412, paras 113–20. The case concerned a specific part of the Norwegian scheme for regionally differentiated social security contributions.

[26] *Konkurrenten I (Oslo Sporveier)* (n 7). The case concerned aid to the municipal bus company in Oslo.

[27] ibid para 46 of the judgment.

[28] ibid para 62.

[29] Jinxed! After submission of this chapter, ESA did lose such a case, specifically Case E-10/22 *Eviny AS v EFTA Surveillance Authority*. The EFTA Court annulled ESA's decision chiefly because ESA had failed to meet its burden of proof as to the existence of an 'advantage'.

cases have been dismissed as inadmissible.[30] One was withdrawn.[31] In the remaining six, the applications were dismissed in full,[32] sometimes with ESA receiving high marks from the EFTA Court for its handling of the formal investigation.[33] ESA also handily won the two actions it has lodged against a Member State for failure to comply with a recovery decision taken pursuant to a formal investigation.[34]

However, for challenges to decisions that ESA adopted without opening a formal investigation, the number of applications dismissed in full, in the span of 30 years, stands at only two: *Private Barnehagers Landsforbund*[35] and the relatively recent *Abelia and WTW*.[36]

For those who might find procedures somewhat tedious – and who might now feel the need to move along – I propose, first, to have a look at the older of these two judgments from a different angle and to move in closer. Because we have here the *pièce de résistance* of our retrospective: the Court's masterpiece:

IV. THE MASTERPIECE: *PRIVATE BARNEHAGERS LANDSFORBUND* – DISSECTING THE NOTION OF AN 'UNDERTAKING'

The applicant in *Private Barnehagers Landsforbund*, the National Association of Private Kindergartens in Norway, had complained to ESA about the public financing

[30] Case E-4/15 *Icelandic Financial Services Association v ESA* [2016] EFTA Ct. Rep 131, Order of the Court of 31 March 2016 (follow-up to Case E-9/04); Case E-19/13, *Konkurrenten.no AS v EFTA Surveillance Authority* [2015] EFTA Ct Rep 52, Order of the Court of 20 March 2015 ('*Konkurrenten III (Sporveien)*') (follow-up to Case E-14/10); Case E-1/17 *Konkurrenten.no AS v EFTA Surveillance Authority* [2017] EFTA Ct Rep 989, Order of the Court of 22 December 2017 ('*Konkurrenten IV (Aust-Agder)*') (concerning aid to bus transport in Aust-Agder county, Norway); and Case E-7/16 *Míla ehf v EFTA Surveillance Authority* [2016] EFTA Ct Rep 903 ('*Míla II*'), Order of the Court of 15 November 2016 (follow-up to Case E-1/13).

[31] Case E-3/03 *Transportbedriftenes Landsforening and Nor-Way Bussekspress AS v EFTA Surveillance Authority* [2004] EFTA Ct Rep 1, Order of the President of 25 February 2004.

[32] Joined Cases E-5–7/04 *Fesil ASA and Finnfjord Smelteverk AS (Case E-5/04), Prosessindustriens Landsforening and Others (Case E-6/04) and The Kingdom of Norway (Case E-7/04) v EFTA Surveillance Authority* [2005] EFTA Ct Rep 117, regarding an electricity tax exemption for energy intensive industries in Norway (it should be noted that certain aspects of the recovery of the aid at issue in this case were only settled at the national level through a judgment of the Supreme Court in December of 2013(!); see Rt 2013 s 1665 *Hydro Søral*); Joined Cases E-4, 6 and 7/10 *The Principality of Liechtenstein, REASSUR Aktiengesellschaft and Swisscom RE Aktiengesellschaft v EFTA Surveillance Authority* [2011] EFTA Ct Rep 16 ('*Captive Insurance*') regarding taxation of captive insurance companies under the Liechtenstein Tax Act; Joined Cases E-10 and 11/11, *Hurtigruten ASA and The Kingdom of Norway v EFTA Surveillance Authority* [2012] EFTA Ct Rep 758, concerning additional funding etc for Hurtigruten's ferry service from Bergen to Kirkenes on the Norwegian coast; Joined Cases E-17/10 and 6/11 *The Principality of Liechtenstein and VTM Fundmanagement v EFTA Surveillance Authority* [2012] EFTA Ct Rep 114 ('*Investment Companies*').on the taxation of investment undertakings under the Liechtenstein Tax Act; Case E-12/11 *Asker Brygge AS v EFTA Surveillance Authority* [2012] EFTA Ct Rep 536, concerning a land sale in Norway, a related option agreement, and whether the agreements were on market terms; and Case E-9/12 *Iceland v EFTA Surveillance Authority* [2013] EFTA Ct Rep 454 ('*Verne*'), regarding whether a sale of real estate in Iceland had been concluded on market terms.

[33] See, eg, *Verne* (n 32) paras 115–22.

[34] See Case E-2/05 *ESA v Iceland (International Trading Companies)* and Case E-25/15 *ESA* v *Iceland (Investment Incentive Scheme)*, which are discussed in further detail below.

[35] Case E-5/07 *Private Barnehagers Landsforbund v EFTA Surveillance Authority* [2008] EFTA Ct Rep 62.

[36] I am not counting *Social Security Contributions* (n 7) as it concerned the validity of proposed appropriate measures in an existing aid case, where initiating a formal investigation was not an option. By the same token, I am also not counting Case E-1/22, *G Modiano Ltd & Standard Wool (UK) Ltd v EFTA Surveillance Authority*, which again concerned existing aid.

of municipal daycare institutions. Kindergartens in Norway were (and still are) largely financed from the public purse, with parents' fees capped at a relatively low monthly figure.[37] The question was whether the financing constituted state aid. At the core of the case was the notion of state aid, which entails that a selective advantage granted from state resources may fall foul of Article 61(1) EEA if it benefits 'undertakings', but not otherwise.

Without opening a formal investigation, ESA dismissed the complaint on several grounds, one of which was that municipal kindergartens were not 'undertakings' within the meaning of Article 61(1) EEA. The EFTA Court was faced with deciding whether this was so and whether ESA faced serious difficulties or doubts in drawing that conclusion, such that the formal investigation procedure would have had to be initiated.

With reference to the definition of an 'undertaking' in Article 1 of Protocol 22 EEA, the Court noted that under EEA competition rules (of which the state aid rules form part), the concept of an 'undertaking' encompasses every entity engaged in 'economic activity', regardless of the legal status of the entity and the way in which it is financed.[38] And so at the outset, municipal kindergartens could well be 'undertakings', provided they would be engaged in 'economic activity'.

The applicant argued that municipal kindergartens would have to be considered as engaged in 'economic activity', seeing as the activity in question could well be carried on by private operators and was in fact carried out by many private operators in Norway, including the applicant's members. Dismissing these arguments with clarity and precision, the Court first set out that:

> When the nature of an activity carried out by a public entity is assessed with regard to the State aid rules, it cannot matter whether the activity might, in principle, be pursued by a private operator. Such an interpretation would basically bring any activity of the State not consisting in an exercise of public authority under the notion of economic activity. It follows that the specific circumstances under which the activity is performed have to be taken into account in order to assess whether the Norwegian municipalities, when offering their kindergarten places, are providing a service as an economic activity or whether they are exercising their powers in order to fulfil their duties towards their population.[39]

The Court then found that the notion of a 'service' within the meaning of the fundamental freedoms may inform the interpretation of the notion of an 'economic activity', which was arguably a novel approach at the time.[40] And with reference to Article 37 EEA and *Humbel*,[41] the Court noted that only services normally provided for remuneration are to be considered as services within the meaning of the EEA

[37] Indeed, compared to mostly everything else in Norway, having your children in kindergarten is positively cheap.

[38] *Private Barnehagers Landsforbund* (n 35) para 78 of the judgment.

[39] ibid para 80.

[40] See OJ Einarsson 'Article 36' in F Arnesen et al (eds), *The Agreement on the European Economic Area: A Commentary* (CH Beck/Hart/Nomos/Universitetsforlaget, 2018) 454, effectively explaining how linking the notion of 'economic activity' under the state aid rules and the notion of a 'service' under free movement law was a novel approach at the time. The approach now seems validated by Brussels through the adoption of the 'NoA', paras 28–30; see below.

[41] Case C-263/86 *Humbel and Edel*, EU:C:1988:451, which concerned free movement of services and freedom of movement for workers. The case centred on access of a worker's child to education provided by the host state and the charging of an enrolment fee which was not charged to domestic students.

Agreement and that the essential characteristic of remuneration lies in the fact that it constitutes consideration for the service rendered.[42]

Applying this to the facts of the particular case was not hard. It had been established that about 80 per cent of the costs of municipal kindergartens were borne by the public purse and that there was no connection between the actual costs of the service provided and the fee paid by the attending children's parents. ESA had also taken into account the municipalities' statutory duty to ensure that sufficient places for children below compulsory school age exist for their population, and that kindergartens in Norway have important social, cultural, educational and pedagogical purposes.[43] The Court could thus conclude, some would say with pointed conciseness, and in any case without doubts:

> [T]hat the element of remuneration is absent in the activity of municipal kindergartens in Norway. The parents' fee which constitutes only a fraction of the true costs of the service cannot be qualified as a quid pro quo vis-à-vis the municipal kindergartens, but only as a contribution to a system which is predominantly funded by the public purse. It is therefore clear that the Norwegian State, when establishing and maintaining a system where every child increases the costs incurred, is not seeking to engage in gainful activity but is fulfilling its duties towards its own population in the social, cultural and educational fields.[44]

The EFTA Court's conclusions here, and the judgment as such, have the unique distinction of being the only EFTA Court case law mentioned in the 2016 Commission Notice on the notion of state aid as referred to in Article 107(1) of the Treaty on the Functioning of the European Union (the 'NoA').[45] They are referenced in para 29 of the NoA, which deals with the notion of undertaking and economic activity in education and which reads as follows:

> The non-economic nature of public education is in principle not affected by the fact that pupils or their parents sometimes have to pay tuition or enrolment fees which contribute to the operating expenses of the system. Such financial contributions often only cover a fraction of the true costs of the service and can thus not be considered as remuneration for the service provided. They therefore do not alter the non-economic nature of a general education service predominantly funded by the public purse.

Given its inclusion in the NoA, the EFTA Court's judgment is regularly relied upon (directly or indirectly) not only by ESA and the EFTA States, but also by the Commission and EU Member States in their assessments of whether various measures may constitute state aid.[46]

[42] *Private Barnehagers Landsforbund* (n 35) paras 80–81.

[43] ibid para 82.

[44] ibid para 83.

[45] [2016] OJ C262, 19 July, p 1. Credit where credit is due: they shall remain nameless bureaucrats for the purposes of this footnote, but thanks go out to a few very dedicated colleagues at ESA who helped ensure that the Court's fine judgment in *Private Barnehagers Landsforbud* ended up *actually* being referenced in the NoA. As required of it, ESA has since also adopted its own 'EFTA(r)ised' version of the NoA, and this version is liberally sprinkled with references to additional ESA Decisions and case law from the EFTA Court (perhaps all those references that did not make it into the Commission's NoA?): [2017] OJ L342, 21 December, p 35.

[46] It also made it into Advocate General Kokott's Opinion of 16 February 2017in the important Case C-74/16 *Congregación de Escuelas Pías Provincia Betania*, EU:C:2017:135, decided by the Grand Chamber. The judgment is also frequently cited in the legal literature.

A particularly interesting instance of the judgment being relied on came in 2012, in connection with the introduction of a new scheme on the financing of *private* kindergartens in Norway. The responsible Norwegian Ministry sought guidance from ESA as to whether the envisaged new legal framework would have to be notified. In response, ESA gave a 'preliminary view'[47] – a comfort letter of sorts – noting, first, the reasoning applied by the Court in finding that the financing of *public* kindergartens did not constitute aid. And then for the slight twist: ESA proceeded to find that the situation for private kindergartens would be no different, with the system foreseeing the same kind of public financing as well as the same caps on fees to be paid by parents. Accordingly, insofar as the provision of services to children and parents is concerned, the private kindergartens are not engaged in 'economic activity' either, and so are also not 'undertakings' within the meaning of Article 61(1) EEA.[48]

V. THE DIFFICULT FOLLOW-UP: *ABELIA AND WTW*

The EFTA Court itself has also built on *Private Barnehagers Landsforbund*, notably in its judgment in *Abelia and WTW*. At the outset, the case concerned the public financing of eHealth and digital health infrastructure in the Norwegian public healthcare system, delivered by a dedicated state enterprise. However, in addition, this state enterprise also provided certain support services in the areas of procurement, information and communication technologies, and archiving. The context was a solidarity-based public healthcare system, once again with largely public financing and very limited end-user fees. However, the support services were provided to the public healthcare administration and not directly to the end users in the healthcare system.

At first glance, this may look very similar to the situation in the *TenderNed* case on electronic procurement platform services.[49] However, there was the difference, in that the services at issue in *TenderNed* were considered connected with the exercise of public powers, whereas such a connection seemed to be lacking for at least some of the support services in *Abelia and WTW*. Perhaps daringly – considering certain statements in the NoA – ESA had therefore taken a slightly different approach in the Decision at issue. Despite statements in the NoA such as 'the fact that a particular service is provided in-house has no relevance for the economic nature of the activity',[50] ESA had concluded that the support services were provided by way of 'genuine self-supply within the public sector' and therefore did not constitute 'economic activity'.[51]

[47] Letter of 3 February 2012, ESA's Document No 622986.

[48] It does not follow that the private operators would not be 'undertakings', eg, when offering their services in say a municipal tender for the operation of a kindergarten. In such a case, the private operator would be providing a 'service' to the municipality even if not providing a 'service' to the end users.

[49] Case T-138/15 *Aanbestedingskalender and Others v Commission* EU:T:2017:675 and, on appeal, Case C-687/17 P *Aanbestedingskalender and Others v Commission*, EU:C:2019:932.

[50] ibid para 14.

[51] Paragraph 135 of ESA's Decision No 057/19/COL. ESA omits any reference to para 14 of the NoA, but does refer to its pre-NoA decisional practice on 'genuine self-supply within the public sector' not constituting 'economic activity'.

ESA's line of argument was built, in part, on an abstraction from *FENIN*.[52] In concrete terms, what follows from *FENIN* is merely that the *purchase* of goods or services is considered non-economic if the sole purpose of purchasing the goods or services is to use them as input into non-economic activity (at the heart of the case was the purchase of medical goods for public hospitals in Spain). The private providers felt that the public buyers abused a dominant position and so were in breach of the competition rules for undertakings, but the Courts did not hold the buyers to constitute undertakings. What the Courts did *not* find was that the *providers* were not undertakings. However, ESA abstracted from the idea arguably underlying *FENIN*, arguing that 'even activities that by themselves could be considered to be of economic nature [*in casu* the support services], but are carried out merely for the purposes of providing another non-economic service, are not of an economic nature'. The key part of the context then became the fact that these services were 'exclusively provided to state or state owned entities charged with health administration' and that the services 'cannot be offered on the market in competition with private companies and are only provided to enable and support the provision of [non-economic] public health administration tasks'.

The EFTA Court apparently did not quite want to speak of *genuine self-supply* within in the public sector and so, whilst upholding ESA's Decision, seemingly wrapped the point in a different mesh of words: the state enterprise does not offer the services on the market, but only within the Norwegian healthcare system,[53] and the state enterprise provides services not for the purpose of offering goods and services as part of an economic activity, but in order for them to be used in the context of non-economic activity.[54] Fortunately, the Court wrapped the point in tightly, because right in the middle is not ESA's *abstraction* from *FENIN*, but an *interpretation* of *FENIN* that – if read in isolation – would go too far: 'The nature of the provision of services must be determined according to whether or not the subsequent use of the services provided amounts to an economic activity.' It cannot be that a provider of goods or services, perhaps a private commercial operator, is not engaged in 'economic activity' (and therefore is not an 'undertaking' and so is not subject to the competition rules) for the one reason that the *buyer's* activity is non-economic. The nature of the *provider's* activity must naturally be determined not only based on the nature of the relevant activity of the buyer, but also by taking into account the specific features of the provider, its provision of goods or services, and the context within which it operates.

In later practice, ESA appeared to deal with the Court's judgment in *Abelia and WTW* in just the right way. There is no more 'genuine self-supply', a term shunned by the Court. And when relying on the Court's judgment on this particular point, ESA made reference not just to that one sentence, but included the full wrapping.[55]

[52] Case T-319/99 *FENIN v Commission*, EU:T:2003:50 and, on appeal, Case C-205/03 P *FENIN v Commission*, EU:C:2006:453.

[53] ibid paras 95 and 97 of the judgment.

[54] ibid para 96.

[55] See ESA Decision No 144/20/COL Municipal eHealth (*Akson*), at fn 33, and ESA Decision No 067/23/COL Organisation of municipal digitalisation services/solutions (*DIF AS*), at fn 38.

A number of other judgments of the EFTA Court also centre on the notion of aid, and various aspects of it, including *Social Security Contributions* (selectivity), *Fesil and Finnfjord* (selectivity), *Captive Insurance* (undertaking/economic activity, selectivity), *Hurtigruten* (the *Altmark* criteria),[56] *Investment Companies* (selectivity), *Asker Brygge* (the market economy operator principle (MEOP)) and *Verne* (MEOP).[57] However, in a retrospective of the Court's state aid case law, they find themselves outshone by *Private Barnehagers Landsforbund* and also the more recent *Abelia and WTW*. We will therefore leave them to one side and glance instead at some of the Court's arguably more esoteric work in the field of state aid. Let us return first, briefly, to the scope of the EEA Agreement.

VI. THE FISH THAT FINALLY CAME BACK AND OTHER SHORT STORIES

Having begun its work in 1994 with a case about fish,[58] *Scottish Salmon Growers*, but having annulled ESA's flawed decision then for lack of reasoning, the particular issue of state aid in the fisheries sector took until 2016 to come back to the Court. In *Marine Harvest*, the Court finally appeared satisfied with ESA's reasoning and could address the substance of a complaint arguing that ESA should enforce the state aid rules of the EEA Agreement in the fisheries sector.

The Court confirmed ESA's approach, an approach that ESA had taken since 1994, maintaining that state aid in the fisheries sector cannot be controlled by ESA.[59] The applicable state aid provisions are the ones set out in Protocol 9 to the EEA Agreement, on trade in fish and other marine products, and these provisions on state aid can only be enforced by the Contracting Parties themselves.

The judgment was important in that it confirmed an important limit to ESA's state aid control.[60] And perhaps this was a *thing* in 2016, a year that also saw a request for an Advisory Opinion to the EFTA Court on the reach of the state aid rules under the EEA Agreement: *Synnøve Finden*.[61] The case centred on whether the *Pedicel* doctrine, from the Court's judgment in *Pedicel AS* v *Sosial- og helsedirektoratet*,[62] should extend to the state aid rules. Specifically, does aid for the *distribution* of dairy products outside the general product scope of the EEA

[56] See Case C-280/00 *Altmark Trans and Regierungspräsidium Magdeburg*, EU:C:2003:415, which concerned compensation for public service obligations.

[57] Only the issues dealt with most prominently are mentioned specifically – some of these cases also touched on other aspects of the notion of state aid, such as effect on trade and competition.

[58] Heading loosely based on the title of the book *Roast Chicken and Other Stories* by Simon Hopkinson, a book that *everyone* should read.

[59] See, eg, ESA Document No 285318, letter of 7 July 2004; and ESA Decision No 176/05/COL and No 729/08/COL. An example can also be gleaned from *ESA v Iceland (International Trading Companies)* (n 34) para 8.

[60] As the Court's judgment came, someone at ESA felt some degree of relief that ESA had not failed to enforce the state aid rules of the EEA Agreement in the fisheries sector for nearly 19 years.

[61] Case E-1/16 *Synnøve Finden AS v Staten v/Landbruks- og matdepartmentet* [2016] EFTA Ct Rep 931.

[62] Case E-4/04 *Pedicel AS v Sosial- og helsedirektoratet* [2005] EFTA Ct Rep. This is discussed by Ólafur Jóhannes Einarsson in ch 16 of this volume.

Agreement fall outside the material reach of Article 61 EEA? Yes, said the Court, applying the *Pedicel* doctrine also in this respect. ESA had argued otherwise,[63] but it probably would have been difficult for the EFTA Court to concur with ESA without effectively overturning *Pedicel*.[64]

VII. YOU NEVER GIVE ME YOUR MONEY

And then there is the question of the money,[65] or recovering the money granted in incompatible aid, where recovery has been ordered by ESA. This, too, is a topic that the EFTA Court has had to address in a number of judgments. *Fesil and Finnfjord* are a prominent example of a Norwegian case where the question of recovery stood front and centre. Perhaps it was also a particularly important case, at least in Norway, with the question of recovery culminating at the national level, years later, in the Supreme Court judgment in *Hydro Søral*.[66] In turn, the Supreme Court judgment informed important provisions on recovery in Norway's new Act on State Aid Procedures, which entered into force on 1 January 2023.[67] Sometimes, case law is a long game.

The Court also had to address issues of recovery, at some length, in its Liechtenstein state aid cases, *Captive Insurance* and *Investment Companies*, again (as in the Norwegian case) to no avail for the applicants.

However, it is the somewhat particular Icelandic cases on recovery that I propose we take a closer look at. There are two of these cases: *ESA v Iceland (International Trading Companies)* and *ESA v Iceland (Investment Incentive Scheme)*. The observant reader will have already noticed that they are particular in the context of state aid, in that they are neither actions for annulment against ESA's decisions nor requests for an Advisory Opinion. They are direct actions against a Member State: Iceland. But they are not the normal infringement cases under Article 31 that follow on from a letter of formal notice and a reasoned opinion. Instead, ESA, in both these cases, relied on the special legal basis found in the second subparagraph of Article 1(2) of Part I of Protocol 3 of the EFTA Surveillance and Court Agreement (SCA), which allows ESA to refer the matter to the EFTA Court directly if an EFTA State fails to comply with a recovery decision:

> If the EFTA State concerned does not comply with this decision within the prescribed time, the EFTA Surveillance Authority or any other interested EFTA State may, in derogation from Articles 31 and 32 of this Agreement, refer the matter to the EFTA Court directly.

[63] ibid para 53 of the judgment. ESA so argued even though its own decisional practice in the field of state aid since *Pedicel* had effectively followed the doctrine from the judgment; see, eg, ESA Decision No 166/08/COL on alleged state aid with regard to the Norwegian reindeer slaughter industry.

[64] And that was perhaps just too much to be hoping for ….

[65] Heading from that song by Lennon/McCartney.

[66] *Hydro Søral* (n 31).

[67] Lov 4 mars 2022 nr 7 om nasjonale saksbehandlingsregler i saker om offentlig støtte (støtteprosessloven) §§ 12–14; see, eg, Prop 212 L (2020–2021) point 7.4.4 on p 53.

In both cases ESA had carried out a formal investigation, following which it had ordered Iceland to recover incompatible aid granted under schemes that Iceland, in full or in part, had failed to notify. When Iceland failed to fully comply with the decisions and to inform ESA of the necessary steps taken within the time limits prescribed, ESA availed itself of this expedited procedure in order to ensure compliance. The fact that Iceland also had not challenged ESA's recovery decisions before the Court within the deadline laid down in Article 36 SCA made the cases particularly difficult for Iceland to argue, but still the Court left little doubt that it would have upheld the decisions in any case. For the keen student of procedures, these little-discussed judgments do contain a few gems of statements from the Court. We learn, for example, that '[a]n excessive length of procedure may indeed render a decision unlawful'.[68] Beyond referencing the principle of good administration[69] and Article 7(6) and (7) of Part II of Protocol 3 SCA, the Court offers no specifics, but at least ESA cannot say that it has not been put on notice!

VIII. A BRIEF NOTE ON COMPATIBILITY

Before drawing our retrospective towards a close with a subject for the aficionados (I will hold you in suspense), a brief note on 'compatibility' is in order. It would be odd to leave it out altogether. The compatibility of aid with the functioning of the EEA Agreement is at the heart of ESA's work on state aid cases and it has not been absent from cases litigated at the EFTA Court. Early examples include *Husbanken II* (services of general economic interest (SGEI)) and *Social Security Contributions* (regional aid). Later examples include *Fesil and Finnfjord* (environmental aid), *HFF* (SGEI) and *Hurtigruten* (rescue and restructuring).

However, compatibility has hardly been at the core of the case law of the EFTA Court overall, and certainly not (or at least not so far) after the seminal Grand Chamber judgment in *Hinkley Point C* in the autumn of 2020.[70] In a nutshell, this judgment redrew the structure of the compatibility assessment as compared to Commission (and ESA) practice going back to the Commission's State Aid Modernisation (SAM) reform of 2012. Whereas the Commission and ESA may still be able to arrive at much the same conclusions as to compatibility, at least in most cases, their analyses must now be conducted differently. By way of an example, on the one hand, they can no longer put the same limits on what objectives may justify state aid; on the other hand, the negative effects of the state aid at issue must be clearly identified and properly weighed against the positive effects.

Pending exciting new judgments on compatibility that eventually surely will come, let us therefore instead move on to the penultimate part of this case law retrospective and look at another exciting issue of state aid in the EFTA pillar.

[68] *ESA v Iceland (International Trading Companies)* (n 34) para 22. Any new case on this today should arguably take due account of Art 41 of the Charter of Fundamental Rights of the European Union.

[69] A principle that in *Hurtigruten* (n 32) para 301 is referred to as 'a fundamental principle of EEA law'.

[70] Case C-594/18 P *Austria v Commission*, EU:C:2020:742 ('*Hinkley Point C*').

IX. EXCITING AID

For state aid lawyers in the EFTA pillar, *existing aid* is still genuinely exciting, even 30 years on. Existing aid can be a lot of things, such as authorised aid or aid with regard to which the limitation period has expired, but the exciting thing is that even today we still see what one might call cases concerning 'existing-existing aid'[71] – that is, cases concerning aid granted under schemes that were put into effect before, and are still applicable after, the entry into force of the EEA Agreement.[72] It was only natural, or at least to be expected, that such cases would make it to the Court in the early years. We saw examples of that with *Husbanken II* and *Social Security Contributions*. Then one would expect these cases to be fewer and farther between. Indeed, the next example of such a case would be *Konkurrenten I (Oslo Sporveier)*, where the main substantive issue was whether to categorise the aid in question as (existing-)existing aid or new aid.[73]

Therefore, it was really rather exciting when *Modiano* landed at the EFTA Court, with the applicants challenging ESA for having dismissed their complaint essentially because ESA considered the aid at issue to constitute existing-existing aid.[74] On the facts, the case concerned something as esoteric as aid to Norwegian sheep farmers and to wool-collecting stations in Norway (yes, wool falls firmly *inside* the product scope of the EEA Agreement). Before the Court, the case raised a number of intriguing issues of Court procedure, but for the state aid aficionado, the exciting bit is the Court's discussion of when alterations to an existing aid scheme may result in new aid. Indeed, the judgment neatly summarises the relevant case law from both sides of Avenue John F Kennedy at Kirchberg and gives a masterclass in how to apply it.[75]

There is just one thing (there is always one thing, of course), and that is the matter of taking procedures seriously (again). Reading the judgment very closely, the reader may be left with the understanding that if there were doubts or serious difficulties concerning the compatibility of an *existing* aid scheme with the functioning of the EEA Agreement, ESA would have to open a formal investigation procedure.[76] Maybe this is reading the judgment *too closely*. Maybe it is reading things into the judgment that are not there. Still, the EFTA Court was very clear in the old *Husbanken II*, and it was arguably a missed opportunity when the Court in *Modiano* did not refer back to its very first (existing-)existing aid case, *Husbanken II*:

> In reviewing cases concerning State aid, it is necessary, in order to determine what procedural rules are applicable, to consider whether the alleged State aid constitutes 'existing aid' or 'new aid' … since the procedural rules are different.

[71] Credit where credit is due: if memory serves, it was Michael Sanchez Rydelski who coined the term.

[72] See Art 1 of pt II of Protocol 3 SCA, in particular subpara (b)(i).

[73] *Fesil and Finnfjord* had a very interesting existing aid background, but ultimately concerned new aid. In *Captive Insurance* (n 32) and *Investment Companies* (n 32), much ink was spilled on existing aid arguments, but the cases clearly concerned (and were dealt with by the Court as) new aid.

[74] *Modiano* (n 36) paras 52–60.

[75] I should note, though, that more than with most other cases discussed in this chapter, your author is arguably not entirely unbiased, having signed the letter to the complainants, which constituted ESA's Decision (full disclosure: the same is true for *Marine Harvest* (n 4)).

[76] This may seem to be implied in paras *Modiano* (n 36) 97–98 and 110.

As regards existing aid, Article 1(1) of the Protocol requires the EFTA Surveillance Authority to keep all such aids in the EFTA States under constant review and to propose to the EFTA State concerned 'any appropriate measures required by the progressive development or by the functioning of the EEA Agreement'. If the EFTA Surveillance Authority considers that an existing aid is incompatible with the EEA Agreement, it must first present the EFTA State concerned with a specific proposal to correct the situation. There is no requirement that formal proceedings be opened before such a proposal is presented. The proposal is not legally binding, but non-compliance enables the EFTA Surveillance Authority to proceed with the contentious procedure provided for in the first paragraph of Article 1(2) of the Protocol.[77]

X. WORDS ON THE OCCASION

We have reached the end of this brief retrospective on the occasion of the EFTA Court celebrating 30 years of state aid case law. That is longer than many might have thought the EEA Agreement would survive, and it has been long enough to build a body of case law with substance and depth. Also, it has been plenty of time for the Court to be criticised for a number of its judgments. Those of us who sometimes engage in a dialogue with the Court, in the courtroom or academically, have come to appreciate how the Court has dealt with that. I think it is fair to say that the Court has stood its ground well, but still with enough of the humbleness famously expressed by Justice Robert H Jackson. In his concurring opinion in *Brown v Allen*,[78] in which the US Supreme Court established that all Federal constitutional claims may be heard through the writ of habeas corpus, he wrote: 'We are not final because we are infallible, but we are infallible only because we are final.' I am confident that the Court will continue to stand firm but humble, and so I take my chances on offering another quote that the EFTA Court may also bear in mind when criticised for its judgments, by this author or others – at times writing with a far sharper pen than in this volume. I am thinking of a quote attributed to Chief Justice Earl Warren, who was appointed just a few months after the judgment in *Brown v Allen* in 1953 and who presided over the 'Constitutional Revolution' in the US of the 1950s and 1960s:

> Everything I did in my life that was worthwhile, I caught hell for.

[77] ibid paras 31–32 of the judgment. Note also paras 35–36. The same follows from the provisions of s 5 'Procedure Regarding Existing Aid Schemes' of pt II of Protocol 3 SCA (Arts 17–19), which are also absent from the judgment in *Modiano*, perhaps confirming that *Husbanken II* was not overruled, but overlooked.

[78] *Brown v Allen*, 344 US 443 (1953).

20

The Evolution of State Control over the Exploitation of Natural Energy Resources

KRISTÍN HARALDSDÓTTIR

I. INTRODUCTION

EU ENERGY POLICY and law has changed dramatically since the signing of the European Economic Area (EEA) Agreement in 1992.[1] In view of the objective of the EEA Agreement to create a dynamic and homogeneous EEA,[2] it is relevant to ask how the evolution of EU law has impacted on the EEA Agreement and Contracting States' energy policy and law in the course of the 30-year lifespan of the EEA. This chapter looks at the evolution from a narrower viewpoint. It aims at explaining how the impact on a Contracting State's control of the exploitation of its natural energy resources (primarily hydrocarbons, wind, hydropower and geothermal) has evolved during this period. It is thus concerned with a topic within EEA law that has proven to be sensitive in the EEA/EFTA States, particularly in Norway and Iceland, and raised questions on the limits of the EEA Agreement.[3]

The analysis is concerned with the evolution of the impact of EU legislative developments on a state's powers to make policy choices and decisions. It is aimed at identifying changes to the impact on a state's powers to decide on those issues over the 30 years of the EEA Agreement. It is not the intention to engage in an analysis of whether they conform to constitutional normative standards on the limits to the

[1] For an account of the development, see K Huhta, 'The Scope of State Sovereignty under Article 194(2) TFEU and the Evolution of EU Competences in the Energy Sector' (2021) 70 *International & Comparative Law Quarterly* 991.

[2] Article 1(1) EEA.

[3] The incorporation of the Third Energy Market Package into the EEA Agreement by way of EEA Joint Committee (JC) Decision No 93/2017 [2019] OJ L36/44 proved controversial. Questions raised by the incorporation concerned the impact on the institutional autonomy of national authorities as well as on a state's powers to control the management of energy resources. For a specific analysis of the EU Third Energy Market Package and its effect on sensitive issues of national resource management relating to public ownership and the building of interconnectors, see H Bjørnebye, 'The Impact of the Third Energy Market Package on National Resource Management' (2019) *Scandinavian Institute of Maritime Law Yearbook (SIMPLY)* 2018 / 519 *MarIus* 199.

transfer of a state's powers. The focus is on EEA-relevant legislation in the area of energy. However, it is not limited to EU legislation already incorporated into the EEA Agreement, but also covers legislation that primarily pursues internal market objectives as well as legislation-promoting renewables. The scope of legislation covered is thus based on presumed relevance. In the chapter reference is made to EEA-relevant acts in both instances.

States' systems for management of the exploitation of natural energy resources are based on a number of political objectives: energy security; the economy; the environment and various social policy objectives. The objectives guide the national legislator and the administration at both the national and regional levels in its decision making. Law and methods for pursuing national policy choices vary between states, but can, in general terms, be divided into three primary categories: (1) property law determining, inter alia, public or private ownership of land and natural resources; (2) administrative law, including methods and procedures for the management of the exploitation of specific resources; and (3) more general plans and rules on, inter alia, land use, protection of the environment and market structure. It is a common feature of those systems that they govern sensitive and important national interests which explains a general reluctance of the Contracting States to accept the incorporation into the EEA Agreement of EU rules which limit a state's control.

Section II discusses the main turning points in EEA-relevant energy law relating to changes in legal processes and legislative competences of the EU. Section III addresses the scope of the EEA Agreement in the area of energy and the widening gap between EU and EEA law in this field. In section IV, the impact of EU law on national policy and decisions on whether to exploit energy resources and in what quantities is addressed. Section V discusses the impact of general principles and the fundamental freedoms as well as EEA-relevant legislation in the area of energy on a state's power to determine requirements for access to energy resources and conditions on the exercise of the activities. Finally, section VI concludes with general remarks.

II. THE DEVELOPMENT OF LEGAL PROCESSES AND LEGISLATIVE COMPETENCES OF THE EU

It is useful for understanding the evolution of EEA law in the area of energy to consider the main drivers of and impediments to legislative changes in EU energy law. In that regard, EU legislative processes and competences are of particular importance. In the overall EU competence structure, energy law has been placed within shared competences. As such, they have been subject to general constraints of a horizontal nature, including the principles of subsidiarity and proportionality.[4] In addition, a diverse group of Treaty provisions are intended to set boundaries to EU competences and limit EU influences on national policy.[5] In the following, we will consider such

[4] Articles 5(3) and 5(4) of the Treaty on European Union (TEU).

[5] For further discussion, see K Haraldsdóttir, 'The Nature of Neutrality in EU Law: Article 345 TFEU' (2020) 1 *European Law Review* 1.

boundaries to legislative actions in the area of energy that may affect the evolution of EU energy law and hence also EEA law.

At the outset, it is pertinent to recall that the negotiations and the signing of the EEA Agreement in 1992 coincided with a turning point in the evolution of EU energy law. The 1992 internal market agenda of the Single European Act (SEA) and changes that the Act brought to institutional structure and legislative processes, with a move from unanimity towards qualified majority voting in the Council, fuelled legislative developments for pursuing internal market objectives, including in the area of energy.[6] The SEA also introduced a special legal basis for legislation pursuing environmental policy.[7] The legal basis was significantly changed by the Maastricht Treaty in 1992, which introduced qualified majority for voting in the Council as a general rule and unanimity as an exception in a similar manner to Article 192(2) of the Treaty on the Functioning of the European Union (TFEU) (ex 175(2) of the EC Treaty (TEC)). Unanimity was required for measures concerning town and country planning, land use and management of water resources, as well as for measures significantly affecting a Member State's choice between different energy resources and general structure of its energy supply.[8]

In the following years, there was a shift from limited and incidental intervention by the EU into states' energy affairs to strategic legislative steps and legal actions aimed at opening public monopoly markets and ensuring equal market access based on the fundamental freedoms and competition rules.[9] As will be further discussed in sections IV and V, in the subsequent 20 years there was a gradual move towards the further harmonisation of EU internal energy market legislation and increased centralisation of the governance of energy affairs, particularly as regards network operations. The legislation was based on Article 114 TFEU (ex 95 TEC). During this period, energy transition was also placed on the agenda with the adoption of legislative measures for promoting renewable energy on the environmental legal basis of Article 192(1) TFEU (ex Article 172(1) TEC).

The entry into force of the Lisbon Treaty in December 2009 can be described as another milestone in EU energy law. As predicted by some legal scholars, the energy-specific legal basis in Article 194 TFEU provided political stimulus for EU energy policy and legal measures.[10] Article 194 TFEU recognises the overall link between the market objectives and need to improve the environment. It adopts a broad approach to the internal market aims, intertwining the functioning of the market, security of the energy supply, energy efficiency and energy saving, and the development of new and renewable forms of energy, as well as the interconnection of energy networks. In

[6] Weiler described the 1992 Agenda and the SEA as an eruption of significant proportions, inter alia, in terms of legislative efficiency: J Weiler, 'Transformation of Europe' (1991) 100 *Yale Law Journal* 2403, 2455–64.

[7] Article 130s EEC (Art 192(1) TFEU).

[8] Article 130s TEC.

[9] The limited legal involvement in the area of energy prior to the shift has also been explained by the political sensitivity of the sector and the national interests involved; see Huhta (n 1) 992.

[10] HS von Sydow, 'The Dancing Procession of Lisbon: Legal Basis for European Energy Policy' (2011) 1 *European Energy Journal* 33, 45; and L Hancher and FM Salerno, 'Energy Policy after Lisbon' in P Eeckhout and S Ripley (eds), *EU Law after Lisbon* (Oxford, Oxford Scholarship Online, 2012) 7 and 36.

addition, it contains a reference to the spirit of solidarity which the Court of Justice of the European Union (CJEU) described, in a case concerning energy security, as a fundamental principle of EU law.[11] The role of this principle in relation to the development of energy resources and how it affects a state's energy rights remain to be clarified.

The political stimulus created by the energy-specific legal basis is reflected in the strategy for a resilient Energy Union published in 2015[12] with five interrelated dimensions: energy security, solidarity and trust; a fully integrated market; energy efficiency; decarbonisation of the economy; and, lastly, research, innovation and competitiveness. This is also reflected in the so-called Clean Energy Package that was based on the five-dimensional approach of the Energy Union, as well as more recent policy and legislative measures particularly aimed at energy security in the Union, and EU climate goals through a transition to renewable energy.[13]

The Lisbon Treaty has also been seen as generally signalling that EU competences have inherent limits.[14] Article 194(2) TFEU is an example of this and reveals EU Member States' scepticism towards increasing centralisation at the EU level of powers concerning energy affairs. The provision recognises a 'State's right to determine the conditions for exploiting its energy resources, its choice between different energy sources and the general structure of its energy supply', but without prejudice to EU competences to legislate on certain sensitive matters in the area of the environment by unanimity in the Council. The outer limits of a state's energy rights remain ambiguous.[15] In sections IV and V, we will consider how a state's energy rights have affected the legislative actions of the EU and thereby also the impact of EU law on the EEA Agreement.

III. THE MATERIAL SCOPE OF THE EEA AGREEMENT AND QUESTIONS OF EEA RELEVANCE

There is no doubt that energy falls under the material scope of the EEA Agreement and that energy legislation with an internal market legal basis is EEA-relevant

[11] Case C-848/19 P *Germany v Poland (Opal Pipeline)* ECLI:EU:C:2021:598. For a discussion of this case and the solidarity principle, see, inter alia, K Huhta and L Reins, 'Solidarity in European Union Law and its Application in the Energy Sector' (2023) 72 *International & Comparative Law Quarterly* 771.

[12] Communication from the Commission, A Framework Strategy for a Resilient Energy Union with a Forward-Looking Climate Change Policy, COM (2015) 80 final.

[13] Communication from the Commission, 'Fit for 55': delivering the EU's 2030 Climate Target on the way to climate neutrality, COM (2021) 550 final. The package consisted of various proposals for changes to the Clean Energy Package legislation and new regulation proposals on alternative fuels. Following the Russian invasion of Ukraine, the Commission proposed further actions to increase the security of supply.

[14] L Azoulai, 'Introduction: The Question of Competence' in L Azoulai (ed), *The Question of Competence in the European Union* (Oxford, Oxford University Press, 2014).

[15] For an analysis of the limits, see, eg, Huhta (n 1) 1000–08, and Huhta and Reins (n 11), as well as K Haraldsdóttir, 'The Limits of EU Competences to Regulate Conditions for Exploitation of Energy Resources: Analysis of Article 192(2) TFEU' (2014) 23 *European Energy and Environmental Law Review* 214–218, and A Johnston and E van der Marel, '*Ad Lucem?* Interpreting the New EU Energy Provision, and in Particular the Meaning of Article 194(2) TFEU' (2013) 22 *European Energy and Environmental Law Review* 181.

and must be incorporated into Annex IV to the EEA Agreement.[16] Nevertheless, the applicability of the main rules of the EEA Agreement to national rules on the management of natural energy resources was a matter of dispute before the EFTA Court in the *Hjemfall* case.[17] In the judgment, the EFTA Court rejected Norway's arguments that the management of essential energy resources fell outside the scope of application of the fundamental rules of the EEA Agreement. It also rejected Norway's arguments to the effect that Article 125 EEA, which mirrors Article 345 TFEU (ex 295 TEC), should, unlike Article 345 TFEU, be interpreted to the effect that rules governing the system of ownership of natural energy resources are exempted from the rules on free movement.

A growing number of EU legislative acts on energy, marked by the EU as EEA-relevant, that have not been incorporated into the EEA Agreement reveal a widening gap between the two systems in the area of energy. This may be explained by the political sensitivity of energy policy matters in general and the inherent tension between national and EU interests in particular. It should also be kept in mind that within the EEA Joint Committee (EEA JC), all decisions to incorporate EU acts into the EEA Agreement must be reached on the basis of unanimity. Another possible influencing factor in the widening of the gap is the integration of different policy areas into legislation adopted on the basis of Article 194 TFEU that may complicate the assessment of the EEA-relevance of individual acts or parts of acts. Regulation 2019/941 on risk-preparedness and management could prove to be an example of this:[18] although clearly intended to strengthen the internal electricity market, it primarily addresses the specific issue of electricity crisis prevention and requires states to cooperate in a 'spirit of solidarity'. Considering the *Opal Pipeline* judgment referred to above,[19] which can be read to the effect that the solidarity principle within Article 194 TFEU imposes rights and obligations on EU Member States as well as EU institutions, it is doubtful that the principle will form part of EEA law in the future.[20]

In principle, decisions of the EEA JC on amendments to the Annexes to the EEA Agreement are politically neutral and are only concerned with the assessment of EEA relevance, ie, whether legislation primarily pursues objectives of the EEA Agreement. Hence, questions concerning the often delicate and sometimes politically sensitive choices made in the EU legislative process are generally not relevant to the assessment of the relevance of EEA legislation in the area of energy. However, the decision-making process within the EEA JC is not entirely disconnected from

[16] Article 24 EEA.

[17] Case E-2/06 *EFTA Surveillance Authority v Norway* [2007] EFTA Ct Rep 167, paras 59–63.

[18] Regulation (EU) 2019/941 of the European Parliament and of the Council of 5 June 2019 on risk-preparedness in the electricity sector and repealing Directive 2005/89/EC [2019] OJ L158, 14 June, 1–21.

[19] *Opal Pipeline* (n 11).

[20] See in this regard Decision of the EEA JC No 93/2017 [2019] OJ L36/44, incorporating the Third Energy Package into the EEA Agreement, including Directive 2009/73/EC concerning common rules for the internal market in natural gas and repealing Directive 2003/55/EC [2009] OJ L211/94. There it is stated that Art 6 of Directive 2009/73, which refers to a duty of Member States to cooperate in order to promote regional and bilateral solidarity aimed at safeguarding security of supply, shall not apply to the EFTA States.

the political realities in the EFTA States. In practice, decisions are reached based on compromises following negotiations between the representatives of the EU and the EEA/EFTA States. According to Article 102(3) EEA, the Contracting Parties shall make all efforts to arrive at an agreement on matters relevant to the Agreement. In particular, the EEA JC shall 'make every effort to find a mutually acceptable solution where a serious problem arises in any area which, in the EFTA States, falls within the competence of the legislator'. Moreover, the EEA JC is subject to the rules of the Agreement concerning the good functioning of the Agreement in Article 102 EEA and the time limits set out therein. Analysis of EEA JC activities in the area of energy sheds light on the position of the EU and EFTA States on the material boundaries of the EEA Agreement. A number of acts in the area of energy which have been marked as EEA-relevant by the EU have not been incorporated into the EEA Agreement. Also, incorporation of important parts of internal market legislation has been delayed, including the so-called Third Energy Market Package, which was delayed for nearly 10 years.[21]

Legislation adopted on the internal market legal basis of Article 114 TFEU (ex Article 95 TEC) is in principle EEA-relevant. In the 30 years since the entry into force of the EEA, Annex IV has grown from nine acts that were primarily related to energy saving and pricing[22] to around 80 acts, the bulk of which concern energy efficiency. Other acts primarily concern the functioning of the internal market, the promotion of renewable energy and the security of the electricity supply. EU legislative acts that concern the security of the supply of gas and oil and/or petroleum products (based on Article 122 TFEU (ex Article 100 TEC)) are in general not EEA-relevant. The same applies to legislation on trans-European energy networks (TEN) based on Article 172 TFEU.[23]

The question of the EEA relevance of EU rules adopted on the environmental legal basis in Article 192 TFEU is less clear-cut. The EEA Agreement recognises, in general, the relevance of environmental rules to the objectives of the Agreement and to the internal market.[24] Pursuant to Article 73 EEA, a state's actions relating to the environment shall have, inter alia, the objectives of preserving, protecting and improving the 'quality' of the environment and ensuring a prudent and rational utilisation of natural resources. In practice, the EEA JC has interpreted the scope of the EEA Agreement in the area of the environment broadly. It is primarily acts that are concerned with nature conservation that have been excluded from its scope. Based on this distinction,

[21] Decision of the EEA JC No 93/2017 [2019] OJ L36/44, which entered into force on 3 October 2019 when constitutional requirements under Art 103 EEA were fullfilled. For an analysis of the concerns in Norway, see Bjørnebye (n 3).

[22] Annex IV to the Agreement as signed in 1992 included nine acts [1994] OJ L1/322.

[23] Regulation (EU) No 347/2013 of the European Parliament and of the Council on guidelines for trans-European energy infrastructure [2013] OJ L115/39 is marked by the EU as EEA-relevant, but is not considered relevant by the EEA/EFTA States: see www.efta.int/eea-lex/32013R0347. Regulation No 347/2013 has now been replaced by Regulation (EU) 2022/869 of the European Parliament and of the Council on guidelines for trans-European energy infrastructure [2022] OJ L152/45, which is still under scrutiny within the EEA JC: www.efta.int/eea-lex/32022R0869. In light of the EEA/EFTA States' position towards Regulation No 347/2013, it is presumed that Regulation 2022/869 is not EEA-relevant for the purposes of this chapter.

[24] Article 1(2)(f) and pt V, ch 3 EEA. Relevant environmental legislation is included in Annex XX EEA.

neither the Birds Directive[25] nor the Habitats Directive[26] was considered EEA-relevant when the EEA Agreement was negotiated. Acts of a mixed nature, in the sense that they include both 'qualitative' and 'quantitative' measures and objectives, have raised questions and complications in the assessment of their relevance to the EEA. The Water Framework Directive (WFD) is an example of this.[27]

IV. POLICY AND DECISIONS ON THE EXPLOITATION OF ENERGY RESOURCES AND IN WHAT QUANTITIES

In the following sections, we will discuss in chronological order EU legislative measures concerned with the exploitation of energy resources and electricity production, and will analyse their impact on state powers to decide as to whether to exploit its energy resources and in what quantities.

A. EU Legislation on the Exploitation of Energy Resources and Electricity Production

The Hydrocarbon Directive[28] was the first legislative act to be added to Annex IV to the EEA Agreement following the entry into force of the EEA Agreement. As explained in the preamble to the Hydrocarbon Directive, its aim is to ensure non-discriminatory access to, and pursuit of, hydrocarbon prospection, exploration and production under conditions which encourage competition and best production of resources in Member States and to reinforce the integration of the internal market.[29] At the same time, the Directive recognises that the Member States retain the sovereign right to determine the areas to be made available for hydrocarbon activities.[30] The Directive thus reflects the legislator's respect for a balance between Member States' interests in retaining control over their natural energy resources and the Community's internal market objective.

The Hydrocarbon Directive was followed by legislation on the opening of electricity and gas markets to competition in 1996,[31] which was incorporated into the EEA

[25] Council Directive 79/409/EEC on the conservation of wild birds [1979] OJ L103/1. This was repealed by Directive 2009/147/EC of the European Parliament and of the Council on the conservation of wild birds (Birds Directive) [2010] OJ L20/7.

[26] Council Directive 92/43/EEC on the conservation of natural habitats and wild fauna and flora (Habitats Directive) [1992] OJ L206/7.

[27] Directive 2000/60/EC of the European Parliament and of the Council establishing a framework for Community action in the field of water policy [2000] OJ L327/1.

[28] Directive 94/22/EC of the European Parliament and of the Council on the conditions for granting and using authorizations for the prospection, exploration and production of hydrocarbons (Hydrocarbon Directive) [1994] OJ L164/3, incorporated into Annex IV to the EEA Agreement by EEA JC Decision No 19/95 [1995] OJ L158/1.

[29] Directive 94/22, recital 6.

[30] ibid recital 4 and Art 2(1).

[31] Directive 96/92/EC of the European Parliament and of the Council concerning common rules for the internal market in electricity (Electricity Directive) [1997] OJ L27/20.

Agreement in 2001.[32] The Electricity Directive covered the production as well as the distribution, transmission and supply of electricity.[33] It required that the production and supply of electricity should be opened up for competition. The Directive was resource-neutral, covering any form of energy sources. Its provisions on electricity generation primarily laid down general rules requiring that authorisations for generation should be based on transparent, objective and non-discriminatory rules, and listed in broad and general terms the public policy objectives on which an authorisation may be based. States retained full discretion as to which sources of energy should be used. This approach remained unchanged in the Second[34] and Third Electricity Directives.[35] The same holds true for the current Electricity Directive that forms a part of the so-called 'clean energy for all package' that is currently under scrutiny in the EEA JC.[36] The package was adopted on the basis of Article 194 TFEU.

B. The Development of Network Infrastructures

There has been a noticeable trend over the past two decades towards centralisation at the EU level of policy and governance of electricity interconnections. The establishment of an Agency for the Cooperation of Energy Regulators (ACER) in Regulation (EC) No 713/2009,[37] whose tasks include, inter alia, to facilitate cooperation of national transmission and distribution system operators and development and to monitor the implementation of network codes and guidelines, is an example of this. Another example is the setting of an overall EU target in the 2018 Governance Regulation[38] for interconnecting at least 15 per cent of installed electricity capacity by 2030.

From the perspective of a state's control of the exploitation of its energy resources, the question is whether powers to decide on the development of new infrastructures have been centralised at the EU and EEA institutional levels. Network infrastructures are undeniably essential for the operation of electricity plants. Hence, their capacity and location may affect decisions on the development of new plants and their location. Other more indirect and remote effects of the centralised management of the operation of electricity networks at the EU and EEA levels that are based on

[32] EEA JC Decision No 168/1999 [2001] OJ L61/223.

[33] The internal market gas directives do not address production activities as they are covered by the Hydrocarbon Directive. Therefore, the gas directives will not be discussed in this chapter.

[34] Directive 2003/54/EC of the European Parliament and of the Council concerning common rules for the internal market in electricity and repealing Directive 96/92/EC (Second Electricity Directive) [2003] OJ L176/37, incorporated into the EEA Agreement by EEA JC Decision No 146/2005 [2006] OJ L53/43.

[35] Directive 2009/72/EC of the European Parliament and of the Council concerning common rules for the internal market in electricity and repealing Directive 2003/54/EC (Third Electricity Directive) [2009] OJ L211/55, incorporated into the EEA Agreement by EEA JC Decision No 93/2017 [2019] OJ L36/44.

[36] Directive (EU) 2019/944 of the European Parliament and of the Council on common rules for the internal market for electricity and amending Directive 2012/27/EU [2019] OJ L158/125.

[37] Regulation (EC) No 713/2009 of the European Parliament and of the Council establishing an Agency for the Cooperation of Energy Regulators [2009] OJ L211/1.

[38] 2018 Governance Regulation, Art 4(d).

delegated legislative measures,[39] which are intended to harmonise the operation of interconnected networks across borders to ensure efficiency and security (including the handling of congestions), will not be discussed here.

As far as the centralisation of powers to develop infrastructures is concerned, it is worth considering the limitation on the competences of the EU legislator in light of the principle of territorial sovereignty of states reflected in the second paragraph of Article 172 TFEU. Based on the judgment of the General Court in the recent *Aquind* case, which concerned the inclusion of a proposed interconnector on the list of projects of common interest based on Regulation EU No 347/2013, it seems clear that the powers of the Commission and other EU institutions to decide on the building of infrastructures within a state's territory would have to be subject to the consent of the state concerned.[40] Moreover, an analysis of Regulation No 713/2009 does not indicate that such powers have been conferred on ACER.[41] No changes in this regard were introduced in the 2019 ACER Regulation.[42]

C. The Promotion of Renewable Energy

EU legislative measures that give priority to certain resources over others are intended to affect the ways in which energy is produced and hence inevitably have an impact on a state's control over its energy mix and the use of its resources.[43] For the past two decades, the EU legislator has set targets for the share of renewable energy resources in the overall energy consumption in the EU and has introduced various measures to promote the use of renewables, including the recognition of different forms of state subsidies.

In 2001, the first renewable energy directive was adopted on the environmental legal basis of Article 175(1) TEC and incorporated into the EEA Agreement four years later.[44] It set an overall EU 12 per cent target for shares of renewable sources. However, the real impact on a state's control was limited, as national targets were

[39] Network codes and guidelines adopted by the Commission on the basis of Art 58 of the 2019 Electricity Market Regulation.

[40] Case T-295/20 *Aquind v Commission* ECLI:EU:T:2023:52, paras 39–44. See also Case C-121/14 *UK v Parliament and Council* ECLI:EU:C:2015:526, Opinion of AG Bot, paras 157–58; and, for an analysis of *Aquind*, see K Huhta, 'T-295/20 *Aquind*: Clarifying the Division of Powers in the EU Energy Sector' (2023) 32 *European Energy and Environmental Law Review* 155.

[41] See in particular Arts 7 and 8. For further discussion on the limits of ACER's powers under the Third Electricity Directive, see Bjørnebye (n 3) 231–34.

[42] It has been argued that ACER's powers were, in general, only extended to a limited extent; see O Stefan and M Petri, 'Too Weak to Be Controlled: Judicial Review of ACER Soft Law' (2018) 37 *Yearbook of European Law* 525, 526–30. See also criticism of changes to the management of structural congestions from central to national level in J Rumpf, 'Congestion Displacement in European Electricity Transmission Systems: Finally Getting a Grip on it? Revised Safeguards in the Clean Energy Package and the European Network Codes' (2020) 38 *Journal of Energy & Natural Resources Law* 409, 434–35.

[43] See Huhta (n 1) 993 and 1001.

[44] Directive 2001/77/EC of the European Parliament and of the Council on the promotion of electricity produced from renewable energy sources in the internal electricity market [2002] OJ L283/33, incorporated into Annex IV to the EEA Agreement by EEA JC Decision No 102/2005 [2005] OJ L306/34.

indicative and states retained wide discretion as to the means used to meet the targets and in the choice of which sources to use.

A more general and ambitious Renewable Energy Directive was adopted in 2009 (RED I) on the basis of Article 192(1) TFEU (then Article 175(2) TEC) and incorporated into the EEA Agreement in 2011 without any adaptations.[45] It introduced a 20 per cent EU target and a binding target for each state that was calculated based on a method laid down in the Directive.[46] As a result, the impact of the binding targets differed between states depending on their resource status and energy supply. In states with a high ratio of fossil fuels or nuclear, it inevitably had a significant effect on the state's control over its energy mix and policy on the use of its resources. However, the margin of discretion left to states as to the choice of means to achieve the targets and in choosing to develop the renewable energy resources most suited to their situation remained wide.[47]

RED I was replaced by Directive (EU) 2018/2001 (RED II), which is currently in force in the EU.[48] It was adopted on the basis of Article 194 TFEU and was still under scrutiny for incorporation into the EEA Agreement by the EEA/EFTA States at the time of writing. Unlike RED I, it did not introduce binding national targets, but an overall EU target of at least a 32 per cent share of renewables in the gross final consumption of energy in the Union in 2030. Pursuant to the 2018 Governance Regulation,[49] states are required to set targets in a 10-year national energy and climate plan. The change from a system of binding targets in RED I was intended to provide states with more flexibility in accordance with their specific circumstances, energy mix and capacity to produce renewable energy.[50] The reversion from binding national targets to overall EU targets restricts the possibility for the Commission to initiate enforcement actions against states. In essence, the measures that the Commission can take based on the 2018 Governance Regulation are limited to recommendations.[51] Despite the increase in the overall renewable energy target in RED II, the methods employed have less impact on a state's control of the exploitation of its energy resources than the binding target in RED I.[52] A possible explanation for the change of approach are the limits imposed on EU legislative competences in Article 194(2) TFEU.

[45] Directive 2009/28/EC of the European Parliament and of the Council on the promotion of the use of energy from renewable sources and amending and subsequently repealing Directives 2001/77/EC and 2003/30/EC [2009] OJ L140/16, incorporated into Annex IV to the EEA Agreement by EEA JC Decision No 162/2011 [2012] OJ L76/49.

[46] The targets for the EEA/EFTA States (other than Liechtenstein, to which the Directive does not apply) were adopted in the incorporating EEA JC Decision No 162/2011.

[47] In this regard see, inter alia, Joined Cases C-215/16, C-216/16, C-220/16 and C-221/16 *Elecdey Carcelen and Others* ECLI:EU:C:2017:705, para 40.

[48] Directive (EU) 2018/2001 of the European Parliament and of the Council on the promotion of the use of energy from renewable resources [2018] OJ L328/81, marked as EEA-relevant but still under scrutiny in the EEA JC: www.efta.int/eea-lex/32018L2001.

[49] Regulation (EU) 2018/1999 of the European Parliament and of the Council of 11 December 2018 on the Governance of the Energy Union and Climate Action [2018] OJ L328/1, marked as EEA relevant but still under scrutiny in the EEA JC: www.efta.int/eea-lex/32018R1999.

[50] RED II, recital 9.

[51] See 2018 Governance Regulation, Arts 31(1) and (3), 32(1) and 34.

[52] Still, the national targets set for 2020 constitute states' minimum contributions: *cf* RED II, Art 3(4).

D. Concluding Remarks

Traditionally, it has been acknowledged in EU law that Member States retain their sovereign power to decide to exploit their energy resources and in what quantities. This rule is based on the principles of international law on territorial sovereignty and a state's permanent sovereignty over its natural resources and still applies. In fact, it was codified in Article 194(2) TFEU. Despite ambiguity about the outer limits of a state's energy rights, it can be concluded from the discussion above that a state's right to determine the conditions for exploiting its energy resources encompasses the decision to exploit its energy resources and the quantities involved.

V. REQUIREMENTS FOR ACCESS TO ENERGY RESOURCES AND THE EXERCISE OF PRODUCTION ACTIVITIES

Exploitation of natural energy resources and the use of land for such purposes are generally subject to land use requirements and a bundle of administrative authorisations at the national and regional levels. In the following sections we will mainly consider the evolution of EEA-relevant legislation on a state's discretion to manage access to and the exploitation of its resources. The legislation builds on the rules on the fundamental freedoms that apply both in EU and EEA law. Insofar as legislation does not lay down more specific rules, the rules on the fundamental freedoms continue to apply. It is thus relevant to give a brief outline of how the fundamental freedom rules impact on a state's discretion in managing the exploitation of energy resources. The discussion focuses primarily on the free movement rules.

A. The Fundamental Freedoms and Market Access

Requirements for authorisation in national law for access to and exercise of economic activities entail restrictions to free movement.[53] In the case of scarce natural resources, such authorisations are generally considered necessary.[54] However, the conditions for obtaining authorisation and to pursue the activities must be based on legitimate objectives and fulfil the requirements of the principle of proportionality. As far as the four freedoms are concerned, it is primarily the assessment of justification for restrictive measures that defines a state's discretion.[55] In that regard, it has been pointed

[53] V Hatzopoulos, 'The Allocation of Limited Authorisations under EU Internal Market Rules' in P Adriaanse et al (eds), *Scarcity and the State I: The Allocation of Limited Rights by the Administration* (Cambridge, Cambridge University Press, 2016) 163.

[54] See, eg, Directive 2006/123 of the European Parliament and of the Council on services in the internal market (Services Directive) [2006] OJ L376/36, Art 12(1). In the words of Hatzopoulos (n 53) 163–66, 'scarce resources not only tolerate but also call for a system of authorization'.

[55] L Azoulai, 'The "Retained Powers" Formula in the Case Law of the European Court of Justice: EU Law as Total Law' (2011) 4(2) *European Journal of Legal Studies* 178, 188–89. See also J Zglinski, 'The Rise of Deference: The Margin of Appreciation and Decentralized Judicial Review in EU Free Movement Law' (2018) 55 *Common Market Law Review* 1341, 1342–43.

out that in certain instances, the CJEU has applied a more 'relaxed regime of justification'.[56] Moreover, it can be inferred from case law of the European courts that schemes for allocation of scarce resources in competitive situations must conform to general principles of non-discrimination, transparency and objectivity as well as proportionality, both in terms of procedural and substantive requirements.[57] These allocation principles reflect the main principles of free movement, competition law and state aid on non-discrimination between economic operators.

The *Hjemfall* case provides a good example of the assessment of justification for restrictions on access to the exploitation of energy resources pursuant to the rules on the four freedoms. The subject matter of the case concerned a concession scheme in Norway for acquiring waterfalls (watercourses) for generating electricity. The scheme was aimed at ensuring public ownership of hydropower resources (waterfalls) and related installations. At the centre of the debate was the question of whether the scheme discriminated between public and private entities and, if so, whether the discrimination could be justified. According to the scheme, private undertakings could only achieve time-limited concessions, whereas public undertakings were granted concessions for an unlimited time. Pursuant to the scheme, property rights to watercourses utilised for energy production and related installations are transferred from private undertakings to the state at a certain time without compensation (system of reversion). The objective of the system of reversion is to ensure public ownership over hydropower resources. The EFTA Surveillance Authority (ESA) claimed that the scheme was discriminatory in nature and violated the freedom of establishment and free movement of capital. In its defence, Norway argued, inter alia, that the objective of ensuring public ownership over essential energy resources was in itself a legitimate justification for the differentiation between public and private undertakings. In the alternative, Norway submitted that public ownership was a means of achieving other legitimate aims, including public security through security of energy supply, public management and control over hydropower resources, environmental considerations and effective collection of economic rent. In its ruling, the EFTA Court found that the differentiation between private and public undertakings restricted the free movement of capital (Article 40 EEA) and the right of establishment (Article 31 EEA). In its assessment of the justification for the restriction, the EFTA Court interpreted Article 125 EEA (which mirrors Article 345 TFEU) to the effect that an 'EEA State's right to decide whether hydropower resources and related installations are in private or public ownership is, as such, not affected by the EEA Agreement'.[58] Based on that, the EFTA Court held that it was legitimate to pursue the objective of ensuring public ownership

[56] Azoulai (n 55). See also Zglinski (n 55) 1351–59, who argues that during the period from 1974 to 2013, there is a gradual shift to an increased number of cases where the CJEU resorts to a more relaxed proportionality assessment which are related to certain policy fields, primarily public and animal health, games of chance, public policy/morality and national security.

[57] For an in-depth analysis of case law on requirements for EU market freedom-based allocation regimes, see F Wollenschläger, 'EU Law Principles for Allocating Scarce Goods and the Emergence of an Allocation Procedure' (2015) 8(1) *Review of European Administrative Law* 205, 216–30. See also Hatzopoulos (n 53). As Hatzopoulos points out, the Services Directive is generally considered to reflect the main principles on allocation requirements.

[58] *EFTA Surveillance Authority v Norway* (n 17) para 72.

over these properties, provided that the objective is pursued in a non-discriminatory, proportionate and consistent manner. The Norwegian system failed the consistency test. In relation to other justificatory grounds put forward by Norway, the EFTA Court found that only ensuring security of supply and protection of the environment were legitimate objectives, but ruled that the contested rules were not necessary to achieve the objectives pursued.

The case is important both in terms of its impact on a state's discretion to pursue the objective of public ownership of essential energy resources and in light of the unprecedented approach of the EFTA Court to accept the objective of public ownership as a justificatory ground for restrictions on the four freedoms. In earlier case law, the CJEU rejected the possibility of interpreting Article 345 TFEU to this effect and in fact maintained this position in its Grand Chamber judgment in the *Essent* case.[59] This author has argued that the difference in the approach of the two courts can be explained by reference to the particularly sensitive sovereignty issues attached to the objects of ownership dealt with by the EFTA Court in the *Hjemfall* case and that hence the judgments are not contradictory.[60]

B. Legislation

The complexity of the administrative authorisation systems within the EEA and the divergent requirements for access to and exercise of economic activities are liable to impede cross-border trade and hence the functioning of the internal energy market.[61] However, in view of the general principle of administrative autonomy of states[62] and the Treaty rules on subsidiarity[63] and proportionality[64] that apply to the delimitation of the legal competences of the EU, the legislator has traditionally been cautious when it comes to harmonisation of authorisation procedures and requirements. Often, legislative provisions add little or nothing to the general rules that follow from case law based on the fundamental freedoms discussed in section V.A above. In the following sections we will consider this further with a view to shedding light on the development of requirements for access to and exercise of exploitation of energy resources, and their impact on a state's discretion.

i. The Hydrocarbon Directive

The Hydrocarbon Directive lays down general rules for granting authorisation for hydrocarbon prospecting, exploration and production of hydrocarbons on a

[59] Joined Cases C-105/12–C-107/12 *The Netherlands v Essent and Others* ECLI:EU:C:2013:677, para 53.

[60] For further discussion on this, see Haraldsdóttir (n 5) 22–23.

[61] See, eg, Directive (EU) 2023/2413 of the European Parliament and of the Council amending Directive (EU) 2018/2001, Regulation (EU) 2018/1999 and Directive 98/70/EC as regards the promotion of energy from renewable sources, and repealing Council Directive (EU) 2015/652 [2023] OJ L2023/2413, recital 20.

[62] On administrative autonomy as a part of the rule of procedural autonomy, see Case 33/76 *Rewe-Zentralfinanz and Rewe-Zentral AG v Landwirtschaftskammer für das Saarland (Rewe)* ECLI:EU:C:1976:188. In EEA law, see Case E-1/04 *Fokus Bank v Norway* [2004] EFTA Ct Rep 11, para 41.

[63] Article 5(3) TEU.

[64] ibid Art 5(4).

non-discriminatory basis with the general objectives of encouraging competition and ensuring the best possible exercise of the activities.[65]

The rules on allocation of authorisations include provisions on how to determine the geographical areas involved and the number of licences as well as their duration,[66] the selection criteria that must in all cases be used[67] and the legitimate objectives that requirements on the exercise of the activities may concern. The list contains national security, public safety, public health, security of transport, protection of the environment, protection of biological resources, the planned management of hydrocarbon resources and the payment of a financial contribution or a contribution in hydrocarbons.[68] The rules provide a certain level of harmonisation, particularly as far as the selection criteria are concerned. Otherwise, they are phrased in general terms and leave considerable discretion to states to pursue the general objectives and fulfil the requirement of non-discrimination irrespective of the nationality of the undertaking.[69]

ii. Directives on the Internal Electricity Market

As mentioned above, all four Electricity Directives have laid down general rules on an open authorisation procedure for the construction of new electricity generating capacity.[70] Only the first Directive gave states the option to choose between the methods employed, ie, the authorisation and tender procedures.[71] The tender procedure option was removed in subsequent directives.[72]

All four directives include generally phrased provisions according to which authorisation procedures must be conducted in accordance with transparent, objective and non-discriminatory criteria in line with the general rules of the fundamental freedoms. In addition, the directives list in general terms the public policy interests that states must consider when determining the criteria. The list in Directive 2009/72 (the Third Electricity Directive) currently in force in the EEA includes the safety and security of the electricity system, installations and associated equipment; the protection of public health and safety; the protection of the environment; land use and siting; the use of public ground; energy efficiency; the nature of the primary sources; the characteristics particular to the applicant, such as technical, economic and financial capabilities; compliance with public service obligations; the contribution to meeting renewable energy targets and the contribution of generating capacity

[65] Directive 94/22, Art 2(2); and Case C-569/10 *Commission v Poland* ECLI:EU:C:2013:425, paras 50–53.

[66] Directive 94/22, Art 4.

[67] ibid Art 5.

[68] ibid Art 6.

[69] See Joined Cases C-364/18 and C-365/18 *Eni and Shell Italia* ECLI:EU:C:2019:938, paras 25 and 35–36.

[70] Directive 96/92, Art 5; Directive 2003/54, Art 6; Directive 2009/72, Art 7; and Directive 2019/944, Art 8. It is not entirely clear whether the rules cover authorisations for exploitation of energy resources. However, there is no doubt that access to exploitation of energy resources for electricity production is not open without obtaining a licence for construction of new capacity.

[71] Directive 96/92, Art 4.

[72] For different explanations, see H Bjørnebye, *Investing in EU Energy Security: Exploring the Regulatory Approach to Tomorrow's Electricity Production* (Alphen aan den Rijn, Wolters Kluwer, 2010) 200–02.

to reducing emissions.[73] The only amendment made to the list by Directive 2019/944 is the addition of 'the alternatives to the construction of new generating capacity, such as demand response solutions and energy storage' as an interest to be considered.[74] The list is generally considered to be exhaustive in nature.[75] However, in view of the broad scope of the interests covered, the list is nearly all-embracing and hence provides states with significant discretion to define the authorisation requirements based on their policy choices. Hitherto no legal actions relating to authorisations for production of electricity have been submitted to the European courts on the basis of the provisions of the Directives on electricity generation.

The first two Electricity Directives did not include any prioritisation for the use of particular resources or types of generation plants. There is some change in that regard in Directive 2009/72 and Directive 2019/944, in which a provision was added requiring states to ensure specific authorisation procedures for small decentralised and/or distributed generation, which take into account their limited size and potential impact.[76] Although general in nature and not directed at any specific resources, the provision signals a push towards, on the one hand, more simplified procedures in accordance with proportionality standards and, on the other hand, prioritisation on behalf of the states for certain forms of electricity generation.

iii. Legislation Promoting Renewable Energy

As discussed above, the prioritisation of renewable energy in EU legislation may impact on a state's control over the exploitation of its energy resources. In addition to the setting of targets and the introduction of supportive measures for development of renewable resources, various requirements intended to ensure simplified and efficient procedures for authorisation of energy plants using renewables have been introduced into the legislation.

RED I, which is still in force in the EEA, lays down generally phrased provisions on the non-discrimination, objectivity, proportionality and necessity of authorisation systems as well as on the need to coordinate and define procedures of different administrative bodies and provide for simplified procedures for smaller projects.[77] RED II includes similar general requirements as RED I.[78] In addition, it lays down stricter procedural rules, requiring, inter alia, designated administrative contact points having the role to guide through and facilitate the entire administrative permit application and granting process,[79] as well as rules on the maximum length of the procedure.[80] In October 2023 amendments were made to RED II aimed at simplifying and coordinating administrative procedures for the development of renewable resources.[81]

[73] Directive 2009/72, Art 7(2).
[74] 2019 Electricity Directive, Art 8(2)(l).
[75] Bjørnebye (n 3) 204.
[76] Directive 2019/944, recital 79.
[77] RED I, Art 13(1).
[78] RED II, Art 15.
[79] ibid Art 16(1) and (2).
[80] ibid Art 16(4).
[81] Directive 2023/2413, recital 24.

Although the amendments are described as procedural in nature, they have substantive characteristics, in particular those concerning states' plans for land use and facilitation of multiple land uses.[82]

From the perspective of the possible impact on a state's control of the exploitation of its energy resources, the amendments have, at the most, an indirect effect in the sense that they encourage prioritisation of renewable resources above other resources. That is of course the whole idea behind the promotion of renewable energy resources and as such is not unexpected. It is rather the method used, instructing land use planning, that is noteworthy in view of how it has been applied in environmental legislation. There, binding qualitative and quantitative rules on nature conservation have been attached to such plans. The Birds Directive and the Habitats Directive are probably the clearest examples of this. Both directives fall outside the scope of the EEA Agreement and hence the Water Framework Directive (WFD),[83] which also includes legally binding objectives and rules attached to management plans, provides a better example.[84] In effect, the legally binding objectives and rules may result in a state's obligation to refuse authorisation for development of an energy production plant if it causes deterioration of the status of the body of water defined in national plans.[85] Consequently, the WFD may have considerable impact on a state's control of the exploitation of its water resources.

The legal development discussed above illustrates a trend towards more detailed and stricter rules intended to coordinate, simplify and speed up authorisation procedures for energy plants using renewables. As far as the insertion of planning obligations into RED II is concerned, it is pertinent to ask whether the trend of imposing stricter administrative obligations on states may in the future develop into binding objectives for land use. The provision in Article 15b stating that states 'shall' favour multiple uses of the identified areas is an indication of this, although the broad and unclear phrasing of the provision would seem to exclude any legal effect. Arguably, however, a state's energy rights, recognised in the second paragraph of Article 194(2) TFEU, would impede such development.[86]

VI. CONCLUDING REMARKS

The aim of this chapter has been to illustrate how the impact of EEA-relevant legislation on a state's control of the exploitation of energy resources has evolved over

[82] ibid recitals 25–27, and new Arts 15b, 15c and 15e inserted into RED II.

[83] Directive 2000/60/EC of the European Parliament and of the Council establishing a framework for Community action in the field of water policy [2000] OJ L327/1, incorporated into Annex XX to the EEA Agreement by EEA JC Decision No 125/2007 [2008] OJ L47/53.

[84] See in particular Art 4.

[85] Case C-461/13 *Bund für Umwelt uand Naturschutz Deutschland* ECLI:EU:C:2015:433, paras 43 and 50.

[86] Arguments have been put forward for a narrow interpretation of the rights on the basis of the objectives pursued to combat climate change in accordance with international law. See M Fehling, 'Energy Transition in the European Union and its Member States: Interpreting Federal Competence Allocation in the Light of the Paris Agreement' (2021) 10 *Transnational Environmental Law* 339. On the narrow interpretation of Art 194(2) TFEU, see also Huhta (n 1) 1007–08.

the 30 years from the entry into force of the EEA Agreement in 1994. The analysis has been confined to the impact on a state's control of whether to exploit its energy resources for energy production and, further, in what quantities, and on its control of access to and exercise of the activities. It has made a distinction between direct and indirect impact, and has left out the more remote indirect impact. Based on the turning point in EU energy legislative competences with the inclusion of Article 194 TFEU as a result of the Lisbon Treaty, it is natural to divide the timeframe into two parts: the first from the entry into force of the EEA Agreement in 1994 until the entry into force of the Lisbon Treaty in late 2009; and the second from that point of time until 2023.

During the first period, EU internal market legislation incorporated into the EEA Agreement was primarily directed at ensuring the functioning of the internal market: non-discriminatory access to and pursuit of energy production, effective market liberalisation and interconnection of electricity markets. Already in the Hydrocarbon Directive, adopted in 1994, a state's control over whether to exploit its energy resources and in what quantities was identified as a matter of state sovereignty. This demarcation of legislative interference into a state's sovereignty was respected in other internal market legislation during this period, both as regards the exploitation of energy resources and the development of infrastructures within a state's territory. During this same period, legislative provisions intended to ensure non-discriminatory access to energy resources and exercise of energy production activities only had a limited impact on a state's discretion beyond what resulted from the rules on the fundamental freedoms in the main part of the EEA Agreement. Hence, the rules on the fundamental freedoms continued to play an important role in shaping a state's powers in this respect. The judgment of the EFTA Court in the *Hjemfall* case was of considerable importance in clarifying a state's discretion under the rules on free movement of capital and freedom of establishment to manage access to the production of electricity through the establishment of a system of public ownership of waterfalls.

It was primarily legislation adopted on the environmental legal basis of Article 175(1) TEC (now Article 192(1) TFEU) that impacted on a state's control of the exploitation of its resources, both in terms of its effect on the prioritisation of which resources should be exploited and on the definition of requirements for their exploitation. RED I was the only EEA-relevant energy legislation that included measures impacting on a state's preferences for the exploitation of its energy resources by introducing nationally binding targets for the overall share of energy from renewable resources of the gross final consumption. Although not specifically directed at energy matters, the WFD can be counted as EEA-relevant legislation that had appreciable impact on a state's control to define the requirements for exploitation of hydropower and geothermal resources.

EU policy and legislative measures in the area of energy following the entry into force of the Lisbon Treaty are shaped by the introduction of the energy-specific legal basis in Article 194 TFEU and its broader and more integrated approach to energy policy and legislation. This is clearly apparent in the Clean Energy Package and the interplay therein between the policy objectives of the internal market, increased interconnections, security of supply and energy transition. The task of identifying the primary objective of EU energy legislative measures from the perspective of EEA relevance has become more complex. In addition, the unclear role of the principle of solidarity in Article 194 TFEU and how it affects EU energy legislation may prove to be an additional complicating factor.

Although the boundaries of a state's energy rights recognised in Article 194(2) TFEU remain unclear, there are some indications of this provision having a restraining effect on the EU legislator. It is safe to conclude that a state's sovereign right to decide whether to exploit its resources and in what quantities, defined during the first period, has now been ring-fenced. The General Court's judgment in the *Aquind* case is also clear on the requirement for a state's consent for the use of its territory for the development of infrastructures within its territory. Arguably, a state's energy rights are also a possible explanation for the change from a binding renewable energy target on each state, as provided for in RED I, to an overall EU target in RED II. As regards access to energy resources open for exploitation and exercise of energy production activities, there has been limited development in EU legislation. The Hydrocarbon Directive remains unchanged and no amendments having an impact on a state's discretion relating to energy production were made by the 2019 Electricity Directive. The role of the fundamental freedoms will thus remain the same. However, there are interesting developments in RED II in the direction of more detailed rules on the planning of land use intended to simplify and coordinate authorisation procedures for the use of renewable energy resources. So far, the rules leave the Member States with considerable discretion, but it will be interesting to follow this trend, particularly in light of Article 194(2) TFEU and a state's territorial sovereignty.

EEA Agreement and Fundamental Rights

21

The EEA Agreement and the ECHR

A Strasbourg Perspective

ARNFINN BÅRDSEN

I. PRELIMINARY POINTS

THE EFTA AND its organs are not High Contracting Parties to the European Convention on Human Rights (ECHR) and they are therefore not as such obliged under Article 1 ECHR to secure the rights and freedoms put forward in it. Any application before the European Court of Human Rights (ECtHR) directed against the EFTA, the EFTA Surveillance Authority (ESA) or the EFTA Court will, inevitably, be deemed to be incompatible, *ratione personae*, with the ECHR, and therefore inadmissible under its Article 35(3)(a). In this sense, the situation when it comes to the EFTA/EEA institutions is analogous to that of the EU and its organs, the Court of Justice of the European Union (CJEU) included, unless and until the EU accedes to the ECHR as envisaged by Article 6(2) of the Treaty on European Union.

However, by the above, very little is said about the impact of the ECHR within EEA law or about the EFTA Court's role in terms of the protection of European fundamental rights, compared to that of the CJEU.[1] On the contrary, this topic raises complex and multi-layered issues – I will touch on only a few of these in this chapter.

It needs to be emphasised at the very outset that according to the preamble to the EEA Agreement, the establishing of a European Economic Area 'will bring to the construction of a Europe based on peace, democracy and human rights'. Thus, even though the EEA Agreement evidently does not have any specific provision pertaining to the protection of fundamental rights, let alone a fully fledged charter of fundamental rights, the EEA Agreement assumes some sort of a link between the functioning of the Agreement and human rights protection at the EU level. Moreover, the ultimate goal of homogeneity between EEA law and EU law within the scope of the EEA Agreement can in practice only be achieved to the extent that EEA law is interpreted

[1] See R Spano, 'The EFTA Court and Fundamental Rights' (2017) 13 *European Constitutional Law Review* 475.

and applied with due regard given to fundamental rights, as protected by EU law. This will, inevitably, include the principle prescribed by Article 52 of the EU Charter on Fundamental Rights, ie, that insofar as the Charter contains rights which correspond to rights guaranteed by the ECHR, the meaning and scope of those rights will be the same as those laid down by the ECHR.

Consequently, and also fully in line with the proviso that pragmatism is key to the maintenance of the EEA Agreement, the EFTA Court has emphasised in cases like *Holship* that fundamental rights 'form part of the unwritten principles of EEA law' and 'that the provisions of the ECHR and the judgments of the European Court of Human Rights (ECtHR) are important sources for determining the scope of these fundamental rights'.[2] Indeed, the EFTA Court has made reference to the case law of the ECtHR on a number of occasions, such as in *Posten Norge*.[3] In general terms, the ECHR and the case law of the ECtHR is either applied as an interpretative aid or, more importantly, is perceived as representing substantive limitations on EEA law.[4]

However, it is still not settled or fully explored what systemic functions fundamental rights have within EEA law, particularly if compared with the role of fundamental rights within EU law on the basis of the EU Charter of Fundamental Rights. This includes the role of the EFTA Court in the *trilateral* set-up of domestic constitutional rights in EEA/EFTA States, EU Charter-based fundamental rights, and human rights and freedoms as defined by the ECHR. In this respect, it should be noted that in hard cases, such as *Holship*, the EFTA Court is inclined not to take a position as to the possible conflict between EEA law taken in isolation on the one hand and fundamental rights on the other hand. Instead, it leaves the issue to be assessed by the national courts.[5] Passing the ball back to the domestic courts in this manner is, evidently, based on the assumption that the domestic courts in EEA/EFTA States shall and will remain the guarantors of fundamental rights, even when implementing EEA law at the domestic level, as also confirmed by the Supreme Court of Norway itself in *Holship*, which emphasised the primacy of constitutional rights before any EEA rights.[6]

Moreover, when assessing the role of the EFTA Court in the context of the protection of fundamental rights, it must be taken into consideration that the EFTA Court is an international court *sui generis* in its creation, in its purpose, in its competence and in its operation, mirroring the one-of-a-kind character of the EEA Agreement itself. Three features may serve as illustrations: first, under the EFTA pillar of the EEA Agreement, there is no formal requirement of domestic direct effect and primacy of EEA law; second, under the Surveillance and Court Agreement (SCA), there is no formal duty for the courts in the EFTA States to refer, through the request for an advisory opinion procedure, any question to the EFTA Court, this avenue being in principle optional; and, third, the EFTA Court's advisory opinions (as opposed to the rulings in direct actions) are indeed advisory, not formally binding.

[2] Case E-14/15 *Holship Norge AS and Norsk Transportarbeiderforbund*, para 123.

[3] Case E-15/10 *Posten Norge AS v EFTA Surveillance Authority*, para 85.

[4] See further S Torp Helmersen, 'The EFTA Court and International Law' (2021) 1 *Oslo Law Review* 30, at 31–37.

[5] *Holship* (n 2) para 123 *in fine*.

[6] HR-2016-2554-P.

In order to explore some elements of the interplay between the EEA Agreement and the ECHR – as seen from Strasbourg – I will address three questions pertaining to state responsibility under the ECHR for the EEA/EFTA States, namely whether these states can be held responsible under the ECHR for the EFTA Court's rulings, either: (1) because of *structural weaknesses relating to the independence and impartiality of the EFTA Court itself*, or (2) as a consequence of the relevant state's *active participation in proceedings before the EFTA Court* (see sections II and III below, respectively); thereafter, I turn to (3) whether an EEA/EFTA State can be held fully responsible under the ECHR for that state's own *implementation of EEA law at a domestic level*. The latter is, at its very core, a question of the applicability of the *Bosphorus* presumption in the context of an EEA/EFTA State's implementation of EEA law (see sections IV–VI below).

II. THE EFTA COURT: AN 'INDEPENDENT AND IMPARTIAL TRIBUNAL'

The characteristics of the EFTA Court, viewed through the prism of Article 6(1) ECHR on the right to have access to a fair hearing before an independent and impartial tribunal established by law, came before the ECtHR for the first time in *Konkurrenten v Norway*.[7] The case was decided by a chamber formation of seven judges. Although the case was not decided by way of a judgment – it is a decision on inadmissibility – *Konkurrenten* may reasonably be considered a landmark ruling, representing a significant development regarding the ECtHR assessment of the EFTA Court.[8]

The company Konkurrenten had applied to the EFTA Court under Article 36(2) of the SCA for the annulment of two decisions by ESA, which had closed the investigation of alleged illegal state aid given by Norwegian authorities to a competing enterprise.[9] Following a detailed examination, concerning the applicant's position in respect of the two contested decisions, and the legal interest required for a company to be granted legal standing in cases and decisions of the type at issue – most notably, that the applicant's market position had been sufficiently substantially, and thus affected by the aid in question – the EFTA Court concluded that the applicant did not have legal standing in respect of either decision. Accordingly, the EFTA Court dismissed Konkurrenten's application for the annulment of the two decisions on the closing of investigation towards the competing enterprise.

In its complaint before the ECtHR, Konkurrenten alleged that Norway was responsible for the denial of 'access to a court', and a sufficiently reasoned decision according to Article 6(1) ECHR, when the EFTA Court had dismissed its application to have the two decisions taken by the ESA annulled. The applicant argued that Norway's responsibility under Article 1 ECHR was engaged because Norway was a party to the SCA and had thereby contributed to creating a system that, according to Konkurrenten, did not sufficiently protect fundamental rights. Norway was also

[7] *Konkurrenten.no AS v Norway* (dec), 28 November 2019, no 47341/15. For the purposes of full disclosure, it should be noted that this author was a sitting judge of the Second Section of the ECtHR that delivered the decision.

[8] M-J Clifton, 'Supplementary Contribution from the EFTA Court' in *National Courts and the Enforcement of EU Law* (The Hague, Congress Publications, 2020), vol 1, at 528 and 530.

[9] Case E-19/13, *Konkurrenten.no v ESA*.

the primary beneficiary of the SCA, insofar as the agreement and the Norwegian implementing legislation meant that an applicant had no other way to seek compensation in the event that the EFTA Court dismissed an application before it. The EFTA Court's dismissal of the applicant's case thus meant that Norway was protected from any compensation claims.

In *Konkurrenten v Norway* before the ECtHR, the Norwegian government submitted that the application effectively targeted the EFTA Court, and that the complaint was therefore incompatible, *ratione personae*, with the provisions of the ECHR. In any event, the EEA Agreement and the SCA offered protection of fundamental rights equivalent to that under the ECHR, and insofar as the complaint could be considered compatible, *ratione personae*, with the ECHR, it was therefore manifestly ill-founded. Also, ESA maintained that under the EEA legal order, there was a system offering protection of fundamental rights equivalent to the protection under the ECHR and that there had not been any manifest deficiencies in the protection of the applicant's rights caused by the standing rules applied by the EFTA Court in the case at hand.

The ECtHR, in its decision, confirmed its reasoning in cases such as *Bosphorus* and reiterated that the ECHR does not prohibit High Contracting Parties from transferring state power to an international organisation in order to pursue cooperation in certain fields of activity, but that they retain liability under Article 1 ECHR in respect of treaty commitments, subsequent to the entry into force of the ECHR.[10] As a result, High Contracting Parties would engage their responsibility under the ECHR should they transfer some of their powers to an international organisation, whose internal litigation mechanisms are manifestly deficient when compared with the requirements under the ECHR.[11]

As for the assessment of the EFTA Court concretely, the ECtHR emphasised that considering the fact that the EFTA Court was set up to operate as a judicial body similar to the CJEU and that the essential procedural principles governing the operation of the EFTA Court were inspired by those of the CJEU, the only starting point could be that there were no such manifest deficiencies.[12] This was, according to the ECtHR, confirmed by specific provisions in the EEA Agreement and the SCA, the EFTA Court's Rules of Procedure and the EFTA Court's case law.

When it then came to whether the applicant had rebutted what the ECtHR called a 'strong presumption' of lack of manifest deficiencies, the ECtHR reiterated that, in respect of Article 6(1) ECHR, the mere fact that an action is found inadmissible on the grounds of lacking legal interest or legal standing does not mean denial of access to a court, provided that the applicant's submissions have been the subject of a genuine examination. In the proceedings at issue, the EFTA Court applied the relevant test for legal standing under the SCA. The applicant was fully involved in the EFTA Court proceedings and had every opportunity to argue the admissibility of its application and to present the EFTA Court with evidence demonstrating that the application met the criteria for legal standing.[13]

[10] *Bosphorus Hava Yolları Turizm ve Ticaret Anonim Şirketi v Ireland*, App No 4593/98, paras 152–53, ECHR 2005-VI (GC).

[11] *Konkurrenten* (n 9) para 39.

[12] ibid para 45.

[13] ibid para 46.

Furthermore, as to the reasons provided by the EFTA Court for its inadmissibility conclusions, the ECtHR reiterated that Article 6(1) ECHR requires courts to adequately state the reasons on which their decisions are based. Without requiring a detailed answer to every argument put forward by a complainant, this obligation nevertheless presupposes that a party to judicial proceedings can expect a specific and express reply to those submissions, which are decisive for the outcome of the proceedings in question. In *Konkurrenten*, the ECtHR was satisfied that the EFTA Court had given detailed reasons as to why the applicant did not have legal standing in accordance with the applicable law.[14]

Against this background, the ECtHR did not consider that there was an appearance of any manifest deficiencies in the protection of the applicant's rights under the ECHR. The complaint from Konkurrenten was, accordingly, considered manifestly ill-founded and therefore inadmissible under Article 35(3) ECHR.[15] For this reason, the ECtHR left open the question of whether Konkurrenten's application was also inadmissible because of non-exhaustion of domestic remedies (a declaratory judgment and/or compensation) or because the case before the EFTA Court did not concern Konkurrenten's 'civil rights and obligations' within the meaning of Article 6(1) ECHR.

The ECtHR's assessment of the EFTA Court and its procedural framework is systemically important, in the sense that the ECtHR recognised the EFTA Court as a court which is in principle, and within the limits of its competence according to the EEA Agreement and the SCA, capable of providing relevant protection of fundamental rights within this rendition of the 'shared responsibility' for the protection of fundamental rights. Indeed, the ECtHR emphasised that the EFTA Court 'is a judicial body, deciding cases on a legal basis, independently and impartially'.[16]

III. RESPONSIBILITY FOR AN EEA/EFTA STATE FOR HAVING ENGAGED IN EFTA COURT PROCEEDINGS

A question that may arise under Article 1 ECHR is whether an EEA/EFTA State may be held responsible for procedural shortcomings at the EFTA Court because that State has actively engaged in the proceedings. Again, the ECtHR's decision in *Konkurrenten* provides important clarification in this respect.

The applicant in *Konkurrenten* argued before the ECtHR that Norway was responsible under Article 6(1) ECHR for alleged procedural shortcomings in the proceedings raised by the company before the EFTA Court, with reference to the fact that Norway had availed itself of its right under the pertinent procedural rules, such as the right of the state as a privileged party to intervene in all cases at the EFTA Court, to submit written and oral observations, in which it had – successfully – argued that the applicant's case was inadmissible. Norway had, according to Konkurrenten, therefore intervened in the proceedings before the EFTA Court in a manner that required liability being attributed to the state under Article 1 ECHR.

[14] ibid para 47.
[15] ibid para 49.
[16] ibid paras 41 and 45.

The ECtHR started its assessment of the applicant's arguments by clarifying that the responsibility under the ECHR may, in principle, be triggered for a High Contracting State which has transferred jurisdiction to an international organisation, and when it concerns proceedings for a reference for a preliminary ruling by a court of that organisation.[17] In this respect, the ECtHR drew a rather general analogy from established case law on the possible responsibility under the ECHR for EU Member States regarding preliminary rulings before the CJEU, such as in *Cooperatieve Producentenorganisatie van de Nederlandse Kokkelvisserij UA*.[18] The ECtHR did not discuss whether the situation may be different, or more nuanced, under the SCA since – contrary to references for preliminary rulings from the CJEU – the advisory opinions from the EFTA Court are indeed advisory, and domestic courts are under no formal or immediate legal obligation to follow them.[19] Implicitly leaving the answer to this question open, the ECtHR instead emphasised the fact that the pertinent proceedings before the EFTA Court concerned the legality of decisions taken by ESA and that proceedings had been initiated directly by Konkurrenten itself with the EFTA Court, in the form of an action for annulment. It was not a matter of a national court in an EEA/EFTA State requesting an advisory opinion of the EFTA Court.[20]

Indeed, it should be noted that in this sense, the situation in *Konkurrenten* was radically different from that in *Cooperatieve Producentenorganisatie van de Nederlandse Kokkelvisserij UA*, since the latter case concerned a reference for a preliminary ruling by the CJEU, where there was an obvious nexus between the proceedings before the CJEU and domestic proceedings. In such situations, it is the domestic court which, finding itself faced with a question of Union law, to which an answer is required in order to give a decision in a pending case before it, seeks the CJEU's assistance in terms of its own choosing. The interpretation which the CJEU then gives of Union law in response to the reference for preliminary ruling is authoritative and cannot be ignored by the domestic court. Such a nexus was non-existent in a situation such as that in *Konkurrenten*, given that it was an action for annulment. The only direct nexus between Norway and the proceedings before the EFTA Court was that Norway made use of the possibilities afforded to the state under the Statute of the EFTA Court and its Rules of Procedure to make written and oral submissions.

The ECtHR rejected the argument of the applicant that responsibility under the ECHR for procedural shortcomings of the EFTA Court could flow from the nature of Norway's submissions in the proceedings before the EFTA Court. In the ECHR's view, the fact that an EEA/EFTA State, in accordance with the relevant procedural rules, avails itself of submitting observations in a case pending before the EFTA Court cannot as such engage the state's responsibility under the ECHR.[21] This was the case irrespective of the state's position on the issue to be decided by the EFTA

[17] ibid para 38.

[18] *Cooperatieve Producentenorganisatie van de Nederlandse Kokkelvisserij UA v The Netherlands* (dec), App No 13645/05, 20 January 2009.

[19] However, see S Magnússon, 'On the Authority of Advisory Opinions: Reflections on the Functions and the Normativity of Advisory Opinions of the EFTA Court' (2010) 13(3) *Europarättslig Tidskrift* 528.

[20] *Konkurrenten* (n 9) para 40.

[21] ibid para 41.

Court or of the quality of its submissions. For the ECtHR, should the EFTA Court have ultimately decided the case along the same lines as was argued in those submissions, it could not in itself trigger the responsibility of the state concerned under the ECHR. In this respect, the ECtHR again emphasised that the EFTA Court was a judicial body, deciding cases on a legal basis, independently and impartially.[22] On those grounds, the ECtHR did not find that Norway was involved in the EFTA Court proceedings in such a manner that could in any way justify attributing responsibility to the state for the compliance of those proceedings with Article 6 ECHR.

IV. THE *BOSPHORUS* PRESUMPTION: A GENERAL OUTLINE

The *Bosphorus* presumption was introduced by the Grand Chamber of the ECtHR in *Bosphorus Hava Yolları Turizm ve Ticaret Anonim Şirketi* and was confirmed by the Grand Chamber in *Avotiņš*, following the Opinion 2/13 of the CJEU[23] on the draft agreement providing for the accession of the EU to the ECHR.[24]

The *Bosphorus* presumption intends, in particular, to ensure that a state party is not faced with a dilemma when it is obliged to rely on the legal obligations incumbent on it as a result of its membership of an international organisation, which is not party to the ECHR and to which it has transferred part of its sovereignty, in order to justify its actions or omissions arising from such membership vis-a-vis the ECHR. It also serves to determine in which cases the ECtHR may, in the interests of international cooperation, reduce the intensity of its supervisory role, as conferred on it by Article 19 ECHR, with regard to observance by the state parties of their engagements arising from the ECHR.[25]

The ECtHR has summarised the key components of this presumption – its scope and application – as established in its case law, as follows.[26]

First, the states which are parties to the ECHR remain responsible under the ECHR for the measures they take to comply with their international legal obligations, even when those obligations stem from their membership of an international organisation, to which they have transferred part of their sovereignty. Absolving the states completely from their responsibility under the ECHR, where they were simply complying with their obligations as members of an international organisation, to which they had transferred a part of their sovereignty, would be incompatible with the purpose and object of the ECHR. Were it to be otherwise, its guarantees could be limited or excluded at will, thereby depriving it of its peremptory character and undermining the practical and effective nature of its safeguards.

Second, action taken in compliance with such international legal obligations is justified where the relevant organisation protects fundamental rights, as regards

[22] ibid para 45.

[23] Opinion 2/13, ECLI:EU:C:2014:2454 (EU Accession to the ECHR II). See KS Ziegler, 'The Second Attempt at EU Accession to the ECHR: Opinion 2/13', in G Butler and RA Wessel (eds), *EU External Relations Law: The Cases in Context* (Oxford, Hart Publishing, 2022).

[24] *Bosphorus* (n 10); *Avotiņš v Latvia* [GC], 23 May 2016, no 17502/07.

[25] See *Michaud v France*, App No 12323/11, para 104, ECHR 2012.

[26] ibid paras 102–03.

both the substantive guarantees offered and the mechanisms controlling their observance, in a manner which can be considered at least equivalent – not identical but 'comparable' – to that for which the ECHR provides. In its case law, the ECtHR has in this respect emphasised that any such finding of 'equivalence' could not be final and would be susceptible to review in the light of any relevant change in fundamental rights protection. If such equivalent protection would be considered to be provided by the organisation, the presumption will be that a state has not departed from the requirements of the ECHR when it does no more than implement legal obligations flowing from its membership of the organisation.

Third, a state will, notwithstanding the presumption described above, be fully responsible under the ECHR for all acts falling outside its strict international legal obligations, notably where it has exercised state discretion. Thus, the application of the *Bosphorus* presumption is indeed subject to the condition that there existed no margin of discretion on the part of the domestic authorities.

Fourth, the presumption of equivalent protection can be rebutted if, in the circumstances of a particular case, it is considered that the protection of rights according to the ECHR was *manifestly deficient*. In such cases, as explained by the ECtHR, the interest of international cooperation would be outweighed by the ECHR's role as a constitutional instrument of European public order in the field of human rights.

Concerning the EU, the ECtHR has made clear that the *substantive protection* of fundamental rights afforded by EU law is equivalent to that of the ECtHR, taking into account the provisions of Article 52(3) of the EU Charter of Fundamental Rights. According to that provision, insofar as the rights contained in the Charter correspond to rights guaranteed by the ECHR, their meaning and scope are the same, without prejudice to the possibility for EU law to provide more extensive protection.[27] The ECtHR has also recognised that the mechanisms provided for by EU law for *supervising* observance of fundamental rights, *insofar as its full potential has been deployed*, also affords protection comparable to that for which the ECHR provides. On this point, the ECtHR has attached considerable importance to the role and powers of the CJEU, even though individual access to the CJEU is far more limited than access to the ECtHR itself under Article 34 ECHR.[28]

V. *KONKURRENTEN v NORWAY*: THE *BOSPHORUS* PRESUMPTION IS INAPPLICABLE IN THE EEA CONTEXT

The *Bosphorus* presumption on equivalent protection of fundamental rights is well suited to the need to organise the coexistence and shared responsibility of two jurisdictions: the ECtHR and the CJEU. The question is then: does this presumption also apply for the EEA/EFTA States within the context of the EEA Agreement?[29]

[27] *Avotiņš* (n 24) para 103.

[28] ibid para 104.

[29] On this, see also DT Björgvinsson, 'The EEA Agreement and Presumption of Equivalent Protection of Human Rights' in JF Kjølbro, S O'Leary and M Tsirli (eds), *Liber Amicorum Robert Spano* (Limal, Anthemis, 2022) 79–90.

Again, the ECtHR's decision in *Konkurrenten* is key, being the first case before the ECtHR addressing the issue. The ECtHR stated:[30]

> 42 … [T]he Court reiterates that it has held that if an organisation to which a Contracting State has transferred jurisdiction is considered to protect fundamental rights in a manner which can be considered at least "equivalent" to that for which the Convention provides, the presumption will be that a State has not departed from the requirements of the Convention when it does no more than implement legal obligations flowing from its membership of the organisation … That presumption applies also as a corollary in cases concerning proceedings internal to the organisation … The protection need not be identical to that provided by Article 6 of the Convention … The presumption can be rebutted if, in the circumstances of a particular case, it is considered that the protection of Convention rights was manifestly deficient …
>
> 43 On this point the Court emphasises that the basis for the presumption established by *Bosphorus* is in principle lacking when it comes to the implementation of EEA law at domestic level within the framework of the EEA Agreement, due to the specificities of the governing treaties, compared to those of the European Union. For the purpose of the present analysis, two distinct features need to be specifically highlighted. Firstly, and in contrast to EU law, there is within the framework of the EEA Agreement itself no direct effect and no supremacy … Secondly, and although the EFTA Court has expressed the view that the provisions of the EEA Agreement 'are to be interpreted in the light of fundamental rights' in order to enhance coherency between EEA law and EU law … the EEA Agreement does not include the EU Charter of Fundamental Rights, or any reference whatsoever to other legal instruments having the same effect, such as the Convention.

Accordingly, the ECtHR is clear that the *Bosphorus* presumption does not generally apply within the context of EEA law, since 'the basis for the presumption established in *Bosphorus* is in principle lacking when it comes to the implementation of EEA law at [a] domestic level within the framework of the EEA Agreement'. The ECtHR referred in this respect to 'the specificities of the governing treaties, compared to those of the European Union', notably that there is 'within the framework of the EEA Agreement itself no direct effect and no supremacy'.[31] The ECtHR's point is perhaps slightly understated. The argument of the ECtHR is that an EEA/EFTA State will in principle never find itself in the dilemma that the *Bosphorus* presumption aims at solving, since the EEA Agreement allows that domestic courts refrain from applying EEA law in order to avoid the violation of fundamental rights as prescribed in the domestic constitution and/or international human rights treaties, such as the ECHR. This position is illustrated by the plenary judgment of the Supreme Court of Norway in *Holship*, emphasising the primacy of constitutional rights before EEA rights:

> Under and pursuant to Article 101, first paragraph, of the Constitution, everyone 'has the right to form, join and leave associations, including trade unions and political parties' … If the boycott against Holship notified by NTF is … protected by Article 101, first paragraph, of the Constitution, any rights derived from the EEA Agreement must yield.[32]

[30] *Konkurrenten* (n 9) paras 42–43.

[31] For a critical analysis of the reasoning in *Konkurrenten*, see HH Fredriksen and S Øby Johansen, 'The EEA Agreement as a Jack-in-the-Box in the Relationship between the CJEU and the European Court of Human Rights' (2020) 5(2) *European Papers* 707.

[32] Judgment 16 December 2016, para 80. An English translation by the Norwegian Supreme Court is available at: https://www.domstol.no/globalassets/upload/hret/decisions-in-english-translation/case-2014-2089.pdf.

This solution, envisaged by the Supreme Court of Norway within the context of EEA law, would, as a matter of principle, not work in the context of EU law. It would undoubtedly be contrary to EU law to perform this kind of constitutional review by a domestic court. In turn, this difference between EU law and EEA law also explains the need for providing protection of fundamental rights within EU law as an extension of the protection of fundamental rights as prescribed by domestic constitutions and under the ECHR, to 'replace' the review by domestic courts under national law. Were it to be otherwise, the requirements of direct effect and primacy of EU law would leave an unacceptable void in the overall protection of fundamental rights.

In *Konkurrenten*, the ECtHR alluded to this structural link between direct effect and primacy on the one side, and the need for equivalent protection of fundamental rights in EU law on the other, recalling that the EEA Agreement does not include the EU Charter of Fundamental Rights or any reference whatsoever to other legal instruments having the same effect, such as the ECHR.[33] In this respect, it should be noted that under EEA law, and in contrast to EU law, such a reference is not a systemic necessity either, since the EEA/EFTA States would not breach their obligations under EEA law should they give priority to fundamental rights. Coherence and homogeneity between EU law and EEA law may, in principle, still prevail as long as domestic courts in EEA/EFTA States continue to protect fundamental rights when implementing EEA law at a domestic level. Indeed, the EFTA Court has made clear that the EEA/EFTA States, and in particular their courts, must not only interpret their national law in a manner consistent with EEA law but are also under an obligation to ensure that the interpretation and application of acts incorporated into the EEA Agreement does not result in a conflict with fundamental rights protected by EEA law.[34]

VI. *HOLSHIP v NORWAY*: CONFIRMATION OF *KONKURRENTEN*, WITH SOME NUANCES ADDED

The applicability of the *Bosphorus* presumption was again addressed and discussed in *Norwegian Confederation of Trade Unions (LO) and Norwegian Transport Workers' Union (NTF)*, often referred to as *Holship*.[35] In this judgment, the ECtHR confirmed *Konkurrenten*'s conclusion that the *Bosphorus* presumption does not apply when an EEA/EFTA State implements EEA law at a domestic level. Moreover, the judgment provided some nuances to the analysis compared to *Konkurrenten*.[36]

In 1970, the applicants, the Norwegian Transport Workers' Union and the Norwegian Confederation of Trade Unions entered into a collective framework

[33] *Konkurrenten* (n 9) para 43. However, see the Charter in EEA law: G Butler and M Meling, 'Horizontal Direct Effect of the Charter in EU Law: Ramifications for the European Economic Area' (2020) 3(2) *Nordic Journal of European Law* 1, https://doi.org/10.36969/njel.v3i2.22389.

[34] Case E-1/20 *Kerim*, para 43.

[35] *Norwegian Confederation of Trade Unions (LO) and Norwegian Transport Workers' Union (NTF) v Norway*, 10 June 2021, App No 45487/17. For the purposes of full disclosure, it should be noted that this author withdrew – having been part of the composition when the case was decided by the Norwegian Supreme Court – from the case at hand.

[36] See also HP Graver, 'The Holship Ruling of the ECtHR and the Protection of Fundamental Rights in Europe', *ERA Forum*, 1 February 2022, https://link.springer.com/article/10.1007/s12027-022-00701-0.

agreement with the Confederation of Norwegian Enterprise, the largest employer organisation in Norway, and the Norwegian Logistics and Freight Association, in respect of a fixed pay scheme for dockworkers at many of the major ports in Norway. Under the terms of the agreement, an office was set up in the port of Drammen, which was responsible for the employment of all permanent workers in that facility. In 2013, Holship Norge AS, a subsidiary of the Danish company Holship Holding A/S, decided to employ four workers at the port who, among other duties, were to load and unload their ships. The company was not a party to the framework agreement. Consequently, the Norwegian Transport Workers' Union decided to organise a boycott of all shipping in Drammen involving Holship. The Union succeeded in obtaining a declaratory judgment of the lawfulness of the boycott from the Drammen City Court. The judgment was upheld by the Borgarting High Court. Holship appealed to the Supreme Court of Norway, which made a request for an advisory opinion from the EFTA Court.[37]

On the case returning from the EFTA Court, in a split decision, the Supreme Court of Norway ruled in *Holship* on 16 December 2016 that the boycott was unlawful. It referred to the judgment of the EFTA Court that Holship's right to freedom of establishment under EEA law might be infringed by the boycott. The right to establishment could justify restrictions of constitutional or ECHR-based human rights. A fair balance had to be struck. The Supreme Court adjudged that giving priority to workers employed via the administration office in the port of Drammen was a restriction on the freedom of establishment. However, EU law and EEA law recognised the protection of workers as a possible reason for restricting freedom of establishment. For the Supreme Court, this justification for restricting freedom was not adequate in the circumstances of the present case. Ultimately, the principal effect of the boycott would have been to limit the access of other operators to the market for loading and unloading services. The Supreme Court concluded that priority of engagement as demanded by the Norwegian Transport Workers' Union was not sufficiently justified and did not satisfy the requirement to strike a fair balance between freedom of establishment and the possible fundamental right to boycott. It thus found the boycott to be unlawful.

Relying on Article 11 ECHR on the freedom of assembly and association, the applicant unions lodged a complaint against the decision to declare their notified boycott unlawful. The ECtHR found that the boycott had sought to protect at least in part the occupational interests of union members in a manner which fell within the scope of Article 11 ECHR and that this provision was accordingly applicable. In addition, it was not contested that there had been a restriction of the trade unions' rights owing to the declaratory judgment finding it unlawful. The question was whether the restriction flowing from the judgment had been necessary in a democratic society, as required under Article 11(2) ECHR.

Before the ECtHR in *Holship*, Norway argued – and in contrast to the ECtHR's conclusion in *Konkurrenten* – that EEA law provided for the protection of fundamental rights in a manner which was similar to the protection provided for by the ECHR, and that there was therefore a presumption of compliance with

[37] *Holship* (n 2).

the ECHR, which was the same as or similar to that set out in *Bosphorus*. This presumption had not been rebutted in the instant case, as there had been no 'manifestly deficient' protection of ECHR rights.

In its judgment, the ECtHR reiterated that if an organisation to which a state has transferred jurisdiction is considered to protect fundamental rights in a manner which can be considered at least 'equivalent' to that for which the ECHR provides for, the presumption will be that a state has not departed from the requirements of the ECHR when it does no more than implement legal obligations flowing from its membership of the organisation. The ECtHR then went on to recall that in *Konkurrenten*, the ECtHR had stated that the basis for the presumption established by *Bosphorus* is in principle lacking when it comes to the implementation of EEA law at a domestic level, within the framework of the EEA Agreement, due to the specificities of the governing treaties compared to those of the EU.

Two distinct features were specifically highlighted. First, and in contrast to EU law, the fact that there is, within the framework of the EEA Agreement itself, no direct effect and no primacy. Second, the EEA Agreement does not include the EU Charter of Fundamental Rights or any reference whatsoever to other legal instruments having the same effect, such as the ECHR. As to the latter, the ECtHR now added a nuance, building on *Konkurrenten*:[38]

> 107 As regards, in particular, the latter feature, the Court observes, however, as clearly stated by the EFTA court in the *Holship* case, that fundamental rights form part of the unwritten principles of EEA law … The respondent Government provided several examples from the EFTA court in this regard. Since this reflects the position which previously pertained under EU law, prior to successive EU Treaty amendments, according to which fundamental rights were first recognised as general principles of EU law, the Court considers that the fact that the EEA agreement does not include the EU Charter is not determinative of the question whether the *Bosphorus* presumption could apply when it comes to the implementation of EEA law, or certain parts thereof.

This indeed echoes the EFTA Court's own statement in *Holship*, ie, that fundamental rights 'form part of the unwritten principles of EEA law' and 'that the provisions of the ECHR and the judgments of the ECtHR are important sources for determining the scope of these fundamental rights'.[39] However, some would find the statement that the current status of the protection of fundamental rights under EEA law 'reflects the position which previously pertained under EU law, prior to successive EU Treaty amendments' to be debatable. While the protection of fundamental rights had to be taken on board in EU law as a decisive extension of the protection of fundamental rights as prescribed by domestic constitutions and under the ECHR, to 'replace' the review by domestic courts. Were it to be otherwise, the requirements of direct effect and primacy of EU law would leave an unacceptable void in the overall protection of fundamental rights. Under EEA law, and in contrast to EU law, such a reference is not a systemic necessity, since the EEA/EFTA States would not breach their obligations

[38] *Norwegian Confederation of Trade Unions (LO) and Norwegian Transport Workers' Union (NTF) v Norway*, 10 June 2021, App No 45487/17) para 107.

[39] *Holship* (n 2) para 123.

under EEA law should they give priority to fundamental rights. Accordingly, an EEA/EFTA State will in principle never find itself in the dilemma that the *Bosphorus* presumption aims at solving, since the EEA Agreement allows that domestic courts to refrain from applying EEA law in order to avoid the violation of fundamental rights as prescribed in the domestic constitution and/or international human rights treaties, such as the ECHR.

In any event, this nuance, and possible change of perspective in the ECtHR's assessment of the nature and level of substantive protection of fundamental rights in EEA law, had no bearing as to the non-applicability of the *Bosphorus* presumption. As per the ECtHR,[40]

> 108 However, given one of the other features of EEA law identified by the Court in the *Konkurrenten.no* decision – the absence of supremacy and direct effect, added to which is the absence of the binding legal effect of advisory opinions from the EFTA Court – and given that the existence of procedural mechanisms for ensuring the protection of substantive fundamental rights guarantees is one of the two conditions for the application of the *Bosphorus* presumption, the Court leaves it to another case, where questions in relation to the procedural mechanisms under EEA law may arise, to review this issue. It therefore proceeds on the basis that for the purposes of this case the *Bosphorus* presumption does not apply to EEA law. The Court is therefore required to determine whether the restriction was necessary for the purposes of Article 11 of the Convention.

This last paragraph is particularly interesting for at least two reasons. First, it confirms that the lack of direct effect and primacy in EEA law is indicative for the inapplicability of the *Bosphorus* presumption, as emphasised in *Konkurrenten*. Second, it announces that the mechanism for the procedural protection of fundamental rights in EEA law may also, in itself, be decisive, with reference to the absence of the binding legal effect of advisory opinions from the EFTA Court. However, the ECtHR left the issue for a possible review in a later case, where questions in relation to the procedural mechanisms under EEA law may arise.

VII. CLOSING REMARKS

In *Konkurrenten*, the ECtHR recognised the legal framework of the EEA Agreement within the EFTA pillar of the EEA, and the institutional and procedural framework of the EFTA Court as being, a priori, compliant with Article 6(1) ECHR. Whilst one can rather safely assume that the EEA/EFTA States will not be held responsible under the ECHR for the EFTA Court's rulings, it is, on the other hand, now also firmly established case law from the ECtHR that the EEA/EFTA States bear full responsibility under the ECHR for their own implementation of EEA law, the *Bosphorus* presumption not being applicable in this context.

Although the ECtHR ultimately concluded that there had been no violation of Article 11 ECHR in *Holship*, this judgment is noteworthy as it illustrates distinctly the implications of the inapplicability of the *Bosphorus* presumption in the EEA/EFTA

[40] *Norwegian Confederation of Trade Unions* (n 38) para 108.

context. In this respect, it should be noted that according to the plenary judgment of the Supreme Court of Norway in the case, any conflict between a right to boycott protected under Article 11 ECHR and the parallel Article 101 of the Constitution of Norway on the one side, and the freedom of establishment as prescribed in Article 31 EEA on the other, should be solved by a rather plain balancing of competing rights:

> The freedom of establishment, as established by Article 31 of the EEA Agreement, is a fundamental freedom in the EEA, and if the right to boycott is protected under Article 101, first paragraph, of the Constitution, these rights must be weighed against each other as part of a consideration of proportionality. This weighing of interests is similar in nature to the one carried out when restrictions are imposed on the freedom of establishment as a result of basic rights forming part of EU and EEA law: just as rights under the EEA Agreement can justify restriction of constitutional or conventional human rights, so can constitutional or conventional human rights justify restrictions of rights under the EEA Agreement.[41]

Moreover, the Supreme Court further explained:

> In considering whether a restriction on the freedom of establishment under the EEA Agreement is justified, I will address how to weigh the freedom of association under Article 11 of the ECHR against the freedom of establishment under Article 31 of the EEA Agreement. In this case, the weighing of the freedom of association pursuant to Article 101, first paragraph, of the Constitution against the freedom of establishment under the EEA Agreement must lead to the same result.[42]

Accordingly, the Norwegian Supreme Court assessed the rights and freedoms under ECHR and the freedoms stemming from the EEA Agreement as being on an equal footing, its task therefore being to strike a balance between competing, commensurable rights. The ECtHR had another view and emphasised the following:[43]

> 117 Firstly, the Court accepts that protecting the rights of others granted to them by way of EEA law may justify restrictions on rights under Article 11 of the Convention … However, it also notes that for a collective action to achieve its aim, it may have to interfere with internal market freedoms such as those at issue in the case before the Supreme Court. As noted by the Borgarting High Court in the present case, creating difficulties for the company in respect of loading and unloading, and the possible negative financial consequences flowing therefrom, would have been an important point of the boycott … In the same way that a right to strike does not imply a right to prevail, the degree to which a collective action risks having economic consequences cannot, therefore, in and of itself be a decisive consideration in the analysis of proportionality under Article 11, paragraph 2 of the Convention … Even when implementing their obligations under EU or EEA law, the Court observes that Contracting Parties should ensure that restrictions imposed on Article 11 rights do not affect the essential elements of trade union freedom, without which that freedom would become devoid of substance.
>
> 118 Secondly, as follows from paragraphs 98 and 110 above, it is primarily for the national authorities, notably the courts, to interpret and apply domestic law, if necessary in

[41] Judgment 16 December 2016, para 85. HR-2016-2554-P (sak nr 2014/2089), *Holship Norge AS, Norwegian Business Association, Confederation of Norwegian Enterprise v Norwegian Transport Workers' Union and Norwegian Confederation of Trade Unions*.

[42] ibid para 87.

[43] *Norwegian Federation of Trade Unions* (n 38), paras 117–18.

> conformity with EU or EEA law, the Court's role being confined to ascertaining whether the effects of such adjudication are compatible with the Convention. As highlighted in the submissions of the applicant unions in the present case, however, there is a risk that a domestic court which finds itself in a position such as that in which the Supreme Court found itself in the present case may balance a right under the Convention against a right under the EEA Agreement in a manner that would generally only be appropriate had the issue before it been a matter of conflicting fundamental rights under the Convention. *From the perspective of Article 11 of the Convention, EEA freedom of establishment is not a counterbalancing fundamental right to freedom of association but rather one element, albeit an important one, to be taken into consideration in the assessment of proportionality under Article 11, paragraph 2.* The risk just referred to is one which, while ensuring full compliance with their obligations under EEA or EU law, domestic courts must seek to avoid. (Emphasis added)

Accordingly, it is in this configuration not a question of balancing competing rights placed on an equal footing, but to assess whether rights under the EEA Agreement can justify an interference with fundamental rights, in this case under Article 11(2) ECHR requiring that the interference was 'necessary in a democratic society'.[44]

The message from the ECtHR in these paragraphs is important as corrective to the Supreme Court's methodology for future cases where the implementation of rights under EEA law might have to be limited because of fundamental rights as protected by the ECHR. Here there is also a clear message to the EFTA Court when it comes to how fundamental rights are expected to operate within and vis-a-vis EEA law, a message that somehow also serves as a reservation to the view that substantive EEA law provides a protection of fundamental rights 'equivalent' to that of the ECHR. The approach of the ECtHR in *Holship* also shows that the non-applicability of the *Bosphorus* presumption in the EEA context opens up, although indirectly, for a slightly more outspoken dialogue with the CJEU on the protection of fundamental rights in Europe, in this particular case, by clarifying the required hierarchical structure of fundamental rights protection as seen from the ECtHR in Strasbourg.

In closing, I recall that European law is dynamic and multi-dimensional, being generated and refined by multiple and complex momentums on a national, international and supranational level. It has been predicted that when the legal history of the early twenty-first century is to be written, history will be a chronicle of courts taking a lead position in clarifying and developing the law and the systems of law, including the protection of fundamental rights. There is also no doubt that the *future* of effective and coherent fundamental rights protection depends heavily on courts taking them seriously, transforming them from normative ideas into legal realities, with an impact on lives in the real world. To do so, courts need to make wise, sustainable and principled choices of legal policy, within the limits of the law and in accordance with the powers vested in the judiciary. The European Courts in Luxembourg and Strasbourg have – alongside European APEX courts – to this end acquired a position that can hardly be overestimated: dedicated to safeguarding and promoting a common European legal order founded on the effective and coherent protection of fundamental rights.

[44] See H Ellingsen, 'Reconciling Fundamental Social Rights and Economic Freedoms: The ECtHR's Ruling in *LO and NTF v Norway (the Holship Case)*' (2022) 59 *Common Marked Law Review* 583.

22

Effective Judicial Protection under the EEA Agreement

HILDE K ELLINGSEN

I. INTRODUCTION

THE AGREEMENT ON the European Economic Area (EEA) serves as the fundamental basis for the relationship between the EEA/EFTA States and the EU. The treaty is of a *sui generis* nature, containing a 'distinct legal order of its own'.[1] One of the key aspects which sets the EEA Agreement apart from traditional trade agreements is that EEA law confers enforceable rights on individuals.[2] Since the provisions of the EEA Agreement benefit individuals and economic operators, the proper functioning of the EEA Agreement depends on their ability to rely on those rights.[3] National courts play a key role in applying EEA law and securing the rights of individuals, and they must ensure access to justice and effective judicial protection of individual EEA rights. The EFTA Court has repeatedly stated that effective judicial protection is a general principle of EEA law.[4]

Effective judicial protection has also been proclaimed by the Court of Justice of the European Union (CJEU) as a general principle of Union law stemming from the constitutional traditions common to the Member States, which has been enshrined in Articles 6 and 13 of the European Convention on Human Rights (ECHR).[5] This principle is now codified in Article 47 of the Charter of Fundamental Rights (hereinafter 'the Charter') which, upon the entry into force of the Treaty of Lisbon, acquired the status of primary law within the EU legal order.[6] The Member States' duty to provide effective judicial protection is also explicitly laid down in Article 19(1) of the Treaty on European Union (TEU), which requires them to 'provide remedies sufficient to ensure effective legal protection in the fields covered by Union law'.

[1] Case E-9/97 *Sveinbjörnsdóttir*, para 59.

[2] FJ Büchel and C Zatschler, 'Judicial Protection in the EEA' in A Biondi and G Sangiuolo (eds), *The EU and the Rule of Law in International Economic Relations* (Cheltenham, Edward Elgar, 2021) 330.

[3] *Sveinbjörnsdóttir* (n 1) para 58.

[4] Case E-15/10 *Posten Norge* para 86; and Joined Cases E-11/19 and E-12/19 *Adpublisher*, para 50.

[5] Case C-222/84 *Johnston* v *Chief Constable of the Royal Ulster Constabulary*, EU:C:1986:206, para 18; and Case C-222/86 *Unectef* v *Heylens*, EU:C:1987:442, para 14.

[6] According to Art 6(1) TEU, the Charter is to have 'the same legal value as the Treaties'.

The EEA Agreement does not include the Charter or a comparable rights instrument, although the preamble to the EEA Agreement does emphasise the right to judicially defend the rights conferred by the Agreement.[7] Since the principle of effective judicial protection lacks an explicit textual basis in the EEA Agreement, the principle has been constructed and developed on the basis of considerations of homogeneity and loyalty. However, the principle of effective judicial protection is less developed in the EFTA Court's case law than in that of the CJEU. The EFTA Court has not defined and clarified the content or scope of the principle, and nor has it provided a clear explanation of the normative and theoretical underpinnings of its case law on effective judicial protection.

This chapter discusses the purview of and limits to the principle of effective judicial protection within the legal framework of the EEA Agreement and the scope of the principle in the domestic legal orders of the EEA/EFTA States. Within the EU, the transformation of the Charter into primary law has had an impact on the protection of rights, by serving as a platform for the evolution of the CJEU's case law. Moreover, the past few years have seen developments in EU constitutional law, with the principle of effective judicial protection being used as a gateway to enforce the rule of law in the Union. In this chapter, how and to what extent the EFTA Court may respond to those developments in the EEA context will be examined, as will the extent to which the 'special relationship' between the EU and the EEA/EFTA States means that a comparable level of effective judicial protection must be ensured in the EFTA pillar of the Agreement.[8]

II. THE PRINCIPLE OF EFFECTIVE JUDICIAL PROTECTION IN EU LAW

EU law provides for various kinds of individual rights, pertaining inter alia to environmental protection, competition policy and consumer protection, and the Member States are obliged to ensure the protection of those rights at the national level. The principle of effective judicial protection in EU law must be seen against the backdrop of this system of decentralised private enforcement, where national courts have become 'functional Union courts'.[9] The CJEU has stated that, together with the Court itself, the Member States are the 'guardians of [the] legal order and the judicial system of the European Union', and they need to ensure the full application of EU law and judicial protection of individual EU rights.[10]

The principle of effective judicial protection is closely related to the principle of effectiveness, which entails that national procedural rules must not render the enforcement of EU law impossible in practice or excessively difficult.[11] The principle of effective judicial protection nevertheless has a different orientation, in that it seeks

[7] See recital 8 of the Preamble.

[8] See Case C-897/19 PPU *Ruska Federacija v IN*, EU:C:2020:262, para 50.

[9] V Trstenjak and E Beysen, 'European Consumer Protection Law: *Curia Semper Dabit Remedium*?' (2011) 48 *CML Rev* 95, 97.

[10] Agreement on the creation of a unified patent litigation system, Opinion 1/09, EU:C:2011:123, paras 66 and 68.

[11] See, for example, Case C-13/01 Safalero, EU:C 2003:170, para 49.

to ensure that individual rights are protected by the courts, whereas the effectiveness principle aims to ensure that national rules do not impede the effective application of Union law. Hence, the latter is a manifestation of the broader principle of *effet utile*, which serves to ensure the full and useful effect of Union law.[12] This principle pervades the entire sphere of Union law, encompassing as it does implementation, enforcement and compliance.[13]

The principle of effective judicial protection – originally a judicial creation – now finds explicit recognition in EU primary law. Pursuant to the first paragraph of Article 47 of the Charter, '[e]veryone whose rights and freedoms guaranteed by the Union are violated has the right to an effective remedy before a tribunal'. The right to effective judicial protection also comprises the right to a fair trial and due process requirements such as the right to be advised, defended and represented, and to obtain legal aid, if necessary (see the second and third paragraphs, respectively).

The CJEU has made use of the principle of effective judicial protection as a means of scrutinising a wide range of domestic enforcement rules concerning access to the courts, due process guarantees applicable during the proceedings and remedies afforded in the case of rights infringements.[14] It is evident from this line of case law that the right to effective judicial protection comprises various facets and both formal and substantive 'sub-rights'.[15] The case law also clearly illustrates that the right to effective judicial protection is not absolute, but may be subject to limitations.

Article 52(1) of the Charter allows for limitations on the exercise of Charter rights insofar as they are prescribed by law, they respect the essence of the right and they comply with the principle of proportionality. Domestic rules and practices may not undermine the very essence of the right to effective judicial protection. That essence 'represents the untouchable core or inner circle of a fundamental right that cannot be diminished, restricted or interfered with'.[16] The CJEU has inter alia stressed that the complete absence of a legal avenue for individuals alleging an infringement of their Union rights is unacceptable, since it impinges upon the very core of the right to effective judicial protection.[17]

The explanations drawn up as a way of providing guidance on the interpretation of the Charter clarify that the first paragraph of Article 47 of the Charter corresponds in essence to Article 13 ECHR, providing for the right to an 'effective

[12] AP Komninos, 'Private Enforcement in the EU with Emphasis on Damages Actions' in D Geradin and I Lianos (eds), *Handbook on European Competition Law: Enforcement and Procedure* (Cheltenham, Edward Elgar, 2013) 236.

[13] F Snyder, 'The Effectiveness of European Community Law: Institutions, Processes, Tools and Techniques' (1993) 56(1) *MLR* 19, 26. The CJEU has developed several mechanisms with a view to ensuring the effectiveness of EU law in the Member States, and groundbreaking cases in the CJEU's history – such as Case C-26/62 *Van Gend & Loos*, EU:C:1963:1 and Case C-6/64 *Costa* v *ENEL*, EU:C:1964:66 on direct effect and primacy, respectively – were grounded on effet utile arguments.

[14] See Case C-73/16 *Puškár*, EU:C:2017:725 (pre-trial obligations and admissibility of evidence) and Case C-30/19 *Braathens Regional Aviation*, EU:C:2021:269 (remedies for non-material damages).

[15] The formal aspects relate to access to the courts, whereas the substantive aspects relate to the outcome of the court's proceedings in terms of effective remedies to prevent and redress rights violations: see, for example, *Puškár* (n 14).

[16] M Brkan, 'The Concept of Essence of Fundamental Rights in the EU Legal Order: Peeling the Onion to its Core' (2018) 14 *European Constitutional Law Review* 332, 333.

[17] Case C-362/14 *Schrems*, EU:C:2015:650; and *Puškár* (n 14).

remedy', whereas the second paragraph thereof largely corresponds to Article 6(1) ECHR, which provides for the right to a 'fair and public hearing within a reasonable time by an independent and impartial tribunal established by law'.[18] The relationship between the ECHR and the Charter is regulated in Article 52(3) of the Charter, which provides that, insofar as the Charter contains rights that correspond to rights guaranteed by the ECHR, the meaning and scope of those rights are to be the same as those laid down by the Convention, although Union law may provide for more extensive protection. Although the right to effective judicial protection under EU law has 'acquired a separate identity and substance … which are not the mere sum of the provisions of Articles 6 and 13 of the ECHR',[19] the guarantees enshrined in these provisions constitute a floor below which the Union must not go.

III. THE PRINCIPLE OF EFFECTIVE JUDICIAL PROTECTION IN EEA LAW

A. Introduction

The EEA Agreement integrates the EEA/EFTA States into the internal market, creating a 'homogenous European Economic Area'.[20] Just as in the EU legal order, the judicial protection of individual EEA rights works in a decentralised system in which national courts effectively function as courts of European law.[21] However, EEA law is not simply a carbon copy of EU law, but rather has 'its own structure and logic'.[22] The EEA legal order differs from the EU legal order in that its objectives are more modest and the depth of integration is less far-reaching than under the EU Treaties.[23] There are also important differences in the judicial architecture of the EEA Agreement, in particular with respect to the required degree of penetration in the domestic legal orders of the Contracting States. This begs the question of whether these distinguishing features entail a difference in the level of effective judicial protection or whether they can be bridged by considerations of homogeneity and loyalty.

Homogeneity and loyalty are cornerstones of the EEA Agreement. The principle of homogeneity finds expression both in the preamble to and in the main part of the EEA Agreement, and entails that identical rules under EU and EEA law are to be interpreted in a uniform manner.[24] Be that as it may, the application of the principle of homogeneity is not restricted to the interpretation of provisions which are identical in substance to parallel provisions of EU law. It also applies to the legal effect of

[18] See Explanations Relating to the Charter of Fundamental Rights [2007] OJ C303, p 17.

[19] Opinion of Advocate General Cruz Villalón in Case C-69/10 *Samba Diouf*, EU:C:2011:102, point 39.

[20] Article 1 EEA.

[21] ME Mendez-Pinedo, 'Constitutional/Judicial Resistance to European Law in Iceland. Sovereignty and Constitutional Identity vs Access to Justice under the EEA Agreement' (2020) 10 *Juridical Tribune* 390, 411.

[22] J Temple Lang, 'The Principle of Sincere Cooperation in EEA Law' in C Baudenbacher (ed), *The Fundamental Principles of EEA Law* (Cham, Springer International, 2017) 74.

[23] Case E-18/11 *Irish Bank* [2012], para 57.

[24] Article 6 EEA requires that provisions of the Agreement be interpreted in conformity with the relevant rulings from the CJEU. See also Art 3(2) of the Surveillance and Court Agreement (SCA), under which ESA and the EFTA Court are bound to pay 'due account' to the principles laid down by the relevant rulings of the CJEU.

EEA law in the legal orders of the EEA/EFTA States, which is so-called effects-based or functional homogeneity.[25] The EFTA Court has explicitly stated that reliance on the principle of homogeneity is needed in order to ensure 'equal access to justice for individuals and economic operators throughout the EEA'.[26]

The requirement of equal access to justice also entails an imperative of reciprocity. It is stated in the preamble to the EEA Agreement that the homogeneous European Economic Area is to be achieved 'on the basis of equality and reciprocity and of an overall balance of benefits, rights and obligations for the Contracting Parties'.[27] Effective judicial protection in both pillars of the EEA Agreement is needed to create a level playing field for citizens and economic operators. In *ESA v Iceland* the principle of reciprocity was proclaimed as a fundamental EEA law principle alongside the principle of homogeneity.[28] Homogeneity and reciprocity are closely connected, and it has been argued that the latter principle is gradually 'emerging into homogeneity's twin sister or brother'.[29] However, the EFTA Court has been silent as to the importance of the reciprocity principle since *ESA v Iceland*, making the legal status of this principle somewhat uncertain.

The principle of homogeneity is also closely related to the principle of loyalty laid down in Article 3 EEA, which places a positive duty on the Contracting Parties to take all measures necessary to ensure fulfilment of the obligations arising from the EEA Agreement, and a negative duty to abstain from any measure which could jeopardise the attainment of the objectives of the Agreement. The EFTA Court has held that the loyalty principle laid down in Article 3 EEA 'mirrors' that of Article 4(3) TEU.[30] The general principle of effective judicial protection in EU law is also anchored in the principle of loyalty. The CJEU has stated – in its post-Lisbon case law as well – that, under Article 4(3) TEU, the courts of the Member States are to ensure judicial protection of a person's rights under EU law and to remedy the unlawful consequences of breach of EU law.[31]

B. The Constitutional Context Surrounding the Principle of Effective Judicial Protection

At the EU level, the principle of effective judicial protection is seen as an aspect of the EU constitutional architecture, together with other legal doctrines central to the EU legal order. As is pointed out in the legal literature, the principle of effective judicial protection is 'embedded in a complex matrix of various other seminal "constitutional" principles of EU law, such as direct effect and primacy'.[32]

[25] HH Fredriksen, 'The EFTA Court', in R Howse et al (eds), *The Legitimacy of International Trade Courts and Tribunals* (Cambridge, Cambridge University Press, 2018) 163.

[26] Case E-14/11 *DB Schenker* [2012], para 78.

[27] Recital 4 of the preamble to the EEA Agreement. See also Case E-3/11 *Sigmarsson* [2011], para 29.

[28] Case E-12/13 *ESA v Iceland*, para 68.

[29] P Speitler, 'Judicial Homogeneity as a Fundamental Principle of the EEA' in Baudenbacher (n 22) 18.

[30] Case E-1/04 *Fokus Bank*, para 41.

[31] See, inter alia, *Puškár* (n 14) para 57; Case C-243/15 *Lesoochranárske zoskupenie VLK*, EU:C:2016:838, para 50; and Case C-316/19 *Commission v Slovenia*, EU:C:2020:1030, para 124.

[32] ME Mendez-Pinedo, 'The Effectiveness of EEA Law and the EFTA Court' (2021) 1 *International Investment Law Journal* 124, 125.

The EEA Agreement does not call for the direct effect or the primacy of EEA law within the domestic legal systems of the EEA/EFTA States.[33] The uniform and effective application of EEA law at a domestic level is nevertheless ensured by doctrines establishing a form of 'quasi-direct effect' and a 'watered-down version' of the primacy principle.[34] First, individuals may rely on a provision of EEA law in domestic proceedings once that provision has been made part of domestic law in accordance with the constitutional and legal traditions of the relevant EEA/EFTA state.[35] Second, national courts are bound to interpret national law as far as possible in conformity with EEA law.[36] Third, Protocol 35 EEA requires the EEA/EFTA States to ensure that implemented EEA rules take precedence over conflicting national legislation. Lastly, an individual has the right to claim damages from the state for infringement of EEA rights.[37] These doctrines complement each other and, together, ensure that EEA law penetrates deeply into the respective domestic legal orders. Although reflecting the *sui generis* legal order of the EEA Agreement, they contribute to ensuring that the legal effects of EEA law at a national level are comparable to that of the EU legal order. The effectiveness and precedence of implemented EEA rules over national law is an inherent part of the EEA Agreement.[38]

The lack of direct effect and primacy under the EEA Agreement cannot in itself justify differences in terms of judicial protection in the EEA. In its seminal *Sveinbjörnsdottir* case, establishing the principle of state liability in the EEA, the EFTA Court anchored the principle in the homogeneity objective, the objective of establishing the right of individuals and economic operators to equal treatment, and the principle of sincere cooperation laid down in Article 3 EEA. In *Karlsson*, it rejected arguments to the effect that state liability reflected the 'supranational' elements of EU law, which are absent in the EEA Agreement.[39] The EFTA Court's reasoning is of relevance beyond the field of state liability. The state liability doctrine can be seen as a reflection of the general principle that every breach of an EU/EEA right 'must carry with it an effective level of redress'.[40] Consequently, the doctrine is an explicit expression of the principle of effective judicial protection. The EFTA Court's stance on state liability – with its functional conception of homogeneity –

[33] See Art 7 EEA; Protocol 35 to the EEA Agreement; and Case E-4/01 *Karlsson*, para 41.

[34] See P Speitler, 'Judicial Homogeneity as a Fundamental Principle of the EEA' in Baudenbacher (n 22) 28; and HH Fredriksen and SØ Johansen, 'The EEA Agreement as a Jack-in-the-Box in the Relationship between the CJEU and the European Court of Human Rights?' (2020) 5 *European Papers* 707, 709.

[35] *Fjarskipti* (n 11) para 24. In Liechtenstein, the EEA Agreement is considered an integral part of domestic law without further action required, whereas in Iceland and Norway, specific implementing measures are required. However, both latter states have incorporated the main part of the EEA Agreement into domestic law.

[36] See Case E-1/07 *Criminal Proceedings against A* [2007], para 39. When interpreting national law, national courts will consider any relevant element of EEA law, whether implemented or not: see *Karlsson* (n 33) para 28.

[37] The principle of state liability was first established in *Sveinbjörnsdóttir* (n 1) and was later upheld in *Karlsson* (n 33).

[38] See, inter alia, Case E-2/12, *HOB-vín* para 122.

[39] *Karlsson* (n 33) paras 26–27.

[40] M Dougan, *National Remedies before the Court of Justice: Issues of Harmonisation and Differentiation* (Oxford, Hart Publishing, 2004) 257, 258.

seems to establish 'a general presumption for judicial protection of EEA-based rights, which, in effect, equals the protection offered in EU law'.[41]

Support for the above-mentioned position can be found in *Koch*, where the EFTA Court stated that EEA/EFTA and EU nationals and economic operators must enjoy 'relying upon EEA law, the same rights in both the EU and EFTA pillars of the EEA', so that the objective of establishing a dynamic and homogeneous EEA is achieved. It stated that access to justice and effective judicial protection are essential elements in the EEA legal framework, and that they depend on EEA/EFTA and EU nationals and economic operators enjoying 'equal access to the courts in both the EU and EFTA pillars of the EEA to ensure their rights which they derive from the EEA Agreement'.[42] The EFTA Court made use of both homogeneity and reciprocity arguments to substantiate the point that the principle of effective judicial protection applies equally under the EFTA pillar of the Agreement.

The integration of the EEA/EFTA States into the internal market was based on the premise that the level of judicial protection should be the same in both the EU and EFTA pillars. The EEA Agreement is an integral part of EU law, and EEA/EFTA nationals thus benefit from the Union principle of effective judicial protection when exercising their EEA rights.[43] A deficiency in the level of judicial protection in the EFTA pillar would affect the position of individuals and economic operators from other EEA States seeking to assert their internal market rights and would be detrimental to the internal market due to a deterrent chilling effect.[44]

Although the EFTA Court has recognised effective judicial protection as a general and unwritten principle of EEA law, this principle is somewhat elusive. Since the EFTA Court has provided only scant details on what the principle requires, pinning down its exact meaning and scope can prove challenging. Nor has it been explicit as to whether it has created an autonomous, EEA-specific version of the right to effective judicial protection, or whether it has transplanted the EU principle to the EEA context. With respect to the principle of state liability, the EFTA Court has stressed that since that principle has a different legal basis in the EEA and the EU, 'the application of the principles may not necessarily be in all respects coextensive'.[45] The EFTA Court's statements on the broader principle of effective judicial protection have not come with such a caveat.

In the following, the presumption of an equal level of protection of EEA-based rights will be examined in greater depth, with a particular focus on whether there may be important differences between the two legal orders such as to justify variations in the purview and content of the principle of effective judicial protection. In section III.C, the *content* of the principle of effective judicial protection in EEA law will be discussed, whereas in section III.D, its *scope* will be discussed.

[41] Fredriksen (n 25) 163–64.

[42] Case E-11/12 *Koch*, paras 116–17.

[43] EU-Canada CET Agreement, Opinion 1/17, EU:C:2019:341, para 117.

[44] Büchel and Zatschler (n 2) 330.

[45] *Karlsson* (n 33) para 30. This was reiterated on HOB-vín (n 38) para 120.

C. The Content of the Principle of Effective Judicial Protection

With the entry into force of the Lisbon Treaty, the principle of effective judicial protection became primary law in the EU. The principle lacks an explicit and formally binding textual basis in the EEA Agreement, which makes the situation different from that which applies in the context of EU law post-Lisbon. In EEA law, the principle of effective judicial protection is anchored in the principle of loyalty laid down in Article 3 EEA, coupled with the principle of homogeneity.

The primary point of reference in the CJEU's case law on effective judicial protection is Article 47 of the Charter. When interpreting this provision, the CJEU builds on its case law predating the entry into force of the Lisbon Treaty.[46] Moreover, the methodology followed by the CJEU in interpreting that Charter provision seems to mirror its traditional methodology in applying the general and unwritten principle of effective judicial protection.[47] It has held that Article 47 of the Charter 'constitutes a reaffirmation of the principle of effective judicial protection' and is thus intended to be of a codifying nature.[48] Despite the CJEU's ostensible affirmations about legal continuity, it seems to have taken a more elaborative approach, providing more detail on what the principle of effective judicial protection requires. In fact, the CJEU has gradually moved in the direction of harmonisation in order to ensure the effective protection of Union rights.[49] Hence, the acquisition of binding force by the Charter arguably marked the beginning of a new phase in the CJEU's case law.[50]

The principle of effective judicial protection clearly precludes certain procedural rules and requires that rules which hinder the effective protection of Union rights be set aside. However, the CJEU has made it clear that that principle also gives rise to *positive obligations* binding on the Member States.[51] The CJEU has taken it upon itself to define measures which must be taken at the Member State level to protect rights under EU law. By developing positive legal standards of national procedure, the CJEU 'concretises the requirements of judicial protection by balancing optimal rights

[46] See, eg, Case C-562/12 *Liivimaa Lihaveis*, EU:C:2014:2229, where the CJEU drew directly on Case C-97/91 *Borelli*, EU:C:1992:491 and Case C-269/99 *Kühne*, EU:C:2001:659.

[47] The permissible limitations laid down in Art 52 of the Charter are largely a codification of the case law of the CJEU pre-dating the Charter: see Case C-292/97 *Karlsson*, EU:C:2000:202; and Explanations Relating to the Charter of Fundamental Rights [2007] OJ C303, p 17.

[48] See, inter alia, Case C-348/16 *Sacko*, EU:C:2017:591, para 31; and Case C-93/12 *Agrokonsulting-04*, EU:C:2013:432, para 59.

[49] See further P van Cleynenbreugel, 'The Confusing Constitutional Status of Positive Procedural Obligations in EU Law' (2012) 5 *Review of European Administrative Law* 81.

[50] A Arnull, 'Remedies before National Courts' in R Schütze and T Tridimas (eds), *Oxford Principles of European Union Law: Volume I: The European Union Legal Order* (Oxford, Oxford University Press, 2018) 1026; and S Drake, 'More Effective Private Enforcement of EU Law Post-Lisbon: Aligning Regulatory Goals and Constitutional Values' in S Drake and M Smith (eds), *New Directions in the Effective Enforcement of EU Law and Policy* (Cheltenham, Edward Elgar, 2016) 27–28.

[51] Whereas a negative obligation means that national provisions which fail to satisfy the requirements of the principle of effective judicial protection must be eliminated, a positive obligation means that new national powers and remedies have to be created: see S Prechal and R Widdershoven, 'Redefining the Relationship between "Rewe-Effectiveness" and Effective Judicial Protection' (2011) 4 *Review of European Administrative Law* 31, 41.

protection with any countervailing objectives of an orderly judicial procedure [and the] outcomes of this balancing crystallise into doctrine'.[52] These positive requirements not only bind the Member States' legislatures and executives, requiring them to establish a system of legal remedies and procedures which ensure respect for the right to effective judicial protection of individuals' rights under EU law, but they also bind Member States' courts. The CJEU has held that Article 47 of the Charter must be seen as sufficiently unconditional and precise so as to be capable of being relied upon before domestic courts without further implementing legislation, including in horizontal disputes between private parties.[53] The application of the principle of effective judicial protection may therefore compel the courts in the Member States to provide for procedures and remedies which do not exist in national law.[54]

When developing positive legal standards, the CJEU has relied heavily on Article 47 of the Charter.[55] Commentators have argued that the establishment of positive standards for national procedures 'highlights a maturation of the EU legal order from a fundamental rights perspective'.[56]

It may well be that the CJEU perceives it as more legitimate to elaborate on what the principle of effective judicial protection requires now that it has a firm legal mandate in the Treaties. In the words of Bonelli, the codification of the principle in primary law stimulated an evolution of the principle, in that it 'offered a platform for the evolution of the [CJEU's] case law'.[57] This platform is lacking in EEA law. The lack of an explicit legal basis in the EEA Agreement may make the EFTA Court more vulnerable to accusations of judicial activism directed at its case law pertaining to procedures and remedies. Moreover, it is not for the EFTA Court alone to determine what the EEA Agreement requires. The EFTA Court is not the supreme and final arbiter of EEA law; rather, it constitutes a part of a wider interpretative community also comprising national courts in the EEA/EFTA States.[58]

Under the terms of the EEA Agreement and the Agreement between the EFTA States on the Establishment of a Surveillance Authority and a Court of Justice (SCA), no provision is made for a preliminary reference procedure for the EFTA Court, as is made for the CJEU. Instead, Article 34 SCA provides for an advisory opinion

[52] V Roeben, 'Judicial Protection as the Meta-norm in the EU Judicial Architecture' (2019) 12(1) *Hague Journal on the Rule of Law* 29, 32.

[53] Case C-414/16 *Egenberger*, EU:C:2018:257.

[54] R Widdershoven, 'National Procedural Autonomy and General EU Law Limits' (2019) 2 *Review of European Administrative Law* 5, 27.

[55] Van Cleynenbreugel states that 'a combined reliance on the principle of sincere co-operation and the binding Charter of Fundamental Rights of the European Union is essential for the Court to legitimise its standard-setting approach to national procedural provisions'; see P van Cleynenbreugel, 'Judge-Made Standards of National Procedure in the Post-Lisbon Constitutional Framework' (2012) 37 *EL Rev* 90, 100.

[56] ibid 99.

[57] M Bonelli, 'Effective Judicial Protection in EU Law: An Evolving Principle of a Constitutional Nature' (2019) 12 *Review of European Administrative Law* 35, 42. See, to similar effect, Drake, who has pointed out that Art 47 of the Charter constitutes a 'more visible and highly legitimate legal basis upon which the Court can develop its standards of fundamental rights protection in relation to the right to an effective remedy': see Drake (n 50) 35.

[58] The term 'final arbiter' stems from M Kumm, 'Who is the Final Arbiter of Constitutionality in Europe? Three Conceptions of the Relationship between the German Federal Constitutional Court and the European Court of Justice' (1999) 36 *CML Rev* 351.

procedure, allowing the courts in the EEA/EFTA States to refer questions on the interpretation of EEA law to the EFTA Court. In further contrast to EU law, nor is there any obligation on national courts of any instance to make a reference to the EFTA Court and the answers, once received, are merely advisory.[59] The relationship between the EFTA Court and the courts in the EEA/EFTA States is, as a result, more 'partner-like'.[60] If the EFTA Court and a Supreme Court of one of the EEA/EFTA States were to disagree as to the correct interpretation of the law, 'the judicial set-up of the EFTA-pillar does not compel either court to fold'.[61] Due to this inherent tension, the EFTA Court tends to be cautious about pushing the boundaries of its judicial mandate.[62]

The EFTA Court must address the issue of effective judicial protection in the post-Charter era in a skilful manner. It may nevertheless shield itself from accusations of judicial activism by relying on Strasbourg case law to develop the content and scope of the principle of effective judicial protection in EEA law. All three EEA/EFTA States are signatories to the ECHR, and the EFTA Court has stressed that the provisions of the ECHR and the case law of the ECtHR are important sources for determining the scope of the fundamental rights enjoyed under EEA law.[63] The Convention rights may accordingly be used as a 'tool to operationalise the principle of homogeneity between EEA and EU law'.[64] The Charter nevertheless enables the EU legal order to offer a higher standard of human rights protection than that which is available under the ECHR. The CJEU has stressed that the autonomy of EU law requires the interpretation of fundamental rights to be 'ensured within the framework of the structure and objectives of the EU'.[65] That autonomy also entails that there is not necessarily a complete overlap between Article 47 of the Charter and Articles 6 and 13 ECHR, although the principle of homogeneity may serve to bridge the gap as and when needed.

The scope and limits of the homogeneity principle are not set in stone. It is submitted that the EFTA Court would indeed stay within the proper scope of its judicial function by relying on considerations of homogeneity to interpret the principle of effective judicial protection in a manner that reflects developments relating to Article 47 of the Charter. The CJEU has not engaged in extensive judicial law-making and developed a full-fledged *jus commune* in the fields of procedures and remedies. Insofar as the CJEU has relied on the Charter to develop judicial standards for national procedure, these standards have not been of such a technical nature as

[59] The Supreme Court of Norway has made it clear that it has the authority and duty to consider independently whether to follow an opinion, but has also emphasised that the opinions should be given 'significant weight' in the interpretation of EEA law. Rt-2000-1811 *Finanger I*; and HR-2016-2554-P *Holship*, para 77.

[60] The term 'partner-like' was used by the EFTA Court in *Irish Bank* (n 23) para 57.

[61] HH Fredriksen, 'Judicial Dialogue in the EFTA Pillar of the EEA: Developments and Challenges (Part 2)' (2019), https://www.efta-studies.org/post/judicial-dialogue-in-the-efta-pillar-of-the-eea-part-2.

[62] Some cases have nevertheless been subject to criticism – for instance, Case E-28/15 *Jabbi* [2016], pertaining to the Citizenship Directive (Directive 2004/38).

[63] See, inter alia, Case E-1/20 *Kerim*, para 43; and Joined Cases E-11/19 and E-12/19 *Adpublisher*, para 50.

[64] R Spano, 'The EFTA Court and Fundamental Rights' (2017) 13 *European Constitutional Law Review* 475, 483.

[65] Accession of the European Union to the European Convention for the Protection of Human Rights and Fundamental Freedoms, Opinion 2/13, EU:C:2014:2454, para 170.

to require the involvement of the legislature. Rather, the standards pertain to the very essence of judicial protection, amounting to the 'untouchable core' of protection.[66] Positive obligations cover, inter alia, the duty to provide for judicial review of administrative decisions and to grant locus standi to right holders. The CJEU held as early as in the seminal *Nold* case that fundamental rights could be subject to certain limits 'on condition that the substance of these rights is left untouched'.[67] The notion of 'essence' of fundamental rights also appears in the case law of the ECtHR, and it should be uncontroversial to accept that it also exists in the EEA context.[68] It is submitted that the EFTA Court would not be acting ultra vires and encroaching on the sovereignty of the Contracting States by acknowledging that the principle of effective judicial protection also entails positive legal obligations pertaining to essential procedural and remedial safeguards.

D. The Scope of Application of the Principle of Effective Judicial Protection

In the CJEU's recent case law, following a constitutional backsliding in some Member States, the principle of effective judicial protection has been used as the legal basis to safeguard the rule of law in the EU. Article 2 TEU enshrines the rule of law as one of the fundamental values of the EU, and the principle of effective judicial protection has become a 'vehicle for the enforcement of the rule of law at the national level'.[69] As a result, the scope of the application of the principle of effective judicial protection has been broadened.

The CJEU has required Member States to ensure that all courts and tribunals within their judicial system that deal with cases in the fields covered by EU law meet the requirements of effective judicial protection. The CJEU has read into this principle certain structural requirements regarding national judiciaries.[70] The focus in this line of case law is not on the effective enforcement of substantive rights, but rather on the general structure of national courts which may adjudicate upon EU law matters.[71] The CJEU's rationale seems to be that, in order to function within the Union's judicial system, national courts must meet certain fundamental requirements.

The seminal case was *Portuguese Judges*, which pertained to the reduction of salaries of judges in Portugal. The CJEU emphasised that the independence of national courts and tribunals serves as a guarantee that EU rights will be protected effectively.[72]

[66] Brkan (n 16) 333.

[67] Case C-4/73 *Nold*, EU:C:1974: 51.

[68] See, inter alia, ECtHR, *Ashingdane v United Kingdom*, App No 8225/78, judgment of 28 May 1985, para 57, where the Court held that although the right of access to the court may be subject to limitations, the limitations 'must not restrict or reduce the access left to the individual in such a way or to such an extent that the very essence of the right is impaired'.

[69] G Gentile, 'Effective Judicial Protection: Enforcement, Judicial Federalism and the Politics of EU Law' (2022) *European Law Open* 128, 130.

[70] F Pastor-Merchante, 'The Overlap between the Principles of Effectiveness and Effective Judicial Protection in Union Law' in Izquierdo-Sans et al (eds), *Fundamental Rights Challenges* (Cham, Springer International, 2021) 211.

[71] Gentile (n 69) 140.

[72] Case C-64/16 *Associação Sindical dos Juízes Portugueses*, EU:C:2018:117, para 41, hereinafter referred to as '*Portuguese Judges*'.

The CJEU relied on Article 19(1) TEU, read in conjunction with Article 2 TEU, rather than Article 47 of the Charter. In its subsequent case law, the CJEU has nevertheless relied on a combined reading of those provisions by proclaiming that Article 19(1) TEU 'requires Member States to provide remedies that are sufficient to ensure effective legal protection, within the meaning in particular of Article 47 of the Charter, in the fields covered by EU law'.[73]

With *Portuguese Judges*, the CJEU broadened the scope of application of the principle of effective judicial protection. Pursuant to Article 51(1) thereof, the Charter applies to the Member States when they are 'implementing EU law'.[74] This corresponds in essence to the scope of application of the general principles of Union law.[75] However, in *Portuguese Judges*, the CJEU held that Article 19(1) TEU has a wider scope of application. Article 19(1) TEU refers to 'the fields covered by Union law', and the provision therefore applies irrespective of whether the Member States are implementing Union law within the meaning of the Charter.[76] This implies that the courts in all Member States must meet the requirements of Article 47 of the Charter not only in situations falling within the scope of EU law, but also at an institutional level.[77] From this perspective, the principle of effective judicial protection 'appears to be detaching itself from its original nature of entitlement in favour of individuals who seek to enforce EU-derived rights'.[78]

This seminal judgment in *Portuguese Judges* has been described as 'truly groundbreaking'[79] and 'being on a par with the Court's judgments in *Van Gend en Loos* and *Costa*'.[80] It is indeed a leap from the traditional principle of effective judicial protection to the CJEU's recent line of case law. As observed in the legal literature:

> *Portuguese Judges* is first and foremost about institutional powers and government structures and not about substantive rights, processes and remedies. The Court essentially held that the values of the Union entail certain institutional guarantees, including judicial independence. National laws must protect those guarantees in relation to national institutions which in abstracto may apply EU law.[81]

The EFTA Court has not had the opportunity to set out its position on the relevance of recent Article 19(1) TEU case law to the EEA context.[82] Whether considerations of homogeneity entail that the CJEU's reasoning applies in EEA law as well is a

[73] See, for example, Case C-824/18 *AB and Others (Appointment of Judges to Supreme Court)*, EU:C:2021:153, para 143.

[74] Case C-617/10 *Åkerberg Fransson*, EU:C:2013:280, para 17.

[75] Case C-206/13 *Siragusa*, EU:C:2014:126, para 35.

[76] *Portuguese Judges* (n 72) para 29.

[77] A van Duin, *Effective Judicial Protection in Consumer Litigation: Article 47 of the EU Charter in Practice* (Cambridge, Intersentia, 2022) 37.

[78] Gentile (n 69) 131.

[79] Bonelli (n 57) 50.

[80] L Pech and D Kochenov, 'Respect for the Rule of Law in the Case Law of the European Court of Justice: A Casebook Overview of Key Judgments since the *Portuguese Judges* Case', SIEPS, Stockholm, 2021–3, available at SSRN: https://ssrn.com/abstract=3850308.

[81] T Tridimas, 'The General Principles of EU Law and the Europeanisation of National Laws' (2020) 13(2) *Review of European Administrative Law* 5, 22.

[82] However, the ECtHR concluded that Iceland had infringed Art 6(1) ECHR in selecting judges for its Court of Appeal: see *Guðmundur Andri Ástráðsson v Iceland* App No 26374/18 (ECtHR Grand Chamber, 1 December 2020).

challenging question. The origin of the CJEU's approach in this new line of case law can be found in the case law relating to the autonomous concept of 'courts or tribunals' under Article 267 of the Treaty on the Functioning of the European Union (TFEU), which has been developed to guarantee the uniform interpretation and effective implementation of EU law.[83] The EFTA Court has interpreted the notion of 'court or tribunal' under Article 34 SCA in a different and more liberal manner, and has allowed for a wider range of bodies to refer cases to it.[84]

However, this difference cannot be decisive. In the EEA context as well, the right to effective judicial protection guarantees the right to an effective remedy before a court *properly speaking*, and the EFTA Court has stressed the importance of having access to a 'tribunal that offers the guarantees provided for by the principle of effective judicial protection'.[85] Moreover, the EFTA Court held in *Nobile* that 'the principle of judicial independence is one of the fundamental values of the administration of justice'.[86] Although that case concerned the composition of the EFTA Court, there is no reason to believe that the EFTA Court would subject national courts to a more lenient standard.

However, the relevant question is in which situations the right to effective judicial protection applies and, in particular, whether the principle extends beyond the protection of individual right holders. The CJEU has consistently held that Article 47 of the Charter restricts the scope of application of the principle of effective judicial protection to situations where the 'rights and freedoms' guaranteed by Union law are at stake.[87] As Roeben points out: 'The animating idea of this fundamental right [to effective judicial protection] is to enforce individual rights and only rights.'[88] The expansion of the principle of effective judicial protection therefore had to be anchored in Article 19(1) TEU. The crux of the CJEU's recent case law relating to Article 19(1) TEU is that it 'turn[s] the requirements of the fundamental right to judicial protection into a standard for the internal legal orders of a State qua its membership of the Union'.[89] If the EEA principle of effective judicial protection is interpreted in accordance with the CJEU's recent case law, it will allow the EFTA Surveillance Authority (ESA) and the EFTA Court to have jurisdiction on a general basis to examine the judicial organisation in the EEA States, over and above safeguarding the protection of individuals' rights under EEA law.

The objective of the EEA Agreement is more modest than under the EU Treaties, and the EEA States do not share the wider political goal of the EU in establishing 'an ever-closer union among the peoples of Europe'.[90] However, the differences do not

[83] See further A Sánchez Frías, 'A New Presumption for the Autonomous Concept of "Court or Tribunal" in Article 267 TFEU' (2023) 19:2 *European Constitutional Law Review* 320.

[84] See Case E-8/19 *Scanteam*, where the EFTA Court deviated from the CJEU's approach in Case C-274/14 *Banco de Santander*, EU:C:2020:17.

[85] See Case E-12/20 *Telenor*, para 77.

[86] Case E-21/16 *Nobile*, decision of the Court of 14 February 2017, para 16.

[87] See Case C-430/21 *RS (Effects of Judgments of a Constitutional Court)*, EU:C:2022:99, para 34. This also covers the right to 'protection against arbitrary or disproportionate intervention by public authorities within the sphere of the private activities of any natural or legal person', which constitutes a general principle of EU law: see Case C-682/15 *Berlioz Investment Fund*, EU:C:2017:373, para 51.

[88] Roeben (n 52) 31.

[89] ibid 40.

[90] Article 1(2) TEU.

extend to its foundation and values. It is stated in the preamble to the EEA Agreement that the relationship between the EU, its Member States and the EFTA States is based on 'long-standing common values and European identity'.[91] Although the EEA Agreement does not contain a provision equivalent to Article 2 TEU, respect for the values listed therein is a precondition for participation in the EEA. The rule of law is 'both a precondition for the will to confer far-reaching substantive rights, and the guarantee that those rights will be enforceable'.[92] The question nevertheless remains as to whether there is a *sufficient legal basis* in EEA law for extending the principle of effective juridical protection beyond the protection of EEA rights.

Article 108 EEA provides that the EFTA Court's competence is limited to 'the application of' the EEA Agreement. In *Fred. Olsen*, the EFTA Court held that 'the fundamental rights guaranteed in the legal order of the EEA Agreement are applicable in all situations governed by EEA law'.[93] The right to effective judicial protection is triggered when an EEA right is at stake, which means that only those seeking the protection of such rights may rely on that principle. Article 3 EEA does not extend the scope of application of EEA law beyond the provisions of the Agreement. The more modest scope of application of the principle of effective judicial protection poses certain challenges for the EFTA Court in its endeavours to achieve homogeneity.

The EFTA Court may cut this Gordian knot by interpreting Article 3 EEA in a manner that encompasses an obligation similar to that laid down in Article 19(1) TEU to 'provide remedies sufficient to ensure effective legal protection in the *fields covered by* Union law'. The latter provision 'turns the subjective right into an objective obligation for Member States to ensure that their judicial systems provide effective judicial protection'.[94] Arguably, Article 3 EEA may entail an obligation to ensure effective judicial protection on a more systemic level. National courts in the EEA States are part of a shared legal order, and they are entrusted with a European mandate. This mandate requires them to establish a legal avenue through which effective implementation of EEA law and the right to effective judicial protection of individuals' EEA rights are ensured. In the words of Roeben, the right to effective judicial protection 'is also the right to a state of affairs, beyond a specific omission or action [and it] generates requirements and standards for general organisation and procedure as well for individual judicial decisions'.[95] It is submitted that the EFTA Court would not be overstepping the limits of its legal mandate if it were to adopt such a position. This is not so much a question of 'competence creep' and undue interference in the judicial systems of the EEA/EFTA States, but rather a matter of ensuring respect for the judicial architecture established by the EEA Agreement. This architecture should at a minimum ensure that individuals and economic operators have access to courts which satisfy basic requirements of independence and impartiality as prescribed by Article 6 ECHR.[96]

[91] See recital 2 of the preamble.

[92] Büchel and Zatschler (n 2) 332.

[93] Joined Cases E-3/13 and E-20/13 *Fred. Olsen*, para 225.

[94] Roeben (n 52) 31. This does not necessarily mean that an individual may invoke this right to have domestic law reviewed in the abstract. The role of the national court is primarily to examine the way in which the law applies to an individual claimant, and not to conduct an abstract review of domestic law.

[95] ibid 40.

[96] See Joined Cases C-542/18 RX-II and C-543/18 RX-II *Simpson and HG*, EU:C:2020:232 paras 72–74.

Deficiencies in the independence and impartiality of an EEA/EFTA State's judiciary will undermine EEA nationals' trust in being able to exercise and enforce their rights,[97] which in turn will jeopardise the functioning of the EEA Agreement. Such deficiencies may also erode ESA's trust in the ability of domestic authorities to enforce EEA law at the national level.[98] The fact that the same fundamental values are shared across the EEA is 'the principal reason why the "self-policing" aspect of the EEA Agreement works, without the need for any cross-pillar checks and balances'.[99]

Systemic or generalised deficiencies in respect of the rule of law in an EEA/EFTA State may also give rise to concerns beyond the field of EEA law. The EEA Agreement constitutes part of a wider fabric of agreements between the EU and the EEA/EFTA States, covering inter alia the Schengen Agreement and the surrender agreement.[100] The CJEU has stressed that these various agreements must be considered in context. In *Ruska Federacija*, the CJEU acknowledged the 'special relationship' between the EU and the EEA/EFTA States, which 'goes beyond economic and commercial cooperation'.[101] The principle of mutual trust underpins these mechanisms, and the EU's trust in other states is based on trust in the structure and functioning of their legal systems.[102] This trust is undermined if there are structural deficiencies, which suggests that the principle of effective judicial protection must apply on a more general basis.

IV. CONCLUSION

Although the principle of effective judicial protection is an integral part of EEA law, the scope and limits of the principle are not clear. It remains to be seen whether the EFTA Court will develop its case law in a manner that fully reflects the case law of the CJEU under Article 47 of the Charter and Article 19(1) TEU.

There are valid reasons for arguing that the content and scope of the principle are the same in EU and EEA law. As regards the content of the principle, the lack of a written legal basis in the EEA treaty framework is not sufficient to rebut the general presumption that the level of judicial protection of EEA-based rights is equivalent to

[97] Büchel and Zatschler (n 2) 330.

[98] See, by way of comparison, Case T-791/19 *Sped-Pro*, EU:T:2022:67, where the CJEU held that compliance with the requirements of the rule of law is a relevant factor that the Commission must take into account for the purposes of determining which competition authority is best placed to examine a complaint regarding an infringement of Arts 101 and 102 TFEU.

[99] Büchel and Zatschler (n 2) 330.

[100] Agreement concluded by the Council of the European Union and the Republic of Iceland and the Kingdom of Norway concerning the latters' association with the implementation, application and development of the Schengen acquis – Final Act [1999] OJ L176, 18 May, p 36; and Agreement between the European Union and the Republic of Iceland and the Kingdom of Norway on the surrender procedure between the Member States of the European Union and Iceland and Norway – Declarations [2006] OJ L292, p 2.

[101] Case C-897/19 *Ruska Federacija v IN*, EU:C:2020:262, para 44.

[102] This was made explicit with respect to the European Arrest Warrant in Case C-216/18 PPU *Minister for Justice and Equality (Deficiencies in the System of Justice)*, EU:C:2018:586, in which the CJEU stated (at para 58) that the high level of trust between Member States on which the European Arrest Warrant mechanism is based is 'founded on the premise that the criminal courts of the other Member States … meet the requirements of effective judicial protection, which include, in particular, the independence and impartiality of those courts'.

the protection enjoyed under EU law. Without an available legal avenue and fundamental procedural and remedial safeguards, EEA rights 'become no more than empty guarantees'.[103] Protection of EEA-derived rights is of paramount importance, due to the system of decentralised implementation and enforcement of EEA law. Since the enforcement of substantive EEA norms lies largely in the hands of the Contracting States, deficiencies in the degree of judicial protection in the EFTA pillar affect not only individual right holders, but also hampers the effectiveness of EEA law more broadly. The principle of effective judicial protection constitutes an essential component of the EEA 'enforcement toolbox'.[104] Private enforcement serves not only the private interest of the individual claimant, but also the public policies embodied in the norm in question.[105] Private parties are largely granted rights with a view to enlisting them as 'private attorneys general', and this function depends on them being able to resort to national courts.

As to the scope of the principle of effective judicial protection, it arguably extends beyond the protection of individual EEA rights to encompass structural requirements for national judiciaries as well. Compliance with the requirements of the rule of law fosters mutual trust between the EEA States. The recognition of a principle of effective judicial protection in keeping with the CJEU's *Portuguese Judges* line of case law would help to bolster that trust by serving as a guarantee that EEA law will be enforced loyally and that the rights recognised by that law will be respected and upheld.

[103] R Craufurd Smith, 'Remedies for Breaches of EC Law in National Courts Legal Variation and Selection' in P Craig and G de Búrca (eds), *The Evolution of EU Law* (Oxford, Oxford University Press, 1999) 296.

[104] The expression is borrowed from Gentile (n 69) 128.

[105] As the EFTA Court held in *Schenker* (n 26) para 132: 'While pursuing his private interest, a plaintiff in such proceedings contributes at the same time to the protection of the public interest.'

23

The Right to Be Heard before Referring to the EFTA Court – And after Receiving the Court's Opinion

WILHELM UNGERANK

THE PROCEDURE TO obtain an advisory opinion from the EFTA Court is regulated in a brief and concise way in Article 34 of the Surveillance and Court Agreement (SCA):[1] where it is necessary for a court of an EEA/EFTA State in pending proceedings to interpret the EEA Agreement, that court may submit questions regarding the correct interpretation to the EFTA Court for an advisory opinion in order to come to a decision. Although all further details are left to the national (procedural) laws of the three EEA/EFTA States – Iceland, Liechtenstein, and Norway – the national courts are obliged to hear the parties of the initial lawsuit before making the request to the EFTA Court for an advisory opinion and also after the advisory opinion has been received. This is due to general principles deduced from the EEA Agreement as well as to the fact that the European Convention on Human Rights (ECHR) applies in all three states.[2]

I. THE LEGAL SITUATION

A. The ECHR

The ECHR of 4 November 1950 has been ratified by Iceland, Norway and Liechtenstein. As is stated in Article 6(1) ECHR, proceedings must be decided *within a reasonable time*. In addition, the ECtHR deduces the right to be heard in court inter alia from Article 6 ECHR ('right to a fair trial'). According to this, the

[1] Agreement between the EFTA States on the Establishment of a Surveillance Authority and a Court of Justice of 2 May 1992.

[2] Parts of this chapter were presented by me on 12 June 2015 during the 'Spring Conference' of the EFTA Court on the topic of 'Fundamental Rights in EEA Law' under the title 'Access to Justice as a Fundamental Right in the EEA? Some Thoughts on the Preliminary Reference Procedure'.

persons concerned by the proceedings have the right to comment *on all points* of the proceedings in question.[3] This is clear from the case law of the ECtHR: the right to be heard has to be an effective right. This includes that the parties to the national proceedings have the right to present the observations which they regard as relevant to their case.

These procedural guarantees apply to criminal and civil proceedings; however, the ECtHR considers the concept 'civil rights and obligations' to have a very broad scope.

All EEA/EFTA States are parties to the ECHR. It is not important whether it is a so-called 'monist' state like Liechtenstein or whether the 'dualistic principle' is applied as it is in Iceland or Norway, since individuals may bring applications against Contracting States concerning all last instance decisions of national courts, alleging that the state violates their rights under the ECHR. Thus, all states have to respect the fundamental principles laid down in Article 6 ECHR, inter alia, first to be heard and second to have the proceedings completed within a reasonable time. There is no exact definition (and there cannot be one) under which circumstances proceedings are done 'within a reasonable time'. However, it is generally understood that a proceeding is conducted within a reasonable time when there is no unreasonable delay.

B. The EEA Agreement

In the Preamble (recital 1) to the Agreement on the European Economic Area of 2 May 1992, the EEA is primarily understood as a contribution to a Europe based on human rights. There is consensus in the case law and the literature that the provisions of the EEA Agreement are to be interpreted and applied in a manner that is consistent with the Contracting Parties' (here Iceland, Liechtenstein and Norway) obligations under the ECHR[4] – and then recital 4 provides for the objective of establishing a dynamic and homogeneous European Economic Area based on common rules, equal conditions of competition and providing for the adequate means of enforcement *including at the judicial level*. In recital 8, the conviction is expressed that individuals will play an important role in the European Economic Area through the exercise of the rights conferred to them by this Agreement and through the *judicial defence of these rights*. Finally, another objective is formulated in recital 15, namely to 'arrive at and maintain in full deference of the independence of the courts a *uniform interpretation and application* of this Agreement and those provisions of Community legislation which are substantially reproduced in this Agreement' and 'to arrive at an *equal treatment of individuals and economic operators* as regards the four freedoms and the conditions of competition' (emphasis added). Pursuant to the *duty of loyalty* laid down in Article 3, the contracting parties have to take 'all appropriate measures, whether general or particular, to ensure fulfilment of the obligations arising out of this Agreement' and 'shall abstain from any measure which could jeopardise the attainment of the objectives of this Agreement'. Finally, Article 108(2) EEA provides

[3] *Kessler Erwin v Switzerland* 10577/04 ECLI:CE:ECHR:2007:0726JUD001057704, paras 29–32.

[4] F Arnesen and HH Fredriksen in F Arnesen et al (eds), *The Agreement on the European Economic Area: A Commentary* (Munich/Oxford/Baden-Baden, CH Beck/Hart Publishing/Nomos Universitetsforlaget, 2018), Preamble, para 11.

that the EFTA States shall establish a Court of Justice ('EFTA Court'). The Article contains no reference to preliminary rulings proceedings – such an option is only provided for in the EEA Agreement (Article 107) with regard to the Court of Justice of the European Union (CJEU).[5]

C. The SCA

In Article 1(a) SCA, the term 'EEA Agreement' is defined as 'the main part of the EEA Agreement, its Protocols and Annexes as well as the acts referred to therein'. In addition to Article 3 EEA, Article 2 SCA contains a separate loyalty clause. It is provided in Article 34 SCA that the EFTA Court may give advisory opinions on the interpretation of the EEA Agreement (as the latter is defined in Article 1 (a)),[6] stating that: 'Where such a question is raised before any court or tribunal in an EFTA State, that court or tribunal may, if it considers it necessary to enable it to give judgment, request the EFTA Court to give such an opinion.' No EEA/EFTA state has made use of the option provided for in Article 34 SCA to limit the right to request such an advisory opinion to courts or tribunals against whose decisions there is no judicial remedy under national law.

D. The Statute of the EFTA Court

Pursuant to Article 20 of the Statute,[7] notice is given to the governments of the EEA/EFTA States, the EFTA Surveillance Authority, the Community (now the Union) and the EC Commission (now the European Commission) of any case pending before the Court. These governments and institutions are entitled to submit statements of case or written observations to the EFTA Court within two months of this notification.

E. Rules of Procedure of the Court (RoP)

Pursuant to Article 37 of the RoP,[8] the court of an EFTA State that suspends its proceedings and refers a case to the EFTA Court is to notify the Court of this decision. Article 20 of the Statute of the EFTA Court provides that the Registrar is to notify the parties and the 30 EEA States, ESA and the European Commission, and invite them to submit written observations. Article 88 RoP provides that the

[5] C Baudenbacher, 'The EFTA Court: Structure and Tasks' in C Baudenbacher (ed), *The Handbook of EEA Law*, 139, 151 et seq (Cham, Springer International Publishing, 2016), considers this to be a merely symbolic provision, which has remained a dead letter (*lettre morte*).

[6] P Christiansen is right where he argues in Arnesen et al (n 4) Art 34 SCA para 5 that the Court also has jurisdiction to interpret the SCA (on the grounds that 'SCA … aiming for a level playing field for economic operators and private individuals throughout the EEA').

[7] Protocol 5 to the SCA.

[8] The current Rules of Procedure entered into force on 1 August 2021: see https://eftacourt.int/the-court/rules-of-procedure/?wpdmdl=7445&ind=1627642570103.

request for an advisory opinion must come with a summary of the case before the national court, including a description of the facts of a case as well as a presentation of the provisions of national law at issue and, where appropriate, the relevant national case law necessary to enable the Court to assess the question to which a reply is sought. In addition, the request must include a statement of the reasons which prompted the referring court to seek the advisory opinion, and of the relationship between the provisions of EEA law and the national legislation applicable to the main proceedings. Pursuant to Article 97 RoP, the interpretation procedure provided for in Article 138 RoP (the Court will interpret its own decision on request if there are any doubts about the decision's meaning or scope) does not apply to advisory opinions of the EFTA Court; rather, it is for the national courts to assess whether they consider that sufficient guidance has been given by an advisory opinion or whether it is required to send a further request for an advisory opinion to the Court.

F. Guidance for Advisory Opinion Requests

The EFTA Court's published Guidance for Advisory Opinion Requests is for guidance[9] only and has no binding or interpretative effect in relation to the provisions governing the advisory opinion procedure. It states that the request should contain a statement of reasons which is succinct but sufficiently complete to give the Court and those who must be notified a clear understanding of the factual and legal context of the main proceedings. The national court should ensure that the request itself includes all the relevant information. Although a national court may request an advisory opinion from the Court as soon as it finds that an opinion on the point or points of interpretation of EEA law is necessary to enable it to give judgment, the national court may find it more appropriate to request the advisory opinion once the national proceedings have reached a stage at which the national court is able to define the legal and factual context of the questions to be referred.

G. National Procedural Law in the EEA/EFTA States

In the present context, Icelandic law can be called exemplary: Article 1(2) of Law Nr 21 of 1994 on Requests for an Advisory Opinion states that whether the party has requested that an advisory opinion be sought under paragraph 1 or the judge considers it required *ex officio*, they shall give the parties an opportunity to be heard before giving a ruling to that effect.[10]

In contrast, neither Norwegian[11] nor Liechtenstein[12] procedural law includes an express provision that the parties of the main proceedings have to be heard before a request for an advisory opinion is submitted to the EFTA Court.

[9] See https://eftacourt.int/the-court/guidance-for-advisory-opinion/?wpdmdl=7446&ind=1627642656131.
[10] S Magnússon, 'Icelandic Courts' in Baudenbacher (ed) (n 5) 287.
[11] TC Poulsen, 'Norwegian Courts' in Baudenbacher (ed) (n 5) 265.
[12] W Ungerank, 'Liechtenstein Courts' in Baudenbacher (ed) (n 5) 299.

II. THE REQUIREMENT TO HEAR THE PARTIES BEFORE SUBMITTING THE REQUEST FOR AN ADVISORY OPINION

A. Common Considerations

With the right to request an advisory opinion from the EFTA Court (Article 34 SCA), the Contracting Parties have provided the national courts – and explicitly also the courts of first instance – with an effective range of instruments, which the national courts have to use very carefully.

Each request for an advisory opinion (unless accelerated (expedited) procedure, as provided by Articles 98 et seq RoP, is requested by the national court and granted by the President of the Court, which happens very rarely)[13] leads to a delay in the main proceedings of (typically) between eight and 12 months,[14] which is in conflict with the right to a conclusion of proceedings within a reasonable time and can only be justified where the request for an advisory opinion is actually necessary (otherwise, the principle of 'justice delayed is justice denied' applies). Requests for advisory opinions in criminal proceedings in which an accused is in pre-trial detention[15] or in which – depending on national procedural law – the interruption of the proceedings resulting from the request will require that the proceedings will have to be repeated, including any adducing of evidence that may already have been carried out,[16] are of special significance in this context.[17] In addition, the request for an advisory opinion will cause additional and not insignificant procedural costs, given that the parties might feel compelled to participate in the proceedings before the EFTA Court in order to safeguard their rights by submitting written statements and taking part in the hearing. Add to this that the EFTA Surveillance Authority, the Commission and all EEA/EFTA and EU Member States have the option to submit written observations and to take part in the hearing before the EFTA Court; however, before doing so, they – that is, more than 30 addressees all over Europe – have to read the request and decide whether they want to take part in the proceedings. Therefore, the decision as to whether a request is submitted and what questions are to be asked must be carefully considered.

However, refraining from submitting a necessary request may also have serious consequences.

First, as the ECtHR has already ruled, when a national court, against whose decisions there is no judicial remedy under national law, refuses a motion to refer a case to another court, it cannot be excluded that such a decision may fall foul of

[13] So far, such a request has only been accepted in Case E-18/14 *Wow Air*; it was declined in Case E-21/16 *Nobile*, Case E-2/18 *Concordia*, Case E-3/19 *Gable* and Case E-5/19 *Criminal Proceedings against F and G*.

[14] P Christiansen in Arnesen et al (n 4) Art 34 SCA para 25.

[15] Under German criminal procedure law, submitting a request to the CJEU may constitute an important reason that prevents judgment from being rendered and permits the continuation of pre-trial detention beyond the six-month maximum (B Schmitt in L Meyer-Goßner and B Schmitt, StPO, 64th edn (Munich, CH Beck, 2021) § 121, para 21b).

[16] 'Entirely new trial' under German criminal procedure law if the maximum terms for interruption have not been complied with (ibid § 229, para 14).

[17] It is perhaps worth noting that an advisory opinion has never been requested where an accused is in pre-trial detention. Should such a request be made, the author regards it as likely that the President would grant a request for accelerated procedure.

the standards of Article 6 (1) ECHR, which provides that in 'determination of his civil rights and obligations … everyone is entitled to a fair and public hearing within a reasonable time by an independent and impartial tribunal established by law'. In particular, this may be the case if the decision to refuse is not reasoned and must therefore be considered arbitrary.[18] In any case, grounds must be provided when denying a party's suggestion that a request for an advisory opinion be submitted; lack of such grounds may constitute a violation of the right to a fair trial (Article 6 ECHR).[19]

Second, there is the danger that if a court of a higher instance receives an appeal of a judgment rendered without obtaining a necessary advisory opinion, it will itself request the EFTA Court to give an advisory opinion. After that opinion has been given, it might have to set aside the decision of the court of first instance and remit the case to that court for renewed decision. This could be, for example, because due to additional legal considerations, supplementary findings of facts are required ('justice hurried is justice buried').[20] This would lead to another delay to the proceedings, which could have been avoided if an advisory opinion had been duly requested.

Third, failure to request an advisory opinion may also constitute a violation of the duty of loyalty under Article 3 EEA and Article 2 SCA, to which national courts

[18] Case E-18/11 *Irish Bank* [2012] EFTA Ct Rep 592, para 64.

[19] *Dhabi v Italy* 17120/09 ECLI:CE:ECHR:2014:0408JUD001712009 (the Italian Court of Cassation had not given any reasons for its decision that the question raised by the applicant should not be referred to the CJEU) and *Georgiou v Greece* 57378/18 ECLI:CE:ECHR:2023:0314JUD005737818 (the Greek Court of Cassation's judgment of 7 June 2018 contains neither a reference to the request made by the applicant nor any reasons why it was considered that the question raised by him did not merit reference to the CJEU); however, see also *Vergauwen v Belgium* 4832/04 ECLI:CE:ECHR:2012:0410DEC000483204 (the Belgian Constitutional Court had given sufficient reasons for not referring the case to the CJEU; in particular, it must be stated why the referral of a question is not considered relevant for the decision, whether the provision of EU law in question has already been interpreted, and whether the application/interpretation of the question whose referral is being discussed is so obvious that it leaves no room for reasonable doubt (the *acte clair* doctrine)).

[20] An example of this is the advisory opinion of the EFTA Court in Case E-7/20 *M and X AG* [2021] EFTA Ct Rep 33. The Court had stated in para 69 that Directive 2001/83/EC on the Community code relating to medicinal products for human use does not apply to any medicinal product which is prepared in a pharmacy in accordance with the prescriptions of a pharmacopoeia and is intended to be supplied directly to the patients served by the pharmacy in question (commonly known as *formula officinalis*). Accordingly, in order to benefit from that exception, a medicinal product had to be prepared 'in a pharmacy', 'in accordance with the prescriptions of a pharmacopoeia' and 'intended to be supplied directly to the patients served by the pharmacy in question'. The Court stated that those conditions were cumulative. It stated in para 71 that although it was for the referring court to ascertain, in the light of the main proceedings, whether the conditions of Art 3(2) of the Directive were fulfilled, it appeared that two of the conditions were not satisfied, as the product at issue in the main proceedings did not appear to have been prepared in accordance with the prescriptions of a pharmacopoeia and had not been intended to be supplied directly to patients served by the pharmacy in question. The referring court (the Liechtenstein Princely Court of Appeal) then set aside the appealed decision of the first instance by judgment of 31 August 2021, file no 15 EU.2019.137-44, and remitted the criminal case to the lower instance for renewed trial and decision. One of the reasons given for doing so (cons. 4.1.3) was that the contested judgment lacked statements on the so-called *formula officinalis* relevant for subsumption. The Court of Appeal stated that the court of the first instance had not made sufficiently precise statements of fact as to the extent of the burnout infusions produced by the pharmacy in Germany in accordance with the defendant's recipe were being administered to patients by himself intravenously in his doctor's practice or delivered directly to patients in Germany, Austria, and Switzerland under the name of the second defendant. Thus, the statement of fact of the contested judgment suffered from a substantial defect, given that the two alternatives listed by the lower instance court (*argumento* 'or') were not equivalent as to their punishability.

are subject. As stated by Carl Baudenbacher: 'One must not forget in this context that the national courts of the EEA/EFTA States are also an integral part of the system of judicial protection established by the EEA Agreement. When applying EEA law they act as European courts.'[21]

B. Case Examples

Only where the parties are heard after the intended questions have been announced and before the request is submitted can the parties safeguard their rights and contribute to the national court deciding 'correctly', that is, either refraining from submitting a request for an advisory opinion or asking questions to the EFTA Court that are relevant for the decision and precisely formulated.[22] This will be illustrated by the following case examples.

i. The Hypothetical or General Question

The EFTA Court does not answer general or hypothetical questions. To give an example, in *Koch*[23] the referring court and the parties to the proceedings before it agreed that the assurance policies in question were unit-linked assurance contracts. Thus, the EFTA Court found that the question as to how the term 'unit-linked policies' should be interpreted was merely hypothetical and refused to answer.[24]

ii. The Already Answered Question

This occurs when a referred question in a request for an advisory opinion has already been answered by the EFTA Court.[25] For example, the first question in *Pucher*[26] ('Does a residence requirement for at least one member of the board of directors of a domiciliary company constitute indirect discrimination?') had in fact already been answered in *Rainford Towning*[27] ('A national provision which requires the managing director of a legal person to reside in the State concerned, constitutes indirect discrimination'). In *Pucher*,[28] the Court made explicit references to its decision in *Rainford-Towning*[29] (but it did not decide by reasoned order as provided for in Article 93 RoP).[30]

[21] Baudenbacher (n 5) 152.

[22] ÓJ Einarsson, 'The Advisory Opinion Procedure and the Relationship between the EFTA Court and the Norwegian Courts: Recent Developments' (2022) 61 *Lov og Rett* 221, 239, underlines that the preferable course of action is to ask the Court concrete questions as it will provide the national court with the *clearest* guidance. This constitutes, as the author writes (at 238), a real 'spirit of cooperation' between national courts and the EFTA Court.

[23] Case E-11/12 *Koch* [2013] EFTA Ct Rep. 272, para 55.

[24] P Christiansen in Arnesen et al (n 4) Art 34 SCA, para 17.

[25] ibid para 16.

[26] Case E-2/01 *Pucher* [2002] EFTA Ct Rep 4.

[27] Case E-3/98 *Rainford Towning* [1998] EFTA Ct Rep 205.

[28] *Pucher* (n 26) para 20.

[29] *Rainford Towning* (n 27) para 30.

[30] At that time Art 97, para 3 RoP.

iii. The Missing Additional Question

In many cases the additional question reads as follows: 'If question 1 is answered in the affirmative, then question 2 is …'

To give an example: in the case of *Paletta I*,[31] the Arbeitsgericht Lörrach/Germany asked if it was 'required to base its decision, in fact and in law, on the findings made by the social security institution of the employee's place of residence concerning the commencement and duration of the incapacity for work?'

The CJEU answered this question in the affirmative, and the Arbeitsgericht Lörrach based its decision on the aforementioned findings.

On appeal by the employer, the Bundesarbeitsgericht submitted another request for a preliminary ruling in the same case and asked if employers are barred from adducing evidence to support a finding of abuse or fraudulent conduct by the worker concerned by the national court, in that although the worker may claim to have become incapacitated for work and has certified such incapacity in accordance with Article 18 of the regulation in question, they may not actually be incapacitated at all. This question was also answered in the affirmative by the CJEU in the case of *Paletta II*.[32]

Had Amtsgericht Lörrach already submitted the question later put forward by the Bundesarbeitsgericht, a delay of two years could have been avoided.

C. Central Thoughts

The EEA Agreement gives rights to individuals, which includes being able to go before the judiciary to assert these rights. But in which situations will the judicial defence of these rights take place? This happens primarily during national proceedings, the so-called main proceedings, when a question arises which has to be answered by an advisory opinion of the EFTA Court. So, the national reference procedure has to be seen in the light of the judicial defence of the rights granted by the EEA Agreement. National courts have to interpret their national procedural law in the light of fundamental rights, especially Article 6 ECHR, to give individuals the possibility to defend the rights which are conferred on them by the EEA Agreement. As has been shown above, this is clearly evident from the Preamble to the EEA Agreement, where reference is made (in recital 4) to adequate means of enforcement of common rules, also at the *judicial level*. It is emphasised in recital 8 that individuals will play an important role in the European Economic Area through the exercise of the rights conferred on them by this Agreement and through the judicial defence of these rights, and finally (recital 15) uniform interpretation and application of the EEA Agreement must be arrived at. The eighth recital is the most important of all of the sixteen recitals of the Preamble.[33] All these objectives particularly concern lawsuits before national courts, where these courts act as European courts[34] and

[31] Case C-45/90 *Alberto Paletta and Others v Brennet AG* ECLI:EU:C:1992:236, [1992] ECR I-03423.
[32] Case C-206/94 *Brennet AG v Vittorio Paletta* ECLI:EU:C:1996:182, [1996] ECR I-02357.
[33] Arnesen and Fredriksen (n 4) Preamble, para 28.
[34] See again Baudenbacher (n 5) 152.

are therefore obliged to provide the parties to the proceedings with the utmost protection of their rights with regard to the application and thus also the interpretation of EEA law. The national courts are therefore obliged to involve the parties as comprehensively as possible before taking the decision whether a request for an advisory opinion is to be submitted and, if so, which questions are to be asked, so that the parties may actually enjoy not only theoretically but also effectively[35] the rights conferred upon them by the EEA Agreement. This is the so-called 'principle of effectiveness', which also requires the effective enforcement of EEA law in national courts.[36] This is in substance the same as what is described by Arnesen and Fredriksen[37] as 'the EEA-based duty of national courts to do whatever lies within their competence to interpret and apply national law in conformity with obligations under the EEA Agreement'.

III. POSSIBLE CONSEQUENCES OF HEARING THE PARTIES

The parties could, for instance:

- inform the court about the question being hypothetical or already answered by the Court (or maybe by the CJEU);
- submit new facts so that the question is no longer necessary;
- submit new legal aspects so that the question is no longer necessary;
- suggest formulating questions differently or suggest referring additional questions;
- abandon the action or appeal, or recognise the claim, which also includes – if admissible under the national procedural law – abandoning or recognising partial claims (ie, if the question relevant under EEA law only relates to part of a claim) or abandon or recognise individual legal aspects (ie, if under national procedural law, the issue of civil law limitation can only be raised as a defence);
- find a way for a settlement: in some cases, the parties may find the way to a settlement instead of waiting 8–12 months for the advisory opinion. It is also possible that the parties do not want to have their case heard by the EFTA Court for whatever reason – for instance, to avoid European case law or 'European publicity'. Here it should be mentioned that Article 89 RoP now provides under special circumstances for anonymity of persons or entities concerned by the case.[38] Currently, the EFTA Court anonymises requests for advisory opinions – for example, where the request is made in the context of criminal proceedings, the cases involve sensitive personal information or when the case has already been anonymised by the referring court.

[35] B Hammermann, 'Liechtenstein: 25 Jahre EWR-Gerichtsbarkeit' (2020) 1 *LJZ* 11, at 12: 'Effective legal protection by the judiciary is therefore an essential element of the legal system of the EEA' (translated).

[36] P Hreinsson, 'General Principles' in Baudenbacher (ed) (n 5) 376.

[37] Arnesen and Fredriksen (n 4) Preamble, para 28, 162.

[38] *cf* Case E-2/23 *A Ltd.*

IV. HOW TO INFORM THE PARTIES

The decision to refer a question is made by the national court.[39] Parties to the national proceedings have no procedural rights (a procedural claim) to have a question referred to the EFTA Court either according to national law in the EEA/EFTA States[40] or under Article 34 SCA.[41]

National courts have to inform parties before an order to refer a question is made. The information has to contain the question and – if this is not clear to the parties – the reasons why it seems to be necessary for the national court to refer:

- Either: if a party raises the need for an advisory opinion, the party will normally formulate the question. So, if an answer to this question seems to be necessary to give judgement in the case, the national court can send the question to the other parties of the proceedings to give a comment. However, a critical position must be taken towards proposals by the parties concerning the wording of the proposed questions – as is correctly pointed out by Fredriksen[42] – given that the parties tend to weave their view of the matter into the way a question is worded.
- Or: if the court finds the referral of a question necessary on its own motion, it has to formulate the question so that the parties can comment on it.

The parties have to know the exact wording of the question that the court wants to refer to the EFTA Court. Otherwise, they cannot comment sufficiently. The right to be heard (Article 6 ECHR) has to be an effective right: the parties to the proceedings have the right to present the observations which they regard as relevant to their case. The parties can only make use of the right to be effectively heard if they know the exact wording and the reasons for the question to be referred, if it is not obvious.

The manner in which the parties are to be heard – ie, whether a hearing is to be carried out or whether the opportunity to submit written statements is sufficient – depends in turn on national procedural law. Under the terms of Article 6 (1) ECHR, written consultation proceedings are sufficient.

[39] *cf* Case C-561/19 *Consorzio Italian Management, Catania Multiservizi SpA v Rete Ferroviaria Italiana SpA* ECLI:EU:C:2021:799, para 55: 'It follows that the determination and formulation of the questions to be put to the Court devolve upon the national court or tribunal alone and that the parties to the main proceedings may not change their tenor.'

[40] S Magnússon, 'Icelandic Courts' in Baudenbacher (ed) (n 5) 287; W Ungerank, 'Liechtenstein Courts' in Baudenbacher (ed) (n 5) 300. In Norway, too, the parties to the proceedings cannot force a request for an advisory opinion by procedural measures; *cf* TC Poulsen, 'Norwegian Courts' in Baudenbacher (ed) (n 5) 265: 'on its own motion … not dependent on an application … a decision to refer or not to refer cannot be challenged on appeal'.

[41] HH Fredriksen, *Europäische Vorlageverfahren und nationales Zivilprozessrecht* (Tübingen, Mohr Siebeck, 2009) 156, fn 133.

[42] ibid 261. There, Fredriksen also refers to Case C-318/00 *Bacardi-Martini* ECLI:EU:C:2003:41, [2003] ECR I-00905, according to which a question submitted for preliminary decision is inadmissible if the national court fails to explain the reasons why it considers answering the question to be relevant for the decision – unless these reasons are clearly evident from the file – and if, being asked about such reasons, it only repeats the pleadings of one of the parties without stating whether it shares that party's point of view.

V. THE OPPORTUNITY TO MAKE A STATEMENT BEFORE THE EFTA COURT IS INSUFFICIENT

The fact that the parties of the main proceedings may (after the request for an advisory opinion has been made) present their positions to the EFTA Court (first by submitting a written statement and then by making an oral submission during the hearing before the Court) is no replacement for being heard by the national court (before the request for an advisory opinion has been made). The EFTA Court will decide on the questions asked by the national court exclusively, doing so on the basis of the facts of the case as presented by the referring court. The parties to the main proceedings are therefore unable to raise and request the answering of any new or different questions in the proceedings before the EFTA Court. Their only opportunity to influence the questions asked is the main proceedings, and they have to do so before the request is made. If the facts of the case and/or the national legal framework stated by the national court in the request are considered to be incorrect in the opinion of a party, and if this is pleaded before the Court in a substantiated manner, the Court may – although without there being any legal claim thereto[43] – ask the national court for clarification pursuant to Article 95(1) of the RoP.[44] All this can be prevented by hearing the parties of the main proceedings before the request for an advisory opinion is made, and it is only hearing the parties which will satisfy the principle of effectiveness.

VI. DIGRESSION: VIEWS ON HEARING THE PARTIES IN GERMAN-SPEAKING EU MEMBER STATES

With regard to Article 267 TFEU, which in this respect raises the same concerns as Article 34 SCA, the literature in Germany and Austria also assumes that there is a duty to hear the parties (before submitting a request for a preliminary ruling to the CJEU).

A. Germany

According to Heß,[45] the protection of the right to be heard in court requires oral proceedings, with a minimum requirement of hearing the parties. In this connection, he also points out that the parties lose the position of being a party in the

[43] *cf* Joined Cases C-482/01 and C-493/01 *Orfanopoulos* ECLI:EU:C:2004:262, [2004] ECR I-05257. The German government disputed the description of national legislation in the two orders for reference (at para 41), the succinct reply to which was that it was not for the Court in the context of a reference for a preliminary ruling to rule on the interpretation of national provisions or to decide whether the referring court's interpretation thereof is correct; rather, the Court had to take account, under the division of jurisdiction between the Community courts and the national courts, of the factual and legislative context, as described in the order for reference, in which the questions put to it were set.

[44] Joined Cases E-11/19 and E-12/19 *Adpublisher AG*, para 37.

[45] B Heß, 'Die Einwirkungen des Vorabentscheidungsverfahrens nach Art 177 EGV auf das deutsche Zivilprozessrecht' (1995) 108(1) *ZZP* 59 and fn 223.

proceedings for a preliminary decision (obviously meaning in the referring proceedings, since these are suspended). It is the opinion of Hüßtege[46] that Article 103 (1) of the German Basic Law (Grundgesetz (GG))[47] requires that the parties be heard before a reference is made. Additionally, Latzel and Streinz[48] base their identical view on Article 103 (1) GG, as does Fredriksen.[49] Middeke[50] also bases the claim for being heard on this provision, but also on the principle of 'effective – in the sense of speedy – legal protection'.

Ultimately, Latzel and Streinz[51] consider it a requirement that the parties to the proceedings also be heard after the preliminary ruling has been received, stating that if the implementation of the CJEU's judgment requires the further clarification of facts, suitable measures must be taken, and that otherwise a time limit for a written submission must be set – the authors explicitly refer to Article 103 (1) of the Basic Law here – and the announcement of the judgment must be scheduled.

No decisions of German courts on the question of hearing the parties in this context can be found.

B. Austria

In Austria, the phase of the main proceedings that lies between the 'occurrence' of questions subject to referral, ie, the time from the receipt of a suggestion by a party (or from the arising of the court's intention *ex officio*, as the case may be) to ask the CJEU for a preliminary ruling, until the dispatch of the decision for referral to the CJEU is called the 'preparatory phase of the proceedings' (*vorbereitendes Verfahrensstadium*).[52] Gamerith[53] has justified the fact that the parties to the proceedings must be heard in this phase of the proceedings before the intended decision for referral, with the argument that Community law must be taken into account by the national court *ex officio*[54] and that the parties must not be surprised by a legal view

[46] R Hüßtege, 'Vorabentscheidungsverfahren nach Art 234 EGV' in W Seitz et al, *Beck'sches Richter-Handbuch*, 2nd edn (Munich, CH Beck Verlag, 1999) 1551, para 13.

[47] 'In the courts every person shall be entitled to a hearing in accordance with law.'

[48] C Latzel and T Streinz, 'Das richtige Vorabentscheidungsersuchen' (2013) 4 *NJOZ* 97, 101, fn 87 with further references.

[49] Fredriksen (n 41) 259. The same author bases the claim of the parties to be heard also on Art 6 ECHR (at 54) and requires that the parties be heard (1) by carrying out oral proceedings on the wording of the order to refer (at 55), and (2) even if no referral is to take place but the decision of the CJEU in parallel proceedings is to be waited for (at 54), and also before a possible withdrawal of the request for a preliminary decision (at 57 et seq).

[50] A Middeke in H Rengeling, A Middeke and M Gellermann (eds), *Handbuch des Rechtsschutzes in der Europäischen Union*, 3rd edn (Munich, CH Beck Verlag, 2014) § 10, para 81.

[51] Latzel and Streinz (n 48) 108.

[52] Bundesministerium für Justiz, decree of 29 August 2019, no BMVRDJ-EU15116/0003-EU/2019, avaialble at: www.ris.bka.gv.at; Kohlegger in HW Fasching and A Konecny (eds), *Zivilprozessgesetze*[3rd] ed II/3 Anh § 190 ZPO para 23, 27 and 50; G Kohlegger, 'Aktuelle Entwicklungen im Vorabentscheidungsverfahren' (1998) *ZfRV*, 89 fn 2.

[53] H Gamerith, 'Das Vorabentscheidungsverfahren nach Art 177 EGV in Wettbewerbssachen' (1995) *ÖBl* 51.

[54] In this context, it should be noted that CJEU has, outside the field of consumer protection, considered the duty of national courts to apply EU law to be relatively limited. See, eg, Joined Cases C-222/05–225/05, EU:C:2007:124 *van der Weerd* and Case C-300/17, EU:C:2018:405 *Hochtief*.

that they have not taken into consideration and that has not been pointed out to them, which means that the national court must discuss the legal view forming the basis for the intention of referral with the parties. Klingler[55] bases the duty to hear the parties before issuing the decision for referral from the right to a fair trial pursuant to Article 6 ECHR.

No opinions can be found on a possible duty to hear the parties in the 'follow-up' stage of the proceedings (*nachbereitendes Verfahrensstadium*), ie, the phase between the referring court receiving the CJEU's answer until the final decision on the matters of Union law, which ultimately may be upon the conclusion of the referring lawsuit.[56]

No decisions of Austrian courts on the question of hearing the parties in this context can be found.

VII. HEARING THE PARTIES AFTER THE REQUEST FOR AN ADVISORY OPINION IS SENT

In special procedural circumstances (for example, when the national law changes or the action is withdrawn), it may be necessary for the referring court to withdraw the request for an advisory opinion. The principles applicable to the withdrawal of a request – which is materially the same as not referring to the Court at all – are identical to those applicable to the decision about submitting a request for an advisory opinion to the Court: the parties also have to be heard before the request is withdrawn, as Fredriksen[57] correctly points out.

VIII. HEARING THE PARTIES AFTER THE OPINION HAS BEEN RECEIVED

The above considerations as to why the parties must be heard before the request for an advisory opinion is made can also be applied to the referring lawsuit, which is to be continued after the advisory opinion has been received (the 'follow-up' phase of the proceedings). An immediate decision on the case by the national court – if permitted at all under national procedural law – would once again violate the right of the parties to be heard in court deduced from Article 6 ECHR. In addition, the criterion of the effective delivery and protection of justice guaranteed by the EEA Agreement applies to this phase of the proceedings too. This can clearly be deduced from Article 97 RoP. Since the so-called 'interpretation proceedings' (Article 138 RoP) are expressly not applicable here, it is for the national court to assess whether it considers that sufficient guidance has been given by an advisory opinion or whether it considers that a further request to the Court is required. Here too, various constellations of facts are conceivable. A question may not have been asked which now, after the advisory opinion has been received, suddenly appears to be relevant. Equally, the advisory opinion may have resulted in the appearance of new aspects of the case, which on the basis of

[55] E Klingler, *Vorabentscheidungsersuchen – Fragen an den EuGH im österreichischen Zivilverfahren* (Vienna, Verlag Österreich, 2018) 105.

[56] Kohlegger (n 52) 89, fn 2.

[57] *cf* Fredriksen (n 41).

the results of the proceedings of the referring lawsuit at the time of referral make a further request for an advisory opinion appear to be necessary. In the main proceedings, it may also have become necessary to consider additional (other) evidence or to broach factual or legal aspects that until that particular time appeared to be of no or little importance. Logically, all of this can only be assessed when involving the parties, which also includes assessments on the basis of the opinion rendered by the EFTA Court. The parties must be able to (partly) waive claims, (partly) acknowledge claims, withdraw appeals or enter into settlement agreements.

Here too, the way in which the parties are to be heard depends on national procedural law, and under Article 6 (1) ECHR, the option to comment in writing is sufficient.

IX. CONCLUSION

Whether or not hearing the parties of the main proceedings (before a court of an EEA/EFTA State submits a request for an advisory opinion) is provided for in national procedural law, such a hearing is required in order to guarantee a fair trial under the terms of Article 6(1) ECHR and in order to provide the parties concerned with the full effectiveness of the rights granted to them by the EEA Agreement. Hearing the parties must not be a mere formality; rather, the national court – which in this case acts as a European court – must be enabled to ask the questions relevant for the decision in order to receive as precise answers as possible from the EFTA Court. Even after the national court has received the advisory opinion, the parties to the proceedings must be heard before any decision on the substance of the case is taken.

24

The EFTA Court's Contribution to Fundamental Rights Protection in the EEA in Competition Law Cases

The Notion of Complex Economic Assessments and Judicial Review

KARIN FLØISTAD

I. INTRODUCTION

Fundamental Rights Protection in the EEA

At the heart of fundamental rights protection in the EEA is that both the three EEA/EFTA States and the EU Member States are parties to the European Convention on Human Rights (ECHR). Many dualist states, such as Norway and Iceland, have incorporated it into their own legal system. The ECHR, monitored by the European Court of Human Rights (ECtHR) in Strasbourg, sets the standard for protecting fundamental rights. Within the EU, the Charter of Fundamental Rights of the European Union (hereinafter the 'EU Charter') adds an additional layer of protection. In *Telenor ASA and Telenor Norge AS*, the EFTA Court reiterated that: 'According to the Court's established case law, fundamental rights form part of the general principles of EEA law.'[1] Hence, fundamental rights protection in the EEA is a multifaceted system, involving the ECHR, the EU Charter and the EEA Agreement.[2]

[1] Case E-12/20 *Telenor ASA and Telenor Norge AS*, judgment of 5 May 2022, para 75. The Court made reference to Case E-1/20 *Kerim*, judgment of 9 February 2021, para 43 to substantiate the reference to fundamental rights forming part of the general principles of EEA law. The concept was also recently presented at conferences opening new research centres regarding the Europeanisation of Norwegian law both in Bergen (UiB) (CENTENOL) and Oslo (UiO).

[2] For a recent general outline of fundamental rights and the EEA, see ÓJ Einarsson, 'Fundamental Rights in the Case Law of the EFTA Court' in JF Kjølbro, S O'Leary and M Tsirli (eds), *Liber Amicorum Robert Spano* (Limal, Anthemis and Eleven International Publishing, 2022).

The aim here is to look more closely at the contribution by the EFTA Court to fundamental rights protection in the EEA in two major competition law cases: the above-mentioned *Telenor* and *Posten Norge*.[3] In particular, the aim is to shed light on the contribution by the EFTA Court to set out in more detail the standard of review regarding the concept of complex economic assessments, involving in-depth analysis of economic data and market analysis, in line with the fundamental right to effective judicial protection, including the right to a fair trial, enshrined in Article 6 ECHR. The boundaries of the principle of effective judicial protection are challenged through the standard according to which the tribunal or court limits the judicial control of so-called 'complex economic assessments' in competition cases.[4]

The argument made is that the EFTA Court has introduced some important clarifications regarding the 'manifest error of assessment' standard, the essence of which is to leave some room for manoeuvre to the administrative authority in competition cases.[5]

This chapter will not address questions regarding any possible differences between the EEA and the EU legal order regarding the extent of fundamental rights protection. On the contrary, in line with the homogeneity objective, this chapter has the aim of equal legal protection based on fundamental rights as a starting point. Hence, contributions by the EFTA Court to clarify and articulate further the fundamental right of judicial protection in the field of competition law is seen as being of interest both in the EEA and in the EU legal order.[6]

This chapter looks at competition enforcement by the EFTA Surveillance Authority (ESA) and judicial control by the EFTA Court. However, it should be mentioned that the Norwegian Supreme Court recently rendered a judgment in a case concerning the prohibition of a merger in which the same limitation regarding judicial review of complex economic assessments was established under national competition law. In this merger case regarding Schibsted ASA and Nettbil AS, both the Competition Authority and the Competition Tribunal in Norway adopted decisions to block the merger. However, both the Court of Appeal and the Supreme Court held that the decision was not justified and therefore annulled it.[7] Regarding the intensity of judicial review, the Supreme Court referred to the judgment of the General Court in *Thyssenkrupp* and held that review of decisions of a competition authority was subject to similar limitations under Norwegian law and in particular that the Court was not to replace the authority's economic assessment with its own.[8] Hence, the courts, also under Norwegian national law, will limit their control regarding complex economic assessments in competition decisions. Given that effective judicial protection is part of the fundamental right to a fair trial under Article 6 ECHR and also

[3] Case E-15/10 *Posten Norge* [2012] EFTA Ct Rep 246.

[4] For a general overview of the principle of effective judicial protection in the context of the EEA Agreement, see HK Ellingsen, ch 22 in this volume.

[5] The rule was developed by the CJEU at the very beginning of competition law litigation in the mid-1960s; see Joined Cases 56/64 and 58/64 *Consten and Grundig v Commission* ECLI:EU:C:1966:41.

[6] Demonstrating the interest by EU academics in the case law of the EFTA Court in this field, see E Barbier de La Serre, 'Standard of Review in Competition Law Cases: *Posten Norge* and beyond' in EFTA Court (ed), *The EEA and the EFTA Court: Decentred Integration* (Oxford, Hart Publishing, 2014) 417.

[7] Gulating lagmannsrett (Gulating Court of Appeal), LG-2021-119638, and Norges Høyesterett (Supreme Court of Norway), HR-2023-02-16.

[8] HR-2023-02-16, para 64, referring to Case T-584/19 *Thyssenkrupp v Commission* ECLI:EU:T:2022:386, paras 276–77 and the case law cited therein.

applies for national systems, the same tension potentially arises in judicial control of national competition decisions in Norway.[9]

II. ARTICLE 6 ECHR: EFFECTIVE JUDICIAL PROTECTION

A. Introduction

As stated above, the principle of effective judicial protection, as part of the right to a fair trial, is enshrined, inter alia, in Article 6 ECHR and is also a general principle of EEA law.[10] The right to a fair trial ensures that individuals facing both civil and criminal proceedings are entitled to a fair and impartial trial. This includes access to an independent tribunal or court, the right to be heard, the right to present evidence and the right to appeal. It is common ground that administrative sanctions in the form of fines are considered criminal sanctions.[11] In competition law a differentiation is often made between the blocking of mergers and administrative fines based on violation of either Article 53 EEA regarding anti-competitive agreements or Article 54 EEA on abuse of dominance and fines for violating stand-still obligations in merger control (eg, 'gun jumping').

According to the case law of the ECtHR, Article 6 ECHR applies in a differentiated manner, depending on the nature of the issue and the degree of stigma carried by certain criminal cases, on the one hand, and on the necessity of the guarantee in question for the requirements of a fair trial, on the other.[12] Thus, to what degree judicial protection inherent in fair trial guarantees applies in a given case must be determined with regard to the weight of the criminal charge at issue. Hence, even competition cases involving fines would generally not amount to 'hard core' criminal law which triggers the full application of the guarantees of Article 6 ECHR and, in particular, the rights accorded to the accused under Article 6(3) ECHR.

B. The Requirement of Full Jurisdiction

Where sanctions in a criminal case are not imposed by a tribunal or court, which fulfils the requirements under Article 6 ECHR, the ECtHR requires that the decision must be reviewed by judicial bodies that have 'full jurisdiction'.[13]

[9] Decisions prohibiting mergers and decisions imposing fines are not identical in terms of the criminal/civil nature of the decision; see the discussion on a sliding scale of requirements depending on this characterisation in section II. B below. See also below on the establishment of the Norwegian Competition Tribunal in 2017, which to some extent will balance the conflicting views with its composition of both lawyers and economists. Throughout the different European systems of judicial/tribunal control of national administrative competition law decisions, the common denominator seems to be this combined permanent composition of lawyers and economists as 'judges'.

[10] *cf* the parallel provision of Art 47 of the EU Charter.

[11] See *Menarini Diagnostics v Italy* App No 43509/08 (ECtHR, 27 September 2011). The Norwegian Competition Tribunal, which was established on 1 April 2017, conducted a study prior to its first case to establish the requirements of Art 6 ECHR for its practice.

[12] See in particular *Jussila v Finland* [GC], ECHR 2006-XIV, para 43; and *Kammerer v Austria* App No 32435/06 (ECtHR, 12 May 2010).

[13] *Schmautzer v Austria* (1995) Series A No 328 A, para 36.

As the institutional set-up of the EFTA side of the EEA mirrors that laid down under EU law, the ESA acts both as an investigator and as a first instance decision maker in the EEA competition enforcement system. Decisions from ESA impose fines on undertakings for infringements of competition law and these are considered criminal penalties under the ECHR. In order to be compatible with Article 6 ECHR, criminal penalties must not necessarily, in the first instance, be imposed by an 'independent and impartial tribunal established by law'. But if criminal sanctions are imposed by an administrative body which does not itself comply with the requirements for independence, the decision of that body must be subject to subsequent control by a judicial body that has full jurisdiction and does in fact comply with those requirements.[14] If this is the case, the competition law procedure as a whole is compatible with the applicable guarantees of the ECHR.[15]

By full jurisdiction, the independent tribunal or court exercising judicial control must have the 'power to quash in all respects, on questions of fact and law, the decision' and 'must have jurisdiction to examine all questions of fact and law relevant to the dispute before it'.[16] The tribunal or court must always establish whether the evidence relied on is factually accurate, reliable and consistent.

The judicial control within the EEA is exercised by the EFTA Court, which clearly satisfies the requirements of an 'independent and impartial tribunal established by law'. In the EEA legal order, the role of the EFTA Court regarding judicial protection against decisions of ESA is provided for by Article 36 SCA.[17] Under that provision, the EFTA Court has jurisdiction to declare decisions adopted by ESA void. Unlike in the EU legal order with both the General Court and the Court of Justice of the European Union (CJEU), there is an absence of a possibility of appeal against judgments in the EEA legal order.[18]

In the national competition enforcement system in Norway, a competition tribunal was established from 1 April 2017 for the subsequent control of sanctions, inter alia, to ensure fulfilment of the requirement for an 'independent and impartial tribunal established by law' having full jurisdiction. Similar independent competition tribunals have been established in national systems for enforcement of competition law in various European states.[19] For more than 20 years, these various national enforcement systems have cooperated in the Association of European Competition Law Judges (AECLJ), including close cooperation with the European Commission.

[14] *Menarini Diagnostics v Italy* App No 43509/08 (ECtHR, 27 September 2011), para 59.

[15] Case C-295/12 P *Telefónica and Telefónica de España v Commission* ECLI:EU:C:2014:2062, para 51 and the case law cited therein.

[16] *Menarini Diagnostics v Italy* App No 43509/08 (ECtHR, 27 September 2011), paras 59, 63 and 64.

[17] The Agreement between the EFTA States on the Establishment of a Surveillance Authority and a Court of Justice.

[18] This absence of appeal under the EFTA enforcement system was examined by the EFTA Court in *Posten Norge*, which stated: 'With regard to Article 2(1) of Protocol 7 ECHR in particular, the applicant has alleged that the absence of a possibility of appeal against the judgments of the Court could pose a problem. However, Article 2(2) of that Protocol excepts from the right to appeal a case in which the person concerned was tried in the first instance by the highest tribunal. Under the relevant treaties of the European Economic Area, the Court is, within its jurisdiction, the highest tribunal.' *Posten Norge* (n 3) para 92.

[19] Since the entry into force of the Icelandic Competition Act, Iceland has had a competition tribunal in place with similar competences to its Norwegian counterpart. Under Art 41 of pt II, ch II of Protocol 4 to the SCA, Liechtenstein is exempted from the obligation to designate a competition authority.

C. The Manifest Error of Assessment Test

As stated in the introduction, the boundaries of the principle of effective judicial protection are tested through the standard according to which the tribunal or court limits the control of so-called 'complex economic assessments' to 'manifest errors of appreciation' (manifest errors test) in competition cases. Even if the scope and meaning of this standard remain unclear and vague, the essence is to leave some room for manoeuvre for the competition authority, even in situations where the authority is both the investigator and the decision maker.

The tension between the need for administrative authorities to exercise a certain amount of discretion in the field of complex economic assessments contrasted with the requirement for effective judicial control is, as mentioned earlier, also found in national law. One proposed solution to balance the conflicting interests can be found in the Norwegian legal order with the Competition Tribunal.[20] It follows from the preparatory works accompanying the Act establishing the Tribunal that a motivating factor was to establish an independent and impartial tribunal established by law with expertise not only in law but also in economics. With this combined expertise, the Norwegian Competition Tribunal has, in the same manner as competition tribunals in general, a different starting point for carrying out a detailed review in competition cases in comparison with courts which are limited to judicial expertise alone. Courts may appoint economic experts as judges, but it is argued here that such temporary solutions are not the same as a tribunal consisting permanently of both legal and economic expertise. This may also explain the number of European competition tribunals also consisting permanently of economists. Similar solutions regarding national control of administrative decisions in the field of competition law can be found in a number of EU Member States as well as in the UK with the Competition Appeals Tribunal (CAT).[21]

D. Increased Fines and Complexity in Administrative Decisions in Competition Law

It is generally acknowledged that the level of fines imposed for breaches of competition law obligations has increased substantially over the years, leading in general to a more criminal-like approach in the field. This fact, combined with the trend of administrative competition law decisions in general to increase both in length and in detail, adds to the burden of challenging the decision for the applicants. Hence, procedural guarantees in the form of judicial review are increasingly important in this field of law as well as increasingly challenging for the applicant to actually invoke. Additionally, it should be noted that very often, the sophistication of the judicial review is in actual fact primarily determined by the sophistication of the applicant's arguments and depends very much on a party's ability to access economic and legal

[20] The Act providing for the Norwegian Competition Tribunal came into force on 1 April 2017.

[21] For an overview of the European competition law tribunal system, see the Association of European Competition Law Judges (AECLJ) website: www.aeclj.com.

expertise. The details of the theory of harm[22] and the quality of evidence supporting the decision may also vary significantly. Faced with this reality, the assessment of the standard of legal review must always have regard to the individual facts of a case, the merits of the case and the evidence presented, as well as the theory of harm, which according to the administrative authorities is of relevance.

E. Substantial Fines in the *Telenor* and *Posten Norge* Cases

In the case law of the EFTA Court analysed in this chapter, the Court has noted that proceedings under Articles 53 and 54 EEA may entail substantial fines.[23] In the *Telenor* case, the fines amounting to €111,951,000 in total were imposed on Telenor for intentional or at least negligent breaches of Article 54 EEA. Given this fact, the Court stated:

> Having regard to the nature of the infringements in question and to the potential gravity of the ensuing penalties, it must be held that the proceedings at hand fall within the criminal sphere for the purposes of the principle of effective judicial protection.

In *Posten Norge*, the fines amounting to €12.89 million were not considered a criminal charge of minor weight.[24] Noting the amount of the charge, including the stigma attached to being held accountable for an abuse of a dominant position, the EFTA Court considered the charge substantial.[25]

In both cases, the EFTA Court stated that the judicial protection inherent in Article 6 ECHR applied given the criminal nature of the sanctions imposed.[26]

With this in mind, the question arises as to how the EFTA Court was able to reconcile the requirement of providing effective judicial review (*cf* section II.B above) with the deferential standard applicable in competition law cases when faced with 'complex economic assessments'.[27] Regarding the standard on how the courts limit their judicial review in competition law cases when faced with 'complex economic assessments', it must be reiterated that the scope and meaning of this rule remain unclear and have varied over the years. In essence, it is described as a manifest error of assessment test. The test has also been described as 'light judicial review'.[28] The EFTA

[22] The term 'theory of harm' is generally used in competition cases as a starting point for the analysis of market behaviour.

[23] Article 53 EEA corresponds to Art 101 of the Treaty on the Functioning of the European Union (TFEU) and Art 54 EEA corresponds to Art 102 TFEU.

[24] *Posten Norge* (n 3).

[25] ibid para 90.

[26] However, the EFTA Court held in *Posten Norge*, based on ECtHR case law, that sanctions such as competition law fines may in the first instance be imposed by an administrative authority, which does not fulfil the requirements of Article 6 ECHR. *Posten Norge* (n 3) para 91.

[27] There are a number of academic analyses of this rule pointing to both its advantages and its limits within the EU literature.

[28] I Forrester, 'A Bush in Need of Pruning: The Luxuriant Growth of "Light Judicial Review"' in CD Ehlermann and M Marquis (eds), *European Competition Law Annual 2009: The Evaluation of Evidence and its Judicial Review in Competition Cases* (Oxford, Hart Publishing, 2011) 407.

Court has formulated this approach within the field of state aid in the *Hurtigruten* case in the following manner:

> Normally, EEA States enjoy a discretion in defining a service of general economic interest mission and the conditions of its implementation, including the assessment of the additional costs incurred in discharging the mission, which depends on complex economic facts. The scope of the control which ESA is entitled to exercise in that regard is limited to one of manifest error. It follows that the Court's review of ESA's assessment in that regard must observe the same limit and that, accordingly, its review must be confined to ascertaining whether ESA properly found or rejected the existence of a manifest error by the EEA State.[29]

Before entering into an analysis of the case law from the EFTA Court, the notion of complex economic assessments will be outlined in more detail below.

III. THE CONCEPT OF 'COMPLEX ECONOMIC ASSESSMENTS'

A. Introduction

The challenge for competition law involves in broad terms how to translate economics into good legal rules. Law is an administrative system with its own functional requirements and in competition cases, a balance must be found regarding precision, risk of error, legal certainty and speed, to name but a few. In this balancing act, we find administrative discretion and the identified need to give enforcers the tools they need.[30] However, the question is how to strike the right balance when deciding which institutions are best at doing what and how to advance in the endeavour to translate economics into law.

B. In-depth Analysis of Economic Data and Market Dynamics

There is no precise definition given by the CJEU of what constitutes complex economic assessments in competition law cases. In the following, an illustration of the predefined framework needed to provide an objective analysis is briefly presented.[31] Economic assessments involve the in-depth analysis of economic data and market dynamics to evaluate the potential anti-competitive effects of certain business practices or proposed mergers.[32] These assessments often rely on vast amounts of data, econometric modelling and economic theory, as well as the need for economic experts

[29] Joined Cases E-10/11 and E-11/11 *Hurtigruten ASA and Norway v ESA*, para 150.

[30] Considerations related to potential under-enforcement in the digital market and significant concentrations were among the drivers for the adoption of sectoral regulation such as the Digital Market Act (DMA) and the Digital Services Act (DSA).

[31] For an insight into the view of a judge at the General Court, see the recent article by J Svenningsen, G Muguet-Poullennec and B Cheynel, 'Judicial Review of Economic Evidence in EU Competition Law: Ready for the Ride?' (2023) 1(1) *Antitrust Chronicle – Judicial Review of Economic Evidence* 14.

[32] As stated above, the blocking of mergers in the enforcement of competition law is generally not considered a criminal sanction.

to analyse and present the data, as these assessments can be highly technical and require specialised knowledge. The key aspects often include the following steps in a competition case:

- Market definition, where complex economic assessments often begin with defining the relevant market, which helps in identifying the boundaries within which competition occurs. This process considers both product and geographical dimensions. Accurate market definition is crucial for determining market power and anti-competitive behaviour.
- Market power evaluation of undertakings is a critical component. It assesses whether a firm or a group of firms can exercise significant influence over price, output or other competitive aspects. High market power can indicate potential antitrust concerns.
- Anti-competitive effects aim to determine whether a specific business conduct or merger could harm competition. This involves analysing pricing strategies, market shares, barriers to entry and other relevant economic factors to gauge potential anti-competitive effects.
- Efficiency defences, on the flip side, consider the potential efficiency gains that could result from certain business practices or mergers. If the efficiencies outweigh the anti-competitive effects, a practice or merger may be deemed pro-competitive.

C. Translating Economics into Good Legal Rules and Enforcement

While complex economic assessments provide vital insights, they must ultimately be translated into statements about facts (eg, foreclosure of as-efficient competitors) that fit into legal rules and interpretations (ie, into facts that become relevant and meaningful when enforcement authorities, tribunals and courts apply the law). The task of competition authorities is to make the final determination based on these assessments, ensuring that they align with the legal standards and objectives of competition law. Hence, complex economic assessments are indispensable tools in competition law. They require a multidisciplinary approach, combining economics, data analysis and legal expertise to assess the competitive landscape and determine the legality of business practices and mergers. These assessments play a crucial role in enforcement by competition authorities to maintain competitive markets and safeguard the interests of consumers. It is in light of the importance of these assessments in competition law cases that the restraint exercised by courts through the application of the manifest error of assessment test must be understood.

However, despite the importance of these complex economic assessments, the standard of judicial review in competition cases is nevertheless a critical component in ensuring the proper functioning of the competition law framework. Judicial review allows undertakings to challenge decisions that may adversely affect their business operations and helps maintain a fair and competitive marketplace. The judicial review process in competition cases aims to uphold the principles of legal certainty, effectiveness and proportionality, and a robust system of judicial review is pivotal to safeguard the rights of businesses and consumers while promoting healthy competition.

D. Justifications for a 'Light Judicial Review'

The reasons generally advanced as a justification of limited judicial review in the EU legal order are the prerogatives of the European Commission to shape the Union's competition policy as well as its expertise in complex economic assessments. Inherent in this concept is the notion that the courts cannot replace the Commission decision with their own. However, the courts must be convinced that the conclusions drawn by the Commission are supported by the facts. There is indeed an in-depth review by the courts of the decision challenged, but within the limitations inherent in the system of legality review. Clearly, the administrative discretion is not without its limitations and it is clear that the EU courts review both the law and the facts of a case and have the power to assess evidence, to annul the contested decision and to alter the amount of a fine.

With this competence in mind, the question remains how to align the margin of discretion in complex economic assessments carried out by the administrative authorities with the requirements of Article 6 ECHR as interpreted by the ECtHR for the courts to have 'full jurisdiction'. In *Menarini*, the notion of full jurisdiction was summarised as entailing a review of whether the administrative authority had 'made appropriate use of its powers'.[33]

Against this background, sections IV and V will be devoted to the contribution resulting from the clarifications made by the EFTA Court in its major competition law judgments in *Posten Norge* and *Telenor*.

IV. *POSTEN NORGE*

A. The Facts

In *Posten Norge*, at issue was whether Posten Norge's pricing practices violated competition rules within the EEA. Posten Norge was the designated universal service provider in Norway and was responsible for providing postal services. The case centred on Posten Norge's pricing strategy, particularly the application of bulk discounts to certain customers, which allegedly resulted in unfair and anti-competitive advantages.

ESA found that Posten Norge's pricing practices were anti-competitive and infringed EEA competition rules, and imposed a fine of €12.89 million. Posten Norge, on the other hand, argued that its practices were in line with its obligations as a universal service provider and did not violate competition rules. The EFTA Court, in its judgment, found that Posten Norge's pricing practices did indeed violate Article 54 EEA. It held, inter alia, that the application of bulk discounts to certain customers had the potential to distort competition by hindering other postal operators' entry into the market and impeding fair competition.

[33] *Menarini Diagnostics v Italy* App No 43509/08 (ECtHR, 27 September 2011), paras 63 and 64.

B. Complex Economic Assessments

ESA submitted in the case that its analysis of the competitive situation constituted a complex economic assessment and that, accordingly, the decision must be upheld unless the Court found that it manifestly erred in the appraisal of the applicant's conduct.[34]

In paragraph 86, the Court held:

> The principle of effective judicial protection including the right to a fair trial, which is inter alia enshrined in Article 6 ECHR, is a general principle of EEA law. It may be noted that expression to the principle of effective judicial protection is now also given by Article 47 of the Charter of Fundamental Rights of the European Union.

The case is significant for several reasons, but not least because it clarified some limits as to the margin of discretion for administrative authorities in cases involving fines and underscored the importance in a criminal case of the presumption of innocence.[35]

On the burden of proof, the Court recalled that it is for ESA to demonstrate the existence of the circumstances that constitute an infringement of Article 54 EEA. Thus, ESA must submit precise and consistent evidence in order to establish the existence of the infringement. The question of whether the evidence is capable of substantiating the conclusions drawn from it by ESA must be answered having regard to the presumption of innocence. Moreover, the Court pointed to Article 6(2) ECHR and the principle of the presumption of innocence to underline that the undertaking must be given the benefit of the doubt.

However, the presumption of innocence does not make it necessary for ESA to present such proof in relation to every aspect of the infringement. It suffices if the body of evidence relied on, 'viewed as a whole, and whose various elements are able to reinforce each other, proves the existence of the circumstances that constitute the infringement in question'.[36]

Regarding judicial review, the EFTA Court starts its reasoning with the traditional view from the case law of the EU courts, according to which review of a complex economic assessment made by ESA, in principle, must be 'confined to verifying whether the rules on procedure and on the statement of reasons have been complied with, whether the facts have been accurately stated and whether there has been any manifest error of assessment or misuse of powers'.[37] The Court continues with the statement that an action for annulment is a review of the legality of acts adopted by ESA. Given the obvious limitations of a court, this means that the legal review has neither the object nor the effect of replacing a full investigation of the case carried out in the context of an administrative procedure. Hence, the Court, when conducting its review of a decision from an administrative authority, cannot substitute its own assessment of a complex economic situation for that of the authority. Finally, the Court states that the decision by ESA will not be void simply because the

[34] *Posten Norge* (n 3) para 83.

[35] The presumption of innocence was found to have been violated in a national competition law case in Norway in the alarm market. See Decision of the Norwegian Competition Tribunal in Case No 2021/1051 *Verisure AS*, in particular point 14.3.

[36] *Posten Norge* (n 3) para 94.

[37] ibid para 95.

Court merely disagrees with the weighing of individual factors in a complex assessment of economic evidence.

As outlined above, assessments in a competition law case often rely on vast amounts of data, econometric modelling and economic theory, and these assessments can be highly technical and require specialised knowledge. This often includes the market definition and the market power evaluation, as well as analysing pricing strategies, market shares, barriers to entry and other relevant economic factors to estimate potential anti-competitive effects.

The EFTA Court considers the situation where, although the Court considers ESA's reasoning to be capable of substantiating the conclusions drawn from the economic evidence, the Court itself comes to a different assessment of a complex economic situation. This could be illustrated, inter alia, by different market definitions.[38] Addressing the situation of different assessments and having regard to the procedure of review of legality, the Court holds that it is precluded from annulling the contested decision 'if there can be no legal objection to the assessment of ESA, even if it is not the one which the Court would consider to be preferable'.[39]

Bearing this in mind, the Court in the subsequent four paragraphs makes some clear statements as to the competence of courts and the strengths of judicial review.

First of all, the Court holds that it must not refrain from reviewing ESA's interpretation of information of an economic nature. The Court must establish:

> [W]hether the evidence relied on is factually accurate, reliable and consistent, [and] also whether that evidence contains all the information which must be taken into account in order to assess a complex situation and whether it is capable of substantiating the conclusions drawn from it.[40]

With reference to the obligations imposed by Article 6 ECHR, the Court holds that it must be:

> [A]ble to quash in all respects, on questions of fact and of law, the challenged decision … Therefore, when imposing fines for infringement of the competition rules, ESA cannot be regarded to have any margin of discretion in the assessment of complex economic matters which goes beyond the leeway that necessarily flows from the limitations inherent in the system of legality review.[41]

Finally, the Court outright rejects the submission from ESA that the Court may intervene only if it considers a complex economic assessment by ESA to be manifestly wrong. The EFTA Court holds: 'Accordingly, the submission that the Court may intervene only if it considers a complex economic assessment of ESA to be manifestly wrong must be rejected.'[42] These two last statements clearly show the EFTA Court's general level of proactivity and give an indication of how the Court interprets its duty. The Court demonstrates the intensity of the judicial review carried out.

[38] For example, in the above-mentioned judgment by the Supreme Court of Norway in *Nettbil/Schibsted*, HR-2023-02-16 (n 7), the Supreme Court disagreed with the market definition adopted by the competition authority.

[39] *Posten Norge* (n 3) para 98.

[40] ibid para 99.

[41] ibid para 100.

[42] ibid para 102.

V. *TELENOR*

A. The Facts

The EFTA Court dismissed an application from Telenor by which it sought to challenge a decision of ESA finding that Telenor had infringed Article 54 EEA. The Court upheld ESA's decision, which had found that Telenor abused its dominant position in the wholesale market for access to and handling of data on mobile networks in a margin squeeze case. ESA's decision found three separate infringements related to instances of margin squeezes imposed by Telenor and imposed separate fines for each of these infringements, which in total amounted to €111,951,000.

The Court did not find that ESA erred when defining the relevant downstream market or the retail market for residential stand-alone mobile broadband. The Court agreed that the conduct constituted an abuse and that ESA did not err in fact and in law when calculating the fines. ESA had provided sufficient evidence to substantiate its conclusions. Neither had ESA erred in its finding that Telenor had abused its dominant position by imposing wholesale tariffs that would entail negative margins for an equally efficient competitor. Regarding the fines imposed, the Court found that Telenor was aware of the essential facts that justified the finding of a dominant position in the relevant market, and an abuse of that position. As such, Telenor could not have been unaware of the anti-competitive nature of its conduct. Consequently, the Court dismissed Telenor's application in its entirety.

B. Complex Economic Assessments

As already mentioned, the EFTA Court took as a starting point that the case falls within the criminal sphere for the purposes of effective judicial protection.[43] Following this observation, the Court makes reference to practice of the ECtHR and the notion of effective judicial protection:

> The review of such a decision must be undertaken by a judicial body that has full jurisdiction for the review in order to comply with the guarantees of the principle of effective judicial protection. Such a body must have the jurisdiction to consider all questions of fact and law relevant to the dispute, and have the power to annul the decision in full, on questions of both facts and law.[44]

Subsequently, the EFTA Court clarified the role of the Court, when hearing an application for the annulment of an ESA decision finding the existence of an infringement of competition law, to be 'to assess whether the evidence and other information relied on by ESA in its decision are sufficient to establish the existence of the alleged infringement'.[45]

Similar reservations as expressed in the *Posten Norge* case are set out in paragraphs 80 and 81, where it is stated 'that the Court should [not] be obliged to

[43] *Telenor* (n 1) para 76.
[44] ibid para 78.
[45] ibid para 79.

undertake of its own motion a new and comprehensive investigation of the file. Judicial review must not lead to the Court substituting ESA's assessment with that of its own'.[46] Furthermore, the familiar phrase from the case law of the EU Courts is reiterated with the Court holding that the:

> [R]eview of complex economic appraisals made by ESA is limited to verifying whether the relevant rules on procedure and on the statement of reasons have been complied with, whether the facts have been accurately stated and whether there has been any manifest error of assessment or misuse of powers.[47]

The Court points to ESA's margin of discretion with regard to complex economic assessments, but limits this margin to 'economic matters' and makes it clear that 'this does not entail that the Court must refrain from reviewing ESA's interpretation of information of an economic nature'.[48]

Again, the EFTA Court reiterates that ESA cannot 'be regarded to have any margin of discretion in the assessment of complex economic matters which goes beyond the leeway that necessarily flows from the limitations inherent in the system of legality review'.[49] In the *Telenor* case, the Court emphasises how the Court must review the decision.

Summing up the scope of judicial control and limiting ESA's margin of discretion, the EFTA Court holds that it must move beyond the establishment of the accuracy of the evidence. It 'must also determine whether that evidence contains all the relevant data that must be taken into consideration in appraising a complex situation and whether the evidence is capable of substantiating the conclusions drawn from it'.[50] It must also review economic evidence and the Court rejects ESA's reference to a 'manifest error of assessment' standard. These statements emphasise detailed judicial control and lay the ground for an intense review by the EFTA Court of competition decisions by ESA.

VI. FINAL REMARKS

Through its judgments in the two major competition law cases in the EEA legal order, *Telenor* and *Posten Norge*, the EFTA Court has contributed with important clarifications on the standard of judicial review. Regarding the concept of complex economic assessments, the EFTA Court has introduced some clear limitations as to the operation of the 'manifest error of assessment' rule. In its statements regarding judicial review, the EFTA Court has given substantial weight to the legal guarantees inherent in the fundamental rights protection of Article 6 ECHR in competition law cases and has shown that the Court takes seriously its own findings that fundamental rights protection is part of the general principles of EEA law.

[46] ibid para 80.
[47] ibid para 81.
[48] ibid para 81.
[49] ibid para 82.
[50] ibid.

The Development and Future of European Integration

25

'Everything Must Change So That Everything Can Remain the Same'[*]

The CJEU and the Temporal Dissonance of Europe 'Then' and 'Now'

JHH WEILER AND ANDREAS P MÜLLER

I. PREMISES, HYPOTHESES AND CLAIMS

Our normative point of departure is simple enough and can be stated in four equally simple propositions:

- The process of European integration, which takes its form in the EU, is one of the noblest endeavours in constructing the relationship among individuals with different national identities, in constructing the relationship of individuals and public authorities and in constructing the relationships among states.
- At the heart of this construct is the Union's constitutional order, which is unprecedented in time and unprecedented in space: There has never been anything even remotely similar in the history of international life, and the Union remains unique in the current global situation.
- The principal credit for the construction of the legal order goes to the Court of Justice of the European Union (CJEU) working in tandem with Member State judiciaries.
- The European construct is a precious asset which is worth protecting and preserving.

It is precisely with these normative premises in mind that one can be – indeed, must be – ever vigilant and ever critical.

In discussing the European constitutional order and the challenges it faces, one must be mindful of the fact that constitutionalism is located at the crossroads of

[*] G Tomasi di Lampedusa, *The Leopard* (Milan, Feltrinelli, 1958).

law and politics. Political issues concerning, say, democratic governance and accountability intrinsically embed within them public law issues. Similarly, the interaction of, say, the CJEU and its national counterparts is of immediate, and at times profound, political significance and has very real political and social ramifications.

In the current circumstance of the Union, the list of issues which could be chosen as 'challenges' is quite long. From the endless array of constitutional challenges the Union faces today, we have picked the two which we believe to be the most profound, the most challenging and the most intractable. Neither of these challenges lends itself to an easy solution.

One of our two picks directly concerns the legal order of the Union. The other concerns its political order. And although we will address them as discrete issues, throughout the analysis the interrelationship between them will be much in evidence.

As regards the legal order, there are striking data to indicate some seismic tremors – surely not yet an earthquake – which prudence suggests should not be brushed aside as 'mere tremors'. We refer, as one may imagine, to a stream – surely not a river – of cases where the very foundation of the legal order, the authority of the CJEU as the final arbiter on issues of European (constitutional) law, has been called into question. We no longer have the luxury of dismissing these as aberrations of one or two recalcitrant courts from recalcitrant Member States – the usual whipping boys of Hungary and Poland. Denmark, the Czech Republic, Italy, France, Romania and of course Germany constitute a broader spectrum. But even if one takes the view, as we do, that we are not facing a true earthquake, a veritable 'revolt of the judicial masses',[1] these cases,[2] we will argue, raise issues which need thinking and rethinking, even if a crisis were not looming.

At the political level, the phenomenon – superficially not of a constitutional dimension – which strikes us as most significant is not just the vagaries of public support for the integration project as evidenced in, say, long-term Eurobarometer data.[3] Even more significant is the normalisation and centralisation of Euroscepticism

[1] J Ortega y Gasset, *La rebelión de las masas* (Madrid, Revista de Occidente, 1930); see also DR Phelan, *Revolt or Revolution: The Constitutional Boundaries of the European Community* (Dublin, Round Hall, 1997).

[2] The most prominent is surely the *PSPP* or *Weiss* decision of the German Federal Constitutional Court, BVerfGE 154, 17. The supremacy of Union law and the role of the CJEU as its arbiter have also been defied by other Member State constitutional or supreme courts: Czech Constitutional Court Pl. ÚS 5/12 *Slovak Pensions XVII/Holubec*; Danish Supreme Court Case 15/2014 *Ajos*; Polish Constitutional Court Case K 3/21; and Romanian Constitutional Court Decision 390/2021. However, the courts of further Member States have established the ability to review Union law on the basis of national (constitutional) law: Belgian Constitutional Court Case 62/2016; Hungarian Constitutional Court Case 22/16 (XII.5). The French Conseil d'État refused to make a reference for a preliminary ruling, leading to infringement proceedings (see Case C-416/17 *Commission v France* ECLI:EU:C:2018:81) and, more recently, developed a novel approach to escaping primacy and the reach of the CJEU concerning national security (see CE Ass, 21 April 2021, Req no 393099). The Spanish Constitutional Court implied it was not bound by a previously requested preliminary ruling from the CJEU (STC 26/2014). The Italian *Taricco* saga is a problematic development as well; see generally A Bobić, *The Jurisprudence of Constitutional Conflict in the European Union* (Oxford, Oxford University Press, 2022).

[3] See CE De Vries, *Euroscepticism and the Future of European Integration* (Oxford, Oxford University Press, 2018).

in Member State politics.[4] When we look at the map of electoral politics (the issues which even mainstream politicians and parties raise on the hustings in the hope of garnering votes),[5] we no longer have the comfort of treating Euroscepticism as epiphenomenal – the usual whipping boys, here too, being Hungary and Poland. Think Marine Le Pen in France, Giorgia Meloni in Italy and the rise of the Alternative for Germany (AfD) in Germany, to give but three examples from founding members of the Union.[6] And of more than anecdotal significance, when a mainstream politician such as Michel Barnier, a former Commissioner, finds it expedient in his electoral bid for the French presidency, in the context of the immigration debate, to propose a referendum in France in order, inter alia, 'no longer [to] be subject to judgments of the CJEU', one gets a sense of how far the political barometer has moved.[7]

The tragedy of Brexit is surely, too, part of that matrix. If we burrow below the surface and try to explore possible reasons for this, political *constitutional* issues are an important factor to consider.

There is a single underlying analytical thesis or hypothesis – based on three claims – which we employ in explaining the emergence of these two challenges:

- Our first claim in setting out this analytical hypothesis is that both the political and legal architectures of the Union were set in the formative years of the Community/Union in the 1950s, 1960s and 1970s. For the sake of convenience, we can refer to this period as the Foundational Era. This historical context causally explains the principal features of those architectures and may also give them a normative justification.

[4] For an early overview, see P Taggart and A Szczerbiak (eds), *Opposing Europe? The Comparative Party Politics of Euroscepticism*, vol 1 (Oxford, Oxford University Press, 2008); M Rooduijn and S van Kessel, 'Populism and Euroskepticism in the European Union' in WR Thompson et al (eds), *Oxford Research Encyclopedia of Politics* (Oxford, Oxford University Press, 2019). A broad perspective may be found in M Kaeding, J Pollak and P Schmidt (eds), *Euroscepticism and the Future of Europe: Views from the Capitals* (London, Palgrave Macmillan, 2021). How realistic an outlook is provided by the Eurobarometer is disputed; see M Höpner and B Jurczyk, 'How the Eurobarometer Blurs the Line between Research and Propaganda', MPIfG Discussion Paper 15/6.

[5] N Brack and N Startin, 'Introduction: Euroscepticism, from the Margins to the Mainstream' (2015) 36 *International Political Science Review* 239; T Persson, C Karlsson and M Mårtensson, 'The Influence of Eurosceptic Challenger Parties on Mainstream Party Behaviour: Is Oppositional Behaviour Contagious?' (2023) 29 *Party Politics* 100. The development of Eurosceptic attitudes is decidedly not a phenomenon found exclusively in right-wing parties; see S Wagner, 'Euroscepticism as a Radical Left Party Strategy for Success' (2022) 28 *Party Politics* 1069.

[6] For France, see D Stockemer, *The Front National in France. Continuity and Change under Jean-Marie Le Pen and Marine Le Pen* (Dordrecht, Springer, 2017); and G Ivaldi, 'Contesting the EU in Times of Crisis: The Front National and Politics of Euroscepticism in France' (2018) 38 *Politics* 278. Regarding Italy, see A Donà, 'The Rise of the Radical Right in Italy: The Case of Fratelli d'Italia' (2022) 27 *Journal of Modern Italian Studies* 775. Concerning Germany, see C Lees, 'The "Alternative for Germany": The Rise of Right-Wing Populism at the Heart of Europe' (2018) 38 *Politics* 295; and Martin Baloge, 'From Brexit to Dexit? Alternative für Deutschland's Euroscepticism on European Debates in the Bundestag' (2021) 29 *Journal of Contemporary European Studies* 552. More generally, see J Sondel-Cedarmas and F Berti (eds), *The Right-Wing Critique of Europe: Nationalist, Sovereignist and Right-Wing Populist Attitudes to the EU* (Abingdon, Routledge, 2022).

[7] P Dallison and E Braun, 'Barnier the Brexiteer? French Candidate Gets Tough with EU on Campaign Trail' *Politico*, 9 September 2021.

In the case of the *legal structure*, we suggest that the key parameter is not just the content of the well-known and endlessly discussed cluster of specific 'heroic' decisions handed down by the Court in that period from *Van Gend & Loos* to *ERTA* and associated jurisprudence.[8] Instead, it is the underlying hermeneutic sensibility of the Court which was formed through, and in turn informed, such decisions. For want of a better term, we would call these the 'Pescatorian hermeneutics'.[9] We will elaborate its lineaments below, but already here, this very nomenclature is sufficiently indicative. And to avoid any misunderstandings, we believe that this hermeneutic sensibility served the Community/Union of those years very well; indeed, it would be a very different – and diminished – Union had the Court adopted a different hermeneutic.[10]

In the case of the *political process*, from the very early days of the Coal and Steel Community, but even more so with the advent of the EEC in that same period of the 1960s and 1970s, we would argue that the fundamental ethos towards governance was functionality, power and legitimation through results.[11] 'Bread and circuses' (*panem et circenses*) is a somewhat less flattering way to describe this approach. Strikingly, the concept of democracy is not even mentioned in the Schuman Declaration, and the nascent Communities operated for decades with little more than symbolic powers vested in the European Parliament.[12] The key debates and contestations then (and to

[8] Case 8/55 *FÉDÉCHAR* ECLI:EU:C:1956:11; Case 26/62 *Van Gend & Loos* ECLI:EU:C:1963:1; Case 6/64 *Costa v ENEL* ECLI:EU:C:1964:66; Case 11/70 *Internationale Handelsgesellschaft* ECLI:EU:C:1970:114; Case 22/70 *Commission v Council (ERTA)* ECLI:EU:C:1971:32. See the essential work of E Stein, 'Lawyers, Judges, and the Making of a Transnational Constitution' (1981) 75 *American Journal of International Law* 1; A-M Burley and W Mattli, 'Europe before the Court: A Political Theory of Legal Integration' (1993) 47 *International Organization* 41; A Stone Sweet and TL Brunell, 'Constructing a Supra-national Constitution: Dispute Resolution and Governance in the European Community' (1998) 92 *American Political Science Review* 63. An overview can be found in T Christiansen and C Reh, *Constitutionalizing the European Union* (London, Bloomsbury, 2009); and A Peters, *Elemente einer Theorie der Verfassung Europas* (Berlin, Duncker & Humblot, 2001).

[9] P Pescatore, *Le droit de l'intégration. Emergence d'un phénomène nouveau dans les relations Internationales selon l'expérience des Communautés Européennes* (Leiden, AW Sijthoff, 1972). On the impact of judges on the development of CJEU hermeneutics, *cf* A Vauchez, *Brokering Europe : Euro-Lawyers and the Making of a Transnational Polity* (Cambridge, Cambridge University Press, 2015).

[10] *cf* A Grimmel, 'Politics in Robes? The European Court of Justice and the Myth of "Judicial Activism"', Europa-Kolleg Hamburg Discussion Paper 2/11 (2011) 7: 'Although the legal decisions can be unhesitatingly characterized as a "quiet revolution" … spearheaded by the ECJ, they have not only been quite consequent and well-founded, but also necessary in light of the historical, local, and functional circumstances.'.

[11] K Featherstone, 'Jean Monnet and the "Democratic Deficit" in the European Union' (1994) 32 *Journal of Common Market Studies* 149, 155; A Moravcsik, 'In Defence of the "Democratic Deficit": Reassessing Legitimacy in the European Union' (2002) 40 *Journal of Common Market Studies* 603. For the term, see D Marquand, *Parliament for Europe* (London, Jonathan Cape, 1979).

[12] Essentially, the Parliament was only able to cast a vote of no confidence concerning the High Authority pursuant to Art 24 of the European Coal and Steel Community (ECSC) Treaty; elections for Members of the European Parlioament (MEPs) were first held in 1979, despite the possibility of direct elections existing since the conclusion of the EEC Treaty in 1957. Faux democratisation in the form of mandatory, but ultimately meaningless, parliamentary consultation was established in Case 138/79 *Roquette Frères v Council (Isoglucose)* ECLI:EU:C:1980:249. Active legitimation for the EP before the CJEU, ie, the capacity to bring an action as an applicant, was only established in Case C-70/88 *Parliament v Council* ECLI:EU:C:1990:217; *cf* M Roos, 'Die informelle Entwicklung einer supranationalen Co-Legislative: Das Europäische Parlament, 1952–1979' in C Henrich-Franke et al (eds), *Grenzüberschreitende institutionalisierte Zusammenarbeit von der Antike bis zur Gegenwart* (Baden-Baden, Nomos, 2019) 411, 422 et seq. For a more positive account, see B Rittberger, 'The Creation and Empowerment of the European Parliament' (2003) 41 *Journal of Common Market Studies* 203; see also A Schäfer, 'Die demokratische Grenze output-orientierter Legitimation' (2006) 29 *Integration* 187.

some extent now) were between intergovernmentalists and Communitarianists, but the flashpoints then (and now) were typically functionalist: what should be done and who should do it?

Pescatorian hermeneutics and governance functionalism are, in this reading, the legal and political double helix of the European constitutional DNA.

- Our second claim, which is perhaps more controversial and certainly contestable,[13] is that despite huge changes in the very ontology of Europe – the Union of today compared to the Community of the Foundational Era is like comparing a 70-year-old person to a 10-year-old child – that original DNA continues to flow in the legal and political bloodstream of the European body politic.
- Our third and final claim is that a legal and political ethos and telos – that original double helix – which developed more than half a century ago and served well then is ill-suited to dealing with the current very different circumstance of the Union and in some respects might even contribute to some of maladies of the body politic. This is what we mean by temporal dissonance. This claim is not merely instrumental – ie, what would functionally be a more efficient political and legal constitutional architecture? It is also normative: what is a more appropriate and, from a value perspective, a more legitimate, way of constructing the constitutional architecture of the Union of the next generation?

On this reading, the principal constitutional challenge facing the Union is, first, to acknowledge this temporal dissonance and, second, in ways which we will outline, to adopt a different ethos and telos. In advancing this hypothesis, we will be, in the eyes of many, clearly laying our heads on the chopping block. There will be no shortage of executioners.

II. THE EUROPEAN CONSTITUTIONAL DNA: THE POLITICAL/LEGAL DOUBLE HELIX

We would like now to flesh out the lineaments of the legal and political double helix.

What is meant by Pescatorian hermeneutics? This is hardly terra incognita and is a field that has been well explored.[14] We content ourselves with a brief and hopefully not overly controversial synopsis.

- In many instances, the Court was (and is) faced, within the zone of legitimate judicial discretion, with an outcome which would either enhance the integration of the Union substantively or make the functioning of the Union more effective.[15]

[13] See in particular as regards the role of the CJEU eg, R Streinz, 'Die Rolle des EuGH im Prozess der Europäischen Integration: Anmerkungen zu gegenläufigen Tendenzen in der neueren Rechtsprechung' (2010) 135 *Archiv des öffentlichen Rechts* 1; J Ziglinski, *Der 'Motor der Integration' schaltet einen Gang runter: Die neue Zurückhaltung des Gerichtshofes der Europäischen Union* (Europe Direct, 2017). An account of a more context-sensitive CJEU is given in C Moser and B Rittberger, 'The CJEU and EU (De-)Constitutionalization: Unpacking Jurisprudential Responses' (2022) 20 *International Journal of Constitutional Law* 1038, 1069–70.

[14] See also R Lecourt, *L'Europe des juges*, 3rd edn (Brussels, Bruylant, 2008).

[15] *cf* Pescatore (n 9) passim.

Dassonville (moving from a discrimination approach to an obstacle approach)[16] is a famous example of the former and *Van Gend & Loos* itself a remarkable example of the latter. Interpretative principles such as effet utile and associate concepts are the doctrinal expression of these decisive impulses.[17]

- As a reflection of this approach, in balancing the classic triumvirate of interpretation – lexical, systematic and teleological – the Court has displayed a marked inclination towards the latter,[18] at times at the expense of the former.[19] *Les Verts*[20] regarding the right/duty of Parliament vis-a-vis third parties is a classic example of this, as is the doctrine of direct effect of directives.[21] To avoid misunderstanding: this, we insist again, is not to say that these decisions were either legally wrong or unwise. They were certainly not 'wrong' and they were wise, but they are a manifestation of a particular hermeneutic sensibility.
- Embedded in *Van Gend & Loos* is an approach which most decidedly places the individual at the centre. This is common and we take it for granted today. However, at the time, it was revolutionary. The norm, then and now – as is still the case today in, say, the World Trade Organization (WTO) – is that individuals were mere objects of such laws. It has been pointed out that instances of this may be found in other international legal regimes,[22] but never on the scale developed by the CJEU, this being an instance where a difference in degree becomes a difference in kind. Opting for a decentralised system of judicial review was important not only conceptually, bringing the Union much closer to being a constitutional state rather than an international (intergovernmental) polity, but it also had major practical consequence consistent with the hermeneutics of effectiveness, in rendering each and every individual affected by Union law a 'private attorney general'[23] and, together with national courts, the principal agents for the enforcement of Union law. As has been argued elsewhere, they could have reached this result by classical

[16] Case 8/74 *Procureur du Roi v Benoît and Gustave Dassonville* ECLI:EU:C:1974:82; see also MP Maduro, 'Der Kontrapunkt im Dienste eines europäischen Verfassungspluralismus' (2007) 42 *Europarecht* 3. Historical context is provided by J Muller, '*Procureur du Roi v Dassonville*: The Judicial Dossier behind the Measure Equivalent to Trade Restriction Formula' (2021) 6 *European Papers* 579.

[17] S Seyr, *Der effet utile in der Rechtsprechung des Europäischen Gerichtshofs* (Berlin, Duncker & Humblot, 2008) 358 et seq; see generally R Streinz, 'Die Auslegung des Gemeinschaftsrechts bzw Unionsrechts durch den EuGH' in S Griller and HP Rill (eds), *Rechtstheorie: Rechtsbegriff – Dynamik – Auslegung* (Vienna, Springer, 2011) 223; and L Tichý, M Potacs and T Dumbrovský, *Effet Utile* (Prague, Charles University, 2014).

[18] An overview and further references can be found in K Lenaerts and JA Gutiérrez-Fons, 'To Say What the Law of the EU is: Methods of Interpretation and the European Court of Justice' EUI Working Paper AEL 2013/9; see also S Brittain, 'Justifying the Teleological Methodology of the European Court of Justice: A Rebuttal' (2016) 55 *Irish Jurist* 134.

[19] For the constitutionalising impact of different methods of interpretation in CJEU jurisprudence, see Moser and Rittberger (n 13).

[20] Case 294/83 *Parti écologiste 'Les Verts' v European Parliament* ECLI:EU:C:1986:166.

[21] Explicitly established in Case 41/74 *Van Duyn v Home Office* ECLI:EU:C:1974:133 and further developed in Case 148/78 *Ratti* ECLI:EU:C:1979:110; see also S Prechal, *Directives in EC Law*, 2nd edn (Oxford, Oxford University Press, 2005) 216 et seq; and M Rasmussen, 'How to Enforce European Law? A New History of the Battle over the Direct Effect of Directives, 1958–1987' (2017) 23 *European Law Journal* 290.

[22] *cf* D Wyatt, 'New Legal Order, or Old?' (1982) 7 *European Law Review* 147.

[23] M Cappelletti, 'Vindicating the Public Interest through the Courts: A Comparativist's Contribution' (1976) 25 *Buffalo Law Review* 643, 661 et seq.

hermeneutic tools of public international law.[24] It is the very fact that the Court used the 'new legal order' vocabulary with the attendant hermeneutic which is so significant.

- As part of this sensibility, it could be argued that cases such as *Bresciani*,[25] where a Member State may not impose a charge for the cost of a justified national health measure whereas the Union may mandate such a charge, shows a greater leniency towards the Union compared to Member States. However, this interpretation is contested.[26]
- A particularly sensitive aspect of this sensibility concerns the limits to the competences and jurisdiction of the Union. It should not surprise us that, as a reflection of the pro-Europa approach, it has been argued, with some cogency here too, that the Court has very rarely[27] struck down a Union measure as ultra vires, and has not developed a robust doctrine of delegated powers and jurisdictional limits.
- The Court has also been extremely 'jealous' in preserving its own prerogatives as the ultimate arbiter of all aspects of Union law, both vis-a-vis national stakeholders (executive, legislative and judicial) and international organisations and other international legal regimes.[28] One may attribute this to 'judicial arrogance', but it derives here too from this double concern with the effective and uniform application of Union law as well as the principle of equality before the law. The two are inextricably linked in this rationale.
- Overall, this may be called legal and logical incrementalism, also characterised as Pescatorian hermeneutics. By this we mean the following: the Court lays down a foundational doctrine, typically informed by the aforementioned features of its hermeneutic sensibility. Once this is in place, as a matter of positivist reasoning, the jurisprudence develops, step by step with, at this point, a compelling doctrinal rationale (since we held A in case X, result B is mandated in case Y). Going back to the Foundational Era, *Van Gend & Loos* and *Costa v ENEL* offer

[24] JHH Weiler, '*Van Gend en Loos*: The Individual as Subject and Object and the Dilemma of European Legitimacy' Jean Monnet Working Paper 10/14 (2014) 3 et seq.

[25] Case 87/75 *Bresciani* ECLI:EU:C:1976:18.

[26] Of particular importance to this contestation is the potential cost of Member States disobeying or overriding judgments, which may influence CJEU decision making; see G Garrett, RD Kelemen and H Schulz, 'The European Court of Justice, National Governments, and Legal Integration in the European Union' (1998) 52 *International Organization* 149; CJ Carruba, M Gabel and C Hankla, 'Judicial Behavior under Political Constraints: Evidence from the European Court of Justice' (2008) 102 *American Political Science Review* 435; and O Larsson and D Naurin, 'Judicial Independence and Political Uncertainty: How the Risk of Override Affects the Court of Justice of the EU' (2016) 70 *International Organization* 377.

[27] Case C-376/98 *Germany v Parliament and Council (Tobacco Advertising I)* ECLI:EU:C:2000:544, in which a strict standard was applied; however, see Case C-380/03 *Germany v Parliament and Council (Tobacco Advertising II)* ECLI:EU:C:2006:772 for a return to a more lax standard; P Craig, 'The ECJ and Ultra Vires Action: A Conceptual Analysis' (2011) 48 *Common Market Law Review* 395; and W Obwexer, 'Kontrolle und Interpretation der Kompetenzverteilung in der EU' in A Gamper et al (eds), *Föderale Kompetenzverteilung in Europa* (Baden-Baden, Nomos, 2016) 693, 733 et seq.

[28] Opinion 1/91 *EEA* ECLI:EU:C:1991:490; Opinion 2/94 *Accession to the ECHR* ECLI:EU:C:1996:140; see also more recently Joined Cases C-402/05 P and C-415/05 P *Kadi and Al Barakaat International Foundation v Commission and Council* ECLI:EU:C:2008:461; and Case C-284/16 *Achmea* ECLI:EU:C:2018:158. See n 2 above regarding the contestation of the CJEU's position in the national dimension.

> the paradigmatic example of this. In *Van Gend & Loos* the Advocate General's Opinion comes down against direct effect.[29] His most cogent argument was simple enough. Since the legal order of the Community (now Union) does not include the supremacy of Community law, to give direct effect would compromise the principle of uniform application and equal protection of Community law. Imagine a situation concerning two national laws enacted after the entry into force of the Treaties. Giving direct effect to a Treaty provision in, say, a case coming from the Netherlands, the Constitution of which does give priority to international law, would not have the same effect in, say, Italy, where the principle of *lex posteriori derogat lex anteriori* would apply in such a situation. Interestingly, in the reasoning of the Court, there is no reference to, or refutation of, this argument by Advocate General Roemer.[30] When, a year later, the Court had to decide the issue of supremacy, it is, naturally enough, an easy doctrinal move to take that very same rationale of Advocate General Roemer and turn it on its head. Since we have direct effect, in the interests of the uniform application of the law and equality of individuals before the law, supremacy becomes logically and legally imperative (and less controversial).

Finally, and bringing together all these features of Pescatorian hermeneutics was *une certaine idée de l'Europe*[31] which it was the role of the Court to preserve and enhance.

We want to conclude this section with three general observations. First, the reader may have noticed that we have avoided the use of the term 'judicial activism'. We belong to that school which finds the term politically useful and legally meaningless.[32] Sometimes the sense which one tries to capture with the term 'activism' is the result of the Court refusing to 'act', as in the case of limiting the jurisdictional reach and scope of Union competences. Our approach, following Barak,[33] is that the zone of legitimate discretion is much wider than positivists (or textualists) imagine. In exercising their discretion, courts must of course act rationally, consistently and in a principled manner. Both in terms of reasoning and of results, we have no criticism of the jurisprudence of the Court in its foundational decisions. We simply point out that its decisions are informed by what we call a specific hermeneutic sensibility which was entirely appropriate at the time. As already explained, we will be arguing that this sensibility, protests of members of the Court notwithstanding, persists and is, arguably, inappropriate in the current circumstance of the Union.

Second, we think the term pro-Europa needs unpacking – there can, after all, be more than one conception of what is 'best' for European integration. We think the

[29] Case 26/62 *Van Gend & Loos* ECLI:EU:C:1962:42, Opinion of AG Roemer; for a historical view, see Morten Rasmussen, 'Revolutionizing European Law: A History of the *Van Gend en Loos* Judgment' (2014) 12 *International Journal of Constitutional Law* 136, 153.

[30] However, the Commission did address the issue of legal certainty directly, which makes the silence of the Court appear even more loud; *cf Van Gend & Loos* (n 29) Opinion of AG Roemer.

[31] P Pescatore, 'The Doctrine of "Direct Effect": An Infant Disease of Community Law' (1983) 8 *European Law Review* 155, 157.

[32] *cf* KD Kmiec, 'The Origin and Current Meanings of "Judicial Activism"' (2004) 92 *California Law Review* 1441, 1476–77; K Roosevelt, *The Myth of Judicial Activism. Making Sense of Supreme Court Decisions* (New Haven, Yale University Press, 2008); see also T Roux, 'Judicial Activism' in JM Smits et al (eds), *Elgar Encyclopedia of Comparative Law* (Cheltenham, Edward Elgar, 2023).

[33] A Barak, *Judicial Discretion* (New Haven, Yale University Press, 1989).

concept underlying the Court's hermeneutic was, to put it crudely, 'more integration' is always better for the overarching project of European integration. An ever-closer union, after all, meant just that – ever closer. In addition, it should also be remembered that precisely in those decisive decades there was no small measure of political stasis. The clearest manifestation of this was the refusal of the Member States to follow the Treaty schedule for the introduction of majority voting as evident by the 'empty chair' crisis and the subsequent 'gentlemen's agreement' consecrated in the Luxembourg Compromise.[34] One can readily see how the Court could have adopted an ethos of 'it needs to be done, and if "they" (the Member States' governments) will not do it, it is our task, as guardians of the Treaties, to fill in the gap'.

Finally, although trite, one cannot emphasise this enough. The entire legal construct, the new legal order, would depend for its success on a relationship of trust (an 'obedience') from national courts, not least the apex courts in the Member States. This is so because when all is said and done, even today, the compliance pull of national courts over the legislative and executive branches of their Member States is far superior to that of international courts and tribunals, including the CJEU. Lose that trust and the whole edifice is endangered both in practical terms and also as a matter of public ethos. The CJEU can climb to the top of the Mount and sermonise about, say, supremacy from here on in. If it does not find willing partners in the national judiciaries, this will be no more than 'a voice crying in the wilderness'.[35] The greatest achievement of the CJEU in its foundational period was its ability, step by step,[36] to gain the confidence and trust of its national counterparts. This is an asset that cannot be squandered.

As regards the political, already mentioned is the functionalist approach to the decision-making process. Attention to process was primarily focused on the relationship between the Commission and the Council, the Union and its Member States, Communitarianism and intergovernmentalism. In contrast to the Court, the political process decidedly did not put the individual at the centre. Regardless of the vicissitudes of the Council and the Commission and Communitarianism and intergovernmentalism, the position of the individual was a black hole. Of course, it is not a totally specious argument to have thought or to have argued that the protection of the individual and, more generally, democratic legitimacy could be achieved or

[34] On this issue, see NP Ludlow, 'Challenging French Leadership in Europe: Germany, Italy, the Netherlands and the Outbreak of the Empty Chair Crisis of 1965–1966' (1999) 8 *Contemporary European History* 231; J-M Palayret, H Wallace and P Winand (eds), *Visions, Votes and Vetoes: The Empty Chair Crisis and the Luxembourg Compromise Forty Years on* (Brussels, Peter Lang, 2006); and Editorial, 'Not Dead Yet: Revisiting the "Luxembourg Veto" and its Foundations' (2017) 13 *European Constitutional Law Review* 1.

[35] Isaiah 40:3 (New International Version, Biblica, 2011).

[36] It would be hard to expect the apex courts of the Member States to accept the supremacy of Union secondary law (eg, *Costa v ENEL*) if this was not accompanied by a jurisprudence which promised review by the CJEU of the compliance of such secondary law with human rights norms such as in Case 29/69 *Stauder* ECLI:EU:C:1969:57; Case 4/73 *Nold* ECLI:EU:C:1974:51; and Case 44/79 *Hauer* ECLI:EU:C:1979:290. See JHH Weiler, 'Eurocracy and Distrust: Some Questions Concerning the Role of the European Court of Justice in the Protection of Fundamental Human Rights within the Legal Order of the European Communities' (1986) 61 *Washington Law Review* 1103; and, more generally, KJ Alter, 'Explaining National Court Acceptance of European Court Jurisprudence: A Critical Evaluation of Theories of Legal Integration' in A-M Slaughter, A Stone Sweet and JHH Weiler (eds), *The European Courts and National Courts* (Oxford, Hart Publishing, 1998) 225.

maintained indirectly through the agency of their governments within the European decision-making process.[37] But this argument, whatever merits it may have, cannot obscure the fact that the emerging legal and political architectures disempowered national parliaments and empowered the executive branch – both ministers and civil servants at the national level. It is, we think, also fair to say that the Commission in that period was more interested in strengthening and consolidating its own power (vis-a-vis, say, the Council) and did not pay particular attention to its own democratic accountability and that of the Community/Union as a whole. We will stick our necks out even further and claim that both governments of the Member States and the Commission shared an unstated, and perhaps even an unnoticed, similar approach to legitimacy: if we do 'the right thing' for our citizens, that is what counts – bread and circuses par excellence. It is hard otherwise to explain the tortuous, multi-decade process of empowerment of the European Parliament. And here an even bolder claim: once attention was given to the so-called democratic deficit of the Union,[38] the notion set in, which all institutional stakeholders shared, that once the European Parliament was empowered, this would close the deficit. The European Parliament was significantly empowered over the decades, but as we will argue below, the democratic deficit remains no less acute today than it was in this foundational period.

III. THE EUROPE OF 'THEN': SOME PUZZLES

Let us take *Van Gend & Loos* as the cornerstone of the entire constitutional structure. Doctrine apart,[39] there is a point which has received somewhat less attention in the literature and yet is central to our argument. Three Member States[40] and Advocate General Roemer himself[41] argued against giving direct effect to the then Article 12[42] of the Treaty. This raises two interesting issues. First, suspend your disbelief and imagine that the Court had followed its Advocate General and the three Member States. Yes, we would be living, most likely, in a very different and impoverished Union compared to the one we have. But we do not believe that at the time there would have been howls

[37] A Moravcsik, 'In Defence of the "Democratic Deficit": Reassessing Legitimacy in the European Union' (2002) 40 *Journal of Common Market Studies* 603, 611 et seq.

[38] An overview can be found in A Follesdal and S Hix, 'Why There is a Democratic Deficit in the EU: A Response to Majone and Moravcsik' (2006) 44 *Journal of Common Market Studies* 533, 534–37.

[39] D Wyatt, 'New Legal Order, or Old?' (1982) 7 *European Law Review* 147; B de Witte, 'Retour à Costa: La primauté du droit communautaire à la lumière du droit international' EUI Working Paper 49 (1983); see also D Edwards, 'Judicial Activism: Myth or Reality? *Van Gend en Loos, Costa v ENEL* and the *Van Duyn* Family Revisited' in AIL Campbell and M Voyatzi (eds), *Legal Reasoning and Judicial Interpretation of European Law: Essays in the Honour of Lord Mackenzie-Stuart* (Trenton, 1996) 29, 36 et seq; and A Cohen, 'Constitutionalism without Constitution: Transnational Elites between Political Mobilization and Legal Expertise in the Making of a Constitution for Europe (1940s–1960s)' (2007) 32 *Law & Social Inquiry* 109, 126–28. A different perspective can be found in Rasmussen (n 29).

[40] The governments of the Netherlands, Belgium and Germany submitted statements to this effect: *cf* Case 26/62 *van Gend & Loos* (n 29) Opinion of AG Roemer; see also European Parliamentary Research Service, '60 Years of *Van Gend & Loos*: Direct Effect of EU Law and a "New Legal Order"' European Parliament Briefing (PE 739.326, 2023).

[41] Note that the Court did not address at all the main argument of AG Roemer.

[42] Article 12 of the EEC Treaty contained a prohibition regarding the introduction of new customs duties and equivalent measures between the Member States. Its successor is the current Art 30 TFEU.

of horror protesting an erroneous and legally aberrational decision; at best, there would have sounded howls of sorrow. In other words, it is meaningless in relation to these cases to talk here about a *legally* 'right' or 'wrong' decision. Both outcomes would be fairly and squarely within the area which Aharon Barak has defined as the zone of legitimate judicial discretion.[43] But this is as clear an illustration as any of what we claimed above was the formation of the CJEU's hermeneutic sensibility which informs the jurisprudence of the Court. These decisions both constituted and subsequently reflected this particular hermeneutic. In deciding these cases the way it did, the Court was not only constituting the legal order of the Community/Union but was also constituting its hermeneutic as the judicial branch of the Community/Union thus constituted. We owe a lot to that sensibility.

No less interesting is the question as to what explains not the decision itself, but its pacific reception by the legal and political orders of the Community of 'then'. After all, we have incidents in the long legal history of the Union when governments of the Member States, even in an earlier period of Community life, did not hide their dissatisfaction with a decision and even took action to 'correct' the Court.[44] If we take the cluster of 'heroic decisions' given in a matter of a decade or so,[45] they were accepted by most, if not all, principal stakeholders, notably national parliaments, national governments and, critically, national judiciaries.[46] The legal constitutional architecture put in place was revolutionary. And yet it was a 'quiet revolution'.[47] How can such pacific acceptance be explained? How can we explain, politically speaking, the 'quiet' in quiet revolution?

A similar question can be asked as regards the political axis of European constitutionalism. Why was the democratic deficit of the Community of the 1950s, 1960s and even 1970s received or tolerated with relative equanimity, both by *la classe politique* and the European populations at large?

Here comes one of the principal artefacts in our overall thesis: the very factors which explain (and justify) the pacific acceptance of the quiet revolution in the

[43] Barak (n 33) 217.

[44] A prominent example can be found in the so-called Barber Protocol adopted in response to Case C-262/88 *Barber* ECLI:EU:C:1990:209. The EU's Common Foreign and Security Policy is a much-discussed area in this context as well; see generally A Arnull, 'Me and My Shadow: The European Court of Justice and the Disintegration of European Union Law' (2007) 31 *Fordham International Law Journal* 1174, 1185 et seq; and SK Schmidt, *The European Court of Justice and the Policy Process: The Shadow of Case Law* (Oxford, Oxford University Press, 2018) 40 et seq, in particular in connection with the requirements of an override in the Europe of 'now'.

[45] There is still debate as to whether the apex courts fully accepted the absolute supremacy of Union law over their constitutional provisions as demanded by the CJEU. But de facto, as a matter of 'constitutional tolerance' (see JHH Weiler, 'Federalism without Constitutionalism: Europe's Sonderweg' in K Nicolaidis and R Howse (eds), *The Federal Vision: Legitimacy and Levels of Governance in the United States and the European Union* (Oxford, Oxford University Press, 2001) 54), the doctrine was not seriously contested until the recent spate of judicial rebellions – see n 2 above.

[46] KJ Alter, *Establishing the Supremacy of European Law: The Making of an International Rule of Law in Europe* (Oxford, Oxford University Press, 2003) in particular ch 5 'Winning Political Support: Why Did National Governments Accept a Judicial Revolution That Transferred Away National Sovereignty?'; and G Barrett, '"Don't You Know They're Talkin' 'Bout a Revolution? (It Sounds Like a Whisper)": The *Bundesverfassungsgericht* Ruling in *Weiss*' in M Belov (ed), *Peace, Discontent and Constitutional Law. Challenges to Constitutional Order and Democracy* (Abingdon, Routledge, 2021) 76 et seq.

[47] JHH Weiler, 'A Quiet Revolution: The European Court of Justice and its Interlocutors' (1994) 26 *Comparative Political Studies* 510.

Foundational Era have largely changed. And the continuing employment of the foundational hermeneutic in a much changed post-foundational EU explains the emergence of the temporal dissonance. If we are concerned with preserving the underlying solidity of the constitutional foundations of the Union, the Court has, more or less radically, to change its underlying hermeneutic sensibility: everything must change so that everything can remain the same.[48] We will suggest in the conclusion to this chapter what this change might consist of.

IV. COMPARING THE 'THEN' AND 'NOW'

We will now set out the 'then' and 'now', which at one and the same time is meant to offer a possible explanation why the foundational hermeneutic was the right hermeneutic for the 'then' period, and perceived as such by the principal political and social stakeholders, and why for the Union of 'now' it is normatively inappropriate and potentially damaging.

A. Size

Size per se is not a trivial parameter. In any process of a 'constitutional settlement', broad consensus is a key requirement for establishing constitutional stability. Just as a matter of numbers, seeking consensus on the 'big issues' is easier with six partners compared to 27 partners.[49] What in our view is critical is that, though lack of consensus has been part of the Community/Union decisional process forever, what is different is that disagreements in the past could largely be attributed to inevitably different assessments by Member States of their respective national interests on discrete issues of policy. In a process that began slowly after enlargement and has increasingly picked up steam, disagreements today do not relate simply to a discrete policy issue, but increasingly to the underlying telos and ethos of the EU. But it is not size alone. There was a much greater homogeneity in the underlying political culture, not least as a result of the historical context which will be explained below, among the original six Member States than there is, necessarily, among the current 27. This is both part of the explanation of the relative pacific acceptance of the quiet revolution as it is a signal that one cannot assume the same kind of public consensus even as regards foundational issues.

B. Historical Context

In the 'old' Europe of 'now', one often witnesses incomprehension and frustration at the failure of 'new' Member States to buy into the supranational ethos of the

[48] Paraphrasing G Tomasi di Lampedusa, *Il Gattopardo* (Feltrinelli, 1958).

[49] This is not a new finding; *cf* J-L Dehaene, D Simon and R von Weizsäcker, *The Institutional Implications of Enlargement: Report to the European Commission* (Brussels, European Commission, 1999).

Foundational Era. It is no longer a national interest which is the spanner in the works, but a nationalist interest – a very different kettle of fish. And here one must recall that it is not only (or even principally) an issue with some of the new Member States, but that this nationalist ethos also informs the new ideological Euroscepticism in both new and old. 'What, they don't remember the awful price that nationalism wreaked on Europe in the cataclysmic Second World War on the ashes of which the European construct was founded?' Historical context can explain a lot. Take as merely one example Poland.[50] It is not as if Poland was spared the ravages of the Second World War. Three million Christian Poles and three million Jewish Poles were slaughtered in that conflagration.[51] But the more immediate historical memory is the subsequent oppression under the communist boot. Part of that oppression was a systematic repression of national identity, one critical manifestation of which, just by way of an example, was the anti-Catholic bias of the Soviet-imposed regime. One hugely powerful sentiment following liberation from communist oppression was the ability to celebrate, to breathe and to realise to the full Polish identity. It is an understandable and, within limits, a legitimate sentiment.[52] And given the West/East cleavage as regards recent historical memory, insisting on the underlying ethos of the 'old' Europe can easily be perceived as a form of intra-European cultural colonial imperialism.

Historical context can also explain (though not justify) the fuel of contemporary nationalist Euroscepticism. It is the simple biological fact that the generation of those, including in the 'old' Europe, both leaders and common citizens, who personally experienced the Second World War is passing away. And here the EU – the winner of the Nobel Prize for Peace – is a victim of its own success. In the heyday of the big debates around the Maastricht Treaty (itself a distant memory), when Kohl and Mitterrand spoke about the need to consolidate the historic elimination of Franco-German enmity, a whole generation of 50 and under might have thought that they were referring to the football World Cup or the Euro competitions.

This *certaine idée de l'Europe*, which downplays national identity and which animated the generation of the Foundational Era, can also be experienced as objectionable and perhaps even inimical by a generation to which the word 'patriotism' and the celebration of a unique and special national identity are no longer anathema – both East and West.

C. Sphere of Competences: A Union Legislative and Administrative Reach

Here is one of the most explosive differences between the Union of 'then' and 'now'. One can start with a simple and uncontroversial legal/political fact. In the 'heroic' era when the Court laid the foundations for the new legal order and developed its foundational hermeneutics, the sphere of Community competences and activities

[50] *cf* O Schmidtke, 'Competing Historical Narratives: Memory Politics, Identity, and Democracy in Germany and Poland' (2023) 12 *Social Sciences* 391.

[51] For this figure and more comprehensive statistics see U.S. Dept. of State, JUST Act Report, 2020, p. 137 et seq.

[52] This is not to say that Poles among themselves do not have fierce debates as to the content and manifestations of Polish identity.

was not only vastly more limited, but also concerned areas which were socially, politically, and culturally far less sensitive. *Van Gend & Loos* and *Costa* may have been constitutionally revolutionary, but one concerned a dispute between the shipping company Van Gend & Loos and the Dutch tax administration relating to the customs duties imposed on a quantity of urea-formaldehyde that Van Gend & Loos imported from West Germany into the Netherlands – in legalese, a measure having equivalent effect to a customs duty. Yawn. The other, an electricity bill, all of 1925 beloved lire (at least it sounds a lot; it actually amounts to less than one euro).[53] Compare this to the Europe of 'now' with the reach of Union activities extending to defence, education, culture, public health, artificial intelligence – write your own list. If one were to engage in a counter-factual 'what if' exercise and try and imagine such an expanded portfolio in the 1960s, the quiet revolution might not have been that quiet after all.

The explosiveness of the competences issue is not simply or even primarily explained by the expanded portfolio. It is fuelled by the perception that there are no hard limits, no clear jurisdictional lines, to the competences of the Union, and by the contested perception that in this area the CJEU has not been, or has not been seen to be, an effective federal policeman – indeed, that it has itself contributed to jurisdictional creep.[54] This is one credible explanation to the judicial tremors mentioned in the opening pages of this chapter. In the context of the famous *Weiss* decision, here is a not untypical comment:

> In fairness to the Karlsruhe court, there really is, as has already been adverted to, a 'who watches the watchman' lacuna in the EU legal order, given the absence of any control over the ECJ's rulings in the matter of competence combined with the difficulty in amending the Treaties. As we have seen, the BVG provided its own answer to this – in effect that it should be for a court – and more specifically, the BVG itself – to control the ECJ, at least as far as Germany was concerned.[55]

As has been endlessly and correctly argued, allowing Member State courts to be the final arbiter in such cases would compromise both the principle of the uniform application of Union law as well as the related principle of equality before the law of individuals subject to that law. But Barrett (who does not endorse this solution) is absolutely right in identifying the underlying motivation informing the decision of the German Federal Constitutional Court.

One way of framing this issue is that there seems to be in the jurisprudence of the Court, not least in its rhetoric (or absence thereof), either a failure to understand or, perhaps, a rejection of the notion that protecting fundamental boundaries in a federal-type polity is as important as protecting fundamental rights.[56]

[53] A Arena, 'From an Unpaid Electricity Bill to the Primacy of EU Law: Gian Galeazzo Stendardi and the Making of *Costa v ENEL*' (2019) 30 *European Journal of International Law* 1017, 1022.

[54] *cf* V Vėlyvytė, *Judicial Authority in EU Internal Market Law: Implications for the Balance of Competences and Powers* (Oxford, Hart Publishing, 2022).

[55] Barrett (n 46) 97.

[56] This is hardly a new concern. *cf* JHH Weiler, 'Fundamental Rights and Fundamental Boundaries: On Standards and Values in the Protection of Human Rights' in N Neuwahl and A Rosas (eds), *The European Union and Human Rights* (The Hague, Kluwer, 1995); and JHH Weiler, 'Limits to Growth? On the Law and Politics of the European Union's Jurisdictional Limits' in *State and Nation: Current Legal and Political Problems before the 1996 Intergovernmental Conference*, IUSEF No 15 (University of Oslo, 1995).

D. The Disappearance of the Political-Legal Equilibrium of the Europe of 'Then'

In our view, another salient factor in explaining the pacific reception of the quiet revolution in the Foundational Era was the emergence of a particular political-legal unstated 'compact' in that period. We still subscribe to the view that the proximity in time between, on the one hand, the decisions of the Court in *Van Gend & Loos* and *Costa* and, on the other hand, the Luxembourg Compromise was not purely coincidental. In the Luxembourg Compromise, the Member States, in a so-called gentlemen's agreement, allowed all Member States to retain a veto power, even on issues which under the Treaties were to be decided by majority voting.[57] Accepting the constitutional revolution (which was both in their interest and also accorded for their moral and ideological commitment to the European construct), but attempting to protect themselves by retaining the power to block any would-be directly effective and supreme legislation with which a Member State could not agree in our view created a productive equilibrium which enabled a smooth digestion of the new legal order. Of course, it came with a cost, notably in the 'constipation' of the decision-making process and its normative dilution to lowest common denominator policies. But perhaps, judged historically, it was a price worth paying for the relatively smooth entrenchment of the new legal order within the Union.

We do not wish to rehearse here the full lineaments of this theory.[58] But if it has any merit, it could offer one explanation why, after the demise of the equilibrium with the entry into force of the Single European Act, coupled with all the factors discussed above, what seemed to be a consolidated constitutional *acquis* is now increasingly contested and under pressure, not least from the apex courts in several Member States.

V. THE POLITICAL: DEMOCRATIC LEGITIMACY AND THE CONSTITUTIONAL ORDER: A BRIEF EXCURSUS

The focus of this chapter so far has been on the challenges to the more explicitly legal and judicial dimensions of the Union's constitutional order with a view as to the appropriate and necessary changes to the hermeneutic sensibility of the Court in the current circumstances of Europe. But as we anticipated in the introduction, constitutional discourse inevitably involves the political too, to which we now turn, albeit in shorthand fashion.[59]

[57] For an overview, see AL Teasdale, 'The Life and Death of the Luxembourg Compromise' (1993) 31 *Journal of Common Market Studies* 567.

[58] See JHH Weiler, 'The Transformation of Europe' (1991) 100 *Yale Law Journal* 2403. For an evaluation of the relevance of this theory in the Europe of today and various critiques, see MP Maduro and M Wind (eds), *The Transformation of Europe: Twenty-Five Years on* (Cambridge, Cambridge University Press, 2017).

[59] The following remarks partially expand upon an earlier perspective. For the full annotated discussion with further references, see JHH Weiler, 'Europe in Crisis: On "Politicial Messianism", "Legitimacy" and the "Rule of Law"' (2012) *Singapore Journal of Legal Studies* 248.

The political element we wish to highlight concerns the democratic woes of the Union. Why should one discuss in this context the democratic woes of the Union for which, it would seem, the Court, on its face, is extraneous?

There are two reasons, the first of which is less important than the second. We certainly do not wish to resurrect the bogeyman of *gouvernement des juges*[60] or to open the stale counter-majoritarian discussion. In the jurisprudence of the CJEU, as is the case in practically the case law of all supreme and constitutional courts, there will often be an element of legislation. Constitutional law professors would be out of a job if this were not the case. Anticipating a point we will make later, we believe that, in the current circumstance of the Union, the Court should abandon one strand of this judicial legislation, namely the hermeneutic reflex, developed in the period of decision-making stasis: that if 'they' don't do it (they being the political organs), we, the Court, should do it, or if they do not do it well, we should fix it.

The more important point is indeed what we consider the overall democratic malaise of the Union to which the Court is indeed extraneous. And yet we believe that if persuaded by our critique of the democratic credentials of the Union, this could also have implications in rethinking a new hermeneutic sensibility.

There is a curious history to the discourse about European democratic legitimacy.

In the Europe of 'then' during the Foundational Era, the democratic credentials, at least the popular democratic credentials of the Union, were extremely weak. The European Parliament was little more than a talking chamber, but this did not seem to trouble many. At least in part, this was a result of the thinking that democratic legitimacy could be assured through Member State representation in the Council (forgetting perhaps that this device resulted in a huge empowerment of the executive branch of the Member States at the expense of national parliaments).[61]

Concern for popular democratic legitimation emerges in the 1970s, at least in part as a result of the constitutional revolution. If Union norms do not have direct effect – ie, are not part of the law of the land which domestic courts must enforce, and even when they are, are not supreme – why should one care about popular democratic legitimation at the Union level? Does anyone care about the democratic legitimation of the stream of norms (notably lacking direct effect and supremacy) emanating from the Council of Europe? However, the other side of this very coin is thought-provoking in the context of the entanglement of law and constitutional politics: can the Court which has attributed direct effect to a large swathe of Union legislation and ascribed to it a robust form of supremacy (even a minor decision of the Union is supreme over Member State constitutions) be totally oblivious to the democratic credentials of legislation to which such constitutional weight has been given?

The result was the awakening of democracy deficit discourse in the 1970s. Such discourse was principally linked to the gap between the rapidly increasing spheres of competences and governance powers of the Union and a concomitant lack of powers of what was perceived as its principal democratising institution – the

[60] E Lambert, *Le gouvernement des juges et la lutte contre la législation sociale aux Etats-Unis. L'expérience américaine du contrôle judiciaire de la constitutionnalité des lois* (Paris, Giard, 1921); in this context, see also C Hillgruber, *Gouvernement des juges – Fluch oder Segen* (Leiden, Brill, 2014).

[61] See n 39 above.

European Parliament. This gap constituted the 'deficit'. As a result, not only were direct elections to the European Parliament instituted in 1979, but the powers of the European Parliament were also progressively enhanced in successive revisions of the Treaties, not least in the last such revision by the Treaty of Lisbon, which itself was but the famous European Constitution repackaged differently.

Now that the Parliament (representing the 'peoples') had become a veritable, if imperfect, co-legislator alongside the Council of Ministers (representing the Member States), the gap was deemed to be closed. Any continued talk of a European 'democracy deficit' could be dismissed as anachronistic at best, or as hypocritical demagoguery of the extreme anti-European left or right.

Typically then, if the issue of democracy in Europe was addressed at all throughout most of the 2010s, attention was given to those Member States experiencing democratic slide or where this is threatened by parties vying to win elections.

But this was, and is, too comforting a narrative, for the rise of populism and turning one's back on some of the most cherished features of liberal democracy at the state level has been, and still is, invariably associated with a heavy dose of Euroscepticism.

Part of the populist narrative can be summed up by the Brexit slogan 'Take back control', shades of which are present in populist discourse in all other Member States, and the worrying truth is that the Union offers an easy target for this (even if one can doubt if at least some of the populist movements are truly concerned with democracy), since the democratic legitimacy of the Union remains, in our view, very far from ideal. In substantiating this position, we need to digress in order to give an all too brief discussion of governance legitimacy.

We would like to suggest the three most important types or forms of legitimacy which have been central to the discussion of European integration:

- Process (or input/throughput) legitimacy – which in the current circumstance can be, with some simplification, be synonymised with electoral democracy. It is easier put in the negative: to the extent that the European mode of governance departs from the habits and practices of democracy as understood in the Member States, its legitimacy will be compromised.
- Result (or output) legitimacy – which, again simplifying matters somewhat, would be a modern version of 'bread and circuses'. As long as the Union delivers 'the goods' – prosperity, stability and security – it will enjoy a legitimacy that derives from a subtle combination of success per se, of success in realising its objectives and of contentment with those results. There is no better way to legitimate a war than to win it.
- Telos legitimacy or political messianism – where legitimacy is gained neither by process nor output, but by promise, the promise of an attractive 'promised land'.[62]

We will now try and illustrate the collapse of all three forms of legitimacy in the current European circumstance.

As regards process legitimacy, there is the persistent, chronic, troubling democracy deficit, which cannot be explained away.

[62] Weiler (n 58) 250 with further references.

First, despite 25 years or more of European citizenship, no veritable European demos, a primordial condition for democracy, has emerged. This became clear in the hard years of the financial crisis and to some extent in the early days of the COVID-19 pandemic. Germans and Dutch and Finns were not saying: 'A bailout as a matter of policy is wrong since, for example, it creates moral hazard by de-responsibilising financial institutions.' Many of them were saying, instead, why should we Germans, or Dutch, or Finns, help those lazy Italians or Portuguese or Greeks, who, in the shameful words of one eurozone leader, were busy spending their money on 'women and drinks':[63] a very visible manifestation of the no-demos thesis of Europe's democracy crisis.

Second, there are failures of democracy which simply make it difficult to speak of governance *by and of* the people. The manifestations of the so-called democracy deficit are persistent and no endless repetition of the powers of the European Parliament will remove them. In essence, it is the inability of the Union to develop structures and processes which adequately replicate, or 'translate', at the Union level even the imperfect habits of governmental control, parliamentary accountability and administrative responsibility that are practised with different modalities in the various Member States. Make no mistake: it is perfectly understood that the Union is not a state. But it is in the business of governance and has taken over extensive areas previously in the hands of the Member States. In some critical areas, such as the interface of the Union with the international trading system, the competences of the Union are exclusive; in others, they are dominant. Democracy is not about states; it is about the exercise of public power – and the Union exercises a huge amount of public power. We live by the credo that any exercise of public power has to be legitimated democratically and it is exactly here that Union process legitimacy fails.

In essence, the two primordial features of any functioning democracy are missing: the grand principles of accountability and representation.

As regards accountability, even the basic condition of representative democracy that at election time the citizens 'can throw the scoundrels out' – that is, replace the government – does not operate in Europe. The form of European governance, governance without government, is, and will remain for a considerable time (perhaps forever), such that there is no 'government' to throw out. Dismissing the Commission by the European Parliament (or approving the appointment of the Commission President) is not quite the same – not even remotely so. And the hostility with which the *Spitzenkandidaten* exercise was initially met by some Member States,[64] and its total disregard in the 2019 election,[65] does not augur well from that quarter.

[63] 'Indignation Grows over Eurogroup Chief's "Drinks and Women" Remarks' (*Euractiv*, 23 March 2017).

[64] *cf* D Dinan, 'Governance and Institutions: The Year of the *Spitzenkandidaten*' (2015) 53(S1) *Journal of Common Market Studies* 93.

[65] Instead of a designated *Spitzenkandidat* from any of the parliamentary political groups, Ursula von der Leyen was voted into office as President of the Commission with just 383 out of 751 votes in favour. For further context, see M Dawson, 'The Lost *Spitzenkandidaten* and the Future of European Democracy' (2019) 26 *Maastricht Journal of European and Comparative Law* 731; P de Wilde, 'The Fall of the *Spitzenkandidaten*: Political Parties and Conflict in the 2019 European Elections' in S Kritzinger et al (eds), *Assessing the 2019 European Parliament Elections* (Abingdon, Routledge, 2020) 37; and B Crum, 'Why the European Parliament Lost the *Spitzenkandidaten*-Process' (2023) 30 *Journal of European Public Policy* 193, 203 et seq.

Likewise, at the most primitive level of democracy, there is simply no moment in the civic calendar of Europe where the citizen can influence directly the outcome of any policy choice facing the Union in the way that citizens can at the national level when choosing between parties which offer clearly distinct programmes. The political colour of the European Parliament only very weakly gets translated into the legislative and administrative output of the Union.

The political deficit, to use the felicitous phrase of Renaud Dehousse,[66] is at the core of the democracy deficit. The Commission, by its self-understanding linked to its very ontology, cannot be 'partisan' in a right-left sense, and neither can the Council, by virtue of the haphazard political nature of its composition. This of course does not mean that the Commission is politically 'neutral'; such neutrality is impossible. So any decision is obviously ideologically laden. But it is always below the surface. It is not openly and accountably a policy at the service of an ideological commitment. Democracy normally must have some meaningful mechanism for expression of voter preference predicated on a choice among options, typically informed by stronger or weaker ideological orientation. That is an indispensable component of politics. Democracy without politics is an oxymoron. And yet that is not only Europe, but it is a feature of Europe – the 'non-partisan' nature of the Commission – which is celebrated. The stock phrase found in endless student textbooks and the like – that the supranational Commission vindicates the European interest, whereas the intergovernmental Council is a clearing house for Member State interests – is, at best, naïve. Does the 'European interest' not necessarily involve political and ideological choices? At times explicit, but always implicit?

Thus, the two most primordial norms of democracy, the principle of accountability and the principle of representation, are compromised in the very structure and process of the Union. It often serves governments (the executive branch) to play the game of European ideological neutrality, thus getting 'cover' from Brussels for politics which would be unacceptable at the national level.

Two deeper and longer-term trends give expression to the above. The first is the extraordinary decline in voter participation in elections for the European Parliament until 2019.[67] In Europe as a whole, the rate of participation barely reached 50 per cent in 2019, with several countries, notably in the East, falling below 30 per cent.[68] The correct comparison is, of course, with political elections to national parliaments, where the numbers are considerably higher. What is striking about these figures is, as noted above, that the decline coincides with a continuous shift in powers to the European Parliament, which today is a veritable co-legislator with the Council.

[66] R Dehousse, 'Constitutional Reform in the European Community: Are There Alternatives to the Majority Avenue?' in J Hayward (ed), *The Crisis of Representation in Europe* (London, Frank Cass, 1995) 118, 123.

[67] The elections in 2019 demonstrated, for the first time since the beginning of direct elections to the European Parliament, a rise in voter participation, halting the continuous and dramatic decline from 61 per cent in 1979 to just 42 per cent in 2014. The 2024 elections will show whether the results of 2019 were a genuine turning point or nothing more than a statistical anomaly, perhaps fuelled by an escape towards Europe in a popular expression of dissatisfaction with national politics. For the corresponding statistics, see European Parliament, '2019 European Election Results' (22 October 2019), www.europarl.europa.eu/election-results-2019/en/turnout.

[68] ibid.

The more powers the European Parliament, supposedly the *vox populi*, has gained, the greater popular indifference to it seems to have developed.

In analysing the legitimacy (and mobilising force) of the EU, in particular against the background of its persistent democracy deficit, political and social science has indeed long used the distinction between process legitimacy and outcome legitimacy (aka input/output, process/result etc). The legitimacy of the Union more generally and the Commission more specifically, even if suffering from deficiencies in the state democratic sense, is said to rest on the results achieved – in the economic, social and, ultimately, political realms. The idea harks back to the most classic functionalist and neo-functionalist theories.

We do not want to take issue with the implied normativity of this position – a latter-day *panem et circenses* (bread and circuses) approach to democracy, which at some level at least could be considered quite troubling. It is with its empirical reality that we want to take some issue. We do not think that outcome legitimacy explains all, or perhaps even most, of the mobilising force of the European construct. But whatever role it played, it is dependent on the *panem*. Rightly or wrongly, many woes of Europe – not least those of economic nature – are attributed to the European construct and manifest in a Polycrisis.[69] So when there suddenly is no bread, and certainly no cake, we are treated to a different kind of circus whereby the citizens' growing indifference turns to hostility and the ability of the Union to act as a political mobilising force seems not just spent, but even reversed. The worst way to legitimate a war is to lose it, and Europe is suddenly seen not as an icon of success, but as an emblem of austerity and thus, in terms of its promise of prosperity, a failure. If success breeds legitimacy, failure, even if wrongly allocated, leads to the opposite.

Therefore, unsurprisingly, there is a seemingly contagious spread of 'anti-Europeanism' in national politics. What was once the province of fringe parties on the far right and left has inched its way into more central political forces. The 'question of Europe' as a central issue in political discourse was for a long time regarded as an 'English disease'. There is a growing contagion in Member States in North and South, East and West, where political capital is to be made among non-fringe parties by anti-European advocacy. The spill-over effect of this phenomenon is the shift of mainstream parties in this direction as a way of countering the gains at their flanks. If we are surprised by this, it is only because we seem to have airbrushed out of our historical consciousness the rejection of the so-called European Constitution, an understandable amnesia since it represented a defeat of the collective political class in Europe by the *vox populi*, albeit not speaking through, but instead giving a slap in the face to, the European institutions.

On some level, the same could have been said 10 and even 20 years ago. The democracy deficit is not new – it is enduring. And how did Europe legitimate itself before it scored its great successes of the first decades?

As we hinted at above, at the conceptual level, there is a third type of legitimation which, in our view, for a long time played a much larger role than is currently acknowledged. In fact, in our view, it has been decisive to the legitimacy of Europe

[69] Cf J Zeitlin and F Nicoli (eds), *The European Union Beyond the Polycrisis?* (Abingdon, Routledge, 2020).

and to the positive response of both the political class and citizens at large. We will also argue that it is key to a crucial element in the Union's political culture. It is a legitimacy rooted in the 'politically messianic'.

In political 'messianism', the justification for action and its mobilising force derive not from process, as in classical democracy, or from result and success, but from the ideal pursued, the destiny to be achieved, the 'promised land' waiting at the end of the road. Indeed, in messianic visions, the end always trumps the means.

Mark Mazower, in his brilliant and original history and historiography of twentieth-century Europe, *Dark Continent*,[70] insightfully shows how the Europe of monarchs and emperors which entered the First World War was often rooted in a political messianic narrative in various states (in Germany, Italy, Russia and even Britain and France). It then oscillated after the First World War towards new democratic orders – that is, to process legitimacy – which then oscillated back into new forms of political messianism in fascism and communism. As the tale is usually told, after the Second World War, Western Europe was said to oscillate back to democracy and process legitimacy. It is here that we want to point to an interesting quirk, which is not often noted.

On the one hand, the Western states, which were later to become the Member States of the EU, became resolutely democratic, their patriotism rooted in their new constitutional values, narratives of glory abandoned and even ridiculed, and messianic notions of the state losing all appeal. Famously, former empires, once defended with repression and blood, were now abandoned with zeal.

And yet, their common venture, European integration, was in our reading a political messianic venture par excellence, the messianic becoming a central feature of its original and enduring political culture. The mobilising force and principle legitimating feature was the vision offered, the dream dreamt, the promise of a better future. Unlike output democracy, which is measured by concrete results, messianism is built on a dream, one often couched in metaphysical goods rather than material ones. The messianic vision found its expression in the Schuman Declaration, which offered a compelling dream of peace, prosperity and a different form of relationships among peoples and states, which was particularly potent in the aftermath of the Second World War. The functionalist messianic vision produced a culture of praxis, achievement, ever-expanding agendas and justification of this, even if it did not correspond to the habits of democracy of and within the Member States.

But part of the very phenomenology of political messianism is that it always collapses as a mechanism for mobilisation and legitimation. It obviously collapses when the messianic project fails – when the revolution does not come. But interestingly, and more germane to the narrative of European integration, even when successful, it sows the seeds of its collapse. On one level, the collapse is inevitable, part of the very phenomenology of the messianic project. Reality is always more complicated, challenging, banal and ultimately less satisfying than the dream which preceded it. The result is not only absence of mobilisation and legitimation, but actual rancour. When, as we saw, output and input legitimacy are in shreds too, the collapse is a veritable *debellatio*.

[70] M Mazower, *Dark Continent: Europe's Twentieth Century* (London, Allen Lane, 1998).

Democracy was not part of the original DNA of European integration. The word was not even mentioned in the Schuman Declaration. It still feels like a foreign implant. With the collapse of the original political messianism, the alienation we are now witnessing is only to be expected. And thus, when failure hits, as in the eurozone crisis, when the *panem* is gone, all sources of legitimacy suddenly, simultaneously collapse.

So, it is not in the immediate – financial/immigration crisis – that we should look for the roots of the current challenges to, and disappointment with, our cherished forms of liberal democracy, but in the long-term hollowing-out processes both pan-European and within the Union governance itself into which the so-called populist forces were able to enter. Populist because popular, and popular because populist.

VI. THE PERSISTENCE OF PESCATORIAN HERMENEUTICS?

Despite a variety of changes in its hermeneutics – for example, a greater sensitivity to cultural and legal diversity among the Member States – we argue that the Pescatorian hermeneutics continue to play a significant role in the contemporary jurisprudence of the Court. We want to illustrate this by three examples highlighting two different strands in these hermeneutics.[71]

One strand is the 'amendment' by the Court of Council legislation in the interest of 'improving' such legislation by a better understanding than the Council itself of what it was trying to achieve by its legislation. Some might think of this as a usurpation of a role that legitimately belongs to the legislative branch. The second is the habit, not least in major jurisprudential departures, to start the ball rolling by laying down a curt apodictic foundation stone, on the basis of which the subsequent legislation is developed, step by step, in a positivist manner.

Whether these examples are typical, or exceptions that prove the rule, we will leave to the judgment of our readers. This analysis will require quite a minute examination of the texts of the decisions and the reasoning therein. *Caveat lector*!

We look first at *Test-Achats*[72] and *Sturgeon*.[73] In the first of the two cases, the Court held, overriding the Council, that allowing Member States to maintain without temporal limitation an exemption from the rule of unisex premiums and benefits in certain insurance policies was incompatible with the objective of equal treatment between men and women, which was the purpose of the Directive in question, and would be incompatible with Articles 21 and 23 of the Charter of Fundamental Rights of the European Union (hereinafter 'the Charter').

In *Sturgeon*, the Court famously held that although the Regulation in question awarded compensation only to passengers whose flight was cancelled and as a result of which they suffered a delay of three hours or more, a similar right under similar

[71] This is a truncated version of a more elaborate argument developed earlier. For the full discussion with further references, see JHH Weiler, 'Epilogue: Judging the Judges – Apology and Critique' in M Adams et al (eds), *Judging Europe's Judges: The Legitimacy of the Case Law of the European Court of Justice* (Oxford, Hart Publishing, 2013) 235.

[72] Case C-236/09 *Association belge des Consommateurs Test-Achats and Others* ECLI:EU:C:2011:100.

[73] Joined Cases C-402/07 and C-432/07 *Sturgeon and Others* ECLI:EU:C:2009:716.

conditions (a three-hour delay or more) would be awarded to passengers whose flight was delayed rather than cancelled.

Relying on the principle of equal treatment, the Court terminated, against the view of the legislator, a provision that was unlimited in time according to which Member States could allow differing actuarial assessments of men and women, in one case, and wrote into the Regulation on passenger compensation, against the views of the Council and the Advocate General, a provision protecting passengers in the case of delay, resulting in three-hour delay being treated as comparable to a case of cancellation.

We want to contextualise both cases in a somewhat different way. *Test-Achats* takes us to the territory of gender equality. We understand discrimination as treating the like in an unlike manner and treating the unlike in a like manner. Of course, critical in any analysis of discrimination will be the comparator chosen to define likeness. Through history and in all cultures, women have suffered discrimination oftentimes of a profound and harmful manner. Even the Enlightenment and the French Revolution made only a little mark on this. Since men and women are biologically different in many ways, and thus 'unlike', it was easy to justify consciously and subconsciously differing treatment, which was mostly detrimental and harmful to women. Given this history, it is a matter of prudential judgment to treat with great suspicion any instance where gender is the selected comparator for likeness with consequent justification of different treatment of women. In the US, for example, gender, like race, is treated as a 'suspect class' of comparator, requiring the strictest scrutiny by the courts. This strategy is not without its dangers. Simply to remove gender as a comparator typically results in treating women in the same way as men are treated. But then it is maleness and male sensibilities which define the norm. Women are treated mostly like men, not men like women. This works in most cases, but can be detrimental to women in others.

And, second, sometimes simply to disregard the biological and other differences may lead to palpable discrimination by treating the unlike as if they were alike. We have separate male and female tennis, football and basketball competitions for obvious reasons. There, gender is legitimately used as comparator (it is not so clear to us why there are separate male and female chess championships). Thus, our default may well be for 'unisex' regulation, but with awareness of these two potential countervailing 'side effects' which might, in the very interests of equality, justify using gender as comparator.

Insurance, both health and life, are particularly sensitive cases. In different societies and cultures, there are statistically marked differences in life expectation between men and women as a class. Typically, women live longer, which in fact for certain policies would result in lower premiums. This is not dispositive as to the question of whether we should allow gender to be a comparator in writing insurance.

We might, for example, find that working-class men live shorter lives than middle or upper middle-class men, or that whites live longer than blacks, and yet as a matter of normative social policy, we may forbid the usage of class or race as insurance comparators. It should be noted that in these two examples, to allow the use of race or class as comparators would result in a detriment to socially disadvantaged categories in many societies.

This is what makes the issue of gender in insurance so tricky. Our basic default suspicion of gender as comparator may justify a presumption in favour of unisex insurance regulation. And the requirement that empirical studies be conducted to correlate differences in, say, insurance premiums and veritable actuarial predictions is also fully justified. But if these substantiate a correlation between verifiable actuarial predictions and differing treatment of men and women, there is a hugely delicate and fraught normative question to be answered, especially given the fact that a wholesale shift to unisex regulation may in certain circumstances be to the detriment of women (and the delight of insurers). We think the more plausible reading of the Directive is that this question was left open, deferred for a later date, because of its delicacy and consequentiality, or even left indefinitely to the discretion of Member States so far as empirical data rather than prejudice informs the actuarial practices.

Paragraph 32 of the *Test-Achats* decision holds that Article 5(2) of Directive 2004/113:

> [W]hich enables the Member States in question to maintain without temporal limitation an exemption from the rule of unisex premiums and benefits, works against the achievement of the objective of equal treatment between men and women, which is the purpose of Directive 2004/113, and is incompatible with Articles 21 and 23 of the Charter.[74]

And yet in our humble opinion, this is a colossal non sequitur, for it begs the question of whether empirically verified actuarial gender differences should, or should not, as a matter of policy, be allowed to serve as a comparator. Articles 21 and 23 of the Charter do not, and cannot, help in this matter. In fact, depending how that difficult question is resolved – and normative arguments can be made one way or another – to annul Article 5(2) of the Directive could have the effect of working against the objective of equal treatment and would violate Articles 21 and 23 of the Charter. Treating the unlike in a like manner is as inimical to equal treatment as treating the like in an unlike manner. There are differences between men and women and it is a deep moral question as to when we should take them into account in allowing different treatment as in allowing pre-natal leave.

At worst, this is a high watermark of Pescatorian hermeneutics. It was highly inappropriate for the Court to arrogate to itself the decision in this matter, the proper forum for which ought to have been democratically accountable politicians. At best, it is unfortunate that this decision was taken by the Court without, it would seem from its decision, fully grasping the depth of the issue involved and unfolding the facets of this problem in a methodological manner.

Part of Pescatorian hermeneutics is, under the guise of simply elucidating the 'real' teleology of the legislator, substituting the Court's normative preferences. To present the decision as simply implementing the teleology of the legislator we find less than convincing.

There is in this case and others like it a second underlying assumption, which comes into sharp relief in the *Sturgeon* decision. The reader will be well advised to reread the magnificent Opinion of Advocate General Sharpston in comparison with

[74] Case C-236/09 *Association belge des Consommateurs Test-Achats and Others* ECLI:EU:C:2011:100, para 32.

the characteristically cryptic decision of the Court. One does not have to agree with every move or conclusion the Advocate General makes to note how much closer she comes to what should be the appropriate role of a court – the Court – when examining legislation.

But for the present purposes, what is more important is the final decision. The Advocate General concludes that it should fall to the legislator to decide on the number of waiting hours which would justify compensation in the case of delay rather than cancellation. The Court, as we know, decided this itself, equating delay with cancellation.

Let us say a word on the merits of this. From a consumer rights perspective, the reasoning of the Court makes perfect sense. If you are entitled to compensation after three hours in the case of cancellation, would it not stand to reason that the same relief will be given in case of a 'merely' delayed flight? What difference does the cause of waiting make? Three stressful hours in a crowded airport are three stressful hours regardless of the cause.

This, of course, is only so if, as is so often the case today, we succumb to the enthrallment of the culture of rights and look at the legislation through that prism alone. But if the perspective is one of responsibility and duty (of the airlines) – and the 'compensation' to the traveller has as a primary objective, or at least a major objective, the penalisation and deterrence of derelict airlines – it is possible at least to imagine that delay and cancellation might be regarded as involving different degrees of dereliction and thus meriting different degrees of sanction and deterrence, in which case the consumer equivalence perspective loses its determinant force and becomes, at best, one factor to be considered. And if there is any merit in this, and even if there is at least some question that this might be at the source of the differentiation, should not this alone point in the direction of the Advocate General rather than the Court? We come to the same conclusion as above. At worst, this decision should have been left to politically accountable bodies; at best, it would be more reassuring if one had the impression that the Court examined the issue in its true complexity.

But one can go even further. Let us assume that in relation to these two cases, our substantive contextualisation and critique are wholly misconceived, as might well be the case. Underlying both cases seems to be the assumption that if the Court can detect 'spot on' what the Council (and Parliament) truly intended in any given piece of legislation, and if the solution adopted in a particular facet violated, say, a general principle of Union law such as equality, then the Court would be doing its duty by interpreting it – effectively amending the legislation – as it did in *Sturgeon* rather than annulling it in whole or in part. After all, what's the harm? If they (the political organs) do not like the judicial decision, they can amend it (provided, of course, they do not violate primary Union law).

This fails to appreciate the major impact such decisions have on the political process, given the rules on majority voting (as well as unanimity, where relevant). It is not fanciful to imagine that in a situation such as *Sturgeon*, you may have mustered the necessary majority for a regulation which compensated for cancellations but not delays and would not have had the requisite majority for a regulation which compensated for both. Since the Court did not follow the Sharpston path, it committed to a judicial amendment that, in effect, nullifies the value inherent in the principle of qualified majority – and a majority required to change the new legislation as 'interpreted' by the Court may well be unattainable too. To put it bluntly, judicial amendment as exemplified in *Sturgeon* may result in legislation for which there might not have been a majority at the time of enactment, and which proves difficult to reverse. This could result in very crass interference in political decision making. There really is a fundamental difference between the following two situations: A. A court saying to the legislature: for legal reasons, you cannot do X, but you can do Y. So X is annulled and you decide if you want to do Y instead. B. A court saying to the legislature: For legal reasons, you cannot do X, but you can do Y. So we will do Y because we think that is what you intended, or because this will cure the legal defect of X.

We tried to explain above the real and present danger that this type of judicial intervention, even if hermeneutically defensible on some teleological assumption, might end up affecting the actual political process, shifting the burden of majority and thus constituting a major judicial encroachment into the very heart of political decision making. But even in instances where this is not the case, it is not clear to us that the *political process* is enhanced by the Court mopping up after the legislator, thereby creating a moral hazard – a little bit like diligent citation-checkers inadvertently encouraging sloppiness in the principal author of an article.[75] It also shifts responsibility to the Court for activity which should really be in the political province.

It is this form of hermeneutics which we believe is no longer justified or accepted in the Union of 'now'.

As we outlined above, a feature of what we call Pescatorian hermeneutics was the laying down of a foundational stone (often apodictic), and then step by step a logical and well-reasoned jurisprudence emerges. We will use the citizenship saga as illustrating the persistence of this in the contemporary jurisprudence of the Court.

We take as our example the 'landmark case' *Ruiz Zambrano*.[76]

Rottmann[77] is the foundation on the basis of which one is to read and understand *Ruiz Zambrano*. How solid are the stones, how clarifying does the reasoning become if the cases are read in sequence?

The founding stone of the founding stone, the legal premise on which the Court reached its conclusion in *Rottmann* was to stress 'once again that 'citizenship of the Union is intended to be the fundamental status of nationals of the Member States'.[78] This is, indeed, the hermeneutic founding stone of that decision. And the Court does stress it again and again in its citizenship jurisprudence. There is hardly a case where this mantra was not repeated. And being so, it should not surprise us that in evenly balanced cases, the Court tilts in favour of the fundamental status.

But the epistemic status of this foundational statement is rather problematic. Intended by whom? And what does 'fundamental status' actually mean and from where does it derive as a legal concept?

[75] For the similar case of courts reinterpreting codified law through a constitutional reading, *cf* A Voßkuhle, 'Theorie und Praxis der verfassungskonformen Auslegung von Gesetzen durch Fachgerichte' (2000) 125 *Archiv des öffentlichen Rechts* 177, 185 et seq.

[76] Case C-34/09 *Ruiz Zambrano* ECLI:EU:C:2011:124.

[77] Case C-135/08 *Rottmann* ECLI:EU:C:2010:104.

[78] K Lenaerts, 'How the ECJ Thinks: A Study on Judicial Legitimacy' (2013) 36 *Fordham International Law Journal* 1301, 1353 et seq.

The innocent reader might come to believe that it is to be found in the Treaty itself. But at least on one reading of the language of the Treaty, it would seem to be in tension, if not in contradiction, with the interpretative criteria of wording, teleology and legislative history.

Following the amendments made by the Maastricht Treaty, Article 8 EC stated: 'Every person holding the nationality of a Member State shall be a citizen of the Union.'

The Treaty of Amsterdam introduced a significant addition, amending this article: 'Citizenship of the Union shall complement and not replace national citizenship.'

Article 20 of the Treaty on the Functioning of the European Union (TFEU) has finally settled on the following: 'Every person holding the nationality of a Member State shall be a citizen of the Union. Citizenship of the Union shall be additional to and not replace national citizenship.'

The fact that the limiting phrase was added to the citizenship clause in response to some serious criticism and public reaction to the initial formulation may, at least to some, argue for a limiting rather than expansive reading, especially when what is at stake are issues, as in *Rottmann*, which precisely pit national and Union citizenship somewhat in opposition to each other.

We would like to repeat that our issue here is not with the actual decision in *Rottmann* or *Ruiz Zambrano*; it is with the reasoning and communicative quality of the internal steps within the decision. In no case to our knowledge has the Court ever explained how it arrives from a Treaty which was amended to include the statement that Union citizenship complements or is additional to national citizenship to its iconic statement about Union citizenship being the *fundamental status* of nationals of the Member States. And, in the same vein, we are unaware of any case in which the Court has explained what it actually means when it talks about the 'fundamental status' of citizenship.

And yet the Court uses this formula as the basis for some of its most important and groundbreaking decisions, such as *Rottmann* and *Ruiz Zambrano*.

This, it is respectfully submitted, is a striking example not of judicial reasoning, but of oracular statement.[79] It is so because we say it is so. And what it means – well you will find out.

The second 'stone' in the *Rottmann* decision is paragraph 42 of the judgment in which the Court explains that, since the decision of the German authorities to annul his naturalisation because of the fraudulent behaviour of Rottmann at the time of his application would render him stateless and thus deprived of his Union citizenship, the matter becomes one of Union law and subject to review by the Court.

We have some sympathy with the Court's approach, and it is certainly less oracular than the 'fundamental status' on which it is based. But this too, as a matter of reasoning, could profit from being, well, more profuse. On one level, it begs the question given the language of the citizenship clause and the priority it seems to give to

[79] The oracular nature is mirrored in the language of the Court as well, in particular concerning the pronounced 'destiny' of Union citizenship as the fundamental status. For the historical development, see O Garner, 'The Existential Crisis of Citizenship of the European Union: The Argument for an Autonomous Status' (2018) 20 *Cambridge Yearbook of European Legal Studies* 116.

Member State nationality. In cases such as *Collins*,[80] a US national, who had never set foot in Ireland and whose connection to the Union was the result of what might only be called the profligate Irish nationality rules, was treated as enjoying all rights without the Court seeming to be concerned at the manner in which nationality is granted, even though such grant is what bestows on the individual the status of Union citizen with all the attendant rights to him or her and, significantly, the attendant duties on all other Member States. That case is predicated on total sovereign discretion of the Member State at the entry gate to Union citizenship. Of course, one may distinguish entry and exit, but it would not require particularly creative lawyering to have taken the opposite tack in *Rottmann*. This hugely complex issue involving Member States, the Union and individuals, sovereign state rights, third countries and responsibilities of individuals weighed against their rights is disposed of in fewer than 100 words. We have seen longer letters to *Le Monde* or the *Frankfurter Allgemeine Zeitung*.

VII. BACK TO THE FUTURE: SOME PROPOSED CHANGES

In order to avoid any misunderstanding, we want to emphasise that our hypothesis, or thesis, is not one which would ascribe responsibility to the Court for the variety of woes which the Union faces, such as the normalisation of Euroscepticism and the like. Our argument is more modest: in the face of a very changed social, political and cultural Europe, a hermeneutic which was suitable for what we call the Europe of 'then' is no longer suitable and may damage the fundamentals of the much-cherished legal order and thus the Europe of 'now'. In our view, change will ensure the continuity and legitimacy of the essentials of the extant construct.

What, then, might be some desirable changes in orientation by the Court in the face of a Union:

- that has grown from six Member States to 27;
- which displays a far greater divergence in the political culture of its Member States;
- in which the consensus about the path of European integration has been shattered and in which Euroscepticism has entered mainstream politics in both West and East;
- in which majority voting (or bargaining in the shadow of the vote) has, thankfully, become the norm in a growing number of sectors; but
- in which policy setting and decision making, regrettably, continues to take place under the cloud of a serious democratic deficit; and
- in which a significant number of apex courts of the Member States, West and East, have displayed a certain lack of confidence in the Court, notably on the issue of creeping jurisdiction?

We emphasise, once again, that we neither believe that this list of 'woes' can be attributed to the Court, nor that the changes we propose will constitute a magic fix to

[80] Case C-138/02 *Collins* ECLI:EU:C:2004:172.

these woes. But we do believe that in this much changed Union, the positioning of the Court should be different from its historical past.

There is nothing radical in this proposition. No less an authority than the historic President of the CJEU, Koen Lenaerts, has suggested that such change is already in the works and that the modern CJEU is following a 'new paradigm',[81] removed from that era and thinking. We want to suggest some changes of orientation and one concrete structural change that may be added to the toolkit of the new paradigm.

The purpose of these suggestions is to preserve the fundamental principles of the legal order encapsulated in the well-known doctrines such as supremacy and direct effect (meaning that Union law is part of the law of the land in the Member States) and to safeguard the position of the CJEU as the ultimate arbiter of the content of this law.

The term 'guardian of the Treaties' is of course an open-ended term, the meaning of which will depend on how one conceives of the underlying telos of the Union. For some, in 'united in diversity', the emphasis is on 'united', while for others it is on 'diversity'. Both approaches are current and legitimate. The Court has to position itself as an impartial adjudicator and needs to be seen as such. Justice must be done and justice must be seen to be done. At this stage in the life of the Union, perception is as important as justice itself. One can argue whether contemporary jurisprudence truly reflects a new paradigm. We believe that the evidence is mixed and can be read in different ways. Some cases point in one direction, others in another. But on the question of perception, the old Pescatorian image is still current among wide swathes of both political and legal stakeholders.

In Europe, the word 'federalism' has become synonymous with centralisation, integration and more unity. In the US, when there are laments about the 'death of federalism', the same word has the exact opposite connotation: federalism means respect for state rights, and checks on centralised governance.[82]

Be that as it may, as regards substance, our Court should in its internal self-understanding shake off the last vestiges of its historical role as an 'engine of integration', of its role as guardian of the Treaties in the sense of accomplishing judicially what the other institutions fail to do politically. It should hesitate much more when interpreting Union legislation before it opts for a maximalist (more integration) rather than a minimalist (less integration) interpretation. Whereas historically it correctly perceived the Member States as in need of disciplining and education in the new logic of the Single Market, it must now review with the same measure of 'suspicion' the institutions of the Union – and be seen to be repositioning itself in this manner.

As regards perception, we can no more than repeat a double Cato's cry. The Court is a victim of the number and style of its judgments. The docket of the Court keeps growing. The number of the cases decided each year grows correspondingly. The result is a dilution of the specific gravity and visibility of its jurisprudence, and, dare we say it, at least in some instances, the quality of the reasoning. The new moves to transfer some of the hallowed preliminary references to the General Court are to be

[81] Lenaerts (n 76) 1309.

[82] *cf* CJ Cooper, 'The Demise of Federalism' (1988) 20 *The Urban Lawyer* 239.

welcomed, but there is still a long road ahead.[83] Giving more responsibility to the General Court is in and of itself a sign of a true maturation of the legal order and also a signal of trust in the General Court, which it has richly earned.

As regards style, though some changes are noted, the decisions often remain apodictic and formalistic. They lack the discursive style of, say, the German Federal Constitutional Court, the UK Supreme Court, the US Supreme Court and like-minded jurisdictions. A more discursive style would allow the Court not only better to elaborate its reasoning in specific cases and specific points of law, but also to explicate the underlying philosophy behind its hermeneutics – possibly leading to more productive exchanges with legal scholarship and improvements in quality.

We are fully aware of the constraints of the Court, which operates on the principle of consensus and which does not allow separate or dissenting opinions. But there is no reason for the Court not to disclose more transparently the contrasting views (without personal attribution) within the judicial decision making, thus assuring its interpretative communities that distinct positions exist and were considered. This muted form of transparency,[84] we would respectfully suggest, would enhance respect for the Court and its decisions.[85]

We come last, but not least, to the issue of jurisdictional creep and the limits to the competences of the Union.[86] This is of direct concern to the CJEU, since it is in this context that some of the most clamorous challenges to the authority of the Court have been raised, but also since it may invite new thinking on the relationship between the European and national judicatures.

There is little point in rehearsing in length, yet again, the all-too-justified laments about the unfortunate decision of the German Federal Constitutional Court of 5 May 2020 in the case of *Weiss* on the public sector asset purchase programme of the European Central Bank (ECB).

Although dealt with in Panzer fashion, the problem the German Federal Constitutional Court faced was real and acute: what is a national constitutional court, which has ultimate responsibility for ensuring the rule of law, human rights and the principles of democracy within its jurisdiction to do, when faced with a Union measure which, in its view, violates these? And what should that court do when a

[83] Cf D Sarmiento, 'Editorial Note: On the Road to a Constitutional Court of the European Union: The Court of Justice After the Transfer of the Preliminary Reference Jurisdiction to the General Court' (2023) 19 Croatian Yearbook of European Law & Policy VII.

[84] While the recent efforts of the European Parliament to have the CJEU publish party statements and observations on the Court's website also intend to increase transparency, such publications by themselves cannot illuminate the judicial reasoning in the same way that improved decisions would – in fact, the Court not engaging with arguments brought forward by the parties would raise more concerns when available for all to see. The changes are detailed in European Parliament, P9_TA(2024)0086 (27 February 2024).

[85] The value of anonymously disclosing contrasting opinions for maturing legal orders should not be underestimated. For a frameweork and analysis on this topic concerning the WTO Appellate Body see PC Mavroidis and EY Kim, 'Dissenting Opinions in the WTO Appellate Body: Drivers of their Issuance & Implications for the Institutional Jurisprudence', EUI Working Paper RSCAS 2018/51.

[86] In the following, we borrow liberally from an earlier proposal. For the full discussion and the extensive commentary it received, see JHH Weiler and D Sarmiento, 'The EU Judiciary after Weiss' (*Verfassungsblog*, 2 June 2020), verfassungsblog.de/the-eu-judiciary-after-weiss; and JHH Weiler and D Sarmiento, 'The Comeback of the Mixed Chamber' (*Verfassungsblog*, 2 October 2023), verfassungsblog.de/the-comeback-of-the-mixed-chamber.

judgment of the CJEU, the guarantor of all those values within the sphere of competences of the Union, legitimates that Union measure in a manner which the national court regards as inadequate?

The matter is at its most acute when at issue is the line delimiting the respective competences of the European Union and its Member States. After all, the Union derives its competences and powers by delegation from its Member States as enshrined in the Treaties, its de facto constitution. So even if procedurally the CJEU is the sole court empowered to pronounce as a matter of Union law on such issues, is it not, at least partially, a matter of national law to define what could constitutionally be delegated? And it is worth remembering that the principle of supremacy operates within the sphere of competences of the Union. An ultra vires norm does not, and should not, enjoy supremacy. But surely one cannot allow these issues to be decided by national courts resulting in an unequal application of Union law within its legal space and compromising the principle of equality before the law of individuals subject to Union law – one outcome in France and another in Latvia, depending on which jurisdiction decided the case?

The matter is further complicated by several additional considerations. First, in its preliminary reference jurisdiction, the CJEU, like several other international and national tribunals, is a court of first and last instance. There is no appeal to a higher court from its decisions. This is an uncomfortable legal situation – after all, *errare humanum est*. We live more comfortably with uncomfortable decisions if they are reviewed and affirmed by a higher court of appeal. In the European Convention on Human Rights system, a decision of a Chamber of the European Court of Human Rights can be appealed to the Grand Chamber with a different composition of judges.[87] But we have already underlined the untenability of each and every national court acting as a court of appeal in matters concerning the delimitation of Union competences.

Second, despite its fundamental and indispensable contribution to European integration, the CJEU has shown itself over the years to have one blind spot. It has not proved to be a strict guarantor in policing the limits to Union competences and jurisdiction. The very limited number of cases in which it has flagged a breach of competence have been the exception that proves a very general rule of broad Union competence. This, as noted above, is probably due to a misconceived vision of federalism, in which the federal vision is (wrongly) associated with a centralist understanding of the Union. The case law of the CJEU can be interpreted as setting a straightforward rule: in the case of doubt, the competence is that of the Union in order to ensure the effet utile of Union law, in the same way that in the logic of fundamental rights, in the case of doubt, the judge must rule for the benefit of individual freedom. This is an ill-sighted approach that rightly raises the concerns of national courts, particularly of those with a more acute sense of the logic of federalism.

How, then, in the long run is one to resolve the structural dilemma of a jurisdictional conflict of this nature? It seems a circle that cannot be squared. And yet with

[87] See Art 43 ECHR.

no solution, the spectre of *Weiss* will continue to hover and threaten the integrity of the Union.

It is for this reason that it was proposed[88] that in the Conference on the Future of Europe (which completed its work in 2022), serious consideration should be given to the establishment of a new appeal jurisdiction – a Mixed Chamber – *within the CJEU*, strictly and narrowly confined to *Weiss*-type cases, where at issue is the delineation of the jurisdictional line between the Member States and the Union.

We believe that this appeal procedure should remain within the province of the CJEU and the obvious forum would be its Grand Chamber.

There can be many permutations to the specific configuration of this new jurisdiction,[89] but underlying all such permutations will be one fundamental principle: it is to be composed by sitting members of the CJEU alongside sitting members of the constitutional or equivalent supreme courts of the Member States. It is this composition, above all else, which will give its decisions an authority and legitimacy which, if enshrined in the Treaties, will be a lot more difficult to contest. True, a determined national court could still dig its heels in, but if the new procedure is enshrined in a Treaty revision which reaffirms the role of the CJEU in deciding such cases, the barrier to such action would be raised very considerably indeed. And it should be noted that it would still be a decision of the CJEU, preserving the principle of the Court being the final arbiter of issues of Union law.

In these limited cases, we propose that the composition should be six judges of the CJEU (although obviously not the judges whose decision is being appealed) and six judges from the constitutional or apex courts of the Member States in a predetermined order reflecting the rich legal diversity of European legal systems. The Mixed Grand Chamber would be presided over by the President of the Court of Justice (the thirteenth judge unless he or she participated in the decision under appeal, in which case another judge of the CJEU, such as a president of a five-judge chamber, would act as replacement). In this proposal the Mixed Grand Chamber would only rule on the distribution of competences between the Union and its Member States, and it would have jurisdiction to declare null and void a Union act – reversing a prior decision of the CJEU validating this – that entails a serious breach of the principle of conferral. The standard of review would be limited to cases of a 'serious breach', in similar terms to the CJEU's jurisdiction in the judicial review procedure, also in line with the standard articulated by the German Federal Constitutional Court itself in its prior jurisprudence (though sadly disregarded in the *Weiss* case itself).

It is our belief that in the current circumstances, the *in dubio mitius* principle should apply. A decision *validating* a contested Union measure should be supported by at least eight judges and perhaps even nine. It seems to us imprudent and

[88] See Weiler and Sarmiento, 'The EU Judiciary after Weiss' (n 81).

[89] The Franco-German Working Group on EU Institutional Reform later made a similar proposal, though in their version the Mixed Chamber would be extraneous to the Court and would be of a consultative nature. We respectfully disagree with the proposed purely consultative nature, as in our view, it would exacerbate the problem if such a Chamber were to make a recommendation contrary to a decision of the Court. See the Working Group report: 'Sailing on High Seas: Reforming and Enlarging the EU for the 21st Century' (Paris/Berlin, 18 September 2023) 28, www.auswaertiges-amt.de/blob/2617322/4d0e0010ffcd8c0079e21329bbbb3332/230919-rfaa-deu-fra-bericht-data.pdf.

counterproductive to validate a Union measure if all six national constitutional court judges in the Mixed Grand Chamber believe it to be ultra vires.

The Mixed Grand Chamber could be seised either by the constitutional or supreme court of a Member State in a *Weiss*-like situation, as well as by a Member State government and/or national parliament within a year from the date of delivery of the CJEU's ruling on the validity of the contested Union act.

Among the constitutional and supreme court judges, participation would be made dependent on a rotation system, but the President of the constitutional or supreme court of the Member State from which the complaint originates should be part of the Member State component of the Mixed Grand Chamber.

The proceedings should allow the intervention of Member States and Union institutions, certainly the Council of the European Union and the European Parliament, to defend their proposal, but also the European Central Bank if the matter concerns any of the areas of Union policy in which it exercises competence.

The workings of this chamber should provide maximum transparency. The hearings should be streamed live and the written submissions of the interveners made public. However, we believe that the question of dissenting opinions is delicate. In principle, they should be possible. But the rules allowing for renewable mandates of the judges of the CJEU make it difficult to preserve their independence if dissents are available. As long as the mandates of the members of the CJEU remain renewable, dissent should not be considered, but should be introduced if the Member States ever decide to amend the current appointment system for judges and Advocates General of the CJEU.

Index